DIRECT AND ALTERNATING CURRENTS

DIRECT AND ALTERNATING CURRENTS

Theory and Machinery

E. A. LOEW

Emeritus Dean of Engineering and Professor of Electrical Engineering
University of Washington

Assisted by

F. R. BERGSETH

Associate Professor of Electrical Engineering
University of Washington

FOURTH EDITION

NEW YORK   TORONTO   LONDON

McGRAW-HILL BOOK COMPANY, INC.

1954

THE MAPLE PRESS COMPANY, YORK, PA.

PREFACE

The aim of this book as set forth in the preface to the first edition remains unchanged. It is to provide a single-volume text covering circuit theory and machinery of direct and alternating currents that is suitable as a text in a first course for majors in electrical engineering and in survey courses for majors in all other branches of engineering. Fundamental principles are stressed throughout, and a solid foundation of basic theory is provided. These are regarded as of far greater importance to the student than a somewhat hazy knowledge of factual details that can have little or no meaning without the support of a substantial theoretical background.

Even a little knowledge of basic principles, preferably associated with its application to commercial machinery, is more meaningful and of far greater lasting benefit to the student than a large collection of more or less unrelated facts concerning the details of machine construction and operation. Moreover, experience indicates that students can gain a good working knowledge of fundamentals in a relatively short time, and without great difficulty. With this background, an understanding of the operating characteristics of electric machines and apparatus may be acquired quite readily with the aid of brief descriptions.

In this edition the rationalized mks system of units is used except where specifically stated to the contrary. The use of this system seemed to make it desirable to change the approach to the subject in the introductory chapters and to rewrite more or less completely the chapters on magnetism, electromagnetism, the magnetic circuit, and the dielectric circuit and capacitance. Several other chapters have also been substantially rewritten, and all the remaining chapters have been thoroughly revised. The chapter on fuses, switches, and lightning arresters has been omitted, as has also most of the chapter on synchronous converters. A new chapter on conversion equipment has been added. This chapter contains a small part of the former discussion on synchronous converters, and new material on the subjects of mechanical and mercury-arc rectifiers, phase converters, and frequency converters.

E. A. Loew

v

CONTENTS

vii

PART II. ALTERNATING CURRENTS

Part I

DIRECT CURRENTS

CHAPTER 1

CURRENT, ELECTROMOTIVE FORCE, AND RESISTANCE

Modern Theory. The *atom* was long regarded as the smallest part of a substance that could exist as a separate entity, but we now know that the atom itself is made up of a number of still smaller particles. According to modern theory the atoms of all substances found in nature are made up of three kinds of subatomic particles: *electrons, protons,* and *neutrons*. Although several other subatomic particles have been identified, these may be disregarded in the present discussion, for one is concerned with them only in natural and artificial radioactivity, and consequently they have no bearing upon the subject matter of this treatise.

The neutrons and protons form a closely packed group, called the *nucleus*. Outside the nucleus and relatively very far from it are the electrons. According to the atomic model proposed by the physicist Niels Bohr in 1913, the atom is regarded as a miniature solar system. The nucleus (sun) is at the center, and about it the electrons (planets) revolve in circular and elliptical orbits. The diameter of the nucleus, considered as a sphere, is of the order of 10^{-12} cm, the diameter of the orbits of the electrons is roughly 10^4 times the diameter of the nucleus, while the diameter of the electron itself is estimated to be 2×10^{-13} cm.

Atoms of ordinary matter contain equal numbers of electrons and protons, but most of the mass of the atom is in the nucleus. The masses of a proton and a neutron are nearly equal, and the mass of each is approximately 1,840 times the mass of an electron.

$$\text{Mass of an electron} = 9.11 \times 10^{-31} \text{ kg}$$
$$\text{Mass of a proton} = 1.67 \times 10^{-27} \text{ kg}$$
$$= \text{mass of a neutron (approximately)}$$

Electric Charge. In addition to the negligibly small gravitational forces existing between them due to their masses, electrons and protons in apparently empty space exert forces on each other. Electrons repel electrons, and protons repel protons, but protons and electrons attract each other. To explain these forces, electrons and protons are said to possess electric *charges*. The charge of a proton is designated as positive $(+)$ and the charge of an electron as negative $(-)$, but the choice of

3

signs is arbitrary. If the interaction between charges is to account for the observed forces, it must follow that positive charges repel positive charges, negative charges repel negative charges, while negative and positive charges attract each other.

All electrons have exactly the same charge, and it is the smallest charge that has ever been observed. The electron may therefore be regarded as the ultimate unit of electric charge. In comparison with the *coulomb*, which is the practical unit of charge used in electrical-engineering computations, the charge of an electron is very small indeed, for the coulomb represents a charge which is the equivalent of the sum of the charges of approximately 6.24×10^{18} electrons.

A normal atom of any substance is electrically neutral, for it exhibits no external electrical properties. The internal forces of attraction and repulsion are in equilibrium. Since a normal atom contains electrons and protons in equal numbers, it follows that each proton has a positive charge equal in magnitude to the negative charge of an electron.

Neutral matter in its normal state is composed of atoms. Since all the internal electrical forces are in equilibrium in a body of this kind, it has no excess or deficiency of electrons, and the body is said to be *uncharged*. It is known from physics as well as from personal experience, however, that the electrical equilibrium of a body may be upset as, for example, by rubbing a glass rod with a silk cloth, or a hard-rubber rod with cat's fur. In each case electrons are withdrawn from one body and collected by the other. The body that gains electrons acquires a *negative charge* because it has a surplus of electrons, while the body that loses electrons acquires a *positive charge* since it has less than its normal quota of electrons. The amount of the net charge which a body has is a measure of the total excess or deficiency in the number of its electrons.

Electric Field about a Small Charged Body. If the air space about a charged body A in Fig. 1 is explored with a unit positive test charge q', it is observed that no matter where the charge is placed, it is everywhere acted upon by a force due to its electrical nature. The space about A is called an *electric field*, by which is meant any space in which an electric charge experiences an electric force of this kind.

The force acting on the test charge varies from point to point in either magnitude or direction or both. It also depends upon the quantity of the test charge. To describe the field at any point the term *field intensity* is used. The field intensity ε at any point is defined as the force acting at the point, per unit quantity of the test charge or, symbolically,

$$\varepsilon = \frac{F}{q'} \tag{1-1}$$

Field intensity and force in this equation are both vector quantities.

There is an energy concept of field intensity, however, which is usually far more useful to engineers than the force concept defined above. Referring again to Fig. 1, let F be the force on q' and let q' be moved radially outward in the direction of the force, a small distance dr. As a result of the force acting over the distance dr, work is done on the charge and the *potential energy (dE) gained* by q', per unit quantity of charge, is

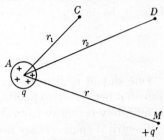

FIG. 1-1. Electric field about an isolated charge.

$$-dE\dagger = F\frac{dr}{q'}$$

But it has already been shown that $\dfrac{F}{q'}$ is the electric field intensity $\mathcal{E}$, so that

$$\mathcal{E}\, dr = -dE$$

or

$$\mathcal{E} = -\frac{dE}{dr} \tag{2-1}$$

$$= -\text{gradient } E \tag{3-1}$$

It appears from this that the field intensity at a point is the *potential gradient* at that point, or it is *the space rate of change of the potential energy per unit of charge*, taken along a given path. If the path of motion is not in the direction of the force, the component of path in the direction of the force ($dr = dl \cos \theta$) must be used.

An electric field is analogous to a gravitational field. In the latter, gravitational mass m replaces q', the gravitational force per unit of mass replaces the electric force per unit of charge, and the field intensity is the gravitational potential gradient, which is directly proportional to the slope of the path.

Potential Difference. The total or absolute potential of a point is the potential energy which a unit charge gains in moving from the edge of the field, where its energy is zero, to the point in question. In Fig. 1 as r approaches infinity the force on q' approaches zero and the gradient $\mathcal{E}$ likewise approaches zero.

If q' is moved from the edge of the field toward A, its potential energy increases from point to point, and the total potential energy it has acquired, per unit of charge, when it reaches M is called the *potential* at M. The potential at M can be found with the help of Eq. (2-1) if the

† The negative sign is used to indicate that the energy gained by q' is negative; that is, energy is lost.

gradient is known as a function of r.† The work is now positive, however, because the test charge is approaching A rather than receding
from it, so

$$dE = \varepsilon\, dr$$

$$E = \int_{\infty}^{r} \varepsilon\, dr$$

One should realize that in this example E is actually the *difference of
potential* between two points, one of which is at M and the other of which
is infinitely far away from A.

Electrical engineers are usually concerned with the potential difference
between two points rather than with the potential of a given point. The
potential difference between the two points C and D in Fig. 1-1, for
example, is

$$E_{CD} = \int_{r_2}^{r_1} \varepsilon\, dr$$

Electric fields are discussed in more detail in Chap. 10.

Electric Lines of Force. As an aid in visualizing an electric field, it
is helpful to represent it by lines, called *electric lines of force*. In the
rationalized meter-kilogram-second system of units [mks (r)] the electric
field due to a charge of Q coulombs is represented by Q dielectric lines of
force—one line for each unit of charge. Consequently, the total number of lines of force (ψ) emanating from a charge of Q coulombs is numerically equal to the charge. The lines are so drawn that everywhere in
the field the direction of a line indicates the *direction*, and the arrowhead
indicates the *sense* along the direction, of the electric force acting on a
positive test charge. In any given medium, the number of lines per
square meter of cross-sectional area taken normal to the flux path is
proportional to the *magnitude* of the force per coulomb of test charge.

---

† The potential at M for the case under discussion is readily evaluated. By
Coulomb's law,

$$F = \frac{qq'}{kr^2}$$

and by Eq. (1-1), $\varepsilon = F/q' = q/kr^2$. Thus $dE = \varepsilon\, dr = (q/kr^2)\, dr$, and the potential
at any point r units of length from A is

$$E = -\frac{1}{k}\int_{\infty}^{r}\frac{q}{r^2}\, dr = \frac{q}{kr}$$

In the rationalized meter-kilogram-second system of units [mks (r)] which is used in
this book, $k = 4\pi\epsilon_r\epsilon_0 = 4\pi\epsilon_r/36\pi \times 10^9 = \epsilon_r/9 \times 10^9$ where

$$\epsilon_0 = 1/36\pi \times 10^9 = 8.854 \times 10^{-12},$$

and ϵ_r is the relative permittivity of the medium in which the dielectric field exists.
($\epsilon_r = 1$ for air or a vacuum.) When q is in coulombs and r is in meters, E in the
last equation above is in volts.

This, by definition, is the magnitude of the *electric intensity* $\mathcal{E}$ or the *voltage gradient* in the direction of the field.   In this manner a complete graphical picture is had which shows the direction, sense, and magnitude of the voltage gradient everywhere in the plane of the field represented.

In Fig. 2-1 are shown (*a*) the outwardly directed radial field about a positive point charge, (*b*) the field in the plane of two equal point charges of opposite sign, (*c*) the field in the plane of two equal point charges of like signs, and (*d*) the field between two oppositely charged metallic plates, in a plane normal to the plates.   In (*a*), (*b*), and (*c*) the gradients are high where the lines are close together and are lower where the lines are farther apart.   In (*d*) the field is *uniform* except for the *fringing* at

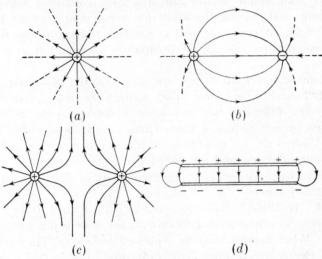

FIG. 2-1. Examples of electric fields.

the outer edges of the plates.   The gradient has the same value at all points between the plates, and the potential rise E from the negative plate to positive plate, with the plates d units of length apart, is

$$E = \int_0^d \mathcal{E} \, dr = \mathcal{E}d$$

Conductors and Insulators.   In a certain class of substances, particularly metals, the outer orbital electrons of an atom appear to be loosely bound to the atom.   One or more of them may become detached from an atom and roam about with random motion.   These are called *free electrons,* and materials which contain large numbers of free electrons are called *conductors.*   The free electrons, which conductors contain in great abundance, may be given a directed motion by establishing an electric field within the conductor, thereby producing an *electric current.*

Most metals and some nonmetals are conductors, but materials generally vary widely in their conducting properties. They may be good conductors, moderately good conductors, or poor conductors, or they may be almost completely nonconducting. Copper, aluminum, and to some extent steel are the conducting materials of which most conductors used in engineering practice are made. Silver is an excellent conductor, but it is too costly to find more than very limited application.

Among the poorer conductors are cast iron, carbon, tungsten, and platinum and a number of metallic alloys. These materials appear to *resist* the movement of electrons; for a given cross-sectional area, higher gradients are required to maintain a given current, and more heat is developed than would be the case if a good conductor material like copper were used, having the same dimensions and carrying the same current. Such materials are used as *resistors*, to convert electric energy to heat, to consume voltage, or to produce illumination as in a lamp filament.

The atoms of many substances are so constituted that their electrons are tightly bound to the atom. They contain few, if any, free electrons, and it is very difficult if not impossible to detach an electron from an atom, even by establishing a very strong electric field within the substance. Under ordinary conditions such materials are more or less completely nonconducting and are called *insulators*.[1] Insulators comprise such substances as rubber, glass, porcelain, wax, shellac, refined mineral oils, and many others.

Current. If a light bulb is connected by copper wires to the terminals of a battery, a current is said to exist in the connecting wires and the filament. What happens may be explained as follows: The battery is a source of electromotive force (emf). It sets up a potential difference between the terminals of the circuit and establishes an axially directed electric field within the wire and the filament, the sense of which is from positive to negative terminal. Both wire and filament contain vast quantities of free electrons. In the presence of the electric field the free electrons are accelerated toward the positive terminal of the battery, but they move only short distances before they collide with other particles of the substance and are slowed down. The accelerating force due to the field has not been diminished, however, so the electrons are again accelerated.[2] In this way the free electrons throughout the copper wires and

---

[1] The insulating properties of an insulator may be destroyed by subjecting it to potential gradients high enough to break it down or "puncture" it. In practice insulators are normally not subjected to gradients high enough to destroy them.

[2] The parts of the atom containing the nuclei and the attached electrons are positively charged and are accelerated toward the negative terminal of the battery. But these are very heavy bodies compared with the free electrons. The velocities which they attain as a result of the action of the electric field are relatively so small that the resultant directed motions of these bodies may be disregarded.

the filament move forward at some average velocity v, each carrying one electron unit of charge q. If there are n free electrons per unit volume of the wire and a is the cross-sectional area, taken normal to the axis, the quantity of electricity (charge) dq which passes over the area in time dt is

$$dq = nav\,dt$$

The time rate of transferring quantity of electricity across the area is called the *current i* or

$$i = \frac{dq}{dt} = nav \qquad \text{electron units of charge/sec}$$

The electric current in a conductor is analogous to a current of water flowing in a pipe. The one is the time rate of transferring a quantity of electricity over the cross-sectional area of a conductor, while the other is the time rate of transferring a quantity of water over the cross-sectional area of a pipe.

Direction of Current. It has been noted that in the external circuit connected to a battery, electrons move *away from the negative terminal and toward the positive terminal*. But long before electrons were known to exist, the *direction of flow* of a current was arbitrarily assumed to be from the positive terminal toward the negative terminal in the external circuit. This has long been and still is the *accepted direction of current flow*. Hence electrons move in a direction opposite to the conventional positive direction of current flow. Fortunately, this anomalous situation causes very little inconvenience.

A stream of electrons that flows always in a given direction comprises

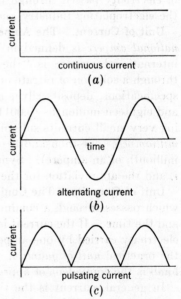

FIG. 3-1. Electric currents.

what is called a *direct current*, and a direct current that does not vary is said to be *continuous*. The direct current supplied by a storage battery is continuous; that supplied by a direct-current generator is also continuous except for a very slight ripple, which, in power applications, is usually of no practical consequence. The current supplied by a rectifier is *pulsating*, while that supplied by an alternating-current generator is *alternating*. These forms of current are illustrated in Fig. 3-1.

The presence of an electric current in a circuit may be detected, and the current may be measured, by a number of different methods. Each method is based upon some *effect* which the current produces under given conditions. One of these effects is called *electrolytic dissociation*. Other effects will be mentioned and discussed in some detail in later chapters.

The properties of most conducting liquids are such that, when a direct current is maintained in them, the constituent elements of the liquid are

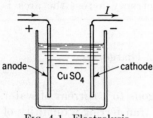

FIG. 4-1. Electrolysis.

separated. If two copper plates (Fig. 4-1) are dipped in a solution of copper sulfate and a direct current is maintained in the liquid, entering at one plate, the *anode*, and leaving at the other, the *cathode*, metallic copper leaves the solution and is deposited on the cathode. Experiment shows that the amount of metal deposited in a given time is proportional to the total quantity of electricity passed through the solution. This principle is the basis of the electroplating industry and is used in the refining of copper.

Unit of Current. The Ampere. The unit of current called the *international ampere* is defined in terms of the effect just described. The international ampere is "the unvarying current which, when passed through a solution of nitrate of silver in water, according to the standard specifications, deposits silver at the rate of one thousand one hundred and eighteen millionths (0.001118) of a gram per second." For measuring very small currents submultiples are often used. These include the *milliampere* (one-thousandth of an ampere) and the *microampere* (one-millionth of an ampere). Symbols used to represent currents are I and i, and the abbreviation for the unit is *amp*.

Unit of Quantity. The Coulomb. The *quantity* of electricity (Q or q) which passes through a conductor is the product of the average current and the time. If the current is unvarying or continuous, the quantity of electricity carried by one ampere in one second is one *coulomb*. This is the practical *unit of quantity*. It has already been stated that the coulomb is the equivalent of approximately 6.24×10^{18} electron charges.

In general, current is the time rate at which quantity of electricity passes along a conductor. If current is in amperes and quantity is in coulombs,

$$i = \frac{dq}{dt} \quad \text{amp} \qquad (4\text{-}1)$$

The quantity passing in dt sec is

$$dq = i\, dt$$

and the total quantity that passes in t sec is

$$Q = \int_0^t i \, dt \qquad \text{coulombs} \qquad (5\text{-}1)$$

Electromotive Force and Resistance.   An *electromotive force* (emf) is that which causes or tends to cause the free electrons in matter to move or be displaced.   Since electrons in motion constitute a current, one may equally well define an emf as that which causes or tends to cause a current to flow.   The electromotive force of a battery or a generator is roughly analogous to the "pressure head" of a centrifugal pump.

Experience with the flow of water in pipes shows that the current which the pipe discharges depends directly upon the pressure head.   It also depends upon the size (area), length, and condition of the interior of the pipe, for the pipe *resists* the flow of water through it.   When subjected to a given pressure head, a small pipe passes less water per second than a large one, a rough one less than a smooth one, a long one less than a short one.   The *resistance* of a pipe depends upon various factors of length, area of cross section, and roughness of the interior.   The *current* which the pipe discharges (in cubic feet per second) *is a function of the head and is inversely proportional to the resistance.*

In a general way, the flow of electric current in wires and other conductors obeys the same law as the flow of water in pipes.   The current that flows in a conductor is directly proportional to the electromotive force (or *voltage*) impressed upon the circuit.   It also depends upon the cross section, length, and kind of conductor.   The conductor is said to *resist* the flow of current through it, and the resistance of a conductor to the flow of electric current, similar to the resistance of a pipe to the flow of water, depends upon the length, the cross-sectional area, and the nature of the conductor material.   For a given impressed voltage, the current in a circuit is small when the resistance is large, and large when the resistance is small.

Ohm's Law.   It has been established experimentally that the analogy pictured above holds true and that, in an electric circuit, *the current is directly proportional to the impressed electromotive force, and inversely proportional to the resistance.*   This statement of fact is called Ohm's law. Briefly, the law states that

$$\text{Current} = \frac{\text{electromotive force}}{\text{resistance}}$$

or

$$I = \frac{E}{R} \qquad (6\text{-}1)$$

where I = current

E = impressed emf

R = resistance of circuit

Equation (6-1) may be put in the alternate forms

$$E = RI \tag{7-1}$$

$$R = \frac{E}{I} \tag{8-1}$$

Equation (6-1) is convenient to use for finding the current in a circuit of known resistance and impressed emf. Equation (7-1) expresses the potential drop due to a known current in a resistance of known value, while Eq. (8-1) is used to find the resistance of a circuit from the measured values of emf impressed across the terminals and the current in the circuit.

These equations apply to any part of a circuit in which the current is everywhere the same, as well as to the circuit as a whole. When they are applied to a part of a circuit, E is the *potential difference* between the ends of the part considered, R is the resistance of the part, and I is the current in it. (It is assumed that the part in question contains no emf.)

The application of Ohm's law to circuits of various kinds is discussed in Chap. 3.

Unit of Resistance. The Ohm. The unit of resistance is called the *ohm*. The *international ohm* is the resistance, at 0 C, offered by a column of mercury of constant cross-sectional area, 106.3 cm long, and weighing 14.4521 g. A secondary resistance standard, called the *Annealed Copper Standard*, is also used to define the ohm. In terms of this standard, the ohm is 58 times the resistance, at 20 C, of one meter length of standard annealed copper wire, having a uniform cross section of one square millimeter.

Commonly used symbols of resistance are R and r. Multiples and submultiples of the ohm are used to measure very large and very small resistances, respectively. The *megohm* is a million ohms, and the *microhm* is one-millionth of an ohm.

Fortunately, the resistances of materials vary over a very wide range. The resistance of a foot of No. 16 lamp cord is about 0.004 ohm; the resistance of a 60-watt, 110-volt lamp filament is about 200 ohms; the resistance of the insulation separating the windings of a motor from the frame (a small fraction of an inch thick) is several megohms. The resistance of a good insulating material is of the order 10^{20} times as large as that of copper.

Unit of Emf. The Volt. With the help of Ohm's law and the definitions of the ampere and the ohm, the unit of electromotive force may readily be defined as follows: The unit of emf, called the *international volt*, is that emf which causes one ampere of current to flow when it is impressed on a circuit having one ohm of resistance. In practice it is usually more convenient to secure the measure of a volt from the emf of a standard cell. The Weston standard cell was adopted by the U.S. Bureau of Standards in 1911 as the standard for the United States, and the 1,000/1,018.3 part of its emf at 20 C is taken as the measure of one international volt.

In addition to the volt, the multiples and submultiples are often used. Voltages above 1,000 are usually expressed in *kilovolts* (kv). Alternating-current generators, for example, operate at rated terminal voltages of 6.6 and 13.2 kv; electric power is transmitted over long distances at voltages ranging from 110 to 330 kv. Very small potential differences are expressed in *millivolts* (mv) or *microvolts* (μv). The potential difference impressed across the terminals of the moving elements of common types of ammeters and voltmeters, for example, is 50 mv at full-scale reading. House lighting circuits operate nominally at 120 volts, electric trolley busses are driven by 600-volt motors, automobile batteries develop an emf of 6 volts, etc.

Symbols commonly used to designate emf, voltage, and potential difference are E, e, V, and v.

Systems of Units. A number of systems of electrical units have been used, but a comprehensive discussion of these is beyond the scope of this book. A brief summary of the principal systems appears in the following paragraphs. (See also Appendix E.) For more complete information the student is referred to one of the standard electrical handbooks.

Electrostatic and Electromagnetic Units. The two systems of units from which most others are derived are the centimeter-gram-second (cgs) *electrostatic units* (esu) and the cgs *electromagnetic units* (emu). These were developed from the fundamental laws of electricity and magnetism relating the various electrical, magnetic, and mechanical quantities involved, and from the assumption that empty space has unit permittivity ($\epsilon_0 = 1$) and unit permeability ($\mu_0 = 1$). (The terms permittivity and permeability are defined in later chapters where they naturally arise in the discussion of related subject matter.)

Practical Units. The cgs electrostatic and absolute electromagnetic units are very useful in discussions involving theoretical analysis, but they are of inconvenient size for making most engineering measurements. To remedy this situation, the so-called "practical" system of units was devised. In this system each unit is derived from the corresponding unit of the absolute electromagnetic system by multiplying the latter by some appropriate power of 10. The units of current, resistance, and emf in the three systems are related as shown in Table I.

International Units. The units of current, resistance, and electromotive force, called the international ampere, ohm, and volt, respectively,

TABLE I. SYSTEMS OF ELECTRICAL UNITS

Unit	Practical	Cgs electromagnetic (absolute)	Cgs electrostatic
Emf.............	Volt	Abvolt = 10^{-8} volt	Statvolt = 300 volts
Current..........	Ampere	Abampere = 10 amp	Statampere = 3.33×10^{-10} amp
Resistance.......	Ohm	Abohm = 10^{-9} ohm	Statohm = 9×10^{11} ohms

have already been defined. It was intended that these and the other units to be derived from them should be, as nearly as possible, equal to the corresponding practical units. It was found, however, that they differ from the practical units by approximately 0.03 to 0.005 percentage point. Accordingly, the practical units, which are based on the cgs electromagnetic units, are substantially, but not exactly, the same as the international units.

Meter-kilogram-second Units. In 1935 the International Technical Commission adopted still another set of units called the meter-kilogram-second (mks) units. This system is based on the absolute electromagnetic units, but employs the meter and the kilogram as the units of length and mass, respectively, instead of the centimeter and the gram. It also introduces a new unit of force called the *newton*, which is equivalent to 10^5 dynes or 0.225 pound. A newton is the force required to give a mass of one kilogram an acceleration of one meter per second per second.

Many of the units in the mks system are substantially the same as the corresponding units in the practical system, although they may be defined differently. These include the ampere, ohm, volt, coulomb, joule, watt, farad, and henry. Others differ from the practical units by various powers of 10.

Rationalized Mks Units. The concepts concerning the electric field were originally developed from a consideration of the field about a point charge in air, the permittivity of which was taken to be unity ($\epsilon_0 = 1$). At a fixed distance from a point charge q the magnitude of the force due to q, acting on another point charge q', is everywhere the same. This suggests the use of a sphere with q at the center, to describe the surface over which the force on q' is constant, thereby introducing the factor 4π into a number of fundamental equations dealing with electrostatics.

The magnetic field about a point magnet pole in air was studied in similar fashion, the permeability of empty space being assumed equal to unity ($\mu_0 = 1$), with the result that a number of the important equations pertaining to the magnetic circuit also contain 4π as a factor.

The process of rationalizing the mks system consists in assigning to the constants ϵ_0 and μ_0, the permittivity and the permeability, respectively, of empty space, values which include the factor 4π and which result in the elimination of the 4π from a number of the more important equations in which it formerly appeared. Some further discussion of this matter appears in later chapters.

The rationalized mks (r) system of units is used throughout this book, except where specifically noted to the contrary.

Problems

1-1. The heating element of an electric range draws 5.2 amp when the impressed potential difference is 120 volts. What is the resistance in ohms of the heating element?

2-1. What voltage is required to maintain a current of 12 amp in a resistance of 30 ohms?

3-1. The winding element of an electric meter, the resistance of which is 4.2 ohms, is designed to carry a current of 0.01 amp at full-scale deflection. The deflection of the needle is directly proportional to the current. What is the voltage drop in the meter winding when the meter indicates one-half full-scale deflection? Express the result in (a) volts, (b) millivolts.

4-1. The insulation resistance of a motor winding (between conductors and machine frame) is 40 megohms. Express the resistance in ohms and microhms.

5-1. A 100-watt 120-volt incandescent lamp has a resistance of 144 ohms at working temperature. What current does the lamp draw from the mains when 120 volts are impressed on its terminals? Express the result in amperes, milliamperes, and microamperes.

6-1. How many coulombs of electricity pass through the lamp filament in Prob. 5-1 in 1 hr of normal use?

7-1. An electron ($q = 1.6 \times 10^{-19}$ coulomb) leaves the cathode (negative electrode) of a vacuum tube at almost zero velocity and is attracted to the plate (positive electrode) by a plate potential of $+250$ volts with respect to the cathode. If the mass of the electron is 9.1×10^{-31} kg, (a) at what velocity does the electron strike the plate? (b) How long does it take the electron to pass from cathode to plate if the separation is 4 mm and the electric field intensity is uniform throughout that distance?

CHAPTER 2

RESISTANCE AND CONDUCTANCE

Resistivity. The electrical resistance of a conductor, similar to the hydraulic resistance of a pipe, as has been pointed out, varies directly with the length and inversely with the cross-sectional area. This relation is expressed by the equation

$$R = \frac{\rho l}{A} \tag{1-2}$$

where l = length of conductor in direction of current

A = area of conductor normal to direction of current

ρ = constant

The constant ρ depends upon the chemical and physical properties and the temperature of the conductor material, and upon the units in which l and A are expressed. It is called the *resistivity* or *specific resistance* of the conductor material.

Equation (1-2) shows that a conductor one unit long and of unit cross sectional area has a resistance equal to the resistivity of the material. It is assumed that the current is uniformly distributed over the cross section, that the length l is measured parallel to the direction of the current flow, and that the area A is taken normal to the direction of the current. Thus, the resistivity of a homogeneous material is the resistance measured between the ends of a sample of the material of unit cross section and unit length. Resistivities are measured in ohm-centimeters, ohm-meters, microhm-millimeters, ohms circular mil per foot,† etc. Values of the resistivities of some of the more commonly used metals and alloys are given in Appendix A.

When the resistivity of a conductor material is known, the total resistance of a conductor made of this material may readily be computed from its dimensions.

---

† Custom has established use of the expression "ohms per circular mil-foot" although the expression is dimensionally incorrect. Nevertheless, for the sake of uniformity, this expression is used hereafter in this book.

Example 1. The resistivity of copper is approximately 0.68×10^{-6} ohm-in. at 20° C. Find the resistance of 1 mile of No. 10 (American wire gage) copper wire. The diameter of No. 10 wire is 0.102 in.

By Eq. (1-2),

$$R = \frac{\rho l}{A} = \frac{0.68 \times 10^{-6} \times 5,280 \times 12}{(3.1416 \div 4)0.102^2} = 5.28 \text{ ohms}$$

Square Mil and Circular Mil. A mil is one-thousandth of an inch. A *square mil* is a unit of area equal to the area of a square with sides one mil long. A *circular mil* is a unit of area equal to the area of a circle one mil in diameter. Thus the mil circle is a circle inscribed in a mil square, as in Fig. 1-2. From this it follows that the *size* of a circular mil is $\pi/4$ times the size of a square mil, while in a given area the *number* of circular mils is $4/\pi$ times the number of square mils.

Fɪɢ. 1-2. Square and circular mils.

Rectangular areas are most conveniently computed in square measure, by taking the product of two adjacent sides. Circular areas, however, are more easily calculated in terms of circular units. For example, the sectional area of a round wire d mils in diameter is

$$\text{Square-mils area} = \frac{\pi d^2}{4}$$

while the number of circular mils in the same area is

$$\text{Circular mils} = \frac{4}{\pi} \times \text{square-mils area} = d^2 \qquad (2\text{-}2)$$

Thus the sectional area of a cylindrical solid, expressed in circular mils, is equal to the square of the diameter in mils. Because of its convenience in computing the areas of round wires, the circular mil has come to be a standard unit of area for conductors of all shapes.

Example 2. (*a*) A certain wire has a diameter of 128 mils (0.128 in.). Find its area of section in circular mils and in square mils. (*b*) The cross section of a conductor is a rectangle 0.032 by 0.125 in. Find its area in square mils and in circular mils.

(*a*) Circular mils $= 128^2 = 16,400$

Square mils $= \frac{\pi}{4} \times 16,400 = 12,880$

(*b*) Square mils $= 32 \times 125 = 4,000$

Circular mils $= \frac{4}{\pi} \times 4,000 = 5,093$

Circular Mil-foot. The circular mil-foot, or simply the *mil-foot*, is a cylinder one mil in diameter and one foot long (Fig. 2-2) It is commonly used as the unit of volume in which resistivities are expressed, as in column 3 of Appendix A. In mil-foot units the resistivity of a given material is the resistance measured between the ends of a cylinder of the material that is one mil in diameter and one foot long. This unit has the same advantage as the circular mil for use in computations involving round wires.

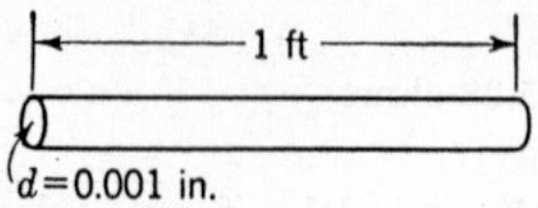

FIG. 2-2. Circular mil-foot.

Example 3. What is the resistance per mile of a round copper wire with a diameter of 102 mils? The resistivity of copper at the assumed temperature is 10.37 ohms/mil-ft.

The resistance of a copper wire 1 mil in diameter and 1 mile long is $10.37 \times 5{,}280$ ohms. The resistance of a wire of the same length but having an area 102^2 times as large is

$$R = \frac{\rho l}{A} = \frac{10.37 \times 5{,}280}{102^2} = 5.26 \text{ ohms}$$

Conductance.   Resistance and conductance are reciprocal terms. The former measures the *opposition* which a circuit offers to the flow of current, while the latter measures the *inducement* which the circuit offers. A good conductor has a high conductance and a low resistance, while a poor conductor has a low conductance and a high resistance. The conductance of a circuit is directly proportional to the area of the conductor and inversely proportional to the length. Like resistance, it also depends upon the chemical and physical properties and the temperature of the conductor material and upon the variation of current density.

If the conductance of a circuit be represented by G and its resistance be represented by R, one may write

$$G = \frac{1}{R} = \frac{A}{\rho l} = \frac{\gamma A}{l} \tag{3-2}$$

where $\gamma = 1/\rho$ is the *conductivity* of the conductor material at a given temperature. The practical unit of conductance is the reciprocal ohm or *mho*.

Example 4. What is the conductance per mile of No. 0 aluminum wire at 20 C? (The diameter of No. 0 wire is approximately 0.325 in.)

From Appendix A the resistivity of aluminum is found to be 17 ohms/mil-ft at 20 C. The cross section of the wire is

$$A = d^2 = 325^2 = 105{,}600 \text{ cir mils}$$

From Eq. (3-2) the conductance of a mile of this wire is found to be

$$G = \frac{105{,}600}{17 \times 5{,}280} = 1.176 \text{ mhos}$$

Conductivity.   The electrical *conductivity* of a material is the conductance, measured between the ends, of a sample of the material which is one unit long and has unit cross-sectional area. It is the reciprocal of resistivity and is represented by the constant γ of Eq. (3-2). Conductivities are expressed in mhos per centimeter, mhos per inch, mhos per meter, etc.

The Annealed Copper Standard is the standard of conductivity of the metals used in metallic conductors. This standard was selected as a result of measurements made by the U.S. Bureau of Standards on commercial wire. At a temperature of 20 C the resistance of a standard annealed copper wire of uniform section, with a sectional area of 1 sq mm and a length of 1 m, is $\frac{1}{58}$ or 0.01724 ohm. This corresponds to a resistance of 10.37 ohms/cir mil-ft at 20 C.

The conductivities of metals are usually expressed in percentage of the Annealed Copper Standard, as illustrated in the following example. The conductivity of commercial hard-drawn copper wire is about 97.3 per cent, while that of aluminum is about 61 per cent.

Example 5. A 1,000,000-cir-mil aluminum cable has a resistance of 0.0177 ohm per 1,000 ft at 25 C. (*a*) What is the conductance of 1,000 ft of this cable? (*b*) What is the percentage conductivity of the material?

(*a*) The conductance of the cable is

$$G = \frac{1}{R} = \frac{1}{0.0177} = 56.5 \text{ mhos}$$

(*b*) Its resistance is

$$R = \frac{\rho l}{A} = 0.0177 \text{ ohm}$$

and

$$\rho = \frac{0.0177 \times 10^6}{1,000} = 17.7 \text{ ohms/mil-ft}$$

In terms of the Annealed Copper Standard the percentage conductivity is 100 times the reciprocal of the resistivity multiplied by the resistivity of copper. The resistivity of copper at 25 C is 10.57. Hence

$$\gamma = \frac{100 \times 10.57}{17.7} = 59.7 \text{ per cent}$$

Variation of Resistance with Temperature. Experiment shows that over ordinary temperature ranges the resistance of a pure metal varies directly with the temperature, as illustrated in Fig. 3-2 for the case of copper. Over a considerable range the metal behaves as though its resistance would be reduced to zero when the temperature reached −234.5 C. Since the usual range of interest runs from perhaps 20 C to a few hundred degrees above zero, a straight-line law of variation may be assumed for the usual condition. It is apparent from Fig. 3-2 that the rule of similar triangles may be applied to find the resistance R_2 of a conductor at any temperature t_2, if the resistance R_1 at some other temperature t_1, and the temperature intercept T_0 of the conductor material are known. (For copper $T_0 = +234.5$ C.) From similar triangles,

$$\frac{R_2}{R_1} = \frac{T_0 + t_2}{T_0 + t_1}$$

$$R_2 = \frac{R_1(T_0 + t_2)}{T_0 + t_1} \tag{4-2}$$

Quantities such as $(T_0 + t_1)$ and $(T_0 + t_2)$ may be called the "apparent absolute temperature" corresponding to the temperatures t_1 and t_2 on the centigrade scale. In terms of this definition, it may be said that the resistance of a given conductor is directly proportional to the apparent absolute temperature.

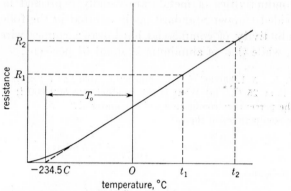

FIG. 3-2. Variation of resistance with temperature.

The temperature intercept T_0 of most pure metals is nearly the same as that of copper. The temperature intercept of aluminum, for example, is 227.5 C.†

Example 6. The resistance of 1,500 ft of No. 12 copper wire at 25 C is 2.43 ohms. Calculate the resistance of the wire when its temperature is 75 C. By Eq. (4-2),

$$R_{75} = R_{25} \frac{234.5 + 75}{234.5 + 25} = 2.43 \times 1.193 = 2.9 \text{ ohms}$$

Temperature Coefficient of Resistance. The resistance-temperature relationship of a given conductor is often expressed in another fashion. If the slope of the straight-line portion of the curve in Fig. 3-2 is designated as m, then from analytic geometry, the equation may be written

$$R_2 = R_1 + m(t_2 - t_1)$$

But

$$m = \frac{R_1}{T_0 + t_1}$$

† Certain alloys such as constantan, a copper-nickel alloy, have relatively flat resistance-temperature curves at ordinary temperatures. Extrapolating the straight-line portion of the curve for constantan results in a temperature intercept of 199,980 C. Nonmetallic conductors do not, in general, have straight-line resistance-temperature relationships. Carbon, for example, exhibits the property of decreasing resistance with increasing temperature.

and therefore

$$R_2 = R_1 + \frac{R_1}{T_0 + t_1}(t_2 - t_1)$$

$$= R_1\left[1 + \frac{1}{T_0 + t_1}(t_2 - t_1)\right]$$

The fraction $1/(T_0 + t_1)$ is usually designated α_1 and is called the *temperature coefficient of resistance*. Thus

$$\alpha_1 = \frac{1}{T_0 + t_1} \tag{5-2}$$

and

$$R_2 = R_1[1 + \alpha_1(t_2 - t_1)] \tag{6-2}$$

Values of the temperature coefficient of resistance for various conductor materials are available in electrical handbooks, and a number are found in Appendix B of this book.

It is important to note that the value of α_1 which appears in Eq. (6-2) must correspond to the temperature t_1 for which the resistance R_1 is known. For example, if R_{20} is the known resistance of a given copper conductor at a temperature of t_{20} (20 C),

$$\alpha_{20} = \frac{1}{234.5 + 20} \text{ or } 0.00393$$

and the resistance R_t of the conductor at any other temperature t is

$$R_t = R_{20}[1 + 0.00393(t - 20)]$$

Example 7. The resistance of 1 mile of aluminum cable used on a transmission line is 0.26 ohm at 20 C. What is the resistance per mile of cable on a hot summer day when the operating temperature of the cable is 110 F? (α_{20} for aluminum is given as 0.00403.)

$$110 \text{ F} = \frac{5(110 - 32)}{9} = 43.3 \text{ C}$$
$$R_t = 0.26[1 + 0.00403(43.3 - 20)] = 0.285 \text{ ohm}$$

If a value of α_a is available, based on a temperature t_a, and it is desired to determine a resistance change based upon the known resistance R_b at some other temperature t_b, one may apply Eq. (5-2) to determine T_0, and subsequently compute the resistance at any desired temperature by applying Eq. (4-2).

Example 8. The resistance of a certain brass specimen is found to be 0.012 ohm when measured at 15 C. α_{20} for brass is known to be 0.0017. What is the resistance of the specimen at 0 C?

$$0.0017 = \frac{1}{T_0 + 20}$$

$$T_0 = 568 \text{ C}$$

$$R_0 = 0.012 \frac{(568 + 0)}{(568 + 15)}$$

$$= 0.012 \times 0.974$$

$$= 0.0117 \text{ ohm}$$

Metallic Conductors.　The important characteristics of good metallic conductors are
1. High electrical conductivity
2. High tensile strength
3. Low density (light weight)
4. Low cost

The metals that possess these qualities to a sufficient degree to make their use economical in the generation, transmission, and utilization of electrical power are copper, aluminum, iron, steel, and certain combinations of these metals, such as copper-clad steel and steel-reinforced aluminum.

Copper wires are used extensively for the conductors of transmission lines, distribution circuits, bus bars, etc.　Copper is used almost exclusively for the windings of electrical generators, motors, transformers, and similar apparatus, and, in general, on all circuits requiring insulation-covered wires.　It is cheaper to insulate copper wire than it is to insulate either aluminum or steel wire, because copper has a higher conductivity than either aluminum or steel and so requires less insulation for a given conductance.　Hard-drawn or medium-hard-drawn copper wires, having a conductivity of about 97.3 per cent, are generally used for transmission and distribution conductors in preference to annealed copper, because of their greater tensile strength.　Tables showing the resistances of copper and aluminum wires and of concentric-lay copper cables are found in Appendixes B and C.

Commercial aluminum has a conductivity of about 61 per cent and a density of about 30 per cent that of hard-drawn copper.　Accordingly, for the same weight, an aluminum conductor of given length has about twice the conductance of the corresponding copper conductor.　On the basis of equal costs for equal conductances, aluminum should sell for about twice the price of copper, but in practice it usually sells for somewhat less than this.　Aluminum wires and cables are now used extensively as conductors for transmission lines.　In this application the larger size of the aluminum cable is often an advantage from the electrical standpoint, although a disadvantage in other respects.　Aluminum bars are sometimes used for bus bars.　Here the larger size is again advantageous, because it facilitates heat dissipation.

The electrical conductivities of soft iron and steel vary from perhaps 10 to 15 per cent that of copper. Steel is about 88 per cent as heavy, but its tensile strength may be as much as eight times as great as that of copper. Both its conductivity and its strength vary over considerable ranges, depending on its chemical and physical properties.

The principal advantages of steel are its cheapness and its strength. It is seldom used as a conductor in power lines, except as a core for aluminum or copper conductors, where its purpose is to furnish added strength. Steel cables are sometimes used as electrical conductors in power circuits where water crossings requiring extra long spans are encountered. Steel cables 2 in. in diameter are used by the city of Tacoma, Wash., in a 6,100-ft span across an arm of Puget Sound. Some additional information on the uses of various kinds of conductors for distribution of power is found in Chap. 31.

Resistance of Cables. Cables are made of varying numbers of small wires twisted together. This gives them a flexibility that solid wires of equal conducting areas do not have. Because the strands are spirally wound to form the cable, the current flowing in a cable follows a spiral path somewhat longer than the cable itself. For this reason the resistance of a cable is slightly larger than that of a cylindrical rod of the same sectional area. Allowance is made for this difference by adding 2 per cent to the resistance of the equivalent solid rod.

Wire and Cable Sizes.[1] In American practice, wire sizes are designated by gage numbers of the American wire gage (A.w.g.), formerly Brown and Sharpe, abbreviated B. & S. Wire sizes run from 1 to 40. There are four sizes larger than No. 1. Beginning with the largest, these are designated as No. 0000, No. 000, No. 00, and No. 0. To give the gage numbers significance, it is convenient to remember that, roughly, No. 10 copper wire has a diameter of 0.10 in., an area of 10,000 cir mils, and a resistance of 1 ohm per 1,000 ft at 20 C. Larger gage numbers, such as 15 and 20, refer to smaller wires, while smaller numbers, such as 2 and 4, refer to larger wires. The circular-mil cross-sectional areas are approximately doubled at intervals of three in the number scale. Thus No. 13 wire has about half the area of No. 10, while No. 7 has about twice the area of No. 10.

Cables are not designated by numbers as are the solid wires but are described by giving their areas of section in circular mils. The smaller cables are designed to have the same sectional areas as the larger sizes of

[1] A table giving the resistance and other pertinent data for copper and aluminum wires of size 0000 and smaller is found in Appendix B. Appendix C contains similar data for concentric-lay copper cables. The allowable current-carrying capacities of cables and wires with various types of insulation, as recommended by the National Electric Code, are given in Appendix D.

solid wires. A 211,600-cir-mil cable has the same area of section as a 0000 wire, etc.

Resistors, Rheostats, and Heaters. The resistance of a circuit opposes the flow of current. Current is maintained in the circuit against this opposition by means of the impressed emf. A part or all of the latter, depending upon the nature of the circuit, is used up in overcoming the voltage drop RI in the resistance. This relation is expressed by Ohm's law, as

$$E = RI$$

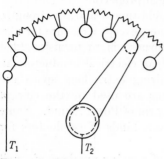

FIG. 4-2. Wiring diagram of a rheostat.

Furthermore, whenever current flows in a resistance, heat energy is liberated. Accordingly, potential drop accompanied by the liberation of heat energy is always associated with a current in a resistance.

When wires or cables are used to transmit electrical energy from one place to another, conductors of low resistance are used in order to minimize these effects, for heat loss and voltage drop then serve no useful purpose and are undesirable. The heat energy liberated is wasted.

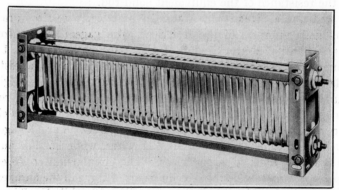

FIG. 5-2. Oven heater. (*Westinghouse Electric Corporation.*)

Often, however, it is desirable (1) to control, limit, or adjust the amount of current in a circuit, or (2) to transform electrical energy into heat energy. In either case conductors of relatively high resistance are used to bring about the desired result.

A resistance used for the purpose described in (1) above is called a *rheostat* or simply a *resistor*. Rheostats are often so constructed that the resistance in the circuit may be varied by turning a lever or knob. Some forms of rheostats and resistors are illustrated in Figs. 4-2 to 7-2. Rheostats are used in radios to adjust the strength of current in the tubes, in the field circuits of motors and generators to adjust the field current, in motors to limit the starting current, etc.

When a resistance is designed and used especially to convert electrical energy to heat energy, the resistor becomes a *heater*. There are a great many applications of domestic and industrial heating. Electric water heaters, electric stoves, and electric space heaters (air heaters) are familiar pieces of equipment. Baking and enameling ovens, heat-treating ovens, and smelting furnaces are forms of equipment in which industrial heating is applied.

Fig. 6-2. Immersion water heater. (*General Electric Company.*)

Resistance Materials. Copper and aluminum have low resistivities and are not suitable materials for rheostats and heaters. The resistivities of iron and steel vary from six to about twelve times that of copper, depending upon hardness and chemical composition. Cast iron is sometimes used for large control resistances, but iron and steel in general are not suitable resistance materials for use at high temperatures because they oxidize too readily. Wires made of alloys of copper and nickel, nickel and chromium, nickel and steel, etc., are generally used where resistance wires are required. Nickel chromium (nichrome) combines high resistivity with noncorrosive properties, which makes it a highly useful resistance material. The approxi-

Fig. 7-2. Resistance units. (*General Electric Company.*)

mate resistivities of some of the more common metallic resistance materials are found in Appendix A.

For extra-high-temperature work, metallic resistors are not suitable. Nonmetallic resistor units have been developed that may be satisfactorily operated up to temperatures of 2500 F. These elements do not corrode and are said to be unaffected by liquids and gases.

Problems

1-2. The table of Appendix B gives the resistances of standard copper and aluminum wires at 25 C. What is the resistance of (a) 1,200 ft of No. 10 copper wire, (b) 10 ft of No. 00 aluminum wire?

2-2. The diameter of No. 0000 wire is 460 mils. Solid copper wire of this size weighs 641 lb per 1,000 ft, while 1,000 ft of aluminum wire of the same cross section weighs 195 lb. Compute the weight in pounds per cubic foot of copper and aluminum.

3-2. (a) Check the answer to Prob. 1-2 by using Eq. (1-2) and ρ_{25} = 10.6 ohms/cir mil-ft. (b) From Appendix B find the ratio of the resistance per unit length of No. 10 copper wire to that of No. 7 copper wire. What is the percentage error made by applying the statement of page 23 to this case?

4-2. The resistivity of standard annealed copper is 10.37 ohms/cir mil-ft at 20 C. What is the resistivity of this material at 20 C (a) in microhm-centimeters, (b) in microhm-inch units?

5-2. The temperature coefficient of resistance of annealed copper at 20 C is 0.00393, while the resistivity of the material is 10.37 ohms/mil-ft. What is the resistivity in ohms circular mil per foot of hard-drawn copper (97.3 per cent conductivity) at a temperature of 50 C?

6-2. From a comparison of the resistances per 1,000 ft of copper and aluminum wires of a given cross section (Appendix B) compute the percentage conductivity of aluminum.

7-2. Compute the cross-sectional area of a round wire having a diameter of 0.325 in. Give results in (a) square mils, (b) circular mils.

8-2. A nichrome ribbon is 0.125 in. wide and 0.015 in. thick. Compute the cross-sectional area in (a) square mils, (b) circular mils.

9-2. The resistance of standard annealed copper is 10.37 ohms/cir mil-ft at 20 C. (a) What is the resistance at 50 C of a copper bus bar 4 in. wide by ⅜ in. thick and 20 ft long? (b) What is the conductance of the bus bar? (c) What is the width of an aluminum bus bar that is ½ in. thick and has the same length and the same total conductance as the copper bar?

10-2. A cylindrical, hollow copper tube has an outside diameter of 1.09 in. and an inside diameter of 0.83 in. What is the area (a) in circular mils? (b) in square mils?

11-2. How many feet long is a piece of the nichrome ribbon specified in Prob. 8-2, the resistance of which is 4 ohms? (Consult the table in Appendix A.)

12-2. Compute the percentage conductivity of nichrome, silver, and tungsten (see Appendix A).

13-2. A german-silver ribbon 0.0625 in. wide has a resistance of 0.25 ohm/ft. How thick is the ribbon (see Appendix A)?

14-2. Compute the resistance of 48 miles of No. 0000 hard-drawn copper wire (97.3 per cent conductivity) at 68 F (consult Appendix B).

15-2. By what percentage does the resistance of a standard annealed copper wire increase when the temperature of the wire is increased from 45 to 148 F?

16-2. Assume the resistivity of aluminum to be 17 ohms/cir mil-ft at 20 C. What is the resistance at 20 C of a single length of No. 10 aluminum wire, the total volume of which is 1 cu ft?

17-2. A coil of fine copper wire is installed in the walls of a gas-engine cylinder for the purpose of measuring the temperature of the inner wall of the engine. The resistance of the wire is 20 ohms at a room temperature of 25 C, while under operating conditions the resistance of the wire rises to 57 ohms. What is the temperature of the cylinder walls?

18-2. The exciting coil of an electromagnet takes 6 amp at 150 volts when the room temperature is 20 C. After the coil has been used continuously for 1 hr, it is found that the current in the coil has decreased to 4.9 amp with the same impressed voltage. Find the average temperature of the winding at the end of the hour.

19-2. The resistance of a certain rheostat increases by 25 per cent when the temperature rises from 25 to 75 C. Find the temperature coefficient of the metal at (a) 0 C, (b) 25 C.

20-2. A certain coaxial cable is formed of No. 10 solid copper wire centered within a metallic sheath of ⅜ in. inside diameter, and the space between conductor and sheath is filled with vinyl, a plastic that has a resistivity of 10^{14} ohm-cm. What is the d-c resistance from conductor to sheath of 1 mile of this cable?

CHAPTER 3

THE ELECTRIC CIRCUIT. COMPUTATION
OF RESISTANCE

As an introduction to this chapter it may be worth while to discuss briefly some of the fundamental concepts that apply to d-c circuits generally.

Consider the circuit shown in Fig. 1-3. It consists of a source of emf, in this case a generator G, connected to a resistance load R through the leads ab and dc. To simplify the discussion the generator and the leads are assumed to have negligible resistance. The terminal voltage $E_{da} = E_{cb}$ is then the voltage impressed on the resistance as indicated in the figure.

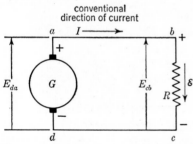

FIG. 1-3. Resistance in series with a source of emf.

In the conductors of a path in the generator armature connecting negative and positive brushes, voltages are generated, the sum of which is the total generated emf, which is ordinarily somewhat more than the terminal voltage of a generator that supplies a load. The generated emf displaces positive charges in the armature conductors in the direction of the positive terminal or in the direction of conventional current flow. Thus, within a source of emf positive charges are displaced and current is said to flow from negative to positive terminal. The net energy gained per unit of positive charge in moving from negative to positive brush is equal to the terminal voltage.

Next consider the resistance R of the load. For reasons of simplicity let it be assumed that the wire comprising the resistance is a length l of straight homogeneous metallic wire across the ends of which the potential difference E_{cb} is impressed as shown in principle in Fig. 2-3. Within the wire a constant axially directed electric gradient ε is established in the positive-to-negative direction. A free positive charge in the wire is acted upon by an electric force $F = q\varepsilon$, directed along the axis toward the negative terminal as shown in Eq. (1-1). If the charge is given a small

28

axial displacement dx in the direction of the force, the work done *on the charge*, per unit of quantity, is $dW = F\,dx/q = \mathcal{E}\,dx = -dE$ [Eq. (2-1)], which is negative.   Over the length l of wire the total work done is $W = \mathcal{E} \int_0^l dx = -E_{cb}$, where $-E_{cb}$ is the *rise* in voltage from b to c in Fig. 1-3.   Actually, of course, this represents a *voltage drop*.   Since, by assumption, the resistance of generator and leads is negligible, the total energy gained in the entire circuit, per unit of positive charge, is $E_{da} - E_{cb} = E_{cb} - E_{cb} = 0$.   This equation is simply a statement of the law of conservation of energy as applied to the circuit.   The case here considered can be extended to cover circuits containing any number of sources of emfs and resistances.   The statement governing the general case is known as Kirchhoff's law of voltages ($\Sigma E = 0$), which is discussed further on page 36.

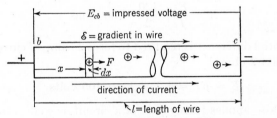

FIG. 2-3. Voltage drop in a resistance.

Finally, to summarize, it is noted that there is a rise of potential from negative to positive terminal in a source and a fall of potential from positive to negative terminal in a sink (a resistance, for example).   An alternate statement is: If one traces through a circuit in the conventional direction of current flow, one encounters a rise of potential in each source and a fall of potential in each sink, and the sum of all the potential rises is equal to the sum of all the potential drops in the circuit.

To avoid confusion it is helpful to indicate the polarity of the terminals of each source in the circuit by $+$ and $-$ signs, and to show the conventional direction of current by arrows.   Plus and minus signs may also be used at the terminals of resistances if desired.

The terms *electromotive force, voltage, voltage drop*, and *potential difference* are often used more or less indiscriminately and not always in conformity with their true meanings.   It should be remembered that an emf is that which causes or tends to cause electric charges to move and is present only in some source of electrical energy, such as a battery, a generator or a motor, etc.   On the other hand, a potential difference or voltage drop (or rise) exists between the terminals of a resistance in which a current flows, regardless of whether or not there is a source of emf between the terminals in question.

Application of Ohm's Law.   Ohm's law states that the current in any continuous-current circuit is equal to the impressed emf divided by the resistance.   To illustrate, let the resistance of the wires leading from the generator to the resistance R in Fig. 3-3 be negligible and let R be 10 ohms.   What is the current in the circuit when the impressed potential difference is 110 volts?

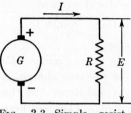

By Ohm's law,

FIG.   3-3. Simple   resistance.

$$I = \frac{E}{R} = \frac{110}{10} = 11 \text{ amp}$$

What is the resistance of an incandescent lamp that draws 2 amp from 120-volt mains?

By Ohm's law,

$$R = \frac{E}{I} = \frac{120}{2} = 60 \text{ ohms}$$

What potential difference is required to force 25 amp of current through a resistance of 4.2 ohms?

$$E = RI = 4.2 \times 25 = 105 \text{ volts}$$

Ohm's law also applies to any part of a circuit as well as to the circuit as a whole.   This is illustrated in the circuit of Fig. 4-3, in which a current

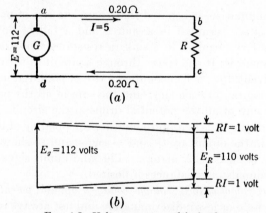

FIG. 4-3. Voltage consumed in leads.

of 5 amp is supplied to an electric heater of unknown resistance R, over a pair of wires, each of which has a resistance of 0.2 ohm.   The potential difference at the generator terminals is 112 volts.

The potential drop in each wire is $RI = 0.2 \times 5 = 1$ volt, *in the direction of current flow.*   With the direction of flow as indicated by the arrow, the potential of b is 1 volt less than that of a, while the potential of c is 1 volt more than that of d. Accordingly, the potential difference impressed on the heater must be $112 - 2$ or 110 volts. By applying Ohm's law to the heater alone, the resistance of the heater is found to be $R = 110 \div 5$ or 22 ohms. As a check, Ohm's law may now be applied to the circuit as a whole. The entire resistance external to the generator is $0.2 + 22 + 0.2 = 22.4$ ohms. The potential difference impressed upon this resistance is that between the generator terminals, or 112 volts. Therefore, the current in the circuit must be $112 \div 22.4$ or 5 amp, which checks the current originally assumed.

The diagram of Fig. 4-3 (b) represents graphically the potential differences across the generator and the heater terminals, as well as the potential drops in the wires. It should be especially noted that the potential of the circuit *falls* in the direction of the current flow, for, as

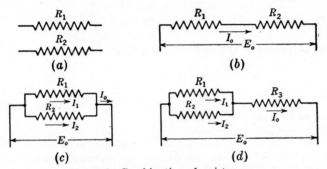

FIG. 5-3. Combination of resistances.

has been shown, the circuit gives up some of its energy. Thus from a to b the potential difference is -1 volt, from b to c it is -110 volts, and from c to d it is -1 volt. Since the circuit receives its energy from the generator, the potential difference between d and a is a *rise* of 112 volts.

If all the above potential differences in the circuit be added algebraically, the sum obtained is zero. This is always the case in any closed circuit.

Types of Circuits. Equivalent Resistance. Conductors may be grouped in various ways. Consider two conductors having the resistances R_1 and R_2 as in Fig. 5-3(a). They may be connected in *series* by joining them end on end as in (b), they may be connected in *parallel* as in (c), or a third resistance R_3 may be joined to the parallel group of (c) to form the *series-parallel* connection of (d). Most combinations of resistances are made up of one or more of such elements.

An important part of the solution of circuits made up of resistances in series-parallel grouping consists in finding a single resistance R_0 which may be substituted for the series-parallel combination without changing the amount of current in the circuit. Such a resistance is called the *equivalent resistance* of the circuit.

Series Circuits. To illustrate the solution of this type of circuit, let it be required to find the resistance R_0 which is equivalent to the three resistances R_1, R_2, and R_3 of Fig. 6-3, connected in series.

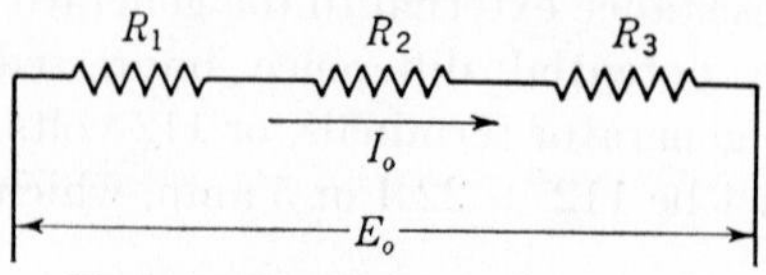

FIG. 6-3. Resistances in series.

In a series connection the current I_0 is common to all parts of the circuit. The impressed potential difference E_0 is used up in forcing the current through the several resistances, and it is equal to the sum of the several potential drops. Thus, by Ohm's law,

$$E_0 = R_0 I_0$$
$$= R_1 I_0 + R_2 I_0 + R_3 I_0$$
$$= I_0(R_1 + R_2 + R_3)$$

Dividing both sides of the last equation by I_0 yields

$$R_0 = R_1 + R_2 + R_3 \tag{1-3}$$

Hence, *the equivalent resistance of a series-connected group is equal to the sum of the series-connected resistances.*

Example 1. The resistance of a 60-watt 120-volt lamp is 240 ohms. The normal current of the lamp is 0.5 amp. (*a*) What is the equivalent resistance of five such lamps in series? (*b*) What voltage must be impressed on a group of five series-connected lamps to force normal current through their filaments?

$$R_0 = 5 \times 240 = 1,200 \text{ ohms}$$
$$E_0 = 0.5 \times 1,200 = 600 \text{ volts}$$

The impressed voltage is also equal to the product of the number of lamps and the voltage consumed per lamp or $E_0 = 5 \times 120 = 600$ volts.

Example 2. An electric heater draws 5 amp from 120-volt mains. The resistance element is made of wire with a resistance of 0.5 ohm/ft at operating temperature. How many feet of wire are required to rewind the heater?

$$R_0 = 0.5l$$

But

$$R_0 = 120 \div 5 = 24 \text{ ohms}$$

Therefore

$$l = \frac{24}{0.5} = 48 \text{ ft}$$

Parallel Circuits. In a parallel circuit the impressed potential difference is the same for each branch, but the line current I_0 divides at the common junction point into its several components. Circuits of this kind are very common.   The resistances in Fig. 7-3, for example, may represent three lamps connected to two leads from a generator.   Since all lamps are connected to the same leads, they each have the same impressed voltage, and the current that each takes is equal to the voltage divided by the resistance of the unit.   The current supplied by the generator is the sum of the currents taken by the three lamps.   Thus

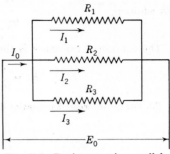

FIG. 7-3. Resistances in parallel.

$$I_0 = I_1 + I_2 + I_3 = \frac{E_0}{R_1} + \frac{E_0}{R_2} + \frac{E_0}{R_3}$$

Dividing both sides of the last equation above by E_0 yields

$$\frac{I_0}{E_0} = \frac{1}{R_0} = G_0 = \frac{1}{R_1} + \frac{1}{R_2} + \frac{1}{R_3}$$

whence

$$R_0 = \frac{1}{G_0} = \frac{1}{(1/R_1) + (1/R_2) + (1/R_3)} \qquad (2\text{-}3)$$

For the case of only two resistances in parallel, Eq. (2-3) reduces to

$$R_0 = \frac{R_1 R_2}{R_1 + R_2}$$

That is, *the equivalent resistance of a parallel-connected group of resistances is equal to the reciprocal of the sum of the reciprocals of the component resistances.*   Since the conductance of a circuit is the reciprocal of its resistance, the equivalent conductance G_0 of a parallel group of conductances is the sum of the component conductances, or

$$G_0 = \frac{1}{R_1} + \frac{1}{R_2} + \frac{1}{R_3} = G_1 + G_2 + G_3 \qquad (3\text{-}3)$$

The equivalent resistance of a parallel circuit is usually most conveniently found by first computing the conductances of the several branches, as in Eq. (3-3).   The reciprocal of the equivalent conductance of the parallel group is then taken to find the equivalent resistance.

Example 3.   (*a*) Find the equivalent resistance of the circuit in Fig. 7-3 when $R_1 = 3$, $R_2 = 4$, and $R_3 = 5$.   (*b*) If the impressed potential difference E_0 is 6 volts, what is the current in each branch and what is the total current?

(*a*) By Eq. (3-3) the conductances of the three branches and the total conductance are

$$G_1 = \tfrac{1}{3} = 0.333 \text{ mho}$$
$$G_2 = \tfrac{1}{4} = 0.250 \text{ mho}$$
$$G_3 = \tfrac{1}{5} = 0.200 \text{ mho}$$

By addition,

$$G_0 \qquad = 0.783 \text{ mho}$$

The equivalent resistance is the reciprocal of the equivalent conductance G_0 or

$$R_0 = \frac{1}{G_0} = \frac{1}{0.783} = 1.28 \text{ ohms}$$

(b) For an impressed potential difference of 6 volts, the several currents are

$$I_1 = \tfrac{6}{3} = 2.0 \text{ amp}$$
$$I_2 = \tfrac{6}{4} = 1.5 \text{ amp}$$
$$I_3 = \tfrac{6}{5} = 1.2 \text{ amp}$$

By addition,

$$I_0 \qquad = 4.7 \text{ amp}$$

By Ohm's law,

$$\frac{E_0}{I_0} = R_0 = \frac{6}{4.7}$$
$$R_0 = 1.28 \text{ ohms}$$

which checks the value previously obtained.

Series-Parallel Circuits. Series-parallel circuits are combinations of series and parallel groups, as illustrated in Fig. 8-3. The equivalent resistance of such a circuit is found by (1) reducing each parallel group to a single equivalent resistance, and (2) adding the equivalent resistances of the several parallel sections to the resistance of the series sections, to find the total equivalent resistance.

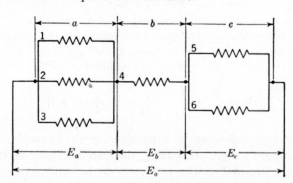

Fig. 8-3. Series-parallel circuit.

Example 4. Let the resistances in Fig. 8-3 have the following values in ohms: $R_1 = 5$, $R_2 = 6$, $R_3 = 8$, $R_4 = 2$, $R_5 = 5$, $R_6 = 7$, and let it be required to find (a) the equivalent resistance of each section of the circuit; (b) the equivalent resistance of the entire circuit; (c) the current input I_0 when the impressed voltage E_0 is 30 volts; (d) the potential drop across each section; (e) the current in each branch.

The solution is carried out in systematic order as follows:

(*a*) The conductances of the left-hand branches are

$$G_1 = \tfrac{1}{5} = 0.200 \text{ mho}$$
$$G_2 = \tfrac{1}{6} = 0.167 \text{ mho}$$
$$G_3 = \tfrac{1}{8} = 0.125 \text{ mho}$$

By addition,

$$G_a \qquad = 0.492 \text{ mho}$$

and

$$R_a = \frac{1}{G_a} = 2.03 \text{ ohms}$$

which is the equivalent resistance of section *a*.

The equivalent resistance of section *b* is 2 ohms.

The conductances of section *c* are

$$G_5 = \tfrac{1}{5} = 0.200 \text{ mho}$$
$$G_6 = \tfrac{1}{7} = 0.143 \text{ mho}$$
$$G_c \qquad = 0.343 \text{ mho}$$

and

$$R_c = \frac{1}{G_c} = 2.92 \text{ ohms}$$

which is the equivalent resistance of section *c*.

(*b*) The total equivalent resistance of the circuit may now be found. It is

$$R_0 = R_a + R_b + R_c$$
$$= 2.03 + 2.00 + 2.92$$
$$= 6.95 \text{ ohms}$$

(*c*) When E_0 is 30 volts, the input current is

$$I_0 = \frac{30}{6.95} = 4.32 \text{ amp}$$

(*d*) By Ohm's law, the potential drops in the several parts of the circuit are

$$E_a = R_a I_0 = 2.03 \times 4.32 = 8.77 \text{ volts}$$
$$E_b = R_b I_0 = 2.00 \times 4.32 = 8.64 \text{ volts}$$
$$E_c = R_c I_0 = 2.92 \times 4.32 = 12.61 \text{ volts}$$

By addition,

$$E_0 = E_a + E_b + E_c \qquad = 30.02 \text{ volts}$$

which checks the impressed voltage very closely.

(*e*) The currents in the several branches may now be found by applying Ohm's law to each part separately. Thus,

$$\frac{E_a}{R_1} = I_1 = E_a G_1 = 8.77 \times 0.200 = 1.75 \text{ amp}$$
$$I_2 = E_a G_2 = 8.77 \times 0.167 = 1.46 \text{ amp}$$
$$I_3 = E_a G_3 = 8.77 \times 0.125 = 1.10 \text{ amp}$$

By addition, to check

$$I_0 = I_1 + I_2 + I_3 \qquad = 4.31 \text{ amp}$$

In branch b the current is the total current I_0, and hence $I_0 = 4.31$ amp.
In branch c the component currents are

$$\frac{E_c}{R_5} = I_5 = E_cG_5 = 12.61 \times 0.200 = 2.52 \text{ amp}$$

$$I_6 = E_cG_6 = 12.61 \times 0.143 = 1.80 \text{ amp}$$

By addition, to check,

$$I_0 = I_5 + I_6 \qquad\qquad = 4.32 \text{ amp}$$

Figure 9-3 is a practical illustration of a series-parallel circuit.

Example 5.   A generator G supplies 30 amp to a motor M and 10 amp to a group of lamps L over a two-wire circuit, each conductor of which has a resistance of 0.15 ohm.   The resistance of the generator armature is 0.20 ohm.   A potential difference of 110 volts is maintained at the terminals of motor and lamps.   Find (*a*) the terminal voltage of the generator, (*b*) the internal (generated) voltage of the generator.

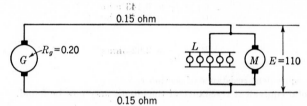

0.15 ohm

$R_g = 0.20$

G L M $E = 110$

0.15 ohm

FIG. 9-3. Generator supplying a load.

Lamps and motor together draw 40 amp from the line.   The voltage drop in the two line wires is therefore

$$RI = 40(0.15 + 0.15) = 12 \text{ volts}$$

(*a*) The generator terminal voltage (E_t) is

$$E_t = 110 + 12 = 122 \text{ volts}$$

(*b*) The potential drop in the generator armature is

$$RI = 0.20 \times 40 = 8 \text{ volts}$$

By adding the potential drop to the terminal voltage of the generator, the induced voltage is found to be

$$E_g = 122 + 8 = 130 \text{ volts}$$

Kirchhoff's Laws.   Kirchhoff's laws, as applied to the d-c circuit, may be stated as follows:

1. *The algebraic sum of all the currents flowing up to any point in a circuit is zero*, or, symbolically,

$$\Sigma I = 0$$

2. *The algebraic sum of all emfs and potential differences in any closed circuit is zero*, or, symbolically,

$$\Sigma E = 0$$

The first law is a statement of the principle of conservation of mass, for it states that at any point in a circuit the amount of electricity flowing into it is equal to the amount flowing out of it, per unit of time. In other words, there is no gain or loss of current anywhere in the circuit.

The second law is a statement of the principle of conservation of energy. Since potential differences and emfs are energy units (page 6), the law states, in effect, that in any closed circuit the algebraic sum of the energies gained per unit quantity of electricity is equal to zero.

Consideration of Fig. 10-3 will clarify the above statements. The generator supplies power to a group of series-parallel connected resistances, the direction of currents in the several parts of the circuit being indicated by arrows. At any point in the circuit, currents are considered to be *positive* when they flow *toward* the point and *negative* when

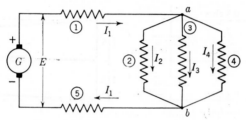

FIG. 10-3. Kirchhoff's laws illustrated.

they flow *away* from the point. Following this notation, Kirchhoff's first law, written for the point a, states that

$$0 = I_1 - I_2 - I_3 - I_4$$

or

$$I_1 = I_2 + I_3 + I_4$$

At the point b, similar results are obtained, for there

$$0 = -I_1 + I_2 + I_3 + I_4$$

and again

$$I_1 = I_2 + I_3 + I_4$$

A statement of the second law may be written for any one of the closed circuits. Since the circuit *gains* energy in the generator and *loses* energy in the resistances, the generated emf is written with a positive sign, while the potential drops in the resistances are written with negative signs. Thus

$$E - R_1 I_1 - R_2 I_2 - R_5 I_1 = 0$$

or

$$E - R_1 I_1 - R_3 I_3 - R_5 I_1 = 0$$

or

$$E - R_1 I_1 - R_4 I_4 - R_5 I_1 = 0$$

The method of applying these laws will be further illustrated.   Let the three-wire circuit of Fig. 11-3 feed two groups of lamps, connected as shown.   There are 25 lamps connected in parallel in one group and 15 lamps similarly connected in the other.   Each lamp has a resistance (assumed constant) of 120 ohms.   The resistance of each line wire connecting generator and lamps is 0.3 ohm.   When the impressed potential difference at the generator is 115 volts between adjacent wires, let it be required to find (1) the current in each line, (2) the potential difference impressed on each group of lamps.

1. First, assume the polarity of the terminals and the direction of current in each part of the circuit.   This is readily done for all parts of the circuit with the possible exception of the middle lead.   Since the resistance of 25 lamps is less than that of 15, it is assumed that some excess

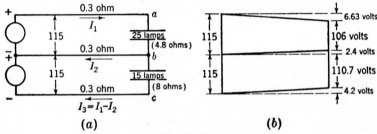

FIG. 11-3. Kirchhoff's laws applied.

current returns to the generator in the middle lead.   If it should turn out that the current in this lead flows in a direction opposite to that assumed, the sign of I_2 would be negative.   It therefore matters little whether the direction is correctly or incorrectly chosen.   If the current in the upper lead is I_1 amp and that in the middle lead is I_2 amp, by Kirchhoff's first law, the current I_3 in the lower lead is $I_1 - I_2$ amp., for at b, $I_1 - I_2 - I_3 = 0$.

Applying Kirchhoff's second law to the upper and lower loops separately yields

$$115 - 0.3I_1 - 4.8I_1 - 0.3I_2 = 0 \tag{4-3}$$
$$115 + 0.3I_2 - 8(I_1 - I_2) - 0.3(I_1 - I_2) = 0 \tag{5-3}$$

From Eq. (4-3) above,

$$I_1 = \frac{115 - 0.3I_2}{5.1} = 22.55 - 0.0588I_2 \tag{6-3}$$

Substituting Eq. (6-3) in Eq. (5-3) yields

$$115 + 0.3I_2 + 8.3I_2 - 8.3(22.55 - 0.0588I_2) = 0$$

or

$$9.088 I_2 = 72.17$$
$$I_2 = 7.94 \text{ amp} \tag{7-3}$$

Substituting Eq. (7-3) in Eq. (6-3) yields

$$I_1 = 22.08 \text{ amp} \tag{8-3}$$

By the first law,

$$I_3 = I_1 - I_2$$

hence,

$$I_3 = 22.08 - 7.94 = 14.14 \text{ amp} \tag{9-3}$$

2. The potential difference across the 25-lamp group is

$$E_{ab} = 4.8 I_1 = 105.98 \text{ volts}$$

and that across the 15-lamp group is

$$E_{bc} = 8 I_3 = 113.12 \text{ volts}$$

The diagram of potential drops in the several parts of the circuit is shown in (b) of Fig. 11-3. There is a fall of potential in the upper wire in the direction from generator to load, while in the middle and lower wires the potential rises in this direction.

Simplification of Networks. Networks containing various combinations of resistances can frequently be simplified.

1. Series-connected resistance elements may be replaced by a single resistance as in Eq. (1-3).

2. Parallel-connected resistance elements may be replaced by a single resistance as in Eq. (2-3).

In applying these rules, however, it is important to remember that Eq. (1-3) holds only for series-connected resistances in all of which the same current exists, while Eq. (2-3) applies only to parallel-connected resistances that have common terminals; that is, branches that are subject to the same potential difference.

3. Frequently networks contain resistances connected in a three-cornered mesh or Δ as in Fig. 12-3(a). Such a mesh may be converted to a three-cornered star or Y, as in Fig. 12-3(b). The reverse conversion from Y to Δ is also possible and may sometimes be advantageously made.

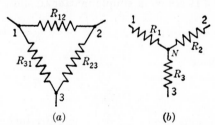

(a)   (b)

Fig. 12-3. (a) Δ-connected and (b) Y-connected resistances.

The equations applying to the conversion from Δ to Y may be derived as follows: Let the Δ-connected group and the equivalent Y be shown in a single drawing, Fig. 13-3. Consider the resistance R_0 between points 1 and 2; via the Y, R_0 is obviously equal to the sum of R_1 and R_2, whereas via the mesh R_0 comprises R_{12} in parallel with $R_{31} + R_{23}$, which reduces to $\dfrac{R_{12}(R_{23} + R_{31})}{R_{12} + R_{23} + R_{31}}$. Since the Y and the mesh are equivalent, each to the other, the resistance between 1 and 2 via the Y must have the same value as the corresponding resistance via the mesh. Thus

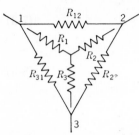

FIG. 13-3. Δ and equivalent Y.

$$R_1 + R_2 = \frac{R_{12}(R_{23} + R_{31})}{R_{12} + R_{23} + R_{31}} = \frac{R_{12}(R_{23} + R_{31})}{D} \qquad (10\text{-}3)$$

where

$$D = R_{12} + R_{23} + R_{31}$$

Similarly,

$$R_2 + R_3 = \frac{R_{23}(R_{31} + R_{12})}{D} \qquad (11\text{-}3)$$

and

$$R_3 + R_1 = \frac{R_{31}(R_{12} + R_{23})}{D} \qquad (12\text{-}3)$$

By subtracting Eq. (11-3) from Eq. (10-3), and adding the result to Eq. (12-3) it readily follows that

$$R_1 = \frac{R_{31}R_{12}}{D} \qquad (13\text{-}3)$$

It is now a simple matter to show that

$$R_2 = \frac{R_{12}R_{23}}{D} \qquad (14\text{-}3)$$

and

$$R_3 = \frac{R_{23}R_{31}}{D} \qquad (15\text{-}3)$$

Equations (13-3) to (15-3), inclusive, enable one to find the three resistances of the equivalent Y when the Δ resistances are given. The corresponding equations which relate the unknown Δ-connected resistances to the three known Y values may be derived as follows:

From Eqs. (13-3), (14-3), and (15-3) form the three products R_1R_2, R_2R_3, R_3R_1 and add. The result is

$$R_1R_2 + R_2R_3 + R_3R_1 = \frac{R_{12}^2 R_{23} R_{31} + R_{23}^2 R_{12} R_{31} + R_{31}^2 R_{12} R_{23}}{D^2}$$

$$N = \frac{R_{12} R_{23} R_{31}(R_{12} + R_{23} + R_{31})}{D^2}$$

$$= \frac{R_{12} R_{23} R_{31}}{D} \tag{16-3}$$

where $N = R_1R_2 + R_2R_3 + R_3R_1$.

Divide Eq. (16-3) by Eqs. (15-3), (13-3), and (14-3) in turn, to obtain

$$R_{12} = \frac{N}{R_3} \tag{17-3}$$

$$R_{23} = \frac{N}{R_1} \tag{18-3}$$

$$R_{31} = \frac{N}{R_2} \tag{19-3}$$

Example 6.   Let a battery with an internal resistance of 0.5 ohm and an open-circuit emf of 100 volts be applied to the network of Fig. 14-3, and let it be required to find the current in each of the resistances shown.

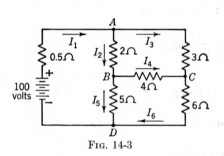

FIG. 14-3

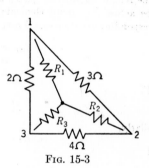

FIG. 15-3

The first step is to indicate the polarity of the battery and to assume the directions of current flow.   If any of the currents are found to be negative in the answer, that fact indicates that *positive* current flows opposite to the assumed reference direction.

From an examination of Fig. 14-3 it is apparent that the network can be solved if one of the three-cornered meshes is converted to its equivalent Y.   It is immaterial whether *ABC* or *BCD* is converted.   Let us take mesh *ABC*.   Redraw this mesh as in Fig. 15-3 for convenience, number the corners 1, 2, 3 to conform with the notation of Eqs. (13-3) to (15-3), and insert the equivalent Y resistances R_1, R_2, and R_3. By Eqs. (13-3) to (15-3), it follows that

$$R_1 = \frac{2 \times 3}{3 + 4 + 2} = 0.67 \text{ ohm}$$

$$R_2 = 1\tfrac{2}{9} = 1.33 \text{ ohm}$$

and

$$R_3 = \tfrac{8}{9} = 0.89 \text{ ohm}$$

Next, redraw the network with the resistances of the equivalent Y put in place of the mesh ABC as in Fig. 16-3. It is now a simple matter to solve this series-parallel circuit. The resistance from N to D is

$$R_{ND} = \frac{5.89 \times 7.33}{5.89 + 7.33} = 3.27 \text{ ohms}$$

and the equivalent resistance of the entire circuit is $3.27 + 0.67 + 0.5$, or 4.44 ohms. By Ohm's law

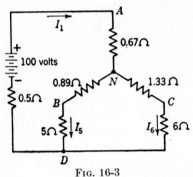

FIG. 16-3

$$I_1 = \frac{100}{4.44} = 22.5 \text{ amp}$$

The potential drop between N and D is

$$E_{ND} = 3.27 \times 22.5 = 73.6 \text{ volts}$$

and

$$I_5 = \frac{73.6}{5 + 0.89} = 12.5 \text{ amp}$$

while

$$I_6 = \frac{73.6}{6 + 1.33} = 10.04 \text{ amp}$$

The remaining currents I_2, I_3, and I_4 may be determined by finding the potential drops across the circuit elements AB, AC, and BC and then dividing these by the corresponding resistances. From Fig. 14-3 it is clear that

$$E_{AB} = 100 - 0.5I_1 - 5I_5$$
$$= 100 - 11.2 - 62.5$$
$$= 26.3 \text{ volts}$$

and

$$I_2 = \frac{26.3}{2} = 13.1 \text{ amp}$$

Similarly,

and

$$E_{AC} = 28.5 \text{ volts}$$

$$I_6 = \frac{28.5}{3} = 9.5 \text{ amp}$$

while

$$E_{BC} = E_{AC} - E_{AB} = 2.2 \text{ volts}$$

and

$$I_4 = \frac{2.2}{4} = 0.55 \text{ amp}$$

Note that all the computed values of current are positive.

Solution of Circuits. General Method.

The solution of circuits is simplified by following systematically a number of successive steps that lead logically to the desired result. These will be outlined in some detail for the greater convenience of the student.

1. Draw a circuit diagram of suitable size that shows all resistances and sources of emf. Internal resistances in sources of emf, such as motors, generators, and batteries, should be shown as separate resistance

elements immediately adjacent to the sources.   These sources may then be considered as resistanceless, and the emf of each will be its internal or generated emf.   If a problem calls for a conductor of given dimensions, its resistance should be computed from the relationship of Eq. (1-2), and the resistance thus found should be inserted in the circuit diagram at the appropriate place.

2. All known values of resistances, currents, and emfs should be inserted in the circuit diagram.   Indicate the polarities of emfs by $+$ and $-$ signs and the assumed directions of currents by arrows pointing in the positive sense of current.

3. Represent the magnitudes of all unknown resistances, currents, and emfs on the circuit diagram by suitable symbols (R_1, E_2, I_0, etc.), and show the assumed polarities of emfs and directions of currents.   The directions of unknown currents and the polarities of unknown emfs may be assumed arbitrarily.   It may, in some cases, turn out that the computed values of some of the quantities are negative.   If this should happen it simply means that the choice of the opposite reference direction would have resulted in a positive quantity.

4. Kirchhoff's law of currents should be applied successively to all junctions of the network to eliminate as many unknowns as possible. It is found, in general, that if there are n junctions, $n - 1$ of them may be used to reduce the number of unknowns; the nth serves merely as a check, since the application of the law of currents to the nth junction results in a redundant equation.

5. Apply Kirchhoff's law of voltages and Ohm's law to a sufficient number of closed loops to solve for the remaining unknowns.   Make certain that each loop employed contains at least one potential difference that does not appear in any other loop, for otherwise the equation of voltages for that loop will contain no new information.

6. Solve the resulting equations simultaneously.

In applying Kirchhoff's law of voltages it is to be remembered that in tracing through a source of emf from negative to positive terminals the potential difference is positive, whereas the terminal potential difference of the source is negative when tracing from positive to negative terminals. If the element through which one traces contains no source of emf, there is a voltage drop in the direction of the current and a voltage rise in the opposite direction.

Example 7.   The application of the general method to the example of Fig. 17-3 illustrates the procedure.   All resistances and the emfs are assumed to be known. Their values have been inserted in the diagram.   The unknown currents are represented by suitable symbols, and their assumed directions are indicated by arrows. To facilitate solution, the six unknown currents are listed at one side of the circuit diagram.

There are four junction points A, B, C, and D, three of which may be used for reducing the number of unknowns; the fourth will serve as a check. The application of Kirchhoff's law of current to junction A yields

$$I_1 - I_2 - I_3 = 0$$

Solve this equation for I_1, list the value obtained beside the diagram, and circle I_1 in the diagram to indicate that it has been eliminated as an unknown, to be solved for when I_2 and I_3 become known. List I_2, I_3 beside the diagram and check them to show that they are unknowns to be retained.

Similar procedure applied to junction B yields

$$I_3 - I_4 - I_5 = 0$$

An inspection of the list shows that I_3 must be retained as one of the unknowns. Accordingly, the equation should be solved for either I_4 or I_5. If I_4 is used, the resulting solution is

$$I_4 = I_3 - I_5$$

This value of I_4 is now listed and circled on the diagram while I_5 is entered and checked as one of the unknowns sought. This leaves only I_6, which, by applying

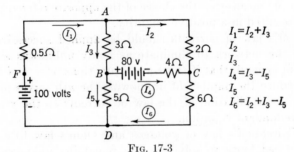

FIG. 17-3

Kirchhoff's law of currents to junction C, is involved in the equation

$$I_2 + I_4 - I_6 = 0$$

But, since I_4 is already available in terms of I_3 and I_5, it may be eliminated from the equation to obtain

$$I_2 + I_3 - I_5 - I_6 = 0$$

from which

$$I_6 = I_2 + I_3 - I_5$$

This value should now be added to the list beside the diagram, and I_6 may be circled to show that it has been eliminated.

As a check, apply Kirchhoff's law of currents to junction D and obtain the equation

$$I_5 + I_6 - I_1 = 0$$

Upon substituting herein the values of I_6 and I_1 listed beside the figure, one finds that

$$I_5 + I_2 + I_3 - I_5 - I_2 - I_3 = 0$$

This equation is identically equal to zero, which indicates that the work thus far is correct in so far as this check is concerned.

Inspection of the diagram discloses that there now remain only three unknown currents; these are the unencircled ones I_2, I_3, and I_5. To solve for them it is necessary to apply Kirchhoff's law of voltages around three suitable loops. The simplest are $ABDF$, ACB, and BCD. It should be noted that each of these contains at least one emf or voltage drop that is not included in either of the other two. As an example of three loops that are unsatisfactory, consider $ABDF$, ACB, and $ACBDF$. The last contains no emf or resistance drop that is not included in the other two; the equation of voltages obtained from this loop could as well be found by adding the equations obtained from loops $ABDF$ and ACB. Accordingly, it provides no new information, which is equivalent to saying that in reality there are only *two* independent equations, while three are needed to solve for the three unknowns.

We may now apply Kirchhoff's law of voltage successively to each of the three loops first proposed. For loop $ABDF$,

$$100 - 0.5I_1 - 3I_3 - 5I_5 = 0$$

which reduces to

$$100 - 0.5I_2 - 3.5I_3 - 5I_5 = 0 \qquad (a)$$

For loop ACB,

$$80 - 2I_2 + 3I_3 + 4I_4 = 0$$

which reduces to

$$80 - 2I_2 + 7I_3 - 4I_5 = 0 \qquad (b)$$

For loop BCD,

$$80 - 5I_5 + 6I_6 + 4I_4 = 0$$

which is equivalent to

$$80 + 6I_2 + 10I_3 - 15I_5 = 0 \qquad (c)$$

Simultaneous solution of the three lettered equations yields the desired currents. From these the remaining values of I_1, I_3, and I_5 readily follow.

The answers are

$$I_1 = 23.6 \qquad I_4 = -12.3$$
$$I_2 = 20.3 \qquad I_5 = 15.7$$
$$I_3 = 3.3 \qquad I_6 = 7.9$$

Note that the sign of I_4 is negative. This means that the positive direction of I_4 is from C to B.

Problems

1-3. When the switch on the heating element of an electric range is on "high," two similar nichrome coils are connected in parallel across a 120-volt circuit. If the current supplied to the heater is 15 amp, what is the resistance of each coil?

2-3. A 10-hp, 220-volt motor has an efficiency of 87 per cent. The location of the motor is 150 ft from the source of supply. The voltage drop in the leads connecting the motor to the supply must not exceed 5 volts per 1,000 ft of single conductor. What is the minimum size of copper wire that may be used?

3-3. A 60-watt 110-volt lamp has a normal current rating of 0.54 amp, while a 40-watt 110-volt lamp has a normal rating of 0.364 amp. Explain what will happen if a 60-watt 110-volt lamp is connected in series with a 40-watt, 110-volt lamp across 220-volt mains. Assume that the filament resistances remain constant.

4-3. Three resistances a, b, and c are connected in parallel. The resistances have the following values in ohms: $a = 2$, $b = 8$, $c = 24$. If the current input to the group is 96 amp, (a) what is the current in each resistance; (b) what is the applied potential difference?

5-3. The insulation resistance of a motor is measured as follows: Connect one terminal of a 600-volt voltmeter to one terminal of a 550-volt supply. Connect the remaining terminal of the voltmeter to the frame of the machine and the second terminal of the supply to the armature circuit of the motor. The resistance of the voltmeter is 600,000 ohms. If the voltmeter reads 17.5 volts, what is the insulation resistance of the motor winding?

6-3. A steel-reinforced aluminum cable has a steel core made of 7 strands of steel wire, each 0.1010 in. in diameter. Over the core are laid 26 strands of aluminum wire each 0.1355 in. in diameter. Assume the conductivity of the aluminum wire to be 61 per cent and that of the steel 10 per cent of the Annealed Copper Standard, the resistivity of which at 20 C is 10.37 ohms/cir mil-ft. Find the resistance at 20 C per mile (a) of the aluminum alone, (b) of the steel alone, and (c) of the entire cable.

7-3. The circuit in Fig. A-3 is made up of a series-parallel arrangement of resistances that have the ohmic values indicated. The potential drop across ab is 14 volts.

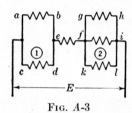

FIG. A-3

Find (a) the equivalent resistance of the sections 1 and 2, (b) the equivalent resistance of the entire circuit, (c) the current in each resistance, (d) the potential drop across each section, and (e) the applied potential difference E. The resistances in ohms, in the several branches, have the following values: $ab = 8$; $cd = 15$; $ef = 2$; $gh = 30$; $fi = 40$; $kl = 25$.

8-3. A load of 75 kw is to be supplied from 440-volt bus bars over a two-conductor copper circuit to a point 800 ft distant from the bus. A potential difference of not less than 420 volts is to be maintained at the load. If the resistivity of the copper at operating temperature is 10.8 ohms/cir mil-ft, (a) what is the resistance of each feeder; (b) what is the area, in circular mils, of the conductor that should be used; and (c) what is the weight of the cable?

9-3. There are two cars on the electric railway of Fig. B-3. Car 1 takes 110 amp, while car 2 takes 80 amp. Find the voltage impressed on each car when the station voltage is 600 volts. (Disregard the resistance of the rail return.)

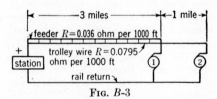

FIG. B-3

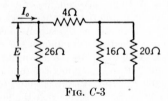

FIG. C-3

10-3. (a) What voltage must be impressed on the circuit of Fig. C-3 to circulate 10 amp in the 4-ohm resistance? (b) What is the total current I_0? (c) What is the resistance of the network?

11-3. The network of Fig. *D*-3 contains the resistances indicated and two batteries, one of 6 volts and one of 12 volts, connected as shown. Disregard the internal resistance of the batteries. The potential difference impressed on the circuit is 60 volts. Find the currents I_1, I_2, I_0.

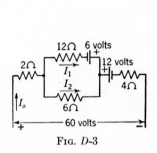

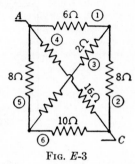

FIG. *D*-3   FIG. *E*-3

12-3. A network of resistances is made up in the form of a rectangle and its two diagonals as in Fig. *E*-3. For convenience of identification, the sides and diagonals are designated by the numbers given in the circles and the resistances have the values indicated. The total resistances of the diagonals three and four are 2 ohms and 16 ohms, respectively. A potential difference of 100 volts is impressed across the ends of diagonal 4. Compute (*a*) the current in each element of the circuit, and (*b*) the resistance between *A* and *C*.

13-3. In Fig. *F*-3, solve for the current in each of the three branches *ab*, *be*, and *bc*.

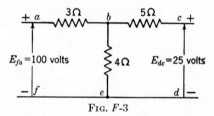

FIG. *F*-3

14-3. Compute the three Y-connected resistances that are the equivalent of the Δ-connected group R_{12}, R_{23}, and R_{31} in Fig. *G*-3. Redraw the circuit connections

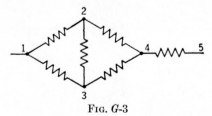

FIG. *G*-3

with the Y-connected resistances substituted. Compute R_0, the total resistance of the circuit between points 1 and 5. The branch resistances have the following values in ohms:

$$R_{12} = 10 \qquad R_{24} = 8$$
$$R_{23} = 4 \qquad R_{34} = 7$$
$$R_{31} = 6 \qquad R_{45} = 3$$

15-3. In Fig. *H*-3 the given voltages of generator and battery are the open-circuit or internal voltages, while the resistances shown adjacent to the symbols of the gen-

Fig. *H*-3

erator and battery in the circuit diagram are the corresponding resistances of generator and battery. Find (*a*) each of the eight currents, (*b*) the terminal voltages of the generator and the battery.

CHAPTER 4

ENERGY AND POWER

Introduction. The age in which we live is characterized by a high degree of mechanization in almost every area of human endeavor where there is work to be done. This is due largely to the availability of vast quantities of low-cost energy and to man's ingenuity in adapting it to his use.

From primitive times until the latter part of the eighteenth century, aside from the energies of moving air and falling water, which had been utilized in a small way, man depended almost entirely upon his own labor and that of his dog, his ox, and his horse to do the work of the world.

About the beginning of the nineteenth century in the United States, and a little earlier in Europe, great changes in methods of production began to take place. These came about chiefly as a result of the introduction of the condensing steam engine which James Watt had succeeded in perfecting by 1782. The steam engine made available for the first time large new sources of mechanical energy. It was soon adapted to every conceivable production activity. Its effect on the growth and mechanization of industry was so far-reaching that this period of rapid development has come to be known as the Industrial Revolution. It was the beginning of the era of mechanization and energy utilization on a grand scale.

Space does not permit, nor is this the proper place to describe, even in the barest outline, the tremendous expansion that has occurred in the United States and elsewhere since 1800 in the utilization and adaptation to man's use of ever-increasing amounts of energy. Work animals have all but completely disappeared from our farms, streets, and highways, and drudgery has been lifted from the shoulders of men everywhere. Wherever work is to be done, mechanical energy, derived principally from fuels or falling water, carries the burden. Man's role has been changed largely from that of laborer to a designer of machines and processes, or a supervisor or director of energy-converting devices. His job demands skill and intelligence, but each year it calls for less and less expenditure of bodily energy.

49

Energy. It is a matter of common experience that energy may be converted from one form to another. In water-power plants the energy of falling water is converted to electrical energy through the medium of water-wheel-driven generators. In steam plants the chemical energy of coal is converted to heat when the coal is burned. Some of the heat liberated is imparted to water, which is turned to steam in boilers. Heat energy is then removed from the steam in turbines, where a portion of it is converted to mechanical energy of rotation. Most of this, in turn, is transformed to electrical energy in turbo-driven generators. At every step some energy is lost as heat, and only about one-fifth of the energy originally present in the coal appears as electrical energy in the output of the generator.

When electrical energy is utilized, the order of conversion is reversed. In the heating element of an electric range all the electrical input is converted to heat. In an incandescent lamp about 98 per cent of the energy is radiated as heat and only 2 per cent appears as light. In a storage battery approximately 90 per cent of the energy supplied to it when charging is stored as chemical energy in the cell; the remaining 10 per cent is lost as heat. In electric motors from 60 to 94 per cent of the energy input, depending upon the size and type of the motor, is converted to the mechanical energy of rotation. The remainder is lost as heat in the motor iron and copper.

Electrical energy may be expressed in terms of volts, amperes, and time. In the discussion of the previous chapter it was shown that the potential difference between any two points of a circuit is the energy gained or lost by a unit quantity of electricity, which is

$$W = EQ \quad \text{joules}$$

By multiplying the right side by t/t and substituting the average current I for Q/t, the above equation reduces to

$$W = EIt \quad \text{joules} \tag{1-4}$$

In Eq. (1-4) E is in volts, I is in amperes, t is in seconds, and energy W is in watt-seconds or joules. Other common units of energy and their relations to one another follow. These relationships are useful when numerical problems need to be solved.

1 joule	$= 10^7$ ergs	$= 1$ watt-sec
1 gram-calorie	$= 4.186$ joules	$= 3.088$ ft-lb
1 ft-lb	$= 1.356$ joules	$= 1.356$ watt-sec
1 Btu	$= 1,055$ joules	$= 778.1$ ft-lb
1 kwhr	$= 3.6 \times 10^6$ joules	$= 2.655 \times 10^6$ ft-lb
1 hp-hr	$= 2.686 \times 10^6$ joules	$= 0.746$ kwhr

Joule's Law. When electrical energy is transformed into heat in the resistance R of a circuit, by the passage of a continuous current I, the heat energy liberated in t sec is directly proportional to the resistance and to the square of the current. This fact was discovered by Joule in 1841 and has since been known as *Joule's law.* The mathematical expression of Joule's law may readily be deduced from Eq. (1-4) and Ohm's law, if the value of E in Eq. (1-4) be interpreted to mean E_r, the voltage drop in the resistance. Since the resistance drop $E_r = RI$, one may substitute RI for E in Eq. (1-4) and obtain

$$W = RI^2 t \qquad\qquad (2\text{-}4)$$

In Eq. (2-4) R is in ohms, I is in amperes, t is in seconds, and the energy loss W is in joules. A unit of energy much used by electrical engineers is the *kilowatthour* (kwhr). In terms of this unit, the heat energy developed in a resistance is

$$W = 0.278 \times 10^{-6} RI^2 t \qquad \text{kwhr} \qquad\qquad (3\text{-}4)$$

Power. Power is the time rate of energy transformation. Large amounts of power are developed when energy is rapidly transformed, and small amounts when it is slowly transformed. When energy is transformed at a constant rate, as in a burning lamp or in a motor under steady load, the power is constant; when it is transformed at a varying rate, as in a motor driving the head saw of a lumber mill or in the cylinders of a gasoline engine, the power is variable. The transformation of a small amount of energy may be associated with the development of a large amount of power if the rate of transformation is very high, as when a bullet is fired from a gun or when a lightning bolt strikes to ground. The power developed by a lightning stroke may be several millions of kilowatts, but the duration of the stroke is only a few millionths of a second, and the total energy expended is so small that its commercial value, could it be utilized, would probably be not more than 2 or 3 cents.

An expression for the electrical power developed by a continuous current of I amp in a circuit in which the emf is E volts may be obtained from Eq. (1-4) by dividing by the elapsed time in seconds. Accordingly, in terms of electrical units, the expression for power is

$$P = EI \qquad \text{watts} \qquad\qquad (4\text{-}4)$$

Equation (4-4) may be used to find the power expended in any circuit for which the impressed voltage and current are known, or in *any part of a circuit* for which the potential drop across the part, and the current in it, are known. Suppose that a circuit contains a resistance R, and let E_r be the voltage drop across the resistance and I be the current. Then, since $E_r = IR$, one may substitute $E_r/R = I$ in Eq. (4-4) and obtain the following equations for the power expended in a resistance:

$$P_r = RI^2 \qquad\qquad (5\text{-}4)$$
$$= \frac{E_r^2}{R}$$
$$= GE_r^2 \qquad\qquad (6\text{-}4)$$

The *watt* may be defined as the power developed when work is done at the rate of one joule per second. It is also the power expended in any part of a circuit wherein one ampere falls through a potential difference of one volt. The *kilowatt* (kw) and *horsepower* (hp) are units of power that are commonly used to measure large amounts of power. These and other units of power, and their relation to one another, are given below.

$$
\begin{aligned}
&1 \text{ watt} &&= 1 \text{ joule/sec} &&= 10^7 \text{ergs/sec} \\
&1 \text{ kw} &&= 1{,}000 \text{ watts} &&= 1.34 \text{ hp} \\
&1 \text{ hp} &&= 746 \text{ watts} &&= 33{,}000 \text{ ft-lb/min} \\
&1 \text{ Btu/min} &&= 17.57 \text{ watts} &&= 778.1 \text{ ft-lb/min} \\
&1 \text{ ft-lb/sec} &&= 1.356 \text{ watts}
\end{aligned}
$$

Energy and Power Calculations. It is often difficult for the student to gain clear concepts of energy and power until he has dealt with a number of more or less familiar situations involving them quantitatively. For this reason the following illustrative examples are included.

Example 1. The heating element of a plate on an electric range draws 10 amp from 120-volt mains. (*a*) How much power does the plate use? (*b*) What is the resistance of the element? (*c*) How many kilowatthours of energy does the plate use when the power is connected continuously for 30 min? (*d*) What is the cost of energy for the 30 min of use, at 6 cents/kwhr?

(*a*) The power expended is

$$P = 120 \times 10 = 1{,}200 \text{ watts}$$

(*b*) The resistance is

$$R = \frac{120}{10} = 12 \text{ ohms}$$

(*c*) The energy used is

$$W = 120 \times 10 \times \tfrac{1}{2} = 600 \text{ watt-hr} = 0.6 \text{ kwhr}$$

(*d*) At 6 cents/kwhr,

$$\text{Cost} = 0.6 \times 6 \text{ cents} = 3.6 \text{ cents}$$

Example 2. (*a*) How long does it take a 3.5-kw electric heater to raise the temperature of a 20-gal tank of water from 50 to 180 F? The tank is assumed to be perfectly insulated. (b) What is the cost of heating the water if the price paid for energy is 2 cents/kwhr? (c) If the supply voltage is 120, what is the resistance of the heater, and how much current does it draw?

(a) 20 gal.
$$= \frac{20 \times 231}{1,728} = 2.673 \text{ cu ft}$$

Weight of water $= 2.673 \times 62.5 = 167.06 \text{ lb}$

Btu required $= 167.06(180 - 50) = 21,718$

1 Btu $= 1.055 \text{ kw-sec} = 2.9305 \times 10^{-4} \text{ kwhr}$

Kilowatthours required $= 21,718 \times 2.9305 \times 10^{-4} = 6.36$

Time required $= 6.36 \div 3.5 = 1 \text{ hr } 49 \text{ min}$

(b) Cost $= 6.36 \times 2 \text{ cents} = 12.72 \text{ cents}$

(c)
$$P = \frac{E^2}{R}$$

$$R = \frac{120^2}{3,500} = 4.11 \text{ ohms}$$

$$I = \frac{3,500}{120} = 29.2 \text{ amp}$$

Example 3. In Fig. 9-3 the generator G supplies power to a motor and a bank of 20 parallel-connected lamps. The two wires over which the load is supplied have resistances of 0.15 ohm each. The internal resistance of the generator is 0.20 ohm. If the lamp-filament resistances are 220 ohms each (assumed constant) and the motor delivers 5 hp and is 85 per cent efficient, find (a) kilowatts input to the motor, (b) kilowatts input to the lamps, (c) current delivered by the generator, (d) potential difference at the generator terminals, (e) emf generated by the generator, (f) power lost as heat in the generator winding, (g) power lost as heat in the line wires. The voltage impressed across the lamps is 110.

(a) Motor input
$$= \frac{5 \times 0.746}{0.85} = 4.39 \text{ kw}$$

(b) Resistance of lamps
$$= \frac{220}{20} = 11 \text{ ohms}$$

Input to lamps
$$= \frac{110^2}{11} = 1.1 \text{ kw}$$

(c) Total input to load $= 5.49 \text{ kw}$

Current in line
$$= \frac{5,490}{110} = 49.9 \text{ amp}$$

(d) Potential drop in leads $= 2 \times 0.15 \times 49.9 = 14.97 \text{ volts}$

Generator terminal voltage $= 110 + 14.97 = 125 \text{ volts (approx.)}$

(e) Generator resistance drop $= 49.9 \times 0.2 = 10 \text{ volts (approx.)}$

Generated voltage $= 125 + 10 = 135 \text{ volts}$

(f) Heat loss in winding is
$$I^2R = 49.9^2 \times 0.20 = 499 \text{ watts}$$

or
$$EI = 10 \times 49.9 = 499 \text{ watts}$$

(g) Heat loss in line wires is
$$I^2R = 49.9^2 \times 0.30 = 747 \text{ watts}$$

or
$$EI = 14.97 \times 49.9 = 747 \text{ watts}$$

Problems

1-4. A 120-volt electric plate has a resistance of 10 ohms when the switch is on "high," 20 ohms on "medium," and 40 ohms on "low." What is the cost of operating the plate 20 min on "high," 30 min on "medium," and $2\frac{1}{2}$ hr on "low" if the energy consumed is billed at 3 cents/kwhr?

2-4. A 50-hp, 220-volt motor having an efficiency of 88 per cent is supplied with power from a generator 200 ft away, over 400,000-cir-mil copper cable. In one year the motor operates the equivalent of 3,000 hr at full load. The cost of energy at the generator is 1.75 cents/kwhr. Find (a) the total cost of energy consumed in one year, (b) the monetary value of the energy lost in the cable during the year.

3-4. A motor is supplied with 85 amp at 500 volts over No. 00 copper wire from a station $\frac{1}{2}$ mile away. The resistance of the wire is 0.42 ohm/mile. What is the efficiency of transmission?

4-4. The internal resistance of a certain type of automobile storage battery is 0.18 ohm. When the battery is charged at the average rate of 4 amp, the required terminal voltage is 6.2 volts. Three batteries and a suitable resistance are connected in series across 110-volt mains, and the batteries are charged at the 4-amp rate for 16 hr. (a) What is the value of the required resistance? (b) How many kilowatt-hours of chemical energy have been stored in each battery at the end of the charging period? (c) What is the percentage efficiency of the process?

5-4. A flatiron with a resistance of 23.5 ohms is operated from a 120-volt circuit. (a) What is the rate of energy consumption in Btu per hour? (b) What is the cost of operating the iron steadily for a period of 4 hr if the energy consumed costs 2.5 cents/kwhr?

6-4. A motor-driven pump on an irrigation project is designed to lift 1,600 cu ft of water per second against a head of 290 ft. If the over-all efficiency of the pumping plant is 80 per cent, what must be the output of the generator required to supply the power for two such pumping units?

7-4. If a 15-ton car in going 3,000 ft down a 5 per cent grade could convert 30 per cent of its stored energy into electrical energy, for how many hours would the energy saved operate a 50-watt lamp?

8-4. The discharge current in a stroke of lightning is 20,000 amp and it lasts for 3 μsec (3/1,000,000 sec). If the potential difference along the stroke is 40,000,000 volts, what would be the monetary value of the stroke if its energy could be sold for 3 cents/kwhr?

9-4. A 12,000-hp waterwheel operates under a head of 420 ft and has an efficiency of 89 per cent. The loss in the penstock is 5 per cent. How many cubic feet of water per second are required?

10-4. A 30,000-kw generator is driven by a steam turbine from coal-fired boilers. The over-all energy efficiency at full load of boilers, turbine, and generator is 22 per cent. (a) How many pounds of coal are burned per kilowatt-hour of energy output if coal has 13,500 Btu of energy per pound? (b) At $6.50 per ton, what is the energy cost of full-load operation for a period of 8 hr?

11-4. In Fig. 11-3, (a) how much power is supplied by each of the generators shown; (b) how much power is lost in the connecting lines; and (c) what is the efficiency of transmission?

CHAPTER 5

MAGNETISM AND THE MAGNETIC FIELD

Historical Background.   It was known to the ancients that the "natural magnet" (magnetite ore) possessed the property of attracting and holding bits of iron.   As early as the first century A.D. the Chinese had some knowledge of bar magnets and were apparently using some form of compass as a guide in desert crossings.   Knowledge of the compass seems to have reached Europe about the tenth century, and by the twelfth century a crude form of compass had come into use.   This greatly stimulated navigation and, in the years that followed, gradually led to wide exploration and discovery.

Until about the second decade of the nineteenth century, electricity and magnetism appeared to be unrelated phenomena, although considerable knowledge had been gained concerning electric charges, electric current, and bar magnets.   In 1819 Oersted discovered that a magnetic needle is deflected when it is brought near a current-carrying wire, and thereby demonstrated that electric current is a source of magnetism. The report of this discovery was immediately followed by experimentation on the part of Biot and Savart and of Ampère, which soon led to the statement of a basic rule known as Ampère's rule, by which the flux density due to a current can be computed in many instances, and 10 years later (1830) the experiments of Faraday and Henry resulted in the discovery of electromagnetic induction.   They showed that a transient current is established in a circuit when a magnet is moved toward or away from it or when the current in an adjacent circuit is changed. Thus in the brief span of about ten years the basic discoveries of electromagnetism were made, and the foundation was laid upon which much of present-day electrical development rests.

Magnetic Field.   A magnetic field is any space in which a magnetic material such as iron or steel tends to become magnetized, or in which the poles of a magnet experience forces due to magnetic causes.   The space near a bar magnet (Fig. 1-5), especially near the poles, and the space around a conductor in which there is a current (Fig. 1-6) are magnetic fields.   The space near the earth's surface is a weak magnetic field, while in the air gaps of commercial motors and generators very strong fields exist.   The presence of a magnetic field can be detected by means of a small magnetic needle or in a number of other ways.

Magnetic Flux.   Magnetic fields are conveniently represented by lines called *lines of induction*.   Fig. 2-5 shows the lines of induction near the poles of a horseshoe magnet, while Fig. 6-5 represents the magnetic field

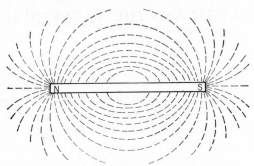

Fig. 1-5. Magnetic field of a bar magnet.

or lines of induction in the air gap of a d-c motor.   The magnetic induction represented by a group of lines of induction taken collectively is frequently referred to as *magnetic flux of induction* or simply as *magnetic flux*.

The lines of induction are so drawn that anywhere in a magnetic field the long axis of a magnetic needle assumes a position of tangency to the

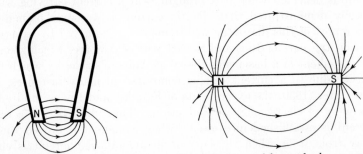

Fig. 2-5. Lines of force of a horseshoe   Fig. 3-5. Lines of force of a bar magnet.
magnet.

lines.   The lines with arrowheads indicate the direction in which a north pole in the field tends to move or in which the north pole of a magnetic needle points.

Experiment shows that, if a magnet is broken at one or more places as in Fig. 4-5, new poles form at the breaks when the pieces are slightly separated.   These poles have approximately the same strength as the original poles.   One concludes from this that lines of induction do not end at the poles of the magnet but continue through the bar to form closed loops.

Magnetic Circuit.   The *path* of the closed loops which comprise the magnetic flux (Figs. 5-5 and 6-5) is called the *magnetic circuit*. The magnetic circuit is analogous to the electric circuit, but there are important differences between the two.   This subject is discussed in greater detail in Chap. 8.

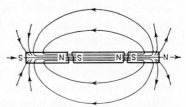

Fig. 4-5. Magnetic lines of force are continuous.

Units of Flux and Flux Density.   The unit of magnetic flux (ϕ) is one line of induction.   In the mks system of units the unit of flux is the *weber*, while in the practical (cgs) system the unit is the *maxwell*.   The weber is a comparatively large unit, while the maxwell is a much smaller one.   They are related as follows:

$$1 \text{ weber} = 10^8 \text{ maxwells}$$

The *flux density* (B) at some point in a magnetic circuit is defined by the equation

$$B = \frac{d\phi}{dA}$$

where dA is an incremental area at the point, taken at right angles to the direction of the flux of induction, and $d\phi$ is the total flux that crosses

Fig. 5-5. Magnetic circuit of a horseshoe magnet.

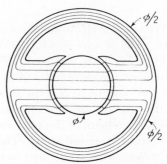

Fig. 6-5. Magnetic circuit of a d-c motor.

dA.   When the flux is uniformly distributed over the total area of section ($d\phi/dA$ is constant), the expression for flux density reduces to

$$B = \frac{\phi}{A} \qquad \text{lines per unit of area}$$

$$= \frac{\text{webers}}{\text{sq m}} \qquad \text{in the mks system}$$

$$= \frac{\text{maxwells}}{\text{sq cm}} \qquad \text{in practical units (gauss)}$$

Magnetomotive Force. A magnetomotive force (mmf) is that which sets up a magnetic field or produces a magnetic flux in a magnetic circuit. It is analogous to the emf of an electric circuit.   Oersted's discovery that a magnetic field is present in the space around an electric current has already been mentioned.   Since the field exists while current flows but disappears when the current is stopped, one concludes that the current causes the magnetic field or, in view of the definition of mmf, that an electric current is a magnetomotive force.

Although it has long been known that a bar magnet or a natural magnet is capable of inducing magnetism in a piece of soft iron, and for this reason may be regarded as a source of magnetizing force, it is now believed that, in the last analysis, all magnets and magnetic circuits owe their magnetism to electric currents.

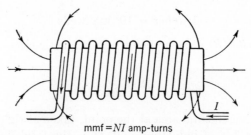

mmf $= NI$ amp-turns

FIG. 7-5. Magnetizing iron with an electric current.

Very strong electromagnets are made by encircling a suitable iron core with a coil of wire in which a direct current is maintained, as illustrated in Figs. 7-5, 14-6, and 16-6.   The mmf of a winding is proportional to the amount of the current I and to N, the number of times the current encircles the core, or to NI, the product of current and turns in the winding. In the mks system of units the unit of mmf (F) is the *ampere-turn* (NI). The ampere-turn is the mmf of a one-turn winding in which one ampere of current is maintained.   The unit of mmf in the practical system is the *gilbert*, which is related to the ampere-turn as follows:

$$1 \text{ amp-turn} = \frac{4\pi}{10} \text{ gilberts} \qquad (1\text{-}5)$$

Magnetic Field Intensity. For purposes of computation it is convenient to define a quantity known as the *magnetic field intensity* (H), also called the *magnetic-potential gradient*. This quantity is the space rate of consuming magnetomotive force in the direction of some assumed path. It is usually desirable to take the assumed path along a line of magnetic induction. On this basis the magnetic field intensity at a point is expressed symbolically, in the mks system of units, as

$$H = \frac{dF}{dl}$$

for the general case or, if the field is uniform (lines of induction parallel), it is

$$H = \frac{F}{l} \quad \text{amp-turns/m}$$

where dl = infinitesimal length of flux path at the point in question

dF = ampere-turns consumed in length dl of path

In case of a uniform field, l is the length in meters over which the consumed mmf is F ampere-turns.

Since the equivalent of one ampere-turn is $4\pi/10 = 1.257$ gilberts, and since in the practical system of units l is in centimeters, the field intensity, in practical units, corresponding to the last of the above equations is

$$H = 1.257 \frac{NI}{l} \quad \text{oersteds or gilberts/cm}$$

In Chap. 1 it was indicated that the electric field intensity could be expressed either as the voltage drop per unit length of path or as the force on a unit charge due to the electric field. In analogous fashion, the magnetic field intensity H was originally described in terms of an alternate definition as the magnetic force experienced by a fictitious unit point north magnetic pole at a given position in the magnetic field.

Magnetic field intensity is sometimes described in terms of *lines of force* which are similar to the lines of induction described previously. Although the two concepts have distinctly different meanings, the terms *lines of force* and *lines of induction* are sometimes loosely used interchangeably.

Relative Permeability. It was explained in Chap. 1 that, to some extent at least, most substances are conductors of electricity, although some are very much better than others. The factor γ, called the *conductivity* of the conductor material, is used to measure the relative conducting ability of a given material in relation to some standard material for which the relative conductivity is unity (100 per cent).

It is possible to establish some magnetic flux in every known kind of substance as well as in empty space (a vacuum), but all except a few materials are said to be nonmagnetic. These are all about equally poor conductors of flux. The term *relative permeability* (μ_r) is used to measure the ability of a given substance to conduct magnetic flux in comparison with empty space, the relative permeability of which is taken as unity ($\mu_r = 1$). Air, glass, wood, wax, etc., and certain nonferrous metals including copper and aluminum have values of μ_r approximately the same as that of empty space.

A number of magnetic materials, principally soft iron and steel, are very much better conductors of flux. Sheet steel, for example, is the material used to form parts or all of most magnetic circuits employed in electrical machines such as motors, generators, and transformers. As conductors of flux, iron and steel may be from several hundred to several thousand times as good as nonmagnetic materials such as air. The value of μ_r for a magnetic material, however, depends not only on the nature of the material itself, but also upon the flux density established in it, or upon what is called the degree of saturation.

This and other related matters are discussed in greater detail in Chap. 8.

Problems

1-5. A current of 10 amp is passed through a coil of 500 turns. What is the magnetomotive force of this coil (a) in ampere-turns, and (b) in gilberts?

2-5. The total magnetic flux from one pole of a certain d-c generator is 0.016 weber, and the flux is distributed uniformly across the surface of the pole face, which is of square shape, 15 cm per side. What is the flux density (a) in webers per square meter, (b) in gauss, and (c) in maxwells per square inch?

3-5. A wooden toroid of circular cross section has a mean diameter of 1 ft. The toroid has a uniformly distributed winding of 2,000 turns in which a current of 5 amp is maintained. Determine the mean field intensity in the core (a) in ampere-turns per meter, (b) in oersteds.

4-5. A certain current in the coil of Prob. 3-5 produces a magnetic flux of 5×10^{-7} weber which threads the coil that encircles the wooden core. If the wooden core is replaced by another core of identical dimensions but of a material that has a relative permeability (μ_r) of 2,000, (a) what flux will then thread the coil? If the cross-sectional area of the toroid is 3 sq in., what is the flux density (b) in gauss, (c) in webers per square meter, and (d) in maxwells per square inch?

CHAPTER 6

ELECTROMAGNETISM

Magnetic Field Due to a Current. Oersted showed that, in the space near a current-carrying conductor, a small compass needle is deflected and that, no matter where it is placed, the axis of the needle assumes a position at right angles to the current. Thus a current produces a magnetic field in the surrounding space.

The field may be further explored by passing a straight wire through a hole in a piece of cardboard and fastening it in a vertical position as in Fig. 1-6. If an upward-flowing current is maintained in the wire and iron filings are sprinkled on the cardboard, they arrange themselves in circles about the wire when the cardboard is tapped lightly. The circles represent the lines of induction set up by the current. The needle of a small pocket compass resting on the cardboard everywhere assumes a position such that its long axis is tangent to the circular field, and its north-seeking pole points with the arrows. When the current is reversed the magnetic field is also reversed and the arrows representing both the current and the field of Fig. 1-6 have to be reversed in order to represent the new conditions.

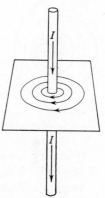

Fig. 1-6. Magnetic field surrounding a current.

Direction of a Current. The accepted conventional direction of current flow is customarily indicated by an arrow, the tip or head of which indicates the positive sense of flow, as in Fig. 1-6. In Fig. 2-6 is shown a view of the two current-carrying conductors of a parallel-sided return loop. The current in *A*, directed away from the reader, is indicated by a cross (+) to represent the tail of the disappearing arrow. The current in *B*, directed toward the reader, is indicated by a dot (•) to represent the point of the approaching arrow. Figure 3-6 shows the field surrounding two equal currents in the same direction.

The direction of a current and the direction of its magnetic field are everywhere at right angles to each other.

61

Right-hand and Right-hand-screw Rules. It is frequently necessary to find the direction (and sense) either of a field due to a known current or of a current which produces a known field. Either of the two following simple rules may be used for this purpose:

1. *Right-hand Rule.* Imagine the current-carrying conductor to be grasped in the right hand with the thumb pointing in the direction of the arrow representing the current. In imagination, the fingers then encircle the conductor in the direction of the lines of induction, with finger tips pointing the same way as the arrowheads.

2. *Right-hand-screw Rule.* Imagine that a right-hand screw is advanced along a conductor in the direction (and sense) of the current. A point on the periphery of the screw then moves in the direction (and sense) of the lines of induction about the current.

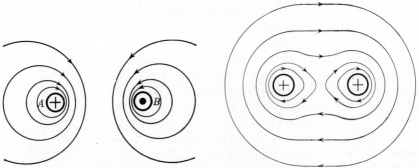

FIG. 2-6. Magnetic field of a return loop.   FIG. 3-6. Magnetic field about two equal currents in the same direction.

It is very important that the student familiarize himself with the use of one or both of these rules.

Ampère's Rule. In the year following Oersted's discovery experiments were performed by Biot and Savart and by Ampère. From these experiments an important rule of electromagnetism, known as *Ampère's rule*, was developed. By applying this rule it is theoretically possible to determine, by computation, the flux density at any point in space, due to a current in a circuit. Actually, however, it is usually not possible to evaluate the flux density except for comparatively few simple shapes and arrangements of conductors.

In symbols, Ampère's rule states that, in empty space,

$$dB = \frac{kI \, dl \sin \theta}{x^2} \tag{1-6}$$

where (Fig. 4-6) dl is an infinitesimal length of a conductor of very small diameter in comparison with the distance OP, dB is the flux density at P due to the current I in dl, θ is the angle between nO, the axis of dl, and the line from dl to P, and k is a constant, the value of which depends upon the units in which the equation is expressed.

In the mks system of units $k = 10^{-7}$, but in the mks (r) system another constant μ_0 is introduced, called the permeability of a vacuum or of "empty space," of such value that $k = \mu_0/4\pi$ or

$$\mu_0 = 4\pi \times 10^{-7} \text{ henry/m} \qquad (2\text{-}6)$$

When $\mu_0/4\pi$ is substituted for k in Eq. (1-6), Ampère's rule becomes

$$dB = \frac{\mu_0 I \, dl \sin \theta}{4\pi x^2} \qquad (3\text{-}6)$$

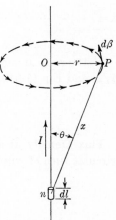

By applying the right-hand rule to Fig. 4-6, one observes that the flux-density vector dB lies in a plane that is perpendicular to the axis of dl and is normal to the plane which contains lines nO and nP. If the latter plane is revolved about the axis of dl, point P describes a circle to which the component vectors dB, corresponding to the different positions of P, are tangent. Thus the circle represents a line of induction passing through P, due to the current in dl.

Fig. 4-6. Flux density due to current in a small length dl of wire.

In following paragraphs the flux density at a point, due to a current, is determined for each of a few simple conductor arrangements.

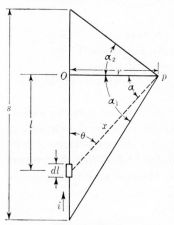

Fig. 5-6. Flux density at a point near a straight round wire due to a current in the wire.

Flux Density at a Point Due to the Current in a Straight Wire.[1] If dl in Fig. 4-6 were part of a straight wire, the axes of dl and of the wire would coincide. In that case, every length dl of the wire produces a component of flux density at P which acts along the same line as every other component, and the total flux density (B) at P is the arithmetic sum of all the components, or

$$B = \frac{\mu_0}{4\pi} \int_{l_1}^{l_2} \frac{I \, dl \sin \theta}{x^2}$$

where the integral is to be taken between the proper limits.

For convenience in solving, the equation is expressed in terms of the independent variable α (Fig. 5-6) by substituting $\sin \theta = \cos \alpha$, $x^2 = r^2 \sec^2 \alpha$, $l = r \tan \alpha$ or $dl = r \sec^2 \alpha \, d\alpha$, and indicating the limits of α corresponding to

[1] The diameter of the wire is assumed to be negligible in comparison with the distance OP in Fig. 4-6.

a wire of length s, to obtain

$$B = \frac{\mu_0}{4\pi} \frac{I}{r} \int_{-\alpha_1}^{\alpha_2} \cos \alpha \, d\alpha$$

$$= \frac{\mu_0}{4\pi} \frac{I}{r} (\sin \alpha_2 + \sin \alpha_1) \qquad (4\text{-}6)$$

If the wire is very long, α_1 and α_2 are both approximately equal to $\pi/2$, and Eq. (4-6) reduces to

$$B = \frac{\mu_0 I}{2\pi r} \qquad \text{webers/sq m} \qquad (5\text{-}6)$$

Flux Density at a Point on the Axis of a Circle. Consider a single circular turn of wire in which the current is I amp, and let it be required

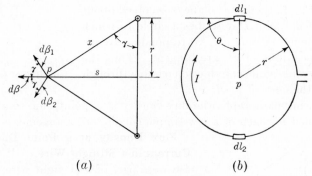

Fig. 6-6. Flux density on the axis of a circular turn of round wire.

to determine the flux density B at any point p on the axis of the coil s meters from the plane of the coil.

Figure 6-6 illustrates the front and side views of the turn, as well as the component vector flux densities dB_1 and dB_2, due to the current in the two diametrically opposite lengths, dl_1 and dl_2 respectively. The resultant vector component dB, which is obtained by adding the vectors dB_1 and dB_2 vectorially, acts along the axis of the coil, and its magnitude is $dB = 2 \, dB_1 \cos \gamma = 2 \, dB_1 \, r/x$.

By Ampère's rule,

$$dB_1 = \frac{\mu_0 I \, dl}{4\pi x^2}$$

since θ in Eq. (3-6) is $\pi/2$ and $\sin \theta = 1$ in the present application. Then

$$B = \frac{2\mu_0 I r}{4\pi x^3} \int_0^{\pi r} dl = \frac{\mu_0 I r^2}{2x^3}$$

or, upon eliminating x by expressing it in terms of s and the constant radius of the circle, the flux density becomes

$$B = \frac{\mu_0 I r^2}{2(r^2 + s^2)^{3/2}} \qquad (6\text{-}6)$$

Flux Density at the Center of a Circular Turn. The flux density at the center of a circular turn is obviously the value derived from Eq. (6-6) for the condition $s = 0$, which is

$$B = \frac{\mu_0 I}{2r} \qquad (7\text{-}6)$$

Flux Density on the Axis of an Air-core Solenoid. In general any straight coil of wire with a closely packed, uniformly distributed winding, usually not more than a few layers deep, is called a *solenoid*. A

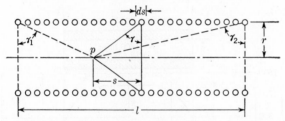

FIG. 7-6. Flux density on the axis of a solenoid.

"long solenoid" is considered to be one for which the ratio of length to diameter is roughly 20 or more.

Let the solenoid of Fig. 7-6 be tightly wound with a single layer of many turns of relatively small wire, and let l be the length of the coil and I be the current in the coil. Then the equivalent current encircling the core in a small length ds of the coil is $\dfrac{NI}{l}\,ds$ amp, and the component of flux density at p due to this current flowing once around the core is found from Eq. (6-6) to be

$$dB = \frac{\mu_0 N I r^2}{2l(r^2 + s^2)^{3/2}}\,ds$$

The flux density at p due to the entire solenoid is found by adding all the components dB, preferably by using γ as the independent variable instead of s. When the above equation is transformed by substituting $s = r \tan \gamma$ and $ds = r \sec^2 \gamma\,d\gamma$, and the integral is formed, the flux density becomes

$$B = \frac{\mu_0 N I}{2l} \int_{-\gamma_1}^{\gamma_2} \cos \gamma\,d\gamma = \frac{\mu_0 N I}{2l}\,[\sin \gamma_2 - \sin (-\gamma_1)] \qquad (8\text{-}6)$$

If the solenoid is a long one and p is not near one of the ends,

$$\gamma_1 = \gamma_2 \cong \frac{\pi}{2}$$

and

$$B = \frac{\mu_0 N I}{l} \qquad \text{webers/sq m} \qquad (9\text{-}6)$$

This equation also applies to a reentrant long solenoid in the form of an anchor ring as in Fig. 3-8.

When p is at one face of the solenoid, either $\sin \gamma_1$ or $\sin \gamma_2$ is zero and

$$B = \frac{\mu_0 N I}{2l} \qquad \text{webers/sq m} \qquad (10\text{-}6)$$

showing that one-half the flux has leaked out.

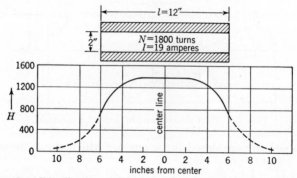

FIG. 8-6. Distribution of field intensity on the axis of a solenoid.

Total Flux of a Solenoid. In a long solenoid the flux density is uniform over the entire cross-sectional area (except near the ends), so the total flux through the solenoid is very nearly

$$\phi = BA = \frac{\mu_0 N I A}{l} \qquad \text{webers} \qquad (11\text{-}6)$$

where A = cross-sectional area, sq m.

Equation (11-6) applies to the reentrant solenoid of large diameter also.

The distribution of the flux density in a rather short solenoid is illustrated in Fig. 8-6.

Example 1. A solenoid 30 in. long consists of 2,500 turns of wire uniformly wound on a hollow fiber cylinder with an outside diameter of 1.5 in. When the current in the winding is 6 amp, what are (a) the flux density at the center of the solenoid, and (b) the total flux?

$$l = 30 \times 2.54 \times 10^{-2} = 0.762 \text{ m}$$

$$A = \frac{\pi \times 1.5^2}{4} \times 2.54^2 \times 10^{-4} = 0.00114 \text{ sq m}$$

$$NI = 2500 \times 6 = 15{,}000 \text{ amp-turns}$$

$$B = \frac{\mu_0 NI}{l} = \frac{4\pi \times 10^{-7} \times 15000}{0.762} = 0.02475 \text{ weber/sq m}$$

$$\Phi = BA = 0.02475 \times 0.00114 = 2.82 \times 10^{-5} \text{ weber}$$

Force on a Conductor in a Magnetic Field. It has been proved by experiment that, in general, a current in a magnetic field experiences a force which tends to move the current at right angles to the field. This principle is used in electric motors to develop a torque, which drives the

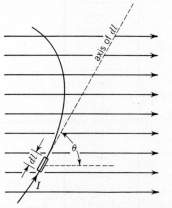

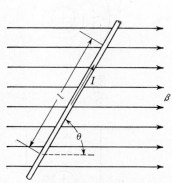

FIG. 9-6. Force on length dl of conductor in a magnetic field.

FIG. 10-6. Force on a straight round conductor of small diameter, the axis of which makes the angle θ with the direction of the magnetic field.

motor and thereby converts electrical energy supplied by the circuit to mechanical energy of rotation. The magnitude of the force developed is proportional to the current I in the conductor, the flux density B of the field, and to the component of the length l of the conductor which is perpendicular to the direction of the field.

In Fig. 9-6 the axis of a short length dl of a conductor, which lies in the plane of the paper, makes an angle θ with the direction of a magnetic field of uniform flux density B. The component force dF on the current in dl is

$$dF = BI \, dl \sin \theta$$

The force is normal to the plane of the paper, and the sense is away from the observer. Every other small section of conductor has a similar component of force.

For the case of a straight wire of length l (Fig. 10-6) the force on the conductor is

$$F = BIl \sin \theta \qquad \text{newtons} \qquad (12\text{-}6)$$

or, when the axis of the conductor is perpendicular to the direction of the field ($\theta = \pi/2$), the force on the conductor is

$$F = BIl \qquad \text{newtons} \qquad (13\text{-}6)a$$
$$= 0.2247BIl \qquad \text{lb} \qquad (13\text{-}6)b$$

where B is in webers per square meter and l is in meters.

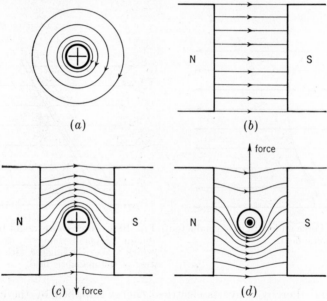

FIG. 11-6. Force on a current which is directed normal to the flux density of a uniform magnetic field.

When the axis of the conductor is parallel to the direction of the field ($\theta = 0$), the force on the conductor is zero.

Force Action of Eq. (13-6) Illustrated. In (a) of Fig. 11-6 is represented the end view of a current directed away from the reader in a straight wire and the associated magnetic field, while in (b) is shown the uniform magnetic field between the poles of a magnet. If the current (a) is placed in the field (b) with the axis of the conductor making a right angle with the direction of the field, the current and the magnetic poles both aid in magnetizing the air gap, and the resultant picture is similar to (c). Below the wire the magnetizing force of the current and the poles are subtractive, while above the wire they are additive. The resultant magnetic field in (c) is that produced by the joint action of the current and the magnetic potential difference impressed across the air gap.

The force on the conductor is in the direction of the weaker field or downward, as indicated. An equal and opposite force acts on the magnetic poles, tending to shove them upward. If the current is reversed as in (d), the forces on the conductor and poles are also reversed.

Rule for Determining Direction of Force. A convenient rule for determining the force action is the following: Apply the right-hand rule to the current, and note on which side of the conductor the magnetizing forces of the current and the field are subtractive. The force on the conductor acts *toward* the weaker field along a line which is perpendicular to the direction of the lines of force in the original field.

Electric Motor. The most common application of the foregoing principle is found in the electric motor. Figure 12-6 is an elementary sketch of a two-pole d-c motor. The motor armature is mounted on a shaft and is free to rotate. On the armature parallel to the shaft are wound many conductors Z or current-carrying wires. These are exposed to flux ϕ of the magnetic field produced by the north and south poles of the motor field structure. The armature conductors or wires are observed to be at right

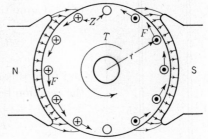

Fig. 12-6. The electric motor.

angles to the air-gap flux. The machine is so constructed that, no matter what the position of the armature, the currents always flow in (+) under one pole and out (•) under the other. In the figure the conductors under the north pole are therefore always forced downward while those under the south pole are forced upward, thus developing the torque that makes the motor run.

Example 2. A motor similar to the one in Fig. 12-6 has 450 conductors, of which there is always a total of 300 under the poles at any instant. The axial length of the conductors exposed to the field flux is 5 in. for each conductor, and at full load the current in the winding is 12 amp. The radius of the armature from center of the shaft to center of the conductors is 3 in. How much torque does the motor develop at full load if the air-gap flux density is 40,000 lines per square inch?

The active length of each armature conductor is

$$l = 5 \times 2.54 \times 10^{-2} = 0.127 \text{ m}$$

and the flux density is

$$B = 40,000/2.54^2 \times 10^{-4} = 0.62 \text{ weber/sq m}$$

Each conductor develops a torque equal to the product of the force on the conductor and the lever arm r. The force per conductor is found from Eq. (13-6)b to be

$$F = 0.2247 \times 0.62 \times 12 \times 0.127 = 0.212 \text{ lb per conductor}$$

The torque produced by the motor is

$$T = 300 \times Fr = 300 \times 0.212 \times \tfrac{3}{12} = 15.9 \text{ lb-perp}\dagger\text{-ft}$$

Force Action between Two Long Straight Parallel Wires.

Assume that the two very long straight parallel wires A and B of Fig. 13-6 carry the continuous currents I_a and I_b respectively, and let the wires be supported r m apart in air which, for the present purpose, may be regarded as empty space. The diameter of the wires is assumed to be very small in comparison with r.

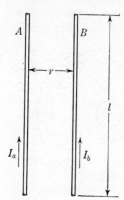

By Eq. (5-6) the flux density at any point r m from A, due to the current I_a, is

$$B_a = \frac{\mu_0 I_a}{2\pi r} \qquad \text{webers/sq m}$$

and from this and Eq. (13-6), the force on B due to the reaction between B_a and I_b is

$$F = \frac{\mu_0 I_a I_b l}{2\pi r} \qquad \text{newtons} \qquad (14\text{-}6)$$

Fig. 13-6. Force between two long straight parallel wires in which currents exist.

This equation is used as the basis for the definition of the unit current (ampere) in the mks (r) system of units. If it be stipulated that the conductors are 1 m apart and that $I_a = I_b = 1$ amp, and if it be recalled that $\mu_0 = 4\pi \times 10^{-7}$, it is at once apparent that the force per meter length of each conductor is $F = 2 \times 10^{-7}$ newton. Accordingly, the *ampere* is defined as that continuous current which, when maintained in each of two infinitely long straight parallel wires of negligible diameter one meter apart in empty space (air), causes each wire to experience a force of 2×10^{-7} newton per meter of length.

Example 3. Two copper-tube bus bars, 6 in. apart, are supported on insulators spaced 4 ft between centers. If, under short-circuit conditions, the equal currents in the busses reach 10,000 amp, how much side thrust does each insulator experience?

$\dagger$ Torque is the product of a force F and a lever arm which is perpendicular to the direction of the force. Hence, the accepted abbreviation:

$$T = \text{force-perp-lever arm}$$

By Eq. (14-6),

$$F = \frac{\mu_0 I_a I_b l}{2\pi r}$$
$$= \frac{2 \times 0.2247 \times 10^{-7} \times 10^8 \times 4}{\frac{1}{2}}$$
$$= 35.95 \text{ lb}$$

Energy Stored in a Magnetic Field.   Consider a uniformly wound air-core or wood-core anchor ring of large diameter in comparison with the diameter of its circular cross section, similar to Fig. 3-8.   Let A be the cross-sectional area of the core, l be the mean length of the ring, and B be the mean flux density in the core when the current in the N turns of the exciting winding is i amp.   Initially, if the winding is excited by impressing a suitable source of d-c emf across the terminals, the current builds up at a varying rate which decreases with time until the steady current I is reached.   During this interval a varying counter emf is induced in the winding by the changing flux linkages, the magnitude of which is (Chap. 7)

$$e = N \frac{d\phi}{dt} = NA \frac{dB}{dt} \qquad \text{volts}$$

and by Eq. (11-6) the exciting current is

$$i = \frac{l\phi}{\mu_0 NA} = \frac{lB}{\mu_0 N}$$

During an infinitesimal interval of time dt, the energy $ei\,dt$ is supplied by the source and stored in the magnetic field.   The amount of this energy is

$$dW = ei\,dt = NA \frac{dB}{dt} \frac{lB}{\mu_0 N} dt = \frac{VB\,dB}{\mu_0}$$

where $Al = V$, the volume of the magnetic field (the core).   The total energy stored when the flux density has built up from 0 to B_1 is

$$W = \frac{V}{\mu_0} \int_0^{B_1} B\,dB = \frac{VB_1^2}{2\mu_0} \qquad \text{joules} \qquad (15\text{-}6)$$

or

$$\frac{W}{V} = \frac{B_1^2}{2\mu_0} \qquad\qquad \text{joules/cu m} \qquad (16\text{-}6)$$

Solenoid with a Soft-iron Plunger.   The flux density within a long air-core solenoid is given by Eq. (9-6).   When a soft-iron plunger is introduced into a solenoid the winding of which is excited with a current, the flux density in the core is much higher than it was when the core was air.   The plunger becomes a magnet and, if the weight of the plunger may be disregarded, is sucked into the coil until it occupies a position of symmetry with respect to the coil.

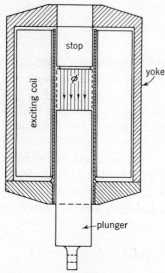

Fig. 14-6. Electromagnet with movable core.

Electromagnets with movable plungers find many applications.   A simple form of such a magnet is illustrated in Fig. 14-6. A stop is provided for the plunger, and there is a return magnetic path through the yoke surrounding the coil.   The stop has the effect of reducing the air gap as the stroke progresses, and it thereby greatly increases the pull which the plunger can exert (Fig. 15-6).

The pull F which the plunger is capable of exerting may be derived with the help of Eq. (9-6) as follows: Assume that the plunger and stop form an air gap l m long and that the plunger is withdrawn an infinitesimal distance dl against the force F of attraction of the stop, without changing the flux density in the gap.   The work done in overcoming the force is then $dW = F\,dl$, and this, in turn, is equal to the additional

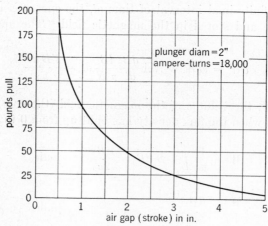

Fig. 15-6. Pull curve of the plunger-type electromagnet of Fig. 14-6.

energy stored in the incremental volume $dV = A\,dl$ of the magnetic field.   Accordingly, by Eq. (16-6),

$$dW = \frac{B_1^2}{2\mu_0} dV = \frac{B_1^2(A \ dl)}{2\mu_0}$$

and since $F = dW/dl$, it follows that

$$F = \frac{B_1^2 A}{2\mu_0} = \frac{\phi_1^2}{2\mu_0 A} \qquad \text{newtons} \qquad (17\text{-}6)$$

When ϕ is in maxwells, A is in square inches, and F is in pounds, the above equation reduces to

$$F = \frac{10^{-6}\phi_1^2}{72.1A} \qquad \text{lb} \qquad (18\text{-}6)$$

The pull curve of Fig. 15-6 was obtained by experiment with an electromagnet of the type illustrated in Fig. 14-6.

Fig. 16-6. Lifting magnet. (*Cutler-Hammer, Inc.*)

Other Uses and Forms of Electromagnets. Electromagnets are used in many forms and are applied in a great variety of ways. All forms of electric motors and generators depend upon magnetic fields for their operation. Industrial motors are often started and otherwise controlled by means of electromagnetically operated switches. Wherever automatic or semiautomatic operations are performed, electromagnets are quite generally used as the medium of control. Large electromagnets are used to move iron and steel in various forms and to collect scrap metal from highways. Telephone receivers utilize electromagnets to transform the electrical energy coming over the telephone wires to the

FIG. 17-6. Magnetic brake. (*Westinghouse Electric Corporation.*)

mechanical energy of sound that finally actuates the eardrum, and telegraph signals are received through the medium of electromagnets. Common forms of electromagnets are illustrated in Figs. 16-6 and 17-6.

Problems

1-6. A small compass is laid on a card through which is passed a conductor carrying a current away from the observer as illustrated in Fig. *A*-6. In which direction does the north-seeking end of the compass needle point in the figure?

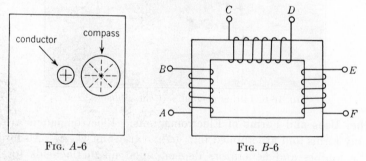

FIG. *A*-6   FIG. *B*-6

2-6. The three coils illustrated in Fig. *B*-6 are wound on the core as shown, and it is desired to so connect the coils in series that their magnetomotive forces are additive. Show how the terminals may be connected to produce the desired result.

3-6. In the picture tube of a television receiver, electrons are shot through a magnetic field by an electron gun. Assume the paths of the electrons to be from left to right, and assume the magnetic flux to be directed away from the observer and at right angles to the path of the electrons. What is the direction of the force tending to deflect the electrons?

4-6. Study the distribution of the magnetic field around a long straight cylindrical conductor due to the current in the conductor. Disregard the effect produced by the return circuit. Determine (*a*) the direction of the resultant force acting on an elementary filament of current, (*b*) the resultant effect of all such forces upon the conductor. (*c*) If the conductor is a column of conducting liquid, what result may follow if the current is very large?

5-6. What is the flux density at the center of a square loop of wire, 5 cm on each side, that carries a current of 50 amp? The loop is assumed to be in air, remote from other objects, and the leads of the coil are assumed to be so close together that their effects on the magnetic field within the square are negligible.

6-6. A counterclockwise current of 24 amp is maintained in a rectangular turn of wire 10 in. long and 4 in. wide. Determine (*a*) the amount and (*b*) the direction of the field intensity at the point of intersection of the two diagonals.

7-6. Two long straight wires (Fig. *C*-6), 3 ft apart, carrying currents of 360 amp each. Find (*a*) the amount and (*b*) the direction of the resultant field intensity at *P*.

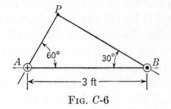

Fig. *C*-6

8-6. A 25-hp motor has an effective armature diameter of 12 in. (see Fig. 12-6) and an axial length of 8 in., and it runs at a speed of 850 rpm. The full-load current in the armature conductors is 48 amp, and the air-gap flux density is 48,000 maxwells/ sq in. The pole faces cover 65 per cent of the armature periphery. If the rotational losses are negligible, how many armature conductors must the motor have?

9-6. Two cables are installed parallel to one another with an axial separation of 6 in. The cables are supported on insulators set 30 in. apart. Rated direct current of 1,000 amp is normally maintained in each of the two parallel-connected cables. (It is assumed that the currents may be regarded as being concentrated along the axes of the cables.) Determine the lateral force in pounds on each insulator pin when a short circuit of fifteen times rated current exists.

CHAPTER 7

GENERATED AND INDUCED VOLTAGES

Electromagnetic Induction. Electromotive forces may be established in the following ways:
1. By electromagnetic induction
2. By chemical action
3. By heating the junction of two dissimilar metals

Of these three, the first is by far the most important. It is the method with which the following discussion is principally concerned and is the only method available for use in the commercial generation of power. The second has a limited application where small amounts of energy are used. All primary batteries, including so-called "dry batteries," employ this principle. The third is used to generate the very feeble emfs employed in the measurement of temperatures by means of thermocouples. A thermocouple is a junction formed of two dissimilar metals by welding them together. When such a junction is heated and the free ends are held at some constant temperature, a difference of electrical potential exists between the free terminals. This potential difference is roughly proportional to the temperature difference between the heated junction and the free ends and so may be used in conjunction with a low-reading voltmeter (millivoltmeter) to indicate temperature.

In 1830, Faraday discovered that an emf is generated in a conductor when the conductor is cut by magnetic lines of force. This was a discovery of very great importance. He found that voltage could be generated in the conductor by moving either the conductor or the flux, or both. In present-day practice this principle is applied in various ways. In d-c generators and motors, revolving conductors cut the stationary flux in the air gap under the field poles; in large a-c generators, the flux from revolving field poles cuts stationary armature conductors; while in transformers, stationary windings link a periodically varying flux produced by an alternating mmf of a stationary winding. When emf is generated by the motion of either the field structure or the conductors, as in a-c and d-c generators, it is called a *generated* emf. When it is produced by a changing flux as in a transformer, it is called an *induced* emf, but this distinction is usually of no great importance.

As a result of his experiments, Faraday announced the law that *the emf induced (or generated) in a conductor by electromagnetic action is proportional to the time rate of change of magnetic linkages or to the time rate of cutting lines of force, as the case may be.* This law, called *Faraday's law*, is probably the most important law in electrical science. It is important, therefore, that the student should have a clear understanding of its meaning.

Generated Voltages. To illustrate the method of generating a voltage by the motion of a conductor, consider Fig. 1-7. Let the total flux enclosed or linked by the coil in the position shown be ϕ webers. When the coil is moved downward, the upper side of the loop cuts across the magnetic lines and generates an emf in the section ab. The remainder of the turn cuts no flux and has no voltage generated in it. The emf generated in ab depends upon the rate at which it cuts the flux from the poles. If the conductor is moved rapidly across the field, the emf generated is large; if it is moved slowly, the emf is small; and as soon as the motion ceases, no lines of force are cut and the emf is zero. If it takes t sec to move ab beyond the lower edge of the field, the *average* emf generated in the turn is

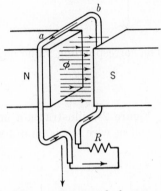

Fig. 1-7. Generated electromotive force. Moving conductor.

$$E_{av} = \frac{\phi}{t} \qquad \text{volts per conductor}$$

In the practical system of units, flux is in maxwells, and since

$$1 \text{ weber} = 10^8 \text{ maxwells}$$

the equation for generated voltage becomes

$$E_{av} = \frac{\phi}{10^8 t} \qquad \text{volts}$$

Thus, when a conductor cuts magnetic flux at the rate of 1 weber or 10^8 maxwells/sec, the emf generated in the conductor is 1 volt. So long as the rate of cutting does not vary, as when the flux in Fig. 1-7 is uniformly distributed over the area and the velocity of the conductor does not change, the voltage is constant. If the field is not uniform, or if the velocity of motion varies, the rate of cutting and the voltage also vary. If the flux ϕ, linking the coil, changes by an infinitesimal amount $d\phi$ during a corresponding interval of time dt, the rate of cutting is $d\phi/dt$

and the instantaneous voltage generated in the coil is

$$e = \frac{d\phi}{dt} \qquad \text{volts}$$

If the single turn in Fig. 1-7 is replaced by a coil of N turns, there are N conductors like ab and each of them cuts the entire flux from the poles when the coil is moved downward as before.   The voltage generated in the upper part of the coil is then N times as much as it was in the first instance, and the average voltage generated in the coil is

$$E_{av} = \frac{N\phi}{t} \qquad \text{volts} \qquad (1\text{-}7)$$

The corresponding value of instantaneous voltage is

$$e = \frac{N\,d\phi}{dt} \qquad \text{volts} \qquad (2\text{-}7)$$

Figure 2-7 illustrates a method of generating an alternating voltage. A coil of wire mn is mounted on a shaft between the poles of a magnet.

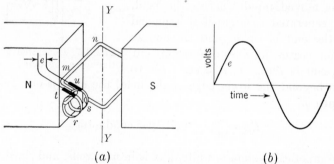

(a)   (b)

FIG. 2-7. Alternating electromotive force.

The ends of the coil are connected to metal rings r and s, called *slip rings*. These are also mounted on the shaft and are fitted with brushes for connection to an external circuit tu.   When the coil is rotated at a constant speed, the sides of the coil cut the lines of force from the poles.   The rate of cutting varies, being greatest when the plane of the coil is in the axis of the poles, for then the coil sides are moving at right angles to lines of induction.   When the plane of the coil is in the YY axis, the conductors are moving parallel to the lines of induction.   The rate of cutting is then zero, and no voltage is generated.   Moreover, the direction of the generated voltage reverses as the coil passes through the YY plane, because the direction of cutting changes.   If the instantaneous voltage is plotted for one revolution of the coil, the curve obtained is the sine wave of Fig. 2-7(b).

Example 1. In Fig. 2-7, 50 turns of wire revolve at a speed of 2,400 rpm. When the plane of the coil lies in the YY plane, called the initial position of the coil, the flux through the coil is 8 milliwebers. What is the average voltage generated in the coil while it turns through one-half revolution from the initial position?

During one-half revolution each side of every turn cuts each line of induction once. Therefore, each turn cuts $2 \times 8 \times 10^{-3}$ weber per half revolution. Since the number of half revolutions per second is $2 \times 2,400/60 = 80$, the average rate of cutting lines of induction, or the average voltage is

$$E_{av} = 50 \times 2 \times 8 \times 10^{-3} \times 80 = 64 \text{ volts}$$

Induced Voltages. An emf may be established in a conductor without moving either the conductor or the poles of a magnet, for the flux of induction which links one or more turns of a coil represents magnetic linkages which may be caused to change by simply varying the ampere-turns which established them. Electromotive forces that are set up in this way are called *induced emfs* as has already been stated.

Whenever the current in a conductor changes, the magnetic field linking it changes also, for the magnetizing force is proportional to the current. Consider the turn of wire in Fig. 3-7, and let the current be directed away from the observer at the top and toward him at the bottom. So long as the current does not change the flux linking the wire remains constant. When the current is increased, however, the number of linkages is increased and when the current is decreased some of the linkages disappear. Experiment shows that in either case emf is induced in the wire. To explain these facts, it is convenient to think of the lines of induction as originating at the axis of the wire, expanding outward when the current builds up, and collapsing on the wire when the current dies down. When the current rises, one side of each closed line cuts across the turn as the lines

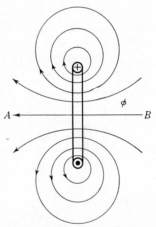

FIG. 3-7. Electromotive force of self-induction.

expand and voltage is induced in the turn in proportion to the rate of cutting. When the current is decreased, the returning lines again cut across the turn and induce a voltage in it, but the direction of the voltage is reversed. An emf induced in a conductor in this way by its own changing magnetic field is called an emf of *self-induction*. Obviously, in a similar manner the magnetic field due to a current in circuit 1 may cut the conductors of a second circuit 2 when the field is changed, as in Fig. 4-7. Voltage is induced in 2 in a given direction when the current in 1 is rising, and in the reverse direction when the current in 1 is falling. The voltage induced in a second circuit by a changing current in the first is called an emf of *mutual induction*.

Direction of Generated and Induced Voltages. When the conductor in which a voltage is generated or induced forms a part of a closed circuit, current flows in the conductor. The direction of the current can always

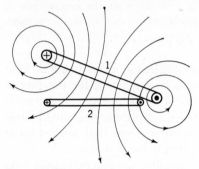

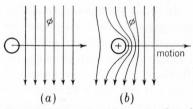

FIG. 4-7. Electromotive force of mutual induction.

FIG. 5-7. Direction of generated emf and current.

be found by the following simple rule, called *Lenz's law*. Lenz's law states that *the current set up by an induced voltage always opposes the motion or change in current which produces it*. The following illustration clarifies the meaning of this law. When the conductor in Fig. 5-7(*a*) moves to the right, the generated voltage establishes a current that flows inward as in (*b*). This current, by its magnetizing action, increases

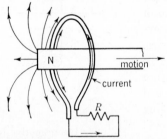

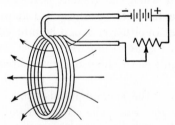

FIG. 6-7. Generated electromotive force. Moving field.

FIG. 7-7. Direction of induced emf.

the strength of field on the right side of the conductor and decreases it on the left side. A force is thereby set up (as in a motor) that tends to move the conductor to the left, thus opposing the motion that generates the voltage. It should be noted that if the circuit is open so that no current can flow, the field remains as in (*a*), no retarding force is developed, and no work is required to move the conductor through the field. When voltage is generated in the coil (Fig. 6-7) by the motion of the magnet to the right, current circulates in the coil in a counterclockwise direction if the circuit is closed. The magnetizing action of the current tends to keep the flux linking the coil from decreasing, and in a manner similar to that described above, a force is set up that tends to prevent the withdrawal of the magnet, thus opposing the motion that generates the voltage. If the coil is free, it moves to the right. In Fig. 7-7, when the current in the coil is decreasing, the induced voltage aids the impressed voltage in maintaining the current in the coil and thus tends to prevent the current from decreasing. When the current in the coil is increasing, the induced emf opposes the impressed voltage and tends to prevent the current from increasing.

Right-hand Rule. The right-hand rule discussed on page 62 may also be used to find the direction of induced or generated voltage and current as follows: *Imagine the conductor to be grasped in the right hand, the fingers pointing in the direction that a line of induction would appear to wrap itself about the conductor when either the flux or the conductor moves, as the case may be. The thumb then points in the direction of the induced emf.* The reader should check the illustrations of the previous paragraph by this rule.

Flux Linkages. Lines of magnetic induction are closed loops or links. If one considers a conductor as being a geometrical line, the current in it always produces magnetic lines that completely surround the current, as in Figs. 3-7, 7-7, and 8-7. One line linking a conductor once is called a *flux linkage* or *flux turn*, while ϕ lines, each linking the conductor once, represent ϕ flux linkages. When a conductor is wound in the form of a coil as in Fig. 8-7, each line, as a rule, links the conductor a number of times. Lines a and a' in the figure each represent one linkage, lines b and b' each three linkages, and lines c and c' and the remaining ones each represent five linkages. The total flux linkages of the coil is obtained by adding those due to all the lines. In the case of the

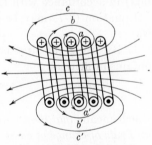

Fig. 8-7. Flux linkages.

figure the total is $N\phi = 43$. In general, when each of ϕ lines links N turns of a conductor the number of flux linkages is $N\phi$. This is equivalent to one line linking the conductor $N\phi$ times or $N\phi$ lines each linking the conductor once. The concept of flux linkages is very useful in the discussion of induced voltages.

Example 2. A solenoid 40 in. long has 2,800 turns of wire wound on a cylindrical wooden core 2 in. in diameter. How many flux linkages does the solenoid have when the current is 5 amp?

The dimensions of the core are

$$\text{Area} = 0.7854 \times 2^2 \times 2.54^2 \times 10^{-4} = 20.26 \times 10^{-4} \text{ sq m}$$
$$\text{Length} = 40 \times 2.54 \times 10^{-2} = 1.016 \text{ m}$$

By Eq. (11-6) on page 66, the flux through the core is found to be

$$\phi = \frac{4\pi \times 10^{-7} \times 2,800 \times 5 \times 20.26 \times 10^{-4}}{1.016} = 35.2 \times 10^{-6} \text{ weber}$$

The number of flux linkages is the product of flux and turns. In a long solenoid each of the lines may be considered as linking all the turns. Hence,

$$N\phi = 2,800 \times 35.2 \times 10^{-6} = 9.85 \times 10^{-2} \text{ weber-turn}$$

This value is only slightly too high, because only the turns near the ends are affected by the lines that leak out through the coil.

Coefficient of Self-induction. A circuit in which a current is maintained cuts the flux from its own magnetic field when the current changes, and the emf of self-induction thereby induced is proportional to the time rate of cutting flux. But, in general, the flux linking a circuit is proportional to the current, so the induced voltage is also proportional to the rate of change of the current. Hence, by Faraday's law,

$$e = -L\frac{di}{dt} = -N\frac{d\phi}{dt} \tag{3-7}$$

where L is the proportionality factor called the *coefficient of self-induction*, or simply, the *self-inductance* of the circuit. The negative signs are used to indicate that the induced voltage opposes the change in current (and flux) in accordance with Lenz's law.

Equation (3-7) may be used to define the inductance in either of two ways:

1. By using the first two terms and solving for the inductance, one obtains numerically

$$L = \frac{e}{di/dt} \tag{4-7}$$

which means *that the inductance of a circuit is the self-induced voltage per unit rate of change of current*. A circuit in which current changing at the rate of one ampere per second induces one volt has an inductance of one henry.

2. If the two right-hand terms of Eq. (3-7) are used, one obtains

$$L = N\frac{d\phi}{di} \tag{5-7}$$

When there is no magnetic material anywhere in the vicinity of the circuit, L is independent of the current and $L\int_0^I di = N\int_0^\phi d\phi$, or

$$LI = N\phi$$

and

$$L = \frac{N\phi}{I} \tag{6-7}$$

From this it may be seen that, in the mks system, *the inductance of a circuit is the number of weber-turns per ampere of current in the circuit.*

This alternate definition of L has the advantage that it may often be used to compute the inductance of a circuit. A circuit in which one ampere produces one weber-turn linkage (or 10^8 maxwell linkages) has an inductance of one *henry.*

Inductance, like resistance, is called a *circuit constant* because, except where magnetic materials are present, it is independent of current and depends only upon the circuit arrangement. A given length of wire has minimum inductance when the wire is straight. The inductance of the same length of wire is increased by winding the wire into a coil. The inductance of a tightly packed coil is proportional to the square of the number of turns.

Unit of Self-inductance. The unit of self-inductance, in both the mks and the practical system of units, is the *henry.* Submultiples of this unit are the *millihenry* and the *microhenry.* For example, the inductance per mile of one conductor of a high-voltage transmission line is about 2 millihenrys, whereas the inductance of the field winding of a 5-hp direct-current motor may be as much as 50 henrys.

Example 3. (*a*) What is the inductance of the wood-core solenoid described in the example on page 81? (*b*) If an iron core is substituted for the wood core, the flux increases to 500 times its former value when the current is 5 amp. What is the self-inductance of the circuit when the iron core is used and the current is 5 amp?

(*a*) From the example on page 81 the number of flux linkages produced by 5 amp (wood core) is found to be 9.85×10^{-2}. From Eq. (6-7) the inductance is

$$L_a = \frac{9.85 \times 10^{-2}}{5} = 0.0197 \text{ henry}$$

(*b*) When iron is substituted for wood, the flux produced by the same current (5 amp) is 500 times the former value. Accordingly, the inductance is 500 times as much as it was before, or

$$L_b = 500 \times 0.0197 = 9.85 \text{ henrys}$$

Coefficient of Mutual Induction. When a circuit 1 is so placed with respect to a second electrically independent circuit 2 that some of the flux from 1 links the turns of 2, an emf of mutual induction is induced in 2 when the current in 1 changes (Fig. 4-7). Experiment shows that this emf is proportional to the rate of change of current in 1, or

$$e_{12} = \frac{-M\, di_1}{dt} \qquad \text{volts}$$

In the above equation, M is the proportionality factor called the *coefficient of mutual induction,* or simply the *mutual inductance* of the circuit, and the minus sign is used to indicate that the current set up in 2 by the emf of mutual induction is in such a direction that it opposes the change of current in 1.   Similar to self-inductance, the mutual inductance of a circuit 2 with respect to 1 is defined as the voltage induced in 2 by unit rate of change of current in 1.   It may also be defined as the flux linkages produced by flux from 1 linking the turns of 2, per ampere of current in 1.   Thus

$$M = \frac{N_2 \phi_{12}}{I_1} \tag{7-7}$$

Mutual inductances are measured in the units already defined for the case of self-inductance, that is, in henrys, millihenrys, etc.

Starting a Current.   The process of starting a current in a circuit is almost exactly analogous to the process of setting a mass in motion. Consider the automobile as a familiar example.   When a car is started, energy is required (1) to overcome the inertia of the mass and (2) to overcome friction.   Let the engine develop a constant torque (constant pull) during the starting period, and assume the friction to be proportional to the velocity of the car.   Since the inertia force is proportional to the acceleration (rate of change of velocity), and the frictional force is proportional to the velocity, the total pull F exerted by the engine is absorbed as follows:

$$F = \text{inertia force} + \text{friction force} = M \frac{dv}{dt} + kv$$

where M = mass of car
$\quad\quad\; v$ = velocity
$\quad\quad\; k$ = constant

When the car first starts to move, the velocity begins at zero and the friction force is negligible.   The pull of the engine is then absorbed in overcoming the force of inertia, and the velocity of the car is increased rapidly.   As the car gains speed, more and more of the pull is absorbed by friction, less and less is available to accelerate the car, and the car gains speed more slowly. Finally, when all the pull developed by the engine is absorbed in overcoming friction, there is no residue left to produce further acceleration and the velocity no longer changes.   A given engine accelerates a light car more rapidly than a heavy one, because the inertia force is less.   The energy developed by the engine during the starting period is partly lost as heat in overcoming frictional resistance and partly stored as kinetic energy in the mass of the car. The latter ($\frac{1}{2}Mv^2$) is again made available when the engine is shut off and the car is allowed to coast to rest.

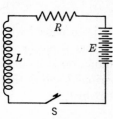

Fig.   9-7. Starting   or stopping a current.

Next consider an electric circuit like the one in Fig. 9-7, containing an inductance L and a resistance R, and let the constant battery emf of E volts be impressed. When current is increasing in the circuit, energy is required (1) to force current through the inductance against the counter emf of self-induction due to the increasing current, and (2) to overcome the resistance of the circuit. The applied voltage is partly balanced by the emf of self-induction and partly consumed in the resistance; that is,

$$E = Ri + L\frac{di}{dt}† \tag{8-7}$$

$$= Ri + N\frac{d\phi}{dt} \tag{9-7}$$

† When this equation is solved and the current is plotted against time, the curve of Fig. 10-7 is obtained. Thus, by separating the variables, changing signs, and multiplying both sides of the equation by R, the equation becomes

$$-\frac{R\,di}{E - Ri} = -\frac{R}{L}\,dt$$

whence, by integration

$$\log_\epsilon (E - Ri) = -\frac{R}{L}t + k \text{ (a constant)}$$

But $i = 0$ when $t = 0$, whence $k = \log_\epsilon E$ and

$$\log_\epsilon \frac{E - Ri}{E} = -\frac{R}{L}t$$

or

$$i = \frac{E}{R}(1 - \epsilon^{-(R/L)t})$$

It is apparent from an inspection of the current equation that the exponent in the last term can be reduced to unity by substituting for t the particular value, $T = L/R$. This value of time is called the *time constant* of the circuit. By making the indicated substitutions and solving one obtains

$$i_T = \frac{E}{R}\left(1 - \frac{1}{2.7183}\right) = 0.632\frac{E}{R}$$

Accordingly, the time constant of an inductive circuit is the time that it takes a direct current to build up from zero to 63.2 per cent of its steady-state value.

The time constant can also be found graphically from a picture or graph of the current curve obtained by means of an oscillograph (see index). The slope of the current curve at time zero may be found mathematically by differentiating the current equation and putting time equal to zero in the resultant solution, thus,

$$\frac{di}{dt} = \frac{E}{L}\epsilon^{-(R/L)t}$$

and

$$\frac{di}{dt_{t=0}} = \frac{E}{L}$$

The slope may also be found graphically by drawing a straight line tangent to the curve of current at time zero. Extend the tangent until it intersects the steady where i = the instantaneous current (Fig. 10-7) corresponding to the velocity of the car. When the switch is first closed, the current starts from zero and the Ri drop is negligible. All the battery voltage must then be balanced by induced voltage, and the current and flux linkages increase rapidly. As the current grows, more and more of the applied voltage is absorbed in the resistance, less and less voltage is available to balance induced voltage, and the current increases more slowly. Finally, when all the applied voltage is absorbed in the resistance, there is no excess available to increase the current further. The current and the flux linkages then no longer change, and there is no emf of self-inductance.

The inductance of the electric circuit is analogous to the mass of the car. With a given impressed voltage applied, the current reaches its steady value sooner in a circuit of small inductance than in one having a large value of L. When L is small, the current rises rapidly because there is little counter emf of self-inductance to retard the action. When L is large, a large counter emf is induced at the beginning and the current must rise slowly. The energy developed by the battery during the starting period is partly lost as heat in the resistance R and partly stored in the inductance of the circuit in the form of energy of the magnetic field. The latter is again returned to the circuit, when the current is stopped by switching out the battery, and appears in the form of an arc across the switch blade when the switch is opened.

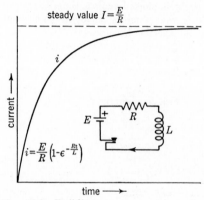

FIG. 10-7. Building up a current in a circuit containing R and L in series. Impressed emf is constant.

Stopping a Current. The automobile analogy holds for stopping a current as well as for starting. In a speeding automobile, kinetic energy

---

current line E/R and from that point drop a perpendicular to the time axis. Let the time thus determined be t_1. By construction it is obvious that the slope of the curve at time zero is then $E/R \div t_1$, from which it follows that

$$\frac{E}{Rt_1} = \frac{E}{L}$$

or

$$t_1 = T = \frac{L}{R}$$

Accordingly, the time constant may also be determined from the slope of the current curve at time zero. Moreover, the inductance of the circuit may be found by taking the product of the time constant and the resistance of the circuit.

is stored in an amount that is directly proportional to the mass and to the square of the speed ($\frac{1}{2}Mv^2$). If an automobile, running at high speed, is stopped too suddenly, as sometimes happens accidentally, the stored energy is suddenly released with disastrous results to both the car and the driver. A much better way to stop a car is to absorb the stored energy gradually in the friction of the brakes and road.

When a current flows in a circuit, energy is stored in the magnetic field in an amount that is directly proportional to the inductance of the circuit and to the square of the current ($\frac{1}{2}LI^2$). When the current is stopped this stored energy is liberated. If the circuit has a large inductance and a moderately large current, it is dangerous to stop the current

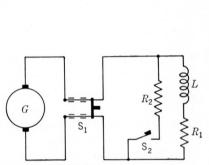

FIG. 11-7. Stopping a current.

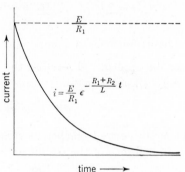

FIG. 12-7. Decay of current in a circuit containing R and L.

suddenly, as by opening a switch. When the switch is opened, the current decreases very rapidly and an emf of self-inductance is induced in the winding that may be high enough to puncture the insulation of the winding. Furthermore, a heavy arc is drawn at the switch blades, in which the energy of the field is liberated as heat, and the operator of the switch may be seriously burned. Circuits such as the field windings of large d-c and a-c generators and motors should never be broken in this way. Instead, the energy stored in the field should be discharged through a resistance as in Fig. 11-7. The switch S_2 is closed an instant before switch S_1 is opened. The emf of self-inductance then establishes a current in the resistances R_1 and R_2 in series, and the stored energy is gradually and safely dissipated. The current falls to zero when the energy of the field has been discharged completely (Fig. 12-7).[1] In practice, S_2

---

[1] The current at any instant of time after S_2 is closed may be found. Since the impressed voltage E has been removed, the equation of equilibrium is

$$0 = Ri + L\frac{di}{dt} \qquad (a)$$

where $R = R_1 + R_2$ in Fig. 12-7. By separating the variables and rearranging, one is usually interlocked with S_1 so that it closes in the process of opening S_1 but before the jaws of the latter are disengaged.

Energy Stored in a Magnetic Field. The amount of energy stored in a magnetic field may be calculated when the inductance of the circuit is known. This may be shown quite simply as follows: Let the inductance of the circuit in Fig. 9-7 be L henrys. When the switch is closed, the current and the flux linking the circuit build up.

A *counter emf* (opposite to the impressed voltage) is induced in the coil as a result of the changing linkages. The counter emf in a circuit due to the self-inductance is

$$e_c = -L \frac{di}{dt} \qquad \text{volts}$$

To overcome this a component of impressed voltage equal to $+L \dfrac{di}{dt}$ must be applied. Therefore the source supplies in dt sec an amount of energy dW such that

$$dW = ei\, dt = Li\, di \qquad \text{joules}$$

When the current reaches its steady value I, the total energy supplied to the inductance of the circuit and stored in the magnetic field is

$$W = \int_0^I Li\, di = \tfrac{1}{2}LI^2 \qquad \text{joules} \tag{10-7}$$

---

obtains

$$\frac{di}{i} = -\frac{R}{L}\, dt$$

and by integration

$$\log_\epsilon i = -\frac{Rt}{L} + k \text{ (a constant)}$$

Let $t = 0$ at the instant when S_1 is opened. Then the current i has the initial value $I = E/R_1$ and

$$\log_\epsilon I = k$$

Hence

$$\log_\epsilon \frac{i}{I} = -\frac{Rt}{L}$$

and

$$i = \frac{E}{R_1} \epsilon^{-\frac{(R_1 + R_2)t}{L}} \tag{b}$$

This is the equation of the curve shown in Fig. 12-7.

The counter emf is

$$e_c = -L \frac{di}{dt} = \frac{E(R_1 + R_2)}{R_1} \epsilon^{-\frac{(R_1 + R_2)t}{L}}$$

Example 4.   The field winding of a small two-pole motor has 800 turns per pole. When the winding is excited with 0.80 amp, the flux per pole is 12.5 milliwebers. (*a*) What is the inductance of the winding?   (*b*) When the field is broken down at a uniform rate in 1.5 sec, what is the voltage induced in the winding?   (*c*) How much energy does the circuit give up when the current is decreased from 0.80 amp to zero?

(*a*)   By Eq. (6-7) the inductance of the circuit is

$$L = \frac{N\phi}{I} = \frac{2 \times 800 \times 0.0125}{0.8} = 25 \text{ henrys}$$

(*b*)   The average voltage is equal to the time rate at which the magnetic linkages are broken down, or

$$E_{av} = \frac{N\phi}{t} = \frac{2 \times 800 \times 0.0125}{1.5} = 13.3 \text{ volts}$$

(*c*)   By Eq. (12-7) the energy given up when the current is reduced to zero is

$$W = \frac{LI^2}{2} = \frac{25 \times 0.8^2}{2} = 8 \text{ joules}$$

Eddy Currents.   When a conductor material is moved relative to a magnetic field, or when it is present in the magnetic field of a varying

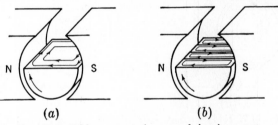

(*a*)   (*b*)

Fig. 13-7. Eddy currents in a revolving iron core.

current, magnetic lines of force cut the material and generate or induce emfs in it.   These emfs set up currents that circulate in large numbers in closed paths (usually short) throughout the solid mass of the material. Because they resemble, in a way, the eddies of swirling water, these currents are called *eddy currents*.   The current in each path is directly proportional to the induced voltage and inversely proportional to the resistance of the path.   Heat energy is liberated in each path proportional to the square of the current in it, and owing to the heat energy developed, the mass quickly becomes hot.

Suppose, for example, that a cylindrical block of steel (Fig. 13-7) is substituted for the armature of a generator and is rotated in the magnetic field.   Electromotive forces are generated in the steel in the axial direction.   If the direction of rotation is clockwise as indicated, the emf generated is away from the observer under the north pole and toward him under the south pole.   Currents circulate in the mass of the steel in circuits similar to the one shown and in the direction of the arrows.   Figure

14-7(*a*) represents the end view of a solenoid with a solid-iron core of rectangular section.   If the winding is excited with an alternating current, or if a direct current is switched on and off repeatedly, emfs are induced in the core in a circumferential direction.   These emfs cause currents to circulate around the core in the indicated direction when the current in the winding is decreasing, and in the reverse direction when the current is increasing.

The heat liberated by eddy currents usually serves no good purpose but actually represents a loss of useful energy.   This energy loss can be reduced to a low value by making it impossible for large currents to circulate.   This is accomplished in two ways:

1. By building up the material out of thin sheets or *laminations*
2. By using material that has a high specific resistance (resistivity)

If the core of Fig. 13-7 is built up with a number of disks as shown in (*b*), and each disk is insulated from its neighbor by a thin coat of shellac,

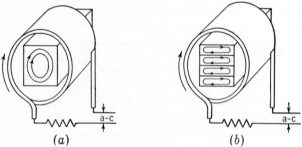

(a) (b)

Fig. 14-7. Eddy currents induced with alternating currents.

the voltage generated in a path is reduced in proportion to the thickness of the disk and the loss is reduced in proportion to the square of the thickness.   In the same way, the loss in the core of the solenoid of Fig. 14-7(*b*) may be reduced by building it up of thin sheets with their long dimensions parallel to the axis of the coil.   The expense of building up a structure increases as the laminations are made thinner, however, and so there is a limit beyond which it is uneconomical further to reduce the loss by reducing the thickness of the laminations.   In the armatures of d-c and a-c motors and generators and in the cores of transformers, punchings of special high-resistance electric steel are used.   Standard sheets are from 0.014 to 0.025 in. thick, depending upon where they are used.

The energy loss due to eddy currents is proportional to the volume of the material affected and to the square of the induced voltage, and is inversely proportional to the resistivity of the material.   Since the voltage is proportional to the rate of cutting lines of force, the eddy-current loss in laminated material is proportional to the square of the maximum flux density, the square of the thickness of laminations, and the square of the frequency.[1] The eddy-current loss in thin laminations may be expressed as

$$P_\epsilon = k_\epsilon \left(\frac{tfB_{max}}{1,000} \right)^2 \qquad \text{watts per unit weight} \qquad (11\text{-}7)$$

where k_ϵ = a factor including resistivity and specific weight of the material

t = thickness of laminations

f = frequency, cps

B_{max} = maximum flux density

Values of k_ϵ are obtained from test data such as those found in Table II on page 105. The value of k_ϵ obviously depends also upon the units in which B_{max} and t are expressed.

Problems

1-7. If the armature of the motor in Prob. 8-6 has 304 armature conductors and one-fourth of these are connected in series in an armature path, what is the voltage generated per path?

2-7. A rectangular coil of wire of 148 turns is 12 in. long and 6 in. wide. The coil is rotated about its long axis of symmetry at a speed of 8 rps in a uniform magnetic field that is normal to the axis. When the plane of the coil is normal to the flux of the field, 0.009 weber threads the coil. Calculate the instantaneous voltage generated in the coil (*a*) when the plane of the coil is parallel to the field; (*b*) when the plane of the coil makes an angle of 45 deg with the direction of the field. (*c*) What is the average voltage generated in the coil between two successive voltage zeros?

3-7. When the coil in Prob. 2-7 is at rest in the 45-deg position, the field is reversed 120 times per second. (*a*) What is the average value of the emf induced in the coil? (*b*) How many flux linkages are there when the flux threading the coil is a maximum?

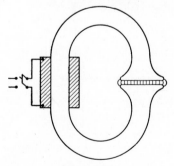

FIG. A-7

4-7. The exciting winding of an electromagnet (Fig. A-7) consists of 2,000 turns of wire having a resistance of 80 ohms. When 120 volts is impressed on the winding

---

[1] The *frequency* of eddy currents, in a direct-current generator or motor, is equal to the number of revolutions per second in a two-pole machine or is equal to $p/2$ times the number of revolutions per second in a p-pole machine.

the air-gap flux is 6.5 milliwebers, while the flux threading the coil is 20 per cent larger.   (a) What is the inductance of the winding in henrys under these conditions? (b) How long after the switch is closed does it take the current to reach 1.2 amp? (The inductance is assumed to remain constant.)   (c) How much energy is stored in the magnetic field when the current is 1.5 amp?   What is the induced voltage (d) at the instant the switch is closed; (e) when the current has risen to 1.2 amp?

5-7. A small, flat, circular exploring coil 2 in. in diameter, consisting of 50 turns of wire, is inserted in the air gap of the electromagnet described in Prob. 4-7 and lies entirely within the gap.   (a) If the air gap is 4 in. square and the exploring coil is open, what voltage is induced in the exploring coil 0.10 sec after the switch of the main winding is closed?   (b) What is the mutual inductance of the exploring coil with respect to the exciting winding of the electromagnet?

6-7. The field winding of a small d-c motor takes 1.2 amp when 120 volts are impressed across the terminals.   If the applied voltage is removed and the field winding is short-circuited on itself at the same instant, a curve like the one in Fig. 12-7 may be obtained photographically by means of an oscillograph.   A tangent drawn to this curve at time zero (the instant of short-circuiting) intersects the time axis at $t = 0.25$ sec.   Find (a) the rate of change of current in amperes per second at zero time, (b) the inductance of the circuit in henrys, (c) the counter emf when the current is 1.2 amp, (d) the counter emf when the current is 0.5 amp, (e) the stored energy remaining in the magnetic field when the current is 0.5 amp.

7-7. The eddy-current loss of No. 29 gage (0.317 mm) electrical steel is 0.357 watt/lb at a frequency of 60 cps for $B_{max} = 10,000$ lines per square centimeter. Calculate k_e, the eddy-current constant, in inch-pound units.

CHAPTER 8

THE MAGNETIC CIRCUIT. MAGNETIC PROPERTIES
OF IRON AND STEEL

Magnetic Circuit Defined. It is possible to establish a magnetic flux in a definite limited path by the use of a magnetic material of high permeability, much as an electric current is established in a conductor. For example, if one side of the wire loop in Fig. 1-8 is passed through the opening in an iron ring, a current in the wire produces a flux of induction in the ring. In Fig. 2-8 a portion of a soft-iron link is wound with a solenoid. When current is maintained in the solenoid, a magnetic flux is set up in the link as indicated. The link and the ring are both closed magnetic paths or *magnetic circuits*. When the region around an electric

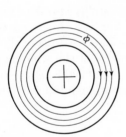

Fig. 1-8. Flux in an iron ring.

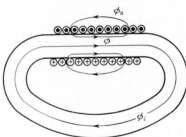

Fig. 2-8. Flux in an iron link.

circuit is air or other nonmagnetic material, the limits of the magnetic circuit are not so definite. In general, however, any space in which closed magnetic lines of force exist is called a magnetic circuit.

It will be recalled that the electrical conductivities of different materials vary widely. Some materials, such as copper and aluminum, have very high conductivities as compared with others like mica or quartz, for mica and quartz are almost perfect insulators at ordinary applied voltages. The best conductor may be as much as 10^{20} times as good as the poorest. The magnetic properties of materials do not vary over the same wide range. All nonmagnetic materials conduct flux, and in about the same degree. There is no material known that may be classed as a

93

magnetic insulator.   Magnetic materials are few in number, and while
some are better conductors of flux than others, under average conditions
the best is only several times as good a conductor of flux as the poorest.
Compared with nonmagnetic materials, the best magnetic material is
only several thousand times as good a conductor of flux under average
conditions.   Magnetic circuits, therefore, cannot be insulated from the
surrounding space as well as electric circuits.   For example, if a coil of
wire is wound around a part of an iron link as in Fig. 2-8 and a current
is maintained in the winding, a flux ϕ_i is established in the iron link.
Not all the flux ϕ through the coil passes entirely around the link, however.   Some flux ϕ_a leaks out of the link and returns through the surrounding air.   The flux ϕ_a leaking
through the air is called the *leakage
flux*.   The total flux through the
coil is the sum of the flux in the
iron and that in the air.

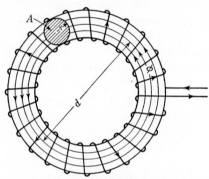

FIG. 3-8. Flux in an anchor ring.

Magnetomotive Force.   Flux is
set up in a magnetic circuit by
maintaining a current in a coil of
wire, the turns of which are wound
around a part or all of the path in
which the flux is to be established,
as in Fig. 3-8, for example.   The
magnetomotive force F is propor-
tional to the product of the number of turns N of the winding and the
current I in it.   In the mks system the unit of mmf is the *ampere-turn*, and
in the practical system it is the *gilbert*.   The total mmf of any winding is

$$F = NI \qquad \text{amp-turns}$$

or

$$F = \frac{4\pi}{10} NI \qquad \text{gilberts}$$

Ohm's Law of the Magnetic Circuit.   The simplest form of a magnetic
circuit is an anchor ring, Fig. 3-8.   Let a circuit of this kind be formed
by winding N turns of wire close together over the entire length of a
wooden ring as shown in the figure.   Since the winding begins and ends
at the same point on the ring, the effect produced is that of a continuous
solenoid.

The flux density on the axis of a long air-core solenoid, due to a current
of I amp in N turns of the winding, Eq. (9-6), has already been found to
be $B = \mu_r\mu_0 NI/l$, and since the relative permeability $\mu_r = 1$ for nonmagnetic materials, $B = \mu_0 NI/l$ holds for wood.   The *field intensity* or
magnetic gradient H, at any point on the axis of a long toroidal solenoid,

has the constant value

$$H = \frac{B}{\mu_0} = \frac{NI}{l} \qquad \text{amp-turns/m} \qquad (1\text{-}8)$$

and the total mmf of the circuit is

$$F = Hl \qquad \text{amp-turns} \qquad (2\text{-}8)$$

The flux density within the core is substantially constant over the entire cross-sectional area A, so the total flux within the core is

$$\phi = BA \qquad \text{webers} \qquad (3\text{-}8)$$

Now let a cast-steel ring be substituted for the wood, and let current and turns remain unchanged. Under these conditions the core flux is greatly increased, because cast steel is a much better conductor of flux than is wood. If μ_r is the relative permeability of the core material at the attained flux density, the latter is μ_r times as much as it is for a nonmagnetic material and the new equation for the flux density is

$$B = \mu_r \mu_0 \frac{NI}{l} \qquad \text{webers/sq m} \qquad (4\text{-}8)$$

The total flux in the core is $\phi = BA = \dfrac{NI\mu_r\mu_0 A}{l}$ webers, and since $F = NI$, the equation for the total flux in the magnetic circuit, for any value of μ_r, may be written as

$$\phi = \frac{F}{l/\mu_r\mu_0 A} \qquad (5\text{-}8)$$

$$= \frac{F}{R} \qquad (6\text{-}8)$$

where l = mean length of flux path, m
A = area of flux path, sq m
R = *reluctance* of the magnetic circuit,

$$R = \frac{l}{\mu_r\mu_0 A} \qquad (7\text{-}8)$$

Thus *in a magnetic circuit the flux is directly proportional to the impressed mmf and inversely proportional to the reluctance of the magnetic circuit.* This law is exactly similar to Ohm's law ($I = E/R$), and for this reason it is often called *Ohm's law of the magnetic circuit.*

The flux that a given mmf sets up in a simple magnetic circuit may be found by applying Eq. (5-8) just as one finds the current in an electric circuit from Ohm's law, provided the relative permeability is known. Usually, however, it is inconvenient to solve for the flux in this way because the value of μ_r varies with the flux density in the core. For this reason problems in magnetic circuits must be solved with the aid of experimental curves (magnetization curves) from which one may either find the relative permeability at any assumed flux density or gain other information that enables one to make a solution. The method commonly used to solve problems in the magnetic circuit is discussed in a future paragraph.

Reluctance and Permeability. The reluctance of a magnetic circuit, like the resistance of an electric circuit, is directly proportional to the

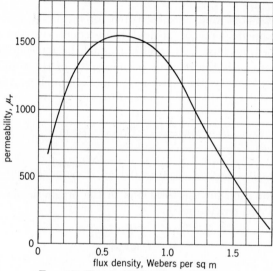

Fig. 4-8. Permeability curve of cast steel.

length of circuit (measured in the direction of flux) and inversely proportional to the cross-sectional area (measured normal to the length) and depends upon the magnetic properties of the material composing the circuit, that is, upon the *relative permeability*.[1] The relative permeability of a magnetic material is not a constant quantity like the conductivity of an electric conducting material but varies widely with the flux density. Figure 4-8, for example, shows that the permeability of cast steel is high for low values of flux density but becomes less and less as B is increased. Other magnetic materials behave in much the same way. The permeability of steel of the quality used in the construction of electric machines usually does not exceed a few thousand under working conditions, and

[1] In the remainder of this book the term "permeability" is often used without a qualifying word or phrase, for convenience in writing. When it is so used, the reference is to relative permeability μ_r and not to the permeability of empty space μ_0.

it may be as low as a few hundred when the flux density is very high. The permeabilities of nickel, cobalt, and chromium are usually less than 50.

The permeability of a magnetic material is analogous to the conductivity of an electric material; it is the magnetic conductance of a unit cube of material in comparison with a standard (air), the permeability of which is taken as unity. The reciprocal of permeability is *reluctivity*, corresponding to the resistivity ρ of the electric circuit. It is usually more convenient to express the reluctance of a magnetic circuit in terms of permeability rather than in terms of reluctivity, however, and the commonly used expression for reluctance is accordingly that given in Eq. (7-8).

Magnetic-potential Difference. The mmf of a magnetic circuit may be applied at a single point in the circuit, as by means of a lumped or concentrated winding [Fig. 6-8(a)], but it is used up piecemeal. Just as in an electric circuit there is a potential drop from point to point in the circuit, so in the magnetic circuit there is a drop of magnetic potential from point to point. The similarity of the electric and magnetic circuits in this respect is brought out in the illustrations of Figs. 5-8 and 6-8.

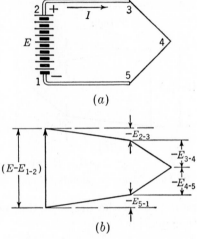

(a)

$$E-E_{1-2}-E_{2-3}-E_{3-4}-E_{4-5}-E_{5-1}=0$$

Fig. 5-8. Electric-potential drops.

In Fig. 5-8(a) current is supplied to an electric circuit by a battery. The conductors composing the circuit are of two sizes. Low-resistance conductors are used between 2-3 and 5-1 and high-resistance conductors between 3-4 and 4-5. In Fig. 5-8(b) the potential drops in the several parts of the circuit are shown. The potential rises in the battery to E volts. This potential difference is used up from point to point in the circuit in forcing the current through the resistance, the rate depending upon the resistance of the conductor and the current. The potential drops E_{3-4} and E_{4-5} in the high-resistance parts are much greater than the drops E_{2-3} and E_{5-1} in the low-resistance parts. The sum of all the drops in the circuit is equal to the voltage impressed, or

$$E = E_{2-3} + E_{3-4} + E_{4-5} + E_{5-1} + E_{1-2}$$

where $E_{1-2} = RI$ drop in battery.

In the magnetic circuit of Fig. 6-8(a) the impressed mmf F is required to maintain the flux ϕ in the circuit, but the mmf required per unit length of circuit is not the same for all parts. From 2 to 3 and from 5 to 1 the cross section is large and the reluctance is low, while from 3 to 4 and from 4 to 5 the area of cross section is less and the reluctance is much higher.

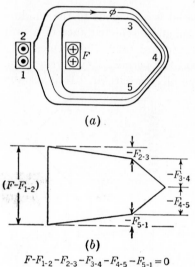

(a)

(b)

$$F-F_{1\text{-}2}-F_{2\text{-}3}-F_{3\text{-}4}-F_{4\text{-}5}-F_{5\text{-}1}=0$$

Fig. 6-8. Magnetic-potential drops.

In Fig. 6-8(b) the magnetic-potential drops in the several parts of the circuit are indicated. The impressed mmf is used up from point to point in the circuit as required to maintain the flux, the rate depending upon the reluctance per meter of path and the flux. The magnetic-potential drops $F_{3\text{-}4}$ and $F_{4\text{-}5}$ in the high-reluctance parts are much larger than the drops $F_{2\text{-}3}$ and $F_{5\text{-}1}$ in the low-reluctance parts, but the sum of the impressed mmf and all the drops in the magnetic circuit is zero, as indicated in the equation

$$F - F_{2\text{-}3} - F_{3\text{-}4} - F_{4\text{-}5} - F_{5\text{-}1} - F_{1\text{-}2} = 0$$

whence

$$F = F_{2\text{-}3} + F_{3\text{-}4} + F_{4\text{-}5} + F_{5\text{-}1} + F_{1\text{-}2}$$

The term $F_{1\text{-}2}$ is the magnetic-potential drop that corresponds to the RI drop in the internal resistance of the battery of the electrical analogue.

Magnetic-potential Drop per Unit Length of Path. Over any part of a magnetic circuit in which the material is the same throughout and the cross section is constant, the amount of magnetizing force required per unit length of path depends upon the flux density. This is apparent from Eq. (4-8), which is readily transformed to

$$H = \frac{NI}{l} = \frac{B}{\mu_r\mu_0} \tag{8-8}$$

The magnetic-potential drop per unit length of path (NI/l) is the magnetic-potential gradient or field intensity H. This value can be obtained experimentally for any magnetic material and for any desired flux density. Curves giving values of B vs. NI/l are available for standard grades of magnetic materials and are called *magnetization curves*. Obviously, when the magnetic-potential difference per unit length of path is known for any given material and flux density, the total magnetizing force required to maintain that flux density throughout a length l of magnetic circuit in the same material is

$$F = \frac{NI}{l} \times l$$

This is the principle that is commonly employed in the design of magnetic circuits of iron and steel. In a future paragraph this principle is applied to the solution of several simple problems.

If an air gap forms a part of a magnetic circuit, the magnetizing force per unit length of gap is found from Eq. (8-8) for the condition $\mu_r = 1$, and the total magnetomotive forces required to maintain a flux density of B webers/sq m in a gap l m long is

$$NI = Bl/4\pi \times 10^{-7} = 79.58 \times 10^4 Bl \qquad \text{amp-turns} \qquad (9\text{-}8)$$

If B' is in gauss (lines per square centimeter) and l' is in centimeters,

$$NI = 0.7958 B'l' \qquad \text{amp-turns} \qquad (10\text{-}8)$$

or if B'' is in lines (maxwells) per square inch and l'' is in inches,

$$NI = 0.3132 B''l'' \qquad \text{amp-turns} \qquad (11\text{-}8)$$

Comparison of Electric and Magnetic Units. The concepts involved in the electric and magnetic units as well as the laws of the electric and magnetic circuits which have been discussed in this and earlier chapters have many points of similarity. Thus magnetomotive force is analogous

ELECTRIC AND MAGNETIC UNITS. BASIC LAWS COMPARED

Electric	Magnetic
E emf	F mmf
I current	ϕ flux
R resistance	R reluctance
γ conductivity	μ permeability
J current density	B flux density
ε electric gradient or field intensity	H magnetic gradient or field intensity

$E = IR$	Ohm's law	$F = \phi R$
$\Sigma E = 0$	Kirchhoff's law of emfs	$\Sigma F = 0$
$\Sigma I = 0$	Kirchhoff's law of currents	$\Sigma \phi = 0$

to voltage, flux to current, reluctance to resistance, etc. These and other corresponding units and fundamental relations are indicated in the accompanying table. It is helpful to keep these in mind.

Magnetization Curves. Curves that show how the flux density in a magnetic material increases when the applied magnetizing force per unit length of path is gradually increased from zero to a high value are called *magnetization curves.* Such curves are drawn from experimental data obtained from sample specimens of magnetic materials. They give all the information necessary to design a magnetic circuit employing the material as a magnetic conductor. The magnetizing force per unit length of path and the flux density corresponding thereto are usually given in either one of two systems of units. When H is in gilberts per centimeter, B is given in lines per square centimeter (gauss). It is often more convenient, however, to have the magnetizing force per unit length of path in ampere-turns per inch and the flux density in lines per square inch, because the dimensions of the magnetic circuit are often in inch units. Both systems of units are used.

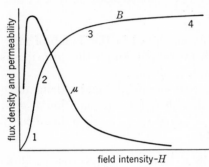

Fig. 7-8. Magnetization and permeability curves.

The form of a typical magnetization curve is illustrated in Fig. 7-8. When a small, gradually increasing magnetizing force is applied, the flux density increases slowly at first. Beyond some point 1, the rate of increase is very much greater and remains nearly constant over a considerable range from 1 to 2. Over this section of the curve the flux density rises in nearly direct proportion to the mmf and the permeability is high and approximately constant. From 2 to 3 the flux density increases at a diminishing rate with increasing mmf, and the permeability falls off rapidly. Increasing the mmf beyond 3 increases the flux density only slowly, for the iron is approaching *saturation* and the permeability is very low. Between 2 and 3, where the slope of the curve changes quite abruptly, is the *knee* of the curve. The ordinary operating range of the material lies below the knee of the curve because, over this range, large increases in flux density are obtained from small increases in mmf. Beyond the knee of the curve relatively large increases in magnetizing force yield only small increases in flux density.

Typical magnetization curves of cast iron, cast steel, and transformer steel are given in Fig. 8-8.

Magnetic Cycle. The iron ring in Fig. 9-8 is uniformly wound with turns of wire through which current is passed to magnetize the iron. The mmf may be changed gradually by adjusting the resistance of the circuit. The resistance is very high when the switch is closed so the

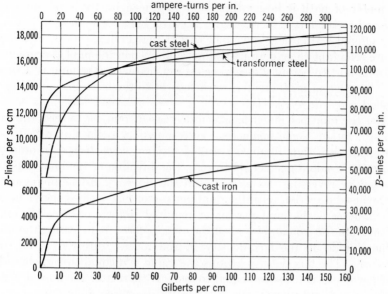

FIG. 8-8. Magnetization curves of commercial iron and steel.

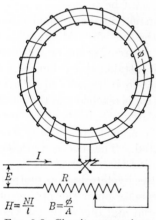

FIG. 9-8. Circuit connections for obtaining hysteresis loop.

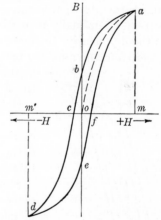

FIG. 10-8. Magnetic hysteresis loop.

mmf is small at the beginning and only a small flux density is produced. As the current is gradually increased from zero by slowly decreasing the resistance of the circuit, the flux density in the core rises according to the curve *oa* (Fig. 10-8), called the *normal magnetization curve*. If the current is decreased after the mmf per meter *H* has reached the value *om*, the *B-H* relation falls according to the curve *ab*. It is found that when the current is decreasing the flux density produced by a given mmf per meter of path is larger than that produced by the same mmf per meter when the flux is increasing. The iron behaves as though its molecules offered a frictional resistance to a change in flux, that is, as though it were reluctant to give up its magnetic flux when the mmf is decreasing and reluctant to permit a flux to be established when the mmf is increasing. This lag of magnetic flux with respect to the mmf that produces it is called *magnetic hysteresis*.

After the mmf per meter has been decreased from *om* to zero, the iron core still retains some magnetism corresponding to the flux density *ob*. The magnetism thus retained is called *residual magnetism*. In order to reduce the residual magnetism to zero, the direction of the mmf must be reversed by reversing the current, and the current must be increased in the reversed direction until the mmf per meter has reached the value *oc*. The value *oc* is the mmf per meter required to force or *coerce* the magnetism from the iron and is called the *coercive force*. Increasing the mmf further builds up the flux density in the reverse direction along the curve *cd*. The flux density attains the value *m'd* equal to *ma* when the mmf per meter reaches *om'* equal to *om*. If thereafter the mmf is again gradually reduced to zero, the flux density decreases along the curve *de*, but the core retains the residual density *oe* at zero mmf. To decrease the flux density further requires that the mmf be reversed by reversing the current. Gradually increasing the current in the original direction causes the flux density to decrease along the line *efa*. At *f* the flux density is zero and the mmf per meter is *of*. Increasing the mmf per meter

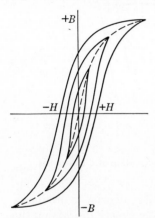

further until it attains the value *om* causes the flux density to increase along the curve until the value *ma* is reached and the magnetic cycle is complete. Each time the mmf is carried through a cycle of values, the flux cycle is repeated. The curve representing this cycle is called the *hysteresis loop*.

The size of the hysteresis loop plotted to a given scale depends upon the nature of the magnetic material and the maximum value of the flux density attained. In Fig. 11-8 three hysteresis loops of a given material are shown, corresponding to three different maximum values of flux density. These curves show

FIG. 11-8. Hysteresis loops of carbon steel.

that the residual flux density and the coercive force, as well as the area, depend upon the maximum flux density attained during the cycle. Soft iron and the sheet steels used in the construction of electric machines, as well as alloys such as perminvar and hypernik, have relatively narrow hysteresis loops, low retentivity, and low coercive force. Hard steel, chromium steel, and alloys of aluminum, nickel, and cobalt as well as cobalt steel, on the other hand, retain considerable flux densities indefinitely, and for this reason they are used in the construction of permanent magnets.

Energy Loss Due to Hysteresis. It has already been shown that energy is stored in a magnetic field. If the field is established in a non-magnetic medium like air, under ordinary conditions the stored energy is all returned to the electric circuit when the field is destroyed. If the field is established in iron, steel, or other magnetic material, however, some energy is lost as heat in the material when the field is built up, and only a part of the stored energy is returned to the circuit when the field is destroyed, the remainder again appearing as heat in the magnetic material.

To explain this loss it is convenient to think of the molecules of the magnetic material as consisting of small magnets. In the normal, unmagnetized state of the material these magnets are assumed to be indiscriminately arranged, but when a magnetizing force is applied, the elementary magnets are turned around so that the axes through their poles tend to align themselves with the field and become parallel to the direction of the lines of force. This motion is resisted by molecular friction, and the work done in overcoming the friction is the hysteresis energy loss appearing as heat while the flux is increasing. When the magnetizing force is decreased, the forces of attraction and repulsion between the poles of the elementary magnets act to return the molecules to their neutral positions. Frictional forces resist this motion as before, and additional heat energy is developed. Moreover, the

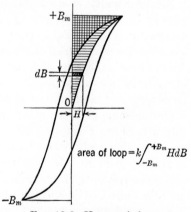

$$\text{area of loop} = k \int_{-B_m}^{+B_m} H dB$$

Fig. 12-8. Hysteresis loss.

friction between the molecular magnets prevents the molecules from completely returning to their neutral positions, with the result that the iron retains some flux even after the magnetizing force has been reduced to zero.

It can be shown that the energy lost in hysteresis when iron is carried once through a complete magnetic cycle is proportional to the area of the hysteresis loop (Fig. 12-8). Dr. Steinmetz found by experiment that for any given material the area of the hysteresis loop (and therefore the loss per cycle) is approximately proportional to the 1.6 power of the maximum flux density (under usual conditions). He also found that for a given maximum flux density the loss per cycle depends upon the nature of the material. When iron is periodically magnetized and demagnetized in alternate directions, as when iron is rotated between the poles of a magnet or when the exciting winding is supplied with alternating current, a continual loss of energy occurs. The power expended as heat then depends upon the number of cycles completed per second in addition to the factors mentioned above.

According to Steinmetz, the power lost in a given volume of magnetic material may be expressed by the equation

$$P_h = kfB_{max}^{1.6} \qquad \text{watts} \qquad (12\text{-}8)$$

where k = constant that depends upon kind of material, volume of material, and units used to measure flux density

f = frequency, cps

B_{max} = maximum flux density

This expression is in very convenient form and is sufficiently accurate for most purposes.

Silicon Steels. Various grades of commercial silicon steels are available in the United States. Typical properties of some of the common grades are given in Table II.

In the preparation of sheet steel various treatments are used such as cold rolling, annealing, pickling, etc. In the selection of a suitable grade of material for a particular application, a number of factors must be considered. Standard and armature grades, for example, are subject to a gradual change in magnetic properties, called *aging*, which results in increasing core losses with use at operating temperatures. Furthermore, they have low resistivities, which makes it undesirable to use them except at low frequencies. High-silicon steels (transformer steel) are nonaging and have relatively high resistivities and low core losses. These sheets are also quite brittle and abrasive to the dies used in making the punchings which form the magnetic circuit. Brittleness and abrasiveness are not seriously objectionable properties in transformer punchings, but for the relatively complex punchings used in the rotors and stators of rotating machines, these properties may be very objectionable because of the high cost of replacing dies. The grades of steel with the lower percentages of silicon—up to 3.5 per cent—are suitable for rotating equipment. Iron losses decrease as the percentage of silicon used increases. Grades with 4 per cent or more of silicon content are used in the cores of large transformers.

Recent developments in winding transformer cores from steel strip have made possible the employment of preferred orientation steels in which a cold reduction process gives greatly improved magnetic properties in the direction of rolling, although at the expense of the properties in a crosswise direction.

Magnetic Alloys. As a result of years of research and experimentation there have been developed certain alloys of iron, nickel, and cobalt that have remarkable magnetic properties which make them superior to the constituent metals for many uses. These alloys have been developed chiefly for use in electrical communication circuits and instruments. Telephone applications require that the magnetic materials used have high permeability at low magnetizing forces together with low hysteresis losses. Certain other situations require constant permeability over the operating range. The alloys known as *permalloy, perminvar,* and *permendur* together meet these requirements. Perminvar, for example, has

TABLE II. PROPERTIES OF TYPICAL ELECTRICAL STEEL SHEETS

Designation of steel sheets	Normal per cent silicon	Core loss, watts/lb, at 10,000 gauss and 60 cps	B, lines/sq in., at $H = 100$ amp-turns/in.	Resistivity, microhm-cm
Standard...................	0	2.1	107,000	15
Armature...................	0.5	1.4	105,000	18
Electrical..................	1.0	1.2	104,000	25
Motor......................	2.5	1.1	100,000	43
Dynamo....................	3.5	0.85	100,000	51
Transformer...............	4.5	0.52–0.72	98,000	62
Preferred orientation				
With grain..............	3.5	0.36	117,000	48–50
Across grain............	3.5	0.70	99,000	

constant permeability at low flux densities and extremely low hysteresis loss. The outstanding property of permendur is high permeability at high flux densities. Permalloy is used in the form of tape helically wrapped on stranded copper conductors in submarine cables, and in powdered form for building the cores of loading coils. Chromium and molybdenum permalloys are used as cores for audio transformers and other apparatus in which high permeability and high specific resistance are required in the core material.

Calculation of Magnetic Circuits. A ring of iron or steel of circular or rectangular shape and cross section constitutes a very simple form of magnetic circuit that is much used. This kind of circuit is called a *series* circuit because all sections of the circuit are traversed by the same flux. When two or more magnetic circuits are separate, but a single magnetizing force is used to set up the flux in all, as in Fig. 15-8, the magnetic circuits are in *parallel*. Various combinations of series and parallel branches are also possible in magnetic circuits, as in electric circuits, and these are called *series-parallel* circuits.

1. *Series Circuit.* To illustrate the method of solving magnetic circuit problems, suppose the circuit of Fig. 13-8 is uniformly wound with 1,500 turns of wire, and let it be required to find the current needed to maintain a flux density of 1.5 webers/sq m (15,000 gauss) in the magnetic circuit. It is assumed that there is no air gap ($l_2 = 0$). The circuit is built of transformer steel sheets punched to the dimensions shown and stacked to a depth to give a net thickness of 5 cm of steel in the stack. The mean length of the magnetic circuit is 1.57 m, and the net cross-sectional area of steel is 25 sq cm.

From the curve of Fig. 8-8 (transformer steel) one finds that to maintain a flux density of 15,000 gauss in transformer steel requires a mmf of 54 amp-turns/in. or 21.3 amp-turns/cm. The mmf of the entire circuit must be $NI = 1.57 \times 2,130$ or 3,350 amp-turns, and the current needed in the winding is $I = 3,350/1,500$ or 2.23 amp.

The total flux in the circuit is $\phi = BA = 1.5 \times 25 \times 10^{-4}$ or 3.75 milliwebers.

Even a very small air gap greatly increases the mmf necessary to

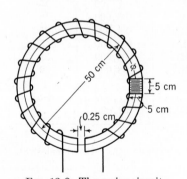

maintain a given flux in a magnetic circuit of given area and length. To illustrate this point, let an air gap $l_2 = 0.25$ cm be cut across the circuit of Fig. 13-8, at right angles to the flux path. Assume that all the flux crosses the air gap in parallel lines (no fringing). To maintain a flux density of 1.5 webers/sq m in the steel, as before, requires substantially the same total mmf as previously (3,350 amp-turns), because the total length of mean path in the steel has been reduced by only 0.25 cm or 0.16 per cent.

Fig. 13-8. The series circuit.

From Eq. (9-8) the magnetomotive force consumed in the air gap is found to be

$$NI = 79.58 \times 10^4 \times 1.5 \times 0.25 \times 10^{-2} = 2,980 \text{ amp-turns}$$

so the total mmf required is $2,980 + 3,350$ or 6,330 amp-turns. Thus the magnetic-potential drop in 0.25 cm of air gap is almost as much as the corresponding drop in 157 cm of steel. Air gaps are required for mechanical clearance in the magnetic circuits of all revolving electrical machines. The foregoing illustration shows why such machines need large numbers of ampere-turns to excite their field windings.

When it is desired to find the flux which results from the application of a given mmf to a magnetic circuit of known dimensions, the problem can readily be solved if the circuit has a constant cross section and the material is of uniform quality, and if its magnetic properties are known.

Example 1. Determine the flux in the ring of Fig. 13-8 (no air gap assumed), when the impressed mmf is 1,225 amp-turns.

The magnetic potential gradient is

$$H = \frac{1,225}{157} \times 2.54 = 19.8 \text{ amp-turns/in.}$$

From the curve of Fig. 8-8 one finds that 19.8 amp-turns/in. establish approximately 14,000 gauss in transformer steel. The total flux in the ring is, therefore,

$$\phi = 25 \times 14,000$$
$$= 350,000 \text{ maxwells}$$
$$= 3.5 \text{ milliwebers}$$

When a circuit is made up of two or more parts in series, differing either in cross-sectional area or in kind of material, it is not possible to solve for the flux in this simple manner. This point is illustrated in the example below.

Example 2. A cast-iron anchor ring has a cross-sectional area of 4 sq in., a mean length of flux path in iron of 35 in., and an air gap 0.25 in. long. Determine the flux set up by an impressed mmf of 3,500 amp-turns. The winding is uniformly distributed and the flux density in the gap is assumed to be uniform.

Assume a number of values of magnetic-potential drop in the air gap, and obtain the corresponding drops in the cast iron by subtracting the drop in the gap from the total in each case. Tabulate the values as shown below, and compute the flux density in the gap and in the iron for each set of assumed conditions. Plot these

Air gap			Cast iron		
NI	NI/in.	B'	NI	NI/in.	B'
1,500	6,000	19,100	2,000	57.2	33,600
2,000	8,000	25,500	1,500	42.8	31,000
2,500	10,000	31,900	1,000	28.6	27,100
3,000	12,000	38,300	500	14.3	21,000

flux densities as ordinates against the ampere-turns drop in the gap as abscissas. Where the curve for the iron crosses the air-gap curve, the flux densities in the gap and in the iron have the same value, and the abscissa corresponding thereto is the number of ampere-turns required for the gap.

When the flux densities in the table are plotted as directed above, the curves cross at a flux density of approximately 28,000 lines per square inch, and at this density there are approximately 2,300 amp-turns absorbed by the air gap (Fig. 14-8). From the curve of cast iron, at a density of 28,500 lines per square inch, the magnetizing force per inch of path is about 34.5 amp turns. The total mmf needed for the iron is

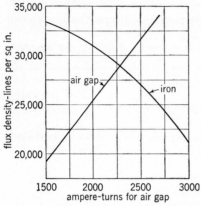

$$NI = 35 \times 34.5 \text{ or } 1,210 \text{ amp-turns.}$$

FIG. 14-8. Curves for example.

Upon adding this number to the number required for the air gap, the total is found to be $2,300 + 1,210 = 3,510$, which checks the impressed ampere turns very closely.

2. *Parallel Circuits.* When two magnetic circuits are in parallel, the same mmf acts on each branch of the circuit. Such a circuit is illustrated in the drawing of Fig. 15-8. If the two parallel branches are exactly alike, as in the figure, a given mmf produces the same flux in each circuit, and it is unnecessary to calculate more than one of them. If they are unlike, as for example, when their lengths or their areas of section are different, or when the branches are made of different materials, the fluxes in the branches are generally unequal. Cut-and-try methods may then have to be used. Occasions for making such calculations, however, seldom arise.

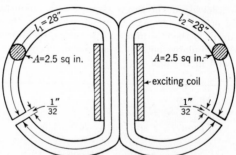

FIG. 15-8. Parallel circuits.

Example 3. The two similar rings of Fig. 15-8 are circular in cross section and are made of cast steel. The area of section of each ring is 2.5 sq in., and the length of the average path is 28 in. Each ring has an air gap of $\frac{1}{32}$ in. How many ampere-turns are needed to maintain a flux of 188,000 lines in each ring?

The flux density in each ring is

$$B'' = \frac{188,000}{2.5} = 75,200 \text{ maxwells/sq in.}$$

From the cast-steel curve of Fig. 8-8, the ampere-turns per inch needed to maintain this flux density in cast steel are about 25, and the total mmf required for the steel section is 28 × 25 or 700 amp-turns. By Eq. (11-8) the ampere-turns required for the air gap are

$$NI = 0.313 \times 75,200 \times \tfrac{1}{32} = 735 \text{ amp-turns}$$

The total number of ampere-turns of the ring must, therefore, be 700 + 735 or 1,435.

3. Series-parallel Circuits. A grouping of series-parallel elements is illustrated in the magnetic circuit of a two-pole motor, shown in Fig. 16-8. The flux from the north pole crosses the air gap, then divides, half of it passing through each half of the armature core. The two paths again join under the south pole. Where the south pole joins the yoke, the flux again divides into two equal parts. One half returns to the north pole after passing through the yoke in a clockwise direction, while the other half passes through the yoke in a counterclockwise direction to the north pole. After passing through the north-pole core, the circuit is completed. Thus, the ampere-turns of the two field windings are in series, and the mmf of each winding needs to be only enough to force the flux through one-half the circuit. One may think of the mmf of the N pole as forcing the core flux through the paths 1-2-3-4-5 and 6-7-8-9-10 to the left of YY, and of the mmf of the S pole as forcing the flux through

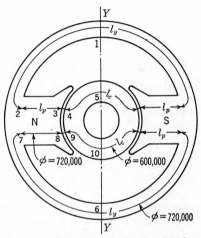

FIG. 16-8. The magnetic circuit of a two-pole motor.

the corresponding paths to the right of YY. If the total flux from the north pole, for example, is split along the center line into two equal parts, indicated by the paths in the drawing, the magnetic-potential drop over each element of one of these paths can be readily computed. Consider the circuit under the north pole, and divide the flux equally between the similar paths 1-2-3-4-5 and 6-7-8-9-10. Since the two paths are in parallel and are exactly similar, a single mmf applied to the north pole supplies equal fluxes over the two paths. Only one path needs to be calculated. The method of making the calculation for either path is exactly similar to that described for the series circuit. The work of making the computations is greatly simplified by tabulating all needed information, such as lengths of the several parts of the circuit, the areas, and the flux densities, in the manner illustrated in the example.

Example 4. The dimensions and other required data pertaining to the magnetic circuit of Fig. 16-8 are given in the tabulation. With the use of the appropriate magnetization curves of Fig. 8-8, calculate the ampere turns required in each field coil to maintain a flux density of 40,000 lines per square inch in the air gap. It is assumed that the air-gap flux is only five-sixths as much as the flux in the pole core,

Symbol	Item	Air gap (air)	Armature core (sheet steel)	Pole core (sheet steel)	Yoke (cast steel)
l'............	Length, in.	0.15	$l_c = 6$	$l_p = 4.2$	$l_y = 22.5$
A'............	Area, sq in.	30	7	16	12
ϕ............	Flux, maxwells	1,200,000	600,000	1,440,000	720,000
B'............	Flux per square inch	40,000	85,700	90,000	60,000
NI/in........	NI per inch	12,520	12	19	12.5
NI............	Ampere-turns	1,880	72	80	282

Total ampere-turns = 2,314 per pole.

owing to leakage of flux from the pole tips. The leakage flux returns to the yoke through the surrounding air space and does not cross the gap.

The calculation is carried out for each part of the circuit (1-2, 2-3, 3-4, 4-5) in the manner described for the series circuit. The ampere-turns per inch for each kind of material used are listed in the line next to the last in the table, while the total for each section is found in the last line. The sum of the ampere-turns in the last line is the total required per pole.

Problems

1-8. The air gap in a magnetic circuit is 6 sq in. in cross section and 0.25 in. long. (a) How many ampere-turns are required to maintain a flux of 240,000 lines across the gap? What is the field intensity in the gap (b) in ampere-turns per inch, (c) in gilberts per centimeter? (Disregard fringing.)

2-8. An air gap 4 sq in. in cross section requires 1,800 ampere-turns to maintain a flux of 80,000 lines across the gap. Determine the length of the gap in inches.

3-8. A wooden anchor ring or toroid has a mean diameter of 12 in. and cross-sectional area of 1.5 sq in. The ring is uniformly wound with 1,200 turns of wire, in which a current of 2 amp flows. Find (a) the field intensity or magnetic gradient in ampere-turns per inch of mean circumference, (b) the magnetic gradient in ampere-turns per meter of mean circumference, (c) the total flux in the ring, (d) the mean flux density in the ring. If the wooden core is replaced by a cast-steel core, the magnetic properties of which are given by the cast-steel curve of Fig. 8-8, (e) what will be the flux in the core when the current is 2 amp; (f) what is the permeability of the steel under these conditions?

4-8. How much current is required to set up a flux density of 110,000 lines per square inch in the cast-steel anchor ring of Prob. 3-8?

5-8. The cast-steel ring of Prob. 3-8 is cut transversely (normal to the circumference) to produce an air gap 0.05 in. long. By the method of trial and error, find the flux set up in the air gap when the current in the winding is 1.2 amp. (Disregard fringing.)

6-8. The hysteresis loss of No. 29 gage electrical steel is 0.958 watt/lb for a flux density of $B_{\max} = 1$ weber/sq m and a frequency of 60 cps. (a) Find the value of the hysteresis constant k for the conditions given (watts per pound). (b) For the same material, frequency, and flux density, find the value of k that will yield the loss in watts per cubic centimeter, (c) in watts per cubic foot. (Steel weighs 490 lb per cu ft.)

7-8. The hysteresis and eddy-current losses in the armature of a generator are 325 and 130 watts, respectively, when the speed is 1,200 rpm. Determine the hysteresis and eddy-current losses (a) when the speed is 1,350 rpm, the flux density remaining the same; (b) when the speed is 1,200 rpm and the flux density is increased 15 per cent.

8-8. The magnetic circuit of Fig. A-8 contains cast iron and cast steel that have the magnetic properties indicated by the respective magnetization curves in Fig. 8-8. The flux crossing the air gap is 0.014 weber and the exciting winding has 1,000 turns. Determine (a) the flux in branch 1, (b) the flux in branch 2, (c) the current in the exciting winding. Assume that all the flux threading the coil crosses the air gap in straight, parallel lines.

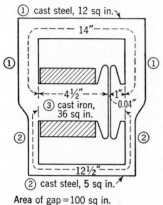

Area of gap = 100 sq in.

Fig. A-8

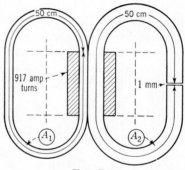

Fig. B-8

9-8. The two cast-steel rings of Fig. B-8 have an exciting mmf of 917 ampere-turns and the total flux in each is 0.0018 weber. Determine the cross-sectional area of each ring. (Assume that the data of the cast-steel curve of Fig. 8-8 apply to the material used and that there is no fringing at the air gap.)

10-8. A relay is constructed as shown in Fig. C-8. The spring exerts a pull of 4 oz to hold the relay contacts open when there is no current in the 5,000-turn exciting coil. When sufficient current is maintained in the coil the relay is pulled shut, the contacts close, and the air gap is reduced from $\frac{3}{32}$ to $\frac{1}{32}$ in. It is assumed that the spring tension is not changed appreciably over this travel, that

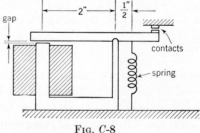

Fig. C-8

the forces of gravity are balanced out, and that the ampere-turns consumed in the steel portions of the magnetic circuit are negligible. The cross-sectional area of the gap is 0.2 sq in. (a) How much current is required to close the relay (pick up)? (b) After the relay is closed, how much current is required to keep it closed (drop out)?

CHAPTER 9

DIRECT-CURRENT AMMETERS AND VOLTMETERS

The power developed or consumed in a d-c circuit can be expressed in terms of current and voltage as $P = EI$, or in terms of either current or voltage and the resistance of the circuit as $P = I^2R$ or $P = E^2/R$. If the resistance is unknown, it can be found by measuring the voltage consumed in it by a current of known value and solving for $R = E/I$. It appears from this that to measure power in a d-c circuit only a voltmeter and an ammeter are required. Hence, these are the instruments most

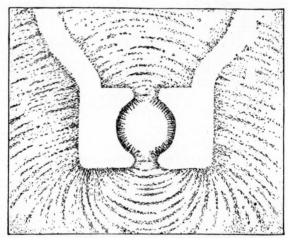

Fig. 1-9. Lines of induction of horseshoe magnet assembly with pole pieces and core. (*Weston Electric Instrument Corporation.*)

often used in d-c measurements. Wattmeters, of course, may also be used to measure power, and watt-hour meters are ordinarily required to measure energy. These meters are discussed in Chap. 22.

Permanent-magnet Moving-coil Instruments. Direct-current ammeters and voltmeters usually are moving-coil instruments of the permanent-magnet type. They operate on the principle of the d'Arsonval galvanometer, which is essentially the following.

In the case of an *ammeter*, the current to be measured, or a known fraction of it, is established in a lightly constructed rectangular coil of wire which is free to turn on its axis.   In the space occupied by the coil sides a radial magnetic field, as in Fig. 1-9, is maintained by a permanent magnet.   The electromagnetic reaction between the coil current and the

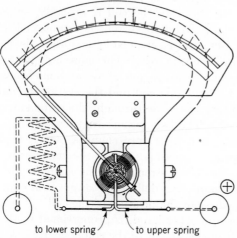

to lower spring   to upper spring

FIG. 2-9. Typical d-c movable-coil system.   (*Weston Electric Instrument Corporation.*)

magnetic field causes the coil to turn against the action of spiral springs, thereby producing a deflection of a needle attached to the coil.   The needle moves over a graduated scale on which the current may be read.

The essential parts of the meter are shown in Fig. 2-9.   A permanent horseshoe magnet, with soft-iron pole pieces, supplies the magnetic field.   The pole pieces are bored out to form a hollow cylinder, coaxially with which is mounted a soft-iron cylindrical core of slightly smaller diameter.   A short air gap of constant length is thus formed between the pole pieces and core.   The air gap reduces the reluctance of the magnetic circuit to a relatively low value, which enables the magnet to retain its magnetism undiminished throughout an indefinite period of years. The core is held in position by nonferrous-metal pieces that are attached to the poles. Surrounding the soft-iron core is a very lightly constructed rectangular aluminum

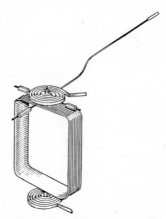

FIG. 3-9. Movable coil. (*Weston Electric Instrument Corporation.*)

frame upon which a coil of fine silk-covered copper wire is wound (Fig. 3-9).   The frame not only serves as a suitable support for the coil but provides a means of damping the motion of the coil and permits the needle to take up its correct position without oscillation. The damping action is due to the reaction between the magnetic field and eddy currents set up in the frame when the frame sides cut the air-gap flux.

The coil is fitted with steel pivots above and below, which turn in jewel bearings. In this way the coil is properly centered and friction is largely eliminated. When a current is established in the winding in the correct direction, the electromagnetic torque developed causes the coil to turn clockwise on its axis. The motion of the coil is opposed by the action of two spiral springs, one above and one below, which are connected between the movable coil and the stationary part of the meter. The springs also serve as leads through which the current is led to and away from the coil. The two springs are spiraled in opposite directions so that the effects of temperature changes, which tend to change the lengths of the springs and thus to alter the zero position of the needle, are neutralized. Since the strength of the magnetic field in the air gap is everywhere the same, the deflecting torque is always proportional to the current, regardless of the position of the coil. The retarding torque of the springs, on the other hand, is proportional to the deflection, and hence the angular displacement of the coil is nearly directly proportional to the current, and the scale is approximately uniform. A lightly constructed balanced aluminum needle, fastened to the coil, measures the angular displacement of the coil and, by means of a suitably calibrated scale with approximately equal divisions, indicates the current in the winding.

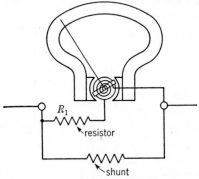

FIG. 4-9. Ammeter with shunt.

Microammeters and Milliammeters. The deflection of a permanent-magnet moving-coil instrument depends upon the number of turns in the coil and upon the coil current. A meter may be designed to measure only a few microamperes at full-scale deflection by providing it with a coil of many turns of very fine wire. Such a meter is called a *microammeter.* Another meter, which differs from the first principally in that it has a movable coil with fewer turns of larger wire, may be designed to give full-scale deflection with a coil current of perhaps 25 milliamperes. The latter then becomes a *milliammeter.*

Ammeters. A milliampere meter may be used with a *shunt* as in Fig. 4-9, to measure currents which are many times as large as the current in the movable coil at full-scale deflection. The shunt is a resistor of low resistance R_s, which is connected in parallel with the meter circuit. The total resistance R_m of the meter circuit is $R_m = R_1 + R_c$, where R_c is the resistance of the movable coil. The current to be measured divides between the meter circuit and the shunt bypass in inverse ratio to their respective resistances. Thus the current in the coil is only the fractional part $R_s/(R_s + R_m)$ of the total metered current. If the resistances of the meter circuit and of the shunt remain constant, the ratio remains constant also, and the meter always indicates correctly the current to be measured. The meter is made direct-reading by providing it with a scale which is calibrated in terms of the metered current instead of the coil current.

Since the movable coil is made of copper wire, the resistance of the coil may change appreciably with changes in temperature. To ensure accuracy of meter readings the meter-circuit resistance must be held substantially constant as stated. This condition is brought about by connecting in series with the coil the resistor R_1, which has several times as much resistance as the coil and is made of a material with a low temperature coefficient of resistance. This has the effect of making the over-all resistance of the meter circuit relatively independent of temperature changes. Resistors which are used as shunts are likewise made of similar materials with low temperature coefficients of resistance and are designed to facilitate radiation. In this way errors due to temperature changes are largely eliminated.

Ammeters for measuring relatively small currents (usually not more than 50 amp) have shunts that are mounted within the case. When large currents are to be measured, the required shunts usually are too bulky to be contained within the housing, or the heat dissipated may be so large as to make self-containment impractical. For the measurement of such currents millivoltmeters with external shunts are used. This application is discussed in a later paragraph.

Millivoltmeters. Although permanent-magnet instruments are essentially current meters, they may also be adapted for use as *millivoltmeters*. To clarify this statement assume, for example, that a given instrument has a meter-circuit resistance R_m of 15 ohms, and let the coil be designed to give full-scale deflection with a current of 10 ma (0.01 amp). Then, by Ohm's law, the voltage E consumed in the meter circuit at full-scale deflection is $E = 10 \times 15$ or 150 mv. Other meter currents less than 10 ma result in proportionally smaller values of consumed voltages, but in every case the deflection is proportional to the millivolts consumed in the meter circuit. Accordingly, the meter scale may be calibrated to read directly the millivolts consumed instead of the coil current, and the instrument, when so calibrated, becomes a *millivoltmeter*.

Voltmeters. The scale of a millivoltmeter may be extended by connecting added resistance in series with the meter-circuit resistance R_m.

By inserting the correct amount of added resistance and providing a suitable scale, the instrument can be converted into a *voltmeter*. The added resistance required to produce full-scale reading when a given impressed voltage is to be measured may be computed.

Let it be required, for example, to determine the added resistance needed, with the millivoltmeter described above, to measure an impressed potential difference of 600 volts at full-scale deflection. By Ohm's law the total resistance R_t between the meter terminals must be such that the product of the meter current at full scale and the total resistance between

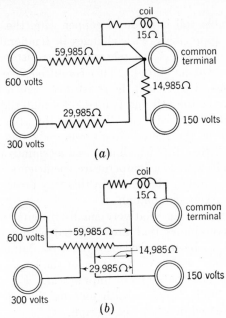

Fig. 5-9. Wiring diagrams of voltmeters.

meter terminals is 600 volts. Thus $0.010 \times R_t = 600$ and $R_t = 60,000$ ohms. Since R_t includes R_1 and the resistance of the coil, which amount to 15 ohms, the added resistance required is $60,000 - 15$ or $59,985$ ohms. The scale of the meter is calibrated to read 600 volts at full-scale deflection.

A given meter may be provided with more than one added resistance and so have a corresponding number of scales, as in Fig. 5-9(a). For convenience in marking the scales it is desirable that the full-scale readings be multiples of each other. Assume, for example, that the 600-volt meter described is to have additional scales of 300 volts and 150 volts. The meter then has one common terminal and three other terminals marked 600, 300, and 150 volts as shown. The added resistance for the 300- and 150-volt scales are those indicated in the figure.

Instead of separate resistances, a single resistance with suitable taps may be used as in Fig. 5-9(*b*). The first arrangement is preferable, however, because it permits separate adjustments to be made of the several resistances, and it has the further advantage that, should one of the resistances burn out, the remaining ones will probably be unaffected.

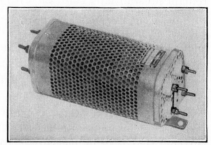

FIG. 6-9. Voltmeter multiplier. (*General Electric Company.*)

Multipliers. The added resistance used with an instrument to adapt it to the measurement of voltage may be housed within the meter case, or all or a part of it may be contained in a separate resistance unit external to the meter, in which case the external resistance is often called a *multiplier* (Fig. 6-9). Multipliers are usually used with standard 150-volt meters and are designed to extend the scale reading by some integral factor such as 5, 10, or 20.

To ensure accuracy, resistors used as added resistance in voltmeters, like the resistors used as shunts for ammeters, must not vary appreciably with temperature changes. For this reason, series resistances are usually made of a copper-nickel alloy which has the desired low temperature coefficient of resistance.

Large Current Measurements with Millivoltmeter and Shunt. It has already been noted that a millivoltmeter indicates the small voltage consumed in the resistance of the meter circuit by the coil current. A low-resistance shunt may be used with a millivoltmeter to measure the shunt current by connecting the terminals of the meter to the terminals of the shunt with two millivoltmeter leads as in Fig. 7-9. The meter then reads the millivolts consumed between the shunt terminals, which is the same as that consumed in the meter, for the shunt and the meter resistances are in parallel. But, since this voltage is proportional to the current in the shunt, the meter scale may be calibrated to read directly

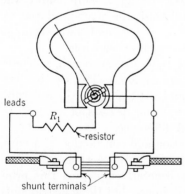

FIG. 7-9. Millivoltmeter with external shunt.

the amperes in the shunt circuit. The shunt should be so designed that the voltage drop in the shunt due to full-rated current is equal to the meter reading in millivolts at full-scale deflection. This assures that the meter needle does not go off scale so long as the rated shunt current is not exceeded.

It is assumed in the foregoing that the meter and shunt resistances remain substantially constant within the limits of the operating temperature range, and that the meter is calibrated with the millivoltmeter leads connected in the meter circuit. To ensure accuracy, the same leads, or similar leads of about the same length, should always be used with the meter. In this application the meter current is usually so small in comparison with the current in the shunt that it may be disregarded. The current in the shunt then becomes, in effect, the current to be metered.

A given millivoltmeter may be provided with several shunts and a corresponding different number of current scales, to extend the range of currents that may be measured. A number of such shunts are pictured

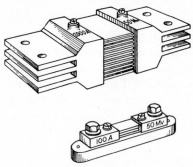

FIG. 8-9. Shunts.

in Fig. 8-9. Assume, for example, that the millivoltmeter previously described is used with shunts to give full-scale readings of 75, 150, and 300 amp. The meter circuit has a resistance of 15 ohms, and full-scale deflection of 150 mv is produced with a coil current of 0.01 amp. The resistance of the 75-amp shunt must then be 0.150/75 or 0.0020 ohm. The 150-amp shunt and the 300-amp shunt have resistances of 0.0010 and 0.00050 ohm, respectively. In the case of the 75-amp shunt the current to be metered at full scale is 75 + 0.01, the error produced by disregarding the meter current is 75.01 − 75 = 0.01 and the percentage error is 100(0.01/75.01) = 0.013 per cent, which is negligible.

Thermal Instruments. The presence of an electric current in a slender wire affects the wire in three ways. It brings about (1) a rise in temperature, (2) an increase in resistance, and (3) elongation of the wire. All these effects have been used, with varying degrees of success, as means of measuring current and potential difference.

Hot-wire instruments employ the elongation and contraction of a wire, due to increasing and decreasing temperatures, to move a pointer over a graduated scale. Both ammeters and voltmeters employing this principle were formerly built and a few are still in use, but these instruments have now been largely superseded by the thermocouple type of instrument. Hot-wire instruments waste relatively large amounts of energy, their readings are affected by room temperature, the zero point is indefinite and requires constant adjustment, and the meter is very sluggish in action. When a new reading is desired, seconds elapse before the needle settles down to the final position.   Owing to these disadvantages, hot-wire meters have largely disappeared from the market.

Thermocouple voltmeters and ammeters utilize a thermocouple that is either in direct contact with (usually welded or soldered) or is immediately adjacent to, but may be insulated from, a slender current-carrying conductor or *heater*.   The leads of the thermocouple are connected to the terminals of a millivoltmeter (or a galvanometer) of the permanent-magnet moving-coil type.   At low values of current the emf developed in the junction of the thermocouple is roughly proportional to the temperature of the heater, which in turn is proportional to the square of the heater current.   At large currents radiation losses cause the curve of voltage to fall below the theoretical "square curve" form.   By proper calibration, such a meter becomes an ammeter; when supplied with a suitable resistance multiplier, it can be used as a voltmeter.

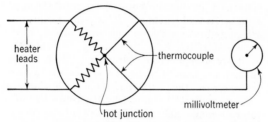

FIG. 9-9. Thermocouple meter.

Ammeters for measuring small currents of 500 ma or less are constructed with heater and thermocouple both enclosed in an evacuated bulb as in Fig. 9-9.   This arrangement eliminates convection currents and increases reliability.   These meters are usually suitable for the measurement of alternating currents of a few milliamperes at audio and radio frequencies.   They have very little inductance or capacitance, although inaccuracies due to the latter become apparent at very high frequencies.

Problems

1-9. The full-scale reading of a millivoltmeter is 50 and the resistance between its terminals is 5 ohms.   Find the resistances of shunts for use with this meter that will give full-scale indications of 25, 50, and 100 amp.

2-9. What resistance must be connected in series with the millivoltmeter of Prob. 1-9 to give full-scale indications of 75, 250, and 500 volts?

3-9. A 1,200-volt voltmeter consists of the millivoltmeter of Prob. 1-9 and sufficient additional series-connected resistance to give full-scale deflection when 1,200 volts is impressed across the meter terminals.   This meter is connected in series with a 1,000-volt supply and the insulation resistance of a motor.   When so connected, the voltmeter reads 5 volts.   Determine the insulation resistance of the motor.

4-9. A No. 0000 copper wire, the resistance of which is 0.05 ohm per 1,000 ft, carries an unknown current.   When the terminals of a millivoltmeter make good electrical contact between two points on the wire 2 ft apart, the meter reads 25 mv. What current flows in the wire?

5-9. The resistance of a millivoltmeter is 3 ohms. It is used with a shunt of 0.0004 ohm to measure a current of 100 amp. How much current flows through the instrument?

6-9. A voltmeter with a full-scale reading of 300 volts and an internal resistance of 18,000 ohms, and an ammeter with a full-scale reading of 3 amp and an internal resistance of 0.08 ohm, are used to measure the resistance of an electromagnet. Meter readings of 250 volts and 0.36 amp are obtained when the ammeter is so connected as to include the voltmeter current. What is (a) the apparent, and (b) the true, resistance of the electromagnet? If the same readings are obtained when the ammeter is reconnected to exclude the voltmeter current, what would be (c) the apparent, and (d) the true, resistance?

7-9. A voltmeter with a full-scale reading of 3 volts and an internal resistance of 300 ohms, and an ammeter with a full-scale reading of 250 amp and an internal resistance of 0.00058 ohm, are used to find the resistance of a series-field winding. Meter readings of 1.2 volts and 200 amp are obtained when the ammeter is so connected as to include the voltmeter current. What is (a) the apparent, and (b) the true, resistance of the series-field winding? If the same readings are obtained when the ammeter is reconnected to exclude the voltmeter current, what would be (c) the apparent, and (d) the true, resistance?

8-9. The sensitivity of a commercial voltmeter is given in terms of "ohms per volt," a figure which when multiplied by the *full-scale* reading of the instrument gives the total resistance of the voltmeter. If a 1,000-ohms/volt instrument is available, how much current will be drawn by the voltmeter (a) when 100 volts is measured on a 150-volt range, and (b) when 150 volts is measured on the same range? (c) Repeat (a) and (b) for a 20,000-ohms/volt instrument.

CHAPTER 10

THE ELECTRIC FIELD. CAPACITANCE

Charging Current. According to modern theory, positive and negative charges of electricity are associated with the atoms of all matter. In the normal state of matter the total positive charge of an atom is equal to the total negative charge and the atom is electrically neutral. In conductor materials, as has been stated, there are many free electrons, which move toward the positive terminal at some average velocity when an emf is applied, thus giving rise to a current of electricity in the conductor when the circuit is closed [Fig. 1-10(a)]. If a circuit is open at one point, as in (b), a small current still exists for a very short time after the switch is closed on a direct source of potential difference. This fact may be verified by inserting a sensitive galvanometer in the circuit, when it is observed that the needle is deflected momentarily at the instant the potential difference is applied. At the instant the switch is closed, the potential of a is higher than that of b, while the potential of c is lower than that of d. The applied potential difference therefore causes electrons to move in the circuit in the direction bacd, and current is established in the opposite direction[1] as indicated by the arrow.

Since the circuit is open, however, electrons cannot move beyond d, so they collect there and quickly lower the potential of d, until it falls to the level of c. In a similar manner, the potential of b is raised as electrons are withdrawn, until it reaches the level of a. When equality is established between the potentials of a and b, and c and d, respectively, the current in the circuit is zero, and the conductors are said to be charged, ab being positively charged and cd being negatively charged. The process of equalizing the potentials in the manner described is called charging and the current that flows during the interval is called the charging current.

---

[1] It should be recalled that the conventional direction of current flow is always opposite to the direction of motion of electrons. In any part of a circuit containing no emf, electrons move toward points of higher potential (from − to +), but according to the approved convention, current flows toward points of lower potential or from + to −.

If the switch is opened after the conductors are charged, the charges remain for a time but gradually leak off, and as they do so the potential difference between the conductors falls, again reaching zero when the charges have completely disappeared. The strength of the charging current depends upon the nature of the circuit, the applied voltage, and the insulation between conductors. At operating voltage the charging current of an ordinary circuit (a lighting circuit, for example) is extremely small indeed. If the circuit is long and the voltage is high, as in case of a 200-mile, 230-kv transmission circuit, the charging current may be 160 amp.

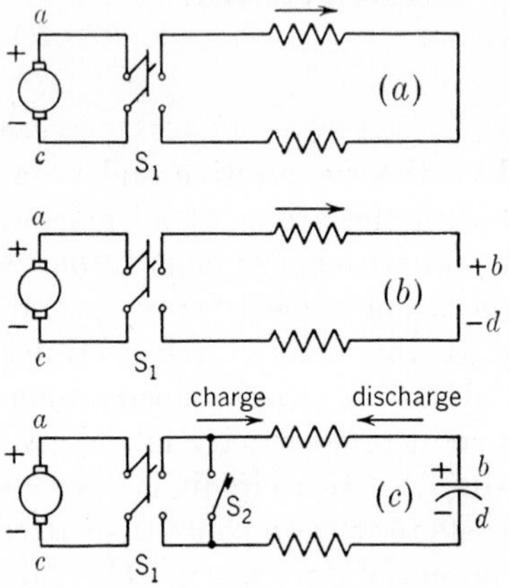

Circuits may be especially designed to have large charging currents by greatly increasing the areas of the terminals and bringing them close together as in (c), for a much larger number of electrons must then be moved to equalize the potentials when the switch is closed. Such a device, consisting of large metal areas separated by a thin sheet of insulating material (air, mica, impregnated paper, etc.), is called a *condenser*. The metal pieces are the *plates* of the condenser and the insulation between them is the *dielectric*. It is of interest to see what happens in the dielectric between the plates of a condenser when voltage is applied to the terminals.

FIG. 1-10. Charging and discharging a condenser.

Displacement Current. If a potential gradient below breakdown is established within an insulating material, the electrons within the atoms of the material are acted on by electric forces which *tend* to separate the electrons from the remainder of their respective atoms, just as in a conductor material under similar circumstances. But, since the bonds that hold electrons to their atoms in insulating materials are very strong yet elastic, the application of an emf does not produce any free electrons but results only in displacing electrons (charges) from their neutral positions.

Refer to Fig. 1-10(c) and note that, at the instant of closing switch S_1, the potential difference across the plates of the condenser rises rapidly at first and then more slowly as the plates become charged, and finally, when the charging process has been completed, the potential difference across the plates becomes constant and equal to the impressed voltage (Fig. 9-10). During this interval electronic charges are being displaced toward the positive plate at varying rates, and since the time rate of displacement of charge is an electric current ($i = dq/dt$), there is a *displacement current* in the dielectric, directed from b to d. At the same time there is an equal conduction current in the connecting wires in the direction $dcab$. Thus, while the voltage is rising, a clockwise current exists throughout the circuit—a displacement current in the dielectric and a conduction current in the conductors. This statement holds for a vacuum capacitor (perfect insulator) as well as for ordinary dielectrics.

If, after the condenser is charged, the voltage is allowed to fall by opening S_1 and closing S_2 simultaneously, the tension in the bonds is released and electrons are returned to their neutral positions (toward the negative plate). During this interval, current flows from d to b in the dielectric and in the direction bS_2d in the external circuit, so long as the voltage falls. The current stops when the voltage no longer changes.

In a continuous-current circuit a perfect condenser is equivalent to an open circuit, except for very short intervals of time while the voltage is being impressed or removed from the circuit. In a-c circuits, however, since the voltage rises and falls continually, a condenser passes current so long as the voltage is applied.

Electric Field. The electric field is discussed briefly in Chap. 1, but it is advantageous at this point to review the principal concepts.

In practice, electrical conductors between which a potential difference is maintained are separated by an insulating material or *dielectric*. Within the dielectric separating two conductors, as well as in the space around them, an *electric field* exists when a potential difference is impressed between the conductors, and electric charges are displaced in the manner already described. The *electric intensity* or *voltage gradient* is the maximum negative space rate of change of voltage ($\varepsilon = -dE/dl$), and the potential difference between any two points in a field is the line integral of the gradient between the two points, or

$$E = -\int \varepsilon \, dl \qquad (1\text{-}10)$$

where dl = elementary component of path taken in direction of gradient.

In the mks (r) system of units the dielectric flux emanating from a charge of one coulomb is one dielectric line. Electric fields are represented by *dielectric flux lines*, also called *lines of displacement flux* (ψ). They are so drawn that the direction of a line at any point represents the direction of the gradient at that point, and the number of lines per unit of normal cross-sectional area of flux path represents the *flux density* $D = \psi/A$, also called the *displacement*, for since $\psi = Q$, the displacement is $D = Q/A$ coulombs/sq m.

The arrowheads on displacement flux lines designate the sense of the gradient; that is, they point out the direction in which a positive charge in the field is urged by the electric force acting.

Parallel-plate Condenser. The simplest form of an electric field is the field between the plates of a parallel-plate condenser (Fig. 2-10).

When a potential difference is impressed, making A positive and B negative, there is a uniform fall of potential in the dielectric from A to B as shown in (b). Since positive charges are displaced in the direction of potential drop in the dielectric, the field can be represented by dielectric flux lines drawn perpendicular to the plates, except at the edges, with arrows pointing toward the negative plate. The voltage gradient is represented by the slope of the line in Fig. 2-10(b) and has the constant value $\mathcal{E} = E/l$. Moreover, since the flux density is proportional to the gradient, D is also constant and the lines of dielectric flux are parallel.

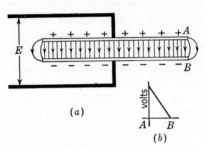

(a)

(b)

FIG. 2-10. The electric field of a parallel-plate condenser.

Permittivity. Assume that a condenser similar to the one in Fig. 2-10 has plates of area A sq m each, which are l m apart, and let a potential difference of E volts be impressed across the condenser terminals, giving rise to the equal charges of $+Q$ and $-Q$ coulombs on the positive and negative plates, respectively. A constant gradient $\mathcal{E} = E/l$ volts/m is set up within the dielectric, and if the medium between the plates is empty space, the flux density or displacement is $D = \epsilon_0\mathcal{E}$, where ϵ_0 is a constant, called the *permittivity of empty space* (which is substantially the same as that of air), the value of which depends only upon the system of units used, as follows:

In the electrostatic system $\quad \epsilon_0 = 1$

In the mks (nr) system $\qquad \epsilon_0 = 10^{11}/C^2$
$$= 1.113 \times 10^{-10}$$

In the mks (r) system $\qquad \epsilon_0 = 10^{11}/4\pi C^2$
$$= 8.854 \times 10^{-12}$$

where C = velocity of light = 2.998×10^{10} cm/sec.

There are a number of materials, however, which are better conductors of dielectric flux than is a vacuum. Several of these are listed in Table III, in the right-hand column of which is given the *relative permittivity* ϵ_r of each material (also called the *dielectric constant*). The relative permittivity of a dielectric material is analogous to the relative conductivity of an electric conductor material or to the relative permeability of a magnetic material, except that the latter is a function of the flux density B whereas ϵ_r is independent of D. The relative permittivity of a vacuum (and approximately of air) is unity. It is the standard to which the value of ϵ_r for any other material is referred.

The significance of this is that, if a dielectric material which has a relative permittivity ϵ_r replaces the vacuum in the condenser mentioned in the first paragraph of this section, the flux density, or the charge dis-

TABLE III. THE DIELECTRIC CONSTANTS OF COMMON MATERIALS

Material	Dielectric constant (ϵ_r)
Air	1
Bakelite	6.6–16
Cloth (varnished)	3.5–5.5
Glass (hard)	5.5–10
Mica	3–6
Paper (impregnated)	2.5–4
Quartz	4.3–5.1
Rubber	2.5–3
Titanium dioxide	90–170
Slate	6–7
Sulfur	4
Vacuum	1

placed per unit of cross-sectional area, is increased by the factor ϵ_r and the displacement is

$$D = \epsilon_r \epsilon_0 \mathcal{E} \tag{2-10}$$

This is the general equation for the displacement at any point in a dielectric where the gradient is $\mathcal{E}$.

Example 1. The area of each plate of a condenser similar to the one in Fig. 2-10 is 100 sq cm, the plates are 0.20 cm apart, and the impressed emf is 1,000 volts. Determine the displacement and the total flux (*a*) when air is the dielectric and (*b*) when glass with a permittivity of $\epsilon_r = 6$ replaces air as the dielectric, the impressed voltage and the physical dimensions of the condenser remaining unchanged.

The electric gradient is

$$\mathcal{E} = \frac{1,000}{0.20 \times 10^{-2}} = 5 \times 10^5 \text{ volts/m}$$

and the displacement for condition (*a*) is

$$D_a = \epsilon_r \epsilon_0 \mathcal{E} = 8.85 \times 10^{-12} \times 5 \times 10^5 = 4.43 \text{ microcoulombs/sq m}$$

whereas for condition (*b*) it is

$$D_b = \epsilon_r \epsilon_0 \mathcal{E} = 6 \times 4.43 = 26.6 \text{ microcoulombs/sq m}$$

The corresponding displacement fluxes are found from the relation $\psi = DA$, whence, since 100 sq cm = 10^{-2} sq m,

$$\psi_a = D_a \times 10^{-2} = 4.43 \times 10^{-8} \text{ coulomb}$$
$$\psi_b = D_b \times 10^{-2} = 2.66 \times 10^{-7} \text{ coulomb}$$

Examples of Electric Fields. The electric field between the parallel plates of a condenser has already been described. The electric fields of several other simple conductor arrangements are shown in Figs. 3-10, 4-10, and 5-10.

The field about a positive point charge of electricity (Fig. 3-10) is radially outward in all directions like the magnetic field about a point north magnetic pole, while the field about a negative point charge is

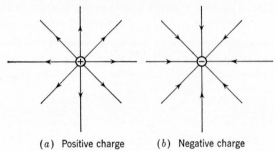

(a) Positive charge   (b) Negative charge

FIG. 3-10. Electric fields about point charges.

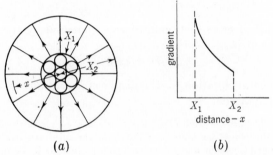

(a)   (b)

FIG. 4-10. The electric field of a single-conductor cable.

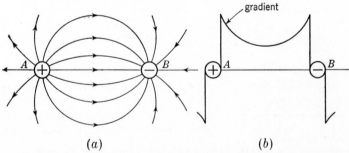

(a)   (b)

FIG. 5-10. The electric field about the return loop of two parallel round wires.

radially inward in all directions, like the magnetic field about a south point pole.

In Fig. 4-10 is shown the electric field between a cylindrical conductor and an outer concentric, cylindrical, conducting sheath. A single-conductor insulated cable with a lead sheath over the insulation has a field of this form. In a plane perpendicular to the axis, the field is radial and the gradient varies inversely with the distance from the axis as shown in (b).

The electric field in the air between two like conductors of a power circuit is circular in form as in Fig. 5-10. In a plane perpendicular to the conductor axes, arcs of circles representing displacement flux begin on the positive conductor and end on the negative conductor. In (b) of Fig. 5-10 is shown the curve of the gradient as a function of distance from the conductor axes. The gradient is seen to reach maximum values at the conductor surfaces, and a minimum value midway between the conductors.

Capacitance. Any two insulated conductors constitute a condenser. When the potential difference impressed between the conductors changes, a charging current is established. Experiment shows that this current is proportional to the rate of change of voltage. Since the flux in the electric field is also proportional to the voltage, the current is proportional to the rate of change of the electric flux. In symbolic language these facts are expressed by

$$i = -C\frac{de}{dt} = -\frac{dQ}{dt} = -\frac{d\psi}{dt} \tag{3-10}$$

where i = current, when voltage changes at rate of de/dt volts/sec and charge changes at rate of $d\psi/dt$ coulombs/sec

C = proportionality factor

The direction of flow of charging current is always such that the charge resulting from it tends to equalize the voltage of the conductors with the impressed voltage in the manner described on a previous page; that is, it tends to prevent the supply voltage from changing. This fact is indicated by the minus sign. The proportionality factor C is called the *capacitance* of the circuit. The capacitance of the circuit depends upon the arrangement of the circuit (area of conductors, distance apart, etc.) and upon the dielectric material between conductors, but it is independent of the voltage applied. For this reason capacitance, like inductance and resistance, is a *circuit constant*.

By solving for capacitance in the above equation, one observes that, numerically,

$$C = \frac{i}{de/dt} \tag{4-10}$$

Accordingly, a circuit has unit capacitance when voltage changing at the rate of one volt per second establishes a charging current of one ampere. This unit of capacitance is called the *farad*. The farad is far too large a unit for ordinary use, however. The capacitances of circuits and condensers ordinarily employed are only small fractions of a farad. For this reason the microfarad (abbreviated μf) is a more convenient unit and is the one generally used. For example, the capacitance per mile between two conductors of a high-voltage power transmission circuit is about 0.007 μf or 7×10^{-9} farad.

Most conductor arrangements are so complicated that it is usually difficult, if not impossible, to calculate their capacitances. In simple conductor arrangements, however, like a parallel-plate condenser or the two parallel wires of a power circuit, the capacitance can be expressed in terms of the circuit dimensions.

Example 2. For the case of a parallel-plate condenser with plates close together, the capacitance may be computed as follows: From Eq. (3-10) by integration,

$$\psi = CE = Q, \text{ or}$$

$$C = \frac{\psi}{E} \tag{5-10}$$

By multiplying Eq. (2-10) by A, the area of a plate, and substituting for $\mathcal{E}$ its constant value E/l, the displacement flux is found to be

$$\psi = DA = \epsilon_r \epsilon_0 \frac{AE}{l} \quad \text{coulombs} \tag{6-10}$$

and from Eqs. (5-10) and (6-10) the capacitance, in mks (r) units, is found to be

$$C = \frac{\epsilon_r \epsilon_0 A}{l} = 8.854 \times 10^{-6} \frac{A}{l} \quad \mu\text{f} \tag{7-10}$$

If l' is in inches and A' is in square inches, the capacitance is

$$C = 0.225 \times 10^{-6} \frac{A'}{l'} \quad \mu\text{f} \tag{8-10}$$

Commercial Condensers or Capacitors. Sometimes it is desirable to introduce capacitance into a circuit for reasons which will be better understood when the student has become familiar with a-c theory. Built-up condensers are used for this purpose. Low-voltage condensers are built with large numbers of metal-foil sheets separated by thin layers of paraffined paper after the manner illustrated in Fig. 6-10. Alternate metal-foil sheets are connected to terminal 1, and the remaining sheets are connected to terminal 2. In this way a very large area of surface is secured, for the effective plate area A_0 is $A_0 = (n - 1)A$, where A is the area of one side of a sheet and n is the number of sheets. The distance separating adjacent sheets is small, so a relatively large flux is produced when voltage is impressed. In this way a large capacitance is obtained from a small volume of material. Condensers are also built with mica, glass, or

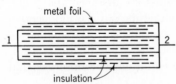

FIG. 6-10. Construction of condensers.

air as the dielectric. Condensers of variable capacitance are built with air as the dielectric and with movable plates, for use in radio circuits.

Low-voltage condensers are widely used in radio, telephone, and television circuits, and in many other less well known applications.

Capacitors which are built to withstand moderately high voltages are used extensively in power systems to supply reactive power to industrial loads that require power-factor correction, to control the voltage of long rural lines and high-voltage transmission circuits, and to increase the economy of operation of long, heavily loaded, high-voltage lines. (These matters are further clarified in later chapters.)

Fig. 7-10. Commercial condensers.

Condensers are used in many other power applications as, for example, in percussion welding, in X-ray machines, in the tripping devices of circuit breakers, in the transformers used with luminous-tube lights, and in single-phase induction motors.

Capacitors for power applications are constructed of alternate thin layers of good-quality linen paper, separated by layers of metal foil. The assembly is vacuum-dried and impregnated with a synthetic liquid called *Askarel* (also called *Inerteen* or *Pyranol*). The use of Askarel is advantageous in this application because it has a high permittivity ($\epsilon_r = 5$, approximately), it does not support combustion, and it does not freeze or crystallize at any temperature experienced in operation.

Various forms of commercial capacitors are illustrated in Fig. 7-10.

Condensers in Series and in Parallel. Condensers in parallel add like resistances in series, while condensers in series add like resistances in

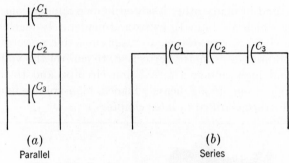

(a)   (b)
Parallel   Series

FIG. 8-10. Condensers in series and in parallel.

parallel (Fig. 8-10). When condensers of capacitances C_1, C_2, and C_3 are connected in parallel, the capacitance C_0 of the group is

$$C_0 = C_1 + C_2 + C_3 \qquad \text{(parallel connection)} \qquad (9\text{-}10)$$

When the same three condensers are connected in series, the capacitance of the group is

$$\frac{1}{C_0} = \frac{1}{C_1} + \frac{1}{C_2} + \frac{1}{C_3}$$

$$C_0 = \frac{C_1 C_2 C_3}{C_1 C_2 + C_2 C_3 + C_3 C_1} \qquad \text{(series connection)} \qquad (10\text{-}10)$$

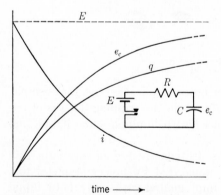

FIG. 9-10. Current, voltage, and counter emf of a condenser being charged through a resistance.

Example 3. (a) What is the capacitance of a 2-μf condenser in parallel with a 3-μf condenser? (b) What is the capacitance of the condensers connected in series?

(a) Parallel connection

$$C_0 = 3 + 2 \text{ or } 5 \ \mu\text{f}$$

(b) Series connection

$$C_0 = \frac{3 \times 2}{3 + 2} \text{ or } 1.2 \ \mu\text{f}$$

Energy Stored in an Electric Field. When an electric field is formed, as by charging a condenser, energy is supplied to the condenser and stored in the dielectric. If a perfect dielectric is assumed, this energy is returned to the circuit when the condenser is discharged by short-circuiting its terminals.   Charging a condenser[1] (Fig. 9-10) is analogous to stretching a weightless spring.   While the spring is being stretched, energy is being stored in the elasticity of the spring.   When the stretching force is released, the spring returns to its natural unstressed position and in so doing releases the stored energy.   When a condenser is charged, the bonds in the atoms of the dielectric are stressed and energy is stored in the dielectric.   When the condenser is discharged (Fig. 10-10), tension in the bonds is released and energy is returned to the circuit.   If a condenser of C farads capacitance is charged in t sec by an emf of E volts, the average charging current is $I_{av} = CE/t$ amp.   This current flows

[1] When a condenser is charged from a battery of voltage E through a resistance R as in Fig. 9-10, the equation of equilibrium of the circuit is

$$E = ri + e$$

where e is the counter emf of the condenser.   By substituting in this equation the value of current from Eq. (3-10) and solving, the voltage of the condenser may be found as follows:

$$E = rC \frac{de}{dt} + e$$

or, after separating the variables and changing sign,

$$-\frac{de}{E - e} = -\frac{dt}{rC}$$

By integration one obtains

$$\log_\epsilon (E - e) = -\frac{t}{rC} + k \text{ (a constant)}$$

Since, when $t = 0$ the voltage of the condenser is zero, $k = \log_\epsilon E$, and

$$e = E(1 - \epsilon^{-t/rC}) \qquad (a)$$

By differentiating Eq. (a) and multiplying the result by C [(Eq. (3-10)], one obtains the current

$$i = \frac{E}{r} \epsilon^{-t/rC}$$

The charge on the condenser is

$$q = \int_0^t i\,dt = \frac{E}{r} \int_0^t \epsilon^{-t/rC}dt = EC(1 - \epsilon^{-t/rC}) \qquad (b)$$

The curves of current, voltage, and charge are shown in Fig. 9-10.   The energy of the charged condenser can be found by taking the integral

$$W = \int_0^\infty ei\,dt$$

which turns out to be

$$W = \frac{CE^2}{2}$$

against the counter emf of the condenser. The counter emf is zero at the beginning (at the instant when the switch is closed) and is equal to the impressed voltage when the condenser is charged. The average value of the counter emf during the charging period is therefore $E/2$ volts. The energy stored is the product of average counter emf, the average current, and the time, or

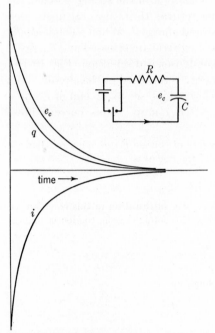

$$W = \frac{E}{2} I_{av}t = \frac{E}{2} \times \frac{CEt}{t}$$

$$= \frac{CE^2}{2} \quad \text{joules} \quad (11\text{-}10)$$

This checks the value already obtained by another method in the footnote on page 131.

It should be noted that the expression for the stored energy in a condenser has exactly the same form as the expressions for stored energy in a spring ($W = \frac{1}{2}kx^2$) and stored energy in the inductance of a circuit ($W = \frac{1}{2}LI^2$).

FIG. 10-10. Current, voltage, and emf of a condenser discharging through a resistance.

Example 4. How much energy is stored in a 12-mf condenser when charged with 1,000 volts?

$$W = \frac{1,000^2 \times 12 \times 10^{-6}}{2} = 6 \text{ joules}$$

Conduction Current and Insulation Resistance. Commercial electric insulation, however good, is never perfect. In addition to the displacement current that exists within a dielectric that is subjected to a varying applied potential difference, there are also *conduction currents* over the surface as well as through the body of the material. Surface conduction takes place through a thin film of moisture with whatever dust or other foreign matter may adhere to it. The current in the surface film is called the *surface leakage current*, and the associated resistance is the *surface insulation resistance*. The resistance of the path over which current is conducted through the body of an insulating material is called the *volume insulation resistance*. Thus, the conduction current comprises both the surface leakage and the conduction current through the body of the material. The former is usually the principal component. Both

depend upon the temperature and the humidity. The surface leakage
also depends upon the nature and extent of the foreign material associated
with the surface film of moisture, that is, upon the cleanliness of the
surface.

Dielectric Loss. When a dielectric is discharged, the energy returned
to the circuit is somewhat less than that supplied to the dielectric upon
charge. The deficiency is due principally to two causes: energy loss in
the insulation resistance and energy loss in the body of the dielectric in
association with what is known as *dielectric absorption*.

On charging a dielectric from a source of constant potential difference,
the current decreases only gradually to the steady state value, which is
the conduction current. On discharging, a current of decreasing magnitude may flow for a long time before the dielectric is fully discharged.
These are manifestations of dielectric absorption. Although the precise
action that takes place within a dielectric has not been fully explained,
it is well known that energy losses do occur within the material when a
dielectric is carried through a cycle of varying potential difference. The
loss associated with absorption is usually the principal loss in a dielectric.

Both absorption and insulation resistance losses are affected by moisture and temperature. The loss characteristic of a dielectric material is
usually expressed in terms of the *loss factor F*. This factor is the product
of the dielectric constant k and the power factor, $\cos \theta$ (page 361). The
power loss in a dielectric that is subjected to the potential difference of
an alternating emf is given by the relation

$$ p = \frac{10^{-12}}{1.8} f \mathcal{E}^2 F \qquad \text{watts/cu cm} $$

where f = frequency, cps

$\quad\ \mathcal{E}$ = electric gradient within dielectric, volts/cm

$\quad\ F$ = loss factor

The total watts loss in a capacitor of C_0 farads geometric capacitance
in vacuo is

$$ P = 2\pi f C_0 E^2 F \qquad \text{watts} $$

where E = effective value of impressed alternating voltage

$\quad\ f$ = frequency, cps

$\quad\ F$ = loss factor

Dielectric Heating. Commercial condensers are used extensively in
the fields of power and communications and in applications involving the
use of vacuum tubes in many types of control circuits. These condensers
are so carefully built that losses are extremely small when they are used

at the voltage and frequency for which they are designed. In most theoretical discussions dielectric losses are disregarded entirely.

It is possible, however, to use the principle of a rapidly varying electric field as a means of heating a dielectric material. Such applications have been made in the plastics industry for curing plastics and for heating the plastic material before it is put into the molds. It has been used in the shoe-manufacturing industry and in the furniture industry for quickly drying the glue used in the manufacture of certain kinds of shoes and in furniture construction. It has also been employed for drying glue in laminated wood structures and for the accelerated curing and drying of expensive woods. Many other applications of this principle will undoubtedly be developed in the future.

The heat liberated in a dielectric by a changing electric field depends on the loss factor of the substance and is proportional to the frequency of the supply and to the square of the impressed voltage. Since each dielectric material has its own loss factor under given conditions of moisture, temperature, etc., it is apparent that to increase the rate of heating one must either raise the impressed voltage or increase the frequency of the supply. For most substances there is a fairly definite limit, however, beyond which it is impractical to raise the voltage for fear of overstressing and puncturing the dielectric material. In the final analysis, then, increasing the frequency remains the only satisfactory way of increasing the rate of heat development in a dielectric. Applications usually employ frequencies ranging from 2 to 100 mc/sec.

Problems

1-10. Ten glass plates, each 10 by 12 by $\frac{1}{16}$ in., are separated by sheets of tin foil and are stacked to make a condenser. The top and bottom plates have sheets of tin foil on their outer sides as well, which sheets form the terminals of the condenser. The glass used has a relative permittivity of 6. Determine (a) the microfarad capacitance of the condenser, (b) the flux density in the glass in coulombs per square meter, (c) the voltage gradient in the glass when 1,000 volts is impressed on the condenser terminals.

2-10. In Prob. 1-10, alternate glass plates are replaced by sheets of Bakelite of the same dimensions as the glass plates but having a permittivity of 10. Determine (a) the microfarad capacitance of the condenser, (b) the voltage gradient in the glass, (c) the voltage gradient in the Bakelite. The impressed emf is 1,000 volts as before.

3-10. Two concentric, hollow spheres are made of spun copper of negligible thickness. The spheres are insulated from each other and are separated by an air gap 0.04 in. long. The capacitance of the condenser formed by the spheres is 1 mf. (a) Compute the mean radius of the spheres in inch units. (b) Suggest how the same capacitance may be obtained with spheres of about one-half the diameter.

4-10. There are available 12 similar condensers of 10 mf capacitance each. What total capacitance results from each of the following connections: (a) 12 condensers in parallel; (b) 12 condensers in series; (c) 6 condensers in series with 6 in parallel; (d) the arrangement shown in Fig. A-10?

5-10. In Fig. A-10 all condensers have the same capacitance. A potential difference of 2,000 volts is impressed across the terminals ac. Determine the potential differences that appear across ad, ae, ab, and bc.

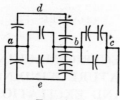

FIG. A-10

6-10. A circuit, comprising a condenser of unknown capacitance and a resistance of 1,600 ohms in series with it, is connected to a 750-volt d-c source through a switch. An oscillogram of the current shows that 0.02 sec after the switch is closed the current has fallen to 0.15 amp. Find (a) the microfarad capacitance of the condenser, (b) the counter emf of the condenser 0.02 sec after the switch is closed.

7-10. When a condenser of C farads capacitance is charged to a potential difference of E volts, its charge is q coulombs. The condenser is subsequently discharged through a resistance of R ohms. Derive the equations of counter emf e, current i, charge q, and power p flowing from the condenser as functions of time.

8-10. A capacitance of 3 μf is connected in series with a resistance of 80 ohms. The capacitance is charged through the resistance by connecting a 120-kv direct-current source of potential across the circuit. (a) How many kilowatt-hours of energy are stored in the capacitance when it is fully charged with 120 kv? (b) What is the charge in coulombs? Determine the following for the instant of time 60 μsec after the switch is closed: (c) the counter emf of the capacitance, (d) the stored energy in kilowatt-hours, (e) the current, (f) the power flowing in the condenser, (g) the power expended in the resistance.

CHAPTER 11

THE DYNAMO-ELECTRIC MACHINE. PRINCIPLE OF OPERATION, ARMATURE WINDING, CONSTRUCTION, AND EXCITATION

Generator Principle. An electric generator is a machine that is used to convert mechanical energy to electrical energy. It consists essentially of a large number of copper conductors and a strong magnetic field which is so arranged that the conductors may be moved in the field. In d-c generators the field is stationary and the conductors are moved, while in a-c generators the conductors are stationary and the field is moved. In either case, however, magnetic lines of force are cut and voltages are generated in the conductors. The conductors are so arranged that they form a circuit in which the voltages are all generated in the same direction. When the circuit is closed, current flows and electric energy may be drawn from the circuit.

The principle upon which the action of the generator depends was briefly discussed in Chap. 7. It was there shown that when the wire loop (Fig. 1-11) is moved downward a part of *cd*, equal in length to the width of a pole face, cuts across the flux in the air gap and generates an emf. When the circuit is closed, current flows around the loop in the direction *adcb*. The direction of both current and emf may be found by the right-hand rule.

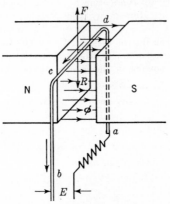

FIG. 1-11. Generator action.

In Fig. 1-11 the vector *R* represents the applied force and the vector *F* is the equal and opposite electromagnetic force developed by the interaction of the current and the magnetic field. In Fig. 2-11 (*a*) an end view of conductor *cd* is shown. The outward-flowing current lies in the magnetic field from the poles. Accordingly, as explained in Chap. 7, an electromagnetic force *F* is developed that tends to move the conductor upward out of the field. This force opposes the motion of the conductor and the work done by the driver in maintaining the electric current is the work it does in overcoming the force F. When the circuit is open as in Fig. 2-11 (b), the generated emf cannot maintain a current (although the emf may be the same as before). There is then no force on the conductor and no energy is required to move the conductor across the field. No work is done when voltage is generated in an open circuit. It is only when the circuit is closed and electrons are moved that a generator is *loaded* and energy is required to drive it, losses neglected.

Motor Principle. An electric motor is a machine that is used to convert electrical energy to the mechanical energy of motion. So far as their construction is concerned, electric motors differ only in minor details from generators. Usually, a given machine can perform as either a generator or a motor, and whether it is one or the other depends upon

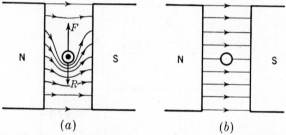

$$(a) \qquad\qquad (b)$$

Fig. 2-11. The resultant magnetic field about conductor cd in Fig. 1-11.

how it is used. When mechanical energy is supplied to the shaft and electrical energy is delivered at the terminals, the machine is a generator. When electrical energy drives the machine and mechanical energy is delivered at the pulley, the machine is a motor. Electric machines that may be operated as either generators or motors are sometimes called *dynamos*, although this term is seldom used by engineers.

In electric motors, current from an outside source is supplied to conductors in a magnetic field. It was shown in Chap. 6 that, when current flows in a magnetic field, there is a force on the current. This force is used in a motor to do mechanical work. The motor principle is further illustrated in Fig. 3-11. The conductor cd lies in the field formed by the poles of a magnet, and current is supplied to the conductor from a battery. The force F is developed, and if the conductor is free or if it is restrained by a resisting force R that is not too great, it moves in the direction of F. In so doing, the force R is overcome through the distance of travel x and mechanical work Rx is done. The electrical energy supplied by the battery is thus converted to mechanical energy of motion and the device constitutes an electric motor. As cd moves upward, a length of conductor equal to the width of the pole face cuts across the magnetic field and generates an emf in exactly the same manner as a generator (Fig. 1-11). In Fig. 3-11, *cd* moves upward, however, while in Fig. 1-11 *cd* moves downward, so the emfs are generated in opposite directions in the two cases *when a given direction of current is assumed.* In the motor the direction of generated emf is opposite that of the impressed voltage and tends to stop the current. For this reason the emf of a motor is called a *counter emf.* The mechanical power developed by the motor is equal to the product of the current and the counter emf of the motor. If the energy losses in the motor are small enough so that they may be disregarded, the power output of the battery is equal to

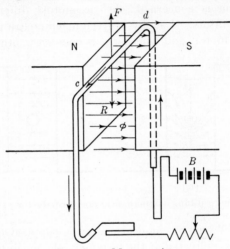

FIG. 3-11. Motor action.

the power developed by the motion of the conductor in overcoming the resisting force *R*.

Ratings of Generators and Motors. A statement of the normal operating limits of each commercial machine is provided by the manufacturer in the form of data stamped on a name plate fastened to the machine frame. These data usually include the output, speed, voltage, and current assigned to the machine by the builder. They constitute what is called the *rating* of the machine, and the various characteristics are spoken of as *rated voltage, rated speed, rated current,* etc. The basis upon which these ratings are founded is discussed briefly in a later chapter. The rated output of a generator is expressed in kilowatts available at the machine terminals, at the voltage and speed specified. A generator with a rating of 25 kw at 125 volts and 1,000 rpm, for example, when driven at a speed of 1,000 rpm and delivering 125 volts at the terminals, supplies an output current of $25,000 \div 125 = 200$ amp. This is the value of current that appears on the name plate.

The rated output of a motor is given in kilowatts or horsepower available at the shaft when the specified voltage is impressed and the motor runs at rated speed. The output of a motor is usually given in horsepower. The motor input is greater than its output because there are certain friction and other heat losses that must be supplied from the electrical input in addition to the useful work which the motor does. A 25-hp 115-volt 800-rpm motor, for example, with an efficiency at rated load of 87.5 per cent, has an input current at rated load of $(25 \times 746)/(115 \times 0.875)$ or 185.3 amp.

Essential Elements of D-c Generators and Motors. In practice, emfs are usually generated in either one of the following two ways:

1. By rotating electric conductors in a stationary magnetic field
2. By rotating a magnetic field past stationary conductors

Direct-current generators and motors generally employ the first of these methods. A number of turns of copper wire or strap are wound in slots on a cylindrical steel core which is mounted on a shaft and may be rotated. The winding and the core constitute the *armature*. Concentric with the armature but separated from it by a small air gap are the concave cylindrical pole faces of the *field magnets*. The field poles embrace about 65 per cent of the armature surface. When the armature revolves, parts of each turn cut the flux from the field poles and generate emfs. These parts are called *armature conductors*. The remaining parts of a turn (in which no voltage is generated) are called the *end connections*.

Since the emf generated in the armature winding of a d-c generator or motor is alternating, while the voltage at the terminals of the machine is direct (always in one direction), the generated wave must be *rectified*. This is accomplished by means of a *commutator* connected between the armature winding and the machine terminals. The commutator is mounted on the same shaft with the armature and revolves with it. Connection is made to the external circuit by means of *brushes* that rest on the commutator and slide on its surface when the armature revolves. Magnetic field, armature, and commutator are the principal elements of all d-c generators and motors. These as well as other parts are described in greater detail in the latter part of this chapter.

Rotational Emf. The field poles north and south and the armature M of a generator are illustrated, in principle, in Fig. 4-11. For the sake of simplicity an armature winding of only one turn is assumed, having the conductors a and b and end connections. The back-end connection is not shown, but the front-end connections are joined to two slip rings f and g. These rings are insulated from each other and from the shaft, and they turn with the armature. When the armature revolves in a clockwise direction, emfs are generated in the conductors in the directions indicated in the figure. The emfs of a and b add around the turn, and their sum is the terminal voltage.

When a is at 1 and b is at 4, the potential difference between terminals [Fig. 4-11(b)] is zero. It rises slowly at first and then more sharply as a and b approach 2 and 5. Thereafter it soon reaches its maximum. The generated voltage then remains constant while a moves from 2

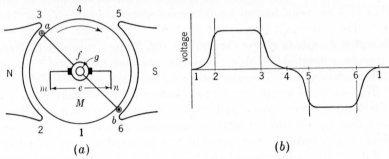

Fig. 4-11. Alternating electromotive force.

to 3 and b moves from 5 to 6. Beyond these points the emf again quickly falls to zero. When the plane of the coil reaches the plane 4-1, the first half revolution is complete. During the next half revolution, a is under the influence of the south pole, while b is under the influence of the north pole, and accordingly the emf of the coil is reversed. All values of emf generated during the first half revolution are repeated, but

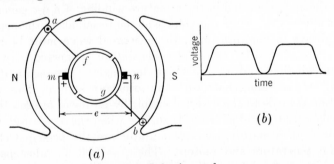

Fig. 5-11. Pulsating emf.

in the reverse direction. Thus when the ends of the coil in the armature are connected to slip rings, the emf generated and the potential difference in the external circuit are both alternating.

Action of the Commutator. A direct potential difference may be obtained at the machine terminals by substituting the single split ring or *commutator* of Fig. 5-11 for the two slip rings of Fig. 4-11. Commutator segments f and g are connected to the conductors a and b and have, respectively, the same potentials.   During the half revolution when a is under the north pole, f is positive and g is negative, while during the next half revolution f is negative and g is positive.   The brushes m and n are fixed in position and rest on the commutator at diametrically opposite points.   They are so placed that they span the gaps between segments at instants when the plane of the coil crosses the axis 4-1 in Fig. 4-11.   In this way brush m always contacts the positive segment while n contacts the negative segment and the potential difference between the terminals (or brushes) is constantly in one direction.

The commutator reverses the connection of the armature coil to the external circuit each time the coil sides (conductors) pass from one pole to the next pole of opposite polarity and in this way rectifies the voltage wave.   The potential difference in the external circuit is the wave shown in Fig. 5-11(b).   This wave is exactly like Fig. 4-11(b) except that alternate loops are rectified.   Figure 5-11(b) is a *direct emf*, and the current that such a wave of voltage establishes is a *direct current*, but because the emf is not constant in value but pulsates, it is called a *pulsating* emf.

In practical machines, pulsations in the terminal voltage are almost entirely eliminated by winding the armature with many turns connected in series between brushes and using a large number of commutator segments.   For example, a certain small (5-kw) generator has 160 turns of wire in the armature winding.   The machine has two poles, so 80 turns are connected in series between brushes in each of two parallel paths, and the sum of the voltages generated in the 80 turns is the terminal voltage.   The coils are commutated one at a time as they cross the axis between poles, and at such times their generated voltages are zero.   The number of turns generating voltage at any instant is always the same and the terminal voltage is constant.

Gramme-ring Winding.   The simplest type of armature winding is the Gramme-ring winding illustrated in Fig. 6-11.   This type of winding was much used at one time but has since been superseded.   The armature core is a hollow cylindrical iron ring or toroid, upon which insulated wire is wound in the form of a continuous spiral.   The armature winding is tapped at regular intervals, and these taps are connected to commutator segments.   There may be one tap for each armature turn, one tap for each two turns, one tap for each three turns, etc.   The number of commutator segments required for an N-turn winding is therefore N, $N/2$, $N/3$, etc., as the case may be.

When the armature revolves emfs are generated in the outer parts of the turns.   By assuming a direction of rotation and applying the right-hand rule, one observes that the emfs are generated in opposite directions around the winding under the poles of opposite signs.   Thus in Fig. 6-11, the emfs generated by that part of the winding lying under the north pole are clockwise, while those generated under the south pole are counterclockwise.

The normal position of the brushes is in the axis AA'. The brushes rest upon the commutator bars that are connected by taps to the con-

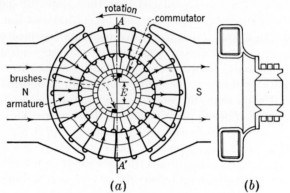

(a)   (b)

FIG. 6-11. Two-pole Gramme-ring winding.

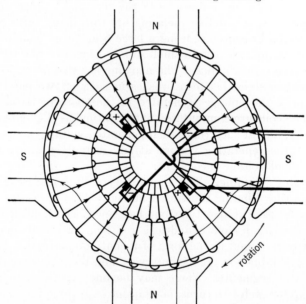

FIG. 7-11. Four-pole Gramme-ring winding.

ductors lying midway between poles. The potential difference between adjacent brushes is therefore equal to the emf generated by the series-connected turns under one pole, that is, by one-half of the armature winding in a two-pole machine, by one-fourth the winding in a four-pole machine (Fig. 7-11), by one-sixth the winding in a six-pole machine, etc.

In this type of winding there are as many sets of brushes as there are poles. Since there is one path through the armature winding between each brush and the next adjacent one, there are also as many parallel-connected paths between machine terminals as there are poles. This is illustrated in Fig. 8-11 for the case of a four-pole machine. In a machine having p poles, the conductors of each path generate the total machine voltage and deliver $1/p$ of the output current.

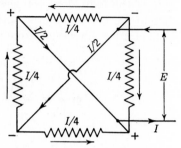

FIG. 8-11. Armature circuits in four-pole Gramme-ring winding.

Example 1. The armature of a 10-kw four-pole Gramme-ring generator is driven at a speed of 1,200 rpm. The axial length of the armature and pole cores is 6 in., and the length of the pole arc is 4 in. The flux density in the air gap under the poles is 45,000 maxwells per sq in. (*a*) How many turns must the armature have to generate 120 volts between terminals? (*b*) When the machine delivers 10 kw to the external circuit, with the field current neglected, how much current flows out at the positive brushes? (*c*) How much current flows in each path of the armature?

(*a*) Area of pole face $\quad$ = pole arc × length of core
$\qquad\qquad\qquad\qquad\quad$ = 4 × 6 or 24 sq in.
$\quad$ Flux per pole $\qquad\qquad$ = 24 × 45,000 × 10^{-5}
$\qquad\qquad\qquad\qquad\qquad$ = 10.8 milliwebers

Since only the upper side of a turn cuts flux, each turn cuts
$$p\phi \times \text{rps} = 4 \times 10.8 \times 10^{-3} \times 1{,}200/60 \text{ webers/sec}$$
and thereby generates
$$E = \frac{4 \times 0.0108 \times 1{,}200}{60} = 0.864 \text{ volt}$$

$\qquad$ Number of turns per path $= \dfrac{120}{0.864} = 139.$

$\qquad\quad$ Total turns required $\quad$ = 4 × 139 = 556
(*b*) Output current $\qquad\qquad$ = 10,000 ÷ 120 = 83.3 amp
(*c*) Current per path $\qquad\quad$ = 83.3 ÷ 4 = 20.8 amp

Continuous Emf and Current. The generated emf of a machine like the one just described is nearly constant in value. Its voltage and the current which it delivers are therefore said to be *continuous*. As the armature of Fig. 7-11 revolves, coils continually pass from south pole to north pole at the top, and from north pole to south pole at the bottom. At the moment a coil is transferred from one pole to the next, its generated emf is substantially zero, however, because it lies in a region of zero flux, and hence its commutation does not materially alter the sum total of the emfs generated in any path of the armature.

Figure 9-11 illustrates how the generated voltage is made up in a machine with six turns per path. The voltage generated in each coil is assumed to be a wave of the shape shown in Fig. 5-11(*b*) and illustrated by the heavy line of Fig. 9-11(*b*). Since the coils are displaced from each other by $^{180}\!/_6 = 30$ electrical degrees,[1] their voltage waves are displaced by the same angle. These waves are shown in Fig. 9-11(*b*) as dotted lines. The total voltage generated per path at any instant is the sum of the individual voltages for that instant as shown in Fig. 9-11(*a*). It may be noted that the total voltage never approaches zero but consists of a large average value plus a small "commutator ripple."

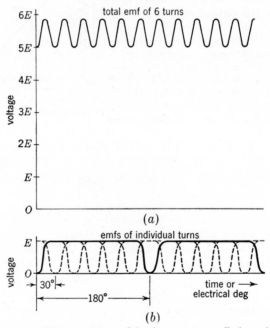

FIG. 9-11. Voltage generated in six armature coils in series.

The example shown in Fig. 9-11 is actually oversimplified, since in commercial machines a large number of turns is used between brushes, and also the brushes often span more than one commutator segment, thus short-circuiting out the turns in the neutral zone. The result is that in most commercial machines the commutator ripple is very much less noticeable than is indicated in the figure, and for most purposes the total voltage may be regarded as truly constant. Only in exceptional circumstances (small generators that supply radio transmitters) is it necessary

---

[1] A single coil generates one positive and one negative loop or one *cycle* of emf for each pair of poles it passes. The angular space through which a coil revolves to generate $^{1}\!/_{360}$ part of a cycle is called an *electrical degree*. In a two-pole machine, 1 space degree = 1 electrical degree; in a four-pole machine, 1 space degree = 2 electrical degrees; etc.

to provide small inductance-capacitance filters to reduce further the residual commutator ripple.

Drum Armature. In a Gramme-ring winding, only the outer portion of each turn cuts the flux from the poles, and so most of the wire on the ring is inactive. Furthermore, the machine must be wound by threading the coils through the eye of the ring, thus requiring much hand labor in winding. Because of these and certain other more or less obvious disadvantages, the Gramme-ring winding is now seldom, if ever, used. To take its place, the *drum-wound* armature has been developed.

The core of a drum armature consists essentially of a cylindrical drum made of suitable electrical steel (Fig. 21-11). The surface of the drum is slotted to receive the winding as illustrated in Figs. 10-11 and 24-11. Formed coils are used (Fig. 11-11); that is, the coils are wound and formed over a template or, in the case of small machines, are pulled into

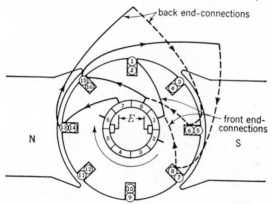

FIG. 10-11. Two-pole lap-wound drum armature.

proper shape before being put in place on the drum. The spread or *pitch* of the coil is made equal to or somewhat less than a pole pitch in order that, when the coil is placed in the slots of the drum, opposite sides of the coil lie under poles of opposite signs and therefore generate voltages which add in the circuit.

For example, in Fig. 10-11, full-pitch coils are used. Inductor 13, lying midway under the north pole, is connected on the back end of the armature to inductor 6 lying midway under the south pole, and hence their generated voltages always add. On the front end of the armature conductors or coil edges 13 and 6 are connected to adjacent commutator segments 7 and 8. All other coils are similarly connected. The number of coil edges over which the back-end connections pass is called the *back pitch*, while the number of coil edges over which the front-end connections pass is the *front pitch*. For example, in Fig. 12-11 the front pitch is 7 and the back pitch is 9.

It should be observed that coil edge 13 lies in the upper part of the slot, while coil edge 6, forming the opposite side of the coil, lies in the lower half of its slot. The same is true of coil edges 15 and 8, 1 and 10, etc. All coils used on d-c machines are made in this way, in order that the front and back end connections, shown solid in the figure, may be above those shown dotted and thus form a satisfactory mechanical structure in the finished machine.

Lap Winding. As already pointed out, the spread of a coil must always be approximately a pole pitch. In practice, it is usually made somewhat less, in order to shorten the end connection. When the armature coils are connected together to form a winding, the same rule holds; that is, the end of a given coil must be connected to the beginning of another, the generated emf of which adds to its own. Thus in Fig. 10-11 edge 13 may be considered as the beginning and edge 6 as the end of the coil

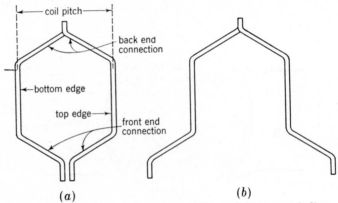

FIG. 11-11. Armature coils for (*a*) lap winding and (*b*) wave winding.

lying midway under the poles. Coil edge 6 should then be connected through the commutator either to coil edge 11 or to coil edge 15, as in the figure; if to the latter, connection is made from coil edge 6 to commutator segment 8, and from segment 8 to coil edge 15. It is observed that the front ends of the coil with edges 13 and 6 end on the adjacent segments 7 and 8, and the coil has the shape shown in Fig. 11-11(*a*). A winding thus connected is called a *lap winding* because it alternately progresses forward and then *laps* back upon itself.

In Fig. 12-11 is represented a *simplex* (simple) lap winding for a four-pole machine with 36 face conductors or coil edges. The slots are not shown, but the coil edges are indicated by the numbered straight lines lying in the position of the air gap. Solid lines represent the upper and dotted lines the lower coil edges. The directions of the generated emfs are indicated by the arrows. By tracing through the winding and noting the directions in which the arrows point, one observes that, if an external circuit were completed between the plus and minus terminals, the induced emfs would cause current to leave the winding at the two plus brushes and to enter the winding at the two minus brushes.

Beginning at the commutator segment 1 and tracing through the winding in the direction of the arrows, the armature path between the

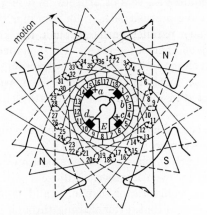

(a) conventional wiring diagram

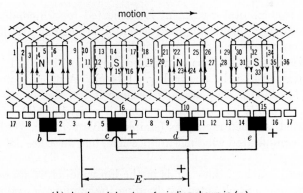

(b) developed drawing of winding shown in (a)

FIG. 12-11. Four-pole lap winding. Front pitch = 7, back pitch = 9.

negative brush b and the positive brush c is readily identified. It includes conductors 1, 10, 3, 12, 5, 14, 7, and 16. Current enters the winding at b and leaves the winding at c. Similarly, the path between the negative brush d and the positive brush c includes the conductors 26, 17, 24, 15, 22, 13, 20, and 11. Accordingly, current flows through the armature winding in a clockwise direction from b to c, and in a counter-clockwise direction from d to c. Thus the current that leaves the wind-

ing through brush c is twice as large as the current in the adjacent armature turns. The current leaving at the positive brush e is likewise made
up of the currents approaching through the winding from brush d on
the left and brush b on the right.

The brushes rest upon the commutator at points where the current
from the armature tends to leave and enter the winding. A six-pole lap-
wound armature requires six sets of brushes, and in general, a machine
with p poles must have p brush sets. Lap windings (of the usual type)
always have as many parallel paths through the armature (between
machine terminals) as there are poles. The conductors in each path
generate the total voltage but deliver only a fraction of the output current. In a four-pole machine, for example, the armature paths are
arranged as illustrated in Fig. 8-11 and each path delivers one-fourth of
the output current.

It should be observed that in Fig. 12-11 the back pitch is 9, the front
pitch is 7, and the average pitch is $(9 + 7)/2$, or 8. In a simple lap
winding, front and back pitches are always odd and differ by 2, while
the average pitch is an even number. Adjacent winding elements are
connected to adjacent commutator segments, and as one traces through
the winding, one observes that, after passing through all the conductors
and commutator bars, one finally reenters the winding at the point of
beginning.

Since each commutator segment is connected to two conductors, the
total number of segments required is equal to one-half the number of
armature conductors in a one-turn winding.

Wave Winding. The type of winding shown in Fig. 13-11 has armature coils shaped like the one in Fig. 11-11(b). A winding made up of
such coils is called a *wave winding* because it has the appearance of a
wave, as may readily be observed by examining Fig. 13-11(b). The winding illustrated is called a *simplex* (simple) wave winding. Other somewhat more complicated windings are possible, but these are not described
here.

The average pitch of the coil, as in the lap winding, is approximately
equal to the quotient obtained by dividing the number of armature conductors by the number of poles. Owing to the fact that both front-end
connections are bent away from the coil axis, however, the termini of
the front-end connections are approximately two pole pitches apart.
For example, in Fig. 13-11 the front ends of the coil that includes conductors 1 and 8 are connected to commutator segments 1 and 7, while
the coil that includes conductors 13 and 20 is connected between segments 7 and 13. Note also that segment 13 is adjacent to segment 1,
the point of beginning. Thus in a four-pole machine with a simplex
wave winding, two coils in series extend around the armature from a

given segment to the adjacent segment. In a six-pole machine three coils are required, in an eight-pole machine four coils, etc., are required to complete the portion of the winding between any segment and the adjacent one.

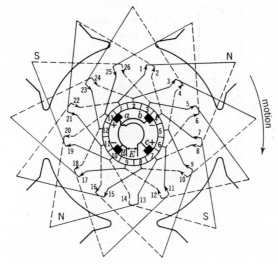

(*a*) conventional wiring diagram

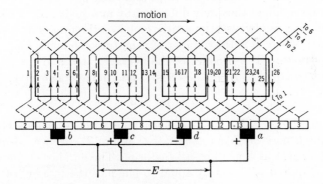

(*b*) developed drawing of winding shown in (*a*)

FIG. 13-11. Four-pole wave winding. Front pitch = 5, back pitch = 7.

A four-pole wave winding with 26 conductors is illustrated in Fig. 13-11. The arrows indicate the directions of the generated emfs, and by tracing through the winding, following the direction of the arrows, one may see that the generated emfs add correctly. The brushes are placed at the points on the commutator where the currents tends to enter or leave the winding. *In this winding only two sets of brushes are required* (although four may be used), because the brushes of like sign are connected in parallel through the winding itself.　Thus brushes d and b are connected together through segment 10, conductor 19, conductor 26, and segment 3; also by segment 4, conductors 7 and 14, and segment 10. The positive brushes are similarly connected.　Accordingly, only two brush sets are necessary.　This is true regardless of the number of poles the machine may have.　If one traces through the winding from a negative brush to the next adjacent positive brush, one observes that the path includes one-half the total number of armature conductors independent of the number of poles the machine may have.　This shows that *a simple wave winding (of the usual type) always has two armature paths only*, between machine terminals.

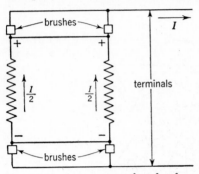

Fig. 14-11.　Armature paths of a four-pole wave-wound machine.

The total voltage of the machine is therefore generated by one-half the armature face conductors, and each armature path supplies half the output current.　The two paths of the armature circuit are illustrated in Fig. 14-11.

In a simplex wave winding the front and back pitches are always odd; they may be equal, or they may differ by any multiple of 2.　The average pitch, however, is always very nearly equal to the quotient Z/p, as has been stated, where Z is the number of armature conductors and p is the number of poles.　The product of the average pitch and the number of poles must be equal to $Z \pm 2$.　Thus, if y is the average pitch,

$$Z = py \pm 2$$

For example, consider a six-pole machine with 70 conductors.　The average pitch may be taken as $(70 + 2)/6$, or 12.　Hence a front pitch of 11 and a back pitch of 13 is satisfactory.　The number of commutator segments required is obviously equal to one-half the number of conductors or 35, and the commutator pitch is equal to the average pitch, which in this case is 12.

Construction of Generators and Motors.　Broadly speaking, d-c generators and motors are built alike, and whether a given machine is one or the other depends primarily upon how it is used.　In other words, these machines are reversible; when mechanically driven to supply an electrical output, the machine is a generator, but when electrically driven to perform mechanical work, it is a motor.　While these broad statements are correct in a general way, it is to be borne in mind that a machine designed as a motor, for example, may perhaps not make the most satisfactory generator, nor does one designed as a generator make the best motor. In either case some changes in the design would probably be desirable to adapt the machine best to meet the new requirements, but its general make-up would remain essentially unchanged. The description of machine parts and structures which follows may therefore be regarded as applying to generators and motors alike.

Frame. The machine *frame* or *yoke* is the circular iron or steel ring to which the pole cores are bolted, as shown in Fig. 15-11. It serves the twofold purpose of supplying the mechanical skeleton for the remainder

FIG. 15-11. Frame with fields in place. G-E d-c motor: 600 hp, 575/1,150 rpm, 600 volts, six poles. (*General Electric Company.*)

of the machine and of providing a good magnetic conductor through which the path of the magnetic flux from the pole is completed. Frames were originally made of cast iron with cast feet for supports. This material is still used for small machines where weight is of little importance. Rolled steel frames of rectangular cross section are used for large machines because this material is more economical. For a given magnetic conductivity its weight is only about 40 per cent as much as that of cast iron. Large frames are usually made in two parts for ease of handling and for convenience of assembly. The two halves are bolted together when the machine is set up. The frame may or may not be horizontally split, depending upon its size. Feet and lugs for bolting

the halves together are welded on the frame.   Pressed-steel feet, bolted
to the frame, are also used for the smaller sizes.

Pole Cores.   The pole cores complete the magnetic circuit between
the armature and yoke, as shown in the cutaway view of the motor in
Fig. 16-11.   They have sometimes been made of cast steel, in which

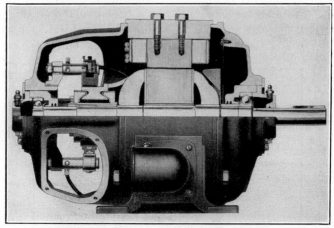

FIG. 16-11. Cutaway view of small motor.   (*General Electric Company.*)

case laminated *pole shoes* are required.   Usually, however, the core is
made of soft sheet-steel punchings of suitable shape (Fig. 17-11) to form
the finished core.   These are stacked and riveted together under pressure.   When punchings with cutaway tips (as in Fig. 17-11) are used,
the punchings are so stacked that pole tips appear alternately at the left

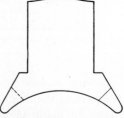

FIG. 17-11. Pole-core punching with one   FIG. 18-11. Punchings stacked to form
tip cut away.   high-reluctance pole tips.

and the right, so that in the completed structure every other tip is
missing as in Fig. 18-11.   In this manner a high magnetic saturation is
produced in the pole tips.   This aids commutation in a manner to be
explained later.   Usually, increased length of air gap under the pole tips
is secured in another way.   The punchings are symmetrical about the
center of the pole core (both tips are present in each punching) but

increased gap length is obtained at the tips by increasing the radius of curvature of the pole arc at these points. The pole cores are usually fastened to the frame by means of bolts as shown in Figs. 15-11 and 16-11.

Field Windings. Field coils for shunt machines consist of many turns of insulated wire wound on suitable frames or spools built up of insulating material (Fig. 19-11). The coils are vacuum-dried, after which they

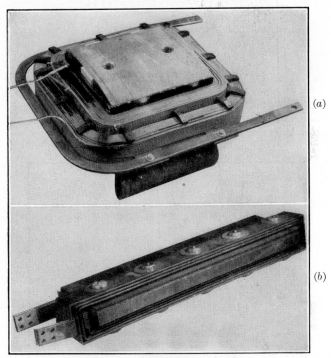

(a)

(b)

FIG. 19-11. Field pole windings.

are impregnated with insulating compound and baked. To assure proper cooling, thin coils that are held away from the pole cores on the ends are used [Fig. 19-11(a)]. For compound machines the series windings are usually made of strap copper, wound on edge to secure better radiation. Bare copper strap is often used. The completed series winding is placed over the shunt windings [Fig. 19-11(a)] but is blocked away from it to facilitate ventilation. Commutating-pole[1] windings [Fig. 19-11(b)] are similar in construction to series windings.

Armature. The *armature core* is built of thin annealed sheet-steel laminations (about 0.014 in. thick), supported in dovetailed grooves, or

---

[1] Interpoles or commutating poles are small poles, located between the main poles, that serve to improve commutation (see Chap. 12).

FIG. 20-11. Armature core showing parts and methods of assembly. (*General Electric Company.*)

FIG. 21-11. Fabricated spider and armature punchings. (*Westinghouse Electric Corporation.*)

with a key on a cast or fabricated *spider* (Fig. 21-11).   The spider itself is keyed to the shaft.   In the fabricated type the armature core is built on bolts which extend through the end plates and keep the laminated core under pressure.   The end plates are shrunk on to the spider arms and are locked in place by means of dowels.

In large machines each layer of the core is made up of several sections (Fig. 21-11), while for small machines a single punching constitutes a layer. The outer periphery of each sheet is punched with slots to receive the armature winding. Details of a slot with armature coils in place are shown in Fig. 22-11. Before the sheets are stacked on the spider they are run through between lacquered rollers, where they receive a thin coating of insulation on each side. This serves to prevent eddy currents from flowing between adjacent sheets in the completed armature core. Laminations are stacked to the required thickness, after which they are put under pressure and are clamped together by means of bolts and end rings. Coil-support rings (shown below the stacked laminations in Fig. 21-11) are fastened to the end rings by means of spokes or

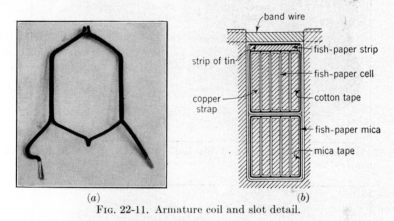

(a)   (b)

FIG. 22-11. Armature coil and slot detail.

welded lugs. Radial vent ducts (shown in Fig. 20-11) are formed in the armature core about every 2.5 in. of its length by the use of special separating laminations at these points. Air entering the machine between the spokes of the spider is thrown out through these ducts by the fanning action of the armature and thus keeps the armature cool.

The armature winding is assembled in a manner illustrated by the partially wound armature of Figs. 24-11. When the winding is complete, the coils are fastened in the slots by wedges driven into the slots over the coils or by high-strength banding wire. The end connections are also fastened to the supporting rings by banding wire.

Commutator. In some respects the commutator is the most important part of a d-c machine. It is made of wedge-shaped hard-drawn copper bars (Fig. 26-11), insulated from each other with thin sheets of high-quality mica. Bars separated by mica punchings are built up into a cylinder which has a circular V-shaped groove on each end. The segments are held together by means of two V-shaped rings that fit into

these grooves (see Fig. 16-11).   Through bolts or stud bolts fasten the
V rings together and clamp the segments in place.   The rings are separated from the copper bars by built-up, V-shaped mica insulation, to
prevent the bars from being short-circuited.   It is now common practice

FIG. 23-11. Assembled 600-kw 600-volt d-c generator. (*Westinghouse Electric
Corporation.*)

FIG. 24-11. Revolving armature of generator or motor in process of winding.   (*General Electric Company.*)

to cut the mica insulation away between bars to a depth of about $\frac{1}{16}$ in.
by means of a special slotting tool.   This is called *undercutting* the mica.
   After the armature is wound, the ends of the armature coils are laid in
slots in the *necks* or *risers* of the commutator segments, provided for the

purpose.   The coil ends are finally soldered to the necks when the winding is complete.

FIG. 25-11.   Revolving armature (partly wound) for G-E d-c generator: 1,750 kw, 500 rpm, 800 volts, 12 poles.   (*General Electric Company.*)

Brushes.   Brushes supported in holders rub upon the commutator and are connected to studs by flexible copper leads called *pigtails*.   They form the connecting link between the armature winding and the external circuit.   All the brush holders and their supporting studs are fastened by arms to a single brush ring, as in Fig. 27-11.   Brushes are usually made of carbon blocks, although for low-voltage machines copper gauze or other low-resistance brushes may be used.   The brushes fit their holders closely, but they

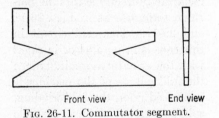

Front view   End view
FIG. 26-11.   Commutator segment.

must not bind; they must be free to follow irregularities in the commutator.   To ensure good contact, they are held against the commutator by springs that apply a pressure of about 1.5 psi of contact area.   The spring tension may be adjusted by means of a ratchet.

Bearings.   The bearings consist of cast-iron shells, made in two halves for the larger sizes and bolted together.   The shells are usually lined with high-grade babbitt and are ring-oiled.

Excitation. The magnetizing ampere-turns that set up the flux in the air gap under the poles are supplied by windings on the pole cores.

Fig. 27-11. Brush rigging. (*Westinghouse Electric Corporation.*)

The required magnetizing force may be obtained in several different ways. Thus suppose it is found that for a given 5-kw, 125-volt generator 2,000 amp-turns per pole are needed at full load. They may be furnished, for example, by winding each pole with 2,000 turns and supplying this winding with 1 amp of current. Such an arrangement employs a large number of turns and a small current. At full load the current output of the above generator is 40 amp. If the machine were wound with 2,000 ÷ 40 turns per pole and the full-load current of 40 amp were passed through this winding, the required 2,000 amp-turns of excitation would likewise be supplied. Obviously, it would also be possible to use two windings, each of which supplies a part of the total excitation.

Generators and motors are classified on the basis of the methods employed to furnish their excitations as follows:

Shunt Machines. The field windings of shunt machines are connected directly across the machine terminals as in Figs. 28-11 and 29-11. The field circuit in this case is in parallel or in *shunt* with the armature circuit. Since the full voltage of the machine is impressed upon the field winding, a large number of turns per pole and a small current are required. Because the current is small, only a small wire is needed, and the total resistance of the field circuit is high. The coils on the several poles are usually connected in series.

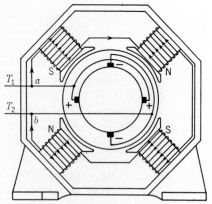

Fig. 28-11. Shunt generator.

A 5-kw 125-volt shunt-connected generator has about 2,000 turns per field spool. When all the spools are connected in series, the field resistance is about 100 ohms and the field current required at rated load is about 1.2 amp.

Separately Excited Machines. The field circuit is sometimes supplied with current from a separate source, as in Fig. 30-11. The machine

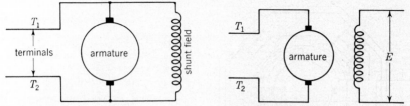

FIG. 29-11. Wiring diagram of shunt-connected generator or motor. Field rheostat not shown.

FIG. 30-11. Wiring diagram of separately excited generator.

is then said to be *separately excited*. The field windings of separately excited machines are usually like those of shunt machines; that is, they are made of many turns of small wire and carry only small currents.

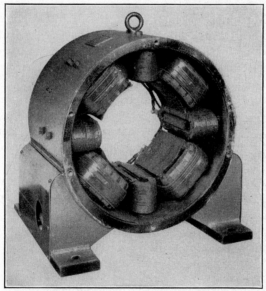

FIG. 31-11. Field of a G-E shunt-wound stabilized d-c motor: 50 hp, 850 rpm, 230 volts. Top and terminal side oblique rear view. (*General Electric Company.*)

Series Machines. In order to secure certain desirable operating characteristics, as in the case of railway motors, it is necessary to supply the field excitation by passing the armature current through the field winding. To accomplish this, the field and armature circuits are connected in *series*, as in Figs. 32-11 and 33-11. Series-connected fields carry much larger currents than do the corresponding or equivalent shunt fields, and hence the series windings have fewer turns, but much heavier copper wire is needed. The series-field resistance is correspondingly low, being usually less than that of the armature.

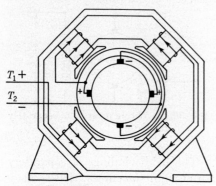

Fig. 32-11. Series generator.

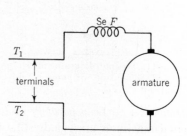

Fig. 33-11. Wiring diagram of a series-connected machine.

Compound Machines. Something of the desirable characteristics of both shunt-connected and series-connected machines may be combined in a single machine by the use of two windings, one shunt-connected and the other series-connected, as in Figs. 34-11 to 36-11. Such a machine is called a *compound machine*. In a compound machine the major portion of the excitation is usually supplied by the shunt field. The shunt field is slightly weaker and the series field is considerably weaker than the fields for the corresponding machine in which the entire excitation is produced either by a single shunt or by a single-series winding, as the case may be.

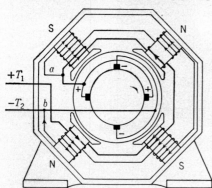

Fig. 34-11. Wiring diagram of a cumulative compound generator.

Compound machines are classified as *long-shunt* and *short-shunt* machines, depending upon which of the two ends of the series-field winding is connected to the shunt field. If terminal 4 of the shunt-field winding is connected to armature terminal T_2, as in Figs. 35-11 and 36-11, the remaining terminal 3 may be connected to the series-field terminal 1, as in Fig. 35-11, or to terminal 2, as in Fig. 36-11. The first of these is called the *short-shunt* connection, while the second is called the *long-shunt* connection. There is comparatively little practical difference between the two.

Compound machines are also classified as *cumulative* and *differential*. In a cumulative compound machine the magnetizing forces of the shunt- and series-field ampere-turns are cumulative; that is, they both tend to set up air-gap flux in the same direction across the gap, as in Fig. 34-11. The machine is differentially connected when the ampere-turns of the shunt winding oppose those of the series winding. This connection would be secured in Fig. 34-11 by reconnecting the series field, so as to

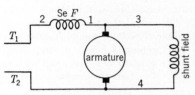

FIG. 35-11. Wiring diagram of a short-shunt compound generator.

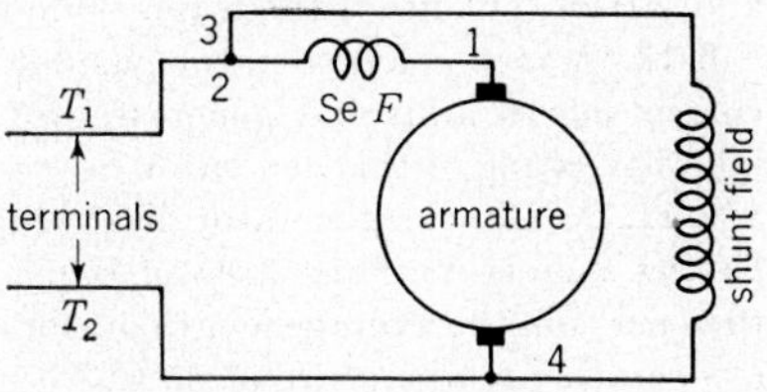

FIG. 36-11. Wiring diagram of a long-shunt compound machine.

pass current through it in the reverse direction, and using the shunt-field connections indicated in the figure.

Problems

1-11. A two-pole, shunt-wound generator has two sets of brushes designated as A and B for purpose of identification. The field winding is so connected that when the generator runs in a clockwise direction, A is positive and B is negative. Call this the initial condition. What is the effect of (*a*) reversing the direction of rotation, (*b*) reversing the shunt-field connections, (*c*) reversing both the direction of rotation and the shunt-field connections? (*d*) Describe the initial direction of the electromagnetic torque developed.

2-11. The machine in Prob. 1-11 is run as a motor by impressing a suitable direct potential difference across the brushes. The field connections and the polarity are the same as in Prob. 1-11, initial condition. Describe the direction of rotation (*a*) under initial conditions, (*b*) when field connections are reversed, (*c*) when the polarity of brushes is reversed, the field connections remaining the same as in the initial condition.

3-11. A single length of strap-copper conductor is just long enough to furnish all the armature turns of a four-pole, simplex lap winding. The resistance of the completed armature winding is 0.164 ohm. Determine (*a*) the resistance per armature path, (*b*) the resistance of the original length of copper strip.

4-11. Draw a double-layer simplex lap winding for a four-pole generator with one turn per winding element and a total of 36 conductors. Use front pitch of 7 and back pitch of 9. Assume clockwise rotation. Indicate the polarity of the poles and the direction of current in the winding elements. Locate the brushes in their correct positions on the commutator.

5-11. Draw a double-layer simplex wave winding for a four-pole generator with one turn per winding element and a total of 58 conductors. Use a front pitch of 15 and a back pitch of 15. Assume clockwise rotation. Indicate the polarity of the poles and the directions of the currents in the armature paths. Use only two brushes and indicate their proper locations on the commutator and their polarities.

6-11. The armature winding of a six-pole wave-wound d-c generator has 1,200 conductors. When the machine is driven at a speed of 500 rpm, the induced emf is 600 volts. The area of each pole face is 39 sq in. Find the average flux density in the air gap.

7-11. An eight-pole wave-wound generator has 600 armature conductors. The flux per pole is 5,000,000 lines and the speed is 250 rpm. (*a*) What is the generated voltage? (*b*) If the machine were lap-wound and had the same number of conductors, what would be the generated voltage? If the armature conductors carry 50 amp continuously without overheating, what is the maximum allowable continuous kilowatt output in (*c*) the wave-wound machine, (*d*) the lap-wound machine?

8-11. A four-pole generator has 336 armature conductors, each of which carries a current of 10 amp and generates 1.5 volts. Determine the terminal voltage and kilowatt rating of this generator (*a*) if wound simplex lap, (*b*) if wound simplex wave.

9-11. A 10-pole generator has 820 armature conductors made of strap copper having a cross-sectional area of 0.072 sq in. The winding is simplex lap with one turn per coil, the average length of coil being 84 in. Compute the armature resistance at operating temperature of 65 C.

CHAPTER 12

ARMATURE REACTION AND COMMUTATION

No-load Field Form. *Field form* is the name given to the curve the ordinates of which represent the flux densities in the air gap of a generator or motor and the abscissas of which are the angles subtended by the corresponding arcs of the armature periphery. When the field circuit is

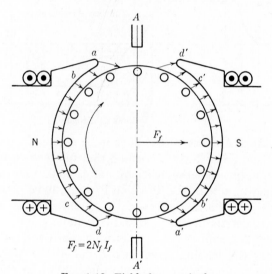

Fig. 1-12. Field alone excited.

excited, but no current flows in the armature circuit, the resulting flux distribution curve obtained is the *no-load field form*. In this case the magnetic-potential drop across the air gap is the same at all points under a pole and the flux density is distributed as in Figs. 1-12 and 2-12.

Between b and c under the north pole and between b' and c' under the south pole, the air gap has a fixed (minimum) reluctance and the flux density has the constant value indicated by the straight portions of the curve in Fig. 2-12. At the tips of the poles, as between ab and cd under the north pole and between $a'b'$ and $c'd'$ under the south pole, the reluctance of the air gap is increased. This may be accomplished by the use of punchings like the one shown in Fig. 17-11 on page 152, and by so stacking them that the spaces left by the missing tips appear alternately to the right and to the left of the core or by using punchings having increased radius of curvature at the tips. Owing to the increased reluctance under the tips, the flux densities at these points fall off rapidly and approach zero. At A and A' the curve passes through zero, for at these points the adjacent poles tend to magnetize the armature equally, but in opposite directions. These points are called the *no-load neutral points* and the axis AA' passing through them is the *no-load neutral axis*. The axis AA' is the normal axis of the brushes.

Because of symmetry in construction, the portions of the curve pertaining to the south pole are exactly like those pertaining to the north pole.

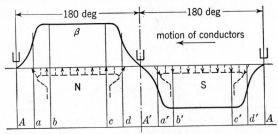

Fig. 2-12. No-load field form.

Armature Cross Ampere-turns. Let it be assumed that the brushes lie on the no-load neutral axis as before, that full-load current circulates in the armature, but that the fields are not excited. The armature current is assumed to flow in the direction it would have if the machine of Fig. 1-12 were acting as a generator. With clockwise rotation the current flows in under the north pole and out under the south pole, as in Fig. 3-12, and the mmf which it sets up magnetizes the armature as shown. Under the leading[1] pole tips d and d' the air-gap flux now crosses the gap in directions opposite to those shown in Fig. 1-12 for the corresponding tips, while under the trailing tips a and a' the flux crosses the gap in the same directions as before. The general direction of the armature mmf F_a is along the axis AA', or at right angles (crosswise) to the field mmf F_f of Fig. 1-12. Because it is due to the armature current and because it magnetizes the armature crosswise, this mmf is spoken of as the *armature cross ampere-turns*. Figure 4-12 is a developed drawing of the arrangement shown in Fig. 3-12. While this figure is drawn for a two-pole machine, it also correctly represents the magnetizing force and the flux distribution for any pair of poles of a multipolar machine.

---

[1] The *leading* pole tip is the tip under which a given armature conductor enters, and the *trailing* tip is the one under which it leaves the region under a pole.

The broken lines show the distribution of armature mmf, while the curve indicates the flux distribution in the air gap.

For a two-pole machine, or per pair of poles of a multipolar machine, the armature cross ampere-turns may be calculated as follows: When the brushes are on the neutral axis, as in Fig. 3-12, all the armature

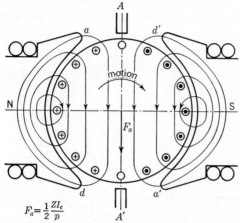

$$F_a = \frac{1}{2}\frac{ZI_c}{p}$$

FIG. 3-12. Current flowing in armature. Field current zero.

ampere-turns aid in magnetizing the armature core crosswise. Hence, if I_c is the current in an armature circuit and Z is the number of armature face conductors ($Z/2$ turns), the total number of ampere-turns on the armature is $ZI_c/2$. If the machine has p poles, $ZI_c/2p$ is the armature cross mmf per pole (across one air gap) and ZI_c/p is the armature cross

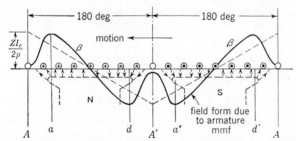

FIG. 4-12. Air-gap flux distribution due to armature mmf alone.

mmf per pair of poles. The paths over which this mmf acts (Fig. 3-12) are as follows: the air gap under pole tip d, the face of the north pole, the air gap under pole tip a, the armature core under the north pole and the similar path under the south pole. But since the reluctances of the iron portions of these paths are negligible with respect to those of the air gaps, the former may be neglected entirely. Accordingly, approximately one-half the armature mmf per pair of poles is used up in forcing the flux across the gap under each pole tip.   This mmf is $ZI_c/2p$ amp-turns, as indicated in Fig. 4-12.

Full Load.   Brushes Shifted.   At the instant when the sides of an armature coil pass through the neutral zones (zones A and A', where the air-gap flux is approximately zero), the coil is transferred from one armature circuit to the next adjacent one by means of the commutator and one of the brushes.   At no load, the neutral zones are in the no-load

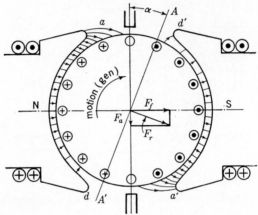

FIG. 5-12.   Current flowing in armature and field excited.   Machine acting as a generator.

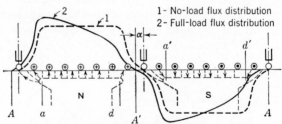

FIG. 6-12.   Air-gap flux distribution due to armature and field mmfs combined.

neutral axis (AA' of Fig. 1-12).   Under full load (Fig. 5-12) the neutral axis is shifted through an angle α.   *If the machine is a generator the shift is forward, or in the direction of rotation.*   A generator, however, rotates counter to the electromagnetic torque developed by the armature current and field flux, while a motor revolves with the torque.   Accordingly, if the machine is a motor with armature and field currents in the directions indicated in Fig. 5-12, it rotates counterclockwise.   *Hence, in a motor, the neutral axis shifts counter to the direction of rotation, or backward.*   In either case, however, the brushes must be shifted[1] into the position

---

[1] In modern machines, auxiliary devices such as commutating poles **or** compensating windings are usually used, which make shifting of the brushes unnecessary.   These will be discussed presently.

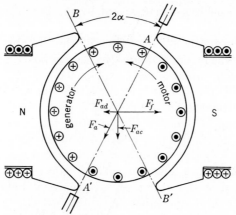

FIG. 7-12. Generator or motor under load with brushes shifted.

of the neutral axis, in order that the armature coils may be commutated at the instant when their sides pass through the neutral zones. The field form for the conditions of Fig. 5-12 is shown in Fig. 6-12.

When the brushes are shifted through the angle α (Figs. 5-12 and 7-12), the direction of the armature current in the conductors included in this angle at A is changed to plus, while at A' the corresponding conductors have their currents changed to minus. The armature ampere-turns represented by the conductors in the angle 2α thus constitute a demagnetizing mmf F_{ad}, as shown in Figs. 7-12 and 8-12(a). For this reason F_{ad} is called the *armature demagnetizing ampere-turns*. The remaining armature ampere-turns, or those included in the angle $360 - 4\alpha$ electrical degrees, constitute the armature *cross ampere-turns F_{ac}*. The resultant mmf of the armature and field combined is obviously less than the mmf of the field alone, and its line of action is shifted in the direction of rotation of the generator. The flux not only is shifted but is less than the corresponding no-load flux of Fig. 1-12 for two reasons:

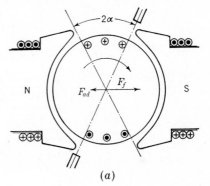

(a)

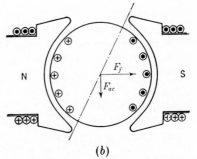

(b)

FIG. 8-12. (a) Armature demagnetizing ampere-turns; (b) armature cross ampere-turns.

1. Because the field is demagnetized by the armature demagnetizing ampere-turns F_{ad}

2. Because the demagnetizing effect of the armature cross ampere-turns F_{ac} reduces the flux more under the leading pole tip than it increases it under the trailing tip, as already explained

The net result is that under load the brushes must be shifted and the emf generated in the windings is reduced.

The magnetizing influence of the armature mmf, resulting in distorting and weakening the field as above described, is called the *armature reaction*.

Neutralizing Armature Reaction. The ill effects of armature reaction may be minimized or almost entirely overcome by making suitable provisions in the design of a machine.

1. *The Length of the Air Gap May Be Increased.* The equivalent gap is usually made longer under the pole tips than elsewhere. This is

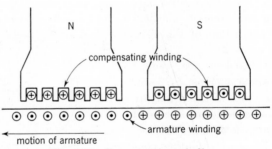

FIG. 9-12. Compensating winding.

accomplished either by cutting off, or chamfering, the pole tips, or by using punchings of the kind illustrated in Fig. 18-11. The use of a long air gap makes the gap reluctance high and requires a strong field mmf to force the flux across the gap. The field ampere-turns in such a machine are usually considerably in excess of the armature ampere-turns. The field is described as a *stiff* field and is not much influenced by armature reaction. On account of the greater equivalent gap length under the pole tips, the influence of the armature cross ampere-turns in shifting the main field is greatly minimized. This principle of design was used quite generally before the advent of interpoles.

2. *The Machine May Be Provided with a Compensating Winding.* This winding is placed in slots in the pole faces of the field, as illustrated in Fig. 9-12, and is connected in series with the armature circuit in such a way that at any point in the gap the current in the compensating winding flows in the direction opposite to the armature current. In this

way, if the compensating winding has the same number of ampere-turns per inch of armature periphery as the armature itself, the mmf of the armature is completely neutralized. The main field is not distorted under load, and the brushes are permanently set in the position that gives best average commutation. This type of construction is expensive and is used only for special applications.

3. *Commutating Poles May Be Used.* Commutating poles are small auxiliary poles mounted on the frame between the main poles. These poles are in reality not used to correct armature reaction, but rather to make satisfactory commutation possible without shifting the brushes, in a manner to be discussed presently. They do not prevent the main field from being distorted by the armature cross ampere-turns, but they do eliminate the demagnetizing ampere-turns, for the latter do not exist when the brushes are at the no-load neutral. These poles introduce great economies into the design of motors and generators, and for this reason they are now quite universally used.

Principle of Commutation. When a d-c armature revolves, the direction of the generated emf in each coil is reversed every time the coil passes from one pole to the next adjacent one. If the armature is loaded, the current in the coils must likewise be reversed. This process of reversal, called *commutation*, is illustrated in the drawings (a), (b), and (c) of Fig. 10-12.

In (a) of this figure, coil G is just passing out from under the trailing tip of the north pole. Current enters this coil from the negative brush by way of segment 2 and passes through the coil in a counterclockwise direction. An instant later, when the armature has turned through an arc corresponding to one-half the width of a commutator segment, coil G is in the neutral axis AA' as shown in (b). Current now enters the winding by way of both segments 1 and 2, thus by-passing coil G entirely. Coil G is temporarily disconnected from the armature circuit and is short-circuited by the negative brush. During the interval of its short circuit, however, this coil lies in the neutral axis where the flux is approximately zero. It therefore cuts no flux, generates no voltage, and has no output current. Figure 10-12(c) shows the position of the coil just a moment after it has passed through the neutral axis. The short circuit on G is removed when segment 2 passes out from under the brush, and current is built up in the coil in a clockwise direction. The conductors of the coil now cut the flux from the south pole and generate voltages which add to those of the other coils under the same pole. Thus while the armature moves progressively through the positions shown in (a), (b), and (c), complete reversal of the current in G is brought about. At the same time, coil H passes from the south pole to the north pole at the bottom of the figure, and its current is reversed in a similar manner with the aid of the commutator segments 7 and 8 and the positive brush.

Effect of Self-inductance. As a matter of fact, commutation is not brought about as simply as the foregoing paragraphs would indicate, for the inductance of the armature coil acts to oppose any change of current from taking place in the coil. The inductance of a coil is analogous to the inertia of matter. The latter opposes any change in the velocity

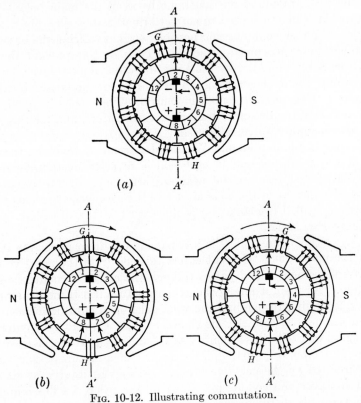

FIG. 10-12. Illustrating commutation.

of a mass, just as the former opposes any change in the current of a circuit. As G approaches the neutral zone, the changing magnetic field due to the falling current induces an emf in the coil which opposes the decrease of current, while when G recedes from AA' the increasing magnetic field due to the rising current induces a voltage which tends to prevent the current from increasing in the coil.

Resistance Commutation. Unless the emf of self-induction is balanced out or neutralized, there is a potential difference between segment 2 and the brush tip [Fig. 10-12 (c)] at the instant when the segment breaks contact with the brush, and sparking results. This is undesirable, because the commutator and brushes are damaged by the burning action of the electric arc formed between segment and brush.

The emf of self-induction may be neutralized as follows:

1. By making use of carbon brushes (brushes having a high contact resistance)

2. By generating in the short-circuited coil an emf approximately equal in value and opposite in direction to the emf of self-induction

3. By combining methods 1 and 2

Method 1, called *resistance commutation*, will now be described. When a coil is undergoing commutation, its terminals are short-circuited by the brush and commutator segments, as in (b) of Fig. 10-12. A circuit is thus formed, consisting of the short-circuited coil, its two leads, parts of the commutator segments under the brush, and the brush itself. The resistance of the contact between copper segment and carbon brush is high as compared with the resistance of the coil and its leads. Approximately, therefore, one may say that all the resistance of the circuit lies in the contacts. Furthermore, the conductance of a contact is proportional to the area of contact, and hence, for a given contact resistance drop, the current passing between a brush and the segments under it divides in proportion to the areas of the contacts. This is illustrated in Fig. 11-12.

Let it be assumed that the current in each armature path is 20 amp, and that the current per brush is therefore 40 amp. In (a) the coil approaching axis AA' is about to begin short circuit. In (b) short circuit has begun. The brush covers one-fourth of the right-hand segment and three-fourths of the left-hand one. Accordingly, the resistances corresponding to these areas are in the ratio of 3:1 and the currents divide in the inverse ratio, or as 1:3. The current in the coil has been reduced by one-half, or to 10 amp, while the commutator has moved the width of one-quarter of a segment. In (c) the commutator has advanced one-half the width of a segment. The contact areas of the two segments under the brush are now each equal to one-half that shown in (a). The current divides equally between the two segments as shown, and the current in the short-circuited coil has fallen to zero. The period of commutation is now one-half over. Figures 11-12(d) and (e) show how the current builds up in the coil during the last half of the period of commutation. In (d) the current in the coil has reached one-half its final value (10 amp); in (e) its final value of 20 amp is reached and commutation is complete.

In the process here described, the current changes at a uniform rate from I_c to $-I_c$ as shown in (f). The induced voltage is constant, since it is proportional to the rate of change of current, or to the slope of the curve. The average voltage required to balance the induced voltage is

$$E_{av} = L\frac{\Delta I}{\Delta t} = L[I_c - (-I_c)] \div T_c = \frac{2LI_c}{T_c} \quad \text{volts}$$

where L = self-inductance and mutual inductance of coil, henrys

$\quad\quad I_c$ = current in one armature path, amp

$\quad\quad T_c$ = time of duration of short circuit, sec

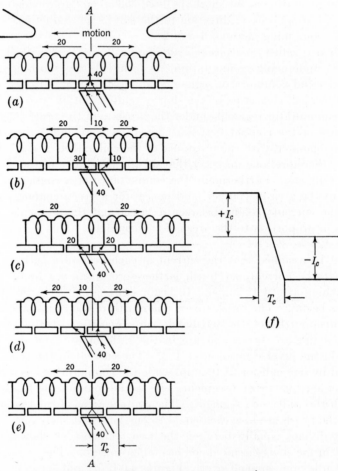

Fig. 11-12. Ideal resistance commutation.

Effect of Shifting the Brushes. The effect of shifting the brushes to some point outside the neutral axis is illustrated in Fig. 12-12. In (b) of this figure the brush is shifted to the left (against the direction of rotation in a generator, or with the direction of rotation in a motor). When the shift is sufficient to bring the short-circuited coil into the field of the trailing pole tip as in (b), an emf is generated in the coil which acts in the same direction as the self-induced voltage. At the instant just before the short circuit begins, this emf is impressed between the leading brush tip and the approaching commutator segment, and sparking takes place. As soon as the short circuit begins, a circulating current is set up in the short-circuited coil, and for a time the current in the coil actually

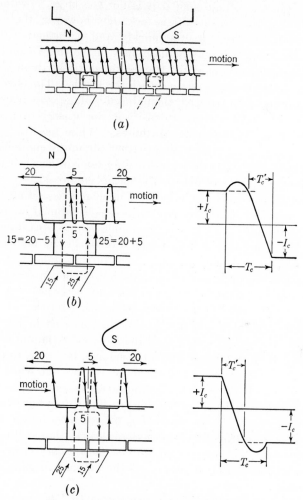

Fig. 12-12. Effect of shifting the brushes.

increases, as shown in the curve to the right. The effective time of commutation is decreased to T'_c, and the induced voltage is increased during the latter part of the period of commutation, because the slope of the current curve (which is proportional to the induced voltage) is now larger than that shown in (c) of Fig. 11-12. The current density in the brush is nonuniform, being largest at the leading tip, where the circulating current adds to the output current, and least at the trailing tip, where they subtract.

When the brush is shifted forward (in a generator) the voltage generated in the short-circuited coil by the flux from the leading pole tip *opposes* the induced voltage, and if it is not too large in value, it aids commutation. If the brush shift is too large, however, the current in the short-circuited coil reverses too quickly, and at the end of the period a larger current than $-I_c$ may actually flow in the coil, as shown in (c). In this case sparking occurs at the trailing brush tip at the instant when the receding segment breaks contact with the brush. The effective time of commutation is again reduced, the induced voltage is increased during the initial period, and the current density in the brush is nonuniform.

Commutation in Noninterpole Machines. While few d-c generators or motors are now being built without either commutating poles or compensating windings (except those designed for low voltages), it is instructive, nevertheless, briefly to discuss the means employed to secure satisfactory commutation in the older type of noncompensated machine.

In these machines the *resistance method* is combined with the *emf method* of commutation. That is, the high contact resistance of the carbon brush is used to aid the current reversal in the manner already described, and, in addition, an emf which further aids the reversal is generated in the coil undergoing commutation. The brushes are shifted through an angle α (forward in a generator and backward in a motor) in order to bring the short-circuited coil into the fringe of the field from the pole tip. The generated emf due to this flux, as seen in Fig. 12-12(c), is opposed to the induced voltage and therefore aids commutation. The brush shift must be made only just large enough, however, to permit the current to attain the correct value $-I_c$ at the instant when the short circuit is broken. If this is done, commutation is sparkless.

It is not always easy to find a suitable brush position, however, because

1. *The induced voltage to be balanced by the generated voltage in the commutating coil is proportional to the armature current*, that is, to the load.

2. *The armature cross ampere-turns cause the resultant field to shift in the direction of rotation (of a generator)*, the amount of shift depending upon the load.

3. *The armature demagnetizing ampere-turns tend to weaken the field*, more and more as the load is increased (page 167).

For each of the above reasons the correct brush position appears farther and farther away from the no-load neutral axis as the load is increased, requiring more and more brush shift. It is, of course, impractical to shift the brush to a new position for each change in load. In practice a suitable fixed brush position is chosen for which commutation is satisfactory at all loads. This position is found by moving the brushes (forward for the generator and backward for the motor) until, at no load, sparking is just about to begin at the trailing brush tip due to the cause illustrated in Fig. 12-12(c). When the armature is loaded and the neutral axis shifts, commutation improves. As the load is further increased and the field continues to shift, however, some load is finally reached beyond which sparkless commutation cannot be secured. In well-designed machines this point is usually well above full load.

From the foregoing it is apparent that noninterpole machines should be so designed that changes in load produce only slight changes in field form. In other words, a *stiff field* should be used. This is accomplished by making the air gap relatively large, especially under the pole tips, and by operating the teeth in the armature punchings at high flux densities. A long gap requires a strong field excitation to maintain the required gap flux. If the field ampere-turns are large as compared with the

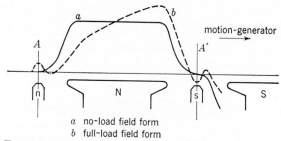

a   no-load field form
b   full-load field form

FIG. 13-12. Field form of a commutating-pole machine.

armature ampere-turns, the latter can have little influence upon the gap flux. By making the equivalent air gap long under the pole tips, the effect of the armature cross ampere-turns is greatly reduced, and only a slight shifting of the field results. Increase in the length of the effective air gap under the pole tips is secured in the manner already described.

Commutating Poles. Commutating poles are small auxiliary poles located in the no-load neutral axis between the main poles of a motor or generator as shown in Fig. 13-12. Their function is to provide a flux of correct sign and of suitable amount to generate in the coil undergoing commutation, the required reversing emf at all loads. The commutating-pole flux is made proportional to the load by connecting the field winding in series with the output circuit. Thus a reversing voltage is generated in the short-circuited coil which is also proportional to the load, as it must be properly to balance the induced voltage, since the latter is proportional to the load current as well.

The polarity of the commutating pole must obviously be the same as that of the main pole toward which the brush would normally be shifted, were the commutating pole omitted. If motion from left to right be assumed (Fig. 13-12), when the machine is a generator, the order of the poles, proceeding in the direction of rotation, is n, N, s, S, n, N, s, etc. When the machine runs as a motor in the same direction as before (assuming that the polarity of the main poles does not change), the interpole current is reversed and the order of polarity is s, N, n, S, s, N, n, etc.

Commutating-pole machines have shorter air gaps and magnetically stronger armatures than non-commutating-pole machines; they are therefore smaller and cheaper, while at the same time commutation is improved. Field distortion is unimportant in these machines, because the proper commutating flux is always supplied by the interpole. The typical field forms for such a machine are shown in Fig. 13-12.

Problems

1-12. What is the effect of field distortion in non-commutating-pole machines? What provision does the designer make to prevent excessive distortion? What is the effect of this upon the size of the machine per unit of output?

2-12. What is the purpose of commutating poles? How does their use affect the output obtained from a machine of given size and speed as compared with a similar non-commutating-pole machine?

3-12. Is it necessary to prevent field distortion in machines with commutating poles? What, if anything, limits the amount of distortion permissible? Explain.

4-12. A four-pole generator with a full-pitch lap-wound armature winding has two turns per armature coil. The length of an armature turn is 30 in., of which 8 in. is embedded in slots and 22 in. is end connections. The flux linking the coil per ampere-conductor is assumed to be 10 lines (maxwells) per inch of embedded length and 1 line per inch of end connection. The speed of the machine is 1,200 rpm, and the rated full-load current output is 40 amp. The commutator has 100 segments and is 8 in. in diameter. Assume that the brush is just wide enough to cover one commutator segment. Determine (a) the sum of the self-inductance and mutual inductance of the short-circuited coil in henrys, (b) the time of commutation, (c) the average value of the reactance voltage in the coil undergoing commutation.

5-12. A six-pole, 275-kw, 550-volt generator has 150 slots with eight conductors per slot. The winding is simplex wave and there are 300 commutator segments. The field current is 10 amp, and there are 3,000 shunt-field turns per pole. At full load the brushes are moved ahead of the neutral axis a distance of four commutator segments. For conditions of rated load, find (a) the cross ampere-turns per pole, (b) the demagnetizing ampere-turns per pole, (c) the net ampere-turns per pole. [Disregard the effect of saturation due to (a).]

6-12. If, in Prob. 5-12, three-fourths of the resultant field ampere-turns is consumed in forcing the air-gap flux across the gap, teeth, and pole faces, what is the resultant mmf (ampere-turns) acting across gap, teeth, and pole face (a) under the leading pole tip, (b) under the trailing pole tip?

CHAPTER 13

OPERATING CHARACTERISTICS OF GENERATORS

Voltage Generated in an Armature of Z **Conductors.** The total voltage generated between the terminals of a generator or motor is the sum of all the voltages generated in the series-connected conductors of one armature path. This was explained in Chap. 11. In the usual lap-wound machine, there are as many parallel paths as there are poles (p_1), and the total voltage is generated in Z/p_1 conductors. In the usual wave winding, there are only two parallel paths and the total voltage is generated in $Z/2$ series-connected conductors.

By Eq. (1-7), page 78, the average voltage generated by a conductor which cuts ϕ webers of flux per second is $E_{av} = \phi/t$ volts. To determine the average voltage generated in the conductors of any armature path, therefore, one has only to calculate the total flux cut per second by all the conductors in the path.

In any d-c generator or motor, let

p_1 = number of poles
p_2 = number of parallel armature paths
ϕ = total air-gap flux per pole, webers
Z = total number of armature face conductors
S = armature speed, rpm

In each armature path there are Z/p_2 conductors, and in one revolution each of these cuts the ϕ webers from each pole once, so each conductor cuts $p_1\phi$ webers per revolution. Since in 1 sec the armature completes $S/60$ revolutions, the total number of lines of force cut per second by each conductor is $p_1\phi S/60$, and the total flux cut per second by all the series-connected conductors of one path is $(Z/p_2)\ (p_1\phi S/60)$ which, by definition, is the average voltage generated per armature path. Therefore, the average generated voltage E_g of any d-c generator or motor is

$$E_g = \frac{p_1 \phi Z S}{p_2 \times 60} \quad \text{volts} \quad (1\text{-}13)$$

While the emf generated by the individual conductors of a path varies from instant to instant according to the flux density in the air gap, the total voltage generated in a path is substantially constant because the number of conductors cutting the flux from a pole is always the same. The average voltage given by Eq. (1-13) is therefore the steady (constant) voltage generated in the armature winding. This equation holds for either Gramme-ring, lap, or wave winding. For simplex windings, in the case of the first two of these, $p_1 = p_2$ and the ratio $p_1/p_2 = 1$, while for the case of the wave winding p_2 is always 2.

Example 1. The armature of a 30-kw 120-volt four-pole generator is driven at a speed of 1,000 rpm. The machine is required to generate 130 volts at full load. The arc of a pole is 7.75 in., and the length of the pole core (parallel to the shaft) is 6 in. The flux density in the air gap is 0.45 milliweber/sq in. (*a*) If the machine is lap-wound, how many face conductors are required? (*b*) How much voltage is generated in each armature path? (*c*) What is the total current output at full load? (*d*) What is the current output per path at full load? A simplex winding is assumed.

(*a*) Area of a pole face = 7.75 × 6 sq in. = 46.5 sq in. The flux per pole is

$$\phi = 46.5 \times 0.45 = 20.92 \times 10^{-3} \text{ weber}$$

By Eq. (1-13),

$$Z \cong \frac{4 \times 60 \times 130}{20.92 \times 10^{-3} \times 1,000 \times 4} = 372 \text{ or } 374 \text{ conductors}$$

(*b*) The entire machine voltage (130 volts) is generated in each path
(*c*) Current output = 30,000/120 = 250 amp
(*d*) Current output per path = 250/4 = 62.5 amp

Saturation Curve of a Generator or Motor. This curve shows how the flux density in the air gap varies when the field excitation is changed from a maximum value to zero. Its experimental determination depends upon the fact that, for constant speed conditions, the generated emf of a generator or motor is proportional to the air-gap flux. This relation follows from Eq. (1-13). In this equation the factor

$$\frac{(p_1 Z)}{(p_2 \times 60)} = Z'$$

is a constant for any particular machine, and hence the equation may be written

$$E_g = \phi Z' S \tag{2-13}$$

When the machine is driven at constant speed, its generated voltage is proportional to the air-gap flux alone, and the generated voltage may be used to measure the flux.

To find the saturation curve, the machine is driven at constant (rated) speed, its field is separately excited, and the armature circuit is open as in Fig. 1-13. An ammeter A is used to measure the field current I_f, and a voltmeter is used to measure the generated voltage E_g.   An adjustable resistance R, capable of safely carrying the field current, is connected in series with the field circuit.   If a series of simultaneous readings of field current and generated voltage is taken as the current is progressively increased from 0 to 125 per cent of normal value, the dotted curve of Fig. 2-13 is obtained. When the field current is progressively decreased from its maximum

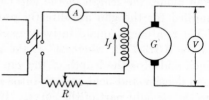

FIG. 1-13. Circuit connections for obtaining data for the saturation curve.

value to zero and a similar series of readings is taken, the plotted readings yield the solid curve of the figure.   The second curve lies above the first because of hysteresis (page 102).

Obviously, since the speed is constant, by Eq. (2-13),

$$E_g = \phi Z'S = k'\phi$$

where $k' = $ constant.   Hence the ordinates may be expressed in terms of flux per pole.   Furthermore, if B_{av} is the average gap density and A_g is the area of the gap per pole, $\phi = B_{\mathrm{av}}A_g$; and since A_g is constant, one may also use B_{av} as the ordinates to the curve.   When values of ϕ or B_{av} are used as ordinates, it is customary to use the field ampere-turns N_fI_f as abscissas, N_f being the turns per pole.

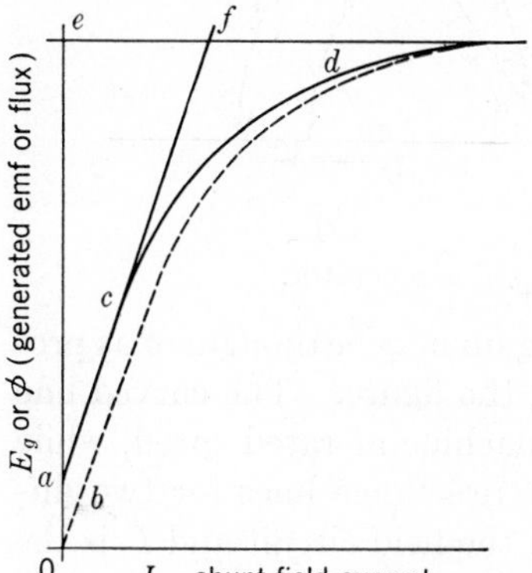

Beginning at d on the curve, the iron portions of the circuit, especially the armature teeth, are somewhat saturated, the permeability is relatively low, and the corresponding number of ampere-turns of excitation required is relatively large.   As the field current is reduced, the saturation decreases, the permeability increases, and the curve falls off rapidly.   From c to a the curve is approximately straight, because over this range the ampere-turns required for the iron portions of the circuit are quite negligible.   The excitation is nearly all used up in forcing the flux across the air gap, so the field ampere-turns are directly proportional to the flux because the reluctance of the air gap is constant.   At a, where the excitation is zero, the poles retain a small amount of residual flux oa.   This enables the machine to build up its own voltage without the aid of a separate source of excitation.

FIG. 2-13. The saturation curve.

E_g or ϕ (generated emf or flux)

I_f , shunt field current

Since the straight part of the curve represents the relation between flux and the field ampere-turns required to force the flux across the air gap alone, the length of the gap can be estimated. The ampere-turns needed for the gap are directly proportional to the length of the gap. This relation is quantitatively expressed in Eq. (11-8) of Chap. 8 as $NI = 0.313B''l''$, where B'' is the gap density in maxwells per square inch and l'' is the length of the gap in inches. Corresponding values of gap density and field ampere-turns may be found from a tangent drawn to the straight part of the curve. If $N_f I_f$ are the field ampere-turns corresponding to a gap flux per pole of ϕ lines, the gap density is $B''_g = \phi/A_g$ and the average length of gap is approximately

$$l''_g \cong \frac{N_f I_f}{0.313B''_g} \quad \text{in.} \tag{3-13}$$

Building Up the Voltage of a Generator.   A self-excited generator, as in Fig. 3-13, must depend upon the residual magnetism of its field poles to

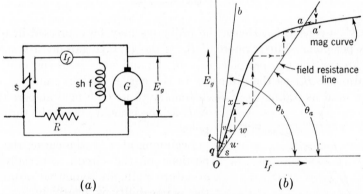

(a)   (b)

Fig. 3-13. Building up the voltage of a generator.

build up its voltage.   The process of building up may be thought of as progressing along the broken line $uvwx$, etc., in the figure.   The curved line represents the magnetization curve of the machine at rated speed, while the straight lines oa and ob are field-circuit resistance lines for two different resistances.   If R_f is the resistance of the field circuit and I_f is the field current when the impressed voltage is E, the equation of the field resistance line is $E = R_f I_f$ and the slope of the line is $R_f = \tan \theta$.   Thus the slope of the line is proportional to the field resistance.

Suppose that the generator is driven at rated speed and that the field resistance is $R_f = \tan \theta_a$.   Even before the switch S is closed, the voltage builds up to the value oq because of the residual magnetism.   When the switch is closed, this voltage sets up a current in the field winding equal to $oq/\tan \theta_a$ or qs, which in turn increases the air-gap flux and thereby raises[1] the generated voltage by the increment st. When the point t is reached, the current again increases to u, which causes the voltage to rise to v, etc., progressively, until the point a is reached. Actually, of course, the voltage builds up along the magnetization curve rather than step-fashion as indicated.

The voltage finally builds up to the point a because at every point on the magnetization curve below a the generated voltage is in excess of that required to maintain the field current corresponding to it, so the latter as well as the generated voltage must continue to increase. Beyond a the generated voltage is everywhere less than that required to maintain the corresponding field current, so the voltage cannot build up beyond a. Should the field resistance be increased to $R_f = \tan \theta_b$, the generator cannot build up beyond the intersection of ob with the magnetization curve, or to a value lying between q and t.

To make a generator build up, therefore, the resistance of the field rheostat (R in the figure) should be decreased gradually until the machine voltage reaches the desired value. Since the contact resistance of the brushes forms a part of the field-circuit resistance, poor brush contact may sometimes prevent a machine from building up its voltage. The usual remedy is to adjust the contact by sanding the brushes or to adjust the spring pressure, or both.

Shunt-generator Characteristics. After its voltage is built up, a generator may be used to supply power to a load, as illustrated in Fig. 4-13. When the line switch is closed, power is supplied to the lamps and the voltage at the terminals drops. With the speed remaining constant, the voltage drops more and more as the load is gradually increased (curve Fig.

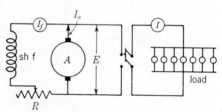

FIG. 4-13. Loaded shunt generator.

5-13). Such a drop in voltage is generally undesirable, particularly when lamps are fed from the circuit. Its causes should be understood, as well as the practical methods used to compensate for it.

There are several reasons for this drop in voltage, as follows:

1. Voltage is required to force the armature current through the resistance of the armature circuit, that is, through the resistance of the brushes

[1] It is assumed that the field circuit is so connected to the armature terminals that any field current, however small, increases the air-gap flux. If, instead, the field current acts to reduce the air-gap flux, the generator voltage builds down from oq toward zero. If there is any doubt as to whether the connection is right or wrong, watch the needle of the voltmeter measuring the terminal voltage at the instant when the switch S is closed. If the needle moves up the scale, the connection is right; if it recedes toward zero, the connection is wrong.

and brush contacts and the resistance of the armature winding. The terminal voltage is the potential difference remaining after the voltage consumed in the armature resistance is subtracted from the generated voltage. Thus if

E_g = generated voltage
E_t = terminal voltage
I_a = armature current
R_a = armature resistance

this relation is expressed symbolically by the equation

$$E_t = E_g - I_a R_a \qquad (4\text{-}13)$$

If the generated voltage were constant, the only drop would be the armature resistance drop, and the terminal voltage would decrease along the

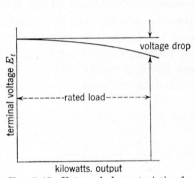

Fig. 5-13. External characteristic of a shunt generator.

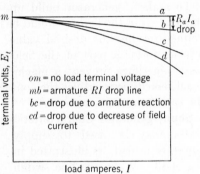

Fig. 6-13. Voltage drops in a shunt generator.

line mb of Fig. 6-13. The difference between the ordinates of this line and the line ma is the armature-resistance drop $R_a I_a$.

Example 2. The armature resistance of a 50-kw d-c generator is 0.0155 ohm. When the generator delivers full-load current of 400 amp at 120 volts, what is the generated voltage?
By Eq. (4-13),

$$120 = E_g - 400 \times 0.0155$$
$$E_g = 120 + 6.2 \text{ or } 126.2 \text{ volts}$$

2. The generated voltage itself decreases with increase of load because the air-gap flux is reduced. When the speed is constant, reference to Eq. (2-13) shows that the generated voltage is proportional to the air-gap flux alone, for

$$E_g = \phi Z'S = k'\phi$$

where S is constant. Accordingly, those factors that affect the air-gap flux—and only those—influence the generated voltage.

It has been shown that the air-gap flux is determined by the resultant magnetizing force F_0, and this in turn is partly due to the field ampere-turns and partly due to the armature ampere-turns.   Both these, therefore, affect the generated voltage as follows:

a. As the load increases, the armature reaction increases.   The resultant flux in the air gap is thereby reduced, less voltage is generated, and the terminal voltage falls off, as indicated by the difference between the ordinates of curves *mb* and *mc* in Fig. 6-13.

b. As the load increases, the above causes 1 and 2*a* gradually reduce the terminal voltage.   The field current is thereby reduced, the air-gap flux is further decreased, and still less voltage is generated.

The several components[1] of voltage drop are shown in Fig. 6-13.   The resultant curve *md*, called the *external characteristic* curve of the generator, shows how the voltage at the terminals falls when the current *I* in the external circuit is increased gradually from no load to full load and beyond.

Effects of Speed and Excitation on the Characteristic Curve.   The degree to which increasing armature reaction and falling field current cause the terminal voltage to drop when the load is increased, depends considerably upon the initial excitation. This is clearly illustrated in the curves of Fig. 7-13.   Curve 1 is the curve of a given machine taken at rated speed. Curve 2 is the curve of the same machine for 75 per cent of rated speed. Since in the second case the speed is only three-fourths of rated value, the air-gap flux per pole (ϕ_2) must be $\frac{4}{3}\phi_1$ if the same no-load voltage is to be obtained. Owing to the shape of the magnetization curve, however [Fig. 3-13 (*b*)], the excitation at no load must be considerably more than four-thirds of that required for

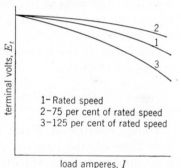

FIG. 7-13. Effect of speed and excitation on the characteristic (external) of a shunt generator.

curve 1.   This means that the field is relatively saturated in the second case and that therefore armature reaction and small reductions in the field current cause relatively small drops in voltage as the load increases. Accordingly, the voltage holds up better and the second curve lies somewhat above the first.

Similarly, when the speed is increased to 125 per cent of rated value, the no-load flux (ϕ_3) is reduced to $\frac{4}{5}\phi_1$, and the no-load field excitation is reduced to an even smaller fraction of that required in the first case.

---

[1] It should be noted that the component *cd* is eliminated when a separate constant-potential source of emf is used to excite the field as in Fig. 30-11.

The field mmf is relatively small, and hence armature reaction and falling field current produce relatively large effects. The terminal voltage therefore falls off more rapidly with increase of load than in the first case, as shown by curve 3 in the figure.

It may be seen from the above that the designer has considerable control over the shape of the curve. If the machine is designed to generate its voltage with a strong field, the curve is relatively flat; if the number of conductors is increased and a weaker field is used, the curve droops more rapidly. The shape of the curve may be further controlled by increasing the excitation with increase of load, as will be pointed out presently.

Regulation. *Regulation* is a term used to describe the amount of change in the voltage of a generator (or in the speed of a motor) that comes about with gradual changes in load. The regulation of a generator is stated by giving the generator full-load voltage and the corresponding no-load voltage measured at the terminals when full load is thrown off, the speed and field-circuit resistance remaining unchanged.

For example, the statement "full-load voltage = 120, no-load voltage = 128" means that the terminal voltage of the generator rises from 120 volts at full load to 128 volts at no load when the load is thrown off, provided rated speed and constant field-circuit resistance are maintained.

Regulation is also sometimes expressed in percentage of full-load voltage as, for example,

$$\text{Regulation} = \frac{100(128 - 120)}{120} \text{ or } 6.67 \text{ per cent}$$

Voltage Control of Shunt Generators. As the reader may already have inferred, the terminal voltage of a shunt generator may be kept constant at all loads with the use of an adjustable resistance, called a field *rheostat*, connected in series with the shunt-field circuit. By adjusting the resistance of the rheostat to suit the load on the machine, changes in terminal voltage with load may be prevented. When the load changes gradually, hand control of the rheostat may be used, although automatic control employing a *voltage regulator* is far more satisfactory.

The terminal voltage may also be controlled automatically by the addition of a series-field winding. This method has the advantages of being automatic, cheap, and generally satisfactory. It is discussed in greater detail in a later paragraph.

Series Generator. The field winding of a series generator is connected in series with the armature winding as in Fig. 9-13. It consists of a few turns of heavy wire, capable of carrying the output current of the machine without overheating.

Series generators cannot be used to supply power to constant-potential systems; and since virtually all power systems are operated at approximately constant potentials, applications in which series generators are used are comparatively rare in American practice. In the past, series machines have been used to supply power at constant current and variable voltage to series-connected arc lights for street lighting. In this

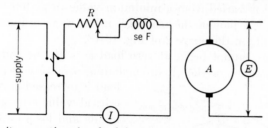

FIG. 8-13. Circuit connections for obtaining the saturation curve of a series generator.

application, however, series machines have been largely replaced by constant-current a-c transformers.

In Europe series-connected generators are sometimes used to supply power to high-voltage constant-current d-c transmission lines. At the points of utilization, series motors, which are connected in series with the line, are used to transform electrical energy into mechanical energy of rotation. This system, known as the *Thury system*, has not been used in the United States.

Series generators are sometimes used as "boosters" to raise the voltage at the ends of long feeders under load. This application will be discussed in greater detail presently.

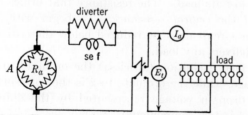

FIG. 9-13. Circuit connections for loading a series generator.

Series-generator Characteristic Curves. The *saturation* curve may be obtained in a manner exactly similar to that already described for the shunt machine, by the use of the circuit connections of Fig. 8-13. The series-connected resistance illustrated in Fig. 8-13 must be capable of safely carrying the maximum current to be used, or about 125 per cent of rated load current. A plot of simultaneous readings of generated voltage and field current, taken at rated speed, yields the magnetization curve 1 of Fig. 10-13.

The *external characteristic curve* represents the terminal voltage as ordinates vs. the load current as abscissas. To obtain data for the curve, the machine is connected to a load as in Fig. 9-13, ammeter and voltmeter being inserted to read the load current I_a and the terminal voltage E_t, respectively. The machine is run at constant (rated) speed, and a series of simultaneous readings of voltage and current is taken while the load is varied from a minimum value to perhaps 125 per cent of rated load. A plot of the readings, using E_t as ordinates and I_a as abscissas, results in the curve 2 of Fig. 10-13.

The readings cannot begin at zero load as with the shunt generator, for if the resistance of the circuit including armature, series field, and load is increased beyond a certain critical value, the generator unbuilds and loses its load entirely. Thus if oa is the resistance line for the circuit the terminal voltage is the ordinate to the curve at a. When the resistance of the circuit is gradually increased, the load falls off along the curve, and a approaches b. When the resistance line finally becomes tangent to the curve, however, operation becomes unstable, and any slight further increase in the resistance causes the machine to unbuild its

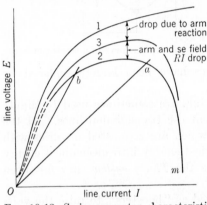

Fig. 10-13. Series-generator characteristic curves.

voltage and to lose its load. The resistance that brings about this condition is called the *critical resistance*. To begin with, therefore, the resistance of the circuit must be reduced below the critical value before the generator delivers any load.

For a given field excitation (abscissa) the ordinate to curve 1 is the generated voltage, while the ordinate to 2 is the corresponding terminal voltage. The drop in voltage represented by the difference between these ordinates has two components:

1. Armature and series-field resistance drops, equal to

$$I_a(R_a + R_{se})$$

2. Armature-reaction drop. That is, the terminal voltage under load is less than it would be if there were no armature reaction, because the demagnetizing effect of the armature ampere-turns reduces the air-gap flux.

These component drops may be separated by drawing the intermediate curve 3, called the *internal characteristic*. This curve—obtained by adding the resistance drop $I_a(R_a + R_{se})$ to the external characteristic curve 2—represents the generated voltage under load as a function of the load current (E_g vs. I_a). The difference between curves 1 and 3 is the reduction in voltage caused by armature reaction.

It should be observed that between a and m a considerable change in resistance brings about only a slight change in load current. Over this

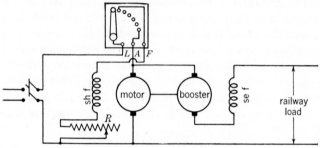

FIG. 11-13. The series booster.

range the voltage decreases rapidly, owing to increasing armature reaction (particularly when the brushes are shifted forward), while the current remains nearly constant. Thus between a and m the machine may be used to supply power to a constant-current variable-voltage circuit, such as a series arc circuit.

Series Booster. The voltage drop in a feeder may be so large that motors fed from the end of it do not receive sufficient power to operate them satisfactorily. This condition may be remedied either by installing additional feeders or by "boosting" the voltage. Other things being equal, the more economical method offers the correct solution.

A fairly common application of the series booster is its use in connection with long feeders on street-railway systems, particularly on outlying sections of lightly loaded lines. The booster is connected in series with the feeder circuit and adds its generated voltage to that of the line. The driving motor

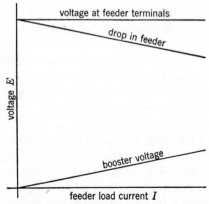

FIG. 12-13. Feeder and booster characteristics.

receives its power from the bus to which the feeder is connected (Fig. 11-13). Since the drop in the feeder is proportional to the feeder current ($E = RI$), it is desirable that the generated voltage of the booster be proportional to the current also. This can be arranged by operating the booster on the rising portion *ob* (Fig. 10-13) of its external characteristic curve. The series field may be provided with a *diverter* or shunt (Fig. 9-13) by means of which the increase in generated voltage between no load and full load may be adjusted to equal the resistance drop in the feeder at full load as illustrated in Fig. 12-13.

Compound Generator. The compound generator has two sources of excitation: one is a shunt-connected field energized from the machine terminals, and the other is a series-connected field energized by all or a definite fraction of the load current. Thus the compound generator combines the rising characteristic of the series generator with the slightly drooping characteristic of the shunt generator and thereby compensates for the voltage drop of the shunt machine. Since the amount of added series excitation may be controlled, the terminal voltage of a compound

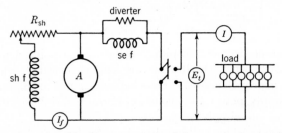

Fig. 13-13. Circuit diagram of a loaded compound generator.

machine may rise with increase of load, as in curve 1 of Fig. 14-13, it may remain approximately constant as in curve 2, or it may droop as in curve 3, depending upon the amount of series excitation that is provided, and upon whether it aids or opposes the shunt-field excitation.

While the series field of a compound machine may be connected either cumulatively or differentially (Fig. 34-11), there is usually no advantage in the latter connection. Unless specifically stated to the contrary, the term "compound generator" is generally understood to mean one that is cumulatively connected.

External Characteristic Curves of Compound Generators. The procedure to be followed in obtaining data for the external characteristic curve of a compound generator is exactly similar to that described for the shunt machine. The diagram of circuit connections to be used is shown in Fig. 13-13 for the *short-shunt* connection. The ammeter used to measure the field current I_f is not required, although it is usually desirable to have a record of the shunt-field current. Speed is held constant at rated value, and the machine is loaded to its rated capacity at rated terminal voltage, the latter being obtained by adjusting the shunt-field rheostat. The load is then thrown off by opening the line switch.

Without altering the setting of the shunt-field rheostat, the load on the machine is now gradually built up from zero to, say, 125 per cent of rated load, and a series of simultaneous readings of load current and terminal voltage is taken.   A plot of these readings, using terminal voltages as ordinates and load currents as abscissas, yields the external characteristic curve.

Degree of Compounding.   The curves of Fig. 14-13 show how the shape of the characteristic curve may be changed by altering the degree of compounding.   When a machine has a relatively strong series field, its terminal voltage at full load may be higher than its no-load voltage.   Such a machine, is said to be *overcompounded* and has a curve like 1.   When the series field is so adjusted that the terminal voltages at full load and at no load are equal, the machine is *flat-compounded* and its curve is like 2. Between no load and full load the voltage rises slightly, but aside from this the terminal voltage is constant throughout the range from

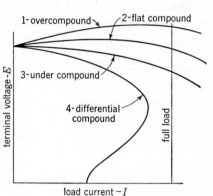

FIG. 14-13. Compound-generator external characteristic curves.

no load to full load.   *Undercompounded* machines are those with series fields that are not strong enough to bring the full-load voltage up to the no-load value, as indicated by curve 3.

When the series field is differentially connected, the ampere-turns of the series field oppose those of the shunt field and the terminal voltage falls off rapidly as indicated by curve 4.   The machine behaves like one having a very large armature reaction, to which it is, in fact, equivalent.

Diverter.   Compound machines are provided with a low-resistance shunt, called a *diverter*, that is connected in parallel with the series-field winding as indicated in Fig. 13-13.   Since a steady current divides between the diverter[1] and the series-field winding in proportion to their

[1] When compound generators are used on circuits that are subject to large sudden changes in load, as, for example, in street-railway service, the current does not divide between the series-field winding and the diverter in proportion to their conductances during intervals of rapid change in load unless the diverter is also provided with a series-connected inductance bearing the same ratio to the diverter-circuit resistance as the inductance of the series field bears to the series-field resistance.   When the diverter circuit is noninductive, the high inductance of the series winding causes more than the normal fraction of the load current to flow in the diverter winding when the current rises rapidly, and less than the normal fraction when the load falls rapidly.   During these intervals commutation is adversely affected, and serious

conductances (inversely proportional to their resistances), the percentage of the output current that passes through the series-field winding may be adjusted by changing the resistance of the diverter. In this way the degree of compounding may be controlled within limits after the machine is built. The diverter is made of german silver or other low-resistance material and is so constructed that the length of the conductor which parallels the field winding may be adjusted, and thus more or less current may be diverted from the series field, as required.

Effects of Speed and Shunt-field Excitation. Much as with shunt generators, the shape of the characteristic curve of a compound generator

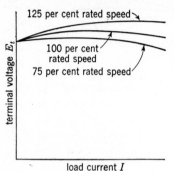

is considerably influenced by the speed at which the machine is driven. When the speed is higher than rated value, the required no-load shunt-field excitation is correspondingly reduced, the magnetic circuit is less than normally saturated, the increase of series-field excitation due to increase of load causes a rapid rise in voltage, and the degree of compounding is increased. When the speed is lower than rated value, the shunt-field excitation must be increased above normal in order to secure the rated no-load voltage; the magnetic circuit is therefore more saturated than normally, the added series excitation of the loaded machine produces less than the normal increase in flux, and the degree of compounding is accordingly decreased. The curves of Fig. 15-13 illustrate what happens.

Fig. 15-13. Effect of speed on the characteristic curves of a cumulative compound generator.

Driving Power for D-c Generators. In present-day practice, it is usually more economical to generate power in large blocks as alternating currents, to transmit and transform it as alternating currents, and finally to convert it to direct currents, than it is to generate the power as direct currents and transmit it as such to the point of use, or than it is to generate it from coal or oil at the point of use. Several factors contribute to this result, principal among which is the fact that the transmission, distribution, and transformation of power in the form of alternating currents are cheaper and far less troublesome than is the case with direct currents. Where direct currents are required, power is usually already available in the form of alternating currents.

Although direct currents are used extensively in industry, they are usually obtained by rectifying alternating currents at the point of appli-

---

sparking may take place. This difficulty is obviated by using a suitable inductance in the diverter circuit.

cation by means of synchronous converters, mercury-arc rectifiers, or motor-generators with a-c motor drives.

Applications of D-c Generators. Shunt generators are used to advantage, in conjunction with automatic regulators, as exciters for supplying the current required to excite the fields of a-c generators. The regulator controls the voltage of the exciter by cutting in and out some of the resistance of the shunt-field rheostat, thereby holding the voltage at whatever value is demanded by operating conditions. This is one of the most important applications of shunt generators.

Shunt machines are also used to charge storage batteries. In this application the voltage should drop off slightly as the load increases, because the voltage of a lead battery is lower when the battery is discharged than when the battery is charged. When it is discharged, however, the battery can stand a larger charging current than when it is charged. Because of its drooping characteristic the shunt generator is admirably suited to battery-charging service, for, in a general way, the voltage curve of the generator has the same shape as the voltage curve of the battery itself. In both cases the voltage rises as the load falls off.

As will appear presently, shunt generators can be operated in parallel without difficulty, and the wiring of parallel-operated shunt machines is quite a bit simpler than the corresponding wiring for compound machines. When a slight drop in voltage is not objectionable, as when a motor load is fed directly from the generator terminals, shunt machines may be used to advantage.

The compound generator is used far more than any other type. It may be built and adjusted automatically to supply an approximately constant voltage *at the point of use*, throughout the entire range of load. This is a very great advantage. It is possible to provide a constant supply voltage at the end of a long feeder by the simple expedient of overcompounding the generator, because the resistance drop in the line is compensated for by the rising characteristic of the generator. When the point of utilization is near the generator, a flat-compounded machine may be used. Compound generators are used to supply power to railway circuits, to the motors of electrified steam railroads, to industrial motors in many fields of industry, to incandescent lamps, elevator motors, etc.

Operation of Generators for Combined Output. The amount of power required by a large system usually exceeds the capacity of a single machine. When this is the case, the load is supplied jointly by two or more machines working together. Even if a single machine large enough to supply the entire load could be obtained, it would still often be advantageous to use two or more smaller units. Such an installation would provide a greater factor of safety in case one of the machines is temporarily out of commission and in need of repairs. Furthermore, the efficiency of a small machine delivering something like full load is greater than that of a large one delivering the same load (but a smaller percentage of its rated output). Accordingly, advantage may be taken of this fact by adding more machines as the load grows, or by removing them from the line when the load decreases.

There are two methods of connecting machines together for combined output corresponding to the two types of circuit connections, namely, *series connection* and *parallel connection*. For the former, series generators are used, and for the latter either shunt generators or compound generators.

Generators in Series. Although series generators were formerly much used to supply a constant current to series arc-lamp circuits for street

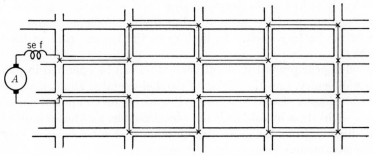

Fig. 16-13. The series arc circuit.

lighting, about the only remaining present-day application of these machines is their use as series boosters on electric-railway feeders. This has already been described. Direct-current arc lamps required a current of about 6.6 amp and a potential difference of about 50 volts. The arcs were all connected in series, as illustrated in Fig. 16-13. A circuit of 50 lamps connected in series required a total potential difference of 50 × 50 or 2,500 volts, which, for the sake of argument, is assumed to be the rated voltage of one machine. A 100-lamp circuit of such arcs could be supplied by connecting two machines in series, for together they would generate the necessary 5,000 volts. The details of operation of this type of circuit need not be discussed further here, for these circuits are now of little commercial importance.

Connecting Shunt Generators in Parallel. Two or more shunt generators may be connected in parallel as in Fig. 17-13 and they operate satisfactorily, dividing the load in proportion to their rated capacities, provided their external characteristic curves are alike.

The machines are connected to the load as follows: Let machine A be brought up to speed, and let its voltage be built up to the required value by adjusting the resistance of its shunt-field rheostat in the usual way. After this is done, its line switch may be closed and its load may be built up to any desired value, as by switching in lamps in the lamp bank. Machine B may now be brought up to speed.   The voltmeter across the terminals should then be observed to see whether the polarity of B corresponds to that of A, for when B's switch is finally closed, the positive terminal of B must be joined to the positive terminal of A and the negative terminal of B to the negative of A.   The reverse connection would cause a large circulating current between the two machines and would lead to disaster unless circuit-breaker protection were provided.   If the polarity is incorrect, the condition should be corrected by reversing the terminals of B at the switch blades and checking with the voltmeter to make sure.

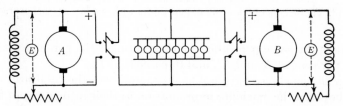

FIG. 17-13. Circuit connections of shunt generators in parallel.

When the correct polarity has been obtained, the voltage of B should be built up to a value a volt or two above that of the bus bars, in order that, when B's switch is closed, B may act as a generator to relieve the load on A rather than as a motor to load it further.   When the voltage has the correct value, B's switch may be closed.   Its load may then be built up to the desired value by increasing its field excitation.

Parallel Operation of Shunt Generators.   The operation of shunt generators in parallel is inherently stable, owing to their drooping characteristics (Fig. 5-13).   With properly governed driving speeds, it follows that if for any reason, such as a momentary fall in its speed, machine A (Fig. 17-13) should suddenly drop a part of its load, thereby shifting it to B, the voltage of A would rise and that of B would fall.   But on account of the increase in its voltage, A regains its lost load as soon as it recovers its speed, and because of the decrease in its voltage B must give it up.   Thus is the original division of load restored.

In order that shunt generators may divide their loads in proportion to their abilities to carry them, they must have similar characteristics; that is, a given percentage of increase in the rated loads of the several machines must cause the same decrease in their terminal voltages, regardless of rated capacities.   This is illustrated in Fig. 18-13 in which the behavior of a 250-kw generator and a 500-kw generator with similar characteristics is pictured.   Since the terminal voltages of both machines must always have the same value, it is clear that their respective loads

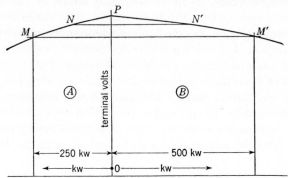

FIG. 18-13. Parallel operation of shunt generators with similar external characteristic curves.

are always the same percentage of their ratings: 100 per cent at M and M', 50 per cent at N and N', and 0 per cent at P.

When the machines have unlike characteristics, the total load cannot divide between the machines in proportion to their ratings except for one value.   Thus the two machines in Fig. 19-13 may have their loads

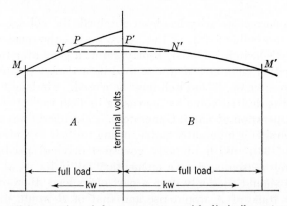

FIG. 19-13. Parallel operation of shunt generators with dissimilar external characteristic curves.

adjusted to the proper ratio at, say, full load for each machine, indicated at M and M', but when the total load falls off to some lesser value, the components are no longer in the correct ratio, as indicated at N and N'. Machine A which has the steeper characteristic, takes more and machine B less than its share of the load.   If the load is decreased far enough, B

will have lost all its load when A still carries a considerable amount, as indicated by the points P and P'. For loads less than PP', machine B becomes a motor.

Parallel Operation of Compound Generators. Undercompounded generators (those with drooping characteristic curves) may be operated satisfactorily in parallel in exactly the same manner as shunt generators, and all the foregoing discussion pertaining to shunt generators applies equally well to them. The parallel operation of overcompounded generators, however, is unstable unless their series fields are put in parallel by means of a low-resistance *equalizer connection*, shown in Fig. 20-13.

Suppose an attempt is made to operate machines A and B of Fig. 20-13 in parallel when the equalizer connection is open. If for any reason (such as a momentary fall in its speed) machine A should lose

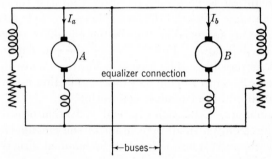

Fig. 20-13. Circuit connections for compound generators operating in parallel.

some of its load and thereby transfer it to B, the series field of A would be weakened while that of B would be strengthened. Because of the rising characteristics (curve 1, Fig. 14-13), the voltage of A would be lowered while that of B would be raised; A would drop more of its load and B would pick it up. This action would become cumulative and would continue until B carried all the load and A carried none, after which A would run as a differential-compound motor receiving power from B. Furthermore, if the degree of overcompounding is sufficient, the ampere-turns of the reversed current through the series field of A will overpower the shunt excitation, the air-gap flux and the electromagnetic torque will be reversed, and A will attempt to drive the prime mover backward.

When an equalizer connection is used, the series fields are connected in parallel and the operation of the machines becomes stable. Just as with shunt generators, however, their characteristic curves must be similar (in the sense already described) if they are to divide the total load in proportion to their rated capacities. Since the drop of potential is now the same across both series fields, the currents in them are always proportional to their conductances regardless of the loads on the machines; any increase or decrease of current through one is accompanied by a corresponding increase or decrease of current through the other. If A should momentarily transfer some of its load to B owing to a fall in speed, current will flow in the equalizer connection from B to A and pass out through the series field of A to the line. The field of A is thereby maintained even though its load has fallen off, and A regains its load as soon as its speed is corrected.

In order that the equalizer may function properly, two important conditions must be fulfilled, namely:

1. The equalizer connection must have a very low resistance.

2. The series fields must have resistances inversely proportional to the ratings of the respective machines.

The first condition is necessary in order that the series fields may always have the same potential difference between their terminals; that is, there must be no appreciable drop in the equalizer connection when an equalizing current flows. For this reason the equalizer connection is made as short as possible. The second condition makes it possible for each of the series fields to receive its proper excitation normally without any current flowing in the equalizer connection.

Rotating Amplifiers. Although the field excitation of a d-c generator ordinarily requires only a small percentage of the machine's output, the excitation power may still be too large to be handled directly by certain types of very sensitive control devices. Very sensitive excitation control may be brought about indirectly by the use of special kinds of d-c generators that require very small amounts of power to control relatively large outputs. These machines, which are in the nature of *rotating amplifiers*, have found wide application in industrial power systems. Three commercial examples of such machines bear the trade names of Amplidyne, Rototrol, and Regulex.

Amplidyne. The Amplidyne is a rotating d-c generator constructed according to rather different principles from those that apply to the machines previously described. The construction is explained in reference to Fig. 21-13, in which four separate illustrations are used to clarify the nature and functions of the several components of voltage and current that are inherent in the operation of this machine. In Fig. 21-13(a) are shown the basic field and armature windings. These are comparable to those of ordinary d-c generators. The field current I_f sets up a magnetomotive force F_1 and a corresponding flux, which causes a voltage e_1 to be generated in the armature conductors when the armature is driven from an external source of power.

Unlike an ordinary generator, the brushes in Fig. 21-13(a) are short-circuited as shown in Fig. 21-13(b). Because of the low armature resist-

ance, a very small field current results in a very large current between
the short-circuited brushes.   The short-circuit current sets up a strong
cross-magnetizing mmf, shown as F_2 in part (b) of the figure.   The magnetic circuit of the machine is so designed that there is an appreciable
component of flux corresponding to F_2, and this flux, in turn, causes a
component of voltage e_2 to be generated between a second set of brushes
spaced 90 electrical degrees from the first set, as illustrated in Fig.
21-13(c).   If a load is connected to the second set of brushes, a current

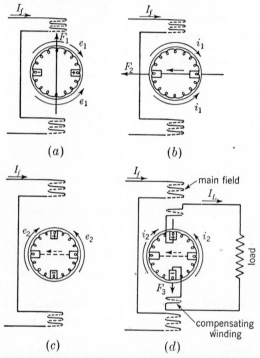

FIG. 21-13. Symbolic representation of Amplidyne.

is set up as shown in Fig. 21-13(d).   Unfortunately, the current i_2 results
in the production of a component of armature-reaction mmf F_3, which
acts counter to the mmf of the original field and tends to demagnetize
it.   In order that an excessive current I_f may not be required to oppose
the demagnetizing action of F_3, a series-connected compensating winding
is provided, which carries the load current.

The net result of the action described in the foregoing is that a *small*
current I_f is able to control a large current and power.   This action is
commonly described by saying that the input current has been *amplified*.

Rototrol or Regulex.   The Rototrol or Regulex is essentially a self-
excited shunt- or series-wound generator with an additional field winding

known as a control winding.   Figure 22-13(a) illustrates the connection diagram for a simple form of this machine, while Fig. 22-13(b) illustrates the saturation curve and field resistance lines.   The representation of the saturation curve differs from that of previous examples in that the region of reversed field current and generated voltage is shown in the third quadrant.   The magnetic circuit is especially designed to have a low hysteresis loss and to produce a saturation curve which closely

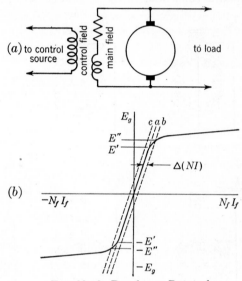

FIG. 22-13. Regulex or Rototrol.

approximates a straight line in the unsaturated region.   Unlike the condition which usually prevails in a self-excited generator, the field resistance is so adjusted that the resistance line coincides with the straight-line portion of the saturation curve, shown by line a in the figure.   This type of operation by itself is unstable, since any point on the resistance line between E' and $-E'$ satisfies the equilibrium conditions, and small random effects cause the voltage to vary unpredictably between the two limits.

If, in addition to the field excitation of line a in the figure, a small current is passed through the control winding, a small increment of ampere-turns ΔNI is added to or subtracted from the mmf of the main field, thereby effectively shifting the field resistance line to the right or left as shown by lines b and c.   In these respective cases the generated voltage starts to build toward E'' or $-E''$ at a rate which depends upon the time constant of the circuit.   In the usual application the current in the control field varies continuously from positive to negative so that the generated voltage does not have time to stray very far from the particular value which it is desired to maintain.

The principles of the above machine may perhaps be better understood by considering a simple application such as the elementary voltage regulator shown in Fig. 23-13. It is assumed that the main generator is supplying a varying load and that it is desired to maintain the output voltage constant at some level E_b. In the regulator shown, the output voltage is connected in opposition to a constant reference voltage E_b (shown as a battery in the figure). If the output voltage E_t of the generator is equal to the desired voltage E_b, there is no net emf around the control field circuit and no current results. If the main generator output voltage E_t rises above the reference voltage E_b, then a current is set up in the control field which is of such direction as to decrease the excitation of the main generator. Conversely, if the generator output

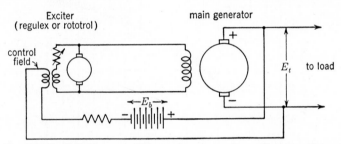

FIG. 23-13. Rotating amplifier used as an exciter-voltage regulator.

voltage E_t drops below the reference voltage, then the current in the control field is reversed and the excitation of the main generator is increased. In practice the output voltage continually *oscillates* or *hunts* about the reference level, but with proper choice of circuit constants the departure from reference level is negligible.

The variations in construction of rotating amplifiers are far too numerous to cover in this section, as are the applications found in many fields. Among the many applications that have been made are those involving control of voltage, current, power, torque, speed, tension, pressure, and position in a wide range of industrial fields, including the heavy machinery of steel mills, public utilities, and paper mills, and the lighter equipment of aircraft.

Problems

1-13. A four-pole shunt generator has pole faces of 32 sq in. area. The flux density in the air gap (assumed to be uniform under the pole faces and zero elsewhere) is 45,000 maxwells/sq in. The armature has 288 face conductors, and the winding is simplex lap. Compute the no-load terminal voltage for speeds of 1,200 and 1,800 rpm.

2-13. A four-pole generator has an armature diameter of 12 in. and a core length of 10 in. (The core length is also approximately equal to the active length of a conductor.)   The flux density in the air gap under the pole is 55,000 maxwells/sq in., and the poles embrace 70 per cent of the armature surface.   (Assume the field form to be a rectangle.)   (*a*) If the average emf generated in a conductor is 3.5 volts, what is the speed in rpm?   (*b*) How much voltage is generated in a conductor lying under a pole face when the speed is 800 rpm?

3-13. The machine in Prob. 2-13 is a 25-kw 220-volt generator, the rated speed of which is 1,500 rpm.   The armature is simplex, lap-wound.   The armature resistance drop at rated load is 6.35 per cent of the rated voltage.   Determine (*a*) the number of armature conductors required, (*b*) the rated armature current in a conductor.   (Disregard the field current.)   If the armature is reconnected to form a simplex wave winding, determine for this condition (*c*) the rated terminal voltage, (*d*) the current in an armature conductor.

4-13. The saturation curve of a 30-kw 125-volt shunt generator is given in Fig. *A*-13.   Ordinates are in percentages of rated voltage, and abscissas are percentages

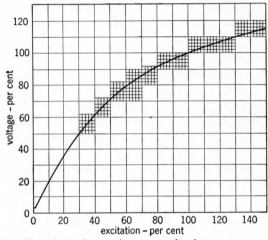

Fig. *A*-13.   Saturation curve of a d-c generator.

of field current that develops rated voltage at rated speed.   Data for the curve were taken with increasing field currents at rated speed of 1,200 rpm.   A field current of 3.8 amp is required at no load and rated speed to produce 125 volts at the terminals. (*a*) Redraw the saturation curve using no-load terminal volts as ordinates and field amperes as abscissas.   For rated speed determine (*b*) the resistance of the field circuit when the generated voltage is 140 volts, (*c*) the minimum field resistance that causes the generator to unbuild.   (Disregard the armature voltage drop due to the field current.)

5-13. (*a*) In Prob. 4-13, what field resistance is required to produce 130 volts at no load and a speed of 1,500 rpm?   (*b*) When the speed is 1,200 rpm, to what voltage does the machine build up if the field resistance is 36 ohms?   (*c*) At 900 rpm, what field resistance will build up the emf to 90 volts?

6-13. A shunt generator for which Fig. *A*-13 is the saturation curve is driven at rated speed.   A suitable voltmeter is connected across the machine terminals.   Before the shunt-field circuit is closed the voltmeter is observed to read 3.5 volts, while after the field is connected across the machine terminals the voltmeter reads only 1.5 volts. The machine voltage does not build up.   Explain the action and suggest a remedy.

7-13. The terminal potential difference of a separately excited generator is 220 volts when it runs at rated speed and delivers rated full-load current of 225 amp. The armature resistance is 0.06 ohm.   When the load is thrown off, the field excitation and speed remaining constant, what is (a) the terminal voltage, (b) the percentage regulation?   (Disregard the effect of armature reaction.)

8-13. Recompute the no-load voltage and the percentage regulation of the machine in Prob. 7-13 on the assumption that armature reaction has the effect of reducing the flux crossing the air gap by 3 per cent of the no-load value when the machine delivers full-load output.

9-13. A 100-kw, shunt generator runs at rated speed and delivers full-load output of 400 amp at a terminal voltage of 250 volts.   The resistance of the armature circuit, including brushes, is 0.04 ohm and the field current is 5.95 amp.   The saturation curve of the machine taken at rated speed has the shape of the curve in Fig. A-13. The generated voltage and field excitation existing at full load, as above, represent, respectively, 100 per cent voltage and excitation in Fig. A-13.   When the load is thrown off, speed and field resistance remaining constant, what is (a) the terminal voltage, (b) the field current?   (c) Compute the percentage regulation.   (Disregard the effect of armature reaction.)

10-13. A shunt generator requires a field current of 5.1 amp to give a no-load terminal voltage of 250 volts.   When the load is increased, while the speed and field resistance are held constant, the terminal voltage falls.   If, however, the terminal voltage is held constant by increasing the field current as the load is increased, it is observed that a field current of 6 amp is required to maintain 250 volts at the terminals when the machine delivers full-load current of 400 amp.   The shunt-field winding has 1,150 turns per pole.   (a) How many series turns per pole are necessary to convert this machine to a short-shunt, flat-compound generator?   (Disregard the RI drop in the series-field winding and select the next larger half turn.)   (b) If 4.5 turns are wound on each pole and the resistance of the entire series winding is 0.005 ohm, what must be the resistance of a diverter connected in parallel with the series field?

11-13. A 50-kw generator A with a regulation of from 125 volts at full-load to 132 volts at no-load is operated in parallel with a 100-kw generator B, the regulation of which is 125 volts at full-load to 130 volts at no-load.   The external characteristics of both machines are assumed to be straight lines.   The excitations of the two machines are so adjusted that each machine delivers its full-load output when the terminal potential difference is 125 volts.   (a) When B delivers 25 kw, what is the load on A?   (b) What is the load on each machine when the terminal potential difference is 127 volts?   (c) When the load on B is zero, what is the load on A?

12-13. Two shunt generators have ratings of 500 and 300 kw.   The regulation of the first machine is 5.5 per cent, while that of the second is 4 per cent.   The external characteristic curves (terminal volts vs. load kilowatts) of both machines are straight lines.   The machines are operated in parallel and their excitations are so adjusted that neither delivers any load when the bus potential difference is 130 volts.   Find (a) the kilowatt output of each machine, and (b) the bus voltage when the combined output of the two machines is 500 kw.

13-13. At the distant end of a railway feeder the trolley voltage is 520 volts.   At this point a series booster is installed that develops a terminal potential difference of 110 volts at full-load current of 100 amp.   The external characteristic of the booster is a straight line.   A No. 00 trolley wire extends for 2 miles beyond the booster location.   A car at the end of the trolley line draws 80 amp.   If the resistance of the trolley wire is 0.46 ohm/mile and the RI drop in the rail return is negligible, what is the trolley voltage at the car?

CHAPTER 14

MOTORS AND THEIR CHARACTERISTICS

The electric motor has already been defined as a machine for converting electrical energy to mechanical energy of motion (usually rotation). The basic principle of such conversion rests upon the experimental fact that, when a current flows in a region occupied by a magnetic field (unless the direction of current and the direction of the magnetic field

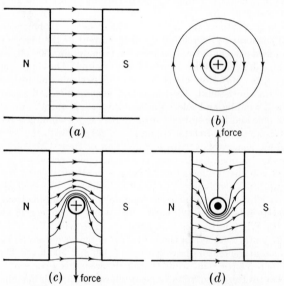

(a)

(b)

(c) ↓force

(d)

Fig. 1-14. The principle of motor action.

are parallel), a reaction is set up which tends to move the current out of the field. When this force is utilized to do mechanical work, the electrical energy of the circuit is changed to mechanical energy of motion, and the arrangement constitutes an electric motor.

Motor Principle Illustrated. The above principle is illustrated in the drawings of Fig. 1-14. In this figure, (a) shows the uniform flux distribution in the air gap of a magnetic circuit, (b) shows the circular magnetic field due to a current flowing in a wire, and (c) shows the resultant field produced when the current-carrying wire of (b) is inserted in the air gap of (a) with the axis of the wire at right angles to the direction of the flux. On the upper side of the wire in (c) the magnetizing forces of the field and of the current in the wire are additive, while on the lower side they are subtractive. This explains why the resultant field is strengthened above and weakened below the wire.

Experiment shows that the wire in (c) has a force on it which tends to move it downward. Thus *the force acts in the direction of the weaker field.* When the current in the wire is reversed, the direction of the force is also reversed, as in (d).

Rule for the Direction of Force. Since the force developed always tends to move the current in the direction of the weaker field, the rule for finding the direction of the force is as follows:

1. Note the direction of the main field.

2. By the right-hand rule (page 62), find the direction of field due to the current alone.

3. Imagine the above two fields to be superimposed and note on which side of the wire the two fields subtract. The wire tends to move in this direction along a line normal to the flux of the main field.

Amount of Force Developed. As has already been shown, experiment teaches that the force on a current-carrying conductor in a magnetic field is proportional to

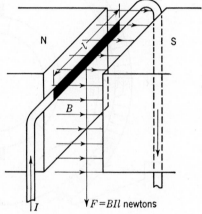

FIG. 2-14. The force on a current.

1. The current
2. The length of the conductor lying in the field
3. The component of the flux density normal to the length of the conductor

In electric machines the conductors are usually so arranged that the flux density in the air gap is normal to the axis of the conductor, as in Fig. 2-14. For such cases, by Eq. (13-6), the force developed is

$$F = BIl \qquad \text{newtons}$$

where B = flux density, webers/sq m

I = current in conductor, amp

l = exposed length of conductor, m

Torque in a Motor. Machines of the type described as generators are also used as motors. When the field of such a machine is excited and a potential difference is impressed upon the machine terminals, the current in the armature winding reacts with the air-gap flux to produce a turning moment or torque which tends to cause the armature to revolve.

The principle upon which this action depends has already been discussed. Its application to the production of torque in a motor is further illustrated in Fig. 3-14. When the brushes are on the neutral axis, all the armature conductors lying under the north pole carry currents in a given direction, while those lying under the south pole carry currents in

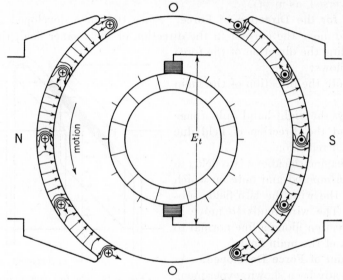

Fig. 3-14. Operation principle of a d-c motor.

the reverse direction. Just as in a generator, the commutator serves to reverse the current in each armature coil at the instant it passes through the neutral axis, so the above relation is always maintained as the armature rotates.

In Fig. 3-14 all conductors under the north pole carry inward-flowing currents which react with the air-gap flux as in (c) of Fig. 1-14 to produce downward-acting forces and a counterclockwise torque. Similarly, the conductors under the south pole carry outward-flowing currents which produce upward-acting forces as in (d) of Fig. 1-14. These forces also give rise to counterclockwise torques. If the air-gap flux is assumed to be radially directed at all points, each of the forces acts tangentially and produces a turning moment equal to the force multiplied by its lever arm—the radial distance from the center of the conductor to the center of the shaft.

The amount of torque developed by each conductor is

$$T = BIlr \qquad \text{newton-perp-m}$$

where r is the lever arm in meters. The component torques produced by the conductors under the north pole add to those produced under the south pole as shown. Accordingly, if the armature has a total of Z conductors, and if the poles cover the fractional part ψ of the armature periphery, the number of active torque-producing conductors is ψZ and the total torque produced by the armature is

$$T = 0.738\psi ZBIlr \qquad \text{lb-perp-ft} \qquad (1\text{-}14)$$

where B = gap density, webers/sq m
$\quad I$ = armature current in a conductor, amp
$\quad\quad$ = armature amperes per path
$\quad l$ = active length of one conductor, m
$\quad r$ = average lever arm of a conductor, m
Equation (1-14) may be reduced to

$$T = 7.04\phi Z' I_a \qquad \text{lb-perp-ft} \qquad (2\text{-}14)$$

where ϕ = air-gap flux per pole
$\quad I_a$ = armature current
$\quad Z'$ = the familiar constant of Eq. (2-13)
In the above equations all terms except B, ϕ, and I depend only upon the design of the machine. Furthermore, since $B = \phi/A$, where A is the area of the air gap, Eq. (1-14) may also be written

$$T = k\phi I_a \qquad (3\text{-}14)$$

where k = constant. Thus the torque of a motor depends only upon the air-gap flux and the armature current. This simple relationship should be kept in mind, for it assists greatly in forming a picture of the behavior of a motor under various conditions of load.

Example 1. A 30-hp 120-volt four-pole lap-wound motor has 440 face conductors, and it draws an armature current of 200 amp from the line at full load. The armature is 6 in. long, the percentage of polar embrace is 65, the air-gap flux density is 45,000 maxwells/sq in., and the mean radius (average lever arm of face conductors) is 5.5 in. How many pound-feet of torque does the motor develop at full load?
In the preceding equations for torque,

$\psi Z = 0.65 \times 440 = 286$ active conductors
$\quad B = 45,000$ lines per square inch
$\quad I = {}^{20}\!{}_{4}^{0} = 50$ amp per armature path
$\quad l = 6$ in.
$\quad r = 5.5$ in.

By Eq. (1-14),

$$T = 0.738 \times 286 \times \frac{45,000(39.37)^2}{10^8} \times 50 \times \frac{6}{39.37} \times \frac{5.5}{39.37}$$
$$= 157 \text{ lb-perp-ft}$$

This is the electromagnetic torque developed by the motor. The pulley torque is somewhat less than the above value because of friction and iron losses in the motor.

Example 2. What torque does the motor in Example 1 develop when the load current is 50 amp? It is assumed that the field excitation remains unchanged.

From Eq. (3-14) it is apparent that, when the air-gap flux remains constant, the torque is proportional to the armature current. Therefore

$$\frac{T_2}{T_1} = \frac{50}{200}$$

and

$$T_2 = \frac{50}{200} \times 157 = 39.2 \text{ lb-perp-ft}$$

Counter Emf. When the armature is free to turn, the torque developed causes it to revolve. In so doing the armature conductors are driven across the air-gap flux just as in a generator, and emf is generated in the

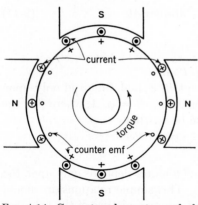

FIG. 4-14. Current and counter emf of a motor.

armature winding. The direction of this emf may be found by the right-hand rule.

In Fig. 4-14 the torque produced by the armature currents there shown is in a counterclockwise direction, and hence rotation is counterclockwise. With this direction of rotation the emfs generated in the conductors under the north pole are directed outward, while the currents in the conductors flow inward. Similarly under the south pole the emfs are directed inward, while the currents flow outward. This relation always exists in a motor; that is, *the generated emf in the motor winding always opposes the impressed voltage* and thereby controls or limits the current in the winding. For this reason the emf generated in a motor armature is called the *counter emf* of the motor.

The emf generated in the winding of a dynamo-electric machine may always be computed from Eq. (1-13), regardless of whether the machine is used as a generator or as a motor. Hence if E_c is the counter emf of the motor,

$$E_c = \frac{\phi Z p_1 S}{p_2 \times 60} = \phi Z' S \qquad (4\text{-}14)$$

where

$$Z' = \frac{Zp_1}{p_2 \times 60}$$

and Z' is constant for any given machine. Accordingly, *the value of E_c depends only upon the air-gap flux and upon the speed.*

When the motor armature is at rest, its counter emf is zero and the current through the armature is limited only by the armature resistance. The armature resistance is very low, however, and if full voltage were impressed upon the motor terminals at standstill, the current would be many times the full-load value. This may be illustrated as follows: A 5-hp 110-volt motor has an armature resistance of about 0.2 ohm. Its rated current is about 40 amp. With full voltage impressed at standstill, the armature current would be $110/0.2 = 550$ amp, or over thirteen times full-load value. This large current would damage the machine. *To protect the motor at starting, therefore, additional resistance must be introduced into the armature circuit,* as will be explained later.

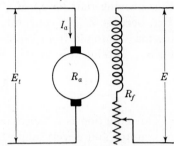

Fig. 5-14. Circuit diagram of a separately excited motor.

When the motor is running, the current in the armature is limited by both the armature resistance and the counter emf. By applying Kirchhoff's law of voltages to the armature circuit of Fig. 5-14, one observes that the impressed voltage is balanced by the sum of the counter emf and the armature-resistance drop. This fact is expressed mathematically by the relation

$$E_t = E_c + I_a R_a \tag{5-14}$$

From this equation the armature current is found to be

$$I_a = \frac{E_t - E_c}{R_a} \tag{6-14}$$

It should be noted also that the counter emf in a motor must always be less than the impressed voltage, because current is required to produce the torque that makes the motor run. The current approaches zero as E_c approaches E_t in value. This is clearly shown by Eq. (6-14).

Example 3. The 5-hp 110-volt motor mentioned above is loaded until its armature current is 40 amp. The armature resistance is 0.2 ohm. What is the counter emf of the motor?

Armature-resistance drop is

$$40 \times 0.2 = 8 \text{ volts}$$

Counter emf is

$$E_c = 110 - 8 = 102 \text{ volts}$$

Relation of Speed and Counter Emf. Equation (4-14) shows that the speed is directly proportional to the counter emf. Solving this equation for speed yields

$$S = \frac{E_c}{\phi Z'} \qquad (7\text{-}14)$$

thus proving that *the speed of a motor is inversely proportional to the field flux,* because Z' is a constant. The speed under any conditions of loading may be found from Eq. 5-14 by substituting $\phi Z'S$ for E_c and solving for S. Making this substitution and solving yields

$$S = \frac{E_t - I_a R_a}{\phi Z'} \qquad (8\text{-}14)$$

This equation is a shorthand statement of the law of speed variation of a motor and is very important.

Example 4. When running light, a motor draws 2.5 amp from 120-volt mains and runs at a speed of 1,250 rpm. The armature resistance is 0.18 ohm. (*a*) When the motor is loaded until its armature current is 30 amp, what is the speed? The impressed voltage and the field excitation remain unchanged. (*b*) If the field flux is reduced to 75 per cent of its no-load value, what is the speed when the armature current is 50 amp?

(*a*) From light-running conditions and Eq. (8-14),

$$\phi_1 Z' = \frac{120 - 2.5 \times 0.18}{1,250} = 0.09564$$

When the motor is loaded, $\phi Z'$ remaining unchanged, the speed is

$$S_1 = \frac{120 - 30 \times 0.18}{0.09564} = 1,198 \text{ rpm}$$

(*b*) Since the excitation is reduced as stated, $\phi_2 Z' = 0.75\phi_1 Z'$ and

$$\phi_2 Z' = 0.75 \times 0.09564 = 0.07173$$

The new speed then is

$$S_2 = \frac{120 - 50 \times 0.18}{0.07173} = 1,547 \text{ rpm}$$

Mechanical Power Developed by Motor Armature. The electrical power delivered to the armature of a motor is all converted to mechanical power of rotation, except for a small amount of heat loss in the armature winding. This may be shown as follows:

Multiplying Eq. (5-14) by the armature current I_a and rearranging yields

$$E_c I_a = E_t I_a - I_a{}^2 R_a \qquad (9\text{-}14)$$

By Eq. (7-14) the left-hand member may be written

$$E_c I_a = \phi Z' I_a \times S = \text{torque} \times \text{speed} \times \text{a constant}$$

as may be seen by reference to Eq. (3-14). Thus the interpretation of Eq. (9-14) is

$$\begin{bmatrix} \text{Mechanical power} \\ \text{developed by the armature} \end{bmatrix} = \begin{bmatrix} \text{electrical power} \\ \text{input to armature} \end{bmatrix}$$
$$- \begin{bmatrix} \text{heat loss in} \\ \text{armature winding} \end{bmatrix} \quad (10\text{-}14)$$

The power available at the pulley for doing useful work is somewhat less than the mechanical power developed by the armature. This is

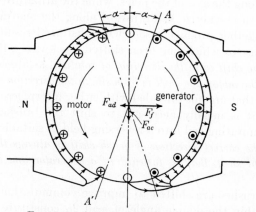

Fig. 6-14. Armature reaction in a motor.

evident, since there are certain mechanical losses (such as bearing and windage friction and iron losses) that must be supplied by the driving power of the motor. These are discussed further in the following chapter.

Example 5. How much mechanical power is developed by the motor of the previous example under conditions (a)? What is the heat loss in the armature winding?

(a) Armature RI drop $= 30 \times 0.18 = 5.4$ volts
Counter emf $\quad E_c = 120 - 5.4 = 114.6$ volts
Mechanical power $\quad = 30 \times 114.6 = 3,438$ watts
Armature copper loss $= 30^2 \times 0.18 = 162$ watts

Armature Reaction and Commutation. The theory of armature reaction and commutation discussed in Chap. 12 applies to d-c motors with only slight modification. This fact has already been mentioned, but it is further illustrated in Fig. 6-14. When the machine in the figure runs as a generator in a clockwise direction, inward emfs and currents are developed in the armature winding under the north pole, while outward emfs and currents are developed under the south pole.   The electromagnetic torque in the armature is counterclockwise, or opposite to the direction of rotation of the generator.   If, however, instead of driving the machine mechanically it is supplied from an outside source *with the same armature current shown in the figure*, the machine is propelled by the electromagnetic torque of its armature.   It then operates as a motor, running in a counterclockwise direction.

Since the armature and field currents in the two cases are assumed to be identical, respectively, the mmfs of these currents remain unchanged and conform to the figure.   The mmf F_f of the field tends to magnetize the armature along the axis of the poles, while the armature cross ampere-turns F_{ac} tend to magnetize it downward along the neutral axis.   Both these acting together produce a somewhat distorted resultant field, the center of density of which has been shifted clockwise. *With respect to the generator, the shift is in the direction of rotation*, as already explained; *with respect to the motor, the shift is opposite to the direction of rotation.*

In machines that are not provided with either interpoles or compensating windings, it is usually necessary to shift the brushes in order to bring the commutating coil into a reversing field of suitable strength (see page 172).   *The correct direction of brush shift is always the same as the direction of field shift, that is, forward in a generator and backward in a motor.*

When the brushes are shifted to improve commutation, the ampere-turns lying within the double angle of lead 2α constitute the armature demagnetizing ampere-turns F_{ad}, which tend to demagnetize the main field and reduce the useful flux, just as in a generator.   The axis of the resultant field is then in the direction of R, the resultant magnetizing force.

Effect of Armature Reaction on Speed and Torque.   The armature ampere-turns are proportional to the armature current and therefore to the load on the motor.   Their effect is to cause the air-gap flux under load to be somewhat less than it would be if armature reaction were not present.   Accordingly, *armature reaction has the effect of decreasing the counter emf* [Eq. (4-14)], *reducing the torque* [Eq. (3-14)], *and increasing the speed* [Eq. (8-14)].

Starting Motors.   A motor at rest has no counter emf.   At starting, therefore, the armature current is limited only by the resistance of the armature circuit, as shown in Eq. (6-14).   The armature resistance is very low, however, and if full voltage were impressed upon the motor terminals at standstill, the resulting armature current would be many times full-load value—usually sufficient to damage the machine.[1] For this reason, additional resistance is introduced into the armature circuit at starting. As the motor gains speed, its counter emf builds up and the starting resistance is cut out.

Figure 7-14 illustrates the correct methods of connecting resistances in the circuits of d-c motors at starting. Figure 7-14(a) shows the correct connection for shunt motors, while Fig. 7-14(b) shows an incorrect method which should be carefully avoided. In order that a motor may start its load, it must develop a large starting torque. This means that

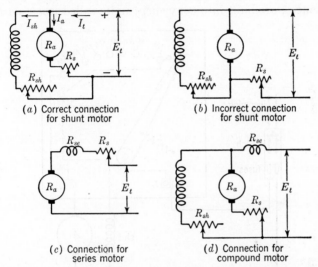

(a) Correct connection
for shunt motor

(b) Incorrect connection
for shunt motor

(c) Connection for
series motor

(d) Connection for
compound motor

Fig. 7-14. Wiring diagrams. Connections for starting d-c motors.

its field should be fully excited. The connection shown in (a) permits full line voltage to be impressed on the shunt field, while in (b) most of the impressed voltage is absorbed in the starting resistance and only a small fraction of it is applied to the field terminals. The starting torque developed in (b) is therefore very low and the motor may not start at all.

The connection for compound motors, shown in (d), is identical with that used for shunt motors except for the addition of the series field.

Example 6. A 10-hp 120-volt shunt motor has an armature resistance of 0.12 ohm. Its full-load armature current is 74 amp. (a) How many times full-load current would the armature draw from 120-volt mains if the motor were connected to the mains without any starting resistance? (b) How much resistance is required to limit the starting current to 150 per cent of full-load current?

[1] Very small d-c motors, either shunt, series, or compound wound, have sufficient armature resistance so that they may be started directly from the line without the use of a starting resistance and without injury to the motor.

(a) Starting current would be 120/0.12 = 1,000 amp. This is 1,000/74 = 13.5 times full-load current.

(b) By Eq. (6-14), since at starting $E_c = 0$, $E_t = I_a(R_a + R)$ and

$$R = \frac{E_t}{I_a} - R_a = \frac{120}{1.5 \times 74} - 0.12 = 0.96 \text{ ohm}$$

This resistance must be capable of safely carrying 120/(0.96 + 0.12) or 111 amp during the starting period.

Shunt-motor Starting Rheostats. Starting resistances of suitable amounts, together with movable contact arms for gradually cutting out the resistances, are built into convenient units called *motor starters*.

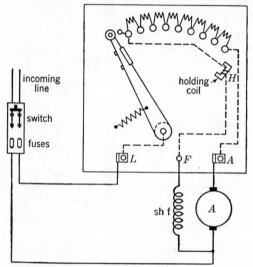

Fig. 8-14. Wiring diagram of three-point starter for shunt and compound motors.

A three-point starter for use with shunt and compound motors is illustrated in Fig. 8-14. This figure also shows how the starter and motor are wired to the power terminals through fuses and switch. One side of the motor armature and one terminal of the shunt field (the lower one in the figure) are connected directly to the line. The remaining side of the line is connected to the line terminal of the starter, which in turn is wired to the hub of the starting lever. The starting resistance units are connected in series between the first and last buttons on the face plate, with intermediate taps connected to buttons as shown. The last button to the right is wired to the armature terminal of the starter, which in turn is connected to the remaining armature lead. The second field terminal is connected to the starter terminal marked *field*.

When the starting lever is moved to contact with the first button, the field is connected directly across the line terminals and is fully energized.

The armature circuit is connected in series with all the starting resistance. As the motor accelerates, the lever is pushed farther to the right, until finally all the starting resistance is cut out and the lever is held in the extreme right position by means of the electromagnet *H*, called the *holding coil*. The winding of the latter is connected in series with the field circuit. If for any reason the line becomes deenergized (loses its voltage), the holding coil lets go of the starting lever, and the latter is returned to the starting position by means of a spring. The motor is thus protected against the possibility of being subjected to full-line voltage without the starting resistance in the circuit. This protective feature is provided by the holding coil, and hence the latter is sometimes called the *no-voltage release*.

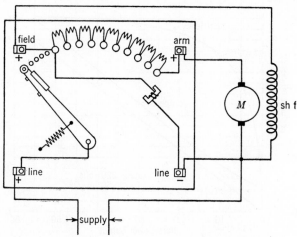

Fig. 9-14. Wiring diagram of a four-point starting box.

The speed of shunt and compound motors may be adjusted by adjusting the field excitation, as is apparent from an examination of Eq. (7-14). When this method of adjustment is used to secure a wide range of speeds, the three-point starter is not satisfactory, for when the field current is reduced below a certain value, the holding coil releases the starting lever. To avoid this a *four-point starter* was developed (Fig. 9-14), in which the holding coil is connected directly across the line and receives its excitation independent of the shunt field.

Characteristic Curves of Shunt Motors. Motor characteristic curves show how the speed and the torque vary with the armature current when the supply voltage remains constant. At no load the counter emf of a shunt motor is nearly equal to the impressed voltage, and the speed has its maximum value (Fig. 10-14). The slight difference between the impressed voltage and the counter emf is sufficient to permit a small current to flow in the armature. This current, reacting with the field flux, produces the torque necessary to supply the no-load losses.

When a load is applied (resisting torque increased), the propelling torque is insufficient to carry the load at the existing speed; hence the speed falls, and since the flux is substantially constant, the counter emf also falls. This allows the armature current and the torque to increase. The speed of the motor continues to fall until the current rises to a value sufficient to produce a torque equal to the resisting torque of the load. Thereafter the speed remains constant at the reduced value until the load is again changed. Thus it is clear that with increase of load the

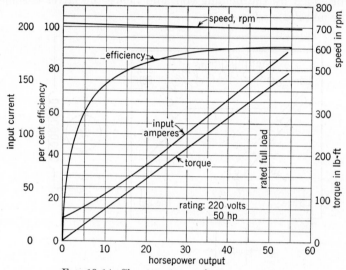

Fig. 10-14. Shunt-motor performance curves.

speed of a shunt motor falls, while the armature current and the torque increase.

The shapes of the torque and speed curves may be predicted from an examination of Eqs. (3-14) and (8-14). By Eq. (8-14) the speed is

$$S = \frac{E_t - I_a R_a}{\phi Z'}$$

Since E_t is constant, the shunt-field current does not change and the air-gap flux is also nearly constant. Accordingly, speed and armature current are the only variables in the above equation, which then is the equation of the drooping straight line shown in Fig. 10-14. Actually, however, armature reaction may bring about a slight reduction of flux as the load increases. For this reason the observed speed under load may be slightly greater than that predicted by the equation, for the speed is inversely proportional to the air-gap flux. If armature reaction is very pronounced, the speed may actually increase slightly under heavy load.

When the flux is constant the torque is directly proportional to the armature current, as shown by Eq. (3-14). The torque curve under these conditions is a straight line of constant slope. The effect of armature reaction is to reduce the torque per ampere of current slightly as the load increases. Therefore under heavy loads the torque increases less rapidly than at light loads, and the torque curve droops slightly as the load is increased.

The starting torque of a shunt motor is determined by the total resistance included between the first and the last notch of the motor starter. This resistance is usually enough to limit the starting current to a value about 25 per cent in excess of full-load current. Hence the starting torque of the motor used with such a starter is somewhat less than 125 per cent of full-load torque.

Shunt motors are used to drive constant-speed equipment such as machine tools for metal and woodworking, the rolls of paper mills, and textile machines.

Speed Regulation. Shunt motors are essentially constant-speed motors; that is, when run with constant field excitation, the change in speed from full load to no load is a small percentage of the full-load speed. (This does not mean, of course, that the speed of a shunt motor cannot be *adjusted* to different values by adjusting the field excitation.) The rules of the AIEE define the *speed regulation* of constant-speed direct-current motors as "the ratio of the difference between rated-load and no-load speeds to the rated-load speed at the final temperature attained at operation under rated-load for the time specified in the rating." Thus, suppose that, when loaded to full load, a given motor runs at a speed of 1,150 rpm. When the load is thrown off, terminal voltage and field resistance remaining unchanged, the speed rises to 1,225 rpm. The speed regulation of the motor, expressed in per cent, then is

$$\text{Regulation} = 100 \, \frac{(1{,}225 - 1{,}150)}{1{,}150} = 6.52 \text{ per cent}$$

Characteristic Curves of Series Motors. In a series motor the armature and field are connected in series as in Fig. 7-14 (c), and the field and armature currents are identical. The air-gap flux increases with the armature current in a manner determined by the magnetization curve of the machine. Over the range covered by the straight-line portion of this curve, the flux is directly proportional to the armature current and may be written as

$$\phi = kI_a \qquad\qquad (11\text{-}14)$$

where k = constant of proportionality.

The fundamental speed equation [Eq. (8-14)] applies to the series motor when written in the form

$$S = \frac{E_t - I_a(R_a + R_{se})}{\phi Z'}$$ (12-14)

where $R_a + R_{se}$ = sum of armature and series-field resistances. In the right-hand member of this equation the numerator decreases slightly and the denominator increases quite rapidly with increasing load current. It is thus apparent that, if the terminal voltage remains constant, the speed of the series motor falls quite rapidly as its load increases. At light loads the armature current and the air-gap flux are both small. The counter emf is then nearly equal to the impressed voltage and the motor runs at high speed. It is impractical to run a series motor without load, for then the speed becomes so high that the motor armature may be destroyed by centrifugal action. For this reason series motors are always permanently connected to their loads by means of gears or direct coupling rather than by belts. The minimum load must be sufficient to keep the speed within safe limits.

Under heavy loads the iron in the magnetic circuit approaches saturation, the rate of increase of flux with loads is reduced, and the speed falls less rapidly. At the very heavy loads armature reaction and saturation both tend to keep the flux from increasing further, and the speed changes slowly (Fig. 11-14).

The torque of a motor is proportional to the product of the air-gap flux and the armature current, as shown by Eq. (3-14); that is,

$$T = \phi I_a \times \text{a constant}$$

At light loads (over the range covered by the straight part of the magnetization curve) the flux is proportional to the armature current. Over this range, therefore,

$$T = k_2 I_a^2$$ (13-14)

where k_2 = constant. Hence the torque curve passes through zero and rises rapidly as the load current is increased. At light loads the curve is a parabola. As more and more load is added, the increasing field ampereturns gradually saturate the magnetic circuit. The air-gap flux then increases at a slower rate than the armature current. The demagnetizing effect of armature reaction also comes into play and acts to keep the flux from increasing as rapidly as it otherwise would. These two influences together cause the slope of the torque curve to increase at a diminishing rate with increasing load; the curve now falls below the theoretical parabola and approaches a straight line.

Typical speed and torque curves of a series motor are shown in Fig. 11-14. Because a series motor develops a high torque at low speed and a low torque at high speed, it is a most satisfactory motor for traction service. With few exceptions, street-railway cars and trolley coaches, as well as the trains of some electrified steam railroads, are hauled by series motors. The high torque at low speed enables a comparatively small motor to start a heavy load. When the starting friction has been overcome, the motor begins to accelerate its load, the counter emf increases, and the current and torque decrease correspondingly, as the speed rises. Railway cars driven by series motors naturally run at high

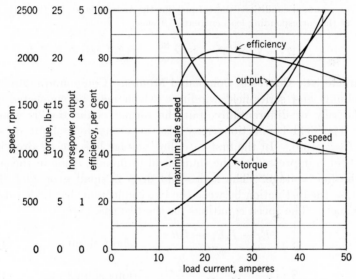

FIG. 11-14. Performance curves of a 5-hp series motor.

speeds over level country or on downgrades. When an upgrade is encountered the load increases and the motor automatically slows down. In so doing it permits the torque to increase to a value great enough to haul the load up the grade at the reduced speed. Under changes in load the speed and the torque of the motor adjust themselves automatically to changing conditions in exactly the manner desired.

Series motors are also much used to drive elevators, cranes, hoists, etc.

Example 7. A 10-hp series motor has an armature resistance of 0.08 ohm and a series-field resistance of 0.07 ohm. When the motor is connected across 120-volt mains and loaded until its armature current is 60 amp, it develops 30 lb-ft of torque and runs at 1,050 rpm. What are the torque and the speed of the motor when the load is increased to 80 amp? Assume the magnetization curve of the motor is a straight line over this range of load.

Substituting the given data in Eq. (12-14) and solving for $\phi Z'$ (called the induction factor) yields

$$\phi_1 Z' = \frac{120 - 60(0.08 + 0.07)}{1,050} = 0.1057$$

The induction factor for the second condition of loading is

$$\phi_2 Z' = {}^{8}\%_{60} \times 0.1057 = 0.1409$$

Solving for the speed for the second condition of loading, with the help of Eq. (12-14), yields

$$S_2 = \frac{120 - 80(0.08 + 0.07)}{0.1409} = 766.5 \text{ rpm}$$

Under the assumed conditions the torques for the two loads are in the ratio of the squares of the corresponding load currents. Hence,

$$T_2 = T_1 \times \frac{I_{a2}{}^2}{I_{a1}{}^2} = 40 \times \frac{80^2}{60^2} = 71.1 \text{ lb-perp-ft}$$

Characteristic Curves of Compound Motors. Compound motors have both shunt- and series-field windings, which may be connected either cumulatively or differentially, but the former connection is generally used. The field connections may also be either long-shunt or short-shunt (page 160). In the first case, line voltage less the RI drop in the series field is impressed on the shunt-field terminals, while in the second it is the line voltage. The series-field drop is small even at full-load output, so the distinction between the two connections has little practical significance. The speed equations for the two cases are

$$S = \frac{E_t - I_a R_a - I_t R_{se}}{\phi Z'} \qquad \text{(short shunt)} \qquad (14\text{-}14)$$

$$S = \frac{E_t - I_a(R_a + R_{se})}{\phi Z'} \qquad \text{(long shunt)} \qquad (15\text{-}14)$$

At no load, the series ampere-turns are negligible and the speed has a definite value determined by the impressed voltage and the amount of shunt-field excitation. When the compounding is cumulative and load is applied, the speed falls and the torque increases. This is due to two causes, as follows:

1. Because the counter emf is decreased owing to the increased RI drop in the armature and series-field windings. That is, the numerator of the fraction which makes up the right-hand member of Eq. (14-14) is reduced, just as in a shunt motor.

2. Because the added ampere-turns of the series field cause the air-gap flux to increase. This enables the machine to generate its required counter emf at a lower speed than would be the case if the series field were disconnected.

For the reason given in 2 above, a given machine, when run as a cumulative compound motor, has a lower speed curve than the same machine has when run as a shunt motor with the same shunt-field excitation. At no load the speeds of the machine are identical in the two cases. The extent to which the speed of the compound motor falls below that of the shunt motor depends upon the *degree of compounding*. Curve 1 of Fig. 12-14 is the speed-load curve of the shunt machine; curve 2 is the curve for a compound machine with a few series turns; while curve 3 shows the effect of increasing the compounding still further. It should be noted that in the above discussion the motors under comparison are assumed to have the same field flux and speed at no load, while the curves are drawn for motors with identical fluxes and speeds at full load.

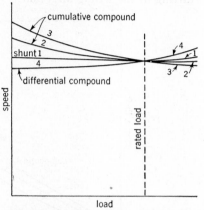

FIG. 12-14. Speed-load curves of shunt and compound motors.

When the machine is differentially compounded the air-gap flux decreases as the load increases, so the motor must speed up to generate the required counter emf, and the speed falls less with increase of load than it does in the case of the shunt machine. If the compounding is sufficient, the speed may increase with increase of load as shown by curve 4.

In a shunt motor the air-gap flux is approximately constant, in a cumulative compound motor it increases, while in a differential compound motor it decreases with increasing load. Since the torque is proportional to the product of flux and armature current [Eq. (3-14)], it follows that, for a given percentage increase in load current, the torque of a cumulative compound motor increases at a greater rate, and the torque of a differential compound motor increases at a lesser rate than the torque of a shunt motor. This accounts for the relative shapes of the torque load curves shown in Fig. 13-14.

Applications of Compound Motors. Cumulative compound motors are used in applications that ordinarily require fairly constant speed drives but in which large sudden fluctuations of load may occur, or in which heavy loads must be started. Rock crushers, shears, punches, and elevators are examples of such loads. Under heavy load the motor slows down enough to permit the torque to increase to the required value without an excessive increase in armature current. When, after starting, the load remains fairly constant, as in the case of elevator drives, the series field may be short-circuited to obtain constant-speed operation.

Differential motors are seldom used, for shunt motors are usually satisfactory for approximately constant-speed applications. Differential motors should be started with the series field short-circuited. When the series field is not disconnected, the starting current may be sufficient to cause the series-field ampere-turns to overpower the shunt-field mmf and thus cause a reversal of field. This would result in the motor's starting in the wrong direction.

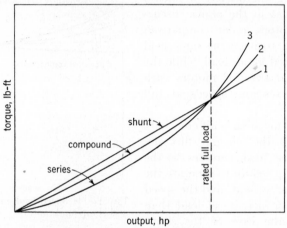

Fɪɢ. 13-14. Comparative torque curves of series, shunt, and compound motors.

Speed Control of Shunt and Compound Motors. It is apparent from an examination of the speed equation

$$S = \frac{E_t - I_a R_a}{\phi Z'}$$

that the speed of a motor may be controlled by any one of the following methods:

1. By adjusting the value of R_a, the resistance of the armature circuit.

2. By adjusting the impressed voltage E_t while the flux ϕ is kept constant.

3. By adjusting the air-gap flux ϕ. This is usually accomplished by changing the current in the field winding.

4. By a combination of two or more of these methods.

Resistance Control. Introducing resistance into the armature circuit increases the voltage drop that a given armature current produces. The counter emf which the motor must generate is thereby reduced and the speed is lowered. The heat loss in the circuit is correspondingly increased, however, and the efficiency of the motor is reduced. The resistance method of speed control is therefore uneconomical and is little used except during the starting period and for experimental work. For experimental work it has the advantage that any speed less than rated speed may be obtained.

Voltage Control. Changing the applied voltage has the same effect on the speed as changing the armature resistance. This method has the advantage of securing the desired change in speed without increasing the losses. If the field flux remains constant, the change in speed is approximately proportional to the change in voltage. In order to make this method available, several different voltages must be provided, as illustrated in Fig. 14-14. The field is permanently connected to a fixed pair of leads, and the several voltages available are impressed upon the armature circuit to obtain the several corresponding speeds. For each

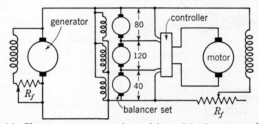

FIG. 14-14. Shunt-motor operation with multivoltage speed control.

voltage a considerable range in speeds may be obtained by adjusting the shunt-field excitation. This method of speed control is known as the *multivoltage system*.

Because of the somewhat extensive equipment that is required to obtain and make available the several voltages, this system of control is expensive. It is usually uneconomical except where a considerable number of motors requiring this method of control are in use.

Field Control. Speed control secured by adjusting the air-gap flux (through the medium of resistance in the shunt-field circuit) is the most commonly used as well as the most economical method of shunt-motor speed control. A considerable range of speed adjustment is possible with stock interpole motors. By building commutating-pole machines with liberally designed magnetic circuits, however, much wider speed ranges are secured. Such motors, called *adjustable-speed motors*, may deliver full-load output at any speed between the highest and the lowest, the latter having ratios as high as 5:1. For example, with maximum excitation a speed of 400 rpm may be obtained, while by reducing the excitation to a low value the same output may be delivered at 2,000 rpm.

The kilowatt rating of an adjustable-speed motor is nearly constant, regardless of the field adjustment used. This means that the motor is capable of delivering approximately rated full-load output at any speed between its highest and lowest without exceeding rated armature current. The reason for this becomes apparent from the following argument: The output of the motor is equal to a constant times the product of torque and speed $(P = kTS)$. The torque, however, is proportional to the product of armature current and flux $(T = k_1\phi I_a)$, so the output may

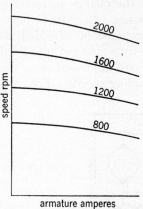

be expressed in terms of flux, armature current, and speed as $P = k_2\phi I_a S$. When the speed is changed by changing the field excitation (thus changing the flux), speed and flux are inversely proportional to each other. The speed is increased in the same ratio as the flux is decreased, and the product of speed and flux is a constant $(S\phi = k_3)$. The constant k_3 may therefore be substituted for $S\phi$ in the expression for power to obtain $P = k_4 I_a$ (approximately). Thus the output of an adjustable-speed motor is proportional to the armature current alone and is independent of speed and excitation. At the lower speeds there is an increase in the field loss owing to the larger field current used, and at the same time the fanning action of the armature is reduced. Both these factors tend to set a somewhat

Fig. 15-14. Speed-load curves of an adjustable-speed shunt motor for four different constant excitations.

lower permissible output limit for the motor at low speeds.

It should also be noted that for any particular adjustment of field excitation the speed remains nearly constant over the entire range from full load to no load, as in any other shunt motor. Thus the speed regulation is good. This is illustrated by the curves of Fig. 15-14. The percentage change in speed accompanying a given change in load is somewhat larger when the motor is adjusted to run at low speed than it is when the speed is high. When the motor is loaded, armature reaction weakens the field, but a given demagnetizing mmf produces a greater percentage change in the flux of a weak field than it does in the flux of a strong field. Accordingly, when the speed is high and the field is weak, armature reaction tends to hold up the speed better under heavy loads than when the speed is low and the field is strong.

The lowest limit of speed is determined by the field excitation which saturates the magnetic circuit. The latter must therefore be designed to carry the large flux corresponding to this speed. For this reason, motors with wide speed adjustments are somewhat larger than stock motors of the same rating and hence are also more costly. The highest practical speed is usually determined by the fact that, when the air-gap flux is reduced beyond a certain minimum value, commutation becomes unsatisfactory. The brushes spark badly. This is due both to the high rate of reversal of the current in the coils undergoing commutation and to the distortion of the main field due to armature reaction.

Non-commutating-pole motors have a relatively narrow range of speed adjustment. In these motors, good commutation demands that the field strength in the commutating zone be maintained at a value which brings about the reversal of current in the short-circuited coil without sparking. When the field is considerably weakened to secure speed adjustment, however, armature reaction acts to reduce the field strength in the commutating zone under load and sparkless commutation becomes impossible.

Problems

1-14. A six-pole lap-wound motor has 432 conductors. The effective armature diameter (the diameter taken to the mid-point of the slots) is 15 in., and the active length of the armature is 4 in. The pole pieces cover 70 per cent of the armature surface and the air-gap flux density is 55,000 lines per square inch. Determine (a) the force in pounds acting on a conductor lying under the poles, (b) the torque in pound-feet when the input to the armature is 240 amp.

2-14. The machine described in Prob. 1-13 is used as a motor. A potential difference of 120 volts is impressed across the terminals; the field flux is adjusted to the value given in Prob. 1-13; and the motor is loaded until the current input to the armature is 40 amp. The resistance of the armature circuit is 0.20 ohm. Determine (a) the counter emf of the motor, (b) the speed, (c) the mechanical power developed by the armature, (d) the power lost in the resistance of the armature circuit.

3-14. If the field resistance is held constant while the terminal voltage impressed on the motor in Prob. 2-14 is increased by 10 per cent, what are (a) the counter emf, (b) the speed, (c) the mechanical power developed by the armature when the armature current is 40 amp? Assume the saturation curve of the motor to be a straight line. (d) What will be the speed when the armature current is reduced to 5 amp?

4-14. A four-pole d-c motor has a wave-wound armature of 256 conductors. The axial length of the pole faces is 4.5 in., and the average distance of the center of the armature conductors from the center of the shaft is 3 in. The armature input current at rated load is 40 amp, and the average flux density in the air gap is 50,000 lines per square inch. If 0.65 of the armature periphery is covered by the pole faces, find (a) the average tangential force in pounds on each armature conductor at rated load, (b) the torque of the motor in pound-feet at rated load, (c) the speed of the armature when the applied potential difference is 125 volts. (The armature resistance is 0.20 ohm.)

5-14. A 70-hp 440-volt shunt motor has a rated current of 135 amp, an armature resistance of 0.18 ohm, and a field resistance of 330 ohms. The motor is required to develop 150 per cent of full-load torque at starting. Determine the total resistance that a suitable starting controller must have on the first step.

6-14. The rated current of an 80-hp 550-volt series motor is 122 amp, the armature resistance is 0.26 ohm, and the field resistance 0.12 ohm. Find the total resistance required on the first step of a controller to give (a) full-load torque, (b) 150 per cent full-load torque. Assume the saturation curve to be a straight line and the armature reaction to be negligible.

7-14. The full-load rated input current of a 20-hp 220-volt shunt motor is 77.5 amp. The resistance of the armature circuit is 0.22 ohm, while the shunt-field resistance is 88 ohms. The motor is started with a four-point starting box similar to the one in Fig. 9-14. The starting operation is assumed to proceed as follows: At the instant the starting lever first makes contact with any button of the starting box, sufficient resistance is included in the rheostat to limit the current to 1½ times full-load value. Contact with each step is maintained only long enough to permit the motor to speed up sufficiently to reduce the current to full-load value. At the instant full-load current is reached the lever is moved forward to the next step of the rheostat. Determine (a) the number of steps, and (b) the resistance between adjacent contacts of the starting rheostat.

8-14. At rated full load a 50-hp 440-volt series motor takes 98 amp from the line and runs at a speed of 450 rpm. The armature resistance, including brushes, is 0.17 ohm, while the series-field resistance is 0.12 ohm. Determine the speed of the motor (a) when the current is 145 amp, (b) when the current is 50 amp. (c) What is the armature current when the speed is 1,100 rpm? Disregard the armature reaction and assume that the saturation curve is a straight line.

9-14. At full load the pulley torque of the motor in Prob. 8-14 is 92 per cent of the electromagnetic torque developed by the armature. Compute the electromagnetic torque and the mechanical power developed by the armature for the conditions of operation specified in (a), (b), and (c) of Prob. 8-14.

10-14. The resistance of the armature (including brushes) of a 10-hp 120-volt shunt motor is 0.11 ohm. The rated full-load input current is 71.5 amp, and the normal field current is 1.8 amp. When the motor is run without load with a field excitation of 1.8 amp, the input current is 5.1 amp and the speed is 1,250 rpm. Disregarding armature reaction, find (a) the speed when the excitation is 1.8 amp and the motor draws rated full-load current, (b) the speed regulation. (c) If armature reaction has the effect of reducing the air-gap flux at full load by 2.5 per cent of the no-load value, what will then be the full-load speed?

11-14. The machine in Prob. 10-14 is supplied with a series-field winding (long shunt) that balances out the effect of armature reaction and, in addition, increases the flux at full load to a value 8 per cent in excess of the no-load value. The resistance of the series field is 0.01 ohm. Assume the shunt-field current is held at 1.8 amp and that the saturation curve is a straight line. When the input current is 71.5 amp, what are (a) the counter emf and (b) the speed? (c) Compare the torque developed by this motor with the torque developed in (c) of Prob. 10-14.

12-14. The motor of Prob. 10-14, when driven as a generator at 1,250 rpm and no load, has the saturation curve shown in Fig. A-13. Excitation of 100 per cent on this curve corresponds to 1.8 amp of field current, while 100 per cent voltage represents the no-load counter emf of the motor in Prob. 10-14. If the machine is operated as a motor from 120-volt mains, what is its speed (a) when the field resistance is 80 ohms and the input current is 70 amp, (b) when the field resistance is 100 ohms and the input current is 30 amp? Disregard armature reaction.

CHAPTER 15

LOSSES, EFFICIENCIES, AND RATINGS

The output of a generator or motor is always less than the input because some of the energy supplied is lost as heat. These losses raise the temperatures of the machine parts above that of the surrounding air until such temperatures are reached that the heat losses are radiated as fast as they are generated. Certain of the losses depend upon the load. The temperature rise therefore depends upon the load also, and the maximum allowable temperature rise determines the maximum permissible load that the machine may carry. The limit of output occurs at the load for which the temperature rise becomes high enough to endanger the insulation of the windings.

Copper Losses. When an electric current of I amp flows in a resistance of R ohms, heat energy is lost at the rate of RI^2 joules/sec, and the power loss is RI^2 watts. Generators and motors have one or more field circuits and an armature circuit in which such losses occur. All resistance losses of this kind are classed as *copper losses*.

1. *Armature Copper Loss.* The armature circuit is made up of the armature winding itself, the brushes, the brush contacts, and the commutator bars under the brushes. The losses in this circuit may be computed when the resistance of the circuit is known. The resistance may be measured with the use of a low-reading voltmeter and an ammeter capable of carrying the rated armature current of the machine. Circuit connections of Fig. 1-15 are used. The field is unexcited and the armature is blocked to keep it from turning.[1] The current in the armature circuit is adjusted to a suitable value by means of an auxiliary resistance connected in series with the circuit. Several readings are taken with the armature in slightly different positions, and the values of resistance computed from these readings are averaged. The brush-contact resistance depends somewhat upon the current. When measuring the armature resistance it is therefore desirable to use a current corresponding, approximately, to the normal working current. If R_a is the average

---

[1] Even though the field is unexcited, a small torque is developed by the reaction of armature current with the residual magnetism of the field poles.

value of the armature resistance measured as above described, the armature copper loss for any current I_a may then be computed from the relation

$$P_a = I_a{}^2 R_a \qquad \text{watts} \qquad (1\text{-}15)$$

2. *Copper Loss in Series and Commutating-pole Field Windings.* The resistance of the series field circuit may be measured with the aid of a low-

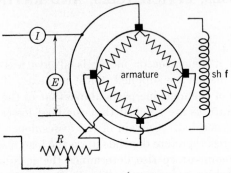

FIG. 1-15. Circuit connections for measuring armature resistance.

reading voltmeter and an ammeter and the wiring diagram shown in Fig. 2-15. The measured resistance of the series-field winding (equal to the impressed voltage divided by the current) includes the resistance of the diverter. If R_{se} is the resistance of the series field and the diverter

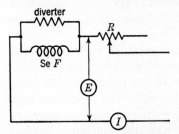

Fig. 2-15. Circuit connections for measuring series-field resistance.

in parallel, while I_{se} is the current in the series field plus that in the diverter, the series-field copper loss is

$$P_{se} = I_{se}{}^2 R_{se} \qquad \text{watts} \qquad (2\text{-}15)$$

The series-field current I_{se} is equal to the armature current when the machine is plain series connected, or when the machine is compound wound and the long-shunt connection is used. When the short-shunt connection is used, the current in the series-field winding is equal to the armature current plus the shunt-field current in a motor and to the armature current less the field current in a generator.

The resistance of the commutating-pole winding may be measured in a manner similar to that described for the series field, and its copper loss may then be computed from an equation similar to Eq. (2-15). The current in the commutating-field winding is the same as the armature current. The armature winding, brushes, and the commutating-field winding are connected in series. Because of this fact, the measured armature resistance usually includes the resistance of brushes and brush contacts and the resistance of the commutating-pole winding as well as the resistance of the armature winding itself.

3. *Shunt-field Copper Loss.* The copper loss in the shunt-field circuit is

$$P_{sh} = E_t I_{sh} = I_{sh}^2 R_{sh} \tag{3-15}$$

where I_{sh} = shunt-field current

R_{sh} = resistance of shunt-field circuit

R_{sh} should include as much of the resistance of the series-connected rheostat as is required to bring the field excitation to the correct value (Fig. 3-15).

Iron Losses. When iron or other magnetic material is subject to the influence of a magnetic field of varying strength, heat is developed therein. The energy that is converted to heat in this way is called *iron loss* or *core loss*.

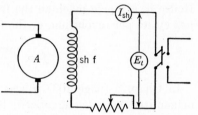

FIG. 3-15. Circuit connections for measuring shunt-field resistance.

1. *Hysteresis Loss.* The armature core of a d-c motor or generator revolves in the magnetic field set up by the field poles. The magnetic circuit is completed through the iron of the core, as shown in Fig. 4-15.

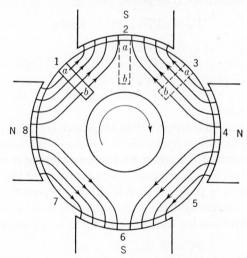

FIG. 4-15. The production of hysteresis loss in the armature core.

Accordingly, the flux through any particular section of the core changes in amount and direction from instant to instant as the armature revolves.

Consider a section of the armature iron indicated by *ab* in Fig. 4-15. In position 1, the flux crosses the section at right angles to the axis *ab* from left to right. When position 2 is reached, flux passes through the section from *b* toward *a*, forming a north pole at *a* and a south pole at *b*. In position 3, the section is again magnetized crosswise, but this time from right to left. In position 4, flux passes through the section parallel to *ab* but in the direction from *a* to *b*, forming a south pole at *a* and a north pole at *b*. By tracing the changes in direction of flux for the remaining positions, one observes that the conditions of magnetization are similar at 1 and 5, 2 and 6, 3 and 7, and 4 and 8. The section passes through one complete cycle of magnetization for each pair of poles. Hence in a *p*-pole machine the frequency of the cyclic change in flux is $p/2$ cycles per revolution, or the frequency is

$$f = \frac{\text{rpm}}{60} \times \frac{p}{2} \qquad \text{cps}$$

In Chap. 8 (page 103) it was shown that, when iron is periodically magnetized and demagnetized, it becomes heated owing to what one may think of as the work done in overcoming the frictional forces between molecules. The continual shifting of the molecular magnets is brought about by the expenditure of energy which appears as heat in the iron. The energy required per cycle of magnetization is proportional to the area of the hysteresis loop and the volume of iron affected, while the rate of energy expenditure (the power lost) is

$$P_h = \eta V f B_{\text{max}}^{1.6} \qquad \text{watts}$$

where f = frequency of cyclic variation

B_{max} = maximum flux density to which iron is subjected

V = volume of iron, cu cm

η = constant the value of which depends upon the quality of iron in the core

It should be noted that frequency in the above equation is proportional to the speed and, for any given machine, volume V is a constant. Therefore *the only two factors that affect the hysteresis loss of a machine are the speed and the flux density in the iron*. The influence of the flux density is the more important of these because it enters the equation to the power 1.6. When the volume and the constant η are combined into a single constant, the expression for hysteresis loss becomes (see page 104)

$$P_h = k_h f B_{\text{max}}^{1.6} \qquad \text{watts} \qquad (4\text{-}15)$$

In the current discussion Eq. (4-15) is included only to indicate the variables that affect the hysteresis loss. This equation is not suitable for computing the hysteresis loss in the armature core because the maximum flux density (in strip *ab* of Fig. 4-15, position 2, for example) is obviously not constant throughout the length *ab*.

While most of the hysteresis loss is developed in the armature core and in the teeth, there is some loss in the pole faces due to the changing flux density caused by the passage of the armature teeth under the pole tips. Armature reaction influences the hysteresis loss only to the extent that it is a factor in determining the magnitude and distribution of flux density in the armature core.

2. *Eddy-current Loss.* Voltage is generated in a conductor which cuts a magnetic field, and if the conductor is part of a closed circuit, an electric current flows.

The steel core of a d-c or a-c generator or motor cuts the flux from the field poles when the rotor revolves, and a voltage is thereby generated in the core in the same direction as the voltages generated in the copper conductors of the adjacent slots. Since steel is an electric conductor, the emfs generated in the core cause currents to circulate in the steel in the manner described on page 89. These currents flow in the resistances of their respective paths and give rise to heat loss ($\Sigma i^2 r$), which is called *eddy-current loss.*

The voltage generated in any eddy-current path is proportional to the length of the conductor that does the cutting (the thickness of a core lamina), to the velocity of motion (or the frequency), and to the maximum flux density of the field. The voltage generated in the path of an eddy may therefore be expressed as the product of these factors and a constant, or

$$e = k_1 t f B_{max} \qquad \text{volts}$$

If r is the resistance of the path over which an eddy flows, the power lost as heat in the eddy is

$$p_\epsilon = \frac{e^2}{r} = k_1 t^2 f^2 B_{max}^2 \qquad \text{watts}$$

The total power lost as heat in the core is evidently proportional to the volume of the core, but since the volume of the core is a constant for any particular machine, the volume may be included in the constant term and the eddy-current loss in the core may be expressed as

$$P_\epsilon = k_\epsilon t^2 f^2 B_{max}^2 \qquad \text{watts} \qquad (5\text{-}15)$$

The constant k_ϵ includes one factor which depends upon the units used and another which is inversely proportional to the resistivity of the core material.

From the above equation it is clear that *in a given machine the eddy-current loss depends only upon the speed and the flux density, and that it varies as the square of each of these factors.*

If a solid armature core were used the eddy-current loss would be so large, and the efficiency of the machine so low, that the device would be commercially impractical. In practice the losses are kept to a low value by using a core built up of thin sheets or laminations of steel (see page 90), which are insulated from each other by a coating of shellac, water-glass, etc. This limits the length of the path [t in Eq. (5-15)] to a low value and thereby greatly reduces the loss. The losses are further reduced by using an electrical steel with high permeability and high electrical resistivity. High permeability decreases the volume, and high resistivity decreases the amount of the eddy currents in a given path. Both serve to reduce the loss.

Some eddy currents are induced in the pole faces as well as in the armature core. These are generated by the tufts of flux entering the teeth as they sweep across the pole faces. In order to keep these losses down to a low value, the pole faces are also made of laminated steel.

Friction Losses. When a machine is running, there are various frictional forces to be overcome, each of which requires a continuous expenditure of energy and results in heating the rubbed parts. There is friction loss in the machine bearings, at the surface of the commutator due to the rubbing of the brushes, and in the armature core due to its fanning action. *These losses depend upon the speed* but are independent of the load on the machine. They are difficult to estimate by direct calculation but may be found by measurement.

Losses Summarized. The following summary of losses will be found convenient:

$$
\text{Losses}\begin{cases}
\text{Electrical}\\
\text{(copper loss)}\end{cases}
\begin{cases}
\text{Armature} & = I_a{}^2 R_a\\
\text{Series field} & = I_{se}{}^2 R_{se}\\
\text{Commutating field} = I_c{}^2 R_c\\
\text{Shunt field} & = E_t I_{sh}
\end{cases}
$$

$$
\begin{cases}
\text{Mechanical}\\
\text{(stray-power loss)}\end{cases}
\begin{cases}
\text{Core loss}\begin{cases}\text{Hysteresis}\\ \text{Eddy currents}\end{cases}\\
\\
\text{Friction}\begin{cases}\text{Bearings}\\ \text{Brushes}\\ \text{Windage}\end{cases}
\end{cases}
$$

The core losses and friction losses are supplied from the mechanical power developed by the machine. They are put into a single group called *mechanical losses* or, more generally, *stray-power losses*. When a generator or motor runs at a fixed speed and generates a given voltage, the stray-power loss is constant regardless of the electrical output or input of the machine, for *speed and flux density are the only two factors that influence the stray-power loss.*

The *electrical losses* are supplied from the electrical power generated by or delivered to the machine, as the case may be. Of these, the shunt-field loss is somewhat, though not entirely, independent of the load, while the remaining electrical losses are nearly proportional to the square of the load current.

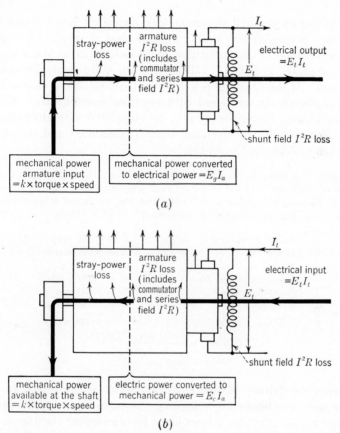

FIG. 5-15. (a) Flow of power through a generator. (b) Flow of power through a motor.

Figures 5-15(a) and 5-15(b) help to picture the energy transformations that take place in generators and motors.

Efficiency. The efficiency of a machine, expressed in percentage, is 100 times the ratio of output to input. This ratio may be found by direct measurement of output and input, by measuring the output and the losses, or by measuring the input and the losses. The following equations correspond to these alternate methods of measuring efficiency:

$$\text{Percentage efficiency} = 100 \frac{\text{output}}{\text{input}} \qquad (6\text{-}15)$$

$$= 100 \frac{\text{output}}{\text{output} + \text{losses}} \qquad (7\text{-}15)$$

$$= 100 \frac{\text{input} - \text{losses}}{\text{input}} \qquad (8\text{-}15)$$

The efficiencies of small motors may be measured directly with the use of a brake to furnish the load. This method is impractical for large machines because of the difficulty of absorbing in a brake the large amount of power involved. Efficiencies are quite generally computed from losses. If the machine is a generator, its electrical output may be easily and accurately measured with electrical instruments. When the losses are known, the efficiency may be computed with the help of Eq. (7-15). For motors, the electrical input is measured and the efficiency is then computed from Eq. (8-15).

Example 1. A 120-volt shunt motor draws 81.7 amp from 120-volt mains. The resistance of armature and commutating-field windings connected in series is 0.10 ohm. The shunt-field current is 1.7 amp and the measured stray-power loss is 480 watts. What is the efficiency of the motor?

$$
\begin{aligned}
\text{Armature current} &= 81.7 - 1.7 = 80 \text{ amp} \\
\text{Motor input} &= 120 \times 81.7 = 9{,}804 \text{ watts}
\end{aligned}
$$

$$
\begin{aligned}
\text{Armature copper loss} &= 80^2 \times 0.10 = 640 \text{ watts} \\
\text{Shunt-field loss} &= 120 \times 1.7 = 204 \text{ watts} \\
\text{Stray-power loss} &= 480 \text{ watts} \\
\text{Total} &= 1{,}324 \text{ watts}
\end{aligned}
$$

$$\text{Efficiency} = \frac{100(9{,}804 - 1{,}324)}{9{,}804}$$

$$= 86.5 \text{ per cent}$$

Efficiency by Direct Measurements. Small motors may be tested with the use of a brake for absorbing the power developed. A prony brake and a pair of scales are required for measuring the torque. The speed is measured with a tachometer, and the electrical input is measured with the use of voltmeter and ammeter.

The prony brake (Fig. 6-15) is used with a hollow brake drum or pulley in which a small amount of water may be held. The energy absorbed by the brake drum is converted into heat, which evaporates the water and keeps the drum cool. The torque of the motor in pound-perpendicular-feet is the length of the lever arm in feet multiplied by the net scale reading F. The latter is the actual reading less the tare. The brake arm should be level so that the downward thrust F is normal to the scale platform.

The dead weight on the scales is found by loosening the brake bands and taking the average of the two scale readings obtained as follows: First, when the motor armature is turned by hand in a clockwise direction and second, when the armature is turned by hand in a counterclock-

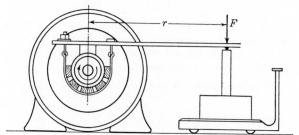

FIG. 6-15. Setup for prony-brake test of a motor.

wise direction. The first reading is the dead weight plus the friction on the brake, while the second is the dead weight less the friction. When the two readings are added and divided by 2, the friction of the drum is eliminated and the result obtained is the tare or zero reading F_0. Under load conditions the net load on the scales is then

$$F = \text{scale reading} - F_0 \quad \text{lb}$$

The electrical input in watts is the product of the impressed voltage E_t and the input current I_t (Fig. 7-15).
The output is obtained from the net scale reading in pounds, the length r of the lever arm in feet, and the measured speed S in revolutions per minute as follows: The torque or turning moment is Fr lb-perp-ft. The work done by the motor in one revolution is $2\pi Fr$ ft-lb, and the work done per minute is $2\pi FrS$ ft-lb. Since a machine that does work

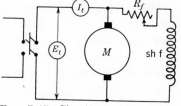

FIG. 7-15. Circuit connections for measuring motor input.

at the rate of 33,000 ft-lb per minute develops 1 hp, the output of the motor is

$$\begin{aligned}
\text{Output} &= \frac{2\pi FrS}{33,000} \\
&= 1.904 \times 10^{-4} Frs \quad \text{hp} \qquad (9\text{-}15) \\
&= \frac{2\pi FrS \times 746}{33,000} \quad \text{watts} \\
&= 1.42 \times 10^{-4} Frs \quad \text{kw} \qquad (10\text{-}15)
\end{aligned}$$

The kilowatt input is $E_t I_t \div 1{,}000$ and the efficiency is

$$\text{Efficiency} = \frac{100 \times 1.42 \times 10^{-4} Frs}{E_t I_t \times 10^{-3}}$$

$$= \frac{14.2 FrS}{E_t I_t} \quad \text{per cent} \tag{11-15}$$

Example 2.   A shunt motor tested by means of a prony brake yields the following data: impressed voltage 117 volts, input current (including input to the shunt field) 81.5 amp, speed 1,250 rpm, length of brake arm 2 ft 9 in, scale reading 20.4 lb, tare 3.5 lb.   Calculate the efficiency of the motor.

$$
\begin{aligned}
\text{Net load on scales} \;&=\; 20.4 - 3.5 = 16.9 \text{ lb.}\\
\text{Torque} \;&=\; 16.9 \times 2.75 = 46.47 \text{ lb-perp-ft}\\
\text{Horsepower output} \;&=\; \frac{2\pi ST}{33{,}000} = \frac{6.28 \times 1{,}250 \times 46.47}{33{,}000}\\
&=\; 11.05 \text{ hp}\\
\text{Kilowatt output} \;&=\; \frac{746 \times 11.05}{1{,}000} = 8.24 \text{ kw}\\
\text{Kilowatt input} \;&=\; 117 \times 81.5 \times 10^{-3} = 9.54 \text{ kw}\\
\text{Efficiency} \;&=\; \frac{8.24}{9.54} \times 100 = 86.4 \text{ per cent}
\end{aligned}
$$

It is usually inconvenient to obtain the efficiency of a generator by direct measurement.   A more convenient method to use is the loss method to be described in the following article.

Efficiency by Method of Losses.   The electrical losses of a generator or motor are computed from the measured resistances of the several electrical circuits and the currents in them.   The armature copper loss is $R_a I_a{}^2$; the series-field loss is $R_{se} I_{se}{}^2$; the shunt-field loss is $R_{sh} I_{sh}{}^2$; etc.

The stray-power loss cannot be calculated readily but must be measured experimentally.   This is easily done.   The stray-power loss depends only upon the speed and the air-gap flux, as has already been noted. These two factors, however, are precisely the variables that determine the generated emf of a generator or motor, for by Eq. (4-14),

$$E_g = \phi Z' S$$

where Z' = constant
ϕ = air-gap flux
S = speed

Therefore to duplicate the stray-power loss of either a generator or a motor for any given set of operating conditions, it is only necessary to make sure that the generated emf and the speed are the same for the two cases.[1]

---

[1] This statement is not exactly true, for it neglects the effect of field distortion caused by armature reaction.   On account of armature reaction, the flux distribution in the armature and pole cores is somewhat altered and core losses are increased.

To obtain the stray power of a generator or motor, the machine is run as a shunt motor without load. The input to the armature alone is measured by means of a voltmeter and an ammeter. Since there is no load on the motor, the output is zero and the entire armature input is converted into heat in the armature. The armature current required to run the motor without load is very small, and the armature I^2R loss is quite negligible. Except for this small amount, the entire armature input is stray-power loss. Suppose, for example, that to measure the stray-power loss of a certain 25-hp motor it is connected as in Fig. 8-15 and is run without load. The armature current read by the ammeter is 9.1 amp when the voltage impressed on the armature terminals is 115 volts. The armature resistance was previously measured and was found to be 0.023 ohm. The input to the armature is

$$EI_a = 115 \times 9.1 = 1,046 \text{ watts}$$

The armature copper loss is

$$I_a{}^2R_a = 9.1^2 \times 0.023 = 1.9 \text{ watts}$$

and the stray-power loss is

$$EI_a - I_a{}^2R_a = 1,044 \text{ watts}$$

Had the armature copper loss been neglected and the total armature input been taken as the stray-power loss, the error would have been only 0.2 per cent.

To illustrate the method further, let it be required to find the efficiency of a generator under the following conditions: A short-shunt compound generator is driven at a speed of 800 rpm and delivers 50 kw to the external circuit at a potential difference of 125 volts. The measured resistances of its several circuits are as follows:

1. Armature resistance, including brushes and commutating-pole winding, 0.021 ohm
2. Series-field resistance, including diverter, 0.002 ohm
3. Shunt-field resistance with rheostat, 24 ohms

In order to find the stray-power loss of the generator, its load is removed and it is run without load as a shunt motor, using the connections of Fig. 8-15. To duplicate the stray-power losses that were developed in the loaded generator, the generated emf and the speed must be duplicated.

These increased losses, together with certain other small "indeterminable" losses, are usually lumped under the head of *load losses* and are assumed to be 1 per cent of the output in large machines. In small machines (machines under 200 hp) these extra losses are neglected entirely in the computation of efficiency.

Line current (I_l) $= \dfrac{50,000}{125}$
$= 400$ amp

Series-field drop ($R_{se}I_l$) $= 400 \times 0.002$
$= 0.8$ volt

Shunt-field impressed voltage $= 125 + 0.8$
$= 125.8$ volts

Shunt-field current (I_f) $= \dfrac{125.8}{24}$
$= 5.23$ amp

Armature current (I_a) $= 400 + 5.23$
$= 405.2$ amp

Armature-resistance drop (R_aI_a) $= 405.2 \times 0.021$
$= 8.5$ volts

Generated voltage (E_g) $= 125.8 + 8.5$
$= 134.3$ volts

Since, when running light as a motor, the R_aI_a drop is negligible, the generated emf is duplicated by adjusting the resistance R in Fig. 8-15 to such a value that the voltmeter connected across the armature terminals reads 134.3 volts. The speed is next adjusted to 800 rpm by means of the rheostat in the shunt-field circuit. When the generated emf and the speed have both been properly adjusted, the

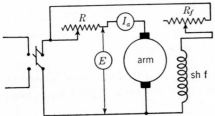

Fig. 8-15. Circuit connections for measuring stray-power losses.

stray-power loss has the correct value. The ammeter reading is found to be 16.2 amp. The efficiency of the generator under load may now be computed as follows:

Armature and commutating-field I^2R loss $= 405.2^2 \times 0.021$
$= 3,448$ watts

Series-field I^2R loss $= 400^2 \times 0.002$
$= 320$ watts

Shunt-field loss (E_fI_f) $= 125.8 \times 5.23$
$= 658$ watts

Stray-power loss $= 134.3 \times 16.2$ (very nearly)
$= 2,175$ watts

Total loss $= 6,600$ watts

Efficiency $= \dfrac{50,000 \times 100}{50,000 + 6,660}$
$= 88.3$ per cent

This method of obtaining the efficiency of a machine has several important advantages over the method of direct measurement:

1. Only a small amount of power is required to make the test.
2. It is applicable to large machines and small machines alike.
3. It has a higher degree of accuracy than the direct method.

A considerable percentage of error may be made in evaluating the stray-power loss, for example, without greatly affecting the accuracy of the computed efficiency, for this loss is itself only a small percentage of the total output of the machine. An error of similar magnitude made in the measurement of total input and output introduces a far greater error in the resultant efficiency computation.

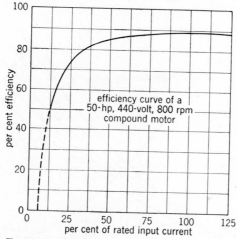

FIG. 9-15. Typical efficiency curve of a motor.

An objection to the method, especially for large machines, lies in the fact that certain "load losses" are absent when the machine is not loaded. These have already been referred to. They amount to about 1 per cent of the output.

A typical efficiency curve of a motor is shown in Fig. 9-15.

Calibrated or "Rated" Motor. It is sometimes desirable to use a shunt motor as a convenient means for measuring the amount of power required to drive another machine under each of a number of different conditions of operation. Obviously, when the motor is used to drive a machine, the input to the latter is the input to the motor armature less the armature losses. The armature losses consist of the I^2R losses of armature and brushes and the stray-power losses. These may be measured as already described, and by subtracting their total from the motor input when loaded, the output is found. A separate determination of losses is required for each load.

When the motor is used repeatedly for such measurements, the computations of output are greatly simplified by the use of a set of curves similar to those of Fig. 10-15 from which the stray-power losses and the armature and brush copper losses may be found for any condition of load, speed, and excitation. A motor for which these curves have been found is sometimes called a *calibrated* or *rated* motor.

To obtain the stray-power curves, the motor is connected as in Fig. 8-15 and is run without load. The field current is adjusted, by means of the shunt-field rheostat, to some suitable value and is then held constant at this value. The armature circuit resistance R is next adjusted

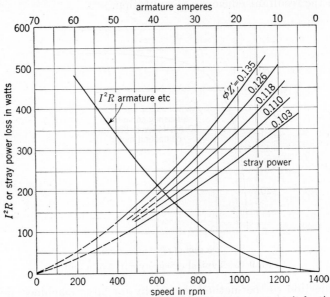

Fig. 10-15. Stray-power and I^2R loss curves for several constant induction factors ($\phi Z' = E_g/S$) vs. speed.

to give the highest probable working speed, and simultaneous readings of armature current, armature voltage, and speed are recorded. From these and the armature resistance the stray-power loss at this speed and excitation may be computed. A series of similar readings for the same excitation and different speeds covering the range from the highest to the lowest probable working speed yields one of the stray-power curves of the figure. Other similar curves are obtained by repeating the process for each of two or more additional values of field current. Three curves usually serve, although five are shown in the figure.

In taking the data of the preceding paragraph it is usually assumed that a constant field current results in a constant flux of excitation, since the effect of armature reaction is ordinarily negligible when running without load.   In plotting the data in the form of curves as in Fig. 10-15 the several curves taken at different values of field current are actually marked in terms of the equivalent flux in the machine $\phi Z'$.   The quantity $\phi Z'$ may readily be found from Eq. (4-14) as

$$\phi Z' = \frac{E_g}{S} = \frac{E_t - I_a R_a}{S} \qquad (12\text{-}15)$$

The actual stray-power losses under load may be found by calculating $\phi Z'$ for the given conditions and entering the proper curve of Fig. 10-15. The effects of armature reaction under load are *therefore* taken into account, which would not be the case if the curves of Fig. 10-15 were marked in terms of the running-light field current.

For convenience in quickly finding the armature output for any assumed condition of load, speed, and excitation, it is desirable to plot the I^2R loss curve for the armature and brushes on the same sheet with the stray-power losses as in Fig. 10-15.   The scales applying to the armature-loss curve are the upper and left-hand ones.

To illustrate the use of the curves, let it be assumed that when the motor is used to drive a machine, the input of which is desired, the armature voltage is 116 volts, the armature current is 50 amp, the armature resistance is 0.134 ohms, and the speed is 950 rpm.   From Eq. (12-15), $\phi Z'$ is 0.115, and from the curves, the stray-power loss is 307 watts and the armature copper loss is 335 watts, so the total armature loss is 642 watts.   The armature input is 116×50 or 5,800 watts; whence, subtracting losses, the output is

$$5{,}800 - 642 = 5{,}158 \text{ watts or } 6.92 \text{ hp}$$

Rating.   The *rating* of a machine is a somewhat arbitrarily specified safe operating limit for the machine, determined in accordance with certain accepted rules and standards applying to it.   It is intended to represent the operating limit which the machine cannot ordinarily exceed for a considerable length of time without in some way damaging it, or at least causing in it an accelerated rate of wear or depreciation in one or more of its parts.

Generators and motors, unless otherwise stated, are assumed to be rated for *continuous* service; that is, their specified loads may be carried for an unlimited period of time without exceeding the limits set by the rules.   Machines that operate on intermittent, varying, or periodic duty are given a *short-time* rating of 5, 10, 15, 30, 60, or 120 min.   A machine with such a rating is guaranteed to carry its rated load continuously for the specified time without exceeding the usual limits.

The principal factors affecting the ratings of motors and generators are heating and commutation. There is no definite maximum load that a machine can carry in the same sense that a 10-qt pail holds a definite amount of water and no more. A machine may exceed its rated load by 25 or 50 per cent, but if the excess load is carried for a considerable length of time, the temperature may rise to a value that causes permanent injury to the insulation. Furthermore, the commutator may spark excessively, and if permitted to continue for long, the burning of commutator and brushes may damage them and thereby shorten their lives as well as increase the cost of their maintenance.

Other factors which may influence rating are voltage regulation, in the case of a generator, and speed regulation, in the case of a motor. The full-load and no-load voltages of generators are usually specified. In the case of motors the specification of full-load and no-load speeds may also be required.

Heating. In the first few pages of this chapter the losses in electric machines were discussed. It was there shown that RI^2 losses are liberated in each of the electric circuits, that is, in the several field windings, in the armature windings, and in the commutator and brushes. In addition, the commutator and brushes, and to a lesser extent the bearings and the armature as a whole, develop friction losses, while the armature core and the pole faces liberate the energy developed by hysteresis and eddy currents. All these energy losses are converted into heat and must be radiated or be carried away by currents of air. In moderate- and large-size machines these losses, in the aggregate, are quite considerable. A 500-kw generator with an efficiency of 91 per cent has an input at full load of 500/0.91 or 550 kw. At full load the machine radiates heat at the rate of 50 kw. This is enough power to maintain two or three six-room houses at a comfortable temperature in winter weather.

Heat energy can flow away from the heated part only by reason of a difference in temperature between it and the surrounding medium. Accordingly, the temperature of a part where losses are liberated must rise until the rate of heat generation in it is equal to the rate at which it loses heat. There is a definite limit of temperature, however, which the armature and field windings of a machine will withstand without deterioration. In order that the maximum output may be secured without overheating, it is therefore necessary, first, that the losses be kept to a minimum and, second, that good facilities be provided for conducting the heat away. The armature and often the field coils are provided with air ducts through which cooling air is circulated by the fanning action of the armature. Large a-c machines are sometimes enclosed and provided with a forced ventilating system.

Ordinarily, however, machines are not enclosed but have free access to the air for cooling. Dirt and dust accumulating in the air ducts impair ventilation and may cause a machine to overheat, even although the rated load is not exceeded.

Altitude is another factor that affects the heating of a machine. The density of air decreases with increase of altitude. For this reason air at sea level is a better cooling medium than air at 3,000 ft elevation, and a machine that ordinarily carries its rated load without overheating may overheat at high altitude. Standard ratings apply to altitudes under 1,000 m (3,300 ft).

Allowable Temperature Rise of Insulation. Excessive temperatures impair and finally destroy the insulating properties of the materials used to insulate the windings and commutators of electric machines. The highest temperature at which an insulating material may be continuously operated without impairing or disqualifying it for continuous service, is taken as the *limiting temperature* for that particular material.

Five classes of insulation are recognized in the standards of the American Institute of Electrical Engineers as follows:

1. *Class O insulation*, consisting of cotton, silk, paper, and similar organic materials, neither impregnated with insulating compounds nor immersed in oil.

2. *Class A insulation*, consisting of cotton, silk, paper, and similar organic compounds when impregnated or immersed in oil; also enamel as applied to conductors.

3. *Class B insulation*, consisting of inorganic materials such as mica and asbestos in built-up forms, using organic binders to hold the parts together.

4. *Class H insulation*, consisting of inorganic materials such as mica and asbestos in built-up forms, using binders composed of silicone compounds.

5. *Class C insulation*, consisting entirely of mica, porcelain, glass, quartz, and similar inorganic materials.

As a result of extensive tests these classes of materials have been assigned the following "hot-spot" or limiting temperatures:

Class	Degrees centigrade
O	90
A	105
B	130
H	180
C	No limit selected

This means that in practice the actual temperature of the insulation shall not exceed the values given in the table.

The temperature measured on the surface of the armature or on the surface of a field spool is somewhat lower than that actually experienced by the embedded conductors. To correct for this difference a "conventional allowance" of 15 C is made. The temperature of "ambient" or surrounding air is taken as standard at 40 C. Hence, when Class A material is used for the insulation of an armature winding, for example, assuming the room temperature at 40 C, the maximum allowable temperature rise for the armature, as measured by thermometer, is 105 − (15 + 40) or 50 C. The commutator, on the other hand, is heated by friction loss liberated as heat on the surface. Its surface temperature is therefore the maximum allowable for the insulation. Hence for class A insulation the temperature rise of the commutator is 105 − 40 or 65 C.

The allowable temperature depends also upon the construction of the machine, whether open or enclosed, etc. The temperature limits for the several parts of d-c motors and generators of various types of construction and insulation are found in the standards of the American Institute of Electrical Engineers, already referred to.

An indication of the temperature of a machine may be obtained with the use of thermocouples or resistances. Large modern machines have thermocouples (or resistances) permanently built into their windings at various places where a knowledge of the temperature is desired. When thermocouples are used, their terminals are connected through a suitable switching device to the terminals of a millivoltmeter mounted on the switchboard. An indication of the temperature of the several parts of a machine may thus be obtained at any time and overheating can readily be avoided. When resistances are used (resistance thermometers), an indication of the temperature of a part of the machine is obtained by comparing the resistance of a resistance element at some known temperature (taken as base) with the resistance of the same element measured while the machine is running. The difference between these two values of resistance is a measure of the temperature rise. Resistance thermometers may be provided with a recording device or they may be of the indicating type. The former give a permanent record of temperature taken at stated intervals of time, while the latter indicate the temperature existing at the moment without recording it.

Silicone Resins as Insulating Compounds. The limiting hot-spot temperature of class H insulation given in the table is a tentative value selected by the American Institute of Electrical Engineers and is subject to revision upward or downward as future experience may indicate. The silicone resins and other silicone compounds are relative newcomers to the field of electrical insulation. Their excellent thermal properties have made possible much higher operating temperatures than were allowable with the organic binders previously available. The use of silicones makes it possible for the manufacturer to reduce the size, weight, and cost of equipment by operating at a higher temperature rise, or alternately to operate at a higher ambient temperature with conventional construction.

Problems

1-15. A 25-kw 230-volt shunt generator runs at a speed of 1,000 rpm. The hysteresis and eddy-current losses are measured at this speed when the field excitation is 1.9 amp. The hysteresis loss is found to be 757 watts, while the eddy-current loss is 450 watts. If the field excitation remains unchanged, what are the hysteresis and eddy-current losses when the speed is (a) 1,250 rpm, (b) 800 rpm?

2-15. Determine the hysteresis and eddy-current losses of the machine in Prob. 1-15 under each of the following conditions: (a) speed 1,250 rpm, field excitation 1.5 amp; (b) speed 800 rpm, field excitation 2.2 amp. Assume the air-gap flux to be directly proportional to the field current.

3-15. The saturation curve of the generator in Prob. 1-15 is the curve of Fig. A-13. On this curve 100 per cent voltage and 100 per cent excitation are 230 volts and 1.9 amp, respectively. Determine the hysteresis and eddy-current losses for the following conditions: (a) excitation 50 per cent and speed 900 rpm, (b) excitation 120 per cent and speed 1,200 rpm, (c) excitation 2.2 amp and speed 800 rpm. Compare the results obtained in (c) with those found in (b) of Prob. 2-15.

4-15. When a certain 900 rpm 220-volt shunt motor delivers its rated output at rated speed and voltage, it draws 288 amp from the line. The resistance of the armature circuit, including brushes and interpole windings, was measured with rated current and found to be 0.047 ohm. The resistance of the field winding is 41.5 ohms. The stray-power losses measured at rated speed and with an excitation that would cause a voltage to be generated equal to the counter emf at rated load were found to be 2,450 watts. Determine (a) the horsepower output of the motor, (b) the torque developed at the pulley, (c) the electromagnetic torque developed by the armature, (d) the percentage efficiency.

5-15. A 200-kw, 250-volt generator is driven at 850 rpm and delivers 800 amp to the line. The total losses are 20.80 kw. Find (a) the horsepower input, (b) the driving torque in pound-feet, (c) the percentage efficiency.

6-15. The following test data apply to a 250-kw 500-volt long-shunt compound generator operating at rated load and speed:

Terminal voltage...	550
Current output, amp....................................	455
Shunt field, amp...	4.3
Resistance of armature, series-field, and interpole windings, ohms...	0.04
Brush drop, volts..	1.9
Iron loss, kw...	5.32
Windage and friction, kw................................	2.85

(a) Assuming terminal voltage constant, calculate the efficiency at the following percentages of rated load: 50, 75, 100, 125. (b) Determine the output at the point of maximum efficiency.

7-15. A 30-hp 120-volt shunt motor draws 212 amp from the line when it delivers rated load at rated speed. The resistance of the armature circuit (including brushes and interpole winding) is 0.038 ohm, while the field resistance is 48 ohms. When the motor is run at rated speed without load, the field resistance remaining unchanged, it draws only 12.6 amp from the line. Compute the stray-power loss of the machine

(a) when running light, as above, (b) at full-load output. (c) Determine the motor efficiency at full load.

8-15. The armature resistance of a 115-volt shunt motor is 0.028 ohm. The resistance of the shunt-field circuit is 29.7 ohms and the stray-power loss is 1,385 watts (assume constant at all loads). Compute the efficiency of the motor for each of the following armature currents: 280, 224, 170, 112 amp. •

9-15. The stray-power loss of a 7½-hp, 120-volt, 1,250-rpm, shunt motor is 425 watts when the motor delivers rated output at rated speed. The resistance of the armature circuit including brushes and interpole windings, is 0.205 ohm. The shunt-field resistance is 89 ohms. For conditions of rated load, voltage and speed find (a) the pulley torque developed, (b) the electromagnetic torque, (c) the motor input, (d) the efficiency.

10-15. The combined resistance of the series-field and armature circuit of an 80-hp 550-volt series motor is 0.24 ohm. When the motor delivers its rated output, the speed is 390 rpm and the stray-power loss is 4,300 watts. Assume the stray-power loss to vary directly with the counter emf and the air-gap flux to vary directly with the load current. Find the motor speed and per cent efficiency for each of the following input currents: 150, 125, 100, 75, and 50 amp.

11-15. A prony-brake test of a motor yields the following readings: terminal potential difference, 125 volts; input current, 220 amp; speed, 1,020 rpm, horizontal length of brake arm from center of shaft to bearing point on scale, 3 ft; scale reading, 54.9 lb. Determine (a) the horsepower output, (b) the kilowatt input, (c) the losses, (d) the efficiency.

CHAPTER 16

ELECTROLYTIC CONDUCTION AND BATTERIES

Types of Conductors. Conductors of electricity may be divided into two general classes, namely:

1. Conductors that are unaffected by the passage of a current through them

2. Conductors that undergo decomposition when electric currents are passed through them

The first of these classes includes the metals, their alloys, and certain other substances like carbon. The laws governing the conduction of electricity through these have already been discussed. The second class includes acids, bases, salt solutions, and fused salts. Conduction through fused salts forms the basis of a number of important electrochemical industries, including the production of aluminum, caustic soda, etc. A discussion of these cannot be given in the limited space here available. Electrical conduction through aqueous solutions of acids, bases, and salts will be considered briefly, however, for this type of conduction is responsible for the electric battery.

Dissociation. Pure water is a good insulator. When a small quantity of an acid, a base, or a salt is added to water, however, it becomes a fairly good conductor. When the added salt, acid, or base goes into solution, it is *dissociated* into separate particles called *ions*. Ions are made up of atoms or groups of atoms but differ from them in that they are electrically charged. When sodium chloride (common salt) is dissolved in water, some of the salt molecules are dissociated into positively charged ions of sodium (Na^+) and negatively charged ions of chlorine (Cl^-). Water has a very high dissociating power. Certain other solvents exhibit the same power but to a much lesser degree. Most acids and bases are dissociated in water, the degree of dissociation being generally dependent upon the strength of the acid or base.

Electrolysis. An acid, base, or salt solution (usually in water) of the kind just described is called an *electrolyte*. When two similar electrodes (Fig. 1-16) are dipped in an electrolyte and a potential difference is impressed on them, current passes through the electrolyte, entering at one terminal, called the *anode*, and leaving at the other, called the *cathode*.

245

The anode is positive (or $+$) with respect to both solution and cathode, while the cathode is negative (or $-$) with respect to the solution and anode. If the electrolyte is a salt solution in water, the negatively charged ions (Cl^-) are attracted by and move up to the anode, while the

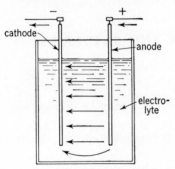

FIG. 1-16. Electrolysis.

positively charged ions (Na^+) move up to the cathode or negative terminal. At the electrodes the charges on the ions are neutralized by the opposite charges of the electrodes and the ions are reduced to the atoms of their respective substances. This process of the decomposition of a solution by the action of an electric current is called *electrolysis*.

The atoms formed at the electrodes are chemically very active and may combine with the electrodes, with the solution, or with any other available substance. If the electrodes and the solution are of such natures that combination cannot take place, then the free substances are liberated. When platinum electrodes are used in the electrolysis of sodium chloride, for example, chlorine gas is liberated at the positive terminal or anode, while at the cathode the sodium first set free immediately reacts with the solution and liberates free hydrogen.

Electromotive Force of Chemical Action. When two dissimilar metals (like copper and zinc) are dipped in a dilute solution of an acid (like sulfuric), a difference of potential is found to exist between them, and if the metals are electrically connected with a piece of copper wire, a current will flow in the circuit (Fig. 2-16). The zinc is gradually eaten away or dissolved in the solution, while at the copper terminal hydrogen gas collects in bubbles and finally breaks away and rises in the air. Any two other dissimilar metals would have shown similar results, except that the potential difference between

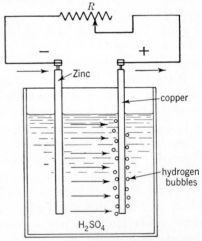

FIG. 2-16. The emf of a cell consisting of zinc and copper electrodes in sulfuric acid.

them, and hence the current flowing, would have been somewhat different in magnitude.

The above phenomenon is the basis for all *primary batteries*. Every metal has a certain *electrolytic solution pressure,* or tendency to go into solution, the measure of which is the emf existing between it and the solution. The potential difference between two dissimilar metals dipped in an electrolyte is a measure of the difference of their electrolytic solution pressures. The various metals and other elements together with their respective potentials with respect to hydrogen taken as zero are shown in Table IV.

TABLE IV. POTENTIALS

Element	Potential against hydrogen electrode, volts
Manganese	+1.075
Zinc	+0.770
Cadmium	+0.420
Iron	+0.344
Cobalt	+0.232
Lead	+0.151
Hydrogen	0.000
Copper	−0.329
Mercury	−0.753
Silver	−0.771
Bromine	−0.993
Chlorine	−1.353

PRIMARY BATTERIES

Primary Cell. A *primary cell* or *battery* is a device working on the principle discussed in the foregoing paragraphs, and used to convert chemical energy into electrical energy. Many types of primary batteries have been used, but few of them survive commercially today. With the present-day wide distribution of electric power and the ease with which direct current for charging storage batteries may be obtained, primary cells have lost their commercial importance. Furthermore, because of the high unit cost of the energy obtained from primary batteries, their use is uneconomical in any application requiring more than a very small amount of power.

To illustrate the general principles of their operation, however, one type will be briefly described. The electrolyte is of dilute sulfuric acid and the electrodes are of copper and zinc as before (Fig. 2-16). Zinc is dissolved because it has a greater tendency than copper to go into solution. It appears in the solution as positive zinc ions, thus leaving the zinc electrode negative. The zinc ions displace some of the hydrogen ions that were originally present in the solution. An electrically equivalent number of hydrogen ions give up their positive charges to the copper plate, thus making it positive. Freed of their charges, the hydrogen ions become free hydrogen atoms, which cling to the copper plate as bubbles.

As the action progresses, the solution adjacent to the copper electrode becomes saturated with hydrogen, which then slowly rises from the plate.

Polarization.   The cell just described is impractical because

1. The hydrogen coating on the copper plate in effect shields the copper electrode and converts it into ions of hydrogen, thereby reducing the effective potential difference between the cell terminals.   This action is known as *polarization*.

2. The hydrogen coating has a high resistance, which greatly increases the internal voltage drop of the cell, reduces its current output, and lowers its efficiency.

To make the cell a practical device, polarization must be either greatly reduced or entirely prevented.   Polarization may be prevented by putting the zinc electrode in a solution of zinc sulfate or dilute sulfuric acid, and the copper electrode in a solution of copper sulfate.   The two solutions are kept separate either by gravity or by means of a porous cup. Then, when the circuit is closed, zinc goes into solution and an electrically equivalent amount of copper is deposited on the copper terminal and polarization is prevented.   This cell, known as *Daniell's cell*, was once much used in telegraphy.

Dry Cell.   The so-called "dry cell" is the most important form of primary battery in use today.   It has the advantage of cheapness, portability, and convenience.   Its many uses in the operation of radio circuits, flashlights, doorbells, ignition circuits, etc., are familiar to all.

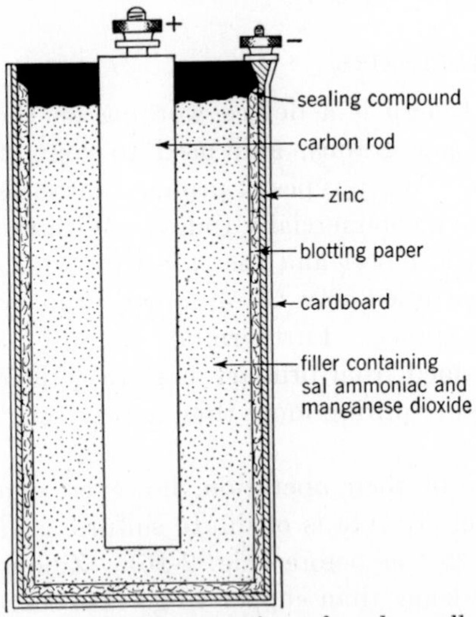

FIG. 3-16. Cross section of a dry cell.

The negative terminal (Fig. 3-16) is a zinc cup, lined with blotting paper to hold moisture.   The positive terminal is a carbon rod, supported in the center of the cup by means of a paste consisting principally of a mixture of ammonium chloride, the electrolyte, manganese dioxide, the depolarizing agent, and powdered carbon, which serves to render the paste more conducting. The manganese dioxide serves to oxidize to water the hydrogen that would otherwise be liberated at the positive terminal.   Manganese dioxide is a poor electrical conductor, however; hence the powdered carbon is added to lower the resistance of the cell.

The "dry battery" is in reality not dry at all, but only relatively so, as may be seen from the above. To prevent drying out, the cell is sealed at the top with some kind of hard wax.

The emf of a dry cell when new is about 1.5 volts. After a time, independent of use, the voltage drops to about 1.4 volts. Dry cells deteriorate with age, and unused batteries are quite worthless when a year and a half old. A new battery, when short-circuited through an ammeter, should deliver from 15 to 20 or 25 amp.

Faraday's Law. The underlying law upon which the action of batteries depends was discovered by Faraday in 1834. Faraday found that, when a current flows through an electrolyte, the amount of chemical action that takes place in a given time is proportional to the total quantity Q of electricity passed. Thus in a primary cell with zinc and copper electrodes, the amount of zinc used up (assuming no secondary reactions) is proportional to the quantity of electricity drawn from the cell. Faraday further found that the weight of the substance deposited or liberated at the electrodes by a given quantity of electricity is directly proportional to the atomic weight m, and inversely proportional to the valence v of the element. In mathematical shorthand, the law may be written as follows:

$$W = \frac{mQ}{96,500v} \qquad g \qquad (1\text{-}16)$$

where m = atomic weight of element

Q = coulombs of electricity passed

v = valence of element

W = weight of element deposited

The constant 96,500, called the *faraday*, is the number of coulombs of electricity required to liberate (or deposit) 1 g equivalent weight of a substance. This is equal to the gram atomic weight of the substance divided by the valence.

As an example, let it be required to calculate the amount of zinc necessary to yield 1 kwhr of electrical energy from dry cells; 1 kwhr is equivalent to $1,000 \times 3,600$ or 36×10^5 watt-sec. If the battery voltage be taken as 1.5 volts, the total quantity of electricity required is found to be $36 \times 10^5 \div 1.5$ or 24×10^5 coulombs. From Eq. (1-16), since zinc has a valence of 2 and an atomic weight of 65.4, the weight of zinc required is found to be

$$W = \frac{65.4 \times 24 \times 10^5}{96,500 \times 2} = 813 \text{ g or } 1.8 \text{ lb}$$

If zinc costs 35 cents/lb, the total cost of zinc alone is 63 cents. To this must be added the far greater cost of the batteries used up (less the cost of the zinc). The cost of 1 kwhr of energy purchased from a typical public utility is about 3 cents. The high unit cost of energy derived from dry cells is thus apparent.

STORAGE BATTERIES

Definitions and Introduction. A *storage battery* is a device in which electrical energy may be converted to chemical energy, stored as chemical energy, and reconverted to electrical energy. Since, generally speaking, the source of its energy is an electric circuit and not the battery itself, such a battery is a *secondary* battery. Primary and secondary cells operate on the same principle with this exception: in the operation of primary cells some of the material in the cell is used up, while in secondary cells the *active material*[1] may be restored to its original form by passing a current through the cell or "charging" it.

Current may be drawn from a storage cell as long as active materials remain in the cell. When used to deliver electrical energy in this way, the cell is said to be *discharging*. The active materials may again be restored, however, by passing a current through the cell in the reverse direction. The cell is then said to be *charging*. If the cell is to be efficient, the chemical energy stored when charging must be nearly equal to the electrical input, and the electrical energy delivered when discharging must be nearly equal to the chemical energy transformed in the cell. In other words, the electrochemical process must be as nearly perfectly *reversible* as possible.

Two types of storage cells are in extensive commercial use. These are the *lead-acid* and the *nickel-alkali* storage cells. They are briefly described in the following sections.

Lead-Acid Cell. *Principle of the Lead Cell.* An "unformed" lead storage cell consists essentially of a suitable container in which two lead plates, separated from each other, are partly immersed in a solution of pure sulfuric acid in water, mixed to a specific gravity of about 1.200. If a direct current is passed in at one plate, through the solution, and out at the other plate, certain chemical changes take place in the cell. On the surface of the positive plate (the one at which the current enters) metallic lead is changed to lead peroxide, while at the surface of the negative plate (the one at which the current leaves) the solid metallic lead is changed to soft spongy lead. Bubbles of hydrogen are given off, principally at the negative plate. These actions take place only at the surface of the plates and cease as soon as the lead in contact with the electrolyte has all been converted. When the action stops, the battery is

---

[1] The active material is that part of the plate or electrode that undergoes chemical change when a battery is being charged or discharged.

charged, and the potential difference between its terminals is about 2.2 volts.

If, when charged, the terminals of the cell are connected through a suitable resistance, the battery will discharge. Current will flow from the positive terminal and enter the battery at the negative terminal for a short time. The lead peroxide on the positive plate and the spongy lead of the negative plate will now both be changed to lead sulfate. In addition, water will be formed in the electrolyte, and the specific gravity of the acid will be lowered.

The cell just described has only a small capacity, owing to the small amount of active material in contact with the electrolyte. By repeatedly charging and discharging the cell, however, the penetration at the plates is increased and more and more active material is formed. This, in fact, is one method of forming the plates of a battery. It and other methods of forming the plates will be briefly discussed in succeeding sections.

The final reaction products produced in a lead cell when charging and discharging, and already described, are conveniently represented by the following symbolic notation:

$$PbO_2 + Pb + 2H_2SO_4 \rightleftarrows 2PbSO_4 + 2H_2O \qquad (2\text{-}16)$$
$$\underset{(+ \text{ plate}) \; (- \text{ plate})}{} \qquad \underset{(+ \text{ and } - \text{ plate})}{}$$

Reading the equation from right to left represents the action when charging, while reading from left to right represents the action when discharging. Of the actual mechanism by which these products are formed at the plates, little is known.

Types of Cells. Two methods are used for forming the active materials on the plates of lead storage cells. The plates formed by these processes are known as the *Planté-type* plate and the *Faure-type* plate.

The Planté type of plate is formed from pure lead by the electrochemical process already described. Lead plates are immersed in an electrolyte of sulfuric acid, and current is passed between them, first in one direction and then in the other. In order to produce a practical device, however, as large an amount of active material as economically possible must be formed on a plate of given weight, and it must be so distributed as to be readily accessible to the electrolyte at all points. To this end, the lead plate is prepared by cutting deep parallel grooves on its two faces, but leaving uncut a checkerboard arrangement of rectangular strips to serve as a supporting framework for the mechanically weakened grooved portions. This framework helps to support the active material in the finished plate and at the same time provides stiffness and prevents buckling of the plate in service.

In the *Manchester* type of plate (Fig. 4-16) a perforated cast grid or framework, made of alloy of lead with from 5 to 12 per cent of antimony, is used to support spirally wound strips of corrugated lead. These are

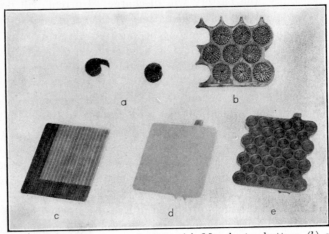

Fig. 4-16. The Manchester type of plate: (*a*) Manchester button; (*b*) section of Manchester positive plate; (*c*) wood separator; (*d*) negative plate; (*e*) positive plate. (*Electric Storage Battery Company.*)

forced into the perforations of the grid and, when formed into lead peroxide, constitute the active material of the positive plate. The lead-antimony grid itself serves as the supporting framework. This type of plate is very rugged and may be used until all the lead in the strips has been transformed into active material.

Planté plates have the advantage of ruggedness and long life. They may normally be expected to operate for between 2,000 and 3,000 complete cycles of charge and discharge. They are more bulky, however, as well as somewhat more costly, than plates made by the Faure process.

In the Faure process a paste of lead oxide or litharge is pressed into a supporting latticed skeleton or framework of cast-lead alloy. Plates thus prepared are then formed by supporting them in the usual electrolyte and passing a current between them. During charging, lead peroxide is formed on the positive plate and spongy lead on the negative plate. The Exide Ironclad type of positive plate (Fig. 5-16) is a particularly

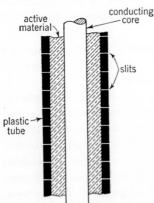

Fig. 5-16. Cross section of tube of positive plate. (*Electric Storage Battery Company.*)

rugged type of pasted plate.   It is much used on trucks and other electric vehicles where the service requirements are severe.   The active material is densely packed about central cores of lead in vertically mounted, slotted plastic tubes.   The tubes serve as containers for the active material, to which the electrolyte gains ready access by way of the slots, while the lead cores serve as conductors to lead the current from the active material to the battery terminals.   The negatives are Exide-type pasted plates.

Pasted plates are lighter and cheaper than Planté plates.   They have a large current output per unit area of plate and a higher overload capacity, but they are also shorter lived.

Construction Details.   Equation (2-16) shows that, when a battery discharges, water is formed at the points of contact of active material and electrolyte.   When the battery is charging, hydrogen is given off at the negative plate and oxygen at the positive plate. Hence the specific gravity of the electrolyte decreases when the battery is discharging and increases when it is charging.   These facts account for certain structural details in the battery itself (Fig. 6-16).   To maintain a high rate of discharge from a given plate area with a constantly weakening electrolyte requires a high degree of accessibility of active material to electrolyte throughout the plate.   Thin plates are better in this respect than thick ones.   For this reason, the thickness of plate used depends somewhat upon the rate of discharge demanded.

Fig.   6-16. Assembled   cell showing   structural   details. (*Electric Storage Battery Company.*)

The specific gravity of the electrolyte varies somewhat also with the service for which the battery is designed.   Vehicle batteries require high discharge rates for starting duty.   They must also have light weight to keep the dead load to a minimum.   Hence, in these batteries, it is desirable to reduce the volume of the electrolyte.   This is accomplished by increasing the strength of the acid used, reducing its volume, and permitting it to work over a wider range of specific gravities between full charge and full discharge of the battery.   The specific gravity of the electrolyte in fully charged vehicle batteries runs up to 1.280 or 1.300. The drop in gravity on discharges varies from 130 to 200 points, depending upon type.   The corresponding range in batteries for stationary service is less—perhaps from 1.230 on charge to from 100 to 120 points below on discharge.

The nominal potential difference between a pair of plates of a lead battery is 2.1 volts. The current drawn from it at its normal rate of discharge depends, among other things, upon the plate area. To build a cell for a given voltage and current rating, therefore, plates are mounted in suitable containers and are connected in series-parallel grouping. The plates in a cell are kept from touching each other by means of *separators* made of wood, rubber, glass, or other suitable material. The plates of stationary batteries are mounted in open, lead-lined wooden tanks or in glass jars. To reduce evaporation and loss of acid in charging, glass plates are used to cover the containers. Vehicle batteries require a more rugged type of construction. The containers for these are made of hard rubber or other similar strong, acidproof material. They are completely sealed except for an opening provided with a screw cap having a small hole or vent in its top. The screw cap provides convenient access to the cell for replenishing the water lost by electrolysis when charging, and the hole in its top serves as a vent through which the gases (oxygen and hydrogen) escape.

Considerable clearance is left between the bottom of the plates and the bottom of the container. This is done to provide space into which the loosely held active material may settle clear of the plates as it falls from them owing to "flaking" and erosion. Short-circuiting of the plates by this material is thereby prevented.

The end plates of a battery are both negative plates and hence the number of plates per cell is *odd*. This construction makes it possible to work both sides of all positive plates in the cell. When a battery charges, lead sulfate on the positive plate is changed to lead peroxide, and the active material of the plate expands. If a positive plate were used on the end of a cell, one of its sides would remain inactive, while the other side would expand and the plate would buckle.

Rating and Output. The rating of a battery is a statement of the ampere-hours that the battery is capable of delivering continuously for a stated time before the terminal voltage falls below a certain fixed minimum, or "final," value. This final voltage differs somewhat with the type of cell and with the rate of discharge. The rating is fixed by the manufacturer. For stationary types of batteries, the rating is usually based on an 8-hr discharge rate. Vehicle batteries are rated on a 6-hr basis. Other times of rating such as 3, 5, and 10 hr are also used. For example, a 320-amp-hr battery, with normal discharge time of 8 hr, will deliver 40 amp continuously for 8 hr before its terminal voltage falls to 1.75, the usual final value. If the discharge time is decreased to 3 hr, the output of the battery is reduced to 80 amp for 3 hr, or to 240 amp-hr. Thus at the higher rate the output of the battery is reduced. The discharge times and outputs of the battery used in the above illustration are given in the following table.

Time of discharge	Discharge rate, amp	Output, amp-hr	Final voltage
8 hr................	40	320	1.75
3 hr................	80	240	1.75
1 hr................	160	160	1.75
1 min.............	400	6.7	1.75

The reason for this reduction of capacity is apparent from the action of the battery. When a lead-acid cell discharges, lead peroxide and spongy lead are changed to lead sulfate at the positive and negative plates, respectively. During the process of change, water is formed throughout the porous active material, and the electrolyte is thereby diluted. The dilution is greatest at the points where the chemical action takes place, and owing to the reduction in strength (specific gravity) of the electrolyte, chemical action is slowed up. Diffusion tends to maintain the electrolyte uniform throughout the cell, but time is required to bring this about. This accounts for the fact that, after a period of rest, a cell that was rapidly discharged is capable of delivering additional energy. A cell that is intermittently discharged has the same rating on rapid as on slow rates of discharge. The loss of capacity with high rates of discharge is somewhat greater for soft thin plates than for hard thick ones.

Lead batteries have large overload capacities. In vehicle batteries, in particular, large overload capacities are required for starting duty. The stationary battery, the discharge characteristics of which are given in the foregoing table, is capable of delivering current for 1 min at ten times its normal discharge rate.

The energy efficiency of a cell also varies with the discharge rate; it is from 50 to 65 per cent at high rates, from 70 to 75 per cent at moderate rates, and about 80 per cent at slow rates of discharge.

Discharge. When fully charged and delivering current at its normal rate, the terminal voltage of a lead-acid cell is about 2.06 volts, regardless of the battery rating. As time goes on, the internal resistance of the cell increases and the terminal voltage falls off. Both the terminal voltage and the rate at which the voltage falls depend upon the rate of discharge, as shown in the typical curves of Fig. 7-16. The upper curve of this figure represents the variation of terminal voltage with time when the battery discharges continuously for 6 hr at its normal rate. The middle curve is for the 3-hr rate and the lower curve for the 1-hr rate. The voltage falls more rapidly at the higher rates because the internal resistance of the cell increases more rapidly.

The condition of charge of a battery may be judged either from a reading of the terminal voltage of the cell, *when it is discharging at a known rate,* or from a measurement of the specific gravity of the electrolyte. At low rates of discharge, however, voltmeter readings are no certain indication because the voltage remains nearly constant until the battery is almost wholly discharged, when it falls rapidly. The open-circuit voltage is no indication of the condition of charge at all. The specific gravity of the electrolyte is a good index of the relative condition of charge. The specific gravity of the electrolyte in the charged battery is known, as is also the number of points through which the gravity drops when the battery is completely discharged. Suppose, for example, that, when a certain battery is fully charged, the specific gravity of its electrolyte is 1.280 and that the drop in density between charge and discharge

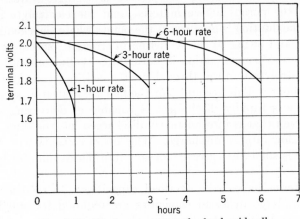

Fig. 7-16. Discharge curves of a lead-acid cell.

is 150 points. At half charge the hydrometer reading should be approximately 1.280 − 0.075, or 1.205.

A discharged battery should not be permitted to stand for long (more than a day) without recharging. When allowed to stand in this condition, some of the lead sulfate changes to a hard form that is difficult to remove by charging. This is known as *sulfating.* Sulfating decreases the output of the battery.

Freezing. Electrolytes freeze at the following temperatures:

Specific gravity at 60 F	Freezing temperature, degrees Fahrenheit
1.100	+19
1.150	+ 5
1.180	− 6
1.200	−17
1.220	−31

The above table shows that in cold weather batteries should not be allowed to become discharged too far in order to guard against freezing.

Furthermore, distilled water should be added at the beginning of the charging period to assure thorough mixing with the electrolyte.

Charging. The method used to charge a battery has little to do with the ability of the battery to function properly. Methods vary widely, depending upon the service in which the battery is employed, the equipment available for charging it, and the amount of supervision given to its operation.

When the source of supply is a shunt or a compound direct-current generator, the battery may be connected to the generator through an adjustable resistance, as shown in Fig. 8-16. Like terminals of the battery circuit and the generator are connected together; that is, positive is connected to positive and negative to negative. The adjustable resistance is used to control the current strength. If a compound generator is used for charging, a circuit breaker with a reverse-current trip should

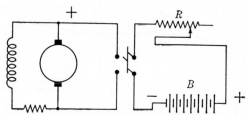

FIG. 8-16. Circuit connections for charging a storage battery.

be used to prevent the possibility of the battery's feeding back through the generator. Alternating current itself cannot be used for battery charging, but rectifiers fed from a-c mains furnish a pulsating unidirectional current that is suitable. This method of charging is much used for isolated batteries.

Batteries are usually charged either from constant-potential mains, using a series-connected resistance as in Fig. 8-16, or from approximately constant-current circuits. The former method requires an impressed voltage of from 2.4 to 3.0 volts per cell. The charging rate is high to begin with but automatically falls off, as the charging proceeds, and reaches a nearly constant value at the end of the charging period. The generated voltage of a present-day automobile generator is nearly constant over the range of usual running speeds, and the usual charging rate is from 10 to 20 amp for the 6-volt starting and lighting batteries of medium-weight cars.

When the rate of charging is constant and equal to the normal discharge rate (for 6 or 8 hr, etc.), the voltage rises rapidly at first, then remains nearly constant in value for the major portion of the charging period, rises rapidly toward the end of the period, and finally reaches a constant value. A typical voltage constant-current recharge curve is shown in Fig. 9-16. The rapid rise in voltage near the end of the charging period is due to two causes: (1) owing to imperfect diffusion, the electrolyte in the pores and on the surface of the active material increases in density more rapidly than elsewhere; (2) the contact resistance between plates and electrolyte is increased by the bubbles of gas that collect on the faces and in the pores of the plates. If the charging rate is decreased toward the end of the charging period, both excessive rise in voltage and excessive gassing will be prevented.

Since the gases liberated on charging consist of hydrogen and oxygen in explosive mixture, flames, lighted matches, cigars, etc., should not be permitted in the vicinity of charging batteries.

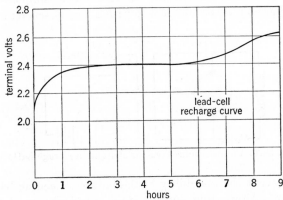

Fig. 9-16. Recharge curve. Charging current constant.

The end of the charging period is reached when the specific gravity of the electrolyte no longer changes. The battery then gasses freely. When the constant-voltage system is used, the charging current also becomes constant; and when the constant-current system is employed, the voltage becomes constant, as the end of the charging period approaches.

Too rapid a rate of charging storage batteries must be avoided, for excessive gassing causes erosion of the active material of the plates. The amount of current that may be employed safely in charging is a function of the number of ampere-hours previously discharged from the battery. One rule of thumb states that a charging current may be used which is numerically equal to the ampere-hours lacking from complete discharge. For example, a 100-amp-hr automobile storage battery that was completely discharged could be charged at an initial rate of 100 amp, but this current must be reduced as the charging progresses. Naturally, considerable time is saved by charging at a variable rate, but care must be used to avoid excessive gassing at all times during the charging period.

Uses of Lead-Acid Batteries. The lead-acid battery has a multitude of applications. Its use for starting and lighting duty on gasoline-engine-driven vehicles of all kinds, including automobiles, motorboats, etc., is too well known to require further comment. These batteries are also used in larger units as the motive power for operating industrial trucks and tractors, mine locomotives, switching engines for use in the terminals of steam roads in large cities, and submarine boats when submerged. Drawbridges are electrically operated by motors fed from batteries.

Batteries are floated on the d-c three-wire Edison networks of power companies, where they serve as stand-by or emergency power plants. Their stored energy is available automatically to pick up the load in case of temporary failure of the usual supply. A typical plant of this kind may supply from 10,000 to 15,000 kw for a period of an hour or so, at 125 volts. Batteries are also used in power stations to operate control circuits and circuit breakers, to excite generator fields, and to light the station in cases of emergency.

Communication and signal circuits are operated by batteries. These include telephone switchboards, telegraph circuits, alarm circuits, and railway signal circuits. Banks, schools, hospitals, and other public buildings must be assured of dependable sources of power for lighting. Batteries are frequently used as emergency power plants in such buildings.

Nickel-Alkaline Cells. In addition to the lead-acid type of storage cell there are other types. The most common is a cell which employs a nickel compound for the positive electrode, an iron or cadmium compound for the negative electrode, and an alkaline solution of potassium hydroxide for the electrolyte. The nickel-cadmium-alkali cell was developed in Europe and has found a considerable market there, but in the United States this type of battery is not well known and is little used. In this country the nickel-iron-alkali cell is generally used in applications which call for nickel-alkaline batteries. The nickel-iron-alkaline cell was developed by Thomas A. Edison and is popularly known as the *Edison cell.* The next few pages are devoted to a further discussion of this cell.

Edison Cell. Description. In this cell the active material of the positive plate is contained in tubes mounted on a grid. The tubes are made of perforated spirally wound strips, cut from nickel-plated iron sheets. The finished tube is about $\frac{1}{4}$ in. in diameter and $4\frac{1}{2}$ in. long and is stiffened by reinforcing rings (Fig. 10-16). The active material of the positive plate is an apple-green oxide of nickel, which is a poor conductor of electricity. Alternate layers of this material and thin flakes of nickel are rammed into the tubes, the flake nickel serving to increase the electrical conductance of the element.

The active material of the fully formed negative plate is finely divided pure iron. It is tamped into pockets made from sheets of perforated nickel-plated iron, the same material that is used for the positives. The pockets are pressed into position in the windows of a suitable nickel-plated steel grid and are corrugated during the mounting operation.

The electrolyte is a 21 per cent solution of potassium hydrate, and the container is a strong welded nickel-plated sheet-steel tank. The plates of like polarity are assembled on a nickel-plated steel rod that is passed through holes in the tops of the grids. Steel washers serve to space the plates properly, and lock washers and nuts on the end of a stack clamp

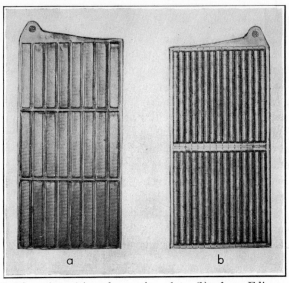

FIG. 10-16. Positive plate (*a*) and negative plate (*b*) of an Edison cell. (*Edison Storage Battery Company.*)

the plates together. A terminal post of nickel-plated steel, fastened to the connecting rod at right angles at the mid-point of the group of plates, forms a terminal of the battery. When assembled, the plates are interleaved as in the lead-acid cell. They are kept from touching each other by means of long hard-rubber pins. The assembly is held together and supported clear from the bottom and sides of the container by grooved hard-rubber frames.

Chemical Reaction. The exact chemical changes that take place in the cell are not completely understood, but they are generally assumed to be represented by the following equation:

$$6NiO_2^+ + 8KOH + 3Fe^- \rightleftarrows 2Ni_3O_4^+ + 8KOH + Fe_3O_4^-$$

Reading from right to left represents charging, and reading from left to right represents discharging. When discharging, the oxide of nickel on the positive plate is reduced to a lower oxide of nickel, and the oxygen thereby set free oxidizes the iron of the negative plate to iron oxide. The reverse process takes place when the battery is charged. The electric current liberates hydrogen at the negative plate, which reduces the iron oxide to iron. The oxygen set free moves over to the positive plate and changes the oxide of nickel from a lower to a higher oxide. It may be observed that oxygen is given up by the positive plate on discharge, and by the negative plate on charging, but that the amount of the electrolyte does not change. No water is formed in the cell, and hence, except for the influence of temperature, the specific gravity of the electrolyte does not change.

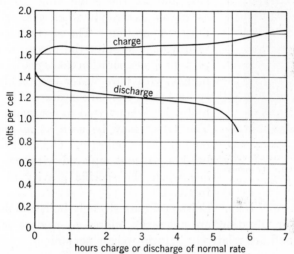

Fig. 11-16. Charge and discharge curves of an Edison cell; 7-hr charge and 5-hr discharge.

Operating Characteristics. Edison cells have a higher internal resistance than lead-acid cells, and hence there is a greater difference between their terminal voltages when charging and discharging. The general shapes of their charge and discharge curves, however, are the same as those of lead-acid cells. Edison cells are rated on the basis of a 5-hr discharge rate. Typical charge and discharge curves are shown in Fig. 11-16. The average voltage on discharge is about 1.2, while the average charging voltage is about 1.7.

Since the specific gravity of the electrolyte does not change with discharge, the condition of charge of an Edison cell cannot be learned from a hydrometer reading. A reading of the terminal voltage of the cell when the battery is discharging at a known rate, however, indicates the charge left in the cell, provided curves for various rates of discharge are

available.   The ampere-hour capacity of the cell does not change with
the rate of discharge, as with lead-acid cells, but the average voltage and
the "final" voltage of discharge vary considerably with the rate.   The

FIG. 12-16. Cutaway view
of Edison cell. (*Edison
Storage Battery Company.*)

watt-hour efficiency also depends upon the rate
of charge or discharge, owing to the increase
in the internal I^2R losses at the higher rates.
Edison cells may be left standing in any condition of charge for long periods of time without doing permanent injury to the cell.

The Edison cell is provided with a vent
controlled by a valve, to permit the escape of
gas, and at the same time to prevent the
escape of electrolyte when gassing and to reduce evaporation.   The electrolyte evaporates
readily, and despite the precautions taken to
prevent it, evaporation takes place and frequent
fillings with pure water are required.   Upon
contact with the carbon dioxide of the air, the
hydroxide is converted to potassium carbonate.
The latter may be seen as a white deposit
on top of the cell case.   Old electrolyte should
be dumped and replaced with *renewal electrolyte* when the specific gravity at 60 F falls
to 1.600.

Advantages and Uses.   Edison cells are strongly built and do not suffer
from shock or vibration, are not easily injured by neglect or abuse, are
long lived, and are relatively light in weight per unit of energy output.
These are among the conspicuous advantages.   The average life of an
Edison cell is about 6 years, or about twice that of the average lead-acid
cell.   Their output per pound of material (*weight efficiency*) varies from
about 8 to 14 watt-hr.   Corresponding figures for the stationary type of
lead-acid cell are from 3 to 5 watt-hr and for traction batteries from 8
to 11.5 watt-hr.   Edison batteries cost on the average about twice as
much as lead-acid cells designed for similar service.

Edison batteries are used to drive delivery trucks, industrial trucks,
and mine locomotives, for laboratory testing, for operating radio sets, etc.

CHAPTER 17

DIRECT-CURRENT DISTRIBUTION

Limitations of D-c Systems. Most energy used in the United States as direct currents is generated and transmitted as alternating currents and is converted to direct currents at or near the point of consumption. The conversion may be effected by means of mercury-arc or other types of rectifiers, synchronous converters, or motor-generators with synchronous motor drive. It should not be inferred from the foregoing that d-c applications are in themselves unimportant. Rather, it should be recognized that it is uneconomical to transmit and distribute power in the form of direct currents except in small amounts over relatively short distances.

It is impractical to build d-c generators of more than a few thousand kilowatts capacity, and the efficiency of the largest unit probably does not exceed 92 per cent. On the other hand, a-c machines delivering 200,000 kw and operating at efficiencies of about 98.5 per cent are now in use. Alternating-current generators are readily insulated to deliver their outputs at several standard voltages ranging from 2,400 to 13,800, while d-c machines built for voltages above 750 are exceptional. Per kilowatt of rated capacity, the a-c generator is also much cheaper than the d-c machine. But the superiority of alternating currents over direct currents as a means of utilizing electrical energy does not lie wholly, or even principally, in the superior economy of the generating machinery, important as this factor is. It is due more particularly to the ease and economy with which the voltage of an a-c circuit can be transformed. This transformation is accomplished by means of a relatively cheap, simple, and highly efficient device, called a *transformer*. With this device it is possible to transform power in the form of alternating currents at a low voltage to an almost equal amount of power at a high voltage. The reverse operation may be performed with the same unit. In d-c machinery there is no equivalent device. The lack of it is a tremendous handicap to d-c systems.

Certain types of service can be performed by direct currents only, while for certain other duties the superiority of the d-c motor makes its use highly desirable, if not absolutely necessary. These constitute the present-day field of d-c application. Generally, direct current is generated at the point of use or is distributed over short distances. Illustrations of the latter are the Edison three-wire systems and the feeder circuits along the right-of-way of electric street railways and electrified steam roads.

Conductor Size as a Function of Voltage. When power is transmitted over a pair of wires, the heat lost in the circuit incidental thereto is directly proportional to the square of the current and to the resistance of the circuit, in accordance with Joule's law. Let the resistance of the circuit be $R/2$ ohms per wire and let the voltage at the receiver end be E (Fig. 1-17). When P kw are delivered, the current in the circuit is $I = 1,000P/E$ amp, and the line loss is I^2R watts. If the receiver voltage is raised to $2E$ volts, the length of line remaining the same, the same amount of power as before is transmitted with a current of $I/2$ amp and the line loss is $I^2R/4$ watts. Doubling the voltage reduces the loss to one-fourth, and similarly quadrupling the voltage reduces the loss to one-sixteenth, etc. In general, when a fixed amount of power is transmitted over a given length of line, the line loss varies inversely as the square of the transmission voltage. Obviously, also, if the loss in the line is limited to a fixed percentage of the transmitted power, the size of wire used in the line construction is inversely proportional to the square of the transmission voltage. Without the use of high voltages, the economical transmission of power over long distances would be impossible. Moreover, the fact that d-c transmission is limited to the short distances already mentioned is a direct consequence of the low voltages at which they are generated and used, coupled with the inability to transform them cheaply.

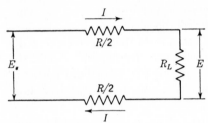

Fig. 1-17. Wiring diagram of loaded two-wire circuit.

Example 1. It is desired to supply 80 kw to a d-c motor located 300 ft distant from the generator bus. The line loss must not exceed 6 per cent of the delivered power. With copper selling at 35 cents/lb, estimate the cost of the copper conductor required to transmit the power at each of the following assumed voltages: 125, 250, and 500. The resistivity of copper is 10.5 ohms/cir mil-ft, and the weight of a piece of 1,000,000-cir-mil copper conductor 1 ft long is 3 lb.

The line loss is 0.06 × 80 or 4.8 kw. For transmission at 500 volts the receiver current is

$$I = \frac{80,000}{500} = 160 \text{ amp}$$

Equating line loss to I^2R and solving for resistance yields

$$R = \frac{4,800}{160^2} = 0.1875 \text{ ohm}$$

This is the resistance of 2×300 or 600 ft of wire, and since $R = \rho l/A$, the area of the wire is

$$A = \frac{10.5 \times 600}{0.1875} = 33,600 \text{ cir mils}$$

Weight of conductor $= 600 \times 33,600 \times 3 \times 10^{-6} = 60.5$ lb
Cost of conductor $= 60.5 \times \$0.35 = \$21.18$
Cost at 250 volts $= (^{500}\!/_{250})^2 \times \$21.18 = \$84.72$
Cost at 125 volts $= (^{500}\!/_{125})^2 \times \$21.18 = \$338.88$

Other Factors Influencing Conductor Size. *If the voltage of a circuit is fixed,* the size of conductor that should be used to transmit a given amount of power over a line of given length depends principally upon the following:

1. Conductor economy
2. Voltage drop allowable
3. Allowable conductor heating—temperature rise
4. Mechanical strength of conductor

If, on the other hand, it is desired to transmit an assumed amount of power over a given length of line at minimum cost and *no restriction is placed on the voltage to be used,* the procedure for finding the most economical conductor would have to be considerably modified.[1] A complete discussion of this case would lead us far beyond the proper scope of this book. The discussion that follows pertains only to the case of a circuit for which the voltage to be used is already known.

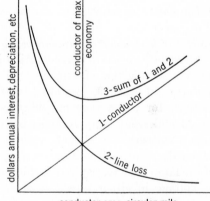

FIG. 2-17. The most economical size of conductor.

The cost of a conductor of given material and of fixed length is proportional to its size. The annual outlay C_1 chargeable to conductors for taxes, interest, and depreciation is therefore directly proportional to the area of the conductor. For a conductor of A cir mils cross-sectional area it may be expressed as

$$C_1 \text{ (dollars)} = k_1 A \qquad \text{(curve 1, Fig. 2-17)} \qquad (1\text{-}17)$$

where $k_1 =$ constant. When a given amount of power is transmitted over a given distance, however, the amount of heat energy lost in the con-

---

[1] See Loew, "Electrical Power Transmission," McGraw-Hill Book Company, Inc., New York, 1927.

ductors during any operating period is inversely proportional to the conductor area. The money value of the heat energy liberated in the line during the time of one year $(I^2R/1000)$(hours in a year $\times$ dollar value of 1 kwhr) may, therefore, be represented by the equation

$$C_2 \text{ (dollars) } = \frac{k_2}{A} \quad \text{(curve 2)} \tag{2-17}$$

where $k_2 = $ constant. The total annual charge, expressed as a function of conductor area, is obtained by adding Eqs. (1-17) and (2-17). It is

$$C_1 + C_2 = k_1A + \frac{k_2}{A} \quad \text{(curve 3)} \tag{3-17}$$

It may be noted that the minimum cost occurs at the value of A for which the ordinates to curves 1 and 2 are equal, that is, where the curves cross. That this must be true can be shown by differentiating Eq. (3-17), equating to zero and solving for A.

The foregoing is the basis for the statement of Kelvin's law, as modified by Gisbert Kapp, which is as follows:

The most economical area of conductor is that for which the annual cost of energy wasted is equal to the interest on that portion of the capital outlay which can be considered proportional to the weight of conductor used.

A second important consideration is the matter of voltage drop in the line connecting the consumer's load and the source of supply. Lamps, motors, and other devices must be supplied with power delivered at the voltages for which they are designed, if they are to perform properly. An incandescent lamp receives excess current when supplied with too high a voltage. Its filament overheats and its life is thereby shortened. When the impressed voltage on the lamp is much below normal, the life of the lamp is increased, but its illumination is unsatisfactory. Extremes of voltage in either direction must be avoided if satisfactory electric service is to be provided. Some latitude is necessarily permissible. For motors, a variation in voltage of perhaps 5 per cent on either side of the mean is allowable. For lighting, the allowable variation is considerably less—perhaps 2 per cent. In some states the allowable variation is fixed by rules of the public-service commissions. In order to keep the voltage drop within the prescribed limits, the size of wire must be so selected that the change in voltage at the receiver or load between maximum load and no load does not exceed the specified amount.

The mechanical strength of a conductor of given material is proportional to its cross-sectional area. This fact sets a limit to the smallest size of conductor it is safe to use on overhead lines. On such lines, conductors smaller than No. 6 hard-drawn copper are seldom used.

Series System. The series system of d-c distribution was formerly much used for street-lighting circuits. Series-connected arcs or incandescent lamps were supplied with power from special d-c series generators. Because of the greater economy obtainable when the a-c system is used, however, series street-lighting circuits in the United States are now everywhere fed from a-c sources through constant-current transformers or mercury-arc rectifiers. (These devices are described elsewhere in this book.) Direct-current series distribution systems are now obsolete in this country.

Multiple or Parallel Systems. In the multiple or parallel system of distribution (Fig. 3-17), lamps, motors, and other loads are connected in parallel between a given pair of wires. In the illustration a compound generator feeds two groups of lamps, L_1 and L_2, a motor M, and a heater R. With the RI drop in the leads neglected, the voltage across

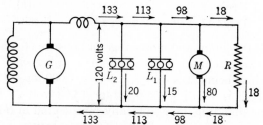

Fig. 3-17. The multiple or parallel system.

the terminals of each of the units is 120. The currents supplied to the several units are indicated, and the current output of the generator is the sum of the currents drawn by the several units, or 133 amp. The terminal voltage is the same for all, but the current drawn by each unit is determined by the resistance of the unit, or by its counter emf and resistance both in case of the motor. Accordingly, the multiple system is a *constant-voltage* variable-current system.

In one form or another this system is almost universally used for the distribution of power in d-c and a-c networks. It has the advantage of flexibility, for any unit may be switched off or on the circuit without disturbing the power supply to the others. In a-c networks, thanks to the transformer, any suitable standard voltage may be employed. The voltage used may thus be adjusted to suit the load on the circuit and the distance of transmission. The principle of conductor economy already discussed may therefore be employed to advantage. In d-c multiple systems, voltages are usually limited to 600 volts for street-railway and interurban service, to 440, 220, and 110 volts for motors, and to 220 and 110 volts for lighting service. (These are nominal or approximate values of voltage and are subject to some variation.) Owing to these relatively low voltages, multiple networks employing direct currents are quite limited in extent. Some typical d-c networks are considered in the following paragraphs.

Two-wire Circuit. The simplest type of multiple circuit is the two-wire circuit illustrated in Fig. 4-17. In this system the voltage of the circuit is approximately equal to the rated voltage of the motors and lamps connected to it. The voltage at the generator is somewhat higher than that at the consumer's load, owing to the RI drop in the leads.

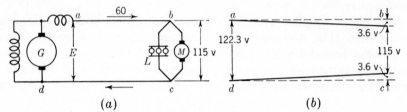

FIG. 4-17. Voltage drops in a two-wire circuit.

For example, if the lamps and motor together receive 60 amp at 115 volts over 150 ft of two-wire line consisting of No. 6 copper wire (the resistance of the two wires being $2 \times 150 \times 0.403 \div 1{,}000$ or 0.121 ohm), the generator voltage is $115 + 60 \times 0.121$ or 122.3 volts. The generator voltage and the line drop are graphically represented in (b).

While 115 volts (approximately) is a satisfactory voltage to use on lamps, small motors, and other small appliances, it is too low a voltage to use for economical power distribution except for small amounts of power over short distances. As a means of retaining the low voltage

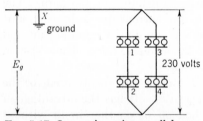

FIG. 5-17. Lamps in series-parallel connection.

at the load and at the same time raising the distribution voltage, the *series-parallel* circuit of Fig. 5-17 may be employed. Lamp units 1 and 2, for example, are connected in series, as are also other units, such as 3 and 4. The same current feeds 1 and 2, 3 and 4, etc., respectively. This arrangement is open to several serious objections, however, that usually make its use impractical. So long as the number of lamps in each of the series-connected groups is the same—lamps of a given size being assumed—the lamps burn satisfactorily. But if one of the lamps in group 1, for example, should burn out, the two remaining lamps in that group would receive too much current, while each of those in group 2 would receive too little current; the voltage drop across group 1 would be too high and that across group 2 would be too low. This unbalanced condition might cause the rest of the lamps in group 1 to burn out, in which case the circuit would then be opened and the lamps in group 2 would go out.   Furthermore, should one of the wires become grounded, as at x for example, a person turning on lights in group 4 might accidentally receive a 230-volt shock, whereas with the two-wire system or with the three-wire Edison system about to be described, a 115-volt shock is the maximum that can be received.

Three-wire Circuit.   The three-wire Edison system of distribution combines consumption at 115 to 120 volts with distribution at from 230 to 240 volts without the inherent disadvantages associated with the series-parallel system just described.   In the Edison system a third or *neutral* wire is run from the generating station, at which point its potential is maintained at a value halfway between the potentials of the two outside wires.   Special generators or balancer sets are used for this purpose.   These are described in a later paragraph.   The lamp loads are connected between each of the outside wires and the neutral wire, as in Fig. 6-17. Motor loads, like the lamp loads, may be connected between the outside wires and neutral, but usually 230-volt motors are used.   These are connected between the two outside wires of the system.

An attempt is made to keep the loads evenly divided between each of the outside wires and neutral.   When the loads are so divided, the current flowing out from the positive bus, and through the lamps and motors connected between the positive wire and neutral, is exactly the amount required to feed the lamps and motors similarly connected between neutral and the negative outside wire.   All the outgoing current returns in the negative wire and none flows in the neutral.   Such a load, called a *balanced load*, is shown in Fig. 6-17.   Usually, however, there is some inequality between the loads on the two sides of the system, in which case the load is *unbalanced*.   The difference between the outgoing current in the positive lead and the return current in the negative lead exists in the neutral wire.   Current returns in the neutral wire when the heavier load is on the positive side, while outgoing current flows in the neutral when the heavier load is on the negative side.   The last-named condition is illustrated in Fig. 7-17.

If the neutral wire of a three-wire system is well grounded, it is unlikely that one making accidental contact with either outside wire would receive more than 120 volts of potential difference impressed across his body, when the potential difference between the outside wires is 240 volts. This is an important advantage of the three-wire system.

Three-wire Edison systems were installed in the business sections of large and moderate-sized cities, such as New York, Chicago, Milwaukee, Seattle, some years before the a-c system came into general use, and most such cities continue to operate them.   An important advantage of d-c systems not previously mentioned is the fact that storage batteries connected in parallel with the generators may be used to supply the load for short periods, at times when the generators fail, and until spare units can be brought into service to pick up the load. By this means some systems have maintained unbroken continuity of service for many years. Such continuity was impossible with a-c systems, particularly in the earlier years when the systems were small and the generating stations feeding them were few in number. More recently a-c facilities have been greatly improved in this respect. For this reason, and because a-c

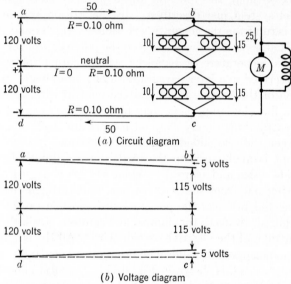

Fig. 6-17. The three-wire Edison system. Balanced load.

systems are perhaps 25 per cent cheaper, most three-wire Edison systems are not being extended as the load grows in the districts served by them.

Voltage Drop in Three-wire Circuits. The fall of potential in a current-carrying wire is in the direction of flow, and the amount of it is proportional to the current. In a balanced three-wire system the neutral carries no current and hence there is no drop of potential in it. If the two outside wires are of the same length and size, the potential drop is the same amount in each and the load voltages are balanced. This condition is illustrated in the voltage diagram of Fig. 6-17(b). The resistance of each wire is assumed to be 0.1 ohm. The drop in each of the outside wires is 5 volts and the potential difference between each outside wire and the neutral at the load end is 120 − 5 = 115 volts.

When the load is unbalanced, as in Fig. 7-17, the potential drops in the leads are unequal. With the assumed loads and resistances shown in the figure, there is a drop of 3.5 volts between generator and load in the positive wire, a drop of 1.5 volts in the neutral wire, and a drop of 5 volts in the negative wire. When proper account is taken of these drops, the load potential difference between positive wire and neutral is found to be 118 volts, while the load potential difference between neutral and negative wire is only 113.5 volts. Thus when the loads on the two sides of the neutral are unequal, the load potential differences are also unbalanced, the heavier load having the lower voltage.

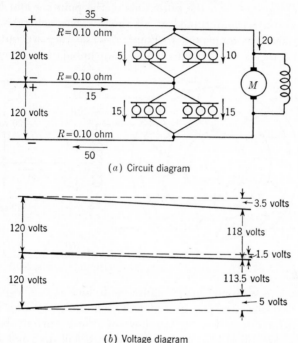

(*a*) Circuit diagram

(*b*) Voltage diagram

FIG. 7-17. The three-wire Edison system. Unbalanced load.

Three-wire Generator. The three-wire generator is a special kind of generator that is used to supply power and to provide the neutral connection for a three-wire Edison system. The form of generator most commonly used is illustrated in principle by the two-pole machine in Fig. 8-17. In addition to commutator and brushes, this machine is provided with a pair of slip rings mounted on the shaft. One of these is connected, by means of a tap, to a point m on the armature winding, and the other is similarly connected to a point n, 180 electrical degrees from m.† Brushes resting on the slip rings are connected to the ter-

---

† A four-pole machine has two taps like m connected to the armature at points 360 electrical degrees apart, and two like n similarly displaced. In general, a p-pole machine has $p/2$ pairs of taps.

minals a and b of an inductance coil the electrical winding of which surrounds a laminated steel core. The alternating emf generated in the armature winding is impressed across the terminals a and b of the inductance coil, its value varying from instant to instant approximately like the ordinates to a sine curve. Only a small alternating current flows in the winding of the coil, however, because the coil has a very high inductance. An inductance coil acts to oppose the passage of a varying or changing current (page 80). The mid-point o of the winding has a potential halfway between the potentials of the points a and b, and this value of potential is maintained at all times. The neutral wire of the three-wire system is connected to point o, while the two outside wires are connected to the d-c brushes. When an unbalance current returns

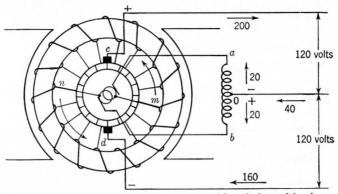

Fig. 8-17. The three-wire generator with unbalanced load.

in the neutral, as assumed in the figure, it divides at o. Approximately one-half of it returns by way of a and the remainder by way of b. The coil offers little opposition to the flow of direct current because the resistance of the coil is low, and an inductance coil does not oppose the flow of an unvarying direct current through it. The current returning by way of a reaches the positive brush by passing through the section mc of the winding, while that returning by way of b passes to the positive brush over the section nc of the armature winding.

Three-wire generators are sometimes used with two separate coils with neutrals electrically connected. Better balancing is secured in this way. Generators so used must be provided with four slip rings, one pair for each coil. One type of three-wire generator has an extra armature winding, which takes the place of the external inductance coils. In such machines the neutral point of the winding is connected to a slip ring, and this ring is the only one required.

Balancer Sets. Three-wire circuits may be supplied with power from a standard 240-volt generator when a balancer set is used to provide the neutral connection.

A balancer set consists of two identical shunt- or compound-wound machines, each of which is designed to generate one-half the voltage between the two outside wires of the three-wire system (120 volts). The two machines have their armatures mechanically coupled or else mounted on the same shaft. The armatures of the two machines, as well as their shunt fields, are connected in series between the two outside wires and the neutral wire of the system is connected to the common point o (Fig. 9-17). When the load is balanced, as in Fig. 6-17, E_g and E_m are equal, and both machines idle as motors. When an unbalance exists, as in Fig. 7-17, with connections as in Fig. 9-17(a) assumed, the voltage on the lightly loaded side is slightly higher than that on the heavily loaded side; M then runs as a motor driving G as a generator. With losses

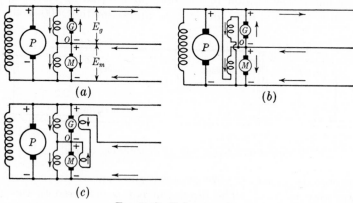

Fig. 9-17. Balancer sets.

neglected, the current input to each M and G is one-half the unbalance current. Actually, the input to the motor exceeds the output of the generator by the amount of the armature losses of the two machines. As the unbalance increases, the motor speed falls off because its load is increased. The generator voltage then falls off because its speed and its field excitation are both decreased. This causes E_g to grow less and E_m to increase, thus shifting the potential of o, nearer the potential of the positive wire.

The balance at all loads is improved by cross-connecting the fields as in (b). As the voltage E_g falls, the motor field is weakened and the motor speeds up. On the other hand, the generator field is strengthened, and because of the increased flux thus produced and the higher running speed, G generates a higher voltage and prevents the potential of o from changing much. The same sort of corrective action is obtained with compound-wound machines connected as in (c). No matter which way the system is unbalanced, the generator is always cumulatively connected, while the motor is differentially connected. The differential action of the motor maintains the speed of the generator, and this, together with the cumulative action of the generator, causes the generated voltage of the latter to be better maintained at all times, thus keeping the voltages on the three-wire system properly balanced.

Street-railway Distribution. A simple street-railway distribution circuit is shown in Fig. 10-17. Only a single station is represented in the figure, but in large railway systems several such stations are located at convenient intervals and all of them feed power into different parts of the network. Owing to the low voltage[1] used, it is uneconomical to transmit power very far from a single station. The illustration in the figure may be considered as one of the component parts of a complete system.

Power enters the station in the form of alternating currents. It is there converted to direct currents at approximately 600 volts. For

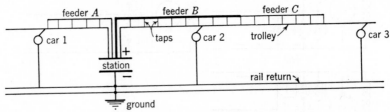

Fig. 10-17. Street-railway distribution system.

this purpose d-c generators, driven by a-c motors, rotary converters, or rectifiers may be used. The direct current is delivered to the station busses shown in the figure. Direct current flows out from the positive station bus, partly over the trolley and partly over heavy copper cables, called *feeders*. In small systems the trolley wire may serve as the only outgoing conductor. The feeders are often supported on the poles from which the trolley wires are suspended and, in the system of feeding illustrated, are always electrically connected or *tapped* to the trolley wire at frequent intervals. Other slightly different systems of feeder connections are also used. Feeders reduce the resistance of the circuit and thereby make it possible to maintain satisfactory voltage near the end of the line. In city systems a maximum voltage drop of about 12 per cent is permissible. Near the station, where the load current is heaviest, large feeders are used. Farther out, the size of feeder may be reduced, and near the end of the line the trolley may serve as the only conductor.

After passing through the motors of the cars, the current returns to the station negative bus by way of the rails, ground, and negative-bus

---

[1] In cities, 600 volts is the standard voltage, while for interurban lines both 600 and 1,200 volts are in use.

ground connection. Absence of a negative feeder is assumed. In order to make the path through the rails continuous and of low resistance, adjacent rail ends are joined together with *bonds* of copper cable. The bonds are short pieces of copper cable which are welded to adjacent rail ends, thus spanning the rail joints. Where bonding is defective, much of the current leaves the rails and passes through ground, buried water mains, underground telephone cables, etc. At the points where the current again leaves the underground paths of pipes, cable sheaths, etc., these structures are damaged by electrolysis. To prevent such electrolytic action by assuring a path of low resistance independent of rails, ground, and conductors buried therein, *negative-return feeders* are installed.

Trolley busses or "trackless trolleys" have supplemented or replaced street railways in a number of our larger cities. These busses employ the d-c series motor for motive power and utilize the same kind of distribution

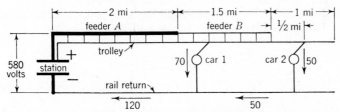

FIG. 11-17. The railway system described in Example 2.

system as do the conventional street railways, but since they require no "tracks" such as street railways use, there is no "rail return" circuit. Instead two trolley wires are used—one representing the outgoing circuit, and the other the return circuit. These are connected to the motor terminals by means of a double trolley mounted on the roof of the bus.

Example 2. The section of the trolley running to the right from the station in Fig. 11-17 is supplemented by two feeders. Feeder A is No. 0000 copper, with a resistance of 0.26 ohm/mile, and it runs 2 miles out from the station. Feeder B is No. 00 copper, with a resistance of 0.41 ohm/mile. It is connected to the end of A and extends 1.5 miles beyond the point of connection. Both feeders are tapped to the trolley at $\frac{1}{4}$-mile intervals. The trolley wire has a resistance of 0.41 ohm/mile and extends for 1 mile beyond the end of feeder B. There are two cars on the line. The first is $2\frac{1}{2}$ miles out from the station and draws 70 amp from the trolley; the second is 4 miles out from the station and draws 50 amp. The station bus voltage is 580. With the resistance of the rail return neglected, what is the voltage between trolley and track at the second car?

The resistances per mile of circuit have the following values:

First 2-mile section:

$$R \text{ per mile} = \frac{R_a R_b}{R_a + R_b} = \frac{0.26 \times 0.41}{0.67} = 0.159 \text{ ohm}$$

Second or 1.5-mile section:

$$R \text{ per mile} = \frac{0.41 \times 0.41}{0.41 + 0.41} = 0.205 \text{ ohm}$$

Third or trolley section:

$$R \text{ per mile} = 0.41 \text{ ohm}$$

In Fig. 11-17 the current in each section of line is shown. The cars are at 1 and 2. The resistance between the first car and the station is

$$R_1 = 2 \times 0.159 + \frac{0.205}{2} = 0.420 \text{ ohm}$$

The resistance between the first car and the second is

$$R_2 = 0.205 + \frac{0.410}{2} = 0.410 \text{ ohm}$$

The RI drop to the first car is 120×0.420 or 50.4 volts.
The RI drop between the first and second cars is 50×0.410 or 20.5 volts.
The total drop to the last car is $50.4 + 20.5$ or 70.9 volts.
The voltage at the last car is $580 - 70.9$ or 509.1 volts.

Problems

1-17. The resistance (hot) of a 40-watt 110-volt tungsten lamp is 303 ohms. A parallel-connected group of four such lamps is connected in series with another similar group of four lamps across 220-volt mains. Find (*a*) the impressed voltage and (*b*) the current of each lamp. Recompute (*c*) the current and (*d*) the impressed voltage for a lamp in each group when one lamp has burned out. Assume the filament resistance to remain constant.

2-17. A 25-hp d-c motor with a full-load efficiency of 88 per cent receives power from a 230-volt constant-potential source 200 ft away. The line drop must not exceed 10 volts when the motor delivers full-load output. (*a*) What is the minimum size of copper wire that may be used? Assume that the resistivity of copper at working temperature is 10.8 ohms/cir mil-ft. (*b*) If rubber-insulated wire is specified, what size of wire should be selected (see Appendix D)?

3-17. The following loads are supplied over a 230-volt feeder 320 ft long: a 20-hp motor with full-load efficiency of 87 per cent; five 5-hp motors with full-load efficiencies of 85 per cent; ten 100-watt lamps. (*a*) Determine the size of rubber-insulated wire that must be used to meet code requirements (see Appendix D). (*b*) Compute the voltage drop in the feeder for the size of wire selected.

4-17. The potential difference impressed between each outside wire and neutral of a three-wire Edison system is 120 volts. Load A connected between the positive wire and neutral draws 240 amp, while load B connected between neutral and the negative wire draws 180 amp. Each of the three wires connecting generator to the load has a resistance of 0.025 ohm. (*a*) Find the voltage impressed upon each load. (*b*) Draw the diagram of voltages.

5-17. Three loads, the terminals of which, for convenience, are designated as *ab*, *cd*, and *ef*, are supplied from the same 600-volt bus. Let *a*, *c*, and *e* be the positive and *b*, *d*, and *f* be the negative terminals of the loads. The terminals of *ab* are connected to the bus terminals by two 1,000,000-cir-mil copper cables, each 2 miles long; the terminals of *cd* are connected to the bus by two 1,000,000-circ-mil copper cables, each 2.5 miles long; the terminals of *ef* are connected to the bus by two 900,000-cir-mil copper cables, each 2 miles long.   In addition, four 500,000-cir-mil copper cables, each 1 mile long, are used to interconnect *a* and *c*, *b* and *d*, *c* and *e*, and *d* and *f*. Load *ab* takes 90 amp; load *cd*, 100 amp; and load *ef*, 80 amp.   Determine the voltage impressed across the terminals of each load.

6-17. A single-track street-railway line extends $3\frac{3}{4}$ miles from the supply.   An overhead trolley of No. 00 copper wire with a resistance of 0.42 ohm/mile extends from the supply station to the end of the line.   Running parallel with the trolley wire for a distance of $2\frac{1}{2}$ miles from the station is a No. 0000 copper feeder with a resistance of 0.26 ohm/mile.   Feeder and trolley are connected together by taps at $\frac{1}{4}$-mile intervals.   A car at the end of the line draws 95 amp, and another 2 miles out from the station draws 110 amp.   These are the only two cars on the line.   If the station bus voltage is 600 volts and the resistance of the rail return is negligible, what is the voltage at each car?

Part II

ALTERNATING CURRENTS

CHAPTER 18

ALTERNATING ELECTROMOTIVE FORCES AND
CURRENTS. FUNDAMENTAL CONCEPTS

Simple Alternator. In an a-c generator, as in a d-c generator, mechanical energy is transformed to electrical energy, but the emf and current supplied at the machine terminals are both alternating instead of direct. A machine of this type may also be used to convert electrical energy, supplied to the machine terminals from an outside source in the form of alternating currents, into mechanical energy of motion. When so used, the machine is called a *synchronous motor*. In other words, a given machine may be employed either as a generator or as a motor, and whether it is one or the other depends entirely upon how it is used. A machine that may be employed in this dual capacity is called an *alternator*.

In Chap. 11 it was shown that the emf generated in the armature of a d-c generator or motor is alternating. When the armature winding of a two-pole d-c generator is provided with taps at diametrically opposite points, and these taps are connected to two slip rings, the alternating emf generated in the winding is made available at the slip-ring brushes and the machine becomes an a-c generator.

The operating principle of a machine of this kind is illustrated in Fig. 1-18. For the sake of simplicity the armature winding of the machine represented in the figure is limited to a single coil (one turn) of wire. When the armature is driven in a clockwise direction at a constant speed, the emf generated in the winding varies periodically according to the ordinates of the curve in (b). The emf generated in the coil side under the north pole is always in the direction away from the observer, while that generated in the side under the south pole is in the opposite direction. The emf between the slip rings is the sum of the emfs generated in the two sides. Its value is nearly constant as long as the coil sides are under the poles, but it falls quickly to zero when the coil sides leave the poles and reverses when the plane of the coil passes the axis *BB*. If the pole tips are not cut back (chamfered), the flux density in the air gap is constant and the shape of the emf wave is approximately rectangular.

Revolving-field Alternator. While in Fig. 1-18 the armature coils rotate and the fields are stationary, it is usually more convenient to build alternators with stationary armatures and revolving fields, as illustrated in Fig. 2-18, and practically all commercial machines are so constructed. The field current is then supplied through slip rings, while the armature is connected to the external circuit through stationary leads as indicated. The shape of the wave generated by the machine in Fig. 2-18 is exactly like that already described for Fig. 1-18.

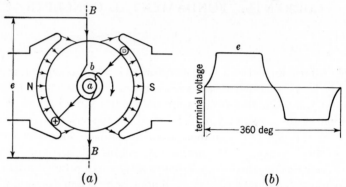

(a)   (b)

FIG. 1-18. A-c generator with revolving armature.   *BB* is the zero time axis.

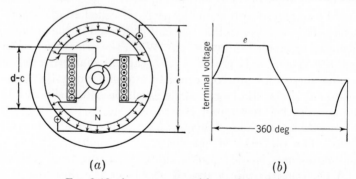

(a)   (b)

FIG. 2-18. A-c generator with revolving field.

Wave Forms. The shape of the emf wave which an alternator generates is largely under the control of the designer, although, for reasons which are discussed in a later chapter, most machines are designed to produce waves that closely approximate the sine shape illustrated in Fig. 7-18. This is particularly true of machines that are used on large power systems.

The shape of the wave readily may be changed by

1. Changing the flux distribution in the air gap
2. Changing the distribution and/or pitch of the winding
3. Combining the methods of 1 and 2.

Figure 2-18 illustrates the type of wave that is generated in a lumped or concentrated winding by a radial revolving magnetic field.   The wave is approximately rectangular.   In Fig. 3-18 the winding is the same but the field distribution is altered by cutting off the tips of the poles.   The wave shape is now trapezoidal.   In Fig. 4-18 the effect of distributing the winding is illustrated.   The field distribution is like that of Fig. 3-18, but the armature winding has three turns spaced 30 deg apart instead

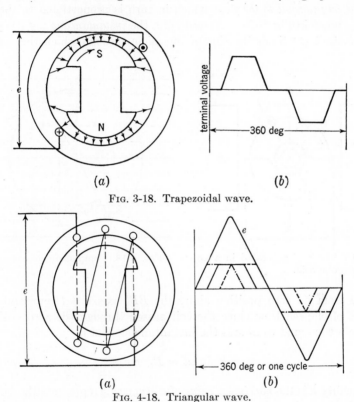

(a)   (b)

Fig. 3-18. Trapezoidal wave.

(a)   (b)

Fig. 4-18. Triangular wave.

of the single turn of Fig. 3-18.   Each turn alone generates a trapezoidal wave just as in Fig. 3-18, but the resultant wave is the sum of the three trapezoidal components 30 deg apart, or it is a wave of triangular shape. By increasing the number of turns and changing the distribution, the shape of the wave may be changed to one closely approaching that of Fig. 7-18.

Sine Wave.   Let the magnetic field in Fig. 5-18 be uniform (lines of force everywhere parallel and flux density constant) and let the coil be rotated at a uniform angular velocity of ω radians per second.   The value e of the generated voltage is constantly changing, for by Faraday's law it depends upon *the rate at which the conductors cut the flux*. When the plane of the coil lies in the axis BB' ($\theta = 0$, π, 2π, etc.), the conductors cut no flux and e is zero. On the other hand, when the plane of the coil lies in the axis of the north-south poles ($\theta = \pi/2$, $3\pi/2$, $5\pi/2$, etc.), the coil sides cut the flux at the maximum rate, and the generated voltage is a maximum. In general, the rate at which the conductors cut the flux at any instant is seen to be *proportional to the component of their velocity normal to the flux*, which in turn is proportional to the sine of θ, as shown in Fig. 6-18. Accordingly, the *instantaneous emf e* is equal to a constant (k) times the sine of the angle through which the coil has

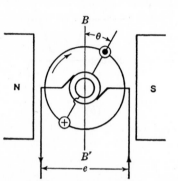

FIG. 5-18. The emf generated in a uniform magnetic field.   FIG. 6-18. Components of velocity.

rotated from its zero position along the BB' axis. If t represents the seconds of elapsed time since the coil passed through the zero position, the angle θ is equal to ωt and the instantaneous emf is

$$e = k \sin \omega t = E_m \sin \omega t \qquad (1\text{-}18)$$

for in reality k is the *maximum value* of e because it represents the voltage at the instant when sin ωt is unity ($\omega t = \pi/2$).

The curve representing the voltage of Eq. (1-18) is a *sine curve*. Such a curve is drawn conveniently by the method indicated in Fig. 7-18. The directed segment of a straight line or arrow, with fixed origin at p and of length E_m, revolves in a counterclockwise direction at a velocity of ω radians per second, and makes one revolution while the generated voltage passes through one cycle. The projections on the Y axis of the tip of the arrow determine the instantaneous values of the voltages. A number of values are shown at o, a, b, c, d, etc. in (b) of the figure. From an examination of the figure it is clear that the voltage curve is represented by the equation $e = E_m \sin \omega t$.

To draw the curve, lay off along the X axis equal angular distances oa, ab, bc, etc., corresponding to suitable angular displacements of the revolving arrow.   After the ordinates at points a, b, c, etc., have been erected, project the free end of E_m for the corresponding positions a', b', c', etc., to meet the ordinates, and draw a curve through the points obtained. The curve thus found is a graphical representation of Eq. (1-18).

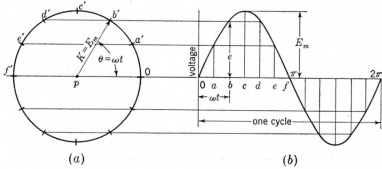

(a) (b)

Fig. 7-18. The sine wave of electromotive force.

Frequency.   The two-pole machines in Figs. 2-18, 3-18, and 5-18 each generate one positive loop and one negative loop per revolution.   Each loop represents one *alternation*, and two alternations constitute one *cycle*, for successive pairs of alternations are just like the first pair.   Multipolar machines (illustrated in Fig. 8-18) generate varying numbers of cycles per revolution, depending upon the number of poles they have.   A four-pole machine generates two cycles per revolution; a six-pole machine, three cycles per revolution; and a p-pole machine, $p/2$ cycles per revolution.

The number of complete cycles which a machine generates in 1 sec is called the *frequency*.   The frequency therefore depends upon both the number of poles and the speed of the machine. In the United States 60 and 25 cps are

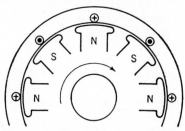

Fig. 8-18. The multipolar generator.

the standard frequencies of power circuits.   Systems supplying combined lighting and power loads usually use 60 cycles, while railway circuits require lower frequencies and usually operate at 25 cycles.

From the above it follows that synchronous machines designed for a particular frequency and with a particular number of poles can run at one speed only.   Thus two-pole 60-cycle alternators generate one cycle per revolution and run at 60 rps, or 3,600 rpm.   Similarly, those with four poles generate two cycles per revolution and must run 60/2 rps or

60 (60 ÷ 2) rpm.   In general, if f is the frequency in cycles per second and p is the number of poles, which is always an even number, the speed of the machine must be

$$\text{Revolutions per minute} = \frac{60f}{p/2} \qquad (2\text{-}18)$$

The possible speeds of 60-cycle machines are 7,200 ÷ p rpm while 25-cycle machines must run at 3,000 ÷ p rpm.

Average Ordinate of Sine Loop.   The average ordinate of any curve is the area under the curve divided by its base.   For one loop of the sine

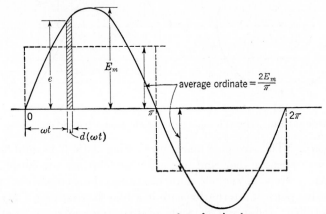

Fig. 9-18. Average value of a sine loop.

curve (Fig. 9-18), the average ordinate is conveniently expressed in terms of the maximum ordinate as follows:

By Eq. (1-18),

$$e = E_m \sin \omega t$$

and in accordance with the above definition the average value of e is

$$\begin{aligned}
E_{av} &= \frac{1}{\pi} \int_0^\pi e \, d(\omega t) \\
&= \frac{E_m}{\pi} \int_0^\pi \sin \omega t \, d(\omega t) \\
&= \frac{E_m}{\pi} \left[-\cos \omega t \right]_0^\pi \\
&= \frac{2E_m}{\pi} \qquad (3\text{-}18) \\
&= 0.636 E_m \qquad (4\text{-}18)
\end{aligned}$$

The average value of the sine curve taken over a cycle is evidently zero, because the area of the negative loop cancels that of the positive one.

Effective Value of a Sine Wave. When a sine wave of emf
on a resistance R, the current is at all times proportional to t.
and the wave of current is also a sine wave. This is evident, for t.
law and Eq. (1-18),

$$i = \frac{e}{R} = \frac{E_m}{R} \sin \omega t = I_m \sin \omega t \qquad (5$$

where the maximum value of the current is $I_m = E_m/R$.

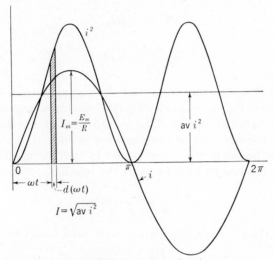

Fig. 10-18. Effective value of a sine wave.

The instantaneous power expended in the resistance is

$$p = Ri^2 \qquad (6\text{-}18)$$

or, from Eqs. (5-18) and (6-18),

$$p = RI_m^2 \sin^2 \omega t \qquad (7\text{-}18)$$

The sine wave of current and the (current)^2 curve are shown in Fig. 10-18.
The *average* power (P_{av}) expended in the circuit is equal to the resistance
times the average ordinate to the i^2 curve, or

$$\begin{aligned}
P_{av} &= \frac{R}{\pi} \int_0^\pi I_m^2 \sin^2 \omega t \, d(\omega t) \\
&= \frac{RI_m^2}{\pi} \int_0^\pi \left[\frac{1}{2} - \frac{1}{2} \cos 2\omega t \right]^\dagger d(\omega t) \\
&= \tfrac{1}{2} RI_m^2 \qquad (8\text{-}18)
\end{aligned}$$

† Since the curve $\cos 2\omega t$ has one positive loop and one negative loop between
0 and π, the value of the expression $\int_0^\pi \cos 2\omega t \, d(\omega t)$ is zero.

Stated in words, Eq. (8-18) says that the average power expended as heat in a resistance of R ohms by an a-c wave of sine shape is equal to one-half the product of the resistance and the square of the maximum current. Suppose next that the same resistance is connected to the terminals of a d-c circuit and that the current is increased until the power loss P in the resistance is the same as before ($P_{av} = P$). If the required strength of the direct current is I amp, the loss in the resistance is RI^2 watts. This loss, by supposition, is equal to P_{av} or

$$RI^2 = \tfrac{1}{2}RI_m{}^2$$

and

$$I = \frac{I_m}{\sqrt{2}} = 0.707I_m \tag{9-18}$$

This means that a sine-shaped wave of alternating current of maximum value I_m produces the same average heating effect as a continuous current with a steady value of only $0.707I_m$ or, expressed in another way, that $0.707I_m$ is the *effective value* of the sine wave of current.

The average power in the resistance could have been calculated from the voltage curve just as well, by using the relation

$$p = \frac{e^2}{R} = \frac{E_m{}^2}{R} \sin^2 \omega t \tag{10-18}$$

in which case the *effective voltage* would have been found to be

$$E = \frac{E_m}{\sqrt{2}} = 0.707E_m \tag{11-18}$$

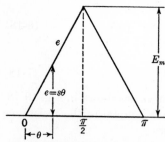

From the above it is apparent that the *effective value of a sine wave is $1/\sqrt{2}$ times its maximum ordinate.*

Effective Values of Other Wave Shapes. For any other curve the effective value is obtained in a manner exactly similar to that described above, that is, by (1) squaring the ordinates of the original curve, (2) finding the average ordinate of the square curve, and (3) extracting the square root of the average ordinate found under (2).

FIG. 11-18. Effective value of a triangular wave.

Because of the method used to find it, the effective value of a curve is sometimes called its *root-mean-square* value, abbreviated rms value.

Example 1. Find the effective value of the triangular wave shown in Fig. 11-18.

Since the wave is symmetrical about the ordinate through $\pi/2$, only one-half of the loop need be considered. Between zero and $\pi/2$ the voltage is

$$e = s\theta$$

where the slope is

$$s = \frac{2E_m}{\pi}$$

Squaring yields

$$e^2 = \frac{4E_m^2}{\pi^2} \theta^2$$

and

$$\text{Av. } e^2 = \frac{4E_m^2}{\pi^2} \frac{2}{\pi} \int_0^{\frac{\pi}{2}} \theta^2 d\theta$$

$$= \frac{8E_m^2}{\pi^3} \left[\frac{\theta^3}{3} \right]_0^{\frac{\pi}{2}}$$

$$= \frac{E_m^2}{3}$$

Accordingly, the effective voltage is

$$E = \sqrt{\frac{E_m^2}{3}} = \frac{E_m}{\sqrt{3}} = 0.578E_m$$

Alternating Volts and Amperes. Alternating-current circuit calculations are conveniently made with the use of effective values of voltage and current for, as has been seen, these quantities are in fact equivalent d-c values. *One a-c ampere (effective value) may therefore be defined as that rms alternating current which, flowing in a given resistance for a given length of time, dissipates therein the same amount of heat as one amp of direct current would dissipate in it in the same length of time.* It is assumed, of course, that no hysteresis or eddy-current losses are present. The reader can readily frame a similar definition for the alternating (effective) volt.

Alternating-current voltmeters and ammeters are usually designed to read effective values, while the oscillograph reads instantaneous values.

Notation. Throughout the remainder of this book the following notation is used for sine-wave currents, voltages, and power:

i, e, p, etc. = instantaneous values of current, voltage, power, etc.
I_m, E_m = maximum current and maximum voltage
I, E = effective values of current and voltage
P = average power

Form Factor. The ratio of the effective value of a wave to its average ordinate is called the *form factor*. For the sine wave this ratio is Eq. (11-18) divided by Eq. (4-18), or

$$\text{Form factor of sine wave} = \frac{\pi}{2\sqrt{2}} \text{ or } 1.11 \qquad (12\text{-}18)$$

For the triangular wave the average value is $\frac{1}{2}E_m$ and the form factor is $0.578 \div 0.5 = 1.156$. In general, peaked waves have high form factors and flat waves have low form factors. The form factor of a rectangular wave is 1, and this is the lowest form factor any wave can have.

Problems

1-18. (a) Draw one cycle of the voltage wave of which the equation is $e = 250 \sin \omega t$. Use voltage as ordinates and ωt as abscissas to the following scales: 100 volts $= 1$ in., π radians $= 2$ in. Determine (b) the effective, and (c) the average, value of the wave.

2-18. Using the same scales and the same set of coordinate axes as in Prob. 1-18, draw the following voltage curves: $e_3 = 100 \sin 3\omega t$ and $e_5 = 50 \sin 5\omega t$. Extend the curves over the angular distance of $\omega t = \pi$.

3-18. Find the number of poles which 60-cycle alternators with the following speeds must have: 900, 720, 514+, 450 rpm.

4-18. Find the correct speeds of 25-cycle generators with the following numbers of poles: 2, 6, 8, 10, 16, 28.

5-18. Sine-shaped current waves have the following maximum values: 200, 150, 80, 65 amp. Determine (a) the effective values, (b) the average values, of the current waves.

6-18. The maximum ordinate of a trapezoidal flux wave is 2.5×10^6 maxwells. The wave has the shape shown in Fig. A-18. Find (a) the average value and (b) the effective value of the flux wave.

7-18. The loops of a periodic voltage wave are semicircles. The average ordinate of the wave is 60 volts. Determine (a) the effective value, (b) the maximum value, and (c) the form factor of the wave.

8-18. The voltage wave $e = 200 \sin \omega t$ is impressed on a resistance of 12 ohms. Determine (a) the effective value of the current and (b) the average power expended in the resistance.

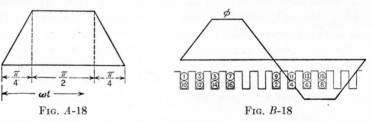

FIG. A-18   FIG. B-18

9-18. The wave of current in a resistance of 8 ohms is an isosceles triangle having an average value of 40 amp. What are (a) the shape of the voltage wave and (b) the effective value of the voltage impressed?

10-18. The air-gap flux wave of a two-pole alternator is the $\frac{1}{3}$ flat-top trapezoid shown in Fig. B-18. The armature winding consists of eight full-pitch coils of one turn each, distributed in eight slots (four slots per pole) spread uniformly over two-thirds of a pole pitch. (The angular distance between adjacent slots in each group is 30 deg.) The conductors are connected in series in the order 1, 2, 3, 4, etc. When a conductor moves under the middle of a pole face (conductors 5 and 7, for example) the voltage generated in it is 10 volts. Draw to scale the voltage wave generated by each turn of the winding and the wave of total voltage appearing between the ends of the winding.

CHAPTER 19

PHASOR REPRESENTATION

Scalar and Vector Quantities. A *scalar* is a quantity that has magnitude only. Illustrations of scalars are 40 acres, 20 min., 5 kwhr, etc. Scalars of like kind are added algebraically like ordinary numbers. A *vector* is a quantity that has direction as well as magnitude, both of which must be given to describe it completely. Force and velocity are common examples.

A vector is represented graphically by a segment of a straight line on which the origin and terminus are indicated. An arrow represents a vector completely when these points are given, or if it may be inferred that the tail is the origin and the tip is the terminus. The length of the arrow from tail to tip represents the magnitude, while the slope of the line and the arrowhead define the direction. A velocity vector is shown graphically in Fig. 1-19. Here the magnitude and direction of a southwest wind with a speed of 30 mph are represented by the arrow *OP*. The four principal points of the compass are indicated in the *XY*

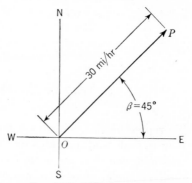

FIG. 1-19. Velocity vector.

plane. Since a southwest wind blows toward the northeast, the velocity is represented by an arrow 30 units long pointing northeasterly, or along a line that is 45 deg in advance of the east-west axis.

Phasors. With minor exceptions, the vectors used in this text are two-dimensional quantities or directed lines in a plane. To distinguish them from the more general three-dimensional vectors and to avoid confusion, the American Standards Association has recommended the use of the term *phasor* to designate such two-dimensional quantities. This practice is followed throughout the remainder of this text. Symbols representing phasors are printed in boldface roman type.

Methods of Representing Sine Waves. In Fig. 7-18 it was shown that the ordinates to a sine curve can be found from the projections along the Y axis of the free end of a revolving arrow (phasor), the length of which is equal to the maximum ordinate of the wave. The wave itself may therefore be represented in any one of three ways:

1. Graphically, by the sinusoidal curve
2. Mathematically, by the equation of the curve
3. Symbolically, by the revolving phasor that generates the curve

To illustrate, assume a sine wave of emf with an effective value of 40 volts. By Eq. (11-18) the maximum ordinate is $E_m = 40 \times \sqrt{2} = 56.5$ volts. If one begins to count time when the curve passes *upward* through zero, the sine curve of Fig. 2-19 correctly represents the voltage by method 1, while the equation $e = E_m \sin \omega t$ is its mathematical representation 2.

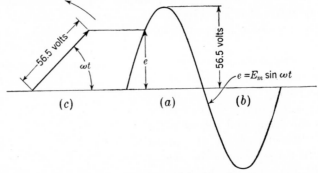

Fig. 2-19. Methods of representing sine waves.

To represent the voltage by method 3, one draws a phasor 56.5 volts long to scale and indicates rotation through an angle ωt in a *counterclockwise direction*, for this is the generally accepted method of measuring a positive angle. One may represent the phasor in any angular position, for it may be stopped in any phase of its rotation. The three methods of representation all appear in Fig. 2-19.

Phasor Diagrams of Sine Waves of the Same Frequency. Sine waves of the same frequency may be shown on the same diagram because the phasors representing the separate waves all revolve counterclockwise at the same velocity and so maintain a fixed position with respect to each other. This is illustrated in Fig. 3-19, in which a voltage e and a current i of the same frequency are shown. The current curve is assumed to pass upward through zero at the instant when $t = 0$, while at the same time the voltage wave has already advanced through the angle α from its zero value. Accordingly, the equation of the current wave is

$$i = I_m \sin \omega t$$

while the voltage wave is represented by

$$e = E_m \sin (\omega t + \alpha)$$

Since the voltage phasor is α radian in advance of the current phasor for all values of ωt, the diagram may be simplified by drawing it as it appears at the instant $t = 0$, as in Fig. 4-19. In this way the angle ωt is eliminated from the diagram.

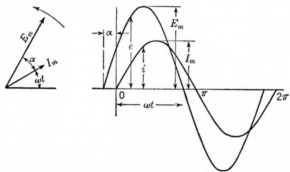

Fig. 3-19. Sine waves of the same frequency.

Sine waves of different frequencies cannot be represented on the same phasor diagram in a still picture because the speed of the revolving phasor has a different value for each of the several waves, and consequently the *phase angles* are constantly changing.

Phase Difference. Since in Fig. 3-19 the voltage wave passes through its zero value in a given direction before the current does, the voltage

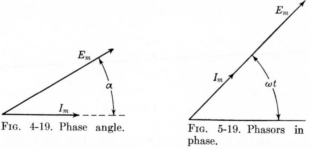

Fig. 4-19. Phase angle.   Fig. 5-19. Phasors in phase.

is said to *lead* the current, or the current *lags* the voltage. Lead or lag is expressed in terms of the angle between the two phasors representing the waves. In the illustration the current lags the voltage by α deg. The angle α is called the angle of *phase difference*, or simply the *phase angle* of the current with respect to the voltage. When the phase angle between two waves is zero (Fig. 5-19), the waves are said to be *in phase* with each other.

Phasors in A-c Theory. Alternating-current circuit calculations involve the addition and subtraction of currents and voltages, just as do d-c circuit calculations. Also, as with d-c circuits, they require that currents and voltages be multiplied together to obtain power, that voltages be divided by circuit constants (resistances in the case of d-c circuits) to obtain current, and occasionally that currents and voltages be squared or raised to some other power, or that the root of some power higher than the first be found. The student is familiar with all these processes involving ordinary numbers such as 100 volts, 16 amp, etc.

It has been shown that sine waves of current and voltage may be represented by phasors, and experience has proved that the calculations involving a-c quantities, such as those enumerated above, can be made most conveniently when the phasor form of notation is used. It is for this reason, and because the laws of a-c circuit theory are better understood and more readily applied when approached from the phasor standpoint, that this method of representation has come into such general use.

The remaining pages of this chapter are devoted to a discussion of the representation and mathematical manipulation of phasors. A few simple processes are illustrated, which the student is urged to master at the outset.

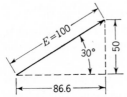

FIG. 6-19. Components of phasors.

Mathematical Representation of Phasors. Let the revolving phasor which represents a sine wave of 100 volts maximum be drawn for the instant when ωt is 30 deg, as in Fig. 6-19. Since the *sense* is always outward from the origin, any symbol or expression which informs the reader concerning the *length* of the phasor and its slope defines the phasor completely.

When rectangular coordinates are used, the phasor is defined by giving its X and Y components. The X component in Fig. 6-19 is 100 cos 30° = 86.6 volts, while the Y component is 100 sin 30° = 50 volts. The complete expression is

$$\mathbf{E} = 86.6 + j50 \qquad (1\text{-}19)$$

in which the boldface $\mathbf{E}$ indicates that the quantity is a phasor, while the symbol $+j$ is prefixed to the 50 to indicate positive direction along the Y axis. This symbol will be further explained shortly. The *length* of the phasor is found from Eq. (1-19) by computing the length of the hypotenuse of the right triangle with sides of 50 and 86.6, thus:

$$E = \sqrt{86.6^2 + 50^2} = 100 \text{ volts} \qquad (2\text{-}19)$$

[In Eq. (2-19) E is a scalar quantity, for it represents length only, and so is printed in lightface italic.] The *slope* of the phasor is defined in terms of the tangent of the angle at the origin as

$$\tan \theta = \frac{50}{86.6}$$

and

$$\theta = 30° \qquad (3\text{-}19)$$

Sometimes it is more convenient to use the *polar* form of expression to represent the phasor. This form of expression combines the *length* of Eq. (2-19) with the *slope* of Eq. (3-19), thus:

$$\mathbf{E} = 100\underline{/30°} \qquad (4\text{-}19)$$

Here the magnitude is given by the number or scalar in the right-hand member, while the slope is given by the angle indicated as shown. Equation (4-19) means a phasor that is 100 units long and has a slope of 30 deg.

The symbol $\underline{/30°}$ or in general $\underline{/\theta}$ designates the positive angle through which the phasor has revolved after passing through the zero or reference axis (usually the X axis). If the angle of the phasor with respect to the reference axis is negative, the angle may be designated either as $\overline{\backslash\theta}$ or as $\underline{/-\theta}$. Both forms are used as, for example, $\mathbf{E} = 80\overline{\backslash\theta}$ or $\mathbf{E} = 80\underline{/-\theta}$.

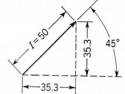

Conversion from Polar to Rectangular Form and Vice Versa. Phasor expressions may be converted from one form to another. Thus a current phasor of length 50 amp, with a slope of 45 deg (Fig. 7-19), expressed as a polar is

Fig. 7-19. Rectangular and polar representations.

$$\mathbf{I} = 50\underline{/45°}$$

The corresponding expression in rectangular form is

$$\mathbf{I} = 50(\cos 45° + j \sin 45°)$$
$$= 35.35 + j35.35 \qquad (5\text{-}19)$$

Equation (5-19) may again be converted to polar form as illustrated in Eqs. (2-19) and (3-19) of the previous article for

$$\text{Length} = I = \sqrt{35.35^2 + 35.35^2} = 50 \text{ amp} \qquad (6\text{-}19)$$

and

$$\theta = \tan^{-1}\frac{35.35}{35.35} = 45° \qquad (7\text{-}19)$$

whence

$$\mathbf{I} = 50\underline{/45°} \qquad (8\text{-}19)$$

Meaning of Symbol j. The letter j in Eqs. (1-19) and (5-19) is a symbol of operation. Just as the symbols $+$, $\times$, $\sqrt{}$, $\int$, etc., are used with numbers to indicate that certain operations are to be performed upon the numbers with which they are associated, so the symbol j is used to indicate rotation of a phasor through 90 deg.

In complex notation, numbers such as 3, 5, −4, etc., are called *real* numbers, and are represented by phasors drawn from the origin along the X axis, to the right if the sign is *positive* and to the *left* if it is *negative*, as in Fig. 8-19.

Prefixing the symbol j to a positive real number has the effect of turning it through an angle of 90 deg from the $+X$ direction. The rotation is counterclockwise for positive values $(+j)$ and clockwise for negative values $(-j)$. For example, the quantity $+3$ (Fig. 8-19) is represented as a phasor 3 units long, in the positive X direction. Multiplying this number by $+j$ yields $+j3$. This is a phasor 3 units long, which appears in the positive Y direction. Similarly, the product $-j2$ represents counterclockwise rotation through 90 deg of the real number 2, and the phasor $-j2$ is a number 2 units long in the negative Y direction.

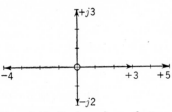

FIG. 8-19. Real and quadrature quantities.

Numbers to which the operator j is prefixed are called *imaginary* or *quadrature* numbers, whereas ordinary numbers like 2, 5, 10 are called real numbers. Phasors usually, though not always, have both real and imaginary components.

Repeated applications of the operator j indicates repeated rotations of 90 deg. Accordingly, the expression $j^2 2$, for example, requires that 2 be revolved through 180 deg from the $+X$ direction in either a clockwise or a counterclockwise direction. The result of the rotation is simply to reverse the phasor $+2$ (or to change the quantity from $+2$ to -2). This is shown as follows: $j^2 2 = (+j)^2 2 = (-j)^2 2 = -1(2)$. Thus, $j^2 = -1$ and $j = +\sqrt{-1}$ while $-j = -\sqrt{-1}$.

By a similar process of reasoning, the equivalent expressions given below are obtained:

$j = 90$ deg counterclockwise rotation $= \sqrt{-1} = -(-j)$

$j^2 = 180$ deg counterclockwise rotation $= (\sqrt{-1})^2 = -1 = (-j)^2$ or $= (+j)^2$

$j^3 = 270$ deg counterclockwise rotation $= (\sqrt{-1})^3 = -\sqrt{-1} = -j$

$j^4 = 360$ deg counterclockwise rotation $= (\sqrt{-1})^4 = +1$

$j^5 = 450$ deg counterclockwise rotation $= (\sqrt{-1})^5 = \sqrt{-1} = +j$

(It should be noted also that $\dfrac{1}{j} = \dfrac{j}{j^2} = \dfrac{\sqrt{-1}}{-1} = -\sqrt{-1} = -j$.)

Addition of Phasors. Phasors lying in the same plane are added according to the parallelogram law. This is equivalent to adding their real and their quadrature components separately and then taking the square root of the sum of their squares to obtain the length of the diagonal.

To illustrate, suppose the two forces

$\mathbf{F}_1 = 10$ lb
    acting at 60 deg with the X axis

and

$\mathbf{F}_2 = 16$ lb
    acting at 30 deg with the X axis

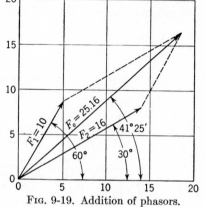

FIG. 9-19. Addition of phasors.

act simultaneously on a body at point 0 (Fig. 9-19). The two acting together are equivalent to a single force $\mathbf{F}_0$, equal to the diagonal of the parallelogram of which $\mathbf{F}_1$ and $\mathbf{F}_2$ are sides, and thus $\mathbf{F}_0$ becomes the *sum* of $\mathbf{F}_1$ and $\mathbf{F}_2$. Expressed in polar form,

$$\mathbf{F}_1 = 10\underline{/60°}$$

and

$$\mathbf{F}_2 = 16\underline{/30°}$$

These expressions are converted to rectangular components by multiplying the length of the phasor in each case by the sine and cosine of the phase angle; whence

$$\mathbf{F}_1 = 10(\cos 60° + j \sin 60°) = 5 + j8.66 \qquad (9\text{-}19)$$
$$\mathbf{F}_2 = 16(\cos 30° + j \sin 30°) = 13.86 + j8 \qquad (10\text{-}19)$$

Adding the real and quadrature components separately yields

$$\mathbf{F}_0 = 18.86 + j16.66 \qquad (11\text{-}19)$$

The amount of this force is

$$F_0 = \sqrt{18.86^2 + 16.66^2} = 25.16 \text{ lb} \qquad (12\text{-}19)$$

and its phase angle is

$$\theta = \tan^{-1}\frac{16.66}{18.86} = 41°\ 25' \qquad (13\text{-}19)$$

It should be observed that these values agree with those obtained graphically in Fig. 9-19, so it is apparent *that phasors are added by separately adding their real and their quadrature components.*

Subtraction of Phasors. Suppose it be required to subtract $\mathbf{F}_2$ from $\mathbf{F}_1$ in Fig. 9-19. This is equivalent to converting the force F_2 from a *pull* at 0 to a *push* at 0, or to a pull in the negative direction. Figure 10-19 is the new diagram which fits this case. It is apparent that $\mathbf{F}_2$ is subtracted by changing its sign and then adding it to $\mathbf{F}_1$ as before.

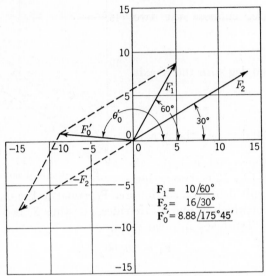

$$\mathbf{F}_1 = 10\underline{/60°}$$
$$\mathbf{F}_2 = 16\underline{/30°}$$
$$\mathbf{F}_0' = 8.88\underline{/175°45'}$$

Fig. 10-19. Subtraction of phasors.

From Eqs. (9-19) and (10-19),

$$\mathbf{F}_1 = 5.0 + j8.66$$
$$-\mathbf{F}_2 = -13.86 - j8.0$$

and accordingly

$$\mathbf{F}_0' = \mathbf{F}_1 - \mathbf{F}_2 = -8.86 + j0.66 \tag{14-19}$$

The amount of this force is

$$F_0' = \sqrt{8.86^2 + 0.66^2} = 8.88 \text{ lb} \tag{15-19}$$

and its phase angle is such that

$$\tan \theta_0' = \frac{0.66}{-8.86} = -0.0745$$

or

$$\theta_0' = 175° 45' \tag{16-19}$$

Thus the difference between two phasors is obtained by changing the sign of the phasor which is to be subtracted—reversing it—and then proceeding as in addition.

Application to Alternating Currents. It is of interest to illustrate the use of phasor addition and subtraction as applied to alternating currents and voltages.

1. *Addition.* In Fig. 11-19 let the sine waves of current i_1 and i_2 be the currents in the branches of a divided circuit, and let them join to produce the current i_0. If the maximum values of the component waves are 10 and 7 amp, respectively, and the phase relations are as shown in the

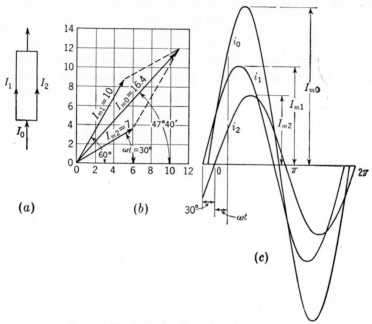

FIG. 11-19. Addition of sine waves of current.

figure, what are the maximum and effective values of the i_0 wave, and what is the phase angle?

The rectangular components of $\mathbf{I}_{m1}$ are

$$\text{Real component of } I_{m1} = 10 \cos 60° = 5.0$$
$$\text{Quadrature component of } I_{m1} = 10 \sin 60° = 8.66$$

or, expressed as a phasor,

$$\mathbf{I}_{m1} = 5.0 + j8.66 \tag{17-19}$$

Similarly,

$$\mathbf{I}_{m2} = 7(\cos 30° + j \sin 30°) = 6.06 + j3.5 \tag{18-19}$$

By adding the real and the quadrature components of Eqs. (17-19) and (18-19) separately, one obtains

$$\mathbf{I}_{m0} = 11.06 + j12.16 \tag{19-19}$$

The phasor I_{m0} in Eq. (19-19) generates the sine wave i_0, which is the sum of the i_1 and i_2 waves. The length of the phasor is

$$I_{m0} = \sqrt{11.06^2 + 12.16^2} = 16.4 \text{ amp} \qquad (20\text{-}19)$$

its phase angle is

$$\theta_0 = \tan^{-1} \frac{12.16}{11.06} = 47° \ 40' \qquad (21\text{-}19)$$

and the effective current is

$$I_0 = \frac{16.4}{\sqrt{2}} = 11.6 \text{ amp} \qquad (22\text{-}19)$$

Since the effective value is equal to a constant times the maximum value, the phasor diagram could as well be drawn using phasors with lengths equal to the effective values of the component currents. The maximum I_{m0} would then be found by multiplying I_0 by $\sqrt{2}$. Phasor diagrams of voltage and current are usually drawn this way, since effective values are usually desired in the results.

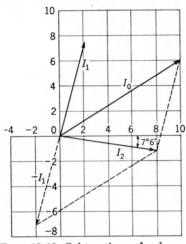

FIG. 12-19. Subtraction of phasor currents.

2. *Subtraction.* In Fig. 12-19 suppose that the total current I_0 and the current I_1 in one branch are

$$I_0 = 10 + j6 \qquad (23\text{-}19)$$

and

$$I_1 = 2 + j7 \qquad (24\text{-}19)$$

and let it be required to find the current I_2 in the remaining branch, all being given in terms of their effective values.

Since $I_2 + I_1 = I_0$, it follows that

$$I_2 = I_0 - I_1$$

or, by subtracting Eq. (24-19) from Eq. (23-19), that

$$I_2 = 8 - j1 \qquad (25\text{-}19)$$

Then

$$I_2 = \sqrt{8^2 + 1^2} = 8.06 \text{ amp} \qquad (26\text{-}19)$$

and its phase angle is

$$\theta = \tan^{-1} \frac{-1}{8} = -7° \ 6' \qquad (27\text{-}19)$$

The maximum value of the wave is $\sqrt{2}$ times its effective value or

$$I_{m2} = 1.41 \times 8.06 = 11.35 \text{ amp} \qquad (28\text{-}19)$$

The phasor $\mathbf{I}_{m2}$ generates a sine wave of current which is equal to the wave generated by $\mathbf{I}_{m0}$ minus that generated by $\mathbf{I}_{m1}$. These waves are not shown in the figure.

Multiplication of Phasors. 1. *Rectangular Form.* Assume **A** and **B** shown in Fig. 13-19, and let it be required to find their product **C**. Expressed in rectangular coordinates,

$$\mathbf{A} = 1 + j3$$
$$\mathbf{B} = 4 + j3$$
$$\mathbf{C} = \mathbf{AB} = 4 + j12 + j3 + j^2 9$$

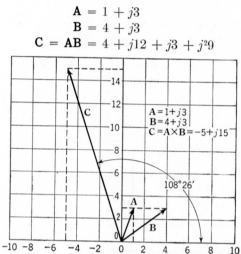

FIG. 13-19. The product of two phasors expressed in rectangular components.

It is to be remembered, however, that $j^2 =$ counterclockwise rotation through $180° = -1$; hence,

$$\mathbf{C} = 4 - 9 + j15 = -5 + j15 \qquad (29\text{-}19)$$
$$C = \sqrt{5^2 + 15^2} = 15.8 \qquad (30\text{-}19)$$
$$\theta = \tan^{-1}\frac{15}{-5} = 108° \ 26' \qquad (31\text{-}19)$$

Accordingly, the polar form of the product is

$$\mathbf{C} = 15.8\underline{/108° \ 26'} \qquad (32\text{-}19)$$

2. *Polar Form.* If the phasors are originally in the polar form, multiplication is greatly simplified, for it can be shown[1] that *the product*

_____

[1] Consider the two phasors

$$\mathbf{A} = A\underline{/\alpha} = A\,(\cos \alpha + j \sin \alpha)$$
$$\mathbf{B} = B\underline{/\beta} = B\,(\cos \beta + j \sin \beta)$$

Their product is

$$\begin{aligned}
\mathbf{AB} &= AB(\cos \alpha \cos \beta + j \sin \alpha \cos \beta + j \cos \alpha \sin \beta + j^2 \sin \alpha \sin \beta) \\
&= AB[(\cos \alpha \cos \beta - \sin \alpha \sin \beta) + j(\sin \alpha \cos \beta + \cos \alpha \sin \beta)] \\
&= AB[\cos (\alpha + \beta) + j \sin (\alpha + \beta)] \\
&= AB\underline{/\alpha + \beta}
\end{aligned}$$

of any two phasors **A** *and* **B** *is a third phasor* **C** *equal in length to* $A \times B$ *and having a slope or phase angle equal to the sum of the angles of* **A** *and* **B**. Thus if

$$\mathbf{A} = A\underline{/\alpha}$$
$$\mathbf{B} = B\underline{/\beta}$$
$$\mathbf{C} = \mathbf{AB} = AB\underline{/\alpha + \beta} \qquad (33\text{-}19)$$

To illustrate, let it be required to find the product of the two phasors **A** and **B** of Fig. 14-19. The polar expressions are

$$\mathbf{A} = 4\underline{/15°}$$
$$\mathbf{B} = 5\underline{/45°}$$

and their product is

$$\mathbf{C} = 20\underline{/60°}$$

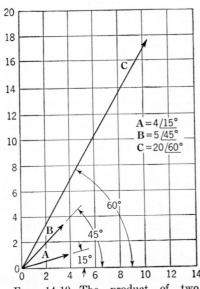

Fig. 14-19. The product of two phasors expressed in polar form.

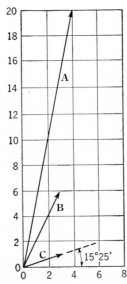

Fig. 15-19. The quotient of two phasors.

Division of Phasors. 1. *Rectangular Form.* Let the given phasors be

$$\mathbf{A} = 4 + j20$$
$$\mathbf{B} = 3 + j6$$

and let it be required to find the quotient $\mathbf{A} \div \mathbf{B}$ (Fig. 15-19). If division is expressed in the usual way, the quotient becomes

$$\mathbf{C} = \frac{4 + j20}{3 + j6} \qquad (34\text{-}19)$$

The next step is to rationalize the denominator by multiplying both terms of the fraction by the conjugate of the denominator, that is, by the denominator with the sign of the quadrature or j term changed. Thus

$$C = \frac{(4 + j20)(3 - j6)}{(3 + j6)(3 - j6)}$$
$$= \frac{12 + j60 - j24 - j^2 120}{9 - j^2 36}$$

or, since $-j^2 = 1$,

$$C = \frac{132 + j36}{45} = 2.9 + j0.8 \tag{35-19}$$

The length of C is

$$C = \sqrt{2.9^2 + 0.8^2} = 3 \tag{36-19}$$

and its phase angle is

$$\theta = \tan^{-1} \frac{0.8}{2.9} = 15° \, 25' \tag{37-19}$$

2. *Polar Form.* Since division and multiplication are reverse processes, it is to be expected that the division of phasors is also simplified when they are expressed in polar form. The process of multiplication being reversed, *the quotient of* **A** ÷ **B** *is found to be* **C**, *with length* A ÷ B *and slope or phase angle equal to the angle of* **A** *minus the angle of* **B**.

To illustrate, let it be required to find the quotient of **C** ÷ **A** in Fig. 14-19. Performing the division according to the above rule yields

$$C = 20\underline{/60°}$$
$$A = 4\underline{/15°}$$
$$B = C \div A = (20 \div 4)\underline{/60° - 15°}$$
$$= 5\underline{/45°} \tag{38-19}$$

Reciprocal of a Phasor. The reciprocal of a phasor is the quotient obtained by dividing unity by the phasor in question. To illustrate, let it be required to find the reciprocal of

$$A = 5\underline{/30°}$$
$$= 5(\cos 30° + j \sin 30°)$$
$$= 4.33 + j2.5$$

The division may be carried out in either polar or rectangular notation. In polar form one obtains

$$C = \frac{1}{A} = \frac{1}{5\underline{/30°}}$$
$$= \frac{1\underline{/0°}}{5\underline{/30°}}$$
$$= \tfrac{1}{5}\underline{/0° - 30°}$$
$$= 0.20\underline{/-30°} \tag{39-19}$$

Reduced to rectangular components, the quotient is

$$\mathbf{C} = 0.20(\cos 30° - j \sin 30°)$$
$$= 0.1732 - j0.100 \tag{40-19}$$

When the division is carried out in rectangular components, the procedure is as follows:

$$\mathbf{C} = \frac{1}{4.33 + j2.5}$$
$$= \frac{4.33 - j2.5}{4.33^2 + 2.5^2}$$
$$= \frac{4.33 - j2.5}{25}$$
$$= 0.1732 - j0.10$$

Reduced to polar form the quotient is

$$\mathbf{C} = 0.2\underline{/-30°}$$

which checks the value previously found.

By generalizing from the above, one concludes that *the reciprocal of a phasor is another phasor, the length and phase angle of which are equal, respectively, to the reciprocal of the length and the negative of the phase angle of the original phasor.*

Conjugate of a Phasor. If a phasor $\mathbf{A} = A\underline{/\phi}$ is turned through the angle $\overline{\backslash 2\phi}$ one obtains a new phasor $\mathbf{A}^* = A\overline{\backslash\phi}$, which is called the *conjugate* of $\mathbf{A}$. Similarly, the conjugate of $\mathbf{D} = D\overline{\backslash\delta}$ is $\mathbf{D}^* = D\underline{/\delta}$. The conjugate of a phasor has the same magnitude as the original phasor and its phase angle is the negative of the original angle.

To denote the conjugate of a phasor, boldface roman type followed by an asterisk is used. Thus, in respect to the above phasors $\mathbf{A} = A\underline{/\phi}$ and $\mathbf{D} = D\overline{\backslash\delta}$ one may write $\mathbf{A}^* = A\overline{\backslash\phi}$ and $\mathbf{D}^* = D\underline{/\delta}$. In terms of rectangular components, since $\mathbf{A} = a_1 + ja_2$ and $D = d_1 - jd_2$, one writes: $\mathbf{A}^* = a_1 - ja_2$ and $\mathbf{D}^* = d_1 + jd_2$.

Powers and Roots of Phasors. Powers and roots of phasors may be evaluated as special cases of multiplication.

If $\mathbf{C} = C\underline{/\gamma} = (A\underline{/\alpha})^n$, the nth power of $\mathbf{A}$ is defined as

$$C\underline{/\gamma} = (A\underline{/\alpha})(A\underline{/\alpha})(A\underline{/\alpha}) \cdots \text{ to } n \text{ terms}$$

which, by the rule for multiplying phasors becomes

$$C\underline{/\gamma} = (A\underline{/\alpha})^n = A^n\underline{/n\alpha}$$

where $C = A^n$
$\gamma = n\alpha$

Similarly, if $\mathbf{D} = D\underline{/\delta} = \sqrt[n]{A\underline{/\alpha}} = (A\underline{/\alpha})^{1/n}$, then by the rule of multiplication

$$D\underline{/\delta} = A^{1/n}\underline{/\alpha/n} = \sqrt[n]{A}\underline{/\alpha/n}$$

where $D = \sqrt[n]{A}$
$\delta = \alpha/n$

Example 1. Evaluate (a) the expression $(2\underline{/15°})^3$ and (b) the expression $\sqrt[3]{27\underline{/90°}}$.
(a) $(2\underline{/15°})^3 = 2 \times 2 \times 2\underline{/15° + 15° + 15°} = 8\underline{/45°}$
(b) $\sqrt[3]{27\underline{/90°}} = \sqrt[3]{27}\underline{/90°/3} = 3\underline{/30°}$

Problems

1-19. Represent the voltage wave $e = 80 \sin (\omega t + \pi/3)$ as (a) a wave in rectangular coordinates, (b) a revolving phasor.

2-19. Represent the following waves of current and voltage on a single diagram: $e = 100 \sin (\omega t + \pi/6)$, $i = 40 \cos (\omega t + \pi/3)$. Draw the curves and the revolving phasors which generate them. Determine the angle of lead or lag of the current with respect to the voltage.

3-19. A circuit consists of three elements connected in series. The phasor voltages consumed in the separate elements are

$$\mathbf{E}_1 = 30 + j40$$
$$\mathbf{E}_2 = 6 + j30$$
$$\mathbf{E}_3 = 20 - j200$$

Determine (a) the phasor impressed voltage, (b) the scalar value of the voltage impressed, (c) the phase angle of the voltage.

4-19. The total current supplied to a branched circuit is $\mathbf{I} = 80 - j60$. There are three parallel branches, the currents in two of which are

$$\mathbf{I}_1 = 20 + j30$$
$$\mathbf{I}_2 = 32 - j65$$

(a) Find the current $\mathbf{I}_3$ in the remaining branch and determine (b) its scalar value and (c) its phase angle.

5-19. A body is acted on by three forces. Two of the forces are

$$\mathbf{F}_1 = 25 - j40$$
$$\mathbf{F}_2 = -30 + j50$$

while the resultant is

$$\mathbf{F}_R = -12 - j32$$

Find (a) the remaining component $\mathbf{F}_3$, (b) its scalar value, and (c) its phase angle.

6-19. Express the following phasors in polar form:

$$\mathbf{F}_1 = 24 - j36$$
$$\mathbf{F}_2 = -32 + j40$$

7-19. Express the current and voltage phasors given below in rectangular form:

$$\mathbf{I} = 40\overline{\underline{\smash{\big\backslash}30°}}$$
$$\mathbf{E} = 120\underline{/20°}$$

8-19. Find the reciprocal of each of the phasors in Prob. 7-19 and express them in rectangular components.

9-19. The phasor power (**P**) expended in a circuit that has the current and impressed voltage given in Prob. 7-19 is the product of **I** and the conjugate of **E**. The conjugate of **E** is

$$\mathbf{E} = 120\underline{\diagdown 20°}$$

Determine the phasor power expended in the circuit and express in rectangular form.

10-19. Find the product of **A** and **B** given below:

$$\mathbf{A} = 120 - j90$$
$$\mathbf{B} = -90 + j60$$

Express the result in (*a*) rectangular and (*b*) polar form.

11-19. Find the reciprocals of

$$\mathbf{F}_1 = 120 + j80$$
$$\mathbf{F}_2 = 0 - j60$$
$$\mathbf{F}_3 = -45 + j20$$

12-19. In a-c circuits with pure sine waves of current and voltage, the quotient obtained by dividing the phasor impressed voltage by the phasor current is called the *phasor impedance* of the circuit. What is the phasor impedance of the circuit in which an impressed potential difference $\mathbf{E} = 110 + j173$ maintains a current

$$\mathbf{I} = 37.6 - j13.7?$$

13-19. The *characteristic impedance* ($\mathbf{Z}_0$) of a transmission line is given by the expression $\mathbf{Z}_0 = \sqrt{\mathbf{Z}/\mathbf{Y}}$ wherein **Z** is called the phasor impedance and **Y** is the phasor admittance of the line. A certain long high-voltage line has the values of **Z** and **Y** given below.

$$\mathbf{Z} = 40 + j160$$
$$\mathbf{Y} = 0 + j11 \times 10^{-4}$$

Determine the characteristic impedance of the line and express in both polar and rectangular form.

14-19. When computations are made of the operating characteristics of long telephone or power transmission lines, it is necessary to know the phasor angle **θ** of the line, which is defined symbolically by the expression

$$\theta = \sqrt{\mathbf{ZY}}$$

Find the phasor angle of the line in Prob. 13-19 and express in rectangular form. (The symbols **Z** and **Y** have the meanings and values assigned to them in Prob. 13-19.)

CHAPTER 20

SERIES CIRCUITS

In constant-potential d-c circuits the resistance alone determines the amount of current that exists in the circuit. In a-c circuits, however, both voltage and current are constantly changing. Varying current induces a counter emf in the inductance of a circuit which tends to prevent the current from changing. Similarly, if a varying potential difference appears across the terminals of a capacitance, it gives rise to a charging current which tends to prevent the voltage from changing.

Accordingly, the applied voltage required to maintain a given alternating current in a circuit that has inductance, capacitance, and resistance in series must contain components of voltage equal in magnitude and

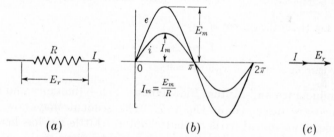

(a) (b) (c)

FIG. 1-20. The voltage and current in a resistance.

opposite in phase, respectively, to the counter emfs of inductance, capacitance, and resistance.

It is the purpose of this chapter to study the series circuit containing various combinations of resistance, inductance, and capacitance, and to develop methods for determining the magnitude and phase of the components of voltage E_r, E_l, and E_c that are required to maintain a current of I amp in the circuit.

Circuit with Resistance Alone. When an alternating voltage e is impressed on a resistance R, the current in the resistance is $i = e/R$ by Ohm's law. From this it follows that, since R is a constant, the current wave has the same shape as the voltage wave (Fig. 1-20). The current and voltage waves both pass through corresponding values at the same time; both pass through zero in a positive direction at the same time, both are zero at the same time, both are maximum at the same time, etc. When this relation exists, the voltage and current are said to be *in phase* with each other. At the instant when maximum values of both voltage and current occur, the impressed voltage is

$$E_m = RI_m$$

If both sides of this equation are divided by $\sqrt{2}$, the left side becomes the effective voltage impressed and the right side becomes the product of the effective current and the resistance, or, in symbols,

$$E_r = RI \tag{1-20}$$

From this equation and the foregoing discussion one concludes that, *when an alternating potential difference of E_r volts (effective) is impressed on a resistance of R ohms, an alternating current of $I = E_r/R$ effective amperes flows in the circuit, and the current is in phase with the impressed voltage.* The phasor representations of impressed voltage and current are shown in (c) of Fig. 1-20.

Example 1. The resistance of a 240-watt incandescent lamp is 60 ohms. (a) How much current does the lamp take when an alternating potential difference of 120 volts (effective) is impressed? (b) What is the phase position of current with respect to voltage?

(a) By Eq. (1-20) the current is

$$I = {}^{120}\!/_{60} = 2 \text{ amp}$$

(b) The current is in phase with the voltage.

Self-inductance and Mutual Inductance. Self-inductance and mutual inductance are discussed in Chap. 7. The student may now find it advantageous to reread parts of that chapter. Little use has heretofore been made of these concepts because in most d-c circuits the current is steady. In a-c circuits the current varies continually and voltages are absorbed in self-inductance and mutual inductance. In dealing with such circuits, it is important to have a clear understanding of the nature of inductance and of its influence upon the flow of alternating currents. For this reason some of the simple facts pertaining to inductance are here reviewed.

It is well known that a current always magnetizes the space around it and that the lines of induction established link the current that produces them (Fig. 2-20). The number of lines linking a current is increased when the conductor is wound in the form of a coil (Fig. 3-20), for then, on the average, each line links several turns and so links the current several times instead of only once, as in Fig. 2-20. The number of linkages is still further increased when the wire is wound on an iron core as in

Fig. 4-20. When the number of lines linking a current is equivalent to ϕ lines each linking the current N times, the total number of flux linkages is $N\phi$. In a circuit like the ones mentioned above, so long as the permeability of the medium in which the flux is established does not change, the

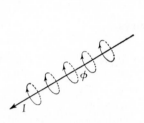

FIG. 2-20. The flux linking a straight current-carrying wire.

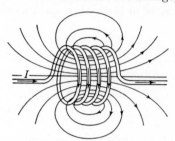

FIG. 3-20. The flux linking a coil of wire.

number of flux linkages is proportional to the current. In the mks system of units, the proportionality factor L is so defined that

$$LI = N\phi$$

or

$$L = \frac{N\phi}{I} \quad \text{henrys} \tag{2-20}$$

The constant L is the *coefficient of self-induction* or simply the *self-inductance* of the circuit. In words it may be stated that when one

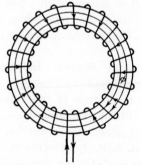

FIG. 4-20. The flux in an iron ring.

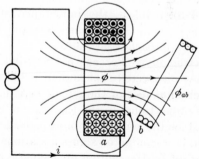

FIG. 5-20. The flux of mutual induction.

ampere of current produces one weber-turn of magnetic linkage with the circuit in which it flows, the self-inductance of the circuit is one henry.

Since 1 weber $= 10^8$ maxwells it follows that, in the practical system of units, 1 amp produces 10^8 (maxwell-turn) linkages with a circuit which has an inductance of 1 henry.

Often two separate circuits are located adjacent to each other and are so formed that a current in one of them [Fig. 5-20(a)] sets up lines of induction that link the other [Fig. 5-20(b)]. If a current of I_a amperes in (a) sets up $N_b\phi_{ab}$ weber-turn linkages with winding (b), the *mutual inductance* of (b) with respect to (a) is

$$M_{ab} = \frac{N_b\phi_{ab}}{I_a} \qquad \text{henrys} \qquad (3\text{-}20)$$

The mutual inductance of (a) with respect to (b) is

$$M_{ba} = \frac{N_a\phi_{ba}}{I_b}$$

and

$$M_{ab} = M_{ba} = M$$

In general, except when magnetic materials are present, both the self-inductance and mutual inductance of a circuit depend only upon the physical properties of the circuit, such as length, whether the conductor is coiled or straight, whether outgoing and return conductors are close together or far apart, etc. Since L and M are usually independent of current and depend only upon the physical nature of the circuit, they are called *circuit constants*.

If a magnetic material forms a part of a magnetic circuit about a current, the inductance of the circuit varies with the current in the circuit. In that case the number of lines of induction that link the circuit per ampere of current, which is the inductance, is directly proportional to the relative permeability of the magnetic material at the given flux density (Fig. 7-8). Hence, the inductance of the circuit is large when the current is small and becomes less and less as the current increases and the core approaches saturation.

Electromotive Forces of Self-induction and Mutual Induction. Faraday discovered that an emf is induced in a circuit by changing the magnetic linkages of the circuit and that the magnitude of the induced emf is proportional to the time rate of change of the linkages.

Most of the emfs heretofore considered are generated either by the motion of a conductor across a stationary field, as in d-c generators and motors, or by the motion of magnetic poles past stationary conductors, as in revolving-field alternators. It was stated in Chap. 7, however, that an emf is *self-induced* in a circuit when current in the circuit changes or varies. The flux of induction linking the circuit changes with varying current and thereby induces emfs therein. Such emfs of self-induction are present in the short-circuited coils of d-c generators and motors during commutation, in the windings of a-c generators, motors, and transformers during normal operation, and to some degree in all a-c circuits.

The emf induced in a circuit by its own changing current is called an *emf of self-induction*. On the other hand, when as in Fig. 5-20, a changing current in a circuit *a* induces an emf in another circuit *b*, the voltage induced in *b* is an emf of *mutual induction*. The emfs of both self-induction and mutual induction oppose the change in current that produces them. Hence, to maintain an alternating current in a self-inductance or mutual inductance requires that a component of impressed voltage be applied which at all times is equal in magnitude and opposite in direction to the voltage induced in the inductance. For this reason the emfs of self-induction and mutual induction are called *counter emfs*.

Current and Induced Voltage in an Inductance. The counter emf induced in the inductance of a circuit is proportional to the rate of change of current or to the rate of change of flux. When current changes at the rate di/dt amp/sec, the flux linkages change at the rate of $Nd\phi/dt$ linkages per second, and by Eq. (3-7), the instantaneous induced voltage is

$$e = -L\frac{di}{dt} = -\frac{Nd\phi}{dt} \qquad \text{volts}$$

The corresponding expression for the average induced voltage is

$$E_{av} = -\frac{LI}{t} = -\frac{N\phi}{t}$$

found on page 78. The minus signs are used to indicate that the induced voltage opposes the change of current, or that it is a counter emf.

Let the circuit (*a*) in Fig. 6-20 have an inductance of *L* henrys and let the resistance be so small that it may be disregarded. A sine wave of current *i* is caused to flow in the inductance by impressing a suitable alternating-voltage wave. The usual shorthand expression for the instantaneous current is then

$$i = I_m \sin \omega t$$

The current constantly changes according to the ordinates of the current curve in the figure, but the *rate of change* varies according to the *slope* of the curve. The counter emf induced at any instant is equal to *L* times the slope of the current curve, but it is positive when the slope is negative and negative when the slope is positive. The emf has its maximum values at 1, 3, and 5, where the slopes of the current wave are steepest, and is zero at 2 and 4, where the slopes are zero. From 1 to 2 and from 4 to 5 the slopes are positive and the counter emfs are negative, while from 2 to 4 the slopes are negative and the counter emf is positive. It is shown below that, if the current wave is sine-shaped as here assumed, the wave of induced emf is a negative cosine wave or, in other words, it is a sine wave that is shifted 90 time degrees to the right of the current wave, as shown by the counter emf curve e_c in Fig. 6-20. Thus if the current wave is sine-shaped, the wave of induced voltage is a sine curve which lags the current by 90 deg.

To maintain the assumed current in the inductance of the circuit requires that the voltage impressed be exactly equal and opposite to the counter emf at every instant of time. This condition is fulfilled by the sine curve e of the figure. This curve is 90 time degrees ahead of the current. Accordingly, *in an inductive circuit the component of impressed voltage required to maintain the current in the inductance leads the current by 90 deg, or the current lags the impressed voltage by the same angle.*

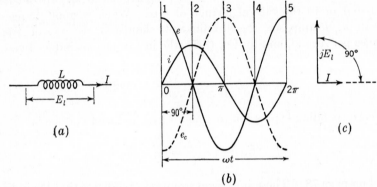

(a)   (b)   (c)

Fig. 6-20. Voltage and current in an inductance.

The counter emf of the inductance is

$$e_c = -L \frac{di}{dt}$$

but since

$$i = I_m \sin \omega t$$

it follows that

$$e_c = -L \frac{d}{dt} (I_m \sin \omega t) = -L\omega I_m \cos \omega t$$

and the maximum value of the counter emf is

$$E_m = L\omega I_m$$

The above relation may be expressed in terms of effective values of voltage and current by dividing both sides by $\sqrt{2}$. Thus

$$\frac{E_m}{\sqrt{2}} = \frac{L\omega I_m}{\sqrt{2}}$$

and

$$E_l = L\omega I = 2\pi f L I \qquad (4\text{-}20)$$

The form of expression in Eq. (4-20) may be simplified by substituting X_l for $2\pi f L$. The quantity

$$X_l = 2\pi f L \qquad (5\text{-}20)$$

is called the *inductive reactance* of the circuit. When this simplification is made, the effective impressed voltage is found to be

$$E_l = X_l I \qquad (6\text{-}20)$$

The form of Eq. (6-20) is exactly similar to that of Eq. (1-20), and inductive reactance, like resistance, is measured in *ohms*. *To force a current of I amp through an inductive reactance of X_l ohms, an impressed voltage of $E_l = X_l I$ volts is required.* In drawing the phasor diagram of current and impressed voltage, it must be remembered that the current lags the voltage 90 deg, as in (b) of Fig. 6-20. If the current phasor is taken as the axis of reference (along the X axis), the impressed voltage must be drawn along the Y axis as in (c) and the phasor equation of the impressed voltage is

$$\mathbf{E}_l = jX_l\mathbf{I} \qquad (7\text{-}20)$$

Example 2. A circuit has 10 ohms of inductive reactance at 60 cycles, and the resistance is negligible. (a) How much current does the circuit draw when its terminals are connected to a 220-volt 60-cycle main? (Sine wave is assumed.) (b) What is the inductance of the circuit? (c) What is the current when the frequency is 25 cycles?

(a) $$I = \frac{E_l}{X_l} = \frac{220}{10} = 22 \text{ amp}$$

(b) $$X_l = 2\pi f L$$
$$L = \frac{X}{2\pi f} = \frac{10}{377} = 0.0266 \text{ henry}$$

(c) $$X_l = \frac{10 \times 25}{60} = 4.17 \text{ ohms}$$
$$I = \frac{220}{4.17} = 52.8 \text{ amp}$$

Resistance and Inductive Reactance in Series. Circuits like the windings of generators, motors and transformers, power lines, etc., contain both resistance and inductive reactance. The resistance and reactance are in series, as in Fig. 7-20. When current flows, two components of impressed voltage are required: one overcomes the resistance drop and the other is the voltage required to balance the counter emf in the inductance. The first is in phase with the current as in Fig. 1-20(c), and the second leads the current by 90 deg as in Fig. 6-20(c). The total impressed voltage is the sum of the two components. In Fig. 7-20(b),

e_r and e_l are the component waves representing the instantaneous voltages absorbed in the resistance and reactance, respectively, while e_0 is the total impressed voltage wave obtained by adding the corresponding ordinates of e_r and e_l.   The effective voltages are shown in the phasor diagram (c). The current phasor is the phasor of reference, the voltage E_r absorbed in the resistance of the circuit is in phase with the current, the voltage E_l absorbed by the reactance of the circuit leads the current by 90 deg, and the impressed voltage $\mathbf{E}_0$ is the sum of $\mathbf{E}_r$ and $\mathbf{E}_l$.

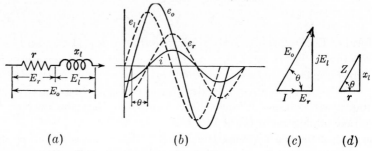

(a) (b) (c) (d)

FIG. 7-20. Resistance and inductive reactance in series.

In phasor notation the component voltages in (c) are represented as follows:

$$\mathbf{E}_r = r\mathbf{I} \qquad \text{(in phase with the current)} \qquad (8\text{-}20)$$
$$\mathbf{E}_l = jx_l\mathbf{I} \qquad \text{(90 deg ahead of the current)} \qquad (9\text{-}20)$$
$$\mathbf{E}_0 = \mathbf{I}(r + jx_l)$$
$$= \mathbf{IZ} \qquad\qquad\qquad\qquad\qquad\qquad (10\text{-}20)$$

The phasor $\mathbf{Z} = r + jx_l$ is called the phasor *impedance* of the circuit. The impressed voltage leads the current by the angle θ, called the *phase angle*, which is defined in terms of its tangent as

$$\tan \theta = \frac{E_l}{E_r} = \frac{x_l}{r} \qquad\qquad (11\text{-}20)$$

The magnitude of the impressed voltage is the hypotenuse of the right triangle of which $\mathbf{E}_l$ and $\mathbf{E}_r$ are sides, or

$$E_0 = \sqrt{(rI)^2 + (x_lI)^2}$$
$$= I\sqrt{r^2 + x_l^2} \qquad\qquad (12\text{-}20)$$
$$= IZ \qquad\qquad\qquad\qquad (13\text{-}20)$$

where $Z = \sqrt{r^2 + x_l^2}$ is the *impedance* of the circuit, measured in *ohms*. If each side of the voltage triangle in (c) is divided by the current, the triangle in (d), called the *impedance triangle*, is obtained.   When drawn to scale, the length of the base is the ohms resistance, the length of the adjacent side is the ohms reactance, and the length of the hypotenuse is the ohms impedance of the circuit. A similar impedance triangle may be drawn for any series circuit.

Example 3. A resistance of 4 ohms is connected in series with an inductance of 0.02 henry. The terminals of the circuit are connected to a 220-volt 60-cycle bus. Find (a) the reactance, (b) the impedance, (c) the current, (d) the voltage consumed in the resistance, (e) the voltage consumed in the reactance, (f) the voltage impressed on the circuit represented as a phasor, (g) the phase angle.

(a) Reactance

$$x_l = 2\pi f L = 2 \times 3.142 \times 60 \times 0.02 = 7.54 \text{ ohms}$$

(b) Phasor impedance

$$\mathbf{Z} = r + jx_l = 4 + j7.54$$

or the scalar impedance is

$$Z = \sqrt{4^2 + 7.54^2} = 8.54 \text{ ohms}$$

(c) Current

$$I = \frac{E}{Z} = \frac{220}{8.54} = 25.8 \text{ amp}$$

(d) Resistance-voltage phasor

$$\mathbf{E}_r = r\mathbf{I} = 4 \times 25.8 = 103.2$$

(e) Reactance-voltage phasor

$$\mathbf{E}_l = jx_l\mathbf{I} = j7.54 \times 25.8 = j194.5$$

(f) Impressed-voltage phasor

$$\mathbf{E}_0 = \mathbf{E}_r + j\mathbf{E}_l = 103.2 + j194.5$$

(g) Phase angle

$$\tan \theta = \frac{194.5}{103.2} = 1.88$$

$$\theta = 62° 0'$$

Capacitance. Capacitance is discussed in Chap. 10, parts of which the student may reread to advantage at this point. In a continuous-current circuit no current exists in a capacitance, except momentarily, at the instant voltage is applied to the circuit or is removed from it. At all other times a condenser is an open circuit, because as has been shown, charging current flows only when the voltage impressed across the terminals of a condenser is *changing*. The current causes charge to collect on the plates and builds up a potential difference that tends to keep the applied voltage from changing and thus to stop the current. The potential difference due to the charge is, therefore, in the nature of a *counter emf* with respect to the impressed voltage. In a-c circuits the voltage is continually changing, and if the circuit contains capacitance, alternating current exists in the capacitance so long as the voltage is impressed. In such circuits, capacitance (where it exists) is just as important a factor in determining the current as is either resistance or inductance.

Whenever two conductors are separated by an insulating material, the conductors and the space between them constitute a *capacitance*. When a potential difference is impressed on the conductors (called the *plates* for convenience), charges of electricity exist on the plates and electric lines of force exist in the insulation between plates. The charge on each plate and the electric flux between plates are proportional to each other, and both are proportional to the impressed voltage. In the rationalized mks system of units the number of coulombs on each plate is numerically equal to the number of electric lines of force (ψ) between plates [see Eq. (5-10)]. The proportionality factor relating voltage and charge or voltage and electric flux is the capacitance C. By Eq. (5-10),

$$C = \frac{\psi}{E} = \frac{Q}{E} \quad \text{farads} \tag{14-20}$$

The capacitance of two conductors or electrodes is a function of the physical arrangement of the conductors and the permittivity of the dielectric. It is ordinarily independent of voltage, current, and frequency. Because it depends only upon the nature of the circuit, as previously explained, and is independent of how the circuit is used, capacitance, like resistance and inductance, is a constant of the circuit.

The capacitance of power-distribution circuits and the windings of motors, generators, and transformers is seldom large enough to be of significance at power frequencies (60 cps). Long power circuits and the circuits of long telephone and submarine cables have large capacitance. The capacitance of a submarine cable, for example, is particularly large because the conductors are long and close together and are insulated from each other by thin layers of insulating materials with high relative permittivities.

Voltage and Current in a Capacitance. Refer to Fig. 8-20, let e be the sine-shaped voltage wave impressed across the terminals of the condenser, and assume the resistance of the circuit to be negligible. The counter emf due to the charges on the plates is represented by the sine wave e_c, for as has been stated, the counter emf is equal in magnitude and opposite in sign to the impressed voltage. The curve of instantaneous current ($i_c = -C\, de_c/dt$) is proportional to the negative of the slope of the counter emf curve or, since $e = -e_c$, it is proportional to the slope of the impressed voltage curve.

Current flows into the condenser at a and out at b during the time intervals 0-1 and 3-4, while the voltage impressed on the condenser is increasing positively. During these intervals the current and the slope of the impressed voltage curve are both positive. During the intervals 1-2 and 2-3 current flows out of the condenser at a and into the condenser at b. During these intervals the impressed voltage increases negatively, and the slope of the impressed voltage curve and the current are both negative. Since the ordinates of the current curve are proportional to the slope of the impressed voltage curve, the zero points of the current curve occur at times of maximum voltage, and maximum currents occur at times of zero impressed voltage.

It is apparent from Fig. 8-20 that *the current alternates at the frequency of the impressed voltage, and that the current curve leads the impressed voltage curve by 90 deg.* If the impressed voltage wave is a sine curve, as here

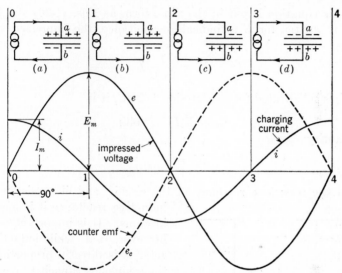

FIG. 8-20. Voltage and current of a condenser. Sine wave of voltage impressed.

assumed, the current curve is a cosine curve. This statement is supported by the following proof.

The mathematical expression for the sine wave of impressed voltage e in Fig. 8-20 is

$$e = E_m \sin \omega t$$

and since $e_c = -e$, the counter emf is

$$e_c = -E_m \sin \omega t$$

by Eq. (3-10), the current in the capacitance is

$$i = -C \frac{de}{dt}$$
$$= -C \frac{d}{dt}(-E_m \sin \omega t)$$
$$= \omega C E_m \cos \omega t$$

This is a sinusoidal curve that is 90 deg ahead of the curve of impressed voltage.

The maximum value of the current is

$$I_m = \omega C E_m$$

But $I_m/\sqrt{2}$ is the effective current and $E_m/\sqrt{2}$ is the effective voltage. Hence, dividing both sides of the foregoing equation by $\sqrt{2}$ yields

$$I = \omega C E = 2\pi f C E \tag{15-20}$$

When this equation is put in the same form as Eqs. (1-20) and (6-20), and E_c is written for E to indicate capacitance, the impressed voltage becomes

$$E_c = \frac{1}{2\pi f C} I$$

or, if X_c is substituted for the fraction $1/2\pi f C$, it is

$$E_c = X_c I \qquad \text{volts} \tag{16-20}$$

The quantity

$$X_c = \frac{1}{2\pi f C} \tag{17-20}$$

is called the *capacitive reactance* of the circuit, and like resistance and inductive reactance it is measured in ohms. It is important to note, however, that, while inductive reactance is directly proportional to the frequency, capacitive reactance is *inversely* proportional to the frequency. Expressed in words then, Eq. (16-20) means that to force a current of I amp through a capacitive reactance of X_c ohms, an impressed voltage of $X_c I$ volts is required.

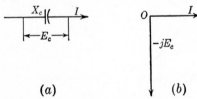

(a)   (b)

FIG. 9-20. Capacitance alone in a circuit.

In drawing the phasor diagram it must be remembered that the current leads the voltage by 90 deg, as in (b) of Fig. 9-20. If the current phasor is taken as reference (along the X axis), the impressed voltage $\mathbf{E}_c$ must be drawn along the Y axis pointing downward, and the equation of impressed voltage is

$$\mathbf{E}_c = -jE_c = -jX_c\mathbf{I} \tag{18-20}$$

Example 4. A circuit with negligible resistance and no inductive reactance has a capacitive reactance of 8 ohms at 60 cycles. When the terminals of the circuit are connected to a 60-cycle 110-volt bus, (a) what is the current? (b) What is the capacitance of the circuit? (c) What is the current when the frequency is 25 cps?

(a) By Eq. (16-20) the amount of the current is

$$I = {}^{110}\!/_8 = 13.75 \text{ amp}$$

(*b*) The reactance is

$$X_c = \frac{1}{2\pi fC} = 8 \text{ ohms}$$

The capacitance is

$$C = \frac{1}{6.28 \times 60 \times 8}$$
$$= 0.000332 \text{ farad}$$
$$= 332 \text{ } \mu\text{f}$$

(*c*) $X_c = {}^{60}\!/_{25} \times 8 = 19.2 \text{ ohms}$

$$I = \frac{110}{19.2} = 5.73 \text{ amp}$$

Circuit with Resistance and Capacitance in Series.

When a resistance and a capacitance are connected in series as in Fig. 10-20 (*a*), the same current flows in both. If the current is taken as the phasor of reference, the impressed potential difference $\mathbf{E}_0$ must obviously contain two components of voltage, $\mathbf{E}_r$ and $\mathbf{E}_c$, such that $\mathbf{E}_r = r\mathbf{I}$ and $\mathbf{E}_c = -jx_c\mathbf{I}$. The first of these is the voltage consumed in the resistance, the second is the voltage consumed in the capacitive reactance, and their sum is the phasor impressed voltage. Accordingly,

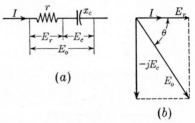

(*a*)

(*b*)

Fig. 10-20. Resistance and capacitance in series.

$$\mathbf{E}_0 = r\mathbf{I} - jx_c\mathbf{I} = \mathbf{I}(r - jx_c) \tag{19-20}$$

where $r - jx_c = $ *phasor impedance* of circuit.

The phase angle of the voltage is obtained from the expression

$$\tan \theta = \frac{-E_c}{E_r} = \frac{-x_c}{r}$$

The amount of the impressed voltage is the hypotenuse of the right triangle of which $\mathbf{E}_r$ and $\mathbf{E}_c$ are sides, or

$$E = I \sqrt{r^2 + x_c^2} \tag{20-20}$$
$$= IZ \tag{21-20}$$

where $Z = \sqrt{r^2 + x_c^2}$ is the *impedance* of the circuit.

Example 5. A resistance of 3 ohms is connected in series with a capacitance of 400 μf. (*a*) How much current does the circuit draw when its terminals are connected to a 110-volt 60-cycle bus? What are (*b*) the voltage across the resistance, (*c*) the voltage across the capacitive reactance, (*d*) the total voltage impressed, represented as a phasor, (*e*) the phase angle, (*f*) the reactance, (*g*) the impedance of the circuit?

(f) The reactance is

$$x_c = \frac{1}{2\pi f C} = \frac{1}{377 \times 0.0004} = 6.63 \text{ ohms}$$

(g) The phasor impedance is

$$\mathbf{Z} = 3 - j6.63$$

and by Eq. (20-20) the impedance is

$$Z = \sqrt{3^2 + 6.63^2} = 7.28 \text{ ohms}$$

(a) Current is

$$I = \frac{E}{Z} = \frac{110}{7.28} = 15.1 \text{ amp}$$

(b) Resistance voltage is

$$\mathbf{E}_r = r\mathbf{I} = 3 \times 15.1 = 45.3$$

(c) Reactance voltage is

$$\mathbf{E}_c = -jx_c\mathbf{I} = -j100.1$$

(d) Impressed voltage is

$$\mathbf{E}_0 = E_r - jE_c = 45.3 - j100.1$$

(e) Tangent of phase angle is

$$\tan \theta = \frac{-100.1}{45.3} = -2.21$$

and

$$\theta = -(65° \ 39')$$

Resistance, Inductance, and Capacitance in Series. Consider a series circuit with the three kinds of circuit constants R, L, and C. Such a circuit is shown in Fig. 11-20.

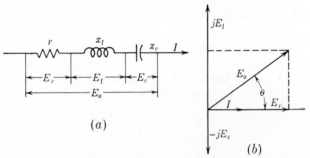

(a)

(b)

Fig. 11-20. Resistance, inductance, and capacitance in series.

In series circuits the current is common to all parts. For this reason phasor diagrams of series circuits usually are drawn with the current phasor laid off on the X axis, as in Figs. 1-20, 7-20, 9-20, and 10-20. According to this procedure, the three components of impressed voltage required in the circuit are

$$\mathbf{E}_r = r\mathbf{I}$$
$$\mathbf{E}_l = +jx_l\mathbf{I} \qquad (22\text{-}20)$$
$$\mathbf{E}_c = -jx_c\mathbf{I}$$

and the total impressed voltage is the phasor sum of these or

$$\mathbf{E}_0 = \mathbf{I}[r + j(x_l - x_c)] \qquad (23\text{-}20)$$
$$= \mathbf{I}(r + jx) \qquad (24\text{-}20)$$

where $x = x_l - x_c$, the total reactance of the circuit, is the algebraic sum of the inductive reactance and the capacitive reactance, and

$$\mathbf{Z} = r + jx$$

is the phasor impedance of the circuit.

From Eq. (23-20) the length of the voltage phasor is found to be

$$E_0 = I \sqrt{r^2 + (x_l - x_c)^2} \qquad (25\text{-}20)$$

while the tangent of the phase angle is

$$\tan \theta = \frac{x}{r} \qquad (26\text{-}20)$$

Equation (24-20) is a statement of Ohm's law in terms of phasors, while Eq. (25-20) is the corresponding scalar equation. If the voltage E_0 were given and the problem were to find the current, the statement of the law in Eq. (25-20) would be put in the form

$$I = \frac{E_0}{\sqrt{r^2 + (x_l - x_c)^2}} \qquad (27\text{-}20)$$

in which the denominator is the impedance of the circuit.

Example 6. A series circuit has the constants $R = 50$ ohms, $L = 0.40$ henry, $C = 35$ μf. When a 220-volt 60-cycle potential difference is impressed on the circuit, find (a) the reactance, (b) the impedance, (c) the current, (d) the voltage consumed by the resistance, (e) the voltage consumed by the inductance, (f) the voltage consumed by the capacitance, (g) the voltage $\mathbf{E}_0$, and (h) the phase angle of the impressed voltage with respect to current. (i) Draw the phasor diagram.

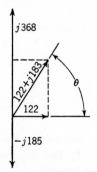

(a) $x_l = 2\pi fL = 377 \times 0.40 = 150.8$ ohms

$\quad x_c = \dfrac{1}{2\pi fC} = \dfrac{10^6}{377 \times 35} = 75.8$ ohms

$\quad x = x_l - x_c = 150.8 - 75.8 = 75.0$ ohms

(b) $Z = \sqrt{r^2 + x^2} = \sqrt{50^2 + 75^2} = 90.1$ ohms

(c) $I = 220 \div 90.1 = 2.44$ amp

(d) $\mathbf{E}_r = 50 \times 2.44 = 122$

(e) $\mathbf{E}_l = j150.8 \times 2.44 = j368$

(f) $\mathbf{E}_c = -j75.8 \times 2.44 = -j185$

Fig. 12-20. Phasor diagram for Example 6.

(g) $\mathbf{E}_0 = 122 + j368 - j185 = 122 + j183$

   $E_0 = \sqrt{122^2 + 183^2} = 220$ volts (which checks the given voltage)

(h) $\tan \theta = {}^{183}\!/_{122} = 1.5$

   $\theta = 56° 20'$

(i) The phasor diagram is given in Fig. 12-20.

Kirchhoff's Law of Voltages.   Equation (23-20) illustrates Kirchhoff's law of voltages (page 36) as applied to a-c circuits.   Accordingly, in terms of phasor voltages the law reads: *In any closed electric circuit* the sum of all generated and induced voltages less the sum of all voltages consumed in impedances is zero or, symbolically,

$$\Sigma E - \Sigma ZI = 0 \qquad\qquad (28\text{-}20)$$

General Series Circuit.   A series circuit may have more than one unit of each kind of circuit constant, as in Fig. 13-20(a).   Such a circuit

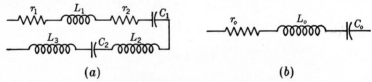

(a)   (b)

Fig. 13-20. Impedances in series.

can always be reduced to an equivalent circuit (b) with only three constants r_0, L_0, and C_0 as follows:

$$r_0 = r_1 + r_2 + r_3 + \cdots \qquad\qquad (29\text{-}20)$$
$${}_lx_0 = 2\pi f L_0 = 2\pi f(L_1 + L_2 + L_3 + \cdots)$$

whence

$$L_0 = L_1 + L_2 + L_3 + \cdots \qquad\qquad (30\text{-}20)$$

Likewise

$${}_cx_0 = \frac{1}{2\pi f C_0} = \frac{1}{2\pi f}\left(\frac{1}{C_1} + \frac{1}{C_2} + \frac{1}{C_3} + \cdots\right)$$

whence

$$\frac{1}{C_0} = \frac{1}{C_1} + \frac{1}{C_2} + \frac{1}{C_3} + \cdots$$

or

$$C_0 = \frac{C_1 C_2 C_3 \cdots}{C_1 C_2 \cdots + C_2 C_3 \cdots + C_3 C_1 \cdots} \qquad\qquad (31\text{-}20)$$

Stated in words, in a series circuit

1. The equivalent resistance r_0 is equal to the sum of the separate resistances.

2. The equivalent inductance L_0 is equal to the sum of the separate inductances.

3. The reciprocal of the equivalent capacitance $1/C_0$ is equal to the sum of the reciprocals of the separate capacitances.

After the equivalent constants r_0, L_0, and C_0 of Eqs. (29-20), (30-20), and (31-20) have been found, the procedure is that described in the previous article and illustrated in the example.

Voltage Resonance. It was observed on page 313 that inductive reactance is directly proportional to the frequency. Accordingly, if in a circuit similar to the one in Fig. 11-20, the frequency is gradually changed from a low value to higher and higher values, x_l varies directly with frequency while x_c varies inversely with frequency. The equivalent reactance x_0 of the circuit as a whole changes from a very large negative value at low frequency to positive values which approach approximate equality with x_l at very high frequencies, as illustrated in Fig. 14-20.

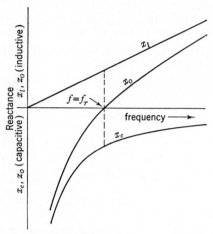

FIG. 14-20. Variation of x_l, x_c, and x_0 with frequency in a series circuit containing resistance, inductance, and capacitance.

At some intermediate frequency f_r, for which $x_l = x_c$ and $x_0 = 0$, the circuit as a whole is purely resistive. At this frequency, called the *frequency of resonance,*

$$2\pi f_r L = \frac{1}{2\pi f_r C}$$

and

$$f_r = \frac{1}{2\pi \sqrt{LC}} \tag{32-20}$$

The variation of the current and the component voltages in a resonant series circuit (Fig. 11-20) are illustrated in Fig. 15-20. The impressed voltage E_0 is held constant while the voltages consumed in r, L, and C vary as shown in the figure. The current reaches its maximum value at about 42 cps, which is the frequency of resonance. At this frequency $x_0 = 0$, $I = E/r$, the power factor is unity, and $E_l = E_c$. At resonant frequency the latter may be several times larger than the impressed voltage for which the circuit insulation is designed, and failure of insulation may result. If the resistance is small, the current at resonant frequency may also be very large.

Resonance in an electric circuit is analogous to the vibration of a reed under the impulse of a deflecting force which is periodically applied at a frequency equal to the natural frequency of the reed. This principle is used in the construction of the vibrating-reed frequency meter.

Summary. 1. In a circuit with resistance alone, in which current is the reference phasor, $\mathbf{E}_0 = r\mathbf{I}$, and the current is in phase with the applied voltage. The magnitude of the current is $I = E/r$.

2. In an inductive circuit containing negligible resistance and capacitance, $\mathbf{E}_0 = +jx_l\mathbf{I}$. The current lags the impressed voltage by 90 deg, the magnitude of the current is $I = E_0/x_l$, and the reactance of the circuit is $x_l = 2\pi fL$.

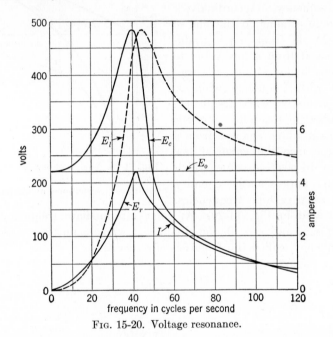

FIG. 15-20. Voltage resonance.

3. In a capacitive circuit which has negligible resistance and inductance, $\mathbf{E}_0 = -jx_c\mathbf{I}$. The current leads the applied voltage by 90 deg, the magnitude of the current is $I = E_0/x_c$, and the reactance is

$$x_c = \frac{1}{2\pi fC}$$

4. In a circuit that has resistance and inductance in series, and negligible capacitance, $\mathbf{E}_0 = \mathbf{I}(r + jx_l)$. The current lags the impressed voltage by the angle $\theta = \tan^{-1} x_l/r$, the magnitude of the current is $I = E_0/\sqrt{r^2 + x_l^2}$, and the impedance is $Z = \sqrt{r^2 + x_l^2}$.

5. In a circuit that has resistance and capacitance in series, and negligible inductance, $\mathbf{E}_0 = \mathbf{I}(r - jx_c)$. The current leads the impressed

voltage by the angle $\theta = \tan^{-1} x_c/r$, the magnitude of the current is $I = E_0/\sqrt{r^2 + x_c{}^2}$, and the impedance is $Z = \sqrt{r^2 + x_c{}^2}$.

6. In any circuit that has resistance, inductance, and capacitance in series,

$$\mathbf{E}_0 = \mathbf{I}[r + j(x_l - x_c)] = I(r + jx_0)$$

where $x_0 = (x_l - x_c)$ is the equivalent reactance of the circuit. Since x_0 is positive when $x_l > x_c$ and negative when $x_l < x_c$, the current lags the impressed voltage in the first case and leads in the second. The phase angle of current with respect to voltage is $\theta = \tan^{-1} x_0/r$. The magnitude of the current is $I = E_0/\sqrt{r^2 + (x_l - x_c)^2}$ and the impedance is $Z = \sqrt{r^2 + (x_l - x_c)^2}$.

Problems

1-20. The voltage wave $e = 150 \sin(\omega t + 45°)$ is impressed on a resistance of 12 ohms. (a) Write the expression for the instantaneous current as a function of time. Determine (b) the effective value of the current, (c) the phase angle of the current wave referred to the voltage wave as reference.

2-20. A series circuit contains a resistance of 12 ohms and an inductance of 0.05 henry. A 60-cycle potential difference of $120/\underline{0}$ volts is impressed upon the circuit. Determine (a) the phasor current, (b) the phase angle of the current with respect to the voltage.

3-20. In the circuit of Prob. 2-20 the frequency of the applied voltage is increased until the current is reduced to one-half its former value. For this condition find (a) the frequency, (b) the phasor impedance, and (c) the phase angle of the current with respect to the voltage.

4-20. Determine the capacitive reactance of a 10-μf condenser at each of the following frequencies: 50, 100, 1,000, and 10,000 cps.

5-20. At what frequency is the reactance of a 15-μf condenser equal to 50 ohms?

6-20. A series circuit has 0.02 henry inductance, 5 μf capacitance, and 10 ohms resistance. A current of 8 amp is produced in the circuit by an impressed potential difference of 120 volts. Determine (a) the frequency, (b) the phasor impedance, (c) the phase angle of the current with respect to the voltage.

7-20. A series circuit comprises a 5-ohm resistance connected to an inductance of 0.025 henry. Determine (a) the 60-cycle impedance, (b) the impressed voltage required to set up a current of 12 amp. (c) Draw the impedance triangle. (d) Referred to the current as reference, express the impressed voltage phasor in rectangular components.

Fig. A-20

8-20. The circuit of Fig. A-20 has these constants: $R_{ab} = 6$ ohms, $R_{cd} = 8$ ohms, $L_{bc} = 0.025$ henry, $L_{de} = 0.012$ henry. A 60-cycle potential difference of 150 volts is impressed across the terminals ae. Determine (a) the total reactance, (b) the total resistance, (c) the current, and (d) the phase angle of the impressed voltage referred to the current. Determine the complex expressions of the voltages (e) between b and e, (f) between a and d.

9-20. A 25-μf condenser is connected in series with the circuit in Fig. A-20. If the impressed potential difference is 150 volts and the frequency is such as to bring the current in the circuit in phase with the applied voltage, what are (a) the frequency, (b) the current, (c) the voltage applied to the condenser terminals, (d) the potential difference across terminals bc ($\mathbf{E}_{bc}$)?

10-20. The voltage $\mathbf{E} = 150 + j180$ is impressed across the terminals of an unknown impedance. The current is $\mathbf{I} = 5 - j4$ amp. Determine (a) the resistance, (b) the reactance, and (c) the scalar impedance.

11-20. The following impedances are connected in series:

$$\mathbf{Z}_1 = 4 + j7$$
$$\mathbf{Z}_2 = 2 + j12$$
$$\mathbf{Z}_3 = 3 - j32$$

Determine (a) the equivalent resistance, (b) the equivalent reactance, (c) the equivalent impedance of the circuit.

12-20. A potential difference of 220 volts is impressed across the terminals of the series-connected impedances of Prob. 11-20. (a) Compute the current in the circuit. With the current taken as reference phasor, determine (b) the phasor voltage consumed in each of the impedances, (c) the impressed voltage phasor, and (d) draw the phasor diagram of current and voltages.

CHAPTER 21

PARALLEL CIRCUITS

Parallel circuits are those in which two or more branches have the same impressed voltage, as in Fig. 1-21(a). The solution of such circuits consists in finding a single *equivalent series circuit* which, with the same impressed voltage, will pass a current of the same magnitude and phase angle as the input current of the branched circuit. In Fig. 1-21, circuit (b) is the equivalent of (a) when a given impressed voltage E_0 produces

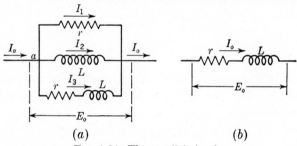

FIG. 1-21. The parallel circuit.

the same total current I_0 in both. This means that the *phasor sum* of the currents in (a) must equal the current in (b) or, mathematically,

$$\mathbf{I}_0 = \mathbf{I}_1 + \mathbf{I}_2 + \mathbf{I}_3 \qquad (1\text{-}21)$$

In parallel circuits, the *impressed voltage* is common to all elements of the circuit, while in series circuits the *current* is common to all elements. In both cases it is convenient to use the common phasor as the phasor of reference. Accordingly, the *current* is the phasor of reference in series circuits and the *impressed voltage* is the phasor of reference in parallel circuits.

Kirchhoff's Laws. In d-c circuits, voltage and current are scalar quantities (ordinary numbers), while in a-c circuits they are complex numbers. The laws governing a-c circuits are identical in form with the laws governing d-c circuits, the only essential difference being that in a-c circuits *phasors* are manipulated (added, subtracted, multiplied, divided, etc.), while in d-c circuits similar operations are performed

327

with scalars.   The solutions of both d-c and a-c circuits are based largely
upon Ohm's and Kirchhoff's laws.   The latter, as applied to effective
values of alternating currents and voltages, may be stated as follows:

1. The phasor sum of all the currents flowing up to any point in a
circuit is zero or, in symbolic language,

$$\Sigma I = 0 \qquad (2\text{-}21)$$

2. The phasor sum of all the emfs in any closed circuit is zero.

The term emfs as here used includes voltages absorbed in impedances
as well as impressed and counter emfs.   With this understanding, the
law may be stated in symbolic language as

$$\Sigma E = 0 \qquad (3\text{-}21)$$

Applications of these laws are illustrated in Fig. 1-21(a).   A statement
of the first law may be written for any point in the circuit where two or
more branches join, as at a.   At a, I_0 is directed toward the point, while
I_1, I_2, and I_3 are directed away from the point.   Hence

$$I_0 - I_1 - I_2 - I_3 = 0$$

or

$$I_0 = I_1 + I_2 + I_3$$

Application of the second law was illustrated in the previous chapter.
In the circuit of Fig. 1-21(a), E_0 is taken as reference phasor and the
voltage equations are

$$E_0 - Z_1I_1 = 0$$
$$E_0 = Z_1I_1$$
$$= Z_2I_2$$
$$= Z_3I_3$$

These laws are very important in the solution of circuit problems and
as an aid to the understanding of electrical theory and the performance
of electrical machinery.

Impedances in Parallel.   In general, each branch of a parallel circuit
consists of an impedance; that is, resistance and inductive reactance
in series, resistance and capacitive reactance in series, or resistance,
inductive reactance, and capacitive reactance in series.   Whatever the
elements making up the impedance of a branch may be, the procedure
for finding the equivalent series circuit is the same in all cases.   The
current in a branch may lag or lead the impressed voltage by any angle
between 90 and −90 deg, depending upon the nature of the impedance.

1. *Inductive Branches.*   Consider the circuit of Fig. 2-21, consisting
of two branches in parallel.   Branch 1 has a resistance r_1 in series with
an inductive reactance x_1, while branch 2 has a resistance r_2 in series

with an inductive reactance x_2.   Accordingly, the current in each branch lags the impressed voltage by an angle less than 90 deg, defined in terms of its tangent as $\tan \theta = x/r$.   Expressed in complex notation, the circuit impedances are

$$\mathbf{Z}_1 = r_1 + jx_1$$
$$\mathbf{Z}_2 = r_2 + jx_2$$

By Ohm's law, the branch currents are

$$\mathbf{I}_1 = \frac{\mathbf{E}_0}{\mathbf{Z}_1} = \frac{\mathbf{E}_0}{r_1 + jx_1} \qquad (4\text{-}21)$$

$$\mathbf{I}_2 = \frac{\mathbf{E}_0}{\mathbf{Z}_2} = \frac{\mathbf{E}_0}{r_2 + jx_2} \qquad (5\text{-}21)$$

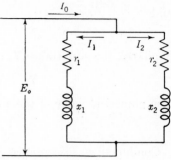

FIG. 2-21. Impedances in parallel. Inductive branches.

The current equations are rationalized by multiplying numerator and denominator of each right-hand member by the conjugate of the impedance (that is, by the denominator with the sign of the imaginary term changed).   Thus

$$\mathbf{I}_1 = \frac{\mathbf{E}_0}{r_1 + jx_1} \times \frac{r_1 - jx_1}{r_1 - jx_1} = \mathbf{E}_0 \left(\frac{r_1}{r_1{}^2 + x_1{}^2} - j\frac{x_1}{r_1{}^2 + x_1{}^2} \right)$$
$$= \mathbf{E}_0(g_1 - jb_1) \qquad (6\text{-}21)$$

$$\mathbf{I}_2 = \frac{\mathbf{E}_0}{r_2 + jx_2} \times \frac{r_2 - jx_2}{r_2 - jx_2} = \mathbf{E}_0 \left(\frac{r_2}{r_2{}^2 + x_2{}^2} - j\frac{x_2}{r_2{}^2 + x_2{}^2} \right)$$
$$= \mathbf{E}_0(g_2 - jb_2) \qquad (7\text{-}21)$$

and, by addition,

$$\mathbf{I}_0 = \mathbf{E}_0[g_1 + g_2 - j(b_1 + b_2)]$$
$$= \mathbf{E}_0(g_0 - jb_0) \qquad (8\text{-}21)$$

In the foregoing expressions,

$$g_1 = \frac{r_1}{r_1{}^2 + x_1{}^2} = conductance \text{ of branch 1}$$

$$g_2 = \frac{r_2}{r_2{}^2 + x_2{}^2} = conductance \text{ of branch 2}$$

$$b_1 = \frac{x_1}{r_1{}^2 + x_1{}^2} = susceptance \text{ of branch 1}$$

$$b_2 = \frac{x_2}{r_2{}^2 + x_2{}^2} = susceptance \text{ of branch 2}$$

$$\mathbf{Y}_1 = \frac{1}{\mathbf{Z}_1} = g_1 - jb_1 = phasor\ admittance \text{ of branch 1}$$

$$\mathbf{Y}_2 = \frac{1}{\mathbf{Z}_2} = g_2 - jb_2 = phasor\ admittance \text{ of branch 2}$$

For the circuit as a whole, the conductance g_0 is the sum of the branch conductances and the susceptance b_0 is the sum of the branch susceptances; that is

$$g_c = g_1 + g_2 \tag{9-21}$$

and

$$b_0 = b_1 + b_2 \tag{10-21}$$

Similarly, the admittance $\mathbf{Y}_0$ of the circuit as a whole is

$$\mathbf{Y}_0 = \mathbf{Y}_1 + \mathbf{Y}_2 = g_0 - jb_0 \tag{11-21}$$

The numerical value of the admittance is

$$Y_0 = \sqrt{g_0^2 + b_0^2} \tag{12-21}$$

Conductance, susceptance, and admittance are measured in reciprocal ohms or *mhos*.

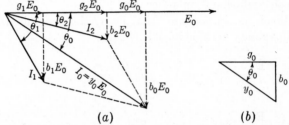

(a)   (b)

FIG. 3-21. (a) Phasor diagram of currents; (b) admittance triangle.

The meanings of the above equations are clarified by referring to Fig. 3-21 which is a phasor diagram of the currents referred to the impressed voltage as reference phasor. From the diagram it is clear that

$$g_1E_0 = \text{in-phase component of current in branch 1}$$
$$g_2E_0 = \text{in-phase component of current in branch 2}$$
$$g_0E_0 = \text{in-phase component of total current}$$
$$b_1E_0 = \text{quadrature component of current in branch 1}$$
$$b_2E_0 = \text{quadrature component of current in branch 2}$$
$$b_0E_0 = \text{quadrature component of total current}$$
$$\mathbf{Y}_0\mathbf{E}_0 = (g_0 - jb_0)\mathbf{E}_0 = \text{total input current (line current)}$$

The line current lags the impressed voltage by an angle of which the tangent is

$$\tan \theta = \frac{b_0}{g_0}$$

The magnitude of the line-current phasor equals the length of the hypotenuse of the right triangle of which the in-phase and quadrature components of current are sides, or

$$I_0 = \sqrt{g_0{}^2 E_0{}^2 + b_0{}^2 E_0{}^2} = E_0 Y_0 \text{ amp}$$

The magnitudes of the component- or branch-current phasors are found in a similar manner.

In Fig. 3-21 the currents are represented by their in-phase and quadrature components. The in-phase components are of the form gE_0, the quadrature components are of the form bE_0, and the sums are of the form YE_0. In each case the three components of current form a right triangle with sides gE_0 and bE_0, and hypotenuse YE_0. If each side of a current triangle be divided by the impressed voltage, the result is a triangle similar to the current triangle with the sides g and b and the hypotenuse Y. The latter is called the *admittance triangle*. Thus, in the admittance triangle, *conductance* is drawn parallel to the impressed voltage, *susceptance* is drawn normal to the impressed voltage (in the direction of the quadrature component of current), and the *admittance* is drawn parallel to the current phasor. An admittance triangle may be drawn for any circuit. In series circuits, however, one usually deals with the impedance rather than the admittance.

A simple series circuit which is the equivalent of the branched circuit of Fig. 2-21 must, obviously, have an impedance such that, when the voltage $\mathbf{E}_0$ (the same as for the branched circuit) is impressed, the line current $\mathbf{I}_0$ (the same as for the branched circuit) will flow. If the impressed voltage is taken as reference phasor, the phasor impedance $\mathbf{Z}_0$ must have the value

$$\mathbf{Z}_0 = \frac{\mathbf{E}_0}{\mathbf{I}_0}$$

and, by Eq. (8-21),

$$\mathbf{Z}_0 = \frac{1}{g_0 - jb_0} \tag{13-21}$$

that is, the *equivalent phasor impedance of the branched circuit is the reciprocal of the total phasor admittance*. To rationalize the right-hand term of Eq. (13-21), numerator and denominator are multiplied by the denominator with the sign of the imaginary term reversed, thus:

$$\mathbf{Z}_0 = \frac{1}{g_0 - jb_0} \times \frac{g_0 + jb_0}{g_0 + jb_0} = \frac{g_0}{g_0{}^2 + b_0{}^2} + j \frac{b_0}{g_0{}^2 + b_0{}^2}$$
$$= r_0 + jx_0 \tag{14-21}$$

The equivalent resistance of the branched circuit is, therefore,

$$r_0 = \frac{g_0}{g_0{}^2 + b_0{}^2} \tag{15-21}$$

The equivalent reactance is

$$x_0 = \frac{b_0}{g_0{}^2 + b_0{}^2} \qquad (16\text{-}21)$$

The numerical value of the equivalent impedance is

$$Z_0 = \sqrt{r_0{}^2 + x_0{}^2} \qquad (17\text{-}21)$$

It should be observed that the equivalent reactance is inductive because the sign of the j term in the equation for Z_0 [Eq. (14-21)] is plus.

Example 1. In the circuit of Fig. 2-21 let the frequency of the impressed voltage be 60 cps and let the circuit constants have the following values in ohms: $r_1 = 4$, $x_1 = 8$, $r_2 = 6$, and $x_2 = 2$. When the impressed voltage E_0 is 120, find (*a*) the admittance of each branch, (*b*) the total admittance of the branched circuit, (*c*) the current in each branch, (*d*) the line current, (*e*) the resistance r_0 and the reactance x_0 of the equivalent simple series circuit.

The current in a branch is the product of impressed voltage and the admittance of the branch [Eqs. (6-21) and (7-21)]. Therefore one proceeds to find the admittance as follows:

$$(a) \quad \mathbf{Y}_1 = \frac{1}{\mathbf{Z}_1} = \frac{1}{4 + j8} = \frac{4}{16 + 64} - j\frac{8}{16 + 64} = 0.05 - j0.10$$

$$\mathbf{Y}_2 = \frac{1}{\mathbf{Z}_2} = \frac{1}{6 + j2} = \frac{6}{36 + 4} - j\frac{2}{36 + 4} = 0.15 - j0.05$$

By addition,

$$
\begin{aligned}
(b) \quad & \mathbf{Y}_0 = \mathbf{Y}_1 + \mathbf{Y}_2 && = 0.20 - j0.15 \\
(c) \quad & \mathbf{I}_1 = \mathbf{E}_0\mathbf{Y}_1 = 120(0.05 - j0.10) = 6 - j12 \\
& I_1 = \sqrt{6^2 + 12^2} = 13.4 \text{ amp} \\
& \tan \theta_1 = {}^{12}\!/_6 = 2 \\
& \theta_1 = 63° \, 24' \\
& \mathbf{I}_2 = \mathbf{E}_0\mathbf{Y}_2 = 120(0.15 - j0.05) = 18 - j6 \\
& I_2 = \sqrt{18^2 + 6^2} = 18.95 \text{ amp} \\
& \tan \theta_2 = {}^6\!/_{18} = 0.333 \\
& \theta_2 = 18° \, 25' \\
(d) \quad & \mathbf{I}_0 = \mathbf{I}_1 + \mathbf{I}_2 = 6 + 18 - j(12 + 6) = 24 - j18 \\
& I_0 = \sqrt{24^2 + 18^2} = 30 \text{ amp} \\
& \tan \theta_0 = {}^{18}\!/_{24} = 0.75 \\
& \theta_0 = 36° \, 54'
\end{aligned}
$$

The phasor diagram of currents corresponding to the above is found in Fig. 4-21.

$$
\begin{aligned}
(e) \quad \mathbf{Z}_0 &= \frac{1}{\mathbf{Y}_0} = \frac{1}{g_0 - jb_0} \\
&= \frac{1}{0.20 - j0.15} = \frac{0.20}{0.20^2 + 0.15^2} + j\frac{0.15}{0.20^2 + 0.15^2} \\
&= 3.2 + j2.4 \\
r_0 &= 3.2 \text{ ohms resistance} \\
x_0 &= 2.4 \text{ ohms inductive reactance} \\
Z_0 &= \sqrt{3.2^2 + 2.4^2} = 4 \text{ ohms}
\end{aligned}
$$

Also

$$Z_0 = \frac{E_0}{I_0} = \frac{120}{30} = 4 \text{ ohms}$$

which checks the value of impedance already found.

2. *Capacitive Branches.* When capacitive circuits are connected in parallel, the currents in the several branches lead the impressed

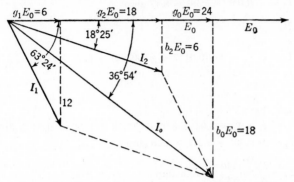

FIG. 4-21. Phasor diagram of currents in Example 1.

voltage, and the line current also leads. The method of computing the admittance, equivalent impedance, currents, etc., is the same as for the inductive circuits.

Example 2. Consider the branched circuit of Fig. 5-21, and let the circuit constants have the following values in ohms at a frequency of 60 cps: $r_1 = 20$, $x_1 = 50$, $r_2 = 60$, $x_2 = 15$. The reactances are capacitive. It is required to find (*a*) the admittance of each branch, (*b*) the total admittance, (*c*) the equivalent impedance, (*d*) the current in each branch and the total current when the impressed voltage is 440 and the frequency is 60 cps, (*e*) the capacitance of each condenser and the capacitance of the equivalent series circuit.

The phasor impedances of the branches are

$$Z_1 = 20 - j50$$
$$Z_2 = 60 - j15$$

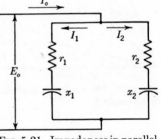

FIG. 5-21. Impedances in parallel. Capacitive branches.

(*a*) The branch admittances are

$$Y_1 = \frac{1}{20 - j50} = \frac{20}{400 + 2,500} + j\frac{50}{400 + 2,500} = 0.0069 + j0.01723$$

$$Y_2 = \frac{1}{60 - j15} = \frac{60}{3,600 + 225} + j\frac{15}{3,600 + 225} = 0.0157 + j0.00392$$

By addition,

(*b*) $Y_0 = Y_1 + Y_2$ $= 0.0226 + j0.02115$

(*c*) The impedance of the equivalent series circuit is the reciprocal of the total admittance; hence,

$$\frac{1}{Y_0} = \frac{1}{0.0226 + j0.02115} = \frac{0.0226}{0.0226^2 + 0.02115^2} - j\frac{0.02115}{0.0226^2 + 0.02115^2}$$
$$= 23.6 - j22.1$$

$r_0 = 23.6$ ohms resistance

$x_0 = 22.1$ ohms capacitive reactance

$$Z_0 = \sqrt{23.6^2 + 22.1^2} = 32.3 \text{ ohms impedance}$$

(d) $I_1 = E_0 Y_1 = 440(0.0069 + j0.01723) = 3.04 + j7.58$

$$I_1 = \sqrt{3.04^2 + 7.58^2} = 8.17 \text{ amp}$$

$$\tan \theta_1 = \frac{7.58}{3.04} = 2.5$$

$$\theta_1 = 68° \, 12'$$

$$I_2 = E_0 Y_2 = 440(0.0157 + j0.00392) = 6.92 + j1.73$$

$$I_2 = \sqrt{6.92^2 + 1.73^2} = 7.13 \text{ amp}$$

$$\tan \theta_2 = \frac{1.73}{6.92} = 0.25$$

$$\theta_2 = 14° +$$

$$I_0 = I_1 + I_2 = 3.04 + 6.92 + j(7.58 + 1.73) = 9.96 + j9.31$$

$$I_0 = \sqrt{9.96^2 + 9.31^2} = 13.6 \text{ amp}$$

Also

$$I_0 = \frac{E_0}{Z_0} = \frac{440}{32.3} = 13.6 \text{ amp}$$

which checks the value already found.

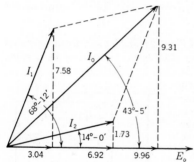

FIG. 6-21. Phasor diagram of currents in Example 2.

(e) When C is expressed in microfarads, the capacitive reactance of a condenser is $x_c = 10^6/2\pi fC$, or, in terms of reactance, the capacitance is $C = 10^6/2\pi fx_c$. For a 60-cycle circuit, $2\pi f = 377$. Accordingly,

$$C_1 = \frac{10^6}{377 \times 50} = 53.1 \ \mu f$$

$$C_2 = \frac{10^6}{377 \times 15} = 177 \ \mu f$$

$$C_0 = \frac{10^6}{377 \times 22.1} = 120 \ \mu f$$

The phasor diagram of currents in the circuit of Fig. 5-21 (pertaining to the foregoing example) is shown in Fig. 6-21.

3. Inductive and Capacitive Branches. The general solution of a branched circuit with any impedances whatever in parallel is now readily understood, for the procedure is exactly the same as that followed in the foregoing examples. In this case the line current either leads, lags, or is in phase with the impressed voltage, depending again upon the nature of the impedances in the branches and their relative values. If the total susceptance is positive $(+jb_0)$ the current leads, if it is negative $(-jb_0)$ the current lags, and if it is zero the current is in phase with the impressed voltage.

Example 3. In the circuit of Fig. 7-21 three impedances are connected in parallel. Each branch contains a resistance in series with a reactance. Branch 1 is inductive, while branches 2 and 3 are capacitive. Expressed in ohms, the resistances are $r_1 = 3$, $r_2 = 4$, $r_3 = 2$ and the 60-cycle reactances are $x_1 = 4$, $x_2 = 5$, $x_3 = 6$. Find the equivalent impedance of the branched circuit (a) when the frequency is 60 cycles,

(b) when the frequency is 25 cycles.   (c) What is the input current in each of the above cases if the impressed voltage is 100?

(a) The admittance of each branch is the reciprocal of the impedance.   Accordingly,

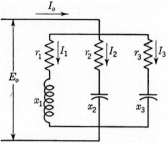

$$\mathbf{Y}_1 = \frac{1}{3 + j4} = \frac{3}{25} - j\frac{4}{25} = 0.120 - j0.160$$

$$\mathbf{Y}_2 = \frac{1}{4 - j5} = \frac{4}{41} + j\frac{5}{41} = 0.0976 + j0.122$$

$$\mathbf{Y}_3 = \frac{1}{2 - j6} = \frac{2}{40} + j\frac{6}{40} = 0.050 + j0.150$$

By addition,

$$\mathbf{Y}_0 = \qquad\qquad = 0.2676 + j0.112$$

Fig. 7-21. Impedances in parallel. Inductive and capacitive branches.

The equivalent impedance is the reciprocal of the total admittance of the branched circuit.   Hence

$$\mathbf{Z}_0 = \frac{1}{\mathbf{Y}_0} = \frac{1}{0.2676 + j0.112} = \frac{0.2676}{0.0840} - j\frac{0.112}{0.0840} = 3.18 - j1.33$$

$r_0 = 3.18$ ohms resistance

$x_0 = 1.33$ ohms capacitive reactance

$\mathbf{Z}_0 = \sqrt{3.18^2 + 1.33^2} = 3.45$ ohms impedance

(b) Inductive reactances are directly proportional while capacitive reactances are inversely proportional to the frequency.   The 25-cycle reactances of the branches, therefore, are

$$x_1 = \frac{25 \times 4}{60} = 1.667 \text{ ohms}$$

$$x_2 = \frac{60 \times 5}{25} = 12 \text{ ohms}$$

$$x_3 = \frac{60 \times 6}{25} = 14.4 \text{ ohms}$$

Using these values of reactance to find the new admittances, one obtains

$$\mathbf{Y}_1 = \frac{1}{3 + j1.667} = \frac{3}{11.8} - j\frac{1.667}{11.8} = 0.254 - j0.1413$$

$$\mathbf{Y}_2 = \frac{1}{4 - j12} = \frac{4}{160} + j\frac{12}{160} = 0.025 + j0.075$$

$$\mathbf{Y}_3 = \frac{1}{2 - j14.4} = \frac{2}{211.4} + j\frac{14.4}{211.4} = 0.0095 + j0.068$$

By addition,

$$\mathbf{Y}_0 = \mathbf{Y}_1 + \mathbf{Y}_2 + \mathbf{Y}_3 = 0.2885 + j0.0017$$

By taking the reciprocal to find the equivalent impedance

$$\mathbf{Z}_0 = \frac{1}{0.2885 + j0.0017} = \frac{0.2885}{0.0992} - j\frac{0.0017}{0.0832} = 3.47 - j0.02$$

$r_0 = 3.47$ ohms resistance

$x_0 = 0.02$ ohm capacitive reactance

$\mathbf{Z}_0 = \sqrt{3.47^2 + 0.02^2} = 3.47$ ohms impedance

(c) In the first case (a),

$$\mathbf{I}_0 = \mathbf{E}_0\mathbf{Y}_0 = 100(0.2676 + j0.112) = 26.8 + j11.2$$
$$I_0 = \sqrt{26.8^2 + 11.2^2} = 29 \text{ amp}$$

Also

$$I_0 = \frac{E_0}{Z_0} = \frac{100}{3.45} = 29 \text{ amp}$$

which checks the value already found.

$$\tan \theta_0 = \frac{11.2}{26.8} = 0.418$$
$$\theta_0 = 22° 42'$$

In the second case (b),

$$\mathbf{I}_0 = \mathbf{E}_0\mathbf{Y}_0 = 100(0.2885 + j0.0017) = 28.8 + j0.17$$
$$I_0 = \sqrt{28.8^2 + 0.17^2} = 28.8 \text{ amp}$$

Also

$$I_0 = \frac{E_0}{Z_0} = \frac{100}{3.47} = 28.8 \text{ amp}$$

which checks the value found above.

$$\tan \theta_0 = \frac{+0.17}{28.8} = +0.0059$$
$$\theta_0 = 0° 20'$$

Series-Parallel Circuits. Series-parallel groupings of impedances, as in Fig. 8-21, are solved by (1) finding the equivalent impedance of

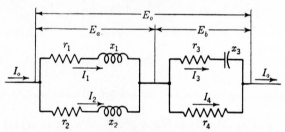

FIG. 8-21. Series-parallel connected impedances.

each parallel group separately, (2) adding the resulting series impedances to find the total.

Example 4. Let the constants of the circuit of Fig. 8-21 have the following values in ohms:

$$r_1 = 3 \qquad x_1 = 5 \text{ (inductive reactance)}$$
$$r_2 = 4 \qquad x_2 = 3 \text{ (inductive reactance)}$$
$$r_3 = 5 \qquad x_3 = 6 \text{ (capacitive reactance)}$$
$$r_4 = 8$$

When the impressed voltage E_0 is 100, find the equivalent impedance of each branch, the total equivalent impedance of the circuit, the current in each branch, the total current, and the voltage consumed in each branch.

For circuit (a),

$$Y_1 = \frac{1}{3 + j5} = \frac{3}{3^2 + 5^2} - j\frac{5}{3^2 + 5^2} = 0.0882 - j0.147$$

$$Y_2 = \frac{1}{4 + j3} = \frac{4}{4^2 + 3^2} - j\frac{3}{4^2 + 3^2} = 0.1600 - j0.120$$

By addition,

$$Y_a = Y_1 + Y_2 = 0.2482 - j0.267$$

$$Z_a = \frac{1}{0.2482 - j0.267} = \frac{0.2482}{0.2482^2 + 0.267^2} + j\frac{0.267}{0.2482^2 + 0.267^2} = 1.87 + j2.01$$

For circuit (b),

$$Y_3 = \frac{1}{5 - j6} = \frac{5}{5^2 + 6^2} + j\frac{6}{5^2 + 6^2} = 0.082 + j0.0983$$

$$Y_4 = \frac{1}{8 + j0} = \frac{8}{8^2 + 0} - j\frac{0}{8^2 + 0} = 0.125 - j0.000$$

By addition,

$$Y_b = 0.207 + j0.0983$$

$$Z_b = \frac{1}{0.207 + j0.0983} = \frac{0.207}{0.207^2 + 0.0983^2} - j\frac{0.0983}{0.207^2 + 0.0983^2}$$

$$= 3.94 - j1.87$$

$$Z_0 = Z_a + Z_b$$

$$= 5.81 + j0.14$$

When the potential difference $E = 100$ volts is impressed on the circuit as a whole, the currents and voltages are

$$I_0 = Y_0 E_0 = \frac{E_0}{Z_0} = \frac{100}{5.81 + j0.14}$$

$$= \frac{100 \times 5.81}{5.81^2 + 0.14^2} - j\frac{100 \times 0.14}{5.81^2 + 0.14^2}$$

$$= 17.25 - j0.42$$

Expressed in polar form,

$$I_0 = 17.3\underline{/-(1° \ 23')}$$

By Ohm's law,

$$E_a = I_0 Z_a = (17.25 - j0.42)(1.87 + j2.01)$$

$$= 33.1 + j33.9$$

$$= 47.4\underline{/45° \ 40'}$$

$$E_b = I_0 Z_b = (17.25 - j0.42)(3.94 - j1.87)$$

$$= 67.1 - j33.9$$

$$= 75.2\underline{/-(26° \ 50')}$$

By Kirchhoff's second law,

$$E_0 = E_a + E_b = 33.1 + 67.1 + j(33.9 - 33.9)$$

$$= 100 + j0$$

$$= 100\underline{/0}$$

which checks the applied voltage. The currents in the several branches are

$$I_{a1} = E_a Y_1 = (33.1 + j33.9)(0.0882 - j0.147)$$

$$= 7.90 - j1.88$$

$$= 8.12\underline{/-(13° \ 24')}$$

$$\mathbf{I}_{a2} = \mathbf{E}_a \mathbf{Y}_2 = (33.1 + j33.9)(0.16 - j0.12)$$
$$= 9.37 + j1.43$$
$$= 9.47\underline{/8°\ 40'}$$

$$\mathbf{I}_{b1} = \mathbf{E}_b \mathbf{Y}_3 = (67.1 - j33.9)(0.082 + j0.0983)$$
$$= 8.83 + j3.82$$
$$= 9.63\underline{/23°\ 23'}$$

$$\mathbf{I}_{b2} = \mathbf{E}_b \mathbf{Y}_4 = (67.1 - j33.9)(0.125 - j0.000)$$
$$= 8.46 - j4.24$$
$$= 9.45\underline{/-(26°\ 37\ )}$$

It should be observed that, by Kirchhoff's first law,

$$\mathbf{I}_0 = \mathbf{I}_{a1} + \mathbf{I}_{a2} = 17.26 - j0.45$$
$$\mathbf{I}_0 = \mathbf{I}_{b1} + \mathbf{I}_{b2} = 17.29 - j0.42$$

both of which check approximately the value of $\mathbf{I}_0$ previously found.

The phasor diagram of currents and voltages is given in Fig. 9-21. In this figure the origin of $\mathbf{E}_b$ as well as that of the currents $\mathbf{I}_{b1}$ and $\mathbf{I}_{b2}$ is O', the free end of $\mathbf{E}_a$, while

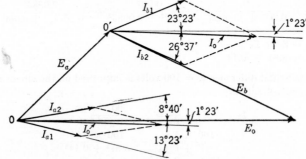

FIG. 9-21. Phasor diagram of currents and voltages in Example 4.

for the (a) circuit the origin is at O. If the two current diagrams were superimposed the I_0 phasors in the upper and lower part of the diagram would, of course, coincide

Sometimes one or more of the branches of a parallel circuit may contain an inductance or a capacitance with negligible resistance in series, or a branch may contain resistance only. In the first case the admittance of the branch has no conductance, while in the second it has no susceptance. The procedure to be followed in solving such a circuit is the same as that used in the foregoing examples.

Example 5. In the circuit of Fig. 7-21 let r_1, x_2, and r_3 be zero, let r_2 be 8 ohms, and let the 60-cycle reactances x_1 and x_3 be 5 and 10 ohms respectively. Find (a) the equivalent 60-cycle impedance of the branched circuit, (b) the phasor input current when the impressed voltage is 100.

(a) The admittances of the three branches are the following:

$$\mathbf{Y}_1 = \frac{1}{0 + j5} = 0.0 - j0.20$$

$$\mathbf{Y}_2 = \frac{1}{8 + j0} = 0.125 - j0.00$$

$$Y_3 = \frac{1}{0 - j10} = 0.00 + j0.10$$

$$Y_0 = 0.125 - j0.10$$

Accordingly, the equivalent impedance is

$$Z_0 = \frac{1}{0.125 - j0.10} = \frac{0.125}{0.0256} + j\frac{0.100}{0.0256}$$

$$= 4.88 + j3.9$$

$$r_0 = 4.88 \text{ ohms resistance}$$

$$x_0 = 3.9 \text{ ohms inductive reactance}$$

$$Z_0 = \sqrt{4.88^2 + 3.9^2}$$

$$= 6.25 \text{ ohms impedance}$$

(b) The input phasor current is the product of the impressed voltage and the admittance of the circuit.

$$I_0 = 100(0.125 - j0.10) = 12.5 - j10$$

$$I_0 = \sqrt{12.5^2 + 10^2} = 16 \text{ amp}$$

Also,

$$I_0 = \frac{E_0}{Z_0} = \frac{100}{6.25} = 16 \text{ amp}$$

$$\tan \theta = \frac{10}{12.5} = 0.80$$

$$\theta = 38° 40'$$

Summary. 1. Kirchhoff's laws state that:

a. At any point in a closed circuit the phasor sum of the currents flowing up to the point is zero. This relation is expressed symbolically by the equation $\Sigma I = 0$.

b. In any closed circuit the phasor sum of all the impressed and absorbed electromotive forces is zero. The symbolic expression for this relation is $\Sigma E = 0$.

2. The phasor admittance of a circuit is the phasor current in the circuit per unit of impressed voltage, that is,

$$Y_0 = \frac{I_0}{E_0} = \frac{1}{Z_0}$$

$= g_0 \pm jb_0$. (The sign of jb_0 is $+$ when the current leads and $-$ when it lags the impressed voltage.)

$g_0 =$ conductance

$\pm jb_0 =$ susceptance

When the phasor impedance Z of a circuit is given, the admittance of the circuit is found by taking the reciprocal of Z:

$$Y = \frac{1}{Z} = \frac{1}{r \pm jx} = \frac{r}{r^2 + x^2} \mp j\frac{x}{r^2 + x^2}$$

$$g = \frac{r}{r^2 + x^2}$$

$$b = \frac{x}{r^2 + x^2}$$

3. When the phasor admittance **Y** of a circuit is given, the phasor impedance is found by taking the reciprocal of **Y**:

$$\mathbf{Z} = \frac{1}{\mathbf{Y}} = \frac{1}{g \pm jb} = \frac{g}{g^2 + b^2} \mp j\frac{b}{g^2 + b^2}$$
$$r = \frac{g}{g^2 + b^2}$$
$$x = \frac{b}{g^2 + b^2}$$

4. When referred to the current as reference phasor, the phasor voltage consumed in a circuit is the product of the scalar current and the phasor impedance, but in general

$\mathbf{E} = (r \pm jx)\mathbf{I}$, the impressed voltage
rI = the component of voltage in phase with the current
xI = the component of voltage in quadrature with the current

5. When referred to the impressed voltage as reference phasor, the phasor current in a circuit is the product of the scalar impressed voltage and the phasor admittance, but in general

$\mathbf{I} = (g \pm jb)\mathbf{E}$
gE = component of current in phase with impressed voltage
$\pm bE$ = component of current in quadrature with impressed voltage

Current Resonance. The reactance of an inductance coil is directly proportional to the frequency, while the reactance of a capacitance is inversely proportional to the frequency. Accordingly, when an inductive circuit is connected in parallel with a capacitive circuit, as in Fig. 10-21, and the frequency of the impressed voltage is increased continuously from a low value to higher and higher values, the impedance of the inductive branch increases, while that of the capacitive branch diminishes. Therefore, if the impressed voltage remains constant, the current in the inductive branch decreases, while the current in the capacitive branch increases as the frequency rises.

The phasor current in each branch is the product of the impressed voltage and the admittance of the branch. To distinguish them, let the inductive branch be designated by subscripts 1 and the capacitive branch by subscripts 2. Then the phasor branch currents are

$$\mathbf{I}_1 = \left(\frac{r_1}{r_1^2 + x_1^2} - j\frac{x_1}{r_1^2 + x_1^2}\right)\mathbf{E}_0 = (g_1 - jb_1)\mathbf{E}_0$$
$$\mathbf{I}_2 = \left(\frac{r_2}{r_2^2 + x_2^2} + j\frac{x_2}{r_2^2 + x_2^2}\right)\mathbf{E}_0 = (g_2 + jb_2)\mathbf{E}_0$$

and the line current is

$$\mathbf{I}_0 = \mathbf{I}_1 + \mathbf{I}_2$$
$$= [g_1 + g_2 + j(b_2 - b_1)]\mathbf{E}_0$$

The reactive component of current in the inductive branch lags the impressed voltage by 90 deg. It is

$$\mathbf{I}_{b1} = -jb_1\mathbf{E}_0$$

The reactive component of current in the capacitive branch leads the impressed voltage by 90 deg. It is

$$\mathbf{I}_{b2} = +jb_2\mathbf{E}_0$$

As the frequency is raised the first of these components decreases, while the second increases. A frequency is finally reached, however, for which

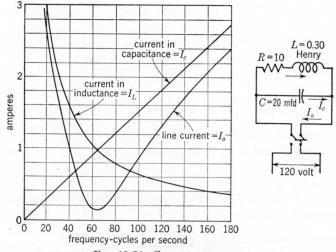

FIG. 10-21. Current resonance.

the magnitudes of the two components are exactly equal. This frequency is called the *frequency of resonance*. At the frequency of resonance the phasor sum of the reactive components of current is zero; no reactive component is present in the input current—for the latter is then

$$\mathbf{I}_0 = (g_1 + g_2)\mathbf{E}_0$$

—and the input current and voltage phasors are in phase with each other. If the resistance of the circuit is small as compared with the reactances (as in Fig. 10-21), the line current is very nearly zero at the resonance frequency. In any case, the current in the line has a minimum value at some frequency very close to the frequency of resonance.

It is possible to solve for the resonance frequency in terms of the circuit constants (R, L, and C), but the resulting expression is not so simple as the corresponding expression for the case of voltage resonance, which was discussed in the preceding chapter.

At the frequency of resonance

$$\mathbf{I}_{b1} + \mathbf{I}_{b2} = j\mathbf{E}_0(-b_1 + b_2) = 0$$

Hence

$$b_1 = b_2$$

and in general

$$\frac{x_1}{r_1{}^2 + x_1{}^2} = \frac{x_2}{r_2{}^2 + x_2{}^2}$$

But

$$x_1 = 2\pi fL = \omega L \quad \text{and} \quad x_2 = \frac{1}{2\pi fC} = \frac{1}{\omega C}$$

so

$$\frac{\omega L}{r_1{}^2 + \omega^2 L^2} = \frac{1/\omega C}{r_2{}^2 + (1/\omega^2 C^2)}$$

Solving for ω yields

$$\omega = \frac{1}{2\pi \sqrt{LC}} \sqrt{\frac{CR_L{}^2 - L}{CR_c{}^2 - L}}$$

where, for ease of identification, $R_L = r_1$ designates the resistance of the inductive branch and $R_c = r_2$ designates the resistance of the capacitive branch.

Resonance is possible in a circuit similar to the one in Fig. 10-21 even though $R_c \neq 0$ provided that the quantity under the second radical sign is positive and, of course, that $\omega \neq 0$.

Problems

1-21. The two impedances $\mathbf{Z}_1 = 2 + j10$ and $\mathbf{Z}_2 = 3 - j15$ are connected in parallel. The current in $\mathbf{Z}_1$ is $\mathbf{I}_1 = 12 - j18$. Find (a) the phasor current in $\mathbf{Z}_2$, (b) the phasor input current.

2-21. A potential difference of 180 volts is impressed upon the following impedances connected in parallel:

$$\mathbf{Z}_1 = 20 + j35$$
$$\mathbf{Z}_2 = 30 + j0$$
$$\mathbf{Z}_3 = 15 + j25$$

Determine (a) the phasor admittance of each branch, (b) the phasor current in each branch, (c) the phasor equivalent impedance of the circuit, and (d) the phasor current input. Use impressed voltage as reference phasor.

3-21. The three impedances given below are connected in parallel. The current in $\mathbf{Z}_2$ is $\mathbf{I}_2 = 6 + j4$. Find (a) the phasor current in each branch, (b) the phasor impressed voltage, and (c) the phasor equivalent impedance of the circuit.

$$\mathbf{Z}_1 = 8 - j10$$
$$\mathbf{Z}_2 = 6 - j8$$
$$\mathbf{Z}_3 = 4 + j2$$

4-21. The equivalent impedance of a parallel circuit consisting of two branches is $\mathbf{Z}_0 = 10.6 - j8.8$. One branch $\mathbf{Z}_1$ consists of a pure resistance of 40 ohms. Find the phasor impedance of the remaining branch.

5-21. The circuit in Fig. A-21 has the resistances and 60-cycle reactances indicated. The current in the upper branch is 5 amp. With this current as reference

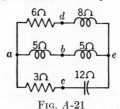

FIG. A-21

phasor find (a) the phasor currents in the remaining two branches, (b) the phasor impressed voltage across ae, (c) the potential difference from b to d, and (d) the potential difference from d to c. (e) Draw a phasor diagram showing these voltages to scale. The source of emf (not shown) is applied at points a and e.

6-21. The 60-cycle impedances

$$\mathbf{Z}_1 = 40\underline{/30°} \qquad \text{and} \qquad \mathbf{Z}_2 = 50\overline{\backslash45°}$$

are connected in parallel across 120-volt mains, the frequency of which may be varied any desired amount. Determine (a) the scalar value of the current in each branch and (b) the total input current for each of the following frequencies in cycles per second: 25, 50, 75, and 100.

7-21. (a) Find the frequency of resonance for the circuit in Prob. 6-21. At this frequency with 120 volts impressed find (b) the current in each branch and (c) the input current.

8-21. The two 60-cycle admittances $\mathbf{Y}_1 = 0.4\overline{\backslash30°}$ and $\mathbf{Y}_2 = 0.5\overline{\backslash60°}$ are connected in parallel. The phasor current in the first admittance is $\mathbf{I}_1 = 20\overline{\backslash53°}$. Find (a) the phasor impressed voltage, (b) the current in the second admittance, and (c) the input current. Express results in rectangular components.

9-21. In the circuit of Prob. 8-21 find the equivalent resistance and the equivalent reactance of the branched circuit.

10-21. Two impedances $\mathbf{Z}_2 = 6 + j3$ and $\mathbf{Z}_3 = 3 - j6$ are connected in parallel (Fig. B-21). Connected in series with this group is a third impedance $\mathbf{Z}_1 = 2 - j4$.

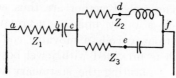

FIG. B-21

The current in $\mathbf{Z}_2$ is $\mathbf{I}_2 = 4 - j8$. Find (a) the phasor current in $\mathbf{Z}_3$, (b) the phasor current in $\mathbf{Z}_1$, (c) the phasor impressed voltage.

11-21. In the circuit of Fig. B-21 find the phasor potential difference (a) between b and d, (b) between b and e.

CHAPTER 22

ALTERNATING-CURRENT METERS

Electrodynamometer. Many portable a-c voltmeters and wattmeters employ the principle of the electrodynamometer illustrated in Fig. 1-22. Two stationary coils G and H are mounted close together on a common axis. The windings of these coils are connected in series in such a manner that, when current is maintained in the circuit, the mmfs of the

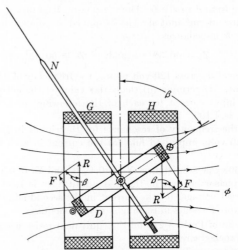

FIG. 1-22. The electrodynamometer.

coils are additive. The coils together are thus equivalent to a short solenoid, within which a fairly uniform magnetic field is produced. Partly within the stationary coils a movable coil D is mounted on a vertical spindle, which is provided with jewel bearings that hold it in position in the space separating the stationary coils G and H. The movable coil is made of a number of turns of fine wire wound on a lightly constructed, hollow cylindrical spool and is designed to carry only a small current. Current is led to and away from the movable coil by spiral springs at the ends of the spindle, similar to those used in the d-c D'Arsonval-type meters described in Chap. 9. The springs also serve to furnish a resisting torque proportional to the angular displacement of the coil from its zero position, thus bringing the needle N to rest at a scale reading proportional to the torque.

When current is passed through the stationary coils, the magnetic field produced within is of the form illustrated in the figure. If at the same time current is also maintained in the movable coil in the direction indicated, a torque is developed which tends to turn the coil in a clockwise direction. In the figure, R is the electromagnetic force tending to move each side of the coil in a direction normal to the field and F is the component of R normal to the plane of the coil. Obviously, then, the torque is equal to the product $2Fr = 2Rr \sin \beta$ where r is the radius of the coil and β is the angle which the plane of the coil makes with a normal to the field.

Dynamometer Used as a Voltmeter. In the dynamometer-type voltmeter the movable coil and the stationary coils are connected in series with a high resistance, as in Fig. 2-22. The stationary coils are made of many turns of fine wire, while the movable coil is made of a smaller number of turns of similar wire. The high resistance is used to limit the current in the circuit to the small value for which the meter is designed and to minimize the effect of the self-inductance of the coil on the accuracy of the meter. The current required to give full-scale reading of the meter (about 0.05 amp) is considerably larger than the corresponding current of the d-c voltmeter employing a permanent magnet. The reason for this is that the flux density in the magnetic field is so much less in the a-c meter. Since the stationary coils and the movable coil are connected in series, the current reverses in both at the same time (as in a series motor) and hence the torque is always in a given direction. Damping is secured by means of a light aluminum vane

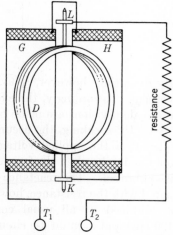

Fig. 2-22. Wiring diagram of the electrodynamometer used as a voltmeter.

(not shown in the figure) which is attached to the moving element. This vane is enclosed in a loosely fitting, airtight box, within which it swings as the coil turns. The air cushion thus provided largely eliminates oscillation and forces the needle to settle down quickly to its final position corresponding to the applied torque.

The scale of the electrodynamometer voltmeter is a nonuniform, modified square-root scale. The instantaneous torque T tending to turn the movable coil is proportional to the product of the flux density B in the field of the stationary coils, the current i in the movable coil, and the sine of the angle between the plane of the movable coil and the normal to the flux density ($\sin \beta$) (see Fig. 1-22). These relations are expressed in symbols as

$$T = kBi \sin \beta$$

where k = constant. Since the stationary coils and the movable coil are connected in series, the flux density is proportional to the current and hence the torque is proportional to the current squared; that is,

$$T = k'i^2 \sin \beta$$

The impedance of the meter circuit is constant, so the current is proportional to the impressed voltage and the torque is proportional to the square of the impressed voltage. Owing to the relatively high inertia of the moving mechanism, the needle cannot follow the instantaneous torque but assumes a position determined by the average torque instead. Thus, if T_{av} is the average torque and e is the instantaneous voltage,

$$T_{av} = k_2(\text{av } e^2) \sin \beta$$

or

$$\text{av } e^2 = \frac{T_{av}}{k_2 \sin \beta}$$

By definition, however, $\sqrt{\text{av } e^2}$ is the effective value of the impressed voltage. Accordingly, the effective voltage will be read by the meter if the scale divisions are made proportional to $\sqrt{T_{av}/\sin \beta}$.

Strictly speaking, the accuracy of these meters is affected by the frequency of the applied voltage, and the highest degree of accuracy is obtained only when the frequency impressed is that for which the meter is calibrated. The reactance of the meter circuit is very small as compared with the resistance, however, so, as a matter of fact, good accuracy is obtained at all usual commercial frequencies (frequencies under 100 cps) and even on d-c circuits. If the meter is to be used to measure voltages of much higher frequencies, it should be recalibrated for the frequency desired.

Dynamometer Used as an Ammeter. The electrodynamometer of the type illustrated in Figs. 1-22 and 2-22 cannot be used conveniently as an ammeter. (In the ammeter the resistance of Fig. 2-22 would, of course, be eliminated.) Two principal difficulties are involved:

1. It is impractical to lead large currents to and away from the moving element, which would require the use of shunts as in d-c meters.

2. It is difficult to use shunts with a-c meters, because in order that the movable coil and the shunt may always divide the current in a fixed

ratio, the impedance ($\sqrt{R^2 + X^2}$) of the shunt and the impedance of the movable coil must have a fixed ratio at all frequencies. To make this possible, the ratio of the resistance to the reactance must have the same value in both moving coil and shunt. These adjustments are hard to make.

Owing to these difficulties, it has usually been found to be impractical to build a-c ammeters employing the principle of the electrodynamometer. Most a-c ammeters are of the moving-vane type, to be described in a later paragraph.

Dynamometer Used as a Wattmeter. The power in a d-c circuit is equal to the product of the impressed voltage and the current. In an a-c circuit, however, while the instantaneous power is equal to the product of instantaneous current and voltage, the *average power* is generally not equal to the product of effective voltage and effective current. Voltmeters and ammeters do not suffice to measure the power in an a-c circuit, therefore, but a special instrument, called a *wattmeter*, must be used.

The usual type of wattmeter operates on the principle of the electrodynamometer. In the wattmeter (Fig. 3-22) the stationary coils G and H are made of a few turns of large wire, suitable for carrying the load current. The coils are connected in series (cumulatively) and the ends of the circuit terminate on the heavy binding posts A_1 and A_2. When the meter is in use, the coils are connected in series with the load, and since there is no iron in the magnetic circuit, the field produced within the coils is proportional to the load current. The circuit through the moving coil and its series-connected resistance is similar to that of the voltmeter and draws only a small current. The terminals of this circuit are V_1 and V_2. When the meter is connected to measure power, the moving-coil circuit is connected across the load terminals as in Fig. 4-22. The current in this circuit is proportional to the applied voltage. For any given position of the moving coil the torque tending to deflect the needle is proportional to the product of the instantaneous voltage (current in the potential coil) and the instantaneous current (flux density set up by the stationary coils), or to the instantaneous power. This is illustrated in Fig. 7-23(b), for example. In this figure the current lags the

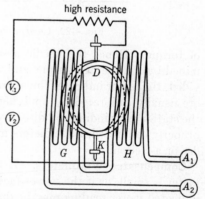

FIG. 3-22. Elementary wiring diagram of a wattmeter.

voltage by the angle $\theta = 45$ deg (cos $\theta = 0.707$), and the instantaneous power, which is proportional to the instantaneous torque of the watt-meter, is shown by the curve p, the average ordinate of which is the average power $P = EI$ cos θ. The latter is the power indicated by the wattmeter.

If the moving element were light enough, the needle of the meter would oscillate in conformity with the instantaneous torque, like the vibrator of an oscillograph. When the power factor[1] is not unity, that is, when the current and the applied voltage are not in phase with each other, the instantaneous torque is negative for a short period of time once during each half cycle. During the negative intervals of torque the needle would move to the left of the zero. In wattmeters the moving element has suffi-cient inertia, however, to keep the needle from following the rapid changes

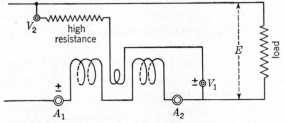

FIG. 4-22. Correct connection of a wattmeter.

of torque. Hence the needle assumes an angular displacement deter-mined by the average torque, and when a suitably calibrated scale is pro-vided, the meter indicates the average power in the circuit. Wattmeters are usually calibrated by applying carefully measured direct current to the stationary winding and direct voltage to the movable winding. When properly calibrated, these meters may be used to measure power in either d-c or a-c circuits.

Compensated Wattmeters. If the power to be measured by a watt-meter is small, or if the power factor is low, an unduly large part of the indicated meter reading may be due to the power loss in the meter itself. Serious inaccuracies may be avoided in such cases by using a *compensated wattmeter.*

It may be observed in Fig. 4-22 that the current in the *current coil* exceeds the load current by the amount of current in the movable *potential coil.* The power indicated by the meter is, therefore, greater than the power consumed by the load by an amount equal to the power consumed in the potential circuit. This error is corrected by supplying the meter with a *compensating winding* connected in series with the potential coil. This winding is made of fine wire (large enough to carry safely the poten-

[1] Power factor is defined on p. 361 and 362.

tial-coil current). The compensating winding and the current coil are wound together, turn for turn. Their turns lie side by side throughout, and each of the windings has exactly the same number. The compensating winding is so connected in series with the potential coil that its mmf and that of the current coil are subtractive. The meter then gives a true indication of the power supplied to the load.

If a separate voltmeter is to be used with the wattmeter to measure the load voltage, a second compensating coil may be provided to compensate for the power consumed by the voltmeter.

Correct and Incorrect Connections. Note that in Fig. 4-22 the terminal V_1 of the potential coil (marked $\pm$) is connected to the side of the line with the current coil in series. This connection, and not the incorrect connection shown in Fig. 5-22, should always be used. There is no appreciable resistance between V_1 and the potential coil, so the potential

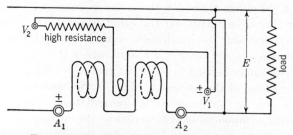

Fig. 5-22. Incorrect connection of a wattmeter.

difference between the current-coil and the potential-coil windings in Fig. 4-22 is negligible. When the connection of Fig. 5-22 is used, however, the potential of the moving coil is approximately the same as that of the line opposite the current coil. The full-line potential difference then exists between the windings of the current coil and the moving element. This potential difference may be sufficient to break down the insulation between the windings and so damage the meter. Even though the insulation may not be damaged, this connection should be avoided because the meter reading will be in error, owing to the electrostatic forces set up between the potential and the current coils.

Under certain conditions of use the reading of a wattmeter may change from positive (deflection of needle to the right) to negative (deflection to the left of zero) when the phase angle of the circuit is varied. To make the meter read in the positive direction again, the relative directions of the currents in the potential and current coils must be reversed. For this purpose a switch is provided to reverse the terminals of the potential coil.

Ratings of Current and Potential Coils. It should be remembered that wattmeters, unlike voltmeters and ammeters, have two electrically independent circuits: one the current element, and the other the potential element.   Each of these has a separate current rating which should not be exceeded.   The allowable maximum impressed voltage of the potential circuit and the allowable maximum current of the current coil are specified by the manufacturer and are marked on either the meter or the case. Care should be exercised not to exceed these values, for it is possible to overload either one or the other of the windings without causing the needle to move beyond the end of the scale.   While a knowledge of the voltage and current in the circuit is not required to measure the power it is usually desirable, nevertheless, to connect a voltmeter and an ammeter in the circuit in order to have a check on the current and voltage applied to the wattmeter.

Var Meters.   Wattmeters measure the product of voltage and the in-phase component of current in a circuit.   Symbolically, this is represented by $P = EI \cos \theta$, where θ is the angle of lag or lead of current I with respect to voltage E and P is the power in watts.   The reactive volt-amperes or *vars* of a circuit, on the other hand, is the product of the impressed voltage and the quadrature component of the current.   It is represented symbolically by $Q = EI \sin \theta$, where Q is the vars.   In general, wattmeters may be used to measure vars by providing suitable means whereby the phase of the voltage applied to the potential coil is shifted 90 deg, thus causing the current in the potential coil to be in phase with the quadrature component of the current in the current coil.   Since the latter is $I \sin \theta$, the meter indication is then proportional to the product $EI \sin \theta = Q$.

The method employed to produce the necessary shift in voltage depends upon the circuit.   In single-phase circuits an impedance network external to the meter is connected in series with the potential coil to produce the shift.   In two-phase circuits quadrature components of voltage may be had by cross-connecting the two phases.   In balanced three-phase circuits a single wattmeter may be used as described in Chap. 24, to measure vars. In general, however, autotransformers are used in three-phase circuits to bring about the required phase shift.

Single-phase Power-factor Meter.   The construction of the single-phase power-factor meter, Fig. 6-22, is similar to that of the single-phase wattmeter shown in Fig. 3-22, except that the moving element of the former has two coils, M and M', spaced 90 deg apart, instead of one. The moving coils are mounted on an axle within the stationary current coil GH.   Coil M is connected in series with a suitable resistance, while M' is connected in series with an inductance.   Hence the current in M is approximately in phase with the impressed potential difference of the load, while the current in M' lags it by 90 deg.

When the power factor of the load is unity, the current in M' is in time quadrature with the field flux of GH and no resultant torque is produced by the reaction between these two. The current in M, however, is in time phase with the field flux; it reacts with the field to produce a torque; and the movable element turns until the position of zero torque is reached. This occurs when the axis of M, normal to the plane of the coil, coincides with the axis of GH. When the power factor is zero there is no torque produced by the reaction of the current in M with the field, since these are now in time quadrature. The current in M', however, does react with the field to produce a torque and the moving assembly again takes up a position of zero torque, which occurs when the axis of M' and GH coincide. For intermediate power factors the position of the moving element is in equilibrium (no torque) when the angular displacement from the position first described is equal to the phase angle. The instrument is made direct

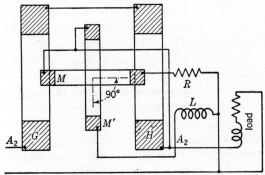

FIG. 6-22. The single-phase power-factor meter.

reading by providing a needle attached to the movable coils and a suitable power-factor scale corresponding to the cosine of the angle of deflection.

Moving-coil Oscillograph. The moving-coil or Duddell oscillograph is an instrument designed on the principle of a galvanometer or moving-coil ammeter in which the moving element is so lightly constructed that, when a small current is passed through it, the deflection secured is proportional to the instantaneous value of the current flowing, even though the current varies rapidly.

The moving element or *vibrator* consists of a single loop of small phosphor-bronze wire suspended between the poles of a magnet and supported by two bridges of nonmagnetic material spanning the pole edges of the magnet. The closed end of the loop embraces a pulley which is held in place by a spring under tension (see Fig. 7-22). The magnets may be of either the permanent or electromagnet type. The vibrator is usually immersed in oil to keep it cool and make it deadbeat. Near the middle of the loop a small, light mirror is cemented to the two wires. The vibrator loop has low inductance and very little inertia and, as mounted.

has a high natural period of vibration—usually about 5,000 cps.   For these reasons it can follow with fidelity the rapidly fluctuating current which actuates it.   A complete oscillograph usually has from three to six vibrator units with which simultaneous measurements of currents, voltages, power, etc., may be made.

Through the medium of prisms and lenses, means are also provided by which a narrow beam of light of high intensity, supplied by an arc lamp

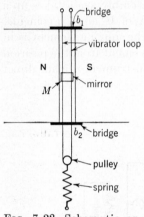

or a concentrated-filament incandescent lamp, strikes the mirror on the moving coil and is reflected through concentrating lenses to a second mirror that oscillates in a plane normal to the motion of the mirror on the moving coil.   From the oscillating mirror the beam of light is reflected on a stationary screen where it appears spread out in the form of a wave. The oscillating mirror moves forward with relatively slow motion, but returns to the starting position rapidly.   This motion is imparted to the mirror through a cam driven by a synchronous motor that is connected to the same supply to which the vibrator or moving coil is connected.   During the return motion of the mirror the source of light is cut off by means of a shutter; hence the spread-out light

Fig. 7-22. Schematic arrangement of poles and vibrator of a moving-coil type of oscillograph.

beam appears on the screen in the form of a wave.   In some designs a revolving mirror is used in place of the oscillating mirror.

Oscillographs of this type are also provided with means for photographing the wave.   For this purpose a film, mounted on a drum in a lighttight box, is used.   The light beam reflected from the vibrator mirror strikes the film directly without striking the cam-driven mirror at all.   When the drum is stationary, the light beam reflected on the film traces out a straight line at right angles to the axis of the film and proportional in length to twice the angular displacement of the vibrator.   When the film is moved, the light beam is spread out on the film in the form of a wave and may be so photographed.

The vibrator elements are electrically connected to the circuit in the manner of voltmeters and ammeters.   The vibrator loop itself is designed to carry only about 0.1 amp.   Accordingly, when a current measurement is to be made, a low noninductive resistance shunt is used to pass the main current, while the vibrator terminals are connected across the terminals of the shunt.   When a voltage wave is to be obtained, suitable high noninductive resistance is placed in series with the vibrator element to limit the current to the proper value.   Since the resistances used are noninductive, the current in the vibrator will always be proportional to and in phase with the current or voltage of the circuit, as the case may be.

Movable-vane Instruments. Ammeters and Voltmeters. In this type of instrument a light strip of iron is fastened to the shaft supporting the needle. Motion of the needle is brought about by the interaction of the magnetic field produced by current in a stationary coil and the iron strip or vane. A number of meters have been developed employing this principle in different ways. In one type of meter the vane is so placed that, when current flows in the coil, the vane tends to assume a position of parallelism with the lines of force in the field. The motion produced is used to indicate the strength of current producing the field. In the Weston meter, about to be described more fully, the repulsion between two polarized strips of iron, one stationary and the other turning on a spindle, is used to obtain a measure of the current in the coil.

The Weston ammeter (model 155) is illustrated in Fig. 8-22, while Fig. 9-22 is a drawing which illustrates the operating principle more fully. A stationary coil, consisting of a few turns of wire of suitable cross-sectional area safely to carry the current for which the meter is designed, produces a magnetic field with intensity proportional to the current. Within the coil and subject to the influence of the magnetic field, two V-shaped, thin cylindrical segments of soft iron are concentrically mounted close together (see Fig. 9-22). One of these (B) is stationary and the other (C) is fastened to an extension of the shaft upon which the needle is supported. When current flows in the exciting coil A, a magnetic field is produced within the coil and the iron segments become polarized, as shown in the side view of the figure.

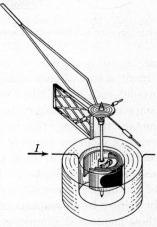

FIG. 8-22. Weston moving-vane a-c ammeter.

Both strips are polarized in the same direction so that, regardless of which way current flows in the coil, corresponding edges of the two strips always have poles of a given sign. When the segments are polarized, a repulsion exists between them. This causes the movable segment and the needle to turn on the spindle. By means of a suitably calibrated scale, the motion is translated into a measure of the current producing the field.

Spiral springs fastened between the shaft and the stationary parts of the meter furnish the necessary resisting torque. The scale divisions are not uniform but are smaller near the ends of the scale than in the middle. The meter reads in a positive direction for either direction of current in the coil. The motion of the needle is freed from oscillation by a damping device. This consists of an aluminum vane (D in Fig. 9-22) which is fastened to an extension of the needle and moves in a closed compartment E. The air in the compartment resists rapid motion of the vane and thus serves to bring the needle to rest gradually and without oscillation. Meters of this type that have been calibrated on a 60-cycle circuit have good accuracy at all ordinary commercial power frequencies.

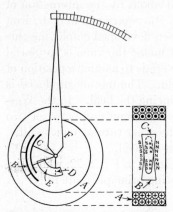

FIG. 9-22. Operating principle of moving-vane ammeter illustrated.

With only slight modification the instrument above described may be used as a voltmeter. Ammeters are connected in series with the load, the current of which is to be measured, while voltmeters are connected across the terminals of the circuit. Ammeters, therefore, must have low-resistance coils, while voltmeters must have a high resistance connected in series with the coil. Moreover, since the current in a voltmeter should be so small as to be negligible in comparison with the current in the metered circuit, a wire of very small cross section may be used. The coil must be wound with many turns of this wire, however, in order to provide the ampere-turns necessary to make the instrument operative. In a voltmeter, therefore, the exciting coil consists of many turns of fine wire, and in series with it a very high resistance is connected. The scale of the meter, of course, is calibrated in volts. In all respects other than those mentioned, ammeters and voltmeters are essentially alike.

Rectifier-type Voltmeter. This meter employs four copper oxide disks or stacks of disks and a permanent-magnet type of d-c millivoltmeter, all connected in a network illustrated in Fig. 10-22. This circuit accomplishes full-wave rectification of the impressed voltage wave.

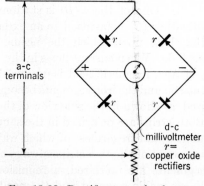

FIG. 10-22. Rectifier type of voltmeter.

The indication of the meter is proportional to the *average value* of the rectified current which, in turn, is proportional to the effective value of the impressed voltage, provided the latter remains sinusoidal in form. If the voltage wave departs from the sine form, the meter reading will be in error.

This meter is designed for use in audio-frequency circuits (up to about 4,000 or 5,000 cps), frequencies that are far beyond the range of the ordinary electrodynamic type of meter. Rectifier-type meters should not be used beyond the upper limit of frequency for which they are designed, because errors may be very large; nor should they be used outside the range of room temperatures over which the meter readings are shown to be accurate.

Multiplying resistance networks are provided to extend the scale of the meter. A typical meter has seven voltage ranges of 2, 4, 10, 20, 40, 100, 200 volts, full scale. For a given multiplier setting it is essential that the input impedance remain substantially constant over the full useful range of scale if a high degree of accuracy is to be secured. The forward resistance of a copper oxide disk varies inversely with the current and is therefore less at high than at low readings. In the high-voltage scales this

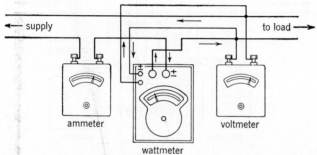

FIG. 11-22. Meter connections for measuring power without instrument transformers.

variation is a negligibly small percentage of the total impedance, but in the lowest voltage scale there may be an increase of as much as 15 per cent, as the current is reduced from full scale to one-fourth scale.

Meter Connections for Measuring Power. As has been mentioned, a voltmeter and an ammeter should also be connected in the circuit when a wattmeter is used to measure the power. The ammeter indicates the current in the current coil of the wattmeter, while the voltmeter indicates the voltage applied to the potential-coil circuit. When the voltage and current of the metered circuit do not exceed the rated values applying to the wattmeter, the meters may be connected directly to the circuit, as in Fig. 11-22. The ammeter and the current coil of the wattmeter are connected in series with the load, while the voltmeter and the potential coil of the wattmeter are connected across the line.

Often it is necessary to measure the power in a circuit with a potential difference larger than that for which the voltmeter and the potential circuit of the wattmeter are designed. Likewise, the current to be metered may be larger than that which either the wattmeter or the ammeter will safely stand.   In such cases potential transformers are used to step the voltage down to a value that may be safely used on the potential coils, and similarly a current transformer is used to reduce the current in the ammeter and the current coil of the wattmeter.   The ratios of transformation of the transformers must be known to translate the meter readings into line values of current, voltage, and power.   Suppose, for example, that the ratio of transformation of the potential transformer is 10:1 and that of the current transformer is 5:1.   The line voltage is then ten times the voltmeter reading, the line current is five times the ammeter reading, and the power is fifty times the wattmeter reading.   These special instrument transformers are described in the chapter on transformers.   The circuit connections for measuring current, voltage, and power with the use of transformers are shown in Fig. 12-22.

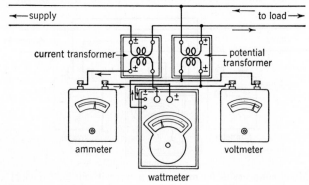

Fig. 12-22. Meter connections for measuring power with instrument transformers.

Frequency Meter.   There are a number of types of meters for indicating frequency.   The meter here described, while not so accurate as some other types, is simple in design and gives indications of frequency correct to within perhaps one-half cycle on commercial power circuits.   It consists essentially of a series of polarized slender steel reeds, fastened securely to a steel frame at the lower ends, loaded at the free ends, and tuned to have a natural period of vibration corresponding to the frequency of the circuit to be measured.   The natural period of each reed differs from the periods of the neighboring reeds by one-half cycle in the instrument shown in Fig. 13-22, and the entire bank covers a range of 10 cycles in 20 equal steps.   Mounted behind the reeds is an electromagnet with a laminated core that alternately attracts and repels the reeds and thus tends to vibrate them at the frequency of the exciting circuit.   The exciting coil is connected to the circuit in series with a suitable resistance which limits the current to the correct amount.   The meter circuit is usually designed for use on 110 volts.   While the electromagnet tends at all times to cause all the reeds to vibrate, that reed the natural period of which corresponds most closely to the frequency of the exciting current of the electromagnet has the largest amplitude of vibration. Usually adjacent reeds vibrate slightly as indicated in the figure.

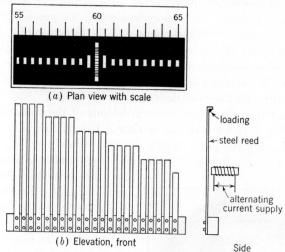

(a) Plan view with scale

(b) Elevation, front

loading

steel reed

alternating current supply

Side

FIG. 13-22. Vibrating-reed frequency meter.

Stroboscope—an Instrument for Measuring Slip. The stroboscope is an instrument that produces an illusion of motion when a moving or rotating body is viewed while it is illuminated by means of a periodically interrupted light. The application of this principle to the measurement of the slip of an induction motor is discussed in the following paragraphs.

Assume a four-pole 60-cycle induction motor and let there be mounted on its shaft a circular sheet-iron disk like the one shown in Fig. 14-22, with four black sectors painted on a white background. (The number of sectors should equal the number of poles of the induction motor.) Let the disk be illuminated by means of a synchronous source of light, either an a-c arc lamp or a high-intensity neon-tube light.

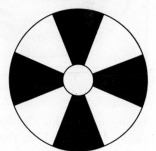

FIG. 14-22. Disk for use with stroboscope.

Lights of these types go out twice during each cycle. Accordingly, if the speed of the revolving disk were synchronous, each sector would move forward exactly one pole pitch into the position of the preceding sector during the time of one alternation of the illumination cycle. At the time of maximum illumination white and black sectors would always occupy

given positions, and hence would appear to stand still.   Actually, the
speed of the rotor is less than synchronous and the sectors move forward
slightly less than one pole-pitch during the time of one alternation.
Thus, during successive intervals of maximum illumination, adjacent sectors are viewed at slightly different positions.   Since the light goes on and
off 120 times per second (in a 60-cycle circuit) the process is continuous
and the sectors appear to travel counter to the direction of rotation of the
motor.   The motor slip is one revolution during the time that a sector
appears to make one complete turn.   Usually it is desirable to view the
disk so that only one sector is viewed at a time.   Then a slip of one revolution occurs when four sectors pass the line of vision.

To measure the slip, count the revolutions of the rotor with a speed
counter during a given interval of time.   Count the number of white
sectors passing a given point during the same time interval.   One-fourth
of this number (for a four-pole machine) is the number of slip revolutions

for the interval.   Add the slip
revolutions to the revolutions of
the shaft to get the revolutions at
synchronous speed.   The percentage slip is 100 times the ratio of
the slip revolutions to the revolutions at synchronous speed for the
interval.

When the slip is large it is usually more convenient to use a single sector because, when a number
of sectors equal to the number of
poles is employed, they appear
to move rapidly and it is difficult
to count them.

FIG.   15-22. The   kilowatthour   meter.
(*Westinghouse Electric Corporation.*)

Watt-hour Meters.   Detailed
descriptions of the types of meters
falling within this classification are beyond the scope of this book.   The
principle upon which their operation depends will, however, be briefly
sketched.

In watthour or kilowatthour meters (Fig. 15-22) the integrated product
of instantaneous power and elapsed time is recorded by pointers moving
over numbered dials much like the face of a clock, but each having only
10 divisions.   Motion of the pointers is brought about through the
medium of a clock mechanism (suitable trains of gears, etc.) that is driven
by a small motor.   (The motor usually operates on the principle of the
induction motor.)   The torque developed in the motor element at any
instant is proportional to the power that is passing through the meter at

that instant; that is, torque is proportional to the product $EI \cos \theta$. Attached to the motor shaft is an aluminum disk that revolves between the poles of a permanent magnet. (In some meters two magnets are used.) In this way, eddy currents are set up in the disk when the meter operates. These currents react with the flux of the permanent magnet (or magnets) to produce a resisting torque that tends to limit the speed of the motor. The resisting torque is proportional to the speed, and hence the driving torque (proportional to the power) increases the speed of the meter until resisting torque and driving torque are exactly equal. When equality of torques is attained, the speed remains constant as long as the power consumed by the load does not change. Thus, the number of revolutions of the meter shaft in a given time is proportional to the elapsed time during which a given power flows, as well as to the power or torque. The registration of the meter is, therefore, proportional to the product of speed and time, or to the product

$$EI \cos \theta \times \text{time} = \text{power} \times \text{time} = \text{energy}$$

When properly calibrated, the dial readings of these meters indicate directly the number of watthours or kilowatthours of energy (as the case may be) transferred through the meter.

Kilowatthour meters are used to measure the energy consumed by customers of a power company, to measure the total energy output of a feeder circuit, etc. Such a meter is installed at the residence of each customer, for example. The meter is usually read once a month by the company's meter reader. The monthly charge for energy consumed is based on the difference between the meter readings of the preceding month and the current month. Both these readings, as well as the difference, are recorded on the monthly bill.

CHAPTER 23

POWER IN SINGLE-PHASE CIRCUITS

Alternating Power. Generally speaking, the power in an a-c circuit varies with time, because the instantaneous current and voltage both vary. The pulsations are very rapid, however, and usually one is interested in the *average* effect produced over a period of time rather than in the instantaneous power developed. Power in a-c circuits is measured by means of wattmeters (page 347) which are so constructed and calibrated that the scale reading indicates the average power developed in the circuit. In a-c circuits just as in d-c circuits, power is measured in *watts* and *kilowatts*.

It has already been observed that, when a sine wave of voltage is impressed on a circuit containing *constant values* of resistance, inductance, and capacitance, or any combination of these, the current wave is a sine wave also. The current wave may be in phase with the voltage wave, or it may lead or lag the voltage wave, depending upon whether the circuit contains resistance only or whether it is capacitive or inductive. If the impressed voltage wave is the sine wave, Fig. 1-23(a),

$$e = E_m \sin \omega t$$

and the phase angle of the current with respect to voltage is $\mp \theta$, the current wave is

$$i = I_m \sin (\omega t \mp \theta)$$

and the instantaneous power in the circuit is the product

$$p = E_m I_m \sin \omega t \sin (\omega t \mp \theta)$$

It can be shown[1] that the product curve is also a sine wave and that, if E

---

[1] From trigonometry, $\sin (\omega t \mp \theta) = \sin \omega t \cos \theta \mp \cos \omega t \sin \theta$. When this expansion is substituted in the power equation, the expression for instantaneous power becomes

$$p = E_m I_m (\cos \theta \sin^2 \omega t \mp \sin \theta \sin \omega t \cos \omega t)$$

From trigonometry also, $\sin^2 \omega t = \frac{1}{2}(1 - \cos 2\omega t)$ and $\sin \omega t \cos \omega t = \frac{1}{2} \sin 2\omega t$. Accordingly (Fig. 1-23), is the effective voltage and I is the effective current, the average value of the product curve or the average power is

$$P = EI \cos \theta \qquad (1\text{-}23)$$

Thus, in terms of effective values, *the power in a single-phase a-c circuit is equal to the product of voltage and current and the cosine of the angle θ.* The

$$p = \frac{E_m I_m}{2}[\cos \theta(1 - \cos 2\omega t) \mp \sin \theta \sin 2\omega t]$$

or, since $E_m/\sqrt{2}$ is the effective voltage E and $I_m/\sqrt{2}$ is the effective current I, one may also write

$$p = EI \cos \theta(1 - \cos 2\omega t) \mp EI \sin \theta \sin 2\omega t$$

Curve 1 represents the first right-hand term, curve 2 represents the second right-hand term, and curve 3 is the sum of 1 and 2, the latter identical with the power curve of Fig. 1-23(a). All these curves are sinusoidal. Curve 1, it should be observed, lies wholly above the X axis and so has no negative ordinates. The average value of this curve represents the power that flows out from the generator and is absorbed in the circuit, as, for example, in producing heat in a resistance or in driving a motor. This kind of power is called *active power*. The average active power is also equal to the height of curve 1 above or below its axis of symmetry mn. The maximum ordinate to curve 1 is the value of the expression $EI \cos \theta(1 - \cos 2\omega t)$ when

$$\cos 2\omega t = -1,$$

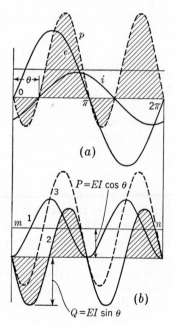

or it is $2EI \cos \theta$, and one-half of this value is the active power. Accordingly, the average active power in the circuit is

$$P = EI \cos \theta \qquad (a)$$

The power represented by curve 2 flows out from the generator into the circuit during one quarter cycle of the voltage wave and *returns* from the circuit to the generator during the next quarter cycle. This is the kind of power that a generator supplies to a condenser or to an inductance coil. The energy supplied to the circuit is stored during one quarter cycle and is returned to the source during the next. These facts will be clarified presently. The fact that the positive loop is exactly like the negative loop indicates that the outgoing power and returning power are equal and that *no power has been expended.* This kind of power is called *reactive volt-amperes,* and like active power, it is measured *by the height of the curve above or below its axis of symmetry.* The axis of symmetry in this case is the X axis. The maximum ordinate of curve 2 is the value

1- $p_r = EI \cos \theta (1 - \cos 2\omega t)$
2- $q = EI \sin \theta \sin 2\omega t$
3- $p = p_r + q$

Fig. 1-23. Active power and reactive volt-amperes.

of the expression $EI \sin \theta \sin 2\omega t$ when $\sin 2\omega t = 1$ or, if Q is used to represent reactive product EI is called the *volt-amperes* of the circuit and cos θ is the *power factor*.

Power Expended in a Resistance.   When a sine wave of voltage is impressed on a resistance (Fig. 2-23), the current and voltage are in phase with each other, the angle θ is zero, cos θ = 1, and the power factor is unity.   Accordingly, the average power expended in a resistance is

$$P_r = EI \qquad\qquad (2\text{-}23)$$

just as in a d-c circuit.   The current in the resistance is $I = E/R$, and the voltage impressed on the resistance is $E = RI$.   By substituting these

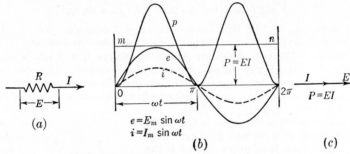

$$e = E_m \sin \omega t$$
$$i = I_m \sin \omega t$$

Fig. 2-23. Power expended in a resistance.

expressions in the equation above, alternate expressions for the power are found to be

$$P_r = \frac{E^2}{R} \qquad\qquad (3\text{-}23)$$

$$= RI^2 \qquad\qquad (4\text{-}23)$$

If the impressed voltage is represented symbolically by the equation $e = E_m \sin \omega t$, the current is $i = (E_m/R) \sin \omega t$ and the instantaneous power is $p = (E_m^2/R) \sin^2 \omega t$.   The curves of e, i, and p are shown in Fig. 2-23.   It is observed that the power curve lies wholly above the X axis; that is, there are no negative values of power.   This means that all the power goes out from the source and none of it returns.   In other words, all the power developed is consumed as heat in the resistance. Such power is called *active power*, and like the power in a d-c circuit, it is measured in *watts* and *kilowatts*.   Since the current and voltage are in phase, the maximum ordinate of the power curve is the product of the

volt-amperes,

$$Q = EI \sin \theta \qquad\qquad (b)$$

Generally speaking, when the term *power* is used without a qualifying adjective, active power is meant.   When speaking of power that comes and goes in a circuit in the manner explained, the power should be referred to as reactive volt-amperes. In this way confusion is avoided.

maximum values of voltage and current or $P_m = E_m I_m$. Half this value is the average height of the power curve, or it is the distance om of the axis of symmetry of the power curve above the X axis. Since

$$E_m/\sqrt{2} = E$$

and $I_m/\sqrt{2} = I$, this distance is $P = EI$, as has already been shown.

Example 1. How much power is expended in the 10-ohm element of an electric heater when a sine wave of potential difference of 110 volts effective value is impressed?

$$I = \frac{E}{R} = \frac{110}{10} = 11 \text{ amp}$$

$$P = EI = 110 \times 11 = 1{,}210 \text{ watts or } 1.21 \text{ kw}$$

Power in an Inductance. When a sine wave of voltage is impressed on an inductive reactance with negligible resistance, the current lags the

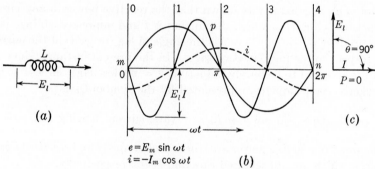

$$e = E_m \sin \omega t$$
$$i = -I_m \cos \omega t \qquad (b)$$

Fig. 3-23. Power in an inductance.

voltage by 90 deg ($\theta = -90$), the power factor is zero (cos $\theta = 0$), and the active power ($EI \cos \theta$) is zero. If the impressed voltage is represented by $e = E_m \sin \omega t$, the current is $i = -I_m \cos \omega t$ and the instantaneous power is the product $p = -E_m I_m \sin \omega t \cos \omega t$. But since $\sin \omega t \cos \omega t = \frac{1}{2} \sin 2\omega t$, $E_m/\sqrt{2} = E$, and $I_m/\sqrt{2} = I$, the instantaneous power is also $p = -E_l I \sin 2\omega t$. The maximum value of this expression is obtained when $\omega t = 45$ deg and hence $P_m = E_l I$.

The current, voltage, and instantaneous power are represented graphically by the curves e, i, and p in Fig. 3-23. The frequency of the power curve is double that of the voltage curve ($2\omega t = 2 \times \omega t$), and the axis of symmetry of p is the X axis. The power curve has one positive and one negative loop each half cycle of the voltage curve. The area of a positive loop is equal to the area of a negative loop, and the sum of their areas is zero, which means that over one cycle the average power is zero. The reason for this is as follows: During the time intervals from 1 to 2 while the current is increasing positively, power is delivered by the generator to the inductance, where energy is stored in the magnetic linkages.   At 2 the current and the stored energy both have attained their maximum values, and the power output of the generator is momentarily zero.   From 2 to 3 the current decreases in value, and the inductance gives up its stored energy and returns it to the generator.   During this interval the inductance delivers power to the generator and the output of the generator is negative.

During the negative half cycle of the current wave the process described above is repeated.   The cyclic interchange of power between the generator and the reactance of the circuit continues as long as the initial circuit conditions and applied voltage remain unchanged.

Since power is exchanged periodically between the generator and the inductance of the circuit but is not consumed, the average power output of the generator is zero, the power in the circuit is said to be reactive, and it is called *reactive power* or, preferably, *reactive volt-amperes*.   In the footnote on page 362 it was shown that the reactive power in any circuit (or part of a circuit) in which the current is I and impressed voltage is E, is the product $EI \sin \theta$, where θ is the angle of lag (or lead) of the current with respect to the impressed voltage.   In the present instance, since the circuit is assumed to be purely inductive, $\theta = 90$ deg (lag), $\sin \theta = 1$, and the reactive volt-amperes, represented by the symbol Q_l, is

$$Q_l = E_l I \sin \theta = E_l I \qquad \text{vars, current lagging} \qquad (5\text{-}23)$$

The units of reactive power are *reactive volt-amperes* and *reactive kilovolt-amperes*, which are abbreviated *vars* and *kvars*, respectively.

In an inductive circuit with negligible resistance the current is

$$I = E_l/X_l$$

and the voltage impressed on the inductance is $E_l = X_l I$.   By substituting these expressions in the above equation for Q_l, alternate expressions for the vars supplied to an inductive reactance are found to be:

$$Q_l = \frac{E_l^2}{X_l} \qquad (6\text{-}23)$$

$$= X_l I^2 \qquad (7\text{-}23)$$

Example 2.   A coil of 0.30-henry inductance and negligible resistance is connected to the terminals of a 120-volt 60-cycle generator.   Assuming a sine wave of voltage, find (*a*) the active power in the circuit, (*b*) the reactive power in the circuit.

(*a*) Because the circuit is purely inductive, the active power expended in the circuit is zero.

(*b*) The reactance of the circuit is

$$X_l = 2\pi f L = 377 \times 0.30 = 113.1 \text{ ohms}$$

The reactive power is

$$Q_l = \frac{E_l{}^2}{X_l} = \frac{120^2}{113.1} = 127.3 \text{ vars, current lagging}$$

Power in an Ironclad Inductive Circuit. Effective Resistance. In many commercial applications, iron is used in conjunction with electric current to obtain a given magnetic flux with a minimum number of ampere-turns. Iron-core electromagnets of all kinds including transformers, generators and motor armatures, and field circuits, etc., are good examples. The simplest case is that of a wire wrapped with many turns about an iron core.

When an alternating emf is impressed on such a circuit, the power is no longer purely reactive. Experience shows that the iron core becomes hot, indicating that some of the energy supplied is converted to heat and does not return to the source each alternate quarter cycle (as in a purely inductive circuit). In other words, the circuit behaves as though it contained both resistance and inductance, even though the true ohmic resistance of the circuit may be negligible. The heat generated in the core is due, of course, to hysteresis and eddy currents. These always exist in iron whenever it is subjected to the influence of a varying magnetic field.

If P is the total power (in watts) consumed in an ironclad circuit and I is the current, the ratio

$$R_{eff} = \frac{P}{I^2}$$

is called the *effective resistance* of the circuit. In general, any circuit in which P watts are consumed when I amp flow is said to have an effective resistance of P/I^2 ohms, irrespective of how the energy is utilized or wasted in the circuit.

Power in a Capacitance. When a sine wave of voltage is impressed on a capacitance with negligible resistance, the current leads the voltage by 90 deg ($\theta = 90$), the power factor is zero ($\cos \theta = 0$), and the active power ($EI \cos \theta$) is zero. If the impressed voltage is again represented by $e = E_m \sin \omega t$, the current is $i = I_m \cos \omega t$ and the instantaneous power is the product $p = E_m I_m \sin \omega t \cos \omega t$. But since $\sin \omega t \cos \omega t$ is equal to $\frac{1}{2} \sin 2\omega t$, $E_m/\sqrt{2} = E$, and $I_m/\sqrt{2} = I$, the instantaneous power is also $p = E_c I \sin 2\omega t$. The maximum value of this expression is obtained when $\omega t = 45$ deg and $P_m = E_c I$.

The current, voltage, and instantaneous power are represented by the curves e, i, and p of Fig. 4-23. The frequency of the power curve is again double that of the voltage curve and the axis of symmetry of the power curve is the X axis. The power curve has one positive and one negative loop each half cycle of the voltage curve. The area of a positive loop is equal to the area of a negative loop and the sum of their areas is zero, which means that the average power in the circuit is again zero.   It should be observed that the power curve in the present instance is identical in form with the power curve in Fig. 3-23 but is displaced 180 deg with respect to it.   If the two power curves are drawn in a single diagram, the loops of Fig. 3-23 are positive when those of Fig. 4-23 are negative, and vice versa.

In Fig. 4-23, during the interval from 0 to 1, while the voltage is increasing positively, power is delivered by the generator to the capacitance, where energy is being stored in the electric field.   At 1 the voltage impressed on the capacitance and the stored energy have both attained their maximum values, and the power output of the generator is momentarily zero.   From 1 to 2 the voltage decreases in value; the capacitance discharges its stored energy and returns it to the generator.   During this

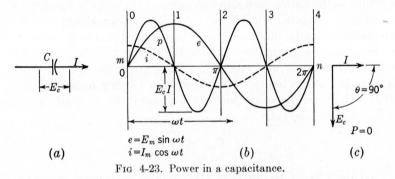

$$e = E_m \sin \omega t$$
$$i = I_m \cos \omega t$$

(a)   (b)   (c)

FIG 4-23. Power in a capacitance.

interval the capacitance delivers power to the generator and the output of the generator is negative.

During each succeeding half cycle of the voltage wave the above described cyclic interchange of power between the generator and the capacitance is repeated.   Since power (and energy) are exchanged periodically between the generator and the capacitance but are not consumed, the average power output of the generator is zero and the power delivered by it is purely reactive.

Similar to the case of the purely inductive circuit, the reactive volt-amperes supplied to a capacitance with negligible resistance is

$$Q_c = E_c I \sin \theta = E_c I \qquad \text{vars, current leading} \qquad (8\text{-}23)$$

Since $\theta = +90$ deg, alternate expressions may be derived in the manner already explained for the inductive circuit.   These are

$$Q_c = \frac{E_c{}^2}{X_c} \qquad \text{vars, current leading} \qquad (9\text{-}23)$$

$$= X_c I^2 \qquad \text{vars, current leading} \qquad (10\text{-}23)$$

Example 3. A 25-μf condenser is connected to the terminals of a 60-cycle 120-volt generator. Assuming a sine wave of voltage, find (*a*) the active power in the circuit, (*b*) the reactive power in the circuit.

(*a*) Because there is no resistance in the circuit (and no other device for absorbing energy), the active power in the circuit is zero.

(*b*) The reactance of the circuit is

$$X_c = \frac{1}{2\pi f C} = \frac{1}{377 \times 25 \times 10^{-6}} = \frac{1}{9,425 \times 10^{-6}} \text{ ohm}$$

The reactive power is

$$Q_c = \frac{E_c{}^2}{X_c} = 120^2 \times 9,425 \times 10^{-6} = 135.7 \text{ vars, current leading}$$

Inductance and Capacitance in Series. When inductance and capacitance are connected in series, the current is the same in both, but the

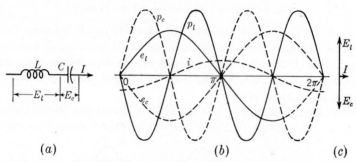

Fig. 5-23. Power in a resonant series circuit.

voltage impressed across the inductance leads the current 90 deg, while the voltage impressed across the capacitance lags the current 90 deg, as in Fig. 5-23. During the time interval when the power loop of the inductive circuit is positive, that of the capacitive circuit is negative. Energy flows from the condenser into the inductance when the condenser discharges and from the inductance into the condenser when the condenser charges. If it so happens that the reactances are equal ($2\pi f L = 1/2\pi f C$), the power loops p_l and p_c will be exactly the same size, and the inductance will supply exactly the power which the capacitance requires and vice versa. This is the condition of *voltage resonance* previously discussed and here illustrated in Fig. 5-23.

When the reactances are unequal, as is usually the case, the difference between the vars required by x_l and x_c must be supplied from an outside source.

Inductance and Capacitance in Parallel. In this case the impressed voltage is common to the two branches, while the two currents are 180 deg out of phase, as illustrated in Fig. 6-23. Again there is an interchange of power between the two parts of the circuit, and when $2\pi fL = 1/2\pi fC$, the power absorbed by the inductance is exactly equal to that given up by the condenser on discharge, and vice versa. No power is supplied from without the circuit after the oscillation is once started. This is the condition of resonance in a parallel circuit already described as *current resonance*.

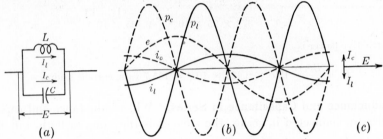

FIG. 6-23. Power in a resonant parallel circuit.

When the susceptances are unequal, the difference between the vars required by the two branches must be supplied from an outside source. Thus if $2\pi fC > 1/2\pi fL$ leading reactive kilovolt-amperes must be supplied, whereas if $2\pi fC < 1/2\pi fL$ lagging reactive kilovolt-amperes must be supplied from the outside source.

Power in an Impedance. The general a-c circuit has resistance as well as reactance, and the current in it leads or lags the voltage by some angle

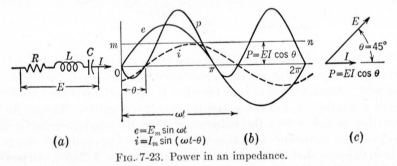

$$e = E_m \sin \omega t$$
$$i = I_m \sin (\omega t - \theta)$$

FIG. 7-23. Power in an impedance.

θ. If the voltage phasor is taken as the phasor of reference, θ is negative when $X_l > X_c$, is positive when $X_l < X_c$, and is zero when $X_l = X_c$. In general, therefore, if the impressed voltage is $e = E_m \sin \omega t$ (Fig. 7-23), the current is $i = I_m \sin (\omega t \mp \theta)$ and the instantaneous power is the product curve

$$p = E_m I_m \sin \omega t \sin (\omega t \mp \theta)$$

In the footnote on page 361 it was shown that for this case the active power is

$$P = EI \cos \theta \qquad (11\text{-}23)$$

and the reactive power is

$$Q = EI \sin \theta \qquad (12\text{-}23)$$

From the form of the above equations it is apparent that active and reactive power may be represented by a right triangle (Fig. 8-23) with acute angle θ, adjacent side P, and opposite side Q because

$$\sqrt{P^2 + Q^2} = EI \sqrt{\cos^2 \theta + \sin^2 \theta} \qquad (13\text{-}23)$$

and

$$\tan \theta = \frac{Q}{P} \qquad (14\text{-}23)$$

Represented in phasor notation, with current leading,

$$\mathbf{P} = P + jQ \qquad (15\text{-}23)$$

The curves of Fig. 7-23 represent instantaneous current i, voltage e, and power p. The power curve has both positive and negative ordinates, which indicates that both active and reactive power exist in the circuit. The average value of the active power is the distance of the axis of symmetry of the p curve above the X axis.

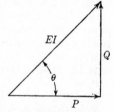

FIG. 8-23. Diagram of phasor power.

Apparent Power, Active Power, Reactive Power. The meanings of these terms may now be summarized to prevent confusion. Assume a circuit as in Fig. 7-23 and let $X_l > X_c$. The current then lags the voltage as in the diagram. By Eq. (13-23) the *apparent power* in the circuit is EI va. The *active power* is $EI \cos \theta$ watts, by Eq. (11-23), the *reactive power* is $EI \sin \theta$ vars, by Eq. (12-23), and the *power* factor is $\cos \theta$. *Power factor is the quantity by which the apparent power must be multiplied to obtain the active power in the circuit.* The expression $\sin \theta$ is called the *reactive factor. Reactive factor is the factor by which the apparent power is multiplied to obtain the reactive power in the circuit.*

Reactive power may be associated with either a leading or a lagging current. When the resultant reactance in the circuit is capacitive, the current leads and Q is designated as *reactive power, current leading.* When the resultant reactance is inductive, the current lags and Q is described as *reactive power, current lagging.*

Example 4. If in the circuit of Fig. 7-23, $r = 4$, $x_l = 10$, $x_c = 2$, and the impressed voltage is 120, find (a) the current, (b) the apparent power, (c) the active power, (d) the reactive power, (e) the power factor.

$$(a) \qquad I = \frac{E}{Z} = \frac{120}{\sqrt{4^2 + 8^2}} = \frac{120}{8.95}$$
$$= 13.41 \text{ amp}$$

(b) $EI = 120 \times 13.41$
$= 1,609 \text{ va}$
$= 1.609 \text{ kva}$

(e) $\cos \theta = \dfrac{r}{Z} = \dfrac{4}{8.95} = 0.447$

(c) $P = EI \cos \theta = 1,609 \times 0.447$
$= 719 \text{ watts}$
$= 0.719 \text{ kw}$

(d) $\sin \theta = \dfrac{8}{8.95} = 0.894$

$Q = EI \sin \theta = 1,609 \times 0.894$
$= 1,439 \text{ vars}$
$= 1.439 \text{ kvars, current lagging}$

It is sometimes advantageous to use the phasor form of power [Eq. (15-23)], as illustrated in the following example.

Example 5. A factory utilizing various forms of electrical equipment has the following loads: (1) 200 kw of unity-power-factor lighting and heating load, (2) 600 kva of electric furnace load taking current at 70 per cent power factor, current lagging, (3) to 150 kva of induction motor load taking current at 80 per cent power factor, current lagging, and (4) 200 kva in synchronous motors taking current at a leading power factor of 85 per cent. Find (a) the total active power required, (b) the total reactive power required, (c) the total volt-amperes, (d) the resultant power factor.

When the several required powers are indicated as phasors of the form $\mathbf{P} = P + jQ$, as in Eq. (15-23), these powers are

$\mathbf{P}_1 = \qquad\qquad\qquad 200 + j000$
$\mathbf{P}_2 = 600(\cos \theta_2 - j \sin \theta_2) = 420 - j428$
$\mathbf{P}_3 = 150(\cos \theta_3 - j \sin \theta_3) = 120 - j90$
$\mathbf{P}_4 = 200(\cos \theta_4 + j \sin \theta_4) = 170 + j105$

By addition,

$\qquad \mathbf{P}_0 = \qquad\qquad\qquad 910 - j413$

(a) $P = 910 \text{ kw}$
(b) $-jQ = -j413 \text{ kvars, current lagging}$
(c) $EI = \sqrt{910^2 + 413^2} = 1,000 \text{ kva}$
(d) $\cos \theta = \dfrac{P}{EI} = \dfrac{910}{1,000} = 0.91$

Phasor Power. Sometimes the voltage impressed upon the terminals of a part of a circuit and the current in it are expressed as phasors, both of which are referred to some reference phasor such as OM in Fig. 9-23. In such a case both the active power and the vars may be determined by taking the product of the current phasor and the conjugate of the voltage phasor.[1] The product $\mathbf{P} = \mathbf{IE}^*$ is called the *phasor power*. The real part

---

[1] From a study of Fig. 9-23 it is apparent that, for the case illustrated, the active power is equal to the algebraic sum of $E_1 I_1$ and $-E_2 I_2$. (The components E_2 and I_2 are in phase opposition, so their product is negative.)

The vars are the algebraic sum of the products $E_2 I_1$ and $E_1 I_2$, in both of which (Fig. 9-23) the current component lags the corresponding voltage component by 90 deg. Hence, both these products are vars, current lagging, and according to the

of this product is the active power and the imaginary part is the reactive vars in the circuit.

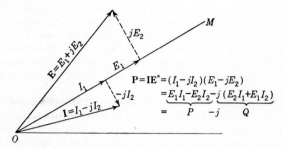

FIG. 9-23. Phasor power. Reference phasor arbitrarily assumed.

To illustrate, consider a circuit in which the current is $I = 4 - j2$ and the impressed voltage is $E = 100 + j45$. The phasor power in the circuit is

$$\mathbf{P} = \mathbf{IE}^* = (4 - j2)(100 - j45)$$
$$= 400 - 90 - j(200 + 180)$$
$$= 310 - j380$$

whence,

$$P = 310 \text{ watts}$$
$$Q = 380 \text{ vars, current lagging}$$

Problems

1-23. A noninductive resistance draws 65 amp from 110-volt mains. Determine (a) the active power expended in the resistance, (b) the vars, (c) the resistance in ohms.

2-23. An ironclad electromagnet with a laminated-steel core draws 8 amp from 120-volt mains. A wattmeter indicates that the power consumed by the magnet is 124 watts. Find (a) the effective resistance, (b) the vars, (c) the power factor.

3-23. When the ohmic resistance of the winding of the electromagnet in Prob. 2-23 is measured with direct current it is observed that to circulate 8 amp requires an impressed emf of only 9.6 volts. Determine (a) the ohmic resistance of the winding, (b) the power consumed in hysteresis and eddy-current losses in Prob. 2-23.

4-23. A resistance of 15 ohms is connected in series with a capacitive reactance of 25 ohms. Sufficient voltage is impressed on the circuit to circulate a current of 4.5 amp. Determine (a) the active power, (b) the reactive power (vars), (c) the total volt-amperes, and (d) the power factor.

5-23. A resistance of 20 ohms and a capacitance of 250 μf are connected in parallel across 120-volt 60-cycle mains. Find (a) the current, (b) the active power, (c) the reactive power, and (d) the power factor of the circuit.

---

notation used in this book, are represented as $-jE_2I_1$ and $-jE_1I_2$, respectively. That is, $-jQ$ represents vars, current lagging, and $+jQ$ represents vars, current leading. (Some authors use $+jQ$ to represent vars, current lagging, and $-jQ$ to represent vars, current leading. No standard notation has been approved.)

6-23. The input to a single-phase, electric-arc furnace is 650 kw, the impressed potential difference is 6.8 kv and the power factor is 0.68. Find (a) the effective resistance, (b) the inductive reactance, (c) the current, and (d) the kva of the furnace.

7-23. The high-voltage winding of a 6,600/220-volt transformer is open while the low-voltage winding is connected to 220-volt mains. An ammeter and a watt-meter are suitably connected to the circuit to measure the current and power input. The ammeter reads 5.8 amp and the wattmeter 440 watts. Determine (a) the active component, (b) the reactive component of the current, (c) the reactive kilovolt-ampere input, (d) the iron loss, and (e) the power factor. Disregard the resistance of the winding.

8-23. At full load the efficiency of a certain 1.5-hp 110-volt, single phase induction motor is 75 per cent, while the power factor is 0.70. What is the current in the current coil of a wattmeter that is used to measure the input to the motor at full load?

9-23. A single-phase induction motor takes 24 amp from 220-volt 60-cycle mains when running at full load. It delivers 4.8 hp under these conditions at an efficiency of 84 per cent. It is desired to bring the power factor of the motor to 0.95, current lagging, by connecting a condenser in parallel with the motor. What capacity of condenser must be used?

CHAPTER 24

POLYPHASE CIRCUITS

Polyphase Machines. The principle of the alternator was briefly discussed in Chap. 18 (pages 281 to 286). It was there shown that such a machine could be constructed with either one or more than one independent circuit. A generator with only one equivalent armature circuit (there may be two parallel paths) is called a *single-phase* machine, while, in general, those with more than one armature circuit are *polyphase* machines. When a generator has two armature circuits spaced 90 electrical degrees apart, as in Fig. 1-24 (here again four coils may form the two circuits), it is a *two-phase* machine. The circuits may be interconnected in various ways, as will be shown, or the terminals of the circuits may be separately brought out to form the four separate terminals of the machine, as in Fig. 2-24. *Three-phase* machines have three separate armature circuits spaced 120 electrical degrees apart. These are usually interconnected internally, as in Figs. 10-24 and 11-24, and only three leads are brought out to form the machine terminals.

The generation, transmission, and utilization of electrical power are largely carried on with the use of polyphase machines and polyphase circuits. Substantially all the power used in the United States is generated by three-phase machines and is transmitted over three-phase lines when transmission is necessary. The vast majority of large motors used for driving machinery are likewise three-phase motors, although two-phase motors and two-phase distribution circuits are sometimes used. Single-phase power obtained from one phase of a polyphase system is used for domestic service—for lighting and for running small motors.

There are good reasons why polyphase machines and polyphase circuits are so generally used. A given generator or motor, when wound for three-phase operation, has a rating of approximately 150 per cent of the rating which the same machine would have if wound for single-phase operation. The corresponding advantage of the two-phase machine over the single-phase machine is about 140 per cent. Thus, per unit of output, the polyphase machine is very much cheaper.

At a given load, polyphase motors develop a constant torque, like a steam turbine, while the torque of a single-phase motor is pulsating, like the torque of a reciprocating engine. It was shown in Chap. 23 (page 360) that the power in a single-phase circuit is pulsating. Since the power output of a single-phase generator or motor is proportional to the product of its torque and speed, it follows that for a given speed the instantaneous torque is proportional to the instantaneous power and it pulsates in the same manner as the power. When the power factor is less than unity, the torque is actually negative twice during a cycle. The single-phase synchronous motor must depend upon its flywheel effect to carry it over the periods when its developed torque is less than that required by the load. The constancy of the torque developed in polyphase motors is demonstrated in the chapter on motors.

With a given transmission or distribution voltage, polyphase circuits transmit a given amount of power at a given percentage loss with the use of a smaller investment in conductor materials than that required for the corresponding single-phase circuit. This is an additional advantage of polyphase systems.

Double Subscript Phasor Notation. In the simpler circuits discussed in the foregoing chapters it is usually quite clear from the circuit diagram how the voltage and current phasors are related. In the case of more involved networks and particularly in polyphase circuits where a number of emfs, consumed voltages, and currents are involved, it is convenient to set up a double-subscript system of notation which identifies each voltage and current and which, when correctly used, indicates the assumed positive sense of each phasor.

In applying the double-subscript notation, all junctions or other points of interest in the network are designated by convenient letters (or numbers). To indicate the phasor emf or consumed potential difference between any two given points such as a and b, for example, the phasor voltage is described as $\mathbf{E}_{ab}$, where the order of the subscripts defines the sense in which the voltage is taken as positive. From this definition it follows that $\mathbf{E}_{ba}$ is the negative of $\mathbf{E}_{ab}$ or

$$\mathbf{E}_{ab} = -\mathbf{E}_{ba}$$

In a similar manner the current in the branch lying between points a and b is described as $\mathbf{I}_{ab}$, where the order of the subscripts again defines the sense in which the current is taken as positive. Here $\mathbf{I}_{ba}$ obviously specifies the negative of $\mathbf{I}_{ab}$ and

$$\mathbf{I}_{ab} = -\mathbf{I}_{ba}$$

Two-phase Voltages and Currents. An illustrative drawing of a two-phase four-pole generator is shown in (a) of Fig. 1-24. It is difficult to show the method of connecting the coil sides together in such a drawing, however, and for this reason the much more convenient developed drawing of (b) is generally used. In this drawing the cylindrical winding is assumed to be unrolled just as a hollow cylinder of paper would be unrolled by cutting it along an element of the cylinder and laying it down flat.

If the field is revolved in the indicated direction and one begins to count time at the instant when the poles are in the positions shown ($\omega t = 0$), the emf in phase B is zero, while that in phase A is a maximum, and as time progresses the waves of (c) are generated. Each wave passes

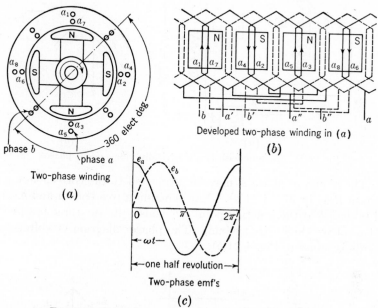

Developed two-phase winding in (a)

(b)

Two-phase winding

(a)

Two-phase emf's

(c)

Fig. 1-24. Two-phase synchronous generator or motor.

through two complete cycles per revolution. The equations of the curves are

$$e_a = E_m \cos \omega t$$
$$e_b = E_m \sin \omega t \qquad (1\text{-}24)$$

Since the windings are alike, the maximum values of the waves are equal. The effective voltages are shown in the phasor diagram of Fig. 2-24(b).

There are a number of ways of connecting these circuits, as follows:

1. The ends of the two windings may be brought out separately to form four terminals, as in Fig. 2-24(a). The windings constitute two independent single-phase circuits. The phasor diagram of voltages and currents is shown in Fig. 2-24(b).

2. The four ends are brought out separately as before, but the windings are interconnected at their centers O, as shown in Fig. 3-24. A fifth wire

may be brought out from the neutral point O. If the circuit is balanced and E is the voltage between any one of the terminals and the neutral conductor, the potential differences available are E between neutral and each corner of the square, $2E$ across each diagonal, and $\sqrt{2}\,E$ across each side of the square in Fig. 3-24(b).

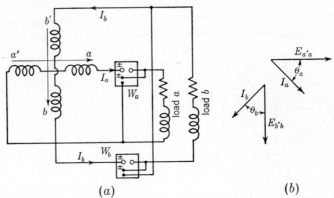

$$(a) \qquad\qquad (b)$$

FIG. 2-24. Machine with two electrically independent phases.

3. The a' end of phase A may be connected to the corresponding end of phase B as in Fig. 4-24(a). The remaining free ends a and b, and a lead taken off at the junction point $a'b'$ constitute the three terminals of the two-phase three-wire system. The phasor diagram of voltages and currents is found in Fig. 4-24(b).

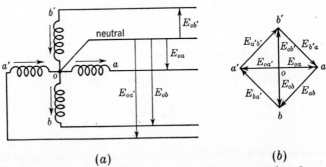

$$(a) \qquad\qquad (b)$$

FIG. 3-24. Machine with two phases interconnected at O.

If the circuit is balanced, $E_{a'a} = E_{b'b} = E$ and $I_a = I_b = I$. If Kirchhoff's law of currents is applied to the junction point $a'b'$, the current flowing outward from $a'b'$ in the neutral wire is $\mathbf{I}_0 = -\mathbf{I}_a - \mathbf{I}_b$. If Kirchhoff's law of voltages is applied by tracing through the phase windings from a to b, the potential difference between the free ends in the ab sense is found to be $\mathbf{E}_{ab} = \mathbf{E}_{aa'} + \mathbf{E}_{b'b}$. From the phasor diagram it is apparent that, if balanced impedances are connected between each lead and the neutral wire, the scalar values of currents and voltages are $I_0 = \sqrt{2}\,I$ and $E_{ab} = E_{ba} = \sqrt{2}\,E$, where $E = E_{a'a} = E_{b'b}$ is the voltage of one phase winding.

4. Each phase winding may be divided into two equal parts by opening the windings at a'' and b'' [Fig. 1-24(b)]. The resulting four coils may then be connected in the form of a four-wire mesh, as in Fig. 5-24(a). When the system is balanced and the voltage of each coil in the mesh is E, the phasor diagram is as represented in (b). The four voltages E (equal to $E_{a'a''} = E_{b'b''}$, etc.) are available on the four sides of the mesh, while between diagonally opposite corners the voltage is $\sqrt{2}\,E$. If the scalar current in each mesh winding is I (equal to $I_{a'a''} = I_{b'b''}$, etc.), the current in each of the four leads is $\sqrt{2}\,I = I_1 = I_2$, etc.

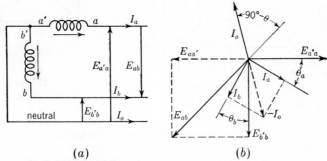

(a)   (b)

Fig. 4-24. The two-phase three-wire circuit.

Power Measurements in Two-phase Circuits. 1. The average power in the network of Fig. 2-24 may be measured by the use of two wattmeters connected as there shown, regardless of whether or not the circuit is balanced. Wattmeter W_a reads $P_a = E_{a'a}I_a \cos\theta_a$ and wattmeter W_b reads $P_b = E_{b'b}I_b \cos\theta_b$, for the circuits are electrically independent.

2. and 4. For these cases three wattmeters must be used and connected as shown in Fig. 5-24(a).

3. The power in a two-phase, three-wire system is measured by two wattmeters connected as in Fig. 6-24, for both balanced and unbalanced loads, for W_a always reads $E_{a'a}I_a \cos\theta_a$ and W_b reads $E_{b'b}I_b \cos\theta_b$. The sum of these readings is the total average power in the network. When the load is balanced, $E_{a'a} = E_{b'b} = E$, $I_a = I_b = I$, and $\theta_a = \theta_b$. Each wattmeter then reads $EI \cos\theta$, and the sum of the two readings is

$$P = 2EI \cos\theta$$

Reactive Volt-amperes in a Two-phase Three-wire Circuit. The reactive volt-amperes in a balanced two-phase three-wire circuit may be measured with a single wattmeter connected as shown in Fig. 7-24. The phasor diagram of voltages and currents is in Fig. 7-24(b). The potential difference impressed on the potential coil of the wattmeter is E_{ba}, the current in the current coil is I_0, and the angle between E_{ba} and I_0 is $90 - \theta$ deg. Accordingly, the wattmeter reads $E_{ba}I_0 \cos (90 - \theta)$.

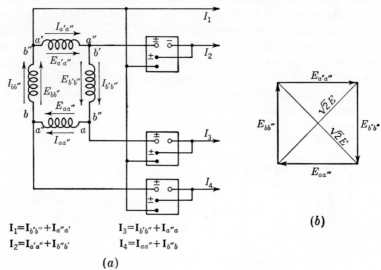

$$I_1 = I_{b'b''} + I_{a''a'} \qquad I_3 = I_{b'b''} + I_{a''a}$$
$$I_2 = I_{a'a''} + I_{b''b'} \qquad I_4 = I_{aa''} + I_{b''b}$$

(a)

(b)

FIG. 5-24. The two-phase mesh connection.

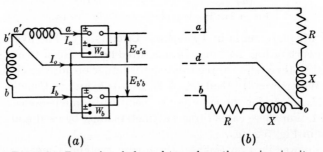

(a)   (b)

FIG. 6-24. Power in a balanced two-phase three-wire circuit.

But $E_{ba} = \sqrt{2}\,E$ and $I_0 = \sqrt{2}\,I$, so the wattmeter reading is $\sqrt{2}\,E \times \sqrt{2}\,I \cos (90 - \theta)$ or

$$Q = 2EI \sin \theta \qquad \text{vars}$$

where Q = reactive volt-amperes in the network. Thus *in a balanced two-phase three-wire circuit, a single wattmeter with current coil connected in the common lead and potential coil terminals connected, one to each of the remaining leads, reads the total reactive volt-amperes in the network.*

Example 1. A balanced two-phase three-wire circuit [Fig. 6-24(*a*)] supplies power to two equal impedances in which $R = 8$ ohms and $X = 3$ ohms. The impedances are connected between outside line conductors and the "third wire" as shown, and the impressed potential difference across each is 110 volts. Determine (*a*) the current in each of the leads *a* and *b*, (*b*) the current in lead *d*, (*c*) the voltage between leads

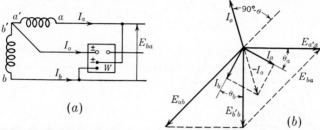

FIG. 7-24. Measurement of vars in a balanced two-phase three-wire circuit.

a and *b*, (*d*) the volt-amperes in the circuit, (*e*) the power factor of the circuit, (*f*) the active power in the circuit, (*g*) the vars in the circuit.

(*a*)
$$I_a = I_b = \frac{110}{\sqrt{8^2 + 3^2}} = 12.88 \text{ amp}$$

(*b*) $\qquad I_d = \sqrt{2} \times 12.88 = 18.2 \text{ amp}$

(*c*) $\qquad E_{ab} = \sqrt{2}\, E = 1.41 \times 110 = 155.1 \text{ volts}$

(*d*) $\qquad 2EI = 2 \times 110 \times 12.88$
$$= 2,834 \text{ va}$$
$$= 2.83 \text{ kva}$$

(*e*) $\qquad \tan \theta = \dfrac{X}{R} = \dfrac{3}{8} = 0.375$
$$\cos \theta = 0.936$$

(*f*) $\qquad P = 2EI \cos \theta = 2,834 \times 0.936$
$$= 2,652 \text{ watts}$$
$$= 2.65 \text{ kw}$$

(*g*) $\qquad Q = 2EI \sin \theta = 2,834 \times 0.351$
$$= 995 \text{ vars}$$
$$= 0.995 \text{ kvars (lag)}$$

In a Balanced Two-phase Circuit the Instantaneous Power is Constant.

This may be proved as follows: The instantaneous voltages are given by Eqs. (1-24). If the power factor is $\cos \theta$, the corresponding instantaneous currents are

$$i_a = I_m \cos (\omega t + \theta)$$
$$i_b = I_m \sin (\omega t + \theta) \qquad (2\text{-}24)$$

where θ may have any value between $-\pi/2$ and $+\pi/2$. From Eqs. (1-24) and (2-24),

$$p_a = E_m I_m \cos \omega t \cos (\omega t + \theta)$$
$$p_b = E_m I_m \sin \omega t \sin (\omega t + \theta)$$

and, by addition,

$$p = E_m I_m \cos \theta \qquad (3\text{-}24)$$

since, from trigonometry, $\cos (\alpha \pm \beta) = \cos \alpha \cos \beta \mp \sin \alpha \sin \beta$. Multiplying and dividing Eq. (3-24) by 2 and simplifying yields

$$p = 2 \frac{E_m}{\sqrt{2}} \frac{I_m}{\sqrt{2}} \cos \theta = 2EI \cos \theta \qquad (4\text{-}24)$$

This shows that the instantaneous power is constant and equal to the average power measured by the wattmeters of Fig. 6-24, for example.

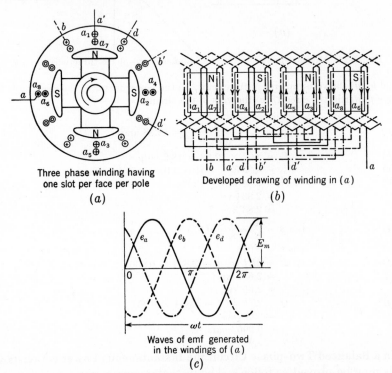

Three phase winding having
one slot per face per pole

(a)

Developed drawing of winding in (a)

(b)

Waves of emf generated
in the windings of (a)

(c)

Fig. 8-24. The three-phase synchronous generator or motor.

Since at a given speed the torque of a machine is proportional to its power output, the above shows that *the instantaneous electromagnetic torque of a two-phase motor or generator does not vary when it carries a balanced load.*

Three-phase Voltages. Figure 8-24(a) illustrates the relative positions of the armature coils which make up the three circuits of a three-phase four-pole generator. Figure 8-24(b) is a developed drawing of the same winding. For the assumed position of the rotor shown in the drawings and a full-pitch winding, phase A occupies the positions under the centers of the poles, starting at a' and ending at a. Phase B starts at b', 120 deg from the start of a'; it progresses around the armature to the right, just as phase A does, and ends at b. Phase D starts 120 deg to the right of the start of phase B, progresses to the right in a manner similar to phase A, and ends at d. Since these three circuits are exactly similar but are spaced 120 electrical degrees apart, the emf waves generated in them when the field revolves are exactly alike in form, but are displaced in time by 120 deg.

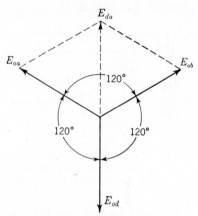

FIG. 9-24. Phasor diagram of balanced three-phase voltages.

If one begins to count time at the instant when the emf in phase A is zero, the instantaneous values of the three voltages are given by the curves of (c) of Fig. 8-24, the equations of which are the following:

$$e_a = E_m \sin \omega t$$
$$e_b = E_m \sin (\omega t - 120°)$$
$$e_d = E_m \sin (\omega t - 240°) \qquad (5\text{-}24)$$

The sum of the above three emfs is always zero. This may be shown by adding the instantaneous voltages in Fig. 8-24(c) or in Eq. (5-24), or by adding the three phasor voltages in Fig. 9-24, where E_{oa}, E_{ob}, and E_{od} represent, respectively, the phasor voltages generated in the start-to-finish sense in the three windings of Fig. 8-24(a) and (b). In Fig. 8-24(c), when ωt is zero, e_a is zero, $e_b = E_m \sin (-120°) = -E_m \sin 60°$, $e_d = E_m \sin 120° = E_m \sin 60°$, and $e_a + e_b + e_d = 0$. When $\omega t = 60°$, $e_d = 0$, $e_a = E_m \sin 60°$, $e_b = -E_m \sin 60°$, and $e_a + e_b + e_d = 0$. When $\omega t = 90°$, $e_a = E_m$, $e_b + e_d = -2E_m \sin 30° = -E_m$, and $e_a + e_b + e_d$ is again zero. Ordinates at any other points yield similar results.

Three-phase Circuit Connections. Δ and Y. The six ends of the three windings in Fig. 8-24(b) may be brought out separately to form three single-phase circuits. In practice, however, the three circuits are usually connected in the form of a network to form a three-phase circuit with only three external leads, or four leads when the neutral connection is brought out, as in Fig. 11-24. Two useful connections of this kind are possible.

1. **Δ Connection.** The circuits may be connected in series to form a closed mesh, as in Fig. 10-24. In this figure the "starts" of the phase

windings are a', b', and d', respectively, and the corresponding "finishes" are a, b, and d. The finish of the first phase is connected to the start of the second, the finish of the second to the start of the third,

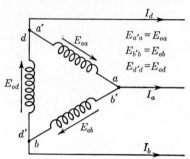

and the finish of the third to the start of the first, as shown in the figure. The order of the phases, of course, may also be ADB instead of ABD, but in both cases the starts and finishes of adjacent windings must be connected together. This type of three-phase circuit is said to be *delta-* or Δ-*connected*. In future diagrams the letters indicating the starts of the phase windings are omitted as in Figs. 11-24 and 12-24.

FIG. 10-24. Δ-connected three-phase network.

It should be observed that, when the voltage phasors of Fig. 9-24 are transferred to the mesh of Fig. 10-24, the arrows all point in the same direction around the mesh, indicating that the voltages are additive.

2. *Y Connection.* When the starts (a', b', and d') of the three-phase windings are connected to a common point O to form a network of the type shown in Fig. 11-24, the system is said to be *star-* or Y-*connected* and the common junction point O is called the neutral point. [Obviously, the finishes (a, b, and d) could also be used to form the neutral, but in that case the phasor voltages to neutral are directed toward the neutral point rather than away from it.] Usually only three wires are used, but sometimes the neutral wire, shown with broken lines in Fig. 11-24, is carried along with the other three leads to form a four-wire three-phase system. Note that the positive sense

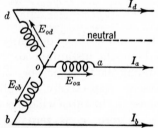

FIG. 11-24. Y-connected three-phase network.

of the voltage in each phase winding of Fig. 8-24 is from start to finish, and since in Fig. 11-24 the starts of these windings are all connected together at the neutral point, the voltages $\mathbf{E}_{oa}$, $\mathbf{E}_{ob}$, and $\mathbf{E}_{od}$ are positive.

Motor and generator windings of three-phase machines, as well as the impedances used as loads in three-phase circuits, are commonly connected either in Δ or in Y. Each connection has certain advantages and disadvantages which determine the choice of circuit for a particular application.

Voltages and Currents in Balanced Δ Systems. In any balanced three-phase system the phasor voltages of the three phases are equal in magnitude and are 120 time degrees out of phase with each other as in Fig. 9-24.

In a Δ connection these voltages add, and since their phasor sum is zero, no current exists in the mesh of a Δ-connected generator, for example, when the external circuit is open, even though normal voltages are generated in the windings. But when balanced three-phase voltages are impressed upon the terminals of a Δ-connected load made up of three equal impedances, as in Fig. 12-24, currents of equal magnitudes exist in the three branches of the Δ, and each current phasor lags (or leads) its respective voltage phasor by the same phase angle, as shown in (b) of the figure. It is also apparent that the line voltages $\mathbf{E}_{ab}$, $\mathbf{E}_{bd}$, and $\mathbf{E}_{da}$ and the corresponding mesh voltages are identical, and since the circuit is balanced, they are all numerically equal. Accordingly, *in a balanced Δ-connected circuit the line voltages and the mesh or coil voltages are numerically*

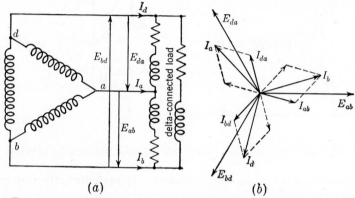

FIG. 12-24. Voltages and currents in a balanced Δ-connected network.

equal. If one represents the former by E and the latter by E_c, one may write

$$E = E_c \tag{6-24}$$

If I is the line current and I_c is the coil current, it is apparent that I is not equal to I_c, for application of Kirchhoff's first law to the junction points of Fig. 12-24(a) shows that *each phasor line current is the phasor difference of the currents in adjacent coils.* Symbolically

$$\begin{aligned}
\mathbf{I}_a &= \mathbf{I}_{da} + \mathbf{I}_{ba} \\
\mathbf{I}_b &= \mathbf{I}_{ab} + \mathbf{I}_{db} \\
\mathbf{I}_d &= \mathbf{I}_{bd} + \mathbf{I}_{ad}
\end{aligned} \tag{7-24}$$

In Fig. 12-24(b) the phasor additions indicated in the above equations are shown. While $\mathbf{I}_{da}$ and $\mathbf{I}_{ab}$ are 120 deg apart, $\mathbf{I}_{da}$ and $\mathbf{I}_{ba}$ are 60 deg apart, and the diagonal of the parallelogram which they form bisects the 60-deg angle. Hence $\mathbf{I}_a$ is 30 deg ahead of $\mathbf{I}_{da}$ and its length is $\sqrt{3}\,\mathbf{I}_{da}$.

The other line currents may be obtained in a similar manner.   Thus if the equal line currents are denoted by I and the equal coil currents by I_c, it follows that

$$I = \sqrt{3}\,I_c \qquad (8\text{-}24)$$

Therefore, *in a balanced Δ-connected circuit the line-current phasor is $\sqrt{3}$ times as long as the coil-current phasor and is displaced from it by 30 deg.*

Voltages and Currents in a Balanced Y System.   In this system the line currents and the currents in the legs of the Y are identical.   This may be seen from Fig. 13-24(a).   Therefore, *in a Y-connected system the*

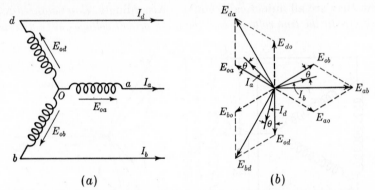

(a)   (b)

FIG. 13-24. Voltages and currents in a balanced Y-connected network.

line currents and the leg currents are equal.   Representing the former by I and the latter by I_c, one may write

$$I = I_c \qquad (9\text{-}24)$$

Using similar notation to represent the voltages, one observes from Fig. 13-24 that the line voltage E is not equal to the leg voltage E_c but that *each phasor line voltage is the phasor difference between the adjacent leg-voltage phasors.*   Using the notation in the figure and applying Kirchhoff's second law to each circuit by tracing through it in the direction indicated, one obtains

$$
\begin{aligned}
\mathbf{E}_{ab} &= \mathbf{E}_{ao} + \mathbf{E}_{ob} \\
\mathbf{E}_{bd} &= \mathbf{E}_{bo} + \mathbf{E}_{od} \\
\mathbf{E}_{da} &= \mathbf{E}_{do} + \mathbf{E}_{oa}
\end{aligned}
\qquad (10\text{-}24)
$$

The phasor additions indicated above are shown graphically in Fig. 13-24(b).   Take $\mathbf{E}_{da}$ as an example.   It is the diagonal of a parallelogram of which the voltages $\mathbf{E}_{do}$ and $\mathbf{E}_{oa}$ are sides.   It therefore bisects the 60-deg angle between $\mathbf{E}_{oa}$ and $\mathbf{E}_{do}$ and leads $\mathbf{E}_{do}$ by 30 deg.   Its length is $\sqrt{3}$ times that of one of the sides.   Similar constructions may be made to find the remaining two voltages.   If the equal line voltages are denoted by E and the equal leg voltages by E_c, it follows that

$$E = \sqrt{3}\, E_c \qquad\qquad (11\text{-}24)$$

Therefore, *in a balanced Y-connected circuit the line-voltage phasor is $\sqrt{3}$ times as long as the leg-voltage phasor and is displaced from it by an angle of 30 degrees.*

Power in Balanced Three-phase Systems. Consider each branch of the balanced Δ-connected system of Fig. 14-24 as a separate single-phase circuit with impressed voltage $E = E_c$, coil current I_c, and the power factor $\cos\theta$. The power in each circuit is $P = E_c I_c \cos\theta$, while the power in the network is

$$P = 3E_c I_c \cos\theta \qquad\qquad (12\text{-}24)$$

By Eq. (6-24) the line voltage is equal to the circuit voltage, and by Eq. (8-24) the line current is $I = \sqrt{3}\, I_c$. After these substitutions are made

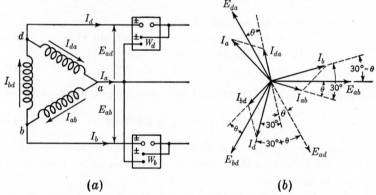

(a)   (b)

FIG. 14-24. Power in a balanced Δ-connected network.

in Eq. (12-24), the total power in the balanced Δ-connected system in terms of line voltage and line current is found to be

$$P = \sqrt{3}\, EI \cos\theta \qquad\qquad (13\text{-}24)$$

When the system is Y-connected, Eq. (12-24) still gives the total power in the network, for E_c is the voltage between line and neutral, while I_c is the coil or leg current. In the Y system, by Eqs. (9-24) and (11-24), the line current $I = I_c$ and the line voltage $E = \sqrt{3}\, E_c$. When these substitutions are made, Eq. (12-24) again yields

$$P = \sqrt{3}\, EI \cos\theta$$

Therefore, *in any balanced three-phase circuit the power is equal to $\sqrt{3}$ times the product of the line voltage, the line current, and the power factor.*

The total volt-amperes of the system are equal to $\sqrt{3}\,EI$ and the power factor is the power divided by the total volt-amperes or

$$\cos \theta = \frac{P}{\sqrt{3}\,EI} \tag{14-24}$$

Power Measurements in Balanced Three-phase Circuits. 1. Δ *Connection.* Two wattmeters, connected as in Fig. 14-24(a), measure the total power in the network. This may be shown as follows: The current in wattmeter W_d is I_d, the impressed potential difference referred to the potential of the common lead a is $\mathbf{E}_{ad}$, and the angle between $\mathbf{E}_{ad}$ and $\mathbf{I}_d$ is $(30 + \theta)$ deg [Fig. 14-24(b)]. The current in wattmeter W_b is I_b; the impressed voltage of the potential coil, referred to the potential of the common lead a, is $\mathbf{E}_{ab}$; and the angle between $\mathbf{E}_{ab}$ and $\mathbf{I}_b$ is $(30 - \theta)$ deg. Accordingly, since $E_{ab} = E_{bd} = E_{da} = E$, and $I_a = I_b = I_d = I$, the readings of the wattmeters are

$$\begin{aligned}
P_d &= EI \cos (30^\circ + \theta) \\
&= EI\,(\cos 30^\circ \cos \theta - \sin 30^\circ \sin \theta) \tag{15-24} \\
P_b &= EI \cos (30^\circ - \theta) \\
&= EI\,(\cos 30^\circ \cos \theta + \sin 30^\circ \sin \theta) \tag{16-24}
\end{aligned}$$

Adding Eqs. (15-24) and (16-24) and substituting $\sqrt{3}/2$ for $\cos 30^\circ$ yields

$$P = P_d + P_b = \sqrt{3}\,EI \cos \theta \tag{17-24}$$

as the sum of the two meter readings. This result is identical with Eq. (13-24), so one concludes that the sum of the two meter readings is the total power in the system.

2. *Y Connection.* Two wattmeters, connected as in Fig. 15-24, measure the total power in the system. The proof of this statement is similar to that given above for the Δ system.

Consider wattmeter W_d. The current in the current coil is $\mathbf{I}_d$, the impressed voltage of the potential coil referred to the potential of the common lead a is $\mathbf{E}_{ad}$, while the angle between $\mathbf{E}_{ad}$ and $\mathbf{I}_d$ is $30^\circ + \theta$, as may be seen from the diagram of Fig. 15-24(b). The current in the current coil of W_b is $\mathbf{I}_b$, the voltage impressed on the potential coil referred to the potential of the common lead a is $\mathbf{E}_{ab}$, while the angle between $\mathbf{E}_{ab}$ and $\mathbf{I}_b$ is $(30^\circ - \theta)$. In a balanced system, $E_{ab} = E_{bd} = E_{da} = E$, and $I_a = I_b = I_c = I$. The readings of the wattmeters therefore are

$$\begin{aligned}
P_d &= EI \cos (30^\circ + \theta) \\
&= EI\,(\cos 30^\circ \cos \theta - \sin 30^\circ \sin \theta) \tag{18-24} \\
P_b &= EI \cos (30^\circ - \theta) \\
&= EI\,(\cos 30^\circ \cos \theta + \sin 30^\circ \sin \theta) \tag{19-24}
\end{aligned}$$

Adding Eqs. (18-24) and (19-24) as before and substituting $\sqrt{3}/2$ for $\cos 30°$ yields

$$P = P_d + P_b = \sqrt{3}\ EI \cos \theta \qquad (20\text{-}24)$$

which is identical with the equation already obtained for the Δ connection.

The difference $P_b - P_d$ [Eq. (16-24) minus Eq. (15-24) or Eq. (19-24) minus Eq. (18-24)] yields

$$P_b - P_d = 2EI \sin 30° \sin \theta = EI \sin \theta \qquad (21\text{-}24)$$

for $\sin 30° = \frac{1}{2}$. But the reactive power in a balanced three-phase network is

$$Q = 3E_cI_c \sin \theta = \sqrt{3}\ EI \sin \theta \qquad (22\text{-}24)$$

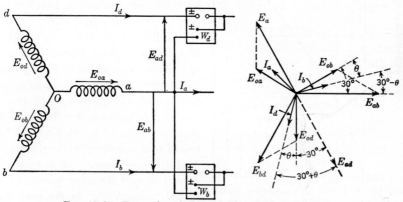

FIG. 15-24. Power in a balanced Y-connected network.

From a comparison of Eqs. (21-24) and (22-24) it follows that the reactive power is $\sqrt{3}$ times the difference of the wattmeter readings or

$$Q = \sqrt{3}\ (P_b - P_d) \qquad (23\text{-}24)$$

The power-factor angle may be obtained from the wattmeter readings alone, for from Eqs. (20-24) and (23-24)

$$\tan \theta = \frac{Q}{P} = \frac{\sqrt{3}\ (P_b - P_d)}{P_b + P_d} \qquad (24\text{-}24)$$

It should be noted, however [Eqs. (15-24) to (19-24)], that the reading of P_b is negative for all negative values of θ larger than 60 deg (power factors less than 50 per cent, current lagging), while over this range P_d is positive. On the other hand, P_d is negative for all positive values of θ larger than 60 deg (power factors less than 50 per cent, current leading), while over the same range P_b is positive. In both the above cases the *difference* (algebraic sum) of the two meter readings must be taken to obtain the total power in the network. For power factors larger than 50 per cent (values of $\theta < 60°$) both readings are positive, and their arithmetic sum is the total power in the system.

At unity power factor ($\theta = 0$) the two meter readings are equal. At 50 per cent power factor, current leading ($\theta = +60°$), W_d reads zero, while at 50 per cent power factor, current lagging ($\theta = -60°$), W_b reads zero.

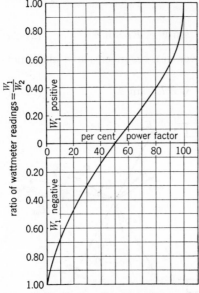

FIG. 16-24. Ratio of wattmeter readings as a function of power factor when two wattmeters are used to measure the power in a balanced three-phase circuit.

The ratios of the readings of two wattmeters W_b and W_d, which are properly connected to read the total power in any balanced three-phase network, are plotted as functions of power factor in Fig. 16-24.

It follows from the above that *in any balanced three-phase, three-wire circuit the total power is the algebraic sum of the readings of two wattmeters, the current coils of which are connected, one each in series with a lead, and the potential coils of which have one terminal each connected to the remaining lead (the one having no current coil in series) and the other terminal connected, respectively, to the lead containing the current coil.* The reactive power is $\sqrt{3}$ times the algebraic difference of the above readings.

Power in Unbalanced Three-phase Circuits. When the circuit is unbalanced, the two wattmeters (Figs. 14-24 and 15-24) still read the total power. This may be shown by using instantaneous values of voltage, current, and power as follows.

Assume a Δ connection as in Fig. (14-24), and let the instantaneous currents and voltages be designated by appropriate subscripts to conform with the drawing. Then the instantaneous current in wattmeter W_d is

$$i_d = i_{bd} - i_{da} \tag{25-24}$$

and its impressed potential difference is e_{ad}. Similarly, the current in wattmeter W_b is

$$i_b = i_{ab} - i_{bd} \tag{26-24}$$

and its impressed voltage is e_{ab}. The instantaneous powers which the two meters read are

$$p_d = e_{ad}i_d$$
$$p_b = e_{ab}i_b$$

and the sum of the meter readings is

$$p = p_d + p_b = e_{ad}i_d + e_{ab}i_b \qquad (27\text{-}24)$$

Upon substituting the values of i_d and i_b from Eqs. (25-24) and (26-24) in Eq. (27-24), the sum of the wattmeter readings is found to be

$$\begin{aligned} p &= e_{ad}(i_{bd} - i_{da}) + e_{ab}(i_{ab} - i_{bd}) \\ &= e_{ad}i_{ad} + e_{ab}i_{ab} + i_{bd}(e_{ad} - e_{ab}) \end{aligned} \qquad (28\text{-}24)$$

It has already been shown that in a three-phase circuit the sum of the instantaneous voltages is zero. Therefore, $e_{ad} + e_{db} + e_{ba} = 0$ and $e_{ad} - e_{ab} = e_{bd}$. Substituting this relationship in Eq. (28-24) yields

$$p = e_{ad}i_{ad} + e_{ab}i_{ab} + e_{bd}i_{bd} \qquad (29\text{-}24)$$

which is the total instantaneous power in the circuit. This shows that the sum of the two wattmeter readings is the total power in the Δ network even when the circuit is unbalanced.

When the Y connection is used (Fig. 15-24), the instantaneous powers read by the wattmeters are

$$p_b = (e_{ao} + e_{ob})i_b$$
$$p_d = (e_{ao} + e_{od})i_d$$

and the sum of the two readings is

$$p = e_{ob}i_b + e_{od}i_d + e_{ao}(i_b + i_d) \qquad (30\text{-}24)$$

By Kirchhoff's law relating to currents, $i_a + i_b + i_d = 0$ or $-i_a = i_b + i_d$. Upon substituting this value of $-i_a$ in Eq. (30-24), the latter becomes

$$p = e_{oa}i_a + e_{ob}i_b + e_{od}i_d \qquad (31\text{-}24)$$

which is the total instantaneous power in the network, as well as the sum of the wattmeter readings.

Measurement of Reactive Power with One Wattmeter. A balanced circuit is assumed. It has already been shown [Eq. (23-24)] that the reactive power in a balanced three-phase system is $\sqrt{3}\,(P_b - P_d)$ where P_b and P_d are the readings of two wattmeters connected as in Figs. 14-24 and 15-24. The same result may be obtained with a single wattmeter when its current coil is connected in series with one lead and its potential-coil terminals are connected across the remaining two leads.

When the circuit is Y-connected as in Fig. 17-24, the current in the meter is I_a, the impressed potential difference is E_{db}, and the angle between I_a and E_{db} is $(90° - \theta)$, as indicated in Fig. 17-24(b). Since $I_a = I$, the

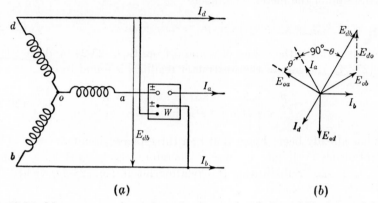

(a)   (b)

Fig. 17-24. Measurement of reactive volt-amperes in a balanced Y-connected circuit with one wattmeter.

line current, and $E_{db} = E$, the line voltage, the wattmeter reads

$$W = EI \cos (90° - \theta) = EI \sin \theta$$

and the reactive power in the network is

$$Q = \sqrt{3}\, W = \sqrt{3}\, EI \sin \theta \qquad (32\text{-}24)$$

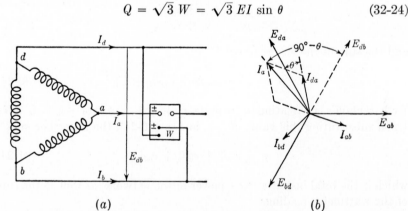

(a)   (b)

Fig. 18-24. Measurement of reactive volt-amperes in a balanced Δ-connected circuit with one wattmeter.

When the circuit is Δ-connected as in Fig. 18-24, the line current is $I_a = I$, the line voltage impressed is $E_{db} = E$, and the angle between I_a and E_{db} is $90° - \theta$. The wattmeter again reads

$$W = EI \cos (90° - \theta) = EI \sin \theta$$

and the reactive power in the circuit is

$$Q = \sqrt{3}\ W = \sqrt{3}\ EI \sin \theta$$

Example 2. Three equal impedances $\mathbf{Z} = 5 + j4$ are connected in the form of a Δ to the three leads of a balanced three-phase circuit. The impressed line voltage is 120. Find (*a*) the current I_c in each branch, (*b*) the line current I, (*c*) the power factor, (*d*) the volt-amperes in the circuit, (*e*) the active power in the circuit, (*f*) the reactive power in the circuit.

(*a*)
$$I_c = \frac{120}{\sqrt{5^2 + 4^2}} = 18.75 \text{ amp}$$

(*b*)
$$I = \sqrt{3} \times 18.75 = 32.48 \text{ amp}$$

(*c*)
$$\tan \theta = \frac{X}{R} = \frac{4}{5} = 0.800$$
$$\cos \theta = 0.782$$

(*d*)
$$\sqrt{3} \times 120 \times 32.48 = 6{,}771 \text{ va}$$
$$= 6.77 \text{ kva}$$

(*e*)
$$P = \text{va} \times \cos \theta = 6{,}771 \times 0.782$$
$$= 5{,}278 \text{ watts}$$
$$= 5.28 \text{ kw}$$

(*f*)
$$Q = \text{va} \times \sin \theta = 6{,}771 \times 0.625$$
$$= 4{,}232 \text{ vars}$$
$$= 4.23 \text{ kvars}$$

Example 3. When the impedances in the previous example are Y-connected and the impressed voltage between lines is $E = 120$, find (*a*) the voltage E_c to neutral, (*b*) the line current I, (*c*) the volt-amperes in the network, (*d*) the power factor, (*e*) the active power, (*f*) the reactive power.

(*a*)
$$E_c = 120 \div \sqrt{3} = 69.4 \text{ volts}$$

(*b*)
$$I = \frac{69.4}{\sqrt{5^2 + 4^2}} = 10.84 \text{ amp}$$

(*c*)
$$\sqrt{3}\ EI = 1.732 \times 120 \times 10.84$$
$$= 2{,}253 \text{ va}$$
$$= 2.25 \text{ kva}$$

(*d*)
$$\cos \theta = 0.782 \text{ (as in previous example)}$$

(*e*)
$$P = \sqrt{3}\ EI \cos \theta = 2{,}253 \times 0.782$$
$$= 1{,}762 \text{ watts}$$
$$= 1.76 \text{ kw}$$

(*f*)
$$Q = \sqrt{3}\ EI \sin \theta = 2{,}253 \times 0.625$$
$$= 1{,}408 \text{ vars}$$
$$= 1.41 \text{ kvars (lag)}$$

By comparing the results of this and the previous example, it is observed that in the Y-connected network the coil current is only $1/\sqrt{3}$ of the coil current in the Δ network, while the volt-amperes, power, and reactive power in the Y system are only one-third of the corresponding values in the Δ system. These conclusions assume the same values of impedances in the legs and the same impressed voltages for the two systems.

Problems

1-24. Three resistances of 36 ohms each are Y-connected to 220-volt three-phase mains. Determine (a) the current in each resistance, (b) the power supplied to the network.

2-24. Three equal impedances of $Z = 36\underline{/30°}$ replace the resistances in Prob. 1-24. Determine (a) the current in each impedance, (b) the power, (c) the kilovars supplied to the network. (d) Draw a phasor diagram showing the line-to-line voltages, the phase voltages, and the line currents.

3-24. A single wattmeter is used to measure the kilovars of the circuit in Prob. 2-24. What is the reading of the wattmeter?

4-24. Three equal impedances of $Z = 36\overline{\underline{\smash{)}40°}}$ are connected in Δ across balanced 220-volt 3-phase mains. Determine (a) the phase currents, (b) the line currents, (c) the kilowatt input, (d) the kilovars input, and (e) the total kilovolt amperes supplied to the network. (f) Draw a phasor diagram showing phase currents, line currents, and impressed voltage.

5-24. The two windings of a 2,000-kva 60-cycle two-phase generator are spaced 90 electrical degrees apart, and each winding generates an emf of 2,300 volts. One end of each winding is connected to a common conductor to form a two-phase three-wire circuit. (a) What is the voltage across the two free ends of the winding? What is the current in (b) the common return, (c) each outside conductor when the machine delivers rated output at 2,300 volts per phase and 0.85 power factor?

6-24. The two windings of the machine in Prob. 5-24 are connected together at their mid-points to form a four-wire two-phase circuit. For rated output of this machine determine (a) the voltages across the terminals, (b) the line currents. (c) Draw a phasor diagram of voltages.

7-24. Corresponding ends of the phase windings of a 5,000-kva 6,600-volt, three-phase generator are connected to a common point while the remaining three ends form the terminals of the machine. (a) What is the voltage of each phase winding? When the machine delivers its rated output at rated voltage and 0.80 power factor, what are (b) the line current, (c) the kilowatts, and (d) the kilovars output? Two wattmeters are connected as in Fig. 15-24, except that potential and current transformers (not shown) are used with the instruments. (e) What is the reading of each wattmeter?

8-24. Two wattmeters are used to measure the power input to a balanced three-phase Δ-connected inductive network. The meter readings are 750 and 1,280 watts. The terminal emf is 120 volts. Determine (a) the power factor, (b) the phase currents, (c) the line currents.

9-24. A single wattmeter is used to find the kilovars in the network of Prob. 8-24. Determine (a) the current in the current coil of the wattmeter, (b) the reading of the instrument, (c) the kilovars.

10-24. Two wattmeters are used to measure the input to a lightly loaded induction motor, the power factor of which is 74 per cent. The sum of the wattmeter readings is 6.5 kw. Determine the reading of each meter.

11-24. Three impedances are Y-connected between the phase wires and neutral of a balanced 220-volt three-phase system with neutral-wire return. The phase wires are designated as a, b, and c, while the neutral wire is o. In leg ao the impedance is $Z_1 = 8 - j0$; in leg bo the impedance is $Z_2 = 6 + j5$; in leg co the impedance is $Z_3 = 8 - j10$. Three wattmeters W_a, W_b, and W_c are used to measure the power taken by the impedances. The current coils of W_a, W_b, and W_c are connected, respectively, in series with a, b, and c, while the potential coils are connected between the respective lines and the neutral wire o. Find (a) the current in each phase winding, (b) the reading of each wattmeter, (c) the total power supplied.

12-24. A three-phase 2,300-volt three-wire feeder supplies a balanced three-phase lighting load of 54 kw at unity power factor, and a balanced three-phase induction motor load of 250 kw at an average power factor of 78 per cent. Determine (a) the current, (b) the kilovolt-amperes, (c) the power factor of the feeder.

13-24. Two wattmeters connected as in Fig. 15-24 are used to measure the power supplied to a balanced three-phase load. If the total input to the load is 150 kva, determine what the indications of the wattmeters are for each of the following power factors: 1.00, 0.90, 0.80, 0.70, 0.60, 0.50.

CHAPTER 25

TRANSFORMERS

Concepts and Definitions. The *transformer* is a stationary device by means of which electrical energy in one circuit is transformed to electrical energy of the same frequency in another circuit. In its simplest form, it consists of two coils of wire insulated from each other and wound on a common laminated sheet-steel core (Fig. 1-25). When the terminals of coil P are connected to a source of power and the terminals of coil S are connected to a load (such as lamps, motors), energy is transferred from circuit 1 to circuit 2 through the medium of the magnetic field in the core. Energy enters the transformer through P, called the *primary*, and leaves it through S, called the *secondary;* thus the direction of energy flow through the transformer is from primary to secondary. Either coil of a transformer may be used as primary or secondary.

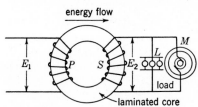

FIG. 1-25. The transformer principle.

Energy may be supplied to a transformer at a voltage E_1 different from the voltage E_2 at which it is delivered to the load. In fact, most transformers are designed for widely different primary and secondary voltages, such as $E_1 = 2,200$, $E_2 = 220$; $E_1 = 50,000$, $E_2 = 2,500$. The coil with the high voltage is called the *high-voltage* winding and the one with the low voltage the *low-voltage* winding. When the high-voltage coil is the primary and the low-voltage coil is the secondary, the transformer is called a *step-down* transformer; when the reverse connection is used, the transformer is called a *step-up* transformer. The ratio of the high-side voltage to the low-side voltage is called the *ratio of transformation*. In the first example cited above the ratio of transformation is 10:1; in the second it is 20:1. Generally speaking, transformers may be designed for any desired ratio of transformation. Common ratios are 5:1, 10:1, 20:1.

Commercial Importance of the Transformer. From the foregoing it is apparent that the important functions of a transformer are twofold, namely:

1. To transfer electrical energy from a circuit of voltage E_1 to another circuit of voltage E_2 (usually different from E_1).

2. To isolate the two circuits from each other.

These make the transformer an extremely important link in the scheme of power transmission and utilization. The transformer makes it possible to generate energy at any suitable voltage, such as 13,000, to transform it to energy at a high voltage, say, 110,000, for transmission to a load center 100 miles or more distant from the generating plant, and there again to deliver it to a distribution system at still a different voltage. Use of a high transmission voltage makes economical power transmission possible. At the same time, through the medium of the transformer, the transmitted energy is delivered to the consumer at a voltage suitable for operating his lights, motors, and other devices with safety, for the low- and the high-voltage circuits are isolated from each other. All these energy transformations are made with a relatively cheap piece of stationary equipment with a high energy efficiency.

Kinds of Transformers. Various descriptive names are applied to transformers to designate the particular kinds of applications for which the transformers are designed. The vast majority of transformers used in commercial power applications receive power from, and deliver power to, circuits with approximately constant potentials. Such transformers are called *constant-potential transformers*. Most constant-potential transformers are *distribution and power transformers;* they are used to deliver relatively large amounts of energy. Others

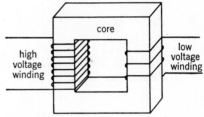

Fig. 2-25. Elementary sketch of a core-type transformer.

supply only the small amounts of energy that are required to excite the potential coils of meters and relays. These are *instrument-potential transformers.* Constant-potential transformers sometimes have only one winding, with taps for primary and secondary connections. Such transformers are called *auto-transformers.* Another type of transformer, called the *constant-current transformer*, receives power from constant-potential mains and delivers it to a constant-current circuit. Their principal application is for supplying power to series street-lighting circuits. Transformers called *regulators* are also used to regulate the voltage of a-c circuits. The current coils of wattmeters, ammeters, and relays are excited by current supplied from *instrument-current transformers.* These have their primaries connected in series with the conductor in which the current is to be metered, and their secondaries in series with the current coil of the meter.

Construction.   The essential elements of all transformers are as follows:

1. Two or more electrical windings insulated from each other and from the core (except in autotransformers).

2. A core, which in the case of single-phase distribution transformers usually comprises cold-rolled silicon-steel strip instead of an assembly of punched silicon-steel laminations such as are used in the larger power-transformer cores.   The flux path in the assembled core is parallel to the direction of the steel's grain or "orientation."   This results in a reduction in core losses for a given flux density and frequency, or it permits the use of higher core densities and reduced size of transformers for given core losses.

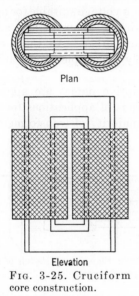

Plan

Elevation

FIG. 3-25. Cruciform core construction.

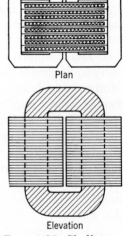

Plan

Elevation

FIG. 4-25. Shell-type construction.

Other necessary parts are a suitable container for the assembled core and windings; a suitable medium for insulating the core and its windings from each other and from the container; suitable bushings for insulating and bringing the terminals of the windings out of the case.

On the basis of the type of core construction used, transformers are classified as *core type* and *shell type*.   In the core type of construction the magnetic circuit is in the form of a single ring (equivalent to two legs and a connecting yoke).   The primary and secondary windings encircle the legs of the core, as in Figs. 2-25 and 3-25.   In the shell type the relative positions of the coils and the magnetic circuit are interchanged; the winding now forms a common ring with which two or more separate magnetic circuits are interlinked, as in Fig. 4-25.   The essential difference between the two types is that the core type has a relatively long magnetic circuit and a short electric one, while the shell type has a short magnetic circuit and a long electric one.

Distribution and power transformers are also classified on the basis of the method used to cool the transformer. For voltages below 25,000, transformers are also built for cooling by means of an *air blast*. Air ducts are provided, leading through windings and core. The transformer is not immersed in oil but is surrounded by a thin sheet-metal case which is open on the ends and through which air is circulated by means of a fan or

Fig. 5-25. (*a*) A 4,000-kva oil-insulated, self-cooled transformer; (*b*) core and coil for the transformer in (*a*). (*Allis-Chalmers Manufacturing Company.*)

blower. Clean air as well as suitable housing is required. The advantage of this type of transformer is its low cost, but the fact that an air-circulating system is required greatly restricts its use.

Small and medium-sized distribution and lighting transformers are of the *self-cooled, oil-immersed* type. The assembled windings and core are mounted in a welded, oiltight steel tank, provided with a steel or cast-iron cover. After the core is in place, the tank is filled with purified, high-quality insulating oil. The oil serves as additional insulation between windings and between windings and core, and to conduct to the case the heat generated by the losses. The case is designed to facilitate radiation.

The losses are roughly proportional to the volume of the core. The volume varies as the cube of a given dimension, while the area of the case varies only as the square. Accordingly, in large sizes the tank surface itself is insufficient to radiate the losses, and additional surface must be provided by means of corrugated tanks or external radiators, as in Fig. 5-25.

Underwriter specifications exclude the use of oil-cooled transformers within buildings unless they are housed in specially constructed, fireproof vaults. To avoid this limitation there has been developed for use in transformers a fireproof cooling liquid called *Askarel*. Manufacturers, however, have applied various trade names to this liquid; the General Electric Company calls it *Pyranol*, while the Westinghouse company's product is *Inerteen*. Transformers that employ this fireproof cooling liquid may be had in all ratings.

Large self-cooled transformers are expensive; a more economical form of construction for large transformers is provided in the *water-cooled, oil-immersed* type. The winding and core are immersed in oil as before, but mounted near the surface of the oil is a cooling coil through which water is circulated. The energy losses are carried off in the cooling water. The largest transformers are constructed in this manner.

Oil-filled transformers are constructed for outdoor use; no housing other than their own is required, and a great saving is thereby effected. They require only periodic inspection.

CONSTANT-POTENTIAL TRANSFORMERS

Elementary Theory. The basic theory of the transformer is not difficult to understand. To simplify matters as much as possible, consider first an *ideal* transformer, that is, one in which the resistance of the windings is negligible and the core has no losses. Let the secondary be open [Fig. 6-25(a)], and let a sine wave of potential difference [e_1, Fig. 6-25(b)] be impressed upon the primary. The impressed potential difference causes an alternating current to flow in the primary winding. Since the primary resistance is negligible and there are no losses in the core, the effective resistance is zero and the circuit is purely reactive. Hence the current wave i_m lags the impressed voltage wave e by 90 time degrees, as shown in Fig. 6-25(b). The reactance of the circuit is very high and the magnetizing current is very small. This current in the N_1 turns of the primary magnetizes the core and produces a flux ϕ that is at all times proportional to the current (if the permeability of the circuit is assumed to be constant) and is therefore in time phase with the current. The flux, by its rate of change, induces in the primary winding a voltage e_{g1} which at every instant of time is equal in value and opposite in direction to e_1. It is called the *counter emf* of the primary. The value which the primary current attains must be such that the flux which it produces in the core is of sufficient value to induce in the primary the required counter emf.

Since the flux also threads the secondary winding, a voltage e_{g2} is induced in the secondary. This voltage is likewise proportional to the rate of change of flux and so is in time phase with e_{g1}, but it may have any value depending upon the number of turns N_2 in the secondary.

The current, flux, and voltages, the instantaneous values of which are represented by the curves of Fig. 6-25(b), are also represented in terms of their respective effective values in the phasor diagram of Fig. 6-25(c).

Modifications of Theory Required by Practical Design. Practical conditions require that certain modifications be made in the foregoing theory.

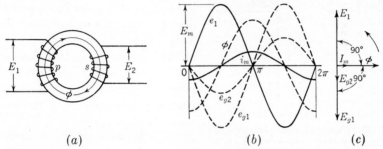

(a)   (b)   (c)

Fig. 6-25. Current, voltage, and flux curves of ideal (no-loss) transformer.

There are iron losses in the transformer core and copper losses in the windings. These are not entirely negligible. Therefore, even when the secondary circuit is open, the input to the primary is not wholly reactive. Accordingly, with open secondary the primary current I_{ex}, called the *exciting current*, must lag the impressed voltage E_1 by some angle $90° - \alpha$ (less than 90 deg) as in Fig. 7-25(a), such that the input to the primary is

$$E_1 I_{ex} \sin \alpha = \text{watts no-load primary copper loss} + \text{core loss} \quad (1\text{-}25)$$

By comparing Figs. 6-25(c) and 7-25(a) it is observed that the principal effect upon the phasor diagram of giving consideration to the iron and no-load copper losses is to shift the no-load current phasor in advance of the flux phasor through the angle α. The exciting current is only a small percentage of the rated primary current, however, so the no-load copper losses are substantially negligible. The core loss (particularly hysteresis loss) is principally responsible for the shift in the current phasor. For this reason the angle α is called the *hysteretic angle of advance*.

It is customary to divide the exciting current into components in phase and in quadrature with the impressed voltage. The in-phase component I_p is called the *active* or *loss component*, while the quadrature component

I_m is the *magnetizing component* of the exciting current. In comparison with the load current [I_{21} of Fig. 7-25(b)] the exciting current is so small that it is usually impractical to represent it to scale in a phasor diagram. Thus I_{ex} is exaggerated in both (a) and (b) of the figure.

Owing to the fact that the permeability of the core varies with the instantaneous value of the exciting current, the wave of exciting current does not have the true sine form. In transformer diagrams an *equivalent sine wave* is used.

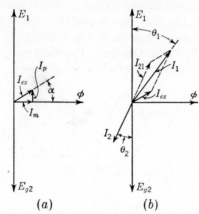

When the secondary is loaded, a secondary load current $\mathbf{I}_2$ [Fig. 7-25(b)] flows. The amount of this current, as well as its phase position, depends upon the nature of the load. This current, flowing in the N_2 turns of the secondary, tends to demagnetize the core and thereby causes the primary current to increase by a component $\mathbf{I}_{21}$, such that the added magnetizing ampere-turns $N_1 I_{21}$ balances the demagnetizing ampere-turns $N_2 I_2$ of the secondary. When the turn ratio is unity the exciting current $\mathbf{I}_{ex}$ is the phasor sum of the primary and secondary currents. The power-factor angle of the primary is somewhat larger than the power-factor angle of the secondary.

FIG. 7-25. Phasor diagrams for commercial transformers: (a) secondary open; (b) secondary loaded. For convenience in drawing the diagram, the turn ratio N_2/N_1 is assumed to be unity.

In practice, the exciting current is only a small percentage of the load current. The primary ampere-turns $N_1 I_1$ are nearly equal to the secondary ampere-turns $N_2 I_2$, and the current $\mathbf{I}_1$ is displaced approximately 180 deg from $\mathbf{I}_2$. Hence, the power-factor angles of the primary and the secondary are substantially equal. The angle α is usually under 30 deg.

Voltage Ratio. When a sine wave of voltage is impressed on the primary of a transformer [e_1, Fig. 6-25(b)], the wave of counter emf e_{g1} must likewise be sinusoidal. The flux wave ϕ is therefore also sine-shaped and is 90 deg behind e_1 and 90 deg ahead of e_{g1} as in the figure. With reference to the figure, the equation of the flux wave may be written as

$$\phi = -\phi_{\max} \cos \omega t \tag{2-25}$$

Then, by Faraday's and Lenz's laws, the emf induced in the N_1 turns of the primary winding is

$$e_{g1} = \frac{-N_1 \, d\phi}{dt} = -\omega N_1 \phi_m \sin \omega t \tag{3-25}$$

where ϕ is in webers. Similarly, the emf induced in the N_2 turns of the secondary is

$$e_{g2} = -\omega N_2 \phi_m \sin \omega t \qquad (4\text{-}25)$$

The maximum values of these voltages are the values of the right-hand members of Eqs. (3-25) and (4-25) for $\sin \omega t = 1$, and since $\omega = 2\pi f$, where f is the frequency of the supply,

$$_{\max}E_{g1} = 2\pi f N_1 \phi_{\max} \qquad \text{volts} \qquad (5\text{-}25)$$

and

$$_{\max}E_{g2} = 2\pi f N_2 \phi_{\max} \qquad \text{volts} \qquad (6\text{-}25)$$

From page 287 the effective value of a sine wave is observed to be $\sqrt{2}/2$ times the maximum value.   Hence the effective values of the primary and secondary induced voltages are, respectively,

$$E_{g1} = 4.44 f N_1 \phi_{\max} \qquad \text{volts} \qquad (7\text{-}25)$$

and

$$E_{g2} = 4.44 f N_2 \phi_{\max} \qquad \text{volts} \qquad (8\text{-}25)$$

The ratio of these voltages is

$$\frac{E_{g2}}{E_{g1}} = \frac{N_2}{N_1} \qquad (9\text{-}25)$$

This ratio, called the *turn ratio*, is approximately equal to the ratio of transformation.

In commercial transformers the induced voltages E_{g1} and E_{g2} differ somewhat, though only slightly, from the corresponding terminal voltages E_1 and E_2.   This is due partly to the resistance drops in the windings and partly to the fact that some of the flux which links the primary winding does not link the secondary.   The ratio of the terminal voltages is therefore slightly different from the turn ratio of a transformer.

Current Ratio.   Transformers have very high efficiencies—from 98 to 99.5 per cent.   Furthermore, as has previously been mentioned, the power factors of primary input and secondary output are approximately equal.   Accordingly, by equating primary input to secondary output and canceling the power factor from both sides of the equation, it follows that, approximately,

$$E_1 I_1 = E_2 I_2$$

or

$$\frac{I_1}{I_2} = \frac{E_2}{E_1} \qquad (10\text{-}25)$$

But since by Eq. (9-25) the voltages are approximately in the ratio of the turns,

$$\frac{I_1}{I_2} = \frac{N_2}{N_1} \qquad (11\text{-}25)$$

In other words, the currents in primary and secondary of a transformer are approximately in the inverse ratio of the corresponding turns.

Leakage Reactance. It has already been pointed out that some of the flux that links the primary of a transformer does not link the secondary, and likewise some of the flux that links the secondary fails to link the primary. This condition is illustrated in Fig. 8-25. All the flux represented by the lines ϕ is common to both windings and induces therein equal voltages per turn. This is sometimes called the *main* or *useful flux*. A much smaller amount of flux ϕ_{L1}, called the *primary leakage flux*, links all or a part of the primary winding but returns through the air and insulation separating primary and secondary windings, without linking the secondary. The linkages of the flux with the turns of the primary ($\Sigma N_1\phi_{L1}$)

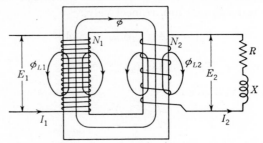

FIG. 8-25. Leakage reactance.

introduce a *leakage reactance* in the primary winding, which absorbs a component of impressed voltage that leads the primary current by 90 deg. This leakage reactance is

$$X_1 = 2\pi f \left[\frac{\Sigma N_1\phi_{L1}}{I_1} \right] = 2\pi f L_1 \qquad \text{ohms} \qquad (12\text{-}25)$$

and the corresponding consumed voltage is

$$E_{x1} = X_1 I_1 \qquad \text{volts} \qquad (13\text{-}25)$$

Similarly, the leakage flux linkages of the secondary ($\Sigma N_2\phi_{L2}$) introduce a leakage reactance of

$$X_2 = 2\pi f \left[\frac{\Sigma N_2\phi_{L2}}{I_2} \right] = 2\pi f L_2 \qquad \text{ohms} \qquad (14\text{-}25)$$

in the secondary winding, and the voltage consumed by it is

$$E_{x2} = X_2 I_2 \qquad \text{volts} \qquad (14\text{-}25)$$

This voltage leads the secondary current by 90 deg.

Generally speaking, leakage reactance is undesirable in transformers because voltages are consumed in it. *It does not appreciably affect the loss in the transformer.* Some special types of transformers, such as current transformers for street-lighting circuits and power transformers designed to supply power to arc furnaces, are especially designed to have high leakage reactances.

The leakage reactance is kept to a low value by interleaving primary and secondary coils. The windings are not mounted on separate legs of the core, as shown for convenience in the diagram of Fig. 2-25, but instead parts of both primary and secondary are wound on each leg. Figure 9-25 shows the winding arrangement on one leg of a core-type transformer with a split low-voltage winding. The winding on the right-hand leg is similarly arranged. The parts of these windings are placed as closely together as

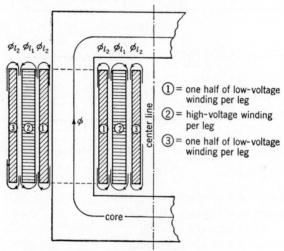

FIG. 9-25. Leakage flux in a core-type transformer.

considerations of insulation and cooling permit. In this way the areas of the leakage paths, and thereby the leakage fluxes, are kept within desirable limits.

Transformer Circuit Diagrams. Both primary and secondary of a transformer contain resistance and inductive reactance, but the two windings are insulated from each other as indicated in Fig. 10-25(a). The exciting circuit is represented by a shunt circuit containing conductance g and susceptance b in parallel as shown. The voltage impressed on the shunt is $E_{g1} = (N_1/N_2)E_{g2}$. If a $1:1$ transformer ratio is assumed, the equivalent circuit is that shown in (b). If the exciting circuit is shifted to the left ahead of the primary impedance as in (c), only small errors appear, and the computations which one must make to solve the circuit are greatly simplified. A similar shift could be made in (a) to yield an approximately equivalent circuit for any two-circuit transformer.

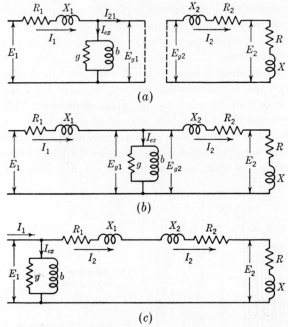

FIG. 10-25. The equivalent circuits of a two-winding transformer.

In the above diagrams,

R = resistance of secondary load

X = reactance of secondary load

R_1 = resistance of primary winding

R_2 = resistance of secondary winding

X_1 = primary leakage reactance

X_2 = secondary leakage reactance

I_1 = primary current input

I_2 = secondary load current

$I_{21} = \dfrac{N_2}{N_1} I_2$ = primary equivalent of secondary load current

g = conductance of exciting circuit

b = susceptance of exciting circuit

$\mathbf{Y} = g - jb$ = admittance of exciting circuit

$\mathbf{I}_{ex} = \mathbf{E}_{g1}\mathbf{Y} \cong \mathbf{E}_1\mathbf{Y}$ = exciting current

$\qquad = I_{ex}(\sin \alpha - j \cos \alpha) = I_p - jI_m$

where α = angle of advance of $\mathbf{I}_{ex}$ with respect to ϕ (Fig. 7-25),

$$I_p = I_{ex} \sin \alpha \qquad (15\text{-}25)$$

and

$$I_m = I_{ex} \cos \alpha \qquad (16\text{-}25)$$

Open-circuit Test.   The exciting current and its components may be obtained experimentally by measuring the input to the transformer with rated voltage and frequency impressed on the primary and with the secondary open.   Connect the transformer as in Fig. 11-25, impress rated voltage at normal frequency on the primary, and read the voltmeter V, the ammeter A, and the wattmeter W.   The wattmeter reads the watts input P, the

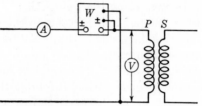

FIG. 11-25. Connections for measuring the exciting current.

voltmeter reads the impressed voltage E_1, and the ammeter indicates the exciting current I_{ex}.   Hence, by Eq. (1-25)

$$P = E_1 I_{ex} \sin \alpha$$

whence

$$\sin \alpha = \frac{P}{E_1 I_{ex}} \tag{17-25}$$

All terms in the right side of Eq. (17-25) are known; hence α is known as is also $\cos \alpha$, and from Eqs. (15-25) and (16-25) the active and reactive components of the exciting current may be found.

Example 1.   The 230-volt winding of a 50-kva 2,300/230-volt 60-cycle transformer is connected to 230-volt mains as in Fig. 11-25, the 2,300-volt winding being open. The meters indicate the following readings: watts = 187, E_1 = 230 volts, I_{ex} = 6.5 amp.   The resistance of the low-voltage winding is 0.06 ohm.   Find (*a*) core losses, (*b*) angle α, (*c*) I_m, (*d*) I_p, (*e*) the percentage exciting current.

(*a*) The copper loss due to the exciting current is $6.5^2 \times 0.06 = 2.5$ watts.   Hence the iron loss is $187 - 2.5$ or 184.5 watts.

(*b*) By Eq. (17-25),

$$\sin \alpha = \frac{187}{230 \times 6.5} = 0.125$$
$$\alpha = 7° 11'$$
$$\cos \alpha = 0.992$$

(*c*) $$I_m = 6.5 \cos \alpha = 6.4 \text{ amp}$$

(*d*) $$I_p = \frac{187}{230} = 0.81 \text{ amp}$$

(*e*) Full-load current is

$$\frac{50,000}{230} = 217.4 \text{ amp}$$

Hence

Percentage exciting current $= 100 \times 6.5/217.4 = 3$ per cent

Phasor Diagram of a Loaded Transformer.   Figure 12-25 is the phasor diagram of a loaded transformer based on the circuit diagram of Fig. 10-25(*b*).   Since the primary and secondary voltages have such widely different values in most transformers, it is customary, when drawing the diagram for illustrative purposes, to assume a turn ratio of 1:1.

In Fig. 12-25 the right half of the diagram pertains to the secondary while the left half pertains to the primary of a loaded transformer. On the secondary side let $\mathbf{E}_2$ be the terminal voltage and let $\mathbf{I}_2$ be the second_ary load current, which is assumed to lag the $\mathbf{E}_2$ by an angle θ_2 such that $\cos \theta_2 = 0.80$. If the secondary load current be taken as reference phasor on the secondary side, it follows that $\mathbf{E}_2 = E_2 \underline{/\theta_2}$ and

$$\mathbf{E}_{g2} = E_2 \cos \theta_2 + R_2 I_2 + j(E_2 \sin \theta_2 + X_2 I_2)$$

where E_{g2} is the voltage induced in the secondary winding by the sinusoidally varying flux ϕ, and R_2 and X_2 are the resistance and the leakage

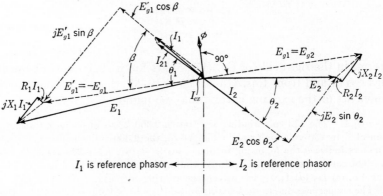

FIG. 12-25. Phasor diagram of a loaded transformer. Turn ratio $= 1:1$. Power factor $= 0.80$, current lagging.

reactance, respectively, of the secondary winding. Moreover, $\mathbf{E}_{g2}$ must lag ϕ by 90 deg, so ϕ leads $\mathbf{E}_{g2}$ by the same angle and its position in the diagram is determined as shown.

It has already been shown that the phasor sum of the secondary ampere-turns $N_2\mathbf{I}_2$ and the primary load ampere-turns $N_1\mathbf{I}_{21}$ is zero. In the present instance, since a 1:1 turn ratio is assumed, it follows that $\mathbf{I}_{21} = -\mathbf{I}_2$. Thus in the phasor diagram pertaining to the primary, $\mathbf{I}_{21} = -\mathbf{I}_2$ is located and the primary current $\mathbf{I}_1$ is found by adding to $\mathbf{I}_{21}$ the exciting current $\mathbf{I}_{ex}$ determined from the open-circuit test. $\mathbf{I}_1$ is taken as the reference. The primary induced voltage $\mathbf{E}_{g1}$ is equal in magnitude to $\mathbf{E}_{g2}$ but appears as a counterelectromotive force in the primary and is thus reversed in sign in the phasor diagram of the primary. The primary impressed voltage $\mathbf{E}_1$ is obviously equal to the sum of $-\mathbf{E}_{g1}$

and the voltage consumed in the impedance of the primary winding or

$$\mathbf{E}_1 = -E_{g1} \cos \beta + R_1 I_1 + j(-E_{g1} \sin \beta + X_1 I_1)$$

where R_1 = resistance of primary winding

X_1 = inductive reactance of primary winding

The angle of lag of the primary current is θ_1.

Equivalent Resistance and Equivalent Reactance. If the small voltage consumed by the exciting current in the impedance of the primary winding be neglected, it may be shown that the circuit diagrams of Fig. 13-25 are electrically equivalent to the circuit diagram of Fig. 10-25. The *equivalent diagrams* of Fig. 13-25 may therefore be used to predict the performance of a transformer.

In any transformer the active power that is lost as heat in the resistances of the primary and secondary windings must obviously be supplied from the circuit to which the primary is connected. If R_1 and R_2 are the primary and secondary resistances, respectively, and I_1 and I_2 are the primary and secondary currents, a portion of the primary input equal to

$$P = R_1 I_1{}^2 + R_2 I_2{}^2 = R_{12} I_2{}^2 + R_2 I_2{}^2 \quad \text{watts}$$

is lost as heat in the windings. If the primary resistance were reduced to zero and the secondary resistance were increased by an amount R_{12} such that the total heat loss in the transformer remained unchanged, then

$$R_{12} I_2{}^2 = R_1 I_1{}^2$$

But since the exciting current is negligible by assumption,

$$I_1{}^2 = \left(\frac{N_2}{N_1}\right)^2 I_2{}^2$$

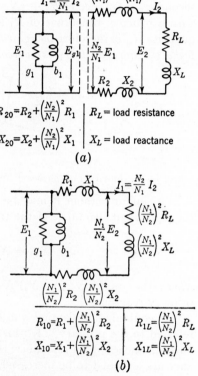

$$R_{20} = R_2 + \left(\frac{N_2}{N_1}\right)^2 R_1 \quad R_L = \text{load resistance}$$

$$X_{20} = X_2 + \left(\frac{N_2}{N_1}\right)^2 X_1 \quad X_L = \text{load reactance}$$

(a)

$$R_{10} = R_1 + \left(\frac{N_1}{N_2}\right)^2 R_2 \quad R_{1L} = \left(\frac{N_1}{N_2}\right)^2 R_L$$

$$X_{10} = X_1 + \left(\frac{N_1}{N_2}\right)^2 X_2 \quad X_{1L} = \left(\frac{N_1}{N_2}\right)^2 X_L$$

(b)

Fig. 13-25. The equivalent circuit of a transformer: (a) referred to the secondary; (b) referred to the primary.

and hence

$$R_{12} = \left(\frac{N_2}{N_1}\right)^2 R_1$$

The total resistance of the secondary would then be

$$R_{20} = R_2 + \left(\frac{N_2}{N_1}\right)^2 R_1 \tag{18-25}$$

This means that a transformer with a primary resistance of zero and a secondary resistance of $R_2 + (N_2/N_1)^2 R_1$ has the same copper loss as one with a primary resistance of R_1 and a secondary resistance of R_2. The quantity R_{20} is therefore *the equivalent resistance of the transformer, referred to the secondary, while R_{12} is the secondary equivalent of the primary resistance.*

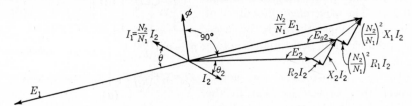

FIG. 14-25. Transformer phasor diagram using equivalent values of R_{20} and X_{20}.

In a similar manner it may be shown that, referred to the secondary, the equivalent reactance of the transformer is

$$X_{20} = X_2 + \left(\frac{N_2}{N_1}\right)^2 X_1 \tag{19-25}$$

where the quantity $(N_2/N_1)^2 X_1$ is the secondary equivalent of the primary reactance.

The equivalent resistance and reactance of a transformer may also be referred to the primary. In this case the secondary is assumed to have no resistance and no reactance, while the primary resistance and reactance are assumed to be increased, respectively, by the amounts

$$R_{21} = \left(\frac{N_1}{N_2}\right)^2 R_2$$

and

$$X_{21} = \left(\frac{N_1}{N_2}\right)^2 X_2$$

Referred to the primary, the equivalent resistance of the transformer is

$$R_{10} = R_1 + R_{21} = R_1 + \left(\frac{N_1}{N_2}\right)^2 R_2 \tag{20-25}$$

while the equivalent reactance is

$$X_{10} = X_1 + X_{21} = X_1 + \left(\frac{N_1}{N_2}\right)^2 X_2$$

The transformer phasor diagram corresponding to the equivalent-circuit diagram of Fig. 13-25(a) is shown in Fig. 14-25.

It is of interest to observe that if the secondary and primary windings have the same current density and the same mean length of turn, the ratio of secondary to primary resistance is equal to the square of the ratio of transformation and the primary and secondary copper losses are equal. These relations may be proved readily.

Let the following symbols be in the mil-foot system of units and let

A_1 = cross-sectional area of primary copper
A_2 = cross-sectional area of secondary copper
l_1 = total length of primary winding
l_2 = total length of secondary winding
R_1 = resistance of primary winding
R_2 = resistance of secondary winding

Then

$$l_2 = \frac{N_2}{N_1} l_1$$

$$A_2 = \frac{N_1}{N_2} A_1$$

$$\frac{l_2}{A_2} = \left(\frac{N_2}{N_1}\right)^2 \frac{l_1}{A_1}$$

$$\frac{R_2}{R_1} = \frac{l_2}{A_2} \div \frac{l_1}{A_1}$$

$$= \left(\frac{N_2}{N_1}\right)^2$$

By Eq. (11-25),

$$\frac{I_2}{I_1} = \frac{N_1}{N_2}$$

hence

$$\frac{I_2^2}{I_1^2} = \left(\frac{N_1}{N_2}\right)^2$$

Accordingly, the ratio of the copper losses is

$$\frac{R_2 I_2^2}{R_1 I_1^2} = \left(\frac{N_2}{N_1}\right)^2 \left(\frac{N_1}{N_2}\right)^2 = 1$$

and

$$R_2 I_2^2 = R_1 I_1^2$$

Under the assumptions stated, the equivalent resistance of the transformer referred to either winding is equal to twice the resistance of that winding. A similar statement holds for the equivalent reactance.

It is customary to express the equivalent resistance and the equivalent reactance of transformers in per cents. The per cent reactance of a transformer is the voltage drop in the equivalent reactance due to rated current, expressed as a percentage of the rated terminal voltage. A similar statement holds for the per cent resistance. Given the transformer rating and the per cent reactance and resistance, the ohms reactance and resistance may be found.

Example 2. A 1,000-kva 13,200-volt to 2,400-volt 60-cycle transformer has 0.73 per cent resistance and 6.8 per cent reactance. Find the equivalent reactance and the equivalent resistance of the transformer in ohms, referred to (a) the high-voltage winding and (b) the low-voltage winding.

(a) The rated current in the high-voltage winding is

$$I_1 = \frac{1,000}{13.2} = 75.8 \text{ amp}$$

Referred to the high-voltage side the reactance drop is

$$X_1 I_1 = 0.068 \times 13,200 = 898 \text{ volts}$$

while the resistance drop is

$$R_1 I_1 = 0.0073 \times 13,200 = 96.3 \text{ volts}$$

hence referred to the high-voltage side the equivalent reactance is

$$X_1 = \frac{898}{75.8} = 11.8 \text{ ohms}$$

and the equivalent resistance is

$$R_1 = \frac{96.3}{75.8} = 1.27 \text{ ohms}$$

(b) The corresponding quantities, referred to the low-voltage side, are

$$I_2 = \frac{1,000}{2.4} = 417 \text{ amp}$$

$$X_2 = \frac{0.068 \times 2,400}{417} = 0.392 \text{ ohm}$$

$$R_2 = \frac{0.0073 \times 2,400}{417} = 0.0420 \text{ ohm}$$

Short-circuit Test. The values of the equivalent resistance and equivalent reactance may be measured experimentally. To do this, one winding—preferably the low-voltage winding—is short-circuited and a reduced potential difference of sufficient magnitude to cause rated current to circulate in the short circuit is impressed on the other winding. Circuit connections are as indicated in Fig. 15-25(a). In transformers of small or moderate sizes the applied potential difference required to circulate rated current under these conditions is usually from 4 to 6 per cent of the rated terminal voltage. Approximately one-half of the applied voltage is used to force the current through the impedance of the primary, so the counter emf generated in the primary is only from 2 to 3 per cent of the rated voltage and the flux is from 2 to 3 per cent of the value it would have under normal operating conditions. The exciting current

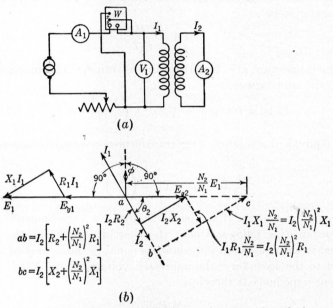

(a)

(b)

Fig. 15-25. The short-circuit test. Equivalent resistance and equivalent reactance.

required to produce this small flux is negligible with respect to the short-circuit current, and accordingly one may assume primary and secondary ampere-turns to be equal; whence

$$I_1 = \frac{N_2}{N_1} I_2$$

The iron losses in the transformer core are proportional to the square of the flux density (approximately), but because the core flux density is very low, the core losses are negligible. Substantially all the power input to the transformer is consumed as copper loss, so the reading of the wattmeter may be equated to the loss in the equivalent resistance of the transformer. If P is the wattmeter reading, the loss in the equivalent resistance of the transformer, referred to the secondary, is

$$P = R_2 I_2{}^2 + \left(\frac{N_2}{N_1}\right)^2 R_1 I_2{}^2.$$

and the equivalent resistance is

$$\frac{P}{I_2^2} = R_2 + \left(\frac{N_2}{N_1}\right)^2 R_1 \tag{21-25}$$

The power factors of the primary and the secondary are substantially equal because the exciting current and the iron losses are negligible.

The power factor may be found from readings of wattmeter, voltmeter, and ammeter to be

$$\cos \theta = \frac{P}{E_1 I_1}$$

from which one may also find the value of tan θ. The reactive power input to the transformer is

$$Q = P \tan \theta = X_2 I_2^2 + \left(\frac{N_2}{N_1}\right)^2 X_1 I_2^2$$

and the equivalent reactance of the transformer, referred to the secondary, is

$$\frac{Q}{I_2^2} = X_{20} = X_2 + \left(\frac{N_2}{N_1}\right)^2 X_1 \tag{22-25}$$

One may also find the equivalent reactance from the known resistance and impedance as follows: Under short-circuit conditions the voltage consumed in the equivalent impedance is equal to the impressed voltage. Referred to the secondary, the impressed voltage is $(N_2/N_1)E_1$ and the equivalent impedance is therefore

$$Z_{20} = \frac{N_2 E_1}{N_1 I_2}$$

But

$$Z_{20}^2 = R_{20}^2 + X_{20}^2$$

Hence

$$X_{20} = \sqrt{Z_{20}^2 - R_{20}^2}$$

Regulation. When the full rated load is thrown off the secondary of a transformer, with the primary voltage assumed to remain constant, the secondary voltage usually changes. One hundred times the amount of this voltage change, divided by the full-load secondary terminal voltage, is the *percentage regulation* of the transformer for rated load and the specified power factor. When no power factor is specified, unity power factor is assumed. Thus if the constant primary voltage is E_1, E_2 is the secondary terminal voltage at full load, and $E_{20} = (N_2/N_1)E_1$ is the secondary terminal voltage when the load is thrown off,

$$\text{Percentage regulation} = \frac{100(E_{20} - E_2)}{E_2} \tag{23-25}$$

For loads of the type usually encountered in practice, the regulation of a transformer is very small. When the power factor of the load is unity, the regulation is of the order of 1 per cent. With lagging currents as well as with leading currents of low power factors, the regulation is greater than with unity-power-factor loads. The reason for this is clearly evident from the way the voltage consumed by the impedance adds to $\mathbf{E}_2$ in the diagrams of Figs. 14-25 and 16-25. When θ_2 is negative (current lagging), $(N_2/N_1)E_1$ is always greater than E_2, and the difference between

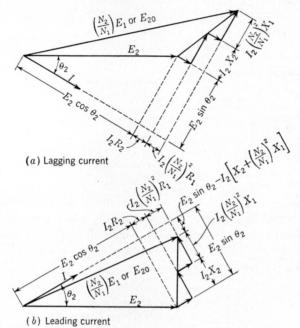

(a) Lagging current

(b) Leading current

FIG. 16-25. Phasor diagram for computing regulation.

them increases as θ_2 increases. When θ_2 is positive (current leading), $(N_2/N_1)E_1$ may be greater than, equal to, or less than E_2. When θ_2 is large, $(N_2/N_1)E_1$ is less than E_2 and the *regulation* is negative. Thus with lagging current E_2 falls with increase of load, while with leading current it may rise as the load increases.

Because of the large amount of space required between windings, high-voltage transformers have higher leakage reactances and greater regulations than low-voltage transformers.

Calculating the Regulation. The regulation for a known load and power factor is conveniently calculated with the aid of a diagram like one of those in Fig. 16-25. In these figures, $\mathbf{E}_2$ is the secondary terminal voltage and $\mathbf{E}_{20}$ is the primary impressed voltage referred to the secondary. The former is resolved into two components, one ($\mathbf{E}_p$) in phase with the current and the other $(\mathbf{E}_q)$ in quadrature with the current. From the diagrams, the first of these is observed to be

$$E_p = E_2 \cos \theta_2 + I_2 \left[R_2 + \left(\frac{N_2}{N_1} \right)^2 R_1 \right]$$
$$= E_2 \cos \theta_2 + I_2 R_{20} \qquad (24\text{-}25)$$

For the case of lagging current the magnitude of the second component is

$$E_q = E_2 \sin \theta_2 + I_2 \left[X_2 + \left(\frac{N_2}{N_1} \right)^2 X_1 \right]$$
$$= E_2 \sin \theta_2 + I_2 X_{20} \qquad (25\text{-}25)$$

while for leading current it is

$$E_q = E_2 \sin \theta_2 - I_2 X_{20}$$

The length of $\mathbf{E}_{20}$ is

$$E_{20} = \sqrt{E_p{}^2 + E_q{}^2}$$
$$= \sqrt{(E_2 \cos \theta_2 + I_2 R_{20})^2 + (E_2 \sin \theta_2 \pm I_2 X_{20})^2} \qquad (26\text{-}25)$$

provided the $\pm$ sign in the second term under the radical is taken to mean plus when the current lags and minus when the current leads. When the power factor is unity, either sign will give the correct result.

The form of Eq. (26-25) can be simplified by dividing each side by E_2 and changing the notation as follows:

$$\frac{E_{20}}{E_2} = \sqrt{(m + r)^2 + (n \pm x)^2}$$

where $m = \cos \theta_2$
$n = \sin \theta_2$
$r = I_2 R_{20}/E_2$
$x = I_2 X_{20}/E_2$

The percentage regulation is the quotient $100 \left(\dfrac{E_{20} - E_2}{E_2} \right)$. By subtracting unity from each side of the above equation and expressing the result in percentage one obtains, after rearranging,

$$\text{Percentage regulation} = \frac{100(E_{20} - E_2)}{E_2}$$
$$= 100[\sqrt{(m + r)^2 + (n \pm x)^2} - 1] \qquad (27\text{-}25)$$

The term under the radical with the double sign is plus for lagging currents and minus for leading currents, as mentioned above.

Example 3. On short-circuit test, with the low-voltage winding short-circuited as in Fig. 15-25, a 50-kva 2,300/230-volt 60-cycle distribution transformer yields the following readings:

$$\text{Watts copper loss} = 620$$
$$E_{20} = 87 \text{ volts}$$
$$I_2 = 217 \text{ amp}$$

Find the regulation (a) at unity power factor, (b) at 0.80 power factor, current lagging, (c) at 0.80 power factor, current leading.

Since an impressed voltage of only 87 volts is required on the high-potential winding to circulate rated current of 50,000/230 or 217 amp in the short-circuited secondary, the flux density in the core is low, the iron losses are negligible, and the wattmeter reading of 620 watts represents the copper losses. Referred to the low-voltage side,

$$R_{20} = \frac{620}{217^2} = 0.0132 \text{ ohm}$$

Referred to the low-voltage side, the impressed voltage is $^{87}\!/_{10}$ or 8.7 volts, and the equivalent impedance is

$$Z_{20} = \frac{8.7}{217} = 0.040 \text{ ohm}$$

The equivalent reactance is

$$X_{20} = \sqrt{0.040^2 - 0.0132^2} = 0.0378 \text{ ohm}$$

By Eq. (26-25) and the above, the regulation at each of the assumed power factors is computed as follows:

(a) Unity power factor:

$$\text{Regulation} = \frac{100[\sqrt{(230 + 217 \times 0.0132)^2 + (217 \times 0.0378)^2} - 230]}{230}$$
$$= 1.3 \text{ per cent}$$

(b) 0.80 power factor (lagging):
Regulation

$$= \frac{100[(\sqrt{(230 \times 0.8 + 217 \times 0.0132)^2 + (230 \times 0.6 + 217 \times 0.0378)^2} - 230]}{230}$$
$$= 3.16 \text{ per cent}$$

(c) 0.80 power factor (leading):
Regulation

$$= \frac{100[\sqrt{(230 \times 0.8 + 217 \times 0.0132)^2 + (230 \times 0.6 - 217 \times 0.0378)^2} - 230]}{230}$$
$$= -1.08 \text{ per cent}$$

Rating. The rating of a transformer is a statement by the manufacturer of the conditions under which it may be operated without exceeding certain limitations, principally concerning temperature rise, insulation, etc. The essential data appear on the name plate.

The temperature rise is determined by the losses and the cooling facilities. The core losses depend upon the impressed voltage and the frequency (pages 228–229); the copper losses depend upon the load current. The rating therefore specifies the output, voltage, and frequency. Output is usually expressed in kilovolt-amperes, for this is equivalent to specifying the load current. A temperature rise of 55 C is standard for class A insulation (page 242). This rise is based on air temperature at 40 C for "air-blast" and self-cooled transformers and on cooling water entering the cooling system at 25 C when water is the cooling medium.

Losses. The losses in a transformer are classified as follows:

1. *No-load Losses.* These consist principally of eddy-current and hysteresis losses in the core (core losses). The factors upon which core losses depend are the frequency and the flux density in the core and these losses are substantially independent of the load. The following equations show how the losses are affected by these variables:

$$P_h = k_h f B_{max}^{1.6} \qquad \text{watts hysteresis loss}$$
$$P_e = k_e f^2 B_{max}^{2} \qquad \text{watts eddy-current loss}$$

In the first equation, however, the exponent of B varies somewhat depending upon the type of steel used. Derivations of these equations are found on pages 89 and 103.

It is important that transformers be operated at the frequency and voltage for which they are designed. A frequency higher than normal lowers the flux density in proportion to the increase in frequency, but the core loss remains approximately constant. A frequency lower than normal increases the flux density and therefore increases the saturation above normal and causes excessive magnetizing current. Hysteresis loss is also increased. Both these result in increased heat loss and reduced efficiency. A voltage higher than normal causes a correspondingly higher core flux density and also results in excessive heating, but a transformer may be operated at 5 per cent above rated voltage without danger of overheating. Operation with less than normal voltage reduces the losses somewhat, but the permissible power output is also reduced approximately in proportion to the reduction in voltage.

No-load losses also include a small copper loss $(I_{ex}^2 R_1)$ due to the presence of the exciting current in the primary resistance, and a small dielectric loss in the insulation. These are usually of negligible amounts.

No-load losses are measured by the wattmeter in the open-circuit test described on page 405.

2. *Load Losses.* These consist principally of I^2R losses in the transformer windings. They are represented by $I^2 R_{eq}$ and are proportional to the square of the load current. Additional losses are caused by induced eddy currents set up in the windings, in the core clamps, in the tank, etc.

The currents are generated by stray magnetic fields and depend upon the load. These losses may amount to as much as 50 per cent of the I^2R loss. Normally they are not over 10 to 20 per cent.

The load losses, including the eddy-current losses just mentioned, are measured by the wattmeter in the short-circuit test described on page 410.

Core losses are kept to a minimum by the use of high-quality annealed electric sheet steel. Sheets 0.014 in. thick are used for 60-cycle transformers, and sheets 0.025 in. thick are used for 25-cycle transformers. Electrical steel has a high permeability, low coercive force, and high electrical resistance. These properties keep eddy-current and hysteresis losses at a low level and reduce temperature rise in the transformer.

Efficiency. The percentage efficiency of a transformer is 100 times the ratio of power output to power input. For reasons discussed under losses, the efficiency should be determined for rated conditions of load, impressed voltage, and frequency, and for the specified power factor. When no power factor is specified, unity power factor is assumed. The voltage wave should approximate the sine shape and temperature should normally be corrected to 75 C.

The efficiency may be calculated from direct measurement of input and output, or from output and losses thus:

$$\text{Percentage efficiency} = \frac{\text{output}}{\text{input}} \qquad (28\text{-}25)$$

$$= \frac{\text{output}}{\text{output} + \text{losses}} \qquad (29\text{-}25)$$

Example 4. The efficiency of a 50-kva 2,300/230-volt 60-cycle transformer is desired for unity-power-factor load. The open-circuit data of the transformer are given in the example on page 405, while the short-circuit data are found in the example on page 415. Find the efficiency of the transformer at (*a*) full load, (*b*) half load.

a. From Example 1 (page 405)

$$\text{Core losses} = 185 \text{ watts}$$

From Example 3 (page 415)

$$\text{Full load } I^2R_{eq} = 620 \text{ watts}$$
$$\text{Total losses} = 805 \text{ watts}$$
$$\text{Efficiency} = \frac{100(50,000)}{50,805}$$
$$= 98.4 \text{ per cent}$$

b. At half load the core loss is the same as at full load, because the flux (and therefore the flux density) depends only upon the impressed voltage. The impressed voltage is constant so the core loss is also constant. At constant impressed voltage the copper loss is proportional to the square of the load current and hence to the square of the output. Accordingly,

$$\text{Core loss} = 185 \text{ watts}$$
$$I^2R \text{ loss} = 620 \div 4$$
$$= 155 \text{ watts}$$
$$\text{Total loss} = 340 \text{ watts}$$
$$\text{Efficiency} = \frac{100(25,000)}{25,340}$$
$$= 98.7 \text{ per cent}^1$$

All-day Efficiency.   *All-day efficiency* is the ratio of energy (kilowatthours) delivered in a 24-hr period divided by energy (kilowatthours) input in the same length of time.   Transformers used on residence-lighting circuits (and distribution circuits generally) are either idle or only lightly loaded during much of the 24-hr period.   However, they must at all times be connected to the line and ready to serve, so that the core losses are being supplied continually.   It is therefore very important that such transformers be designed for minimum core loss.   The copper losses are relatively less important, since they depend on the load.   Because they are lightly loaded much of the time, distribution transformers are designed for relatively large full-load copper loss and have their maximum power efficiencies at light loads.   This design results in improved all-day efficiency for these transformers.   Power transformers, on the other hand, are loaded more or less continuously and are designed for full-load copper losses equal to about twice the no-load losses.

To find the all-day efficiency, it is necessary to know how the load on the transformer varies from hour to hour.   The quotient obtained by dividing the energy output by the energy output plus the energy losses over a 24-hr period yields the efficiency expressed as a decimal fraction. Practical calculations are facilitated by the use of a *load factor*.

Preferred Voltages.   Certain voltages have become nominally standard for different sections of transmission or distribution systems.   Preferred secondary or utilization voltages are 120, 240, 480, 600, and 2,400, while preferred primary-distribution voltages are 480, 600, 2,400, 2,400/ 4,160 Y, 4,800, 7,200, 7,620/13,200 Y, 14,400, 25,000, 34,500, 46,000, and 69,000.   The preferred voltages at which power is transmitted over greater distances are 46,000, 69,000, 92,000, 115,000, 138,000, 161,000, 196,000, 230,000, 287,000, and 345,000.   Transmission and distribution voltages are chosen with reference to conditions of economy and standardization.   Heavy power circuits require high voltages, particularly if they are many miles long.   Preferred service voltages for lighting and small motors are 240 and 120 volts.   Other common low voltages are 480 and 600.   Large motors may be operated at voltages of 2,400, 4,800, or 7,200.

---

[1] It should be observed that the efficiency at half load is higher than the full-load efficiency. Distribution transformers have their maximum efficiencies between quarter load and half load, while power transformers usually are most efficient at about 70 per cent load.   The reason for this is explained in the following section.

Transformers are designed to transfer power between circuits with a variety of voltages, and so a variety of transformer ratios are required. Common ratios for distribution circuits are from 2,400 to 240/120 and from 2,400 to 480/240 volts.

Polarity. The rules of the American Institute of Electrical Engineers provide for the marking of transformer leads in a uniform manner in order to facilitate the making of proper connections. In accordance with these rules the high-voltage leads appearing on the outside of the case are marked H_1, H_2, etc., and the low-voltage leads are marked X_1, X_2, etc.

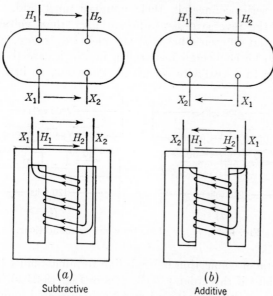

(a) Subtractive   (b) Additive

FIG. 17-25. Transformer polarity: (a) subtractive; (b) additive.

The order of the markings is so chosen that "when H_1 and X_1 are connected together and voltage is applied to the transformer, the voltage between the highest numbered H lead and the highest numbered X lead shall be less than the voltage of the full high-voltage winding."

When H_1 and X_1 are adjacent, as in Fig. 17-25(a), and the adjacent ends of the high-voltage and low-voltage windings (H_1 and X_1) are connected together, the voltage between the two remaining leads is less than the voltage of the high-potential winding. The *polarity* of the transformer is then said to be *subtractive*. When H_1 and X_1 are diagonally opposite each other, as in Fig. 17-25(b), connecting a high-voltage lead to the adjacent low-voltage lead (H_1 to X_2) results in the addition of the induced voltages. The voltage between the two remaining leads is then larger than the voltage of the full high-potential winding and the polarity of the transformer is *additive*.

Transformers with leads that are properly marked in accordance with the foregoing rules may be connected together for parallel operation or for operation in three-phase circuits without difficulty.

Single-phase Circuit Connections.   Standard distribution transformers receive power from 2,400-volt circuits and deliver it to 240- or 120-volt circuits.   The low-voltage winding consists of two equal coils, each wound for 120 volts.   The secondaries may be connected in series for operation on either a two-wire 240-volt system or a three-wire 240/120-volt system, as shown in Fig. 18-25(a).   When· the secondaries are cumulatively series-connected, their voltages must add.   If they are connected in the reverse order (differentially), their voltages subtract and the potential difference between outside wires is zero.   The secondaries may also be connected in parallel, in which case the transformer delivers power to a two-wire circuit at 120 volts, as in Fig. 18-25(b).

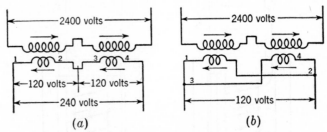

Fig. 18-25. Single-phase transformer connections.

When the parallel connection is used, like terminals must be connected together.   Thus, if the order 1, 2, 3, 4 as in Fig. 18-25(a) is the correct series connection, then terminals 1 and 3 are connected to one side of the 120-volt line and 2 and 4 to the opposite side, to make the correct parallel connection.   If either the terminals 3 and 4 or 1 and 2 were reversed, a 240-volt short circuit would exist in the secondary.   Corresponding polarities may be found either from a wiring diagram furnished with the transformer or by test.   The current output at full load with connection (b) is double that in (a).

While the voltages mentioned are standard, some variations from standard exist in all systems.   In order to make it possible to obtain approximately correct voltages for the lamps and motors on the low-potential circuits, some adjustment in the transformer ratio must be possible.   This adjustment is provided by means of taps as illustrated in Fig. 19-25.   Thus 2,400-volt distribution transformers may have two taps, of approximately 5 per cent each.   These make it possible to secure the normal secondary voltage, even though the feeder voltage may have dropped or risen by 5 per cent.

Two-phase Circuit Connections. Two-phase systems were formerly much used but are now practically obsolete. Three-phase systems are standard and only remnants of old two-phase systems remain. These are supplied from three-phase systems with the use of single-phase transformers.

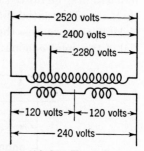

FIG. 19-25. Transformer with taps.

In two-phase systems, two types of connections are used. These are the three-wire system and the four-wire system illustrated in Figs. 20-25 and 21-25, respectively. Of these the four-wire system is by far the more common. The four-wire system is essentially two separate single-phase systems with voltages and currents, respectively, 90 time degrees out of phase. In the three-wire system the current in the common lead is $\sqrt{2}$ times the current in one of the outside wires, while the potential difference between the outside mains is $\sqrt{2}$ times the potential difference between the common wire and one of the outside wires. This is apparent from the phasor diagram Fig. 20-25(*b*), for by Kirchhoff's law of voltages $\mathbf{E}_a - \mathbf{E}_b = \mathbf{E}_0$, and by his law of currents $\mathbf{I}_a + \mathbf{I}_b = \mathbf{I}_0$.

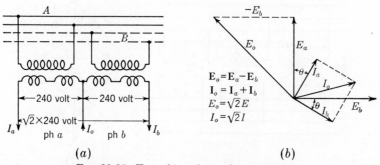

$$\mathbf{E}_0 = \mathbf{E}_a - \mathbf{E}_b$$
$$\mathbf{I}_0 = \mathbf{I}_a + \mathbf{I}_b$$
$$E_0 = \sqrt{2}\,E$$
$$I_0 = \sqrt{2}\,I$$

(*a*)   (*b*)

FIG. 20-25. Two-phase three-wire connection.

Three-phase Connections. Three-phase transformations may be made with the use of properly connected single-phase transformers. These connections are in extensive commercial use. The most frequently used connections are the following:

> Primary Y—secondary Y
> Primary Δ—secondary Δ
> Primary Δ—secondary Y, or vice versa
> Primary and secondary open Δ
> Primary T—secondary T

In the following discussion, balanced loads are assumed.

connection. Figure 22-25 illustrates this connection, which is sometimes, though infrequently, used. The line phasor potential differences are the dotted lines $\mathbf{E}_{ab}$, $\mathbf{E}_{bc}$, and $\mathbf{E}_{ca}$ in (b), corresponding to the three equal potential differences of a three-phase generator. The potential differences across the primary windings are $\mathbf{E}_{oa}$, $\mathbf{E}_{ob}$, and $\mathbf{E}_{oc}$, the potential of the point o being the same as that of the points 2, 4, and 6, while a,

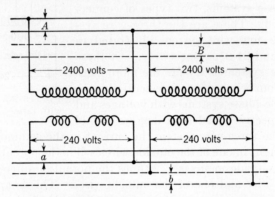

FIG. 21-25. Two-phase four-wire connection.

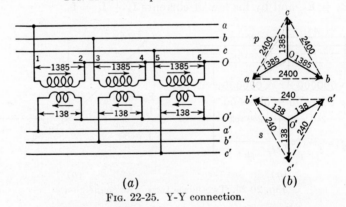

(a)   (b)

FIG. 22-25. Y-Y connection.

b, and c have, respectively, the same potentials as 1, 3, and 5. By Kirchhoff's law of voltages,

$$\mathbf{E}_{ab} + \mathbf{E}_{bo} + \mathbf{E}_{oa} = 0$$

or

$$\mathbf{E}_{ab} = \mathbf{E}_{ob} - \mathbf{E}_{oa}$$

where $\mathbf{E}_{ob}$ means $-\mathbf{E}_{bo}$. Similarly,

$$\mathbf{E}_{bc} = \mathbf{E}_{oc} - \mathbf{E}_{ob}$$

and

$$\mathbf{E}_{ca} = \mathbf{E}_{oa} - \mathbf{E}_{oc}$$

Since the induced voltage in the secondary of a transformer is always
180 time degrees out of phase with the impressed voltage, $a'b'$, $b'c'$, and
$c'a'$ are drawn in opposite directions to ab, bc, and ca, respectively, in the
phasor diagram of voltages.

When the line voltage is 2,400, the voltage across a primary winding is
$2,400 \div \sqrt{3}$, that across a secondary winding is $2,400/(10\sqrt{3})$, and the
secondary line voltage is

$$\frac{2,400 \sqrt{3}}{10 \sqrt{3}} = 240$$

The current I_c in the transformer coil is the same as the line current I_2.

2. Δ-Δ *Connection.* This is a very common connection. Full line
voltages are impressed on the primary windings. Since the phasor sum
of the three line voltages is zero, no 60-cycle current circulates in either

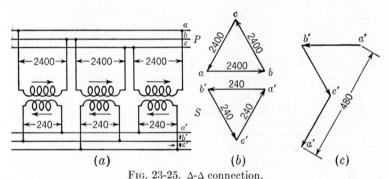

FIG. 23-25. Δ-Δ connection.

the primary or secondary delta mesh. The secondaries must be so connected that when one of the vertices is open, the potential difference
between the open ends is zero. Should one of the secondaries, as, for
example, $c'a'$, be reversed, the phasor diagram of secondary voltages
would be as in (c) (Fig. 23-25) and the potential difference between the
open ends would be 480 volts. Closing the mesh would then result in
a very large circulating current.

The current in a transformer coil is the line current divided by $\sqrt{3}$.

3. Δ-*Y and Y-*Δ *Connections.* These are combinations of the two foregoing connections. In Fig. 24-25 the primary is Δ-connected and the
secondary is Y-connected; the transformer ratio is 20:1. Underground
systems are fed from 2,400-volt mains with this connection. They
employ a fourth wire connected to the neutral of the low side. The
voltage between one line and neutral is 120, while the line voltage is 208.
Single-phase service is supplied from the 120-volt line to neutral connections, while three-phase service is supplied from the outside wires. When
the neutral wire has the same cross section as the three outside wires,

a saving of 56 per cent is made in the cost of copper as compared with a 120-volt single-phase system.

If the primary had been connected in Y and the secondary in Δ, the primary coil voltage would have been 2,400 ÷ $\sqrt{3}$ or 1,385 volts and the secondary coil voltage would have been 1,385 ÷ 20 = 69.2 volts. Thus, in effect, the use of these connections makes it possible to raise or lower the transformation ratio by the factor $\sqrt{3}$. It should also be observed that the secondary line voltages are not in phase opposition with the corresponding primary line voltages but are displaced therefrom by 30 deg. A bank of Y-Δ- or Δ-Y-connected transformers may therefore not be paralleled with a Δ-Δ or a Y-Y bank, even though the voltages and frequency have the correct numerical values.

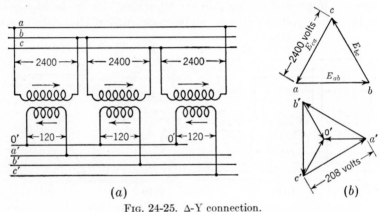

(a) (b)

Fig. 24-25. Δ-Y connection.

4. *Open-Δ or V Connection.* Three-phase service may be supplied with only two single-phase transformers either by means of the *open-Δ* or *V connection*, or by means of the T connection, which is not described in this edition. Either of these may be substituted for a Δ-connected bank with one transformer out of commission. The open-Δ connection, however, is far more commonly used than the T connection.

The open-Δ connection is illustrated in Fig. 25-25. If the internal impedance drop be neglected, the potential difference E_{ca} across the open primary terminals c and a is the same as though the third transformer were actually connected, and similarly for the secondary. With this connection, however, the current in each of the transformer coils is the line current, which at unity power factor is 30 deg out of phase with the transformer voltage (page 383). On unity power-factor load, therefore, the transformers themselves operate at a power factor of cos $\theta = \sqrt{3}/2$, or only 86.6 per cent. Hence, with the capacity of the Δ-connected bank taken as 100 per cent, the full-load output of the V-connected bank of two transformers is only $\frac{2}{3} \times \sqrt{3}/2 \times 100$ or 57.8 per cent.

Three-phase Transformers. It has been shown that voltage transformations from three-phase to three-phase may be accomplished with (usually) three interconnected single-phase transformers, The identical functions can also be performed by a single unit, called a *three-phase transformer*, in which three interlinked magnetic circuits are combined

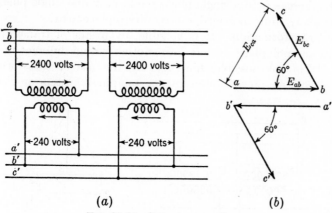

(*a*)   (*b*)

FIG. 25-25. Open-Δ connection.

with three interconnected groups of primary and secondary windings in the manner illustrated schematically in Fig. 26-25. For the sake of simplicity, only one set of windings is shown in each drawing. Actually, the coils of each primary and secondary winding are interleaved in a manner similar to those shown in Figs. 3-25 and 4-25. Primary and secondary

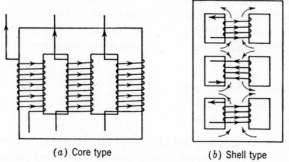

(*a*) Core type   (*b*) Shell type

FIG. 26-25. Three-phase transformers: (*a*) core type; (*b*) shell type.

windings may be connected to the primary and secondary three-phase networks, respectively, by Y-Y, Y-Δ, Δ-Y, or Δ-Δ connection as desired, or as conditions may require. Two general kinds of three-phase transformers are recognized, similar to single-phase transformers, depending upon the relative arrangements of windings and cores. These are the *core type* and the *shell type* illustrated in the figure.

A three-phase transformer of a given capacity and voltage rating costs substantially less than an equivalent bank of three single-phase transformers of the same capacity and voltage class. For this reason there is a growing tendency to prefer three-phase units. A disadvantage is that in case of failure of a three-phase transformer, the entire unit must be replaced, whereas with a single-phase bank, only one single-phase transformer is likely to be damaged and require replacement.

Phase Transformation. It is possible, by means of transformers, to transform one polyphase system into another with a different number of phases. It is not possible, however, by the use of transformers, to transform a single-phase system into a polyphase system or vice versa.

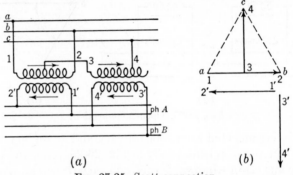

(a)   (b)

FIG. 27-25. Scott connection.

The power in a polyphase system is constant, while that in a single-phase system is pulsating (pages 361 and 379). Hence, such transformations require energy storage sufficient to make up the difference. Of this the transformer is incapable. Rotary machines are required to make such transformations. Some of the more common phase transformations are

1. Three-phase to six-phase
2. Three-phase to two-phase
3. Two-phase to six-phase

A discussion of these is beyond the scope of this book. The method of transforming from three-phase to two-phase, using the familiar *Scott connection*, will be mentioned briefly.

Scott Connection. In the Scott connection two transformers are used to transform power either from three-phase to two-phase, or vice versa. The coils connected to the three-phase side are provided with taps at the center and at 86.7 per cent of the full winding, as in Fig. 27-25(a). One end (3) of the transformer winding 3-4 is connected to the center tap of 1-2 to form the T connection, as in Fig. 27-25. The terminals of 1-2 and the 86.7 per cent tap of 3-4 are connected to the three-phase lines a, b, and c. Since the transformer primary voltages $E_{1\text{-}2}$ and $E_{3\text{-}4}$ are 90 deg out of phase, the corresponding secondary voltages are likewise 90 deg out of phase. Both secondary windings have the same number of turns, and hence the secondary voltages are equal. A balanced two-phase system is therefore formed by the secondaries.

Autotransformers. Autotransformers have certain parts of the primary and secondary windings in common, as shown in Fig. 28-25. This at once gives rise to certain important advantages as well as certain disadvantages.

Figure 28-25 illustrates a 20-kva autotransformer. The high-voltage winding comprises all the N_1 turns between 1 and 3, and the secondary winding has N_2 turns, or all the turns between 2 and 3. If the exciting current and the internal impedance drops are neglected, the primary and secondary ampere-turns are equal, and

$$\frac{I_2}{I_1} = \frac{N_1}{N_2} = \frac{E_1}{E_2}$$

just as in an ordinary potential transformer. Any secondary voltage E_2 between zero and E_1 may be obtained by simply moving the tap 2 to the desired location. In the illustra-
tion, 2 is halfway between 1 and 3, and so E_2 is half E_1. Since the primary and the secondary windings are common between 2 and 3, one may think of the primary current I_1 as flowing downward between 1 and 3, while the secondary current flows upward from 3 to 2. Accordingly, over the common section 3-2 there flows upward the difference between I_2 and I_1, or 45.5 amp, in the illustration. The 91 amp of secondary

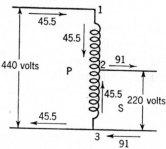

Fig. 28-25. Autotransformer supplying a 20-kva load.

output is made up of 45.5 amp supplied by the secondary and 45.5 amp supplied directly from the primary. Thus only half the energy output of the transformer is actually transformed; the other half passes over directly from the primary without passing through the secondary. The capacity of transformer required in the illustration is therefore only 10 kva, or one-half the output.

Autotransformers are cheaper than ordinary transformers of the same capacity, and they have better regulation, better efficiency, and less exciting current. These transformers may not be used to supply power to the ordinary distribution circuits, however, for since primary and secondary are electrically connected, they are unsafe. They are used to tie together transmission or distribution circuits of slightly different voltages, as, for example, an 11,000-volt system with a 13,200-volt system. They may also be used for obtaining partial line voltages for starting induction and synchronous motors with squirrel-cage windings.

Induction Regulators. The induction regulator is really a special type of potential transformer with primary winding mounted on a cylindrical

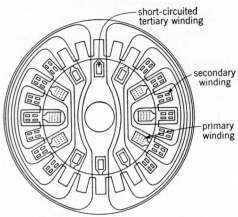

FIG. 29-25. Single-phase voltage regulator.

core that may be turned on its axis. The secondary winding is stationary. Both windings are mounted in slots, much as are the windings of an induction motor. A small air gap separates the stator from the rotor.

Regulators of this type are used to regulate the voltage on single-phase feeder circuits. Voltage drop in the feeder is compensated for by the voltage induced in the secondary of the regulator. The principle of

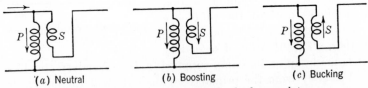

(a) Neutral   (b) Boosting   (c) Bucking

FIG. 30-25. Circuit connections for feeder regulator.

operation is illustrated in Fig. 29-25, while the electrical connections to the regulated feeder are shown in Fig. 30-25. Maximum voltage is induced in the secondary when the primary is in the position shown in Fig. 29-25, while, if the primary is turned through an angle of 90 deg from the position shown, the induced voltage in the secondary becomes zero. Turning the primary through an angle of more than 90 deg (but less than 180) causes the direction of the secondary voltage to be reversed.

The primary is connected between the two wires of the feeder, the voltage of which is to be regulated, while the secondary is connected in series with one of the feeder wires. Thus the voltage of the secondary may be added to or subtracted from the feeder voltage in any desired amount from zero to the maximum for which the regulator is designed. When the feeder voltage is too low, the regulator boosts it; when it is too high, the regulator bucks it down. The action is made automatic by means of a contact-making voltmeter on the feeder circuit, which controls a motor that drives the movable core upon which the primary is wound. Thus the core is turned either forward or backward the exact distance required to maintain constant voltage at the point of control for all loads.

Step-type Voltage Regulators. It was noted in Fig. 19-25 that transformers are often provided with taps for adjustment of turns ratio. Connections to these taps are ordinarily made with so-called *no-load tap changers*, that is to say, the switching apparatus provided for tap changing is intended for operation only when the transformer is deenergized. It is possible to design switching apparatus suitable for tap changing under load, and this equipment is used on a wide variety of transformer apparatus. One very common application of equipment for tap changing under load is illustrated in Fig. 31-25. An autotransformer is supplied with a number of taps permitting an adjustment of output voltage over a range of perhaps from 10 per cent over to 10 per cent under normal voltage. The tap-changing equipment is controlled by an automatic device which regulates voltage at some point on the power system. This apparatus is known as a *step-type voltage regulator*.

The sequence of operations of a typical load tap changer may be seen from a study of Fig. 31-25. Note that in (a) both leads, x and y, of the small autotransformer T_2 are connected to the highest tap of the main transformer T_1. Since T_2, called the *preventive autotransformer*, is center-tapped and the load current divides equally between the two halves, there is no net excitation on this core. The output voltage is approximately that of the highest tap.

In Fig. 31-25(b) contact y of T_2 has dropped to the next lower tap while x remains on the original position. The transformer T_2 now acts as a voltage divider, and the output voltage is approximately midway between that of the upper two taps.

In Fig. 31-25(c) the tap-changing cycle has been completed; both x and y are connected to the second tap, and the output voltage is approximately that of the lower tap. It is important to note that at no time during the tap-changing cycle is the load current interrupted, although for a short instant during the changing operation the current is carried by only half the preventive autotransformer and a small impedance drop is introduced into the circuit.

The actual switching is ordinarily done by an oil-immersed switch. In the larger sizes the actual interruption in lines x and y may be made by small auxiliary oil circuit breakers. Since step-type voltage regulators may be insulated according to the same practices that are used for other

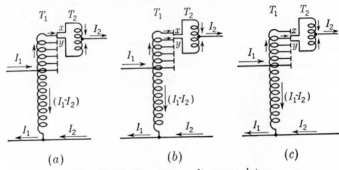

Fig. 31-25. Step-type voltage regulator.

transformers, they are suitable for operation on higher-voltage circuits than are induction regulators.

Constant-current Transformers. Constant-current transformers receive energy from constant-potential mains and deliver energy to constant-current circuits. Thus they serve as a means of supplying power to a series circuit from a constant-potential source. They are used principally to furnish power for the circuits of arc or incandescent street lighting.

In a series circuit the current is constant and the load is changed by changing the impressed voltage. This is accomplished in a constant-current transformer by varying automatically the equivalent leakage reactance to suit the load.

The principle of operation is illustrated in Fig. 32-25. One coil is stationary while the other one is movable, and its weight is partly balanced by a counterweight (W). Either coil may

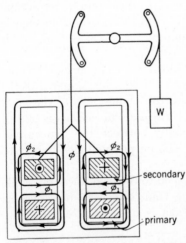

Fig. 32-25. Constant-current transformer.

usually be the movable coil. The openings through the coils are much larger than the core. This permits a large leakage flux to be set up through the coils when currents are maintained in them, as shown in the figure.

From the figure it is also apparent that a mechanical force of repulsion exists between the coils. This force tends to drive the movable coil upward on the core, and owing to the counterweight, a relatively small force produces motion. At maximum load the movable coil is close to the stationary one and the voltage induced in the former is a maximum. When the secondary load is reduced by cutting out some of the lamps in the series circuit, the current in the remaining units increases momentarily. This causes the force of repulsion to increase. The floating coil then moves upward and thereby increases the equivalent leakage reactance of the transformer, reduces the secondary voltage, and brings the current back to normal. The coil comes to rest when the terminal voltage is properly reduced to suit the lesser number of lamps and the current attains its correct constant value.

These transformers are built to receive power from 2,400-volt primaries and to deliver a constant current of from 4 to 10 amp, although 6.6 amp is the current most commonly used. The maximum secondary voltage is usually under 5,000. These transformers regulate automatically at all loads to within about 1 per cent of constant secondary current.

Instrument Transformers. Instrument transformers are made for use with metering instruments and control devices such as voltmeters, ammeters, watthour meters, and relays. They transform only small amounts of energy and are of two kinds, namely, *potential transformers* and *current transformers*.

Voltmeters and the potential coils of wattmeters, watthour meters, relays, etc., are usually designed for about 120 volts. In the case of voltmeters and wattmeters this corresponds to full-scale reading. When it is desired to measure higher voltages, as, for example, 2,400 volts, a *potential transformer* with a suitable turn ratio is used—in this case 20:1. The high-voltage winding is connected to the line of which the voltage is to be measured, while the low-voltage winding is connected in series with the potential coil of the meter (Fig. 33-25). The scale of the meter may be marked to indicate the voltage on the primary; in this case the combination of transformer and instrument comprises a direct-reading unit. In the above application the transformer serves the dual purpose of stepping the voltage down to a value suitable for the meter and at the same time insulating the meter from the high-voltage line and making it safe to handle.

The current coils of ammeters, wattmeters, watthour meters, and the relays used in a-c circuits are ordinarily not operated directly from circuits with potentials exceeding 120 volts. Moreover, ammeters and the current coils of wattmeters are usually designed for full-scale deflections with a low current of about 5 amp. When larger values of current are to be measured, or when the circuit voltage is too high for safe operation with direct connection to the meter, *current transformers* are used to secure the correct value of current for the meter and to insulate it from the high-voltage line.

The primary of the transformer consists of one or more turns, while the secondary usually has a considerably larger number of turns. The turn ratio depends upon but is not exactly equal to the ratio of the current in the line to the current in the meter at full-scale reading. The primary is connected in series with the circuit to be metered, and the secondary is connected in series with the meter (Fig. 33-25). The voltage induced in the secondary must be only just enough to force the required current through the combined impedance of the secondary and the meter coil, called its load or "burden." This is a very low voltage, and hence the transformer flux is also low. The flux, however, is produced by an excitation equal to the difference between the primary and

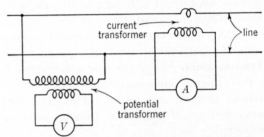

Fig. 33-25. Wiring diagrams for current and potential instrument transformers.

the secondary ampere-turns. When the instrument is disconnected from the secondary, the secondary ampere-turns disappear, the net excitation and therefore the core flux increase greatly, and the secondary voltage rises correspondingly. The voltage then may be high enough to break down the insulation. For this reason, before the burden on the secondary is removed, the secondary winding should be short-circuited.

Current instrument transformers, as pointed out above, do not have a turn ratio exactly equal to the ratio of the currents, because the secondary voltage required depends upon the impedance of the load. These transformers are calibrated with their burdens connected, and if they are used with a greatly different burden, the indication of the meter is incorrect.

Problems

1-25. The maximum value of the sinusoidal flux wave in the core of a 60-cycle transformer is unknown. The voltage generated in the 200-turns of the low-potential winding is 440. What is the maximum value of the core flux?

2-25. The core of a 60-cycle 2,200/220-volt transformer has a gross area of cross section of 12 sq in. of which 90 per cent is steel. The maximum flux density in the core is 75,000 maxwells per sq in. If the flux wave is sine-shaped, how many turns are required in (a) the high-voltage winding, (b) the low-voltage winding?

3-25. A 50-kva 60-cycle 11,500/230-volt lighting transformer has iron losses of 385 watts and full-load copper losses of 675 watts. Compute the efficiency of the transformer at $\frac{1}{4}$, $\frac{1}{2}$, $\frac{3}{4}$, and full load and plot the efficiency curve.

4-25. If the transformer in Prob. 3-25 operates on the 24-hr schedule given below, what is the all-day efficiency?

> 1 hr at full load
> 3 hr at $\frac{3}{4}$ load
> 8 hr at $\frac{1}{2}$ load
> 8 hr at $\frac{1}{4}$ load
> 4 hr at no load

5-25. The input to a 30-kva 60-cycle 6,600/220-volt transformer is measured with 220 volts impressed on the low-voltage winding and with the high-voltage winding open. The current is found to be 9.7 amp, while the power input is 184 watts. Find (a) the active and (b) the reactive component of the exciting current, (c) the hysteretic angle of advance. (d) Draw the no-load phasor diagram.

6-25. The iron loss of a 25-kw 13,200/220-volt 60-cycle transformer is 256 watts. The resistance of the low-voltage winding is 0.015 ohm, while that of the high-voltage winding is 55 ohms. Compute (a) the equivalent resistance of the transformer referred to the high-voltage side, (b) the efficiency at full load, (c) the load for which the efficiency is a maximum. Unity power factor load is assumed.

7-25. Estimate the iron losses of the transformer in Prob. 6-25 for an impressed potential difference of (a) 10 per cent over rated voltage, (b) 10 per cent under rated voltage.

8-25. A certain 750 kva 66/6.6-kv. transformer has 1.1 per cent resistance and 6.3 per cent reactance. Compute (a) the reactance and (b) the resistance in ohms referred to the 66-kv side.

9-25. Compute the percentage regulation of the transformer in Prob. 8-25 (a) for 80 per cent power factor, current lagging, (b) for 90 per cent power factor, current leading.

10-25. A 4,000-kva 60-cycle 66/6.6-kv transformer is tested with the 6.6-kv winding short circuited and with sufficient voltage impressed upon the high-potential terminals to circulate rated current of 60.6 amp. The input is found to be 28 kw, while the impressed voltage required is 4.2 kv. Find (a) the percentage resistance and reactance, (b) the regulation at unity power factor, and (c) the regulation at power factor of 0.80, current lagging.

11-25. A 25-hp 230-volt three-phase 60-cycle induction motor is supplied with power from 2,300-volt feeders through a bank of three similar Δ-Δ-connected 2,300/230-volt transformers. Assume that when the motor operates at rated voltage and delivers rated output, its power factor is 87 per cent, its efficiency is 88 per cent, and the transformer efficiencies are 98.3 per cent. For conditions of rated output of the motor, determine (a) the current in the high-voltage windings of the transformers, and (b) the line current on the high-voltage side of the transformer bank.

12-25. A factory has 40 kw of heating load and 250 kw of induction motor load at 0.85 power factor. The heating load is divided equally among the three phases. Power is supplied to the load at 220 volts, three-phase, from a 6.6-kv line. Determine both high- and low-side current ratings of suitable transformers for this service if they are (a) Y-Δ connected, (b) Δ-Δ connected, (c) open-Δ connected. It is assumed that the transformers operate at rated load.

13-25. A total load of 750 kw is supplied from a 13.2 kv three-phase line to two-phase induction motors operating at 440 volts. The average power factor of the motor load is estimated to be 0.85, while the estimated average efficiency is 0.88. Specify the current and voltage of both primary and secondary windings of the two Scott-connected transformers that have a total rating just sufficient to supply the induction-motor load.

14-25. Two 50-kva 2,300/230-volt transformers are open-Δ or V connected to supply a balanced three-phase load at 0.85 power factor, current lagging. How much load in kilowatts can the transformers supply without exceeding their rated capacities?

CHAPTER 26

POLYPHASE INDUCTION MOTORS

Induction Motors. *General.* The induction motor is a simple, reliable, rugged, and relatively cheap a-c motor. Because of its many good qualities, it is widely used where small or moderate-size a-c motors are required. Several different types are available to meet the varying demands of practical operation. Polyphase motors for operation on two-phase or three-phase circuits are built in sizes ranging from fractional horsepower motors to motors developing several thousands of horsepower. The vast majority of single-phase motors are small motors suitable for operation from the ordinary lighting circuit. On account of the vast numbers of these smaller motors that are now required, however, they are of great commercial importance.

Construction. All induction motors consist essentially of two parts, namely, an outer, stationary, hollow, cylindrical structure built of slotted laminated sheet-steel punchings, called the *stator* (Fig. 1-26), and an inner cylindrical core, called the *rotor*, which is also built of laminated sheet-steel punchings, usually with partially enclosed slots, and is mounted on a spider and provided with a shaft. When properly assembled, the rotor is free to turn within the stator, for it is separated therefrom by a small air gap. The width of the air gap is made as small as mechanical clearance permits in order to reduce to a minimum the ampere-turns required to set up the necessary flux in the gap.

The stator has a winding similar to the armature winding of the corresponding polyphase generator. Two separate interconnected windings, as illustrated in Fig. 4-26(*b*), are used for the two-phase motor, and three separate windings, which may be either Y- or Δ-connected, are used for the three-phase motor, as illustrated in Fig. 6-26(*b*). The function of the stator winding is to provide the air-gap flux and to supply to the rotor the power necessary to drive it.

The electrical circuit of the rotor may be either one of two distinct types, regardless of the kind of stator winding used. The simplest type of rotor is the so-called *squirrel-cage rotor* illustrated in Fig. 2-26. It has a large number of parallel connected conducting bars made of aluminum, copper, or alloys of these metals, which are embedded in the partially

Fig. 1-26. Stator of 300-hp three-phase induction motor. (*Allis-Chalmers Manufacturing Company.*)

Fig. 2-26. Squirrel-cage rotor for 250-hp induction motor. (*Allis-Chalmers Manufacturing Company.*)

enclosed slots on the periphery of the rotor. To secure a tight fit and to prevent movement of the bars with respect to the core, the squirrel-cage winding is sometimes formed of oversize copper bars of correct size and length, which are pressed into the slots. At both ends of the rotor all bars are connected solidly to end rings by electric welding or brazing.

In some rotors bars and end rings are cast to form a single integral structure. Perhaps 90 per cent of all induction motors are of the squirrel-cage type.

For reasons which will appear later, certain kinds of drives require a motor which has a *wound rotor* rather than a "cage" winding. For this purpose, in place of bars and end rings, the rotor is provided with a

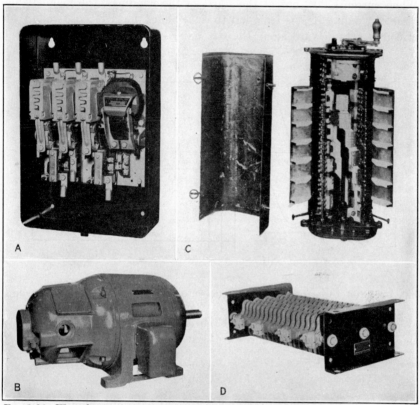

A   C

B   D

Fig. 3-26. Wound-rotor induction motor (*b*), with primary magnetic switch (*a*), hand-operated secondary drum switch (*c*), and starting resistor (*d*). (*General Electric Company.*)

polyphase winding, similar to that used in the stator circuit. The ends of the winding are connected to slip rings, mounted on the shaft. A means is thus provided for connecting the rotor winding to an external circuit (see Fig. 3-26). The purpose of this arrangement is to permit the introduction of additional resistance during the starting period.

Revolving Magnetic Field in Two-phase Motors. The stator of any two-phase two-pole motor has two windings with axes 90 space degrees apart, as illustrated in principle in Fig. 4-26(*b*).

S_a and S_b are the starts and F_a and F_b the finishes of windings A and B, respectively. If F_a and F_b are connected together to form the common lead O, then when O, S_a, and S_b are connected to the three wires of a three-wire two-phase system as shown, two-phase currents exist in the windings. Since the circuits are symmetrical in all respects, the currents are equal and 90 time degrees apart, as illustrated in Fig. 4-26(a). When currents flow out at the starts of the windings, the magnetizing force of winding A acts from left to right along the AA' axis, while that of coil B acts upward along the BB' axis. Since the mmf of each coil

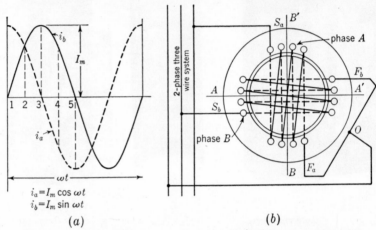

$$i_a = I_m \cos \omega t$$
$$i_b = I_m \sin \omega t$$

$$(a) \qquad\qquad\qquad (b)$$

FIG. 4-26. Stator winding (in principle) and currents of a two-phase induction motor.

at any instant is proportional to the current in it, from Fig. 4-26(a), the instantaneous ampere-turns are seen to be

$$\begin{aligned} f_a &= F_m \cos \omega t \\ f_b &= F_m \sin \omega t \end{aligned} \qquad (1\text{-}26)$$

where $F_m = NI_m$, value of mmf when current has its maximum value I_m
$\qquad N$ = number of turns in each coil

Substantially all the mmf of each phase winding is consumed in the reluctance of two air gaps and the associated teeth of the stator and rotor punchings. If l' is the length of the equivalent air gap, the maximum value of the magnetic gradient in the equivalent gap due to the ampere-turns of one phase winding is

$$H_m = \frac{NI_m}{2l'} \qquad (1\text{-}26)a$$

The air-gap instantaneous magnetic gradients due to the ampere-turns of the two phases are *space phasors*, the magnitudes of which *vary with time* in accordance with the fluctuations of the phase currents. Expressed as time functions, the *magnitudes* of these are

$$h_a = H_m \cos \omega t$$
$$h_b = H_m \sin \omega t \tag{1-26}b$$

For the assumed positive directions of currents in the phase windings, the instantaneous magnetic field intensity h_a acts from left to right along the X axis while h_b acts upward along the Y axis. The space-phasor magnetic gradients may therefore be represented as

$$\mathbf{h}_a = H_m(\cos \omega t)\underline{/0}$$
$$\mathbf{h}_b = H_m(\sin \omega t)\underline{/\pi/2} \tag{1-26}c$$

By expressing these in rectangular components and adding, the resultant air-gap magnetic field intensity is found to be

$$\mathbf{h}_0 = H_m(\cos \omega t + j \sin \omega t) \tag{2-26}$$
$$= H_m\underline{/\omega t} \tag{3-26}$$

If constant permeability of the magnetic circuit be assumed, the air-gap flux is obviously proportional to the resultant magnetic field intensity in the gap, so that the resultant phasor flux can be represented by an equation that is exactly similar in form to Eq. (3-26), or as

$$\boldsymbol{\phi} = \phi_m\underline{/\omega t} \tag{4-26}$$

Equation (4-26) shows that, for constant permeability, the amount of air-gap flux produced by the resultant field intensity is constant and equal in magnitude to the maximum flux which the mmf of one phase winding would set up if acting alone, and that the flux phasor revolves in space at the constant angular velocity ω.

Figures 4-26 and 5-26 are intended to show graphically in step-by-step fashion how the revolving magnetic field is produced in the air gap of a two-phase motor. The two-phase currents in (a) of Fig. 4-26 are assumed to be applied to the two windings shown in (b). It is assumed further, that the current i_a flows in the winding of phase A while i_b flows in the winding of phase B, and that the winding terminals are so connected to the sources of supply that when the currents in (a) of Fig. (4-26) are positive, currents flow *in* at the finishes and *out* at the starts of the corresponding phase windings in (b). When the currents become negative, the reverse directions apply.

In the upper part of Fig. 5-26 the motor structure and windings of Fig. 4-26(b) are redrawn to show the currents in the two-phase windings for the four different time angles 0, 45, 90 and 135 deg corresponding to 1, 2, 3, and 4 of Fig. 4-26(a). The stator currents corresponding to these four times give rise to corresponding components of magnetic intensities h_a and h_b, the magnitudes of which are found from the projection on the Y axis of the phasors a and b in the time-phasor diagram of the lower part of the figure.   (The lengths of a and b are each equal to H_m.)   Thus, at time zero, the field intensity due to the mmf of phase A is a maximum while that due to phase B is zero, as in $(a)'$.   When the elapsed time is that corresponding to $\omega t = 45$ deg as in $(b)'$, the component field intensities due to the two phases are equal and the magnitude of each is 70.7 per cent of the maximum, while for the instant of time corresponding to $\omega t = 90$ deg the intensity due to phase A has fallen to zero and that due to phase B has risen to maximum value, as in $(c)'$. For any given instant of time the components of intensities due to the two phases are added to give the resultant shown in the space-phasor

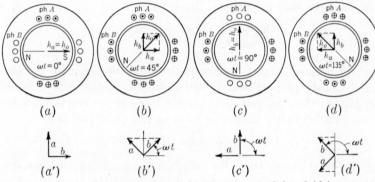

(a) (b) (c) (d)

(a') (b') (c') (d')

FIG. 5-26. Diagrams illustrating the production of a revolving field in a two-phase motor.

diagrams in the upper parts of Fig. 5-26.   These figures show that the resultant field intensity phasor is of constant length and that it rotates at the angular velocity ω in the case of the two-pole machine. Since $\omega = 2\pi f$, the number of revolutions per second of the revolving field in a two-pole machine is equal to the frequency in cycles per second.   This corresponds to a speed of 60 rps or 3,600 rpm for a 60-cycle circuit.   In general, the revolving field of any 60-cycle machine with $p/2$ pairs of poles rotates at a speed of $3,600 \div p/2$ or $7,200/p$ rpm.

Revolving Field in a Three-phase Motor.   The stator of a three-phase induction motor is wound with three separate windings, spaced 120 electrical degrees apart.   For a two-pole motor an electrical degree is equal to a space degree, so for this case the windings are also 120 space degrees apart, as shown in Fig. 6-26(b).   The back connections of the windings are omitted for the sake of clarity.   The circuits are either Y- or Δ-connected, and when fed from a three-phase supply, they carry three-phase currents as illustrated in Fig. 6-26(a).

Assume that the windings in Fig. 6-26(b) are so connected to the supply circuit that when the phase current in (a) is *positive* the currents in the windings flow *in* at the starts and *out* at the finishes. For negative currents in (a) the currents in the phase windings are reversed. When current flows in the assumed positive directions in the three windings, the corresponding mmfs establish component phasor magnetic field intensities in the air gap, the directions and positive senses of which are indicated by the shafts and points, respectively, of the associated arrows. The phasor field intensities due to positive currents in phases A, B, and C have the directions of the arrows AA', BB', and CC' in Fig. 6-26(b).

Note, however, that at no time do the currents in the three phases all have the same sign. Two may be positive and one negative or two may

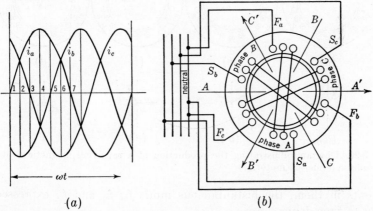

(a) (b)

Fig. 6-26. Stator winding (in principle) and the currents of a Y-connected three-phase induction motor.

be negative and one positive, except when one is zero, in which case the two remaining ones have opposite signs. This means that the sense of one of the magnetic field intensities is always reversed with respect to the other two as shown in Fig. 7-26.

In Fig. 7-26, (a'), (b'), (c'), and (d') are the time-phasor diagrams of the three-phase currents corresponding to the angles indicated by 1, 2, 3, and 4 of (a) of Fig. 6-26. Since the magnetizing force of each coil is proportional to the current in it, the diagrams also represent the instantaneous values of the magnetic field intensities of the three coils for $\omega t = 0$, 30, 60, and 90 deg. In (a), (b), (c), and (d) of Fig. 7-26 the structure of the motor, including the three stator windings, is indicated. The instantaneous magnetic field intensity of each coil, taken from (a'), (b'), (c'), and (d'), respectively, is transferred to the corresponding upper figure and is laid off on the appropriate axis in a *positive direction* when the current is *positive*, and in a *negative direction* when the current is *negative*.

The diagrams in *a, b, c,* and *d* are *space phasor diagrams* of air-gap magnetic field intensities, the components of which are added to find the resultant air-gap intensity. The resultant is observed to be a phasor of constant length that revolves at a fixed speed of $2f/p$ rps, where f is the frequency of the supply in cycles per second and p is the number of poles.

The above relations are shown mathematically as follows: From Fig. 6-26(a), since the mmfs of the coils are proportional to the instantaneous

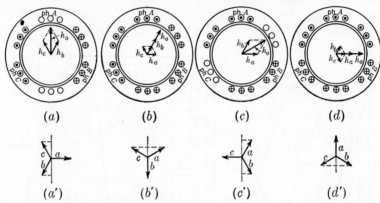

Fig. 7-26. Diagrams illustrating the production of a revolving magnetic field in a three-phase induction motor.

currents in them, the instantaneous mmfs f_a, f_b, and f_c, expressed in terms of time degrees, are

$$f_a = F_m \sin \omega t$$
$$f_b = F_m \sin (\omega t - 120°)$$
$$f_c = F_m \sin (\omega t - 240°)$$

(5-26)

where F_m = maximum value of the mmf of a single coil
$$= NI_m$$
N = number of turns in a phase winding
I_m = maximum current in a phase winding

The component magnetic field intensities are proportional to the magnetomotive forces of the three phases. If H_m is the maximum intensity in the air gap due to the mmf of one phase winding when the current in it is a maximum (I_m), one may write

$$H_m = \frac{NI_m}{2l'}$$

where l' = length of equivalent air gap

Accordingly, the *magnitudes* of the component magnetic field intensities vary with time just as the mmfs do. Expressed as functions of time, they are

$$h_a = H_m \sin \omega t$$
$$h_b = H_m \sin (\omega t - 120°) \qquad (5\text{-}26)a$$
$$h_c = H_m \sin (\omega t - 240°)$$

In the *space-phasor diagrams* of the upper part of Fig. 7-26 the component magnetic field intensities due to the three mmfs are laid off on the appropriate axes AA', BB', and CC' for each of four time angles ωt, beginning with zero in the figure at the left and progressing to 90 deg by 30 deg intervals. In each diagram, as in (a) for example, the magnitudes of the three component space phasors are found from the corresponding time-phasor diagram (a'), immediately below. The resultant intensity is the phasor sum of the three component intensities. It appears in each of the diagrams (a), (b), (c), and (d) in correct magnitude, direction, and sense. An examination of successive diagrams reveals that the resultant is constant in length but revolves in space at the same angular velocity as the phasors of the time diagrams do.

The three component space phasors as well as their resultant may be expressed mathematically in terms of their rectangular components as functions of time. Expressed in this form, the equations of the three *space phasors* are

$$\mathbf{h}_a = H_m(\cos 0 + j \sin 0) \sin \omega t$$
$$\mathbf{h}_b = H_m(\cos 240° + j \sin 240°) \sin (\omega t - 120°) \qquad (6\text{-}26)$$
$$\mathbf{h}_c = H_m(\cos 120° + j \sin 120°) \sin (\omega t - 240°)$$

Upon expanding Eqs. (6-26) and adding, one finds the resultant air-gap magnetic field intensity to be

$$\mathbf{h}_0 = \mathbf{h}_a + \mathbf{h}_b + \mathbf{h}_c$$
$$= \tfrac{3}{2}H_m(\sin \omega t + j \cos \omega t)$$
$$= \tfrac{3}{2}H_m\underline{/90° - \omega t} \qquad (7\text{-}26)$$

Equation (7-26) is the equation for the resultant air-gap magnetic field intensity in (a), (b), (c), and (d) of Fig. 7-26. It shows that the magnitude of the resultant magnetic field intensity is constant and equal to $\tfrac{3}{2}$ of the maximum field intensity of one of the three windings, and that it revolves at an angular velocity of ω for a two-pole machine. Furthermore, for the arrangement of winding and sequence of phases shown, the rotation is in a negative or clockwise direction. The direction of rotation may be reversed by changing the sequence of phases. This may be done by interchanging any two of the three leads as, for example, S_a and S_b in Fig. 6-26.

Multipolar Polyphase Machines. In a two-pole machine with a full-pitch winding, the opposite sides of a coil constituting one of the phase

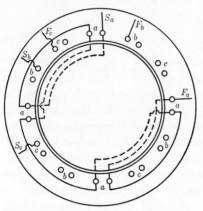

windings are 180 space degrees apart, as shown in Figs. 4-26 and 6-26. In a four-pole machine the opposite coil sides are 90 space degrees apart, while in a p-pole machine they are $360/p$ deg apart. In general, the phase windings are $180/p$ space degrees apart in two-phase machines and $240/p$ deg apart in three-phase machines. This is illustrated for the case of the four-pole three-phase motor in Fig. 8-26. Wiring connections for phases B and C are omitted to simplify the drawing, but they are exactly similar to those shown for phase a.

FIG. 8-26. Stator winding of a three-phase four-pole motor. Connections are shown for phase A only.

In Fig. 9-26(b), when read from left to right, the figures show the positions of the four poles corresponding, respectively, to the angles indicated by 1, 2, 3, and 4 of Fig. 9-26(a). It is apparent from these figures that

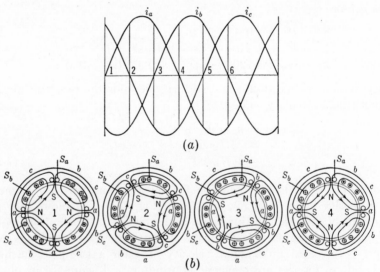

FIG. 9-26. The revolving field of a three-phase four-pole motor.

the speed at which the field of a four-pole machines revolves is $f \div 2$ rps where f is the frequency of the applied voltage in cycles per second. Thus for a 60-cycle four-pole machine, the speed of the field is

$$60 \div \tfrac{1}{2} \times 4 = 30 \text{ rps}$$

or 1,800 rpm. Similarly, for a p-pole machine the speed of the rotating field is

$$\text{Speed} = f \div \frac{p}{2} \text{ rps} \tag{8-26}$$

$$= 60f \div \frac{p}{2} \text{ rpm}$$

$$= \frac{120f}{p} \text{ rpm} \tag{9-26}$$

Theory of Motor at Standstill. The distribution of the revolving flux in the magnetic circuit of a two-pole squirrel-cage motor is pictured in Fig. 10-26. A developed drawing of the same field is shown in Fig. 11-26, in which the flux densities in the air gap are represented by the ordinates to the sine curve marked β.

The revolving field is represented by a gliding motion of the flux curve at a speed equal to that of the field.

When the field moves to the right as shown, the air gap flux sweeping past the rotor conductors generates in them voltages proportional to the flux densities in which they lie. The directions of the generated emfs are found by the right-hand rule to be *outward* under the north pole and *inward* under the south pole. The distribution of emfs is indicated by the curve e. These emfs cause currents to circulate in the rotor bars

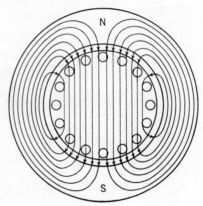

Fig. 10-26. Flux distribution in the air gap of a two-pole motor.

that are directly proportional to the emfs and inversely proportional to the impedances of their paths.

Since the rotor is stationary, the frequency of the rotor current is the same as that of the stator. Under these conditions the reactance of a squirrel-cage rotor is several times as high as the rotor resistance, and therefore the rotor current lags the generated voltage by a large angle θ_2, determined by the relation

$$\theta_2 = \tan^{-1} \frac{X_2}{R_2} \tag{10-26}$$

where X_2 = reactance of rotor circuit at standstill
R_2 = resistance of rotor

The distribution of the rotor currents around the periphery of the rotor may accordingly be represented by the sine curve i_2, lagging the emf by the angle θ_2 as shown ($\theta_2 = 45$ deg in the illustration). The effective value of the current at standstill is equal to the effective voltage E_2 divided by the rotor impedance at standstill; that is,

$$I_2 = \frac{E_2}{\sqrt{R_2{}^2 + X_2{}^2}} \tag{11-26}$$

The directions of the rotor currents are indicated by the dots and crosses. These currents, reacting with the air-gap flux, cause the conductors to receive side thrusts, as shown in Fig. 11-26. For any particular conductor the thrust is proportional to the product of the current

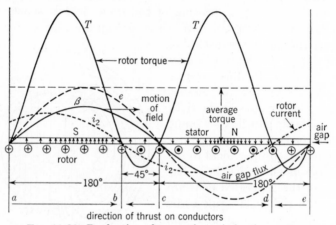

FIG. 11-26. Production of torque in an induction motor.

and the flux density in which it lies. If the forces on the conductors are plotted, using positive ordinates to indicate thrusts to the right, the thrust curve T of the figure is obtained. The forces on conductors in belts ab and cd are to the right, while those in belts bc and de are to the left. It is apparent that so long as θ_2 is less than 90 deg [and Eq. (10-26) shows that this is always the case, since R_2 is never zero] the resultant thrust is always to the right.

The resultant thrust, indicated by the average ordinate to the thrust curve, multiplied by its lever arm, constitutes the *starting torque* of the motor. Thus the thrust curve is actually a torque curve to another scale and is usually so designated.

Since the average value of the product of two sine waves is the product of their effective values multiplied by the cosine of the angle between them, the torque T is

$$T = kI_2 \, \phi \cos \theta_2 \tag{12-26}$$

where k = constant

I_2 = effective value of rotor current

ϕ = effective value of gap flux

Influence of θ_2 on the Torque per Ampere of Current. Figure 12-26 shows how the resultant torque per ampere of current is increased by reducing the angle θ_2 and hence increasing the power factor of the rotor. In wound-rotor motors the reduction in angle may be brought about conveniently by increasing the rotor resistance. This principle is used to increase the starting torque, as will presently be shown. T_0 shows the resultant torque in the two cases.

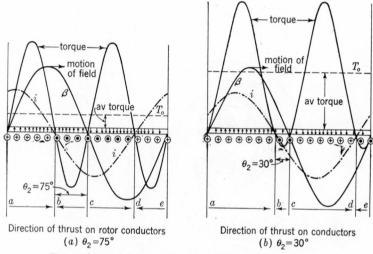

Direction of thrust on rotor conductors
(a) $\theta_2 = 75°$

Direction of thrust on conductors
(b) $\theta_2 = 30°$

FIG. 12-26. Variation of torque with rotor power factor.

The power factor of a motor of given voltage and horsepower rating varies inversely with the number of poles because the magnetizing current is nearly directly proportional to the number of poles. For this reason, especially in small sizes, two-pole and four-pole motors are most common. In special applications, where low speeds are required, a supply of appropriate low frequency is provided.

Starting Torque of Squirrel-cage Motors. Squirrel-cage motors are so constructed that it is not convenient to introduce additional resistance in the rotor circuit at starting. The designer may build a squirrel-cage motor with relatively high or relatively low starting torque, however, by choosing conducting materials of correspondingly high or low resistivities, but high starting torques secured in this way are always obtained at the expense of greater heating and some loss in efficiency, due to the higher rotor copper losses under running conditions.

The starting torque may be improved considerably by the use of deep rotor slots and bars. This construction results in a high apparent resistance and a low reactance at starting, and a low resistance and a high reactance at running speeds. The large apparent resistance is due to the "skin effect," which at standstill frequency crowds the current into the upper parts of the rotor bars, thereby increasing the current density in the upper part and increasing the I^2R losses. Near synchronism, the rotor frequency becomes the slip frequency and the skin effect is negligible.

The impedance of the motor circuit at standstill is sufficient to limit the starting current to about five times normal value, but the effective starting torque produced is seldom more than 150 per cent of the running

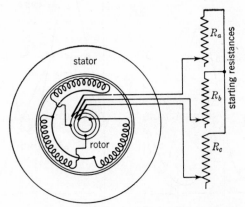

Fig. 13-26. Wound rotor with starting resistance.

torque at full load, owing to the low power factor of the motor at starting. There are many motor applications in which little or no load is connected to the motor at starting, the load being thrown on after the motor is up to speed. For these the squirrel-cage motor is very satisfactory and is to be recommended because it is cheap, rugged, and simple to operate.

Improved Starting Torque of Wound-rotor Motor. As previously mentioned, the rotor of this motor has a two-phase or a three-phase winding in which the ends are brought out to slip rings, as illustrated in principle in Fig. 13-26. By means of brushes, the internal winding may be connected to external resistances during the starting period, thus improving the power factor of the rotor circuit, and increasing the starting torque per ampere of rotor current in the manner previously explained.

There is a definite limit, however, to the increase in torque which can be secured in this way. This is best seen from a study of Eq. (12-26). When the value of I_2 from Eq. (11-26) is substituted, and it is remembered that $\cos \theta_2 = R_2/\sqrt{R_2{}^2 + X_2{}^2}$, Eq. (12-26) becomes

$$T = \frac{k\phi E_2 R_2}{R_2{}^2 + X_2{}^2} \tag{13-26}$$

In Eq. (13-26) the torque is a maximum when $R_2 = X_2$ and, of course, cannot be increased beyond this value. This occurs when θ is 45 deg. At this angle the rate of increase of torque due to increased power factor obtained by adding resistance is exactly balanced by the rate of decrease of torque due to decreasing current resulting from increasing the rotor impedance.

The starting resistances are connected to suitable rheostat contacts so that they may be cut out after the motor has come up to speed. This type of motor develops full-load torque at starting with full-load current. It is generally used where heavy loads are to be started.

Starting Conditions. If the rotor is free to turn and the resisting torque of the load is less than the propelling torque developed by the interaction between the rotor currents and the stator magnetic field at standstill, the rotor revolves in the direction of the magnetic field. As the speed increases, the rate at which the stator flux is cut by the rotor conductors decreases. Hence, the slip s, which is defined in the next topic "Running Conditions," the rotor generated voltage sE_2, and the rotor frequency f_2 all decrease proportionately.

Since the reactance sX_2 of the rotor winding is proportional to the rotor frequency $(sX_2 = 2\pi f_2 L_2)$, reducing the rotor frequency causes the rotor reactance and the rotor impedance to decrease. Thus, even though the rotor generated voltage is decreasing, the rotor current does not decrease as rapidly as it would if the impedance remained constant. Furthermore, if the rotor resistance is less than the standstill reactance, decreasing the frequency improves the rotor power factor. For these reasons the rotor continues to accelerate after the motor has started, until the maximum or "break-down" torque is reached. Thereafter the rotor torque decreases and the rotor gains speed more and more slowly until the exact speed is attained for which the resisting torque of the load and the net propelling torque of the rotor are equal (Fig. 14-26).

If there were no load on the motor and if friction and other rotor losses were reduced to zero, the motor would continue to accelerate until its speed and that of the revolving field were equal. This theoretically maximum speed is called the *synchronous speed*, for at this speed the rotor and the field would revolve "together in time." Actually, the final no-load speed is slightly less than synchronous speed, and just enough less so that the emf generated in the rotor circuit is exactly the right amount to supply enough current to produce a propelling torque equal to the resisting torque of the rotor and the mechanical losses combined.

Running Conditions. It has been seen that the running speed is always less than synchronous speed. This speed differential, when expressed as a decimal fraction of the synchronous speed, is called the *per unit* (pu)

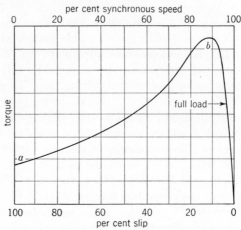

FIG. 14-26. Torque-speed curve of a squirrel-cage motor.

slip, and 100 times the per-unit slip is the *percentage slip*. Accordingly, the slip is

$$s(\text{pu}) = \frac{\text{synchronous speed} - \text{rotor speed}}{\text{synchronous speed}} \qquad (14\text{-}26)$$

$$s \text{ (per cent)} = 100s(\text{pu})$$

For example, a four-pole 60-cycle motor that runs at 1,750 rpm has a slip of

$$s = \frac{1,800 - 1,750}{1,800} = 0.0277 \text{ pu} \qquad (15\text{-}26)$$

$$= 2.77 \text{ per cent}$$

At standstill the rotor frequency f_2 is equal to f_1, the stator frequency, but during running the frequency of the rotor is reduced to sf_1, called the *slip frequency*. This has the effect of reducing the rotor reactance from X_2 to sX_2 and thereby increasing the power factor of the rotor circuit. Because of the slip, the rotor voltage is reduced to sE_2, and the rotor current is therefore

$$I_2 = \frac{sE_2}{\sqrt{R_2{}^2 + s^2X_2{}^2}} \qquad (16\text{-}26)$$

while the power-factor angle of the rotor circuit is

$$\theta_2 = \tan^{-1}\frac{sX_2}{R_2} \qquad (17\text{-}26)$$

a very much smaller angle than the standstill angle of Eq. (10-26).

The rotor input[1] is $E_2I_2 \cos \theta_2$, of which the part $sE_2I_2 \cos \theta_2$ appears in the form of electrical energy and is converted to copper loss, while the remainder appears as the mechanical energy of rotation, which carries the load and supplies the rotor friction losses. That the entire *electrical* input to the rotor is converted to copper loss may be shown by multiplying Eq. (16-26) through by I_2R_2 and substituting $\cos \theta_2$ for the fraction $R_2 \div \sqrt{R_2{}^2 + s^2X_2{}^2}$. When this is done, Eq. (16-26) becomes

$$I_2{}^2R_2 = sE_2I_2 \cos \theta_2 \qquad (18\text{-}26)$$

Solving Eq. (18-26) for the slip yields

$$s = \frac{I_2{}^2R_2}{E_2I_2 \cos \theta_2} \qquad (19\text{-}26)$$

which shows that the slip is numerically equal to the ratio of the rotor copper loss to the rotor input. If friction and windage be neglected, copper loss is the only rotor loss when running. With windage and friction neglected, the rotor output is

$$\text{Rotor output} = E_2I_2 \cos \theta_2 - sE_2I_2 \cos \theta_2$$
$$= (1 - s)E_2I_2 \cos \theta_2$$
$$= (1 - s) \text{ (rotor input)} \qquad (20\text{-}26)$$
$$\frac{\text{Rotor output}}{\text{Rotor input}} = \frac{1 - s}{1}$$
$$= \frac{\text{rotor speed}}{\text{synchronous speed}} \qquad (21\text{-}26)$$

No-load Phasor Diagram per Phase. In Fig. 15-26 and the following diagrams, the motor under discussion is assumed to be three-phase Y-connected, and all quantities represented, such as current, voltage, power developed, etc., are the "per-phase" values.

Consider a three-phase induction motor that has balanced rated voltages E_1 per phase impressed on the stator winding, and runs without load (Fig. 15-26). Under these conditions the stator input per phase must supply (1) one-third of the active power consumed by the stator and rotor losses ($E_1I_{ex} \cos \theta_0$), and (2) one-third of the vars ($E_1I_{ex} \sin \theta_0$)

[1] Students often find it difficult to establish the validity of this expression. A little thought and reference to Fig. 16-26 should help to clarify matters.

Let us speak in terms of values per phase and assume, for the sake of simplicity, that the stator and rotor windings have the same number of turns per phase. The rotor input is equal to the stator output, since no losses occur in the air gap. The stator output is, obviously, equal to the product of the component $-\mathbf{E}_2$ of the stator voltage consumed by the stator counterelectromotive force $\mathbf{E}_2$, the stator equivalent $\mathbf{I}_{2-1}$ of the rotor current $\mathbf{I}_2$ and the cosine of θ_2, which is the angle of phase difference between $\mathbf{E}_2$ and $\mathbf{I}_2$. The scalar product is $P = E_2I_2 \cos \theta_2$.

necessary to maintain the air-gap revolving magnetic field. In these expressions θ_0 is the angle of lag of the exciting current with respect to $\mathbf{E}_1$.

Since the rotor is unloaded, rotor and stator copper losses are both relatively small, and substantially all the power input to the stator is consumed in the stator core losses and the rotor windage and bearing friction losses. The sum of these two comprises the so-called "constant losses" of the motor. Both are nearly independent of the motor load. The rotor core losses under running conditions are negligibly small because the rotor frequency is only a small fraction of the stator frequency.

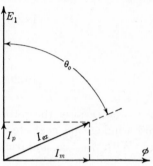

FIG. 15-26. Induction-motor no-load phasor diagram in per-phase values.

Thus, in Fig. 15-26, when a voltage of $\mathbf{E}_1$ per phase is impressed on the stator, a flux ϕ is established in the air gap. Just as in a transformer, this flux is an alternating one which changes at such a rate as to induce in the stator windings a counter emf oppositely directed and nearly equal to $\mathbf{E}_1$, but differing therefrom sufficiently to permit the current $\mathbf{I}_{ex}$, called the *exciting current*, to flow in the stator leads. The phasor sum of $\mathbf{E}_1$ and the counter emf is $\mathbf{Z}_1\mathbf{I}_{ex}$, the voltage consumed in the impedance of the stator. The current automatically adjusts itself to a magnitude and phase position such that its quadrature component, called the *magnetizing current*, is sufficient to produce the required flux, and its active component is sufficient to supply the motor losses. Since the magnetizing current required depends largely upon the length of air gap, the latter is made as small as safe mechanical clearance permits and a relatively heavy shaft is used to provide the necessary stiffness.

Phasor Diagram for Any Load. When the motor is loaded, the rotor current, given by Eq. (16-26), is

$$I_2 = \frac{sE_2}{\sqrt{R_2{}^2 + s^2 X_2{}^2}}$$

Dividing the numerator and denominator by the slip yields

$$I_2 = \frac{E_2}{\sqrt{(R_2{}^2/s^2) + X_2{}^2}} \tag{22-26}$$

Since $R_2/sX_2 = (R_2/s) \div X_2 = \cot \theta_2$, the current may be expressed in terms of the fixed standstill reactance and the rotor power-factor angle, as follows:

$$I_2 = \frac{E_2}{X_2 \sqrt{\cot^2 \theta_2 + 1}} = \frac{E_2}{X_2} \sin \theta_2 \qquad (23\text{-}26)$$

Equation (23-26) is the polar equation of a circle. It defines the rotor current per phase in terms of the rotor *induced voltage* (E_2) per phase at standstill and the rotor power-factor angle θ_2, as illustrated in Fig. 16-26. The rotor standstill voltage is induced by transformer action of the flux ϕ cutting the turns of the rotor winding as in a transformer. Consequently, in the diagram E_2 lags ϕ by 90 deg or it is substantially in phase opposition to E_1. The rotor current per phase at standstill is the value of I_2 obtained from Eq. (22-26) for 100 per cent slip $[s(pu) = 1]$. This value is represented by $_mI_2$ in the figure and is the maximum value of current that can exist in the rotor when rated voltage E_1 per phase is impressed on the stator. The corresponding angle of lag of the maximum rotor current is $_m\theta_2 = \tan^{-1} X_2/R_2$. Under running conditions other values of current $\mathbf{I}_2$ and angle θ_2 apply, depending upon the load.

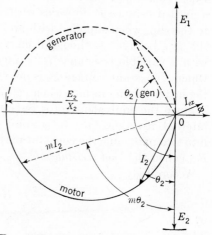

FIG. 16-26. Locus of the rotor current of an induction motor.

If the exciting current under load is assumed to be the same as that under no load, then, under running conditions, the stator ampere-turns are increased over the no-load value by an amount equal to the secondary ampere-turns. For a 1:1 ratio of turns between stator and rotor, this condition is represented on the diagram by reversing the rotor-current phasor and adding it to the stator current at no load. This is accomplished for all loads by rotating the semicircle through 180 deg about the point O, and then sliding the origin at O along the current phasor $\mathbf{I}_{ex}$ in Fig. 16-26 to its end, as shown in Fig. 17-26. In the diagram, $\mathbf{I}_{2\text{-}1}$ is the primary equivalent of the rotor current, $\mathbf{I}_{ex}$ is the no-load stator current (the *exciting* current), $\mathbf{I}_1$ is the resultant stator

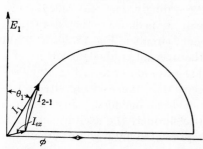

FIG. 17-26. Locus of the stator current of an induction motor.

current, and θ_1 is the stator power-factor angle. When data are available for drawing the diagram of Fig. 17-26, the performance of the motor may be calculated from the diagram to an accuracy sufficient for most practical purposes.

Approximate Circuit Diagram Corresponding to Fig. 17-26. From Eqs. (16-26) and (22-26) one observes that the rotor circuit, comprising a fixed resistance R_2 in series with a variable reactance sX_2 proportional to the slip, when supplied with an impressed voltage sE_2 proportional to the slip, behaves as though it consisted of a fixed reactance X_2 in series with a variable resistance R_2/s, inversely proportional to the slip, upon which a constant voltage E_2 is impressed. One may therefore substitute the latter for the former when considering the behavior of the rotor.

Since the equivalent rotor resistance R_2/s can never be less than the internal resistance R_2, it is convenient to divide the rotor resistance into two parts, one the constant part R_2 and the other a variable quantity R_L, called the *load resistance*.

Accordingly

$$\frac{R_2}{s} = R_2 + R_L$$

or

$$R_L = R_2 \frac{(1 - s)}{s} \tag{24-26}$$

and the equivalent rotor-circuit diagram is that given in Fig. 18-26.

In a motor with a 1:1 ratio of stator to rotor turns, and disregarding the flux leaking out between stator and rotor windings, the voltage E_2 may be regarded as both the counter emf of the stator and the impressed emf of the rotor at standstill, since these voltages are equal in magnitude

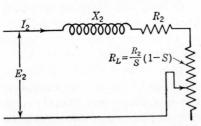

FIG. 18-26. Equivalent rotor circuit in per-phase values.

and are in phase with one another. Accordingly, one may add the primary impedance to the rotor equivalent circuit of Fig. 18-26 to obtain the over-all equivalent circuit of a 1:1 ratio motor as in Fig. 19-26 except that the exciting circuit has not been included. Just as in a transformer, the exciting circuit is represented by a shunt circuit the constants of which are such that g_0E_1 is the active component of the exciting current and b_0E_1 is the reactive component of the exciting current or the magnetizing current. The complete approximate equivalent-circuit diagram (Fig. 19-26) results from the addition of the shunt exciting circuit and the equivalent series circuit representing stator and rotor impedances and rotor load resistance.

To be strictly correct, the exciting circuit should be connected so as to receive the impressed voltage E_2, but the circuit is greatly simplified and little error is introduced by using the connection shown. For three-phase machines it is convenient to regard all voltages as the line-to-neutral values of a Y-connected motor, regardless of how the motor is actually connected. The resistances and reactances are then the values per phase—one-half the values measured between two leads—and the currents are the values measured in the leads. The diagram constructed on this basis represents one phase of the motor.

Construction of Circle Diagram. The diagram of Fig. 17-26 may be constructed from experimental data as follows:

1. *No-load Data.* Connect the motor to the mains and insert watt-meters, ammeters, and a voltmeter to measure the input watts, amperes, and impressed voltage. Bring the motor up to speed and run without

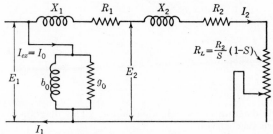

FIG. 19-26. Approximate equivalent circuit per phase, of an induction motor with a 1:1 turn ratio.

load. Since the power factor is less than 50 per cent, the difference of the two wattmeter readings (for the case of three-phase motors) is the input, equal to $3E_1I_0 \cos \theta_1$. From the readings taken the no-load angle θ_1 is computed, and $E_1 = E/\sqrt{3}$ and I_0 may be laid off to suitable scales as in Fig. 20-26. The point M is thus located.

2. *Locked-rotor Data.* Lock the rotor to prevent it from turning (by means of a brake or other convenient device). Reduce the impressed voltage to a value such that when the switch is closed the currents registered by the ammeters are about 1.50 normal full-load values. Read wattmeters, ammeters, and voltmeter as before. Take two or three additional sets of readings at progressively lower voltages. Compute the power-factor angle and plot the currents to the scale of I_0. Calculate the locked-rotor current which would flow at normal impressed voltage by multiplying the observed current by the ratio of rated voltage ÷ impressed voltage. Draw a straight line through the plotted points and the origin O, and extend it to the locked-rotor current at full voltage, indicated by P (Fig. 20-26). Since M and P are points on the circle,

the chord MP may be drawn, and by erecting a perpendicular bisector to it, the center of the circle may be found at Q, on the diameter MN.

3. *Stator Resistance.* With direct current measure the resistance between each pair of stator leads and average the computed resistances obtained from the three sets of readings. One-half the result thus obtained is R_1, the resistance per phase of the stator winding (assumed to be Y-connected).

Performance Curves from Circle Diagram. The performance curves may be calculated from the approximate circle diagram with sufficient accuracy for most purposes.

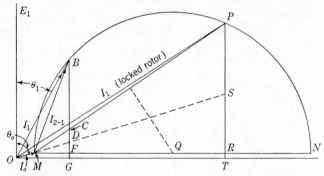

Fig. 20-26. Circle diagram of an induction motor. This diagram may be used for computing performance curves.

At standstill the stator current is OP, and $3E_1 \times PT$ is the motor loss, of which $3E_1 \times RT$ represents iron losses, windage, and bearing friction.[1] These losses are assumed to be constant. Subtracting the constant losses from the total leaves $3E_1 \times PR$ as the sum of the stator and rotor copper losses. The stator copper losses may be computed from the stator current OP and the measured resistance R_1 per phase. At standstill

$$3(E_1 \times PR - OP^2 \times R_1) = \text{rotor copper loss} = 3E_1 \times PS$$

In this way the point S is found, and the line MS is located. For any other load current, such as OB, the rotor copper loss is approximately $3E_1 \times CD$, while the stator loss is approximately $3E_1 \times DF$.

From the diagram, other data necessary to the calculation of the performance may now be found. To simplify the notation, let $3E_1 \div 1,000 = k$ and let power be given in kilowatts. Then, if BG, BD, BC, etc., are measured to the current scale,

[1] While the windage and bearing friction losses are zero at standstill but are substantially constant under running conditions, these losses can be included in the diagram as a part of the core loss by increasing the conductance of the exciting circuit (Fig. 20-26) by a suitable amount.

Stator input $\qquad = k \times BG$
Rotor input $\qquad = k \times BD$
Rotor output $\qquad = k \times BC$
Rotor copper loss $\qquad = k \times CD$
Stator copper loss $\qquad = k \times DF$
No-load or constant losses $\quad = k \times FG$
Total loss at given load $\qquad = k \times CG$
Efficiency $=$ output $\div$ input $= BC \div BG$
Power factor $\qquad = BG \div OB$
Slip, per cent $\qquad = 100(CD \div BD)$
Speed, rpm $\qquad = (1 - s)(\text{synchronous speed, rpm})$
Torque, lb-perp-ft $\qquad = (7{,}040k \times BC) \div \text{rpm}$
$\qquad\qquad\qquad\qquad\qquad = (7{,}040k \times BD) \div (\text{synchronous rpm})$

The performance curves of a 2-hp 220-volt three-phase motor are found in Fig. 21-26.

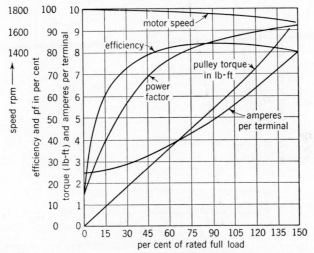

Fig. 21-26. Performance curves of a 220-volt 2-hp three-phase induction motor.

Speed Characteristics of Induction Motors. The induction motor is essentially a constant-speed motor with a slightly dropping characteristic curve, like that of the d-c shunt motor (Fig. 21-26). At no load, since little torque is required, the rotor speed is nearly equal to that of the revolving field, but as the load increases the slip must increase in order that additional emf may be developed to supply the larger rotor current required to carry the increased load. By Eq. (9-26) the speed of the revolving field is $120f_1/p$, while by Eq. (21-26) the rotor speed is $(1 - s)(\text{synchronous speed})$, and by combining these relations the rotor speed is seen to be

$$\text{Rotor speed} = \frac{120f_1}{p} (1 - s) \qquad (25\text{-}26)$$

Motors usually are built with a fixed number of poles and operated from a circuit of fixed frequency; hence Eq. (25-26) readily accounts for the shape of the speed curve, for in it slip is the only variable.

Speed Control of Induction Motors. The possible methods of speed control are suggested by Eq. (25-26) above. They include

1. Control of rotor slip
2. Control of supply frequency
3. Control of number of poles
4. Combinations of the above

1. *Control by Changing Slip.* Introducing resistance into the rotor circuit increases the slip for a given motor load, since, owing to the larger

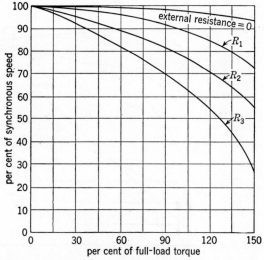

Fig. 22-26. Speed-torque curves of a wound-rotor motor for several values (R_1, R_2, R_3, etc.) of rotor-circuit resistances.

rotor impedance, an increased rotor emf is required to supply the necessary current, and additional emf can be generated only at the sacrifice of speed. By this method, as shown by curves, R_1, R_2, R_3, etc., of Fig. 22-26, any torque up to the *breakdown* value may be developed at any speed less than that indicated on the speed-torque curve of the motor taken with all the external resistance cut out. (Such a curve is the top curve of Fig. 22-26 for torques up to 150 per cent load.) This method of speed control is open to the objection that the introduction of resistance increases the copper loss and reduces the efficiency.

By the use of auxiliary machines it is possible to introduce counter emfs into the rotor circuit to take the place of resistance drops, and thus to bring about changes in slip and speed without the use of resistance. This method has the advantage of providing a wide adjustment in speed without serious reduction in efficiency. Its use is limited, however, to very special applications that use large amounts of power in a single unit.

2. *Control by Changing Frequency.* This method of control is impractical for most applications because the frequency of the supply system must remain fixed. In special cases where the motor load is the only load connected to the generators, the speed of the prime movers may be varied to change the supply frequency and thus change the motor speed. The range over which the speed may be varied in this way, however, is limited by the range of economical speeds of the driver. This method of control has been applied to a limited extent in ship propulsion.

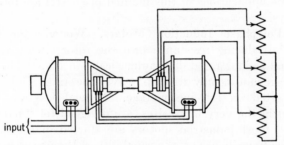

Fig. 23-26. Wound-rotor motors connected in tandem.

3. *Control by Changing Number of Poles.* When this method of control is used, the stator is provided either with two separate windings connected to form the two desired numbers of poles, or with a single winding used in conjunction with a switch, by means of which the circuit may be changed to form either p_1 or p_2 poles, depending upon the connection used. In the latter case the windings are often Y-connected for one speed and Δ-connected for the other, in order to secure the best operating characteristics in the motor. The number of speeds obtainable in this way is usually limited to two in order to keep the winding from being too complicated.

4. *Control by Tandem Connection.* Where multiple speeds are desired, motors are sometimes operated in *tandem* or cascade. When so used, two motors are rigidly coupled to the same shaft or are otherwise mechanically linked, as by means of gears. The stator winding of the first is connected to the mains in the usual way, while that of the second stator is fed from the rotor winding of the first, as shown in Fig. 23-26. If the two machines are designed for the same voltage, as is usually the case, the turn ratio of stator to rotor of the first machine should be unity.

The second rotor may have a cage winding or a polyphase winding like its stator. In the latter case the rotor circuit of the second motor is connected to slip rings in the usual way, in order that resistance may be introduced while starting and for securing additional speed control when running.

The motors may be so connected that both tend to run in the same direction, or the phase rotation of one motor may be reversed, thus tending to make it rotate in the reverse direction. In either case the set will run after it is started, but in the latter case no starting torque is developed, and for this reason this connection is little used. If the first machine has p_1 poles and the second has p_2 poles, the synchronous speed of the set is that of a motor with $p_1 + p_2$ poles for the first case and $p_1 - p_2$ poles for the second. If p_1 and p_2 are not equal, four synchronous speeds are possible, two with tandem operation and one for each motor separately. Some applications of this method of control are found in European railways.

Starting Polyphase Induction Motors. Wound-rotor motors are started by introducing resistance into the rotor circuit as previously described, and as illustrated diagrammatically in Fig. 13-26.

Squirrel-cage motors may draw up to five times rated load current when they are started on full-line voltage. Nevertheless, most induction motors, even in the very large sizes, are designed for "across-the-line" starting, and most industrial motors are started in this manner. In certain applications, however, the capability of the power-supply system may not be adequate to permit across-the-line starting without causing an objectionable dip in voltage due to large starting current and the relatively large line impedance. In such cases motors are started on reduced voltage obtained by the use of a *compensator* or autotransformer (Fig. 24-26), that is provided with taps by means of which a fraction of the line voltage may be supplied to the motor at starting. When the motor is up to speed the starting lever is switched to the running position, full-line voltage is impressed, and the autotransformer is disconnected. The transformer taps and motor leads are connected to the contact points of a switch so that connections can be quickly shifted from the starting to the running position.

Applications. Induction motors are available with torque characteristics suitable for a wide variety of loads. The standard motor has a starting torque of about 120 to 150 per cent of full-load torque. Such motors are suitable for most applications. For starting loads such as small refrigerating machines or plunger pumps operating against full pressure or belt conveyers, high-torque motors with a starting torque of twice normal full-load torque, or more, are used. For driving machines that use large flywheels to carry peak loads, such as punch presses and shears, a high-torque motor with a slip at full load up to 10 per cent is available. The high slip permits enough change in speed to make possible the proper functioning of the flywheel. By the use of a wound-rotor motor with suitable controller and external resistances connected in series with the rotor winding, it is possible to obtain any value of starting torque up to the maximum breakdown torque. Such motors are well adapted as constant-speed drivers for loads that have large friction loads to overcome at starting.

Classification of Motors. Squirrel-cage induction motors are manufactured in large numbers, particularly in sizes up to 200 hp, and therefore a great deal of thought has been given to standardization among the

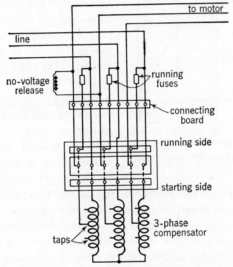

FIG. 24-26. Wiring diagram of three-phase starting compensator.

manufacturers. Motors are classified and standardized with regard to various of their electrical and mechanical features by the National Electrical Manufacturers Association (NEMA).

Motors are classified according to their degree of enclosure. The following are a few, but not all, of the classifications of enclosures: open, dripproof, splashproof, totally enclosed fan-cooled, explosion-proof, and waterproof.

As has been illustrated in preceding paragraphs, the relations of starting torque, slip, and starting current are subject to considerable variation under the control of the designer through such devices as high rotor resistance, deep-bar rotors, double-cage rotors, etc. Certain broad classifications of these designs have been designated by NEMA as follows:

Design A................. Normal torque, normal starting current
Design B................. Normal torque, low starting current
Design C................. High torque, low starting current
Design D................ High slip
Design F................. Low starting torque, low starting current

Typical speed-torque curves for these designs are shown in Fig. 25-26. Most motor manufacturers offer designs in the above categories in their

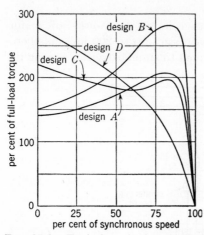

FIG. 25-26. Typical squirrel-cage-motor speed-torque curves.

catalogues. Application of the proper motor to the job involves a consideration of the speed-torque curves of the motor as compared with the speed-torque demands of the load. For example, a centrifugal pump requires only a low starting torque, and a motor of design A or B would probably suffice. On the other hand, a crusher or conveyor may require a starting torque considerably in excess of full-load torque, and a motor of design C would be indicated. A load with a large flywheel effect requires a motor such as design D in order that advantage may be taken of the stored energy in the flywheel by allowing the load to decelerate without drawing excessive current.

The general details of classification and standards are too lengthy for treatment in a work of this nature, and the reader is referred to the applicable standards for further information in this regard.

Induction Generator. Electrical machines are generally reversible and may perform either one of two functions:

1. Convert mechanical energy to electrical energy
2. Convert electrical energy to mechanical energy

In the first case the machine is a *generator*, and in the second it is a *motor*. The induction machine heretofore described as an induction motor is no exception to this rule. Its operation as a motor has been discussed, and it remains briefly to describe its behavior as a generator.

Let a polyphase machine of this type be connected through its stator winding in the usual way to a power system of large capacity, the energy of which is supplied by synchronous machines, and let the induction machine be mechanically driven in the direction of its revolving field. When the machine runs at its motor no-load speed (the speed which it would maintain when run as a motor at no load), the driver does no work.

All the losses are supplied by the electrical circuit through the stator, and the performance of the machine is that described for the motor at no load. The phasor diagram for this case is that of Fig. 15-26.

Next let the machine be driven at a speed of a few per cent above synchronous speed. The air-gap flux is substantially the same as it was when the machine ran as a motor, for with the impedance drop of the stator neglected, it must generate in the stator winding the same emf as before, namely, a counter emf which is approximately equal to the impressed voltage. But the latter has in no way changed, and so the flux, too, must have remained approximately constant. This means that the magnetizing component of the stator current remains unchanged and is correctly represented by the quadrature component of OM in Fig. 20-26 or by OA in Fig. 26-26. Because the rotor speed is above that of the revolving field, the slip is now negative and Eq. (17-26) becomes

$$\theta_2 = \tan^{-1}\left(-\frac{sX_2}{R_2}\right)$$

which indicates that the rotor current I_2 (shown in the upper semicircle of Fig. 16-26) lags the rotor induced voltage by an angle greater than 90 deg. Equation (23-26) plotted for this condition yields the semicircle shown dotted in Fig. 16-26, which is the locus of the rotor current for negative slips. Since the stator winding must provide a number of ampere-turns equal and opposite to the ampere-turns of the rotor winding, in addition to its no-load ampere-turns, the total stator current per phase for any load (assuming a 1:1 turn ratio) is represented by adding to the no-load current phasor a phasor equal to the reversed rotor-current phasor. This is done for all loads by superimposing on the no-load phasor diagram of Fig. 15-26 the dotted semicircle of Fig. 16-26 rotated through 180 deg. Thus, in the approximate circle diagram of Fig. 20-26, the stator equivalent of the rotor current, for the machine operating as described, is found on the lower half of the circle drawn on the diameter MN, not shown in the figure.

These relations are shown in the circle diagram of Fig. 26-26, in which **OA** is the magnetizing current supplied by the line, just as in the case of motor operation, **MB′** is the stator equivalent of the rotor current, and **OB′** is the stator current. The active component AM of the exciting current supplies the no-load losses and is furnished by the induction machine. Since the stator current now flows counter to the impressed voltage, it is evident that the machine operates as a generator and delivers power to the circuit. It should be observed that the machine has no means of exciting itself but receives its excitation from the line. One or more synchronous machines must therefore always be connected to the

circuit to which the induction generator delivers power.   The frequency
of the system, too, is determined by the synchronous machines, while the
load which the induction machine de-
livers depends upon the excess of its
speed over that of the revolving field,
or upon the slip.   Because the machine has no frequency of its own,
it is said to be *asynchronous* or
"without synchronism."

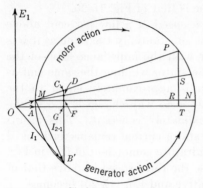

FIG. 26-26. Circle diagram of an induction generator.

The approximate performance characteristics of the machine may be
predicted from the circle diagram of
Fig. 26-26, in the manner already
described for the motor on page 456,
except that what appeared as *input*
to the motor becomes *output* for the
generator, and vice versa.   Because of the limited application of this
type of generator, a detailed discussion of its operating characteristics
as distinct from the motor is omitted.

Problems

1-26. At rated output an eight-pole 60-cycle induction motor runs at a speed of
865 rpm.   Determine (a) the percentage slip, (b) the speed of the revolving field in
revolutions per second.

2-26. A four-pole 25-cycle induction motor has a full-load slip of 3.5 per cent.
Determine for full-load conditions (a) the speed of the rotor in revolutions per minute,
(b) the speed of the revolving field in revolutions per second, (c) the frequency of the
rotor current.

3-26. A 10-hp 120-volt three-phase 60-cycle induction motor has a full-load efficiency of 86 per cent, a power factor of 87 per cent, and runs at 1,750 rpm.   Determine
(a) the number of poles, (b) the percentage slip, (c) the line current, (d) the current
in each stator phase winding if the stator is Δ-connected.

4-26. The 10-hp motor in Prob. 3-26 has 630 watts stray power loss (iron, windage,
and friction loss).   The full-load stator and rotor copper losses are 286 and 304 watts,
respectively.   Determine the resistance of a stator phase winding (a) if the motor is
Y-connected, (b) if the motor is Δ-connected.   (c) What is the resistance between
a pair of leads in (a) and in (b)?   (d) Compute the efficiency of the motor at 1.25
full load on the assumption that the power factor remains unchanged.

5-26. A 25-hp three-phase four-pole 440-volt 60-cycle induction motor is started
on the 60 per cent taps of a Y-connected compensator.   At the instant of starting
the motor current is 68.7 amp.   (a) What is the line current?   (b) What current
does the motor take when it is connected directly across the line at starting?   (c)
Estimate the rated current of the motor.

6-26. A 220-volt three-phase 60-cycle six-pole induction motor with a Y-connected
stator winding takes 43.2 kw from 220-volt mains at full load.   The input current is
125 amp per terminal.   When the motor is run without load at rated voltage the
input is 2.75 kw.   From short-circuit test the copper losses are known to be 2.95 kw

at rated load current. The stator resistance measured between two leads is 0.06 ohm. For conditions of full load determine (a) the output in kilowatts and horsepower, (b) the pulley torque in pound-feet, (c) the percentage efficiency, (d) the stator copper loss, (e) the rotor copper loss, (f) the power factor, (g) the slip, (h) the speed in revolutions per minute.

7-26. The following data pertain to a 100-hp 2,300-volt 60-cycle three-phase eight-pole induction motor with a Y-connected stator.

a. Running without load.

$$\begin{array}{ll} \text{Impressed emf} & = 2{,}300 \text{ volts} \\ \text{Current per terminal} \quad = \quad 5.8 \text{ amp} \\ \text{Wattmeter readings} \quad W_1 = \quad 8.22 \text{ kw} \\ \qquad\qquad\qquad\qquad W_2 = \quad -4.80 \text{ kw} \end{array}$$

b. Short-circuit test.

$$\begin{array}{ll} \text{Impressed emf} & = 560 \text{ volts} \\ \text{Current per terminal} \quad = \quad 34.2 \text{ amp} \\ \text{Power input} \qquad W_1 = \quad 15.3 \text{ kw} \\ \qquad\qquad\qquad\quad W_2 = -2.0 \text{ kw} \end{array}$$

Construct a circle diagram for this motor to a scale of 1 in. = 20 amp and from it determine, for a current of 25 amp per terminal, the following: (a) the no-load losses, (b) the copper loss at 25 amp input, (c) the equivalent resistance of the motor per phase, referred to the primary, (d) the output in horsepower, (e) the percentage slip, (f) the power factor, (g) the torque, (h) the speed in revolutions per minute, (i) the efficiency. Assume the copper loss to be divided equally between stator and rotor.

CHAPTER 27

ALTERNATORS

Introduction. The *a-c generator* is the generating unit that serves as the medium through which the energies of coal, oil, gas, and water are made available in electrical form for transmission and distribution in modern power networks. The driving unit may be a steam engine, an oil engine, or a gas turbine for a small, isolated plant. Power networks generally, however, are supplied by steam-turbine- and water-wheel-driven units of much larger sizes.

One of the most remarkable developments of the present century is the tremendous industrial expansion that has taken place. This growth continues unabated. It produces an ever-increasing demand for electrical energy to meet the needs of industry and the requirements of an expanding population. This has resulted in large increases in the number and size of steam and hydraulic turbogenerators, transformers, motors, and other allied equipment and devices that are manufactured annually; in improvements in the design and efficiencies of electric machinery generally, and in increased over-all economy of power-system design and operation. The result has been that the ever-growing demand for electrical energy has been supplied with little or no increase in the cost per kilowatthour to the consumer, despite the fact that prices of most commodities have more than doubled.

Elementary Concepts. An a-c generator has a magnetic circuit that interlinks a system of field coils and a system of armature coils, much like a d-c machine. Imagine a two-pole d-c generator with a ring winding and with its commutator removed. What remains of the rotating element is a helical winding on a hollow cylinder, the whole being mounted on a suitable spider and shaft. If the winding is tapped at three points 120 deg apart [Fig. 1-27(a)] and these taps are connected to three slip rings mounted on the shaft, the rotor becomes the armature of a three-phase generator. When the fields are excited with direct current in the usual way and the armature is driven at constant speed, three-phase alternating current of constant frequency may be collected from brushes resting on the slip rings. If the armature is tapped at only two diametrically opposite points, the machine is a single-phase generator; if four equally spaced taps are used, it is a two-phase generator.

Revolving-field Generator. The type of generator described in the foregoing paragraph is called a *revolving-armature* type of generator. This type of construction is now seldom used, for reasons which will soon appear. The same end may be attained by placing the armature winding on an external stationary, hollow cylindrical ring within which the field poles are concentrically mounted on a shaft, as in Fig. 1-27(*b*). The armature winding is provided with taps as before, but since it is stationary, no slip rings are required to connect it to the external circuit. The field structure is the rotor; hence the field winding must be supplied with direct current through movable contacts. Two slips rings and a set of brushes are required. This construction is now almost universally

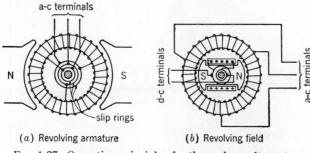

(*a*) Revolving armature   (*b*) Revolving field

FIG. 1-27. Operating principle of a three-phase alternator.

used, even in small machines. Machines of this type are called *revolving-field generators*.

Among the principal advantages of the revolving-field type are the following:

1. The armature windings are more easily braced to prevent deformation under the mechanical stresses due to short-circuit currents and centrifugal forces.

2. The armature winding must be insulated for a high voltage, while the voltage of the field circuit is low (125 or 250 volts). It is much easier to insulate the high-voltage winding when it is mounted on the stationary structure.

3. Only a small amount of power at low voltage is handled by the slip-ring contacts.

4. It is easier to build and properly balance high-speed rotors when they carry the field structure.

All synchronous a-c generators and motors require direct current for excitation. Excitation is supplied by a d-c generator called an *exciter*. The capacity of the exciter is only a small percentage of the rated capacity of the alternator. The exciter may be directly connected to the shaft of the alternator, or it may be driven by a separate electric motor, water wheel, or small turbine. Large power stations usually have several exciters employing different methods of drive as insurance against the failure of excitation.

Rotor. The revolving-field structure is usually called the *rotor*. Rotor construction depends somewhat upon how the machine is to be driven and upon the speed at which it must run. Low- and moderate-speed rotors have projecting (salient) poles, with cores bolted to a heavy steel ring of good magnetic quality (Fig. 2-27). In high-speed machines the cores are dovetailed to the spider and are locked by means of keys. The spider usually is made of cast steel, except for high-speed machines;

FIG. 2-27. Rotor of a generator showing poles, shaft, slip rings, etc. (*General Electric Company.*)

these use laminated steel structures. Extra-heavy rims are used in spider construction in order to secure the maximum moment of inertia (WR^2) consistent with good design. This feature is particularly important in engine-driven generators, for the driving torque of an engine is pulsating. The rotors of water-wheel-driven generators are designed to withstand double speed in order to provide against the possibility of wrecking them by centrifugal action, should the governing mechanism or gate control fail.

The pole faces are sometimes slotted to receive the copper bars of a *grid* or *damper* winding. Bars embedded in these slots are short-circuited by connecting them all together at both ends by short-circuiting rings. These windings serve to minimize momentary fluctuations in speed and thus improve the parallel operation of generators, especially of those driven by prime movers with a pulsating torque.

The field coils of all but the larger slow- and moderate-speed machines are made of copper wire wound on the core in such a way that the wire is directly exposed to the air. In large machines the coils are made of copper strap wound on edge; heat-resisting material is used to insulate each turn from the next. Only a single (shunt) winding is used, since voltage control is effectively secured by means of an automatic regulator.

Modern large steam-driven generators employ the steam turbine as the prime mover. These run at very high speeds and have very large outputs per pound of material employed; 60-cycle two-pole generators run at 3,600 rpm, while four-pole machines run at 1,800 rpm. The rotors of such machines are cylindrical in form and carry their field windings in slots cut in the rotor core parallel to the shaft. The poles are *nonsalient;* that is, they do not project out from the surface of the core. Such a machine is called a *round rotor* machine. The cores of two-pole machines are generally made of a single forging, an extension on either end of which forms the shaft. The use of the cylindrical construction is necessary in high-speed machines because of the great mechanical stresses in the rotor. Better balance and quieter operation are also secured. Moreover, windage losses increase rapidly with the speed; high-speed, salient-pole machines would have very high windage losses, but in the cylindrical type of construction these losses are greatly reduced.

Stator. The armature or *stator* consists essentially of a cast-iron or a welded-steel frame supporting a slotted ring made of soft laminated sheet-steel punchings, in the slots of which the armature coils are assembled. Figure 3-27 shows the stator of a synchronous motor. The stator of a generator is similarly constructed. The laminations are annealed and are insulated from each other by a thin coating of oxide and an enamel, as in d-c machines, transformers, etc. Open slots are used, permitting easy installation of stator coils and easy removal in case of repair. Suitable spacing blocks are inserted at intervals between laminations to leave radial air ducts, open at both ends, through which cooling air may circulate. The coils are shaped much like the coils of a d-c generator, the two sides of the coil being approximately a pole pitch apart.[1] All coils are alike, and therefore interchangeable. They are insulated before being inserted in the slots and are further protected by a horn-fiber slot lining. When in place on the armature, the coils are connected together in groups to form a winding of the required number of phases, three-phase Y-connected windings being common.

---

[1] Coil pitches considerably less than a full pole pitch and as low as two-thirds pole pitch are common, particularly in machines with a small number of poles. This construction is used to secure a suitable wave shape and to shorten the end connections of the coils.

A fractional rather than an integral number of slots per pole is often used in order to eliminate harmonics in the wave form.

Because of their high speeds, turbogenerators have far larger outputs and larger losses per unit of weight than do water-wheel- or engine-driven generators. To provide suitable facilities for carrying off the losses and cooling the machine with clean washed air, as well as to reduce the noise, the entire structure is enclosed and is provided with a forced system of ventilation. Enormous quantities of cooling air are necessary for large

Fig. 3-27. Synchronous motor stator showing frame of welded steel plates. (*General Electric Company.*)

machines. In many cases hydrogen is used instead of air to cool turbogenerators. It absorbs heat more readily and entails less windage friction loss because it is lighter.

Armature Winding. The type of winding most generally used is a double-layer winding of the kind illustrated in the wiring diagram of Fig. 5-27. The coils are of the same shape as those used in d-c generators, but they are grouped differently. Other types of windings are used but to a lesser extent.

The fundamental principle of a three-phase winding is illustrated in Fig. 4-27, which shows a one-turn single-layer full-pitch winding for a four-pole generator. In Fig. 4-27(*b*) all conductors with a given subscript belong to a given circuit. Thus, each circuit is composed of four coil sides: circuit a starts at 1_a and finishes at 4_a; circuit b starts at 1_b and finishes at 4_b; circuit c starts at 1_c and finishes at 4_c. Adjacent conductors of a given circuit are connected together on the ends, as indicated in the developed wiring diagram [Fig. 4-27(b)]. When a full-pitch winding is used, as in the illustration, all conductors forming a given circuit generate voltages that add directly for all positions of the rotor. When the pitch is either less than or more than one pole pitch, the generated emfs of one half of a circuit oppose those of the other half for certain positions of the rotor.

The voltages generated in the three circuits are 120 time degrees apart in the order a, b, c. When the terminals of the windings are connected together as follows: F_a to S_b, F_b to S_c, F_c to S_a, the three-phase winding is

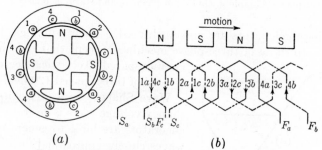

(a)   (b)

Fig. 4-27. Single-layer three-phase stator winding.

Δ-connected (page 381). Leads from the three points of connection form the machine terminals. If either the three starts S_a, S_b, S_c or the three finishes F_a, F_b, F_c be connected together, the remaining three unconnected ends form the terminals of a Y-connected generator.

It should be observed that the armature winding of a three-phase a-c generator (or motor) is similar to the stator winding of a three-phase induction motor.

The diagram of Fig. 4-27 is intended merely to illustrate the principle of the three-phase winding. In practice the winding generally has two coil sides in a slot, as in a d-c machine. Furthermore, the total available winding space on the slotted stator ring is much more economically utilized when the winding is distributed over the entire inner surface of the ring instead of being confined to a few slots. Accordingly, each armature circuit generally occupies several slots per pole, as in Fig. 5-27. This figure shows one phase winding of a double-layer three-phase winding, with three slots per phase per pole. The connections for making up three-phase Y- and Δ-connected circuits are the same as those described above.

Single-phase machines are required for a few industrial uses. They are usually obtained from three-phase Y-connected machines by using only two legs of the Y. The remaining leg is left idle.

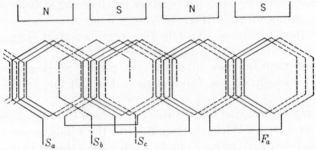

FIG. 5-27. Full-pitch, double-layer winding of a four-pole machine with three slots per phase per pole. Complete winding of phase *A* and starts of phases *B* and *C* are shown.

Two-phase generators are not much used. Their windings, however, are similar to those of three-phase machines, except that they have two circuits spaced 90 electrical degrees apart instead of three spaced 120 deg. apart.

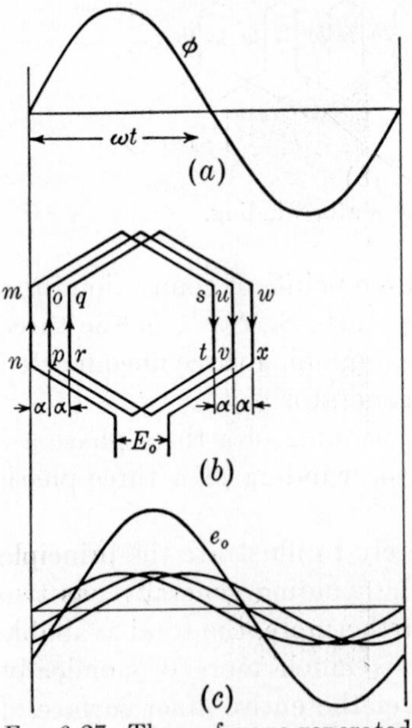

Wave Shape. In a-c circuits a sine-shaped voltage wave is desirable, and a-c generators are built to generate voltage waves closely approximating this shape. The shape of the field form or air-gap flux distribution curve, the distribution of the winding, the amount of the winding pitch, and the use of either a whole number or a fractional number of slots per phase per pole are all factors which influence the wave shape. Designers have learned how to combine these factors to produce the desired result.

Figure 6-27 illustrates how some of these factors are combined to generate a wave of suitable shape. In (c) of this figure is shown the wave generated by a full-pitch winding (b) with three slots per phase per pole, when the field form is sine-shaped as shown in (a); Fig. 7-27 shows the wave generated by the same coils when the field form is trape-

FIG. 6-27. The emf wave generated in a full-pitch winding distributed in three slots per phase per pole. A sine-shaped field form is assumed.

zoidal. Since the pitch of the coil is 180 electrical degrees, opposite coil sides, such as *mn* and *st*, *op* and *uv*, etc., generate equal voltages that add

in the circuit.   Hence the shape of the voltage wave generated by each
turn is the same as that of the field form shown in (a).   In Fig. 6-27 each
turn generates a sine wave of voltage, but the component waves of the
three turns are displaced from each other by the angular distance between adjacent slots (20 deg in the illus-
tration).   Hence the resultant wave is the
sum of three equal component sine waves
spaced 20 deg. apart.   This sum curve is
also sine-shaped.

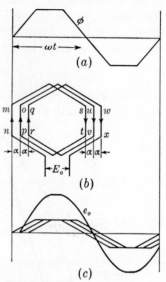

The trapezoidal field form in Fig. 7-27
conforms more nearly to the shape to be
expected in practice, but it too yields a
voltage wave that is approximately sine-
shaped.   The shape of curve can be made
to approach the sine form very closely by
suitably choosing the pitch and the spread
or distribution of the winding.

Magnitude of Generated Voltage. Consider a p-pole generator with a field form
of sine shape, as in Fig. 6-27(a).   Let the
flux per pole crossing the air gap be ϕ
webers, and assume a rotative speed of S
rpm or $S/60$ rps.   In the time of one revolution ($60/S$ sec), each armature conductor
(mn, for example) cuts the flux from p
poles, or a total of $p\phi$ webers, thereby
generating an emf of *average* value

Fig. 7-27. The emf wave generated in a full-pitch winding distributed in three slots per
phase per pole.   A trapezoidal
field form is assumed.

$$E_{av} = \frac{p\phi S}{60} \qquad \text{volts} \qquad\qquad (1\text{-}27)$$

By Eq. (2-18), page 286, the speed of a p-pole generator is

$$S = \frac{120f}{p} \qquad \text{rpm}$$

By substituting this value of S in the above equation of emf the *average*
generated voltage per conductor, in terms of frequency, is found to be

$$E_{av} = 2f\phi \qquad \text{volts}$$

The wave of emf is sine-shaped by assumption.   The effective value E
of a sine wave of emf may be found from the average ordinate by multiplying the latter by the form factor ($\pi/2 \sqrt{2} = 1.11$).   Hence the effec-

tive value of the generated voltage per conductor is

$$E = 2.22f\phi \qquad \text{volts} \qquad (2\text{-}27)$$

The voltage generated in a single turn of a full-pitch winding is equal to the arithmetic sum of the voltages in the two conductors composing it; the voltages in the two coil sides are equal and add directly because the pitch is 180 deg. Accordingly, the voltage per turn of such a winding is twice the value given in Eq. (2-27), or for a coil of N turns it is

$$E = 4.44f\phi N \qquad \text{volts} \qquad (3\text{-}27)$$

A comparison of this equation with Eq. (7-25) on page 401 shows that the two are identical. This means that when ϕ lines cut N turns at a

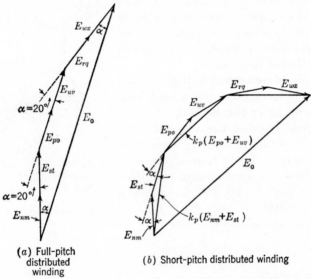

(a) Full-pitch distributed winding

(b) Short-pitch distributed winding

Fig. 8-27. Phasor diagrams illustrating the effect of distribution and pitch of winding upon resultant emf.

frequency f ($2f$ times per second), the voltage generated is always that given by Eq. (3-27), regardless of whether the cutting is due to speed action or to transformer action. This result is, of course, to be expected.

Distribution Factor and Pitch Factor. When the $2N$ coil sides forming the N coils of a winding are not bunched but are distributed over several slots, as in Fig. 5-27, the voltages generated in the turns of adjacent slots are out of phase by an angle equal to the angular slot pitch α ($\alpha = 20$ deg in Fig. 8-27). Accordingly, while in a full-pitch winding the voltages in the coil sides nm and st add arithmetically, as do also the two components of every other coil, the total voltage E_0 generated by the three coils is not $3E$ but is only $E + 2E\cos 20° = 0.96 \times 3E$; that is, the components are added at the angle α, as in the diagram of Fig. 8-27(a). The resultant voltage is less than the arithmetic sum of the coil voltages and may be expressed by the relation

$$E_0 = 4.44k_d f\phi N \qquad \text{volts}$$

in which k_d ($= 0.96$ in the figure) is a constant, called the *distribution factor*. The value of k_d depends upon the distribution and is always less than unity except in a bunched winding. It can be shown quite readily (Fig. 8-27) that if s is the number of slots per phase per pole, which is equal to the number of phasors to be added, the distribution factor is

$$k_d = \frac{\sin s\alpha/2}{s \sin \alpha/2}$$

It should now be apparent that shortening the pitch of the coil has the same effect as distributing the winding. Thus, when the coil pitch is one slot less than full pitch, the emfs in the two sides of a coil are also out of phase by the angle α. The component voltages of a single coil must then be added as phasors also; the voltage of a turn is no longer $E_{nm} + E_{st}$ as in (a) of Fig. 8-27 but becomes $k_p(E_{nm} + E_{st})$ as in (b). The constant k_p is called the *pitch factor*, and its value can never exceed unity. The voltage equation for a short-pitch distributed winding is therefore

$$E_0 = 4.44k_d k_p f\phi N \qquad \text{volts} \qquad (4\text{-}27)$$

Rotating Armature Mmf. In Fig. 9-27 is shown one phase winding of a three-phase stator with two slots per phase per pole. The winding is full pitch. The remaining two circuits are similarly wound. The second begins at S_2 and ends at F_2, while the third begins at S_3 and ends at F_3. When the rotor is driven at constant speed in a clockwise direction, emfs are generated in the stator windings in the directions and amounts indicated by the dots and crosses. If the winding is suitably connected to a balanced three-phase unity-power-factor load, the dots and crosses also represent the currents in the conductors. Under the tips of the poles the generated emfs are smaller than under the centers, as indicated by the reduced sizes of the crosses and dots.

The generated emfs in the conductors under the poles always bear the relations indicated in the figure, regardless of the position of the rotor. As the rotor turns to the right, the positions of the belts of crosses and dots follow the rotor, shifting from slot to slot as the rotor revolves. Even though the armature winding is stationary, the phasor magnetizing force produced by the ampere-turns is constant in amount and revolves at the same speed and in the same direction as the rotor itself; it maintains a fixed position with respect to the rotor so long as the power factor and the load do not change. The field produced by these ampere-turns is called the *revolving field* of the stator. This same sort of thing happens in the stator of an induction motor (page 437).

Electromagnetic Torque. By applying the rule for force action (page 67) it is observed that the reaction between the stator currents and the air-gap flux under each pole is such as to produce forces on the stator conductors which tend to turn them to the right in the direction of the revolving rotor. The stator cannot move, however, and since action and reaction are equal and opposite, there is an equal and opposite torque on the rotor, which tends to turn it to the left. The amount of this

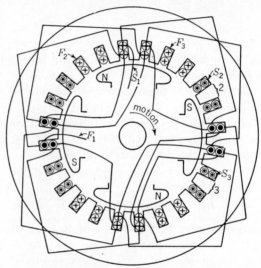

FIG. 9-27. Partially wound full-pitch three-phase stator.

torque depends upon the current strength, the field strength, and the power factor. With losses neglected, the power supplied to the rotor, when the machine is loaded, is the power expended by the prime mover in overcoming this torque.

Motor Action. Obviously, the stator may be supplied with three-phase power from an external source, and when it is so supplied, phase belts are produced similar to those in the figure. These set up a revolving field just as in the stator of a generator. Let the rotor be driven in the same direction and at the same speed as the revolving field of the stator, and assume its excitation and its position with respect to the stator to be such that the emfs which its poles generate in the stator conductors are at all instants approximately equal in value and opposite in direction to the impressed voltages. At all times when the rotor occupies this position with respect to the stator, the rotor and the stator fields are in synchronism; that is, they revolve together in time. Then in the figure the dots and crosses represent the generated (counter) emfs, while if the dots and crosses are replaced by crosses and dots, respectively, the bands of crosses and dots will represent the impressed voltages as well as the currents flowing in the conductors when the power factor is unity. Since these currents are everywhere opposite in direction to the corresponding generator currents represented in the figure, they react with the air-gap flux to produce a force that tends to turn the stator to the left and the rotor to the right. The electromagnetic torque developed therefore tends to drive the rotor in the same direction as does the prime mover. If the latter is disconnected, the rotor continues to run at synchronous speed and to carry a load connected to its shaft. An alternator used in

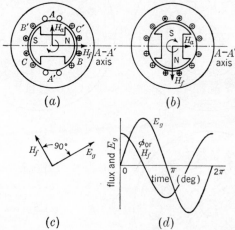

(a) (b)

(c) (d)

FIG. 10-27. Diagram showing time-phase relationships of air-gap flux and generated emf in armature coil.

this manner becomes a *synchronous motor*. A more detailed discussion of the behavior of this motor is found in the following chapter.

Relation between Generated Voltage and Flux in Armature. The voltage generated in the armature winding and the armature current depend upon the resultant air-gap flux. This flux, in turn, is produced by the resultant magnetomotive force, that is, by the armature and field mmfs acting together. If the space distribution of these magnetomotive forces in the air gap be assumed to be sine-shaped, the waves of voltage and current are also sine-shaped and it is possible to represent them as phasors on the same diagram. Thereby a very convenient method is provided for studying the effects of armature reaction.

To make the procedure clear, consider the simplified drawing of a two-pole three-phase generator operating with the armature circuit open (no armature reaction) as in Fig. 10-27. In the position of the rotor shown in (a), the space position of the magnetic gradient $\mathbf{H}_f$ in the air gap due to the field ampere-turns coincides with the axis of coil AA'; the field flux links the coil AA' and the voltage in the coil is zero. At the instant shown in (b), the rotor has moved forward through 90 space degrees; the magnetic gradient along the axis of the coil AA' and the flux linking the coil have fallen to zero, while the generated voltage in AA' has risen to its maximum value. Both the flux linking AA' and the voltage in AA' vary at the same frequency. The time required for the rotor to move from

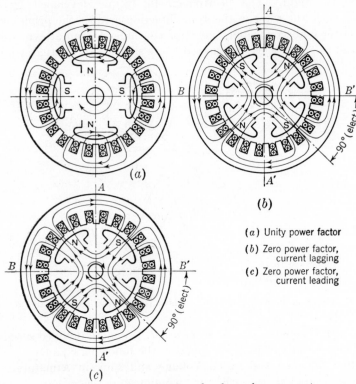

(a) Unity power factor

(b) Zero power factor, current lagging

(c) Zero power factor, current leading

Fig. 11-27. Armature reaction of a three-phase generator.

the position shown in (a) to the position shown in (b) is the time of one-quarter cycle. Since the flux linking AA' was maximum and the voltage zero in position (a) and one-quarter cycle later the flux linking AA' is zero while the voltage in AA' is maximum, and both flux and voltage waves are sinusoidal, they may obviously be represented as in (c) or in rectangular coordinates as in (d). Time is counted from the instant that the axis of the poles coincides with the axis of the coil AA'.

Armature Reaction of Polyphase Synchronous Machines. In respect to armature reaction, all polyphase synchronous machines behave alike. In the discussion that follows, a three-phase machine is used to illustrate the principles involved, and all currents, voltages, and magnetomotive forces refer to per-phase values. Three general cases are considered: (1) load current is in phase with the generated voltage E_g, (2) current lags E_g, and (3) current leads E_g.

1. *Current in Phase with* E_g. When the currents and generated voltages in the phase windings are, respectively, in phase with each other, the dots and crosses in Fig. 11-27(a) represent the magnitudes and space positions of armature mmfs with respect to the poles *for all positions of the rotor*. As in the stator winding of an induction motor (page 439), *the resultant mmf of the revolving field is constant in value*. Its magnetizing effect on the field poles is the same as though the belts of armature currents were d-c belts which always occupy the indicated positions (and distribution of current magnitudes) with respect to the poles. These mmfs tend to magnetize the poles crosswise, similar in manner to the action of the ampere-turns of a d-c machine with brushes aligned on the neutral axis. The ampere-turns tend to reduce the air-gap flux density under the leading pole tip of the generator and to increase it under the trailing tip. If the effect of saturation is small, the decrease of flux under the leading pole tip and the increase of flux under the trailing tip nearly offset one another. The result is that the magnitude of the generated voltage under load is nearly the same as it was under no-load conditions. The principal effect of removing the load (and thereby the armature reaction) is to shift the generated voltage backward from E_o to E_g as in Fig. 12-27.

In Fig. 12-27 is shown the phasor diagram of armature current I_a, generated voltage under load E_g, open-circuit voltage E_o, and the phasor magnetomotive

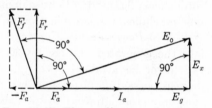

FIG. 12-27. Phasor diagram of voltages and magnetomotive forces for the condition of E_g in phase with I_a.

forces due to the field F_f, the armature F_a and the resultant of these two F_r. By assumption, the *generated voltage* E_g is in phase with the current I_a. This is the voltage generated per phase by the flux of the resultant magnetomotive F_r, which is due to the combined action of the armature and field ampere-turns per pole. The resultant magnetomotive force F_r is composed of two components, namely, the field magnetomotive force F_f and the armature magnetomotive force F_a, and it leads E_g by 90 deg.

The armature magnetomotive force is proportional to the armature current and is in phase with it. If the field mmf is kept constant and the armature current is reduced to zero, the armature mmf disappears and the field mmf alone remains. The field mmf is the difference $F_r - F_a$

or F_f.   Under these conditions (open circuit) the voltage E_o, called the *open-circuit voltage*, is generated, and E_o lags F_f by 90 deg.   Thus, for the assumed condition the effect of armature reaction is to alter slightly the magnitude of the resultant mmf and to shift both F_r and the induced voltage E_g backward in phase.   The change in voltage produced by armature reaction is E_x.

One other fact of importance should be noted.   At unity power factor the axis along which the armature ampere-turns act is in space quadrature with the axis of the field poles (Figs. 10-27 and 11-27).   This is called the *quadrature axis*.   In salient-pole machines the reluctance of the magnetic circuit along the quadrature axis is much larger than that along the axis of the poles (the *direct axis*).   Accordingly, at unity power factor the armature ampere-turns produce much less change in the resultant flux of a salient-pole machine than they would produce if they acted along the direct axis.   For this reason, even at full load, the armature mmf does not greatly affect the generated voltage when the power factor is near unity.   In round rotor machines, such as are used with steam turbines, the reluctance is approximately the same along all axes.

For many purposes the disparity between the direct- and quadrature-axis reluctances may be neglected in computations involving salient-pole machines.   In most of the discussions that follow, the so-called "round-rotor theory" is used.   For use in making more precise analyses of salient-pole machines, the two-reaction method may be applied.[1]

2. *Zero Power Factor, Current Lagging.*   When the armature current lags the generated voltage by 90 electrical degrees (a condition which can never be attained exactly), the rotor has advanced 90 electrical degrees beyond its position in Fig. 11-27(a) before the currents in the conductors adjacent to the axes AA' and BB' reach their maximum values.   The armature mmfs now act along the direct axis counter to the field mmf and directly demagnetize the poles, thereby reducing the flux and causing a drop in the generated voltage.   If the same generated voltage as in case 1 is to be maintained, the field excitation must be increased.

The phasor diagram of mmfs, generated voltage, and current is shown in Fig. 13-27.   The internal voltage E_g is generated by the flux produced by the resultant mmf F_r.   If the field mmf is kept constant and the armature current is reduced to zero, the generated voltage rises to the open-circuit value E_o.

3. *Zero Power Factor, Current Leading.*   For this condition the armature current is assumed to lead the generated voltage by 90 electrical

---

[1] See any standard textbook on a-c machinery or A. E. Knowlton (ed.), "Standard Handbook for Electrical Engineers," 8th ed., pp. 661–670, McGraw-Hill Book Company, Inc., New York, 1949.

degrees and the currents in the conductors adjacent to the axes AA' and BB' reach their maximum values when the rotor is 90 electrical degrees behind the position shown in Fig. 11-27(a). The armature mmfs now magnetize the poles and thereby increase the air-gap flux and the generated voltage. If the same voltage as in case 1 is to be maintained, the field excitation must be reduced.

Figure 14-27 is the phasor diagram for the case of zero internal power factor, current leading. In this case the field and armature mmfs both act together along the direct axis to produce the resultant mmf $\mathbf{F}_r$. The generated emf is $\mathbf{E}_g$, which again lags $\mathbf{F}_r$ by 90 deg. When the armature current is reduced to zero, the resultant mmf becomes the field mmf $\mathbf{F}_f$ and the generated voltage falls to the open-circuit value $\mathbf{E}_o$.

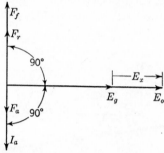

Fig. 13-27. Phasor diagram of voltages and magnetomotive forces for the condition that E_g leads I_a by 90 deg.

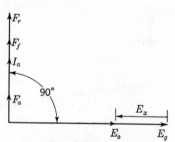

Fig. 14-27. Phasor diagram of voltages and magnetomotive forces for the condition that E_g lags I_a by 90 deg.

In a synchronous motor the armature currents are reversed (180 deg out of phase) with respect to the generator currents. Therefore at unity power factor the motor armature mmf weakens the trailing pole tips and strengthens the leading tips. Similarly, with leading currents armature reaction weakens the field as in Fig. 11-27(b), while with lagging currents armature reaction strengthens the field as in (c). If the counter emf is to remain unchanged, the field excitation must be strengthened for leading currents and weakened for lagging currents.

4. *Power Factor neither Zero nor Unity.* Under usual operating conditions the current leads or lags the internal voltage by some angle θ less than 90 deg. The phasor diagrams of mmfs, armature current, and voltage then take the forms shown in Fig. 15-27. When the current lags, as in (a), the armature mmf acts partly along the direct axis to decrease the resultant magnetization and partly along the quadrature axis to distort the field. When the current leads, as in (b), the direct-axis component of armature mmf acts to increase the resultant magnetization, while the quadrature component distorts the field as before. In each case the

field mmf is the phasor difference between the resultant mmf and the armature mmf. If the magnetic circuit is unsaturated so that the flux produced by a given mmf is proportional to the mmf, it is clear that

a. The armature ampere-turns due to the in-phase component of current act along the quadrature axis. In a salient-pole machine, owing to the high reluctance of the magnetic circuit along this axis, the resultant flux is not greatly changed, but the voltage wave is shifted and somewhat distorted.

b. The armature ampere-turns due to the quadrature component of current act along the direct axis. They result in decreasing the flux proportional to the armature current when the current lags and in increasing the flux proportional to the current when the current leads.

If the field current is held constant and the load current is reduced to zero, the voltage generated in the armature will change from E_g to E_o,

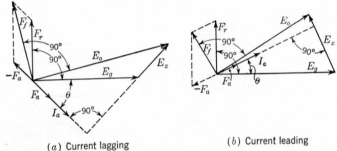

(a) Current lagging   (b) Current leading

FIG. 15-27. Phasor diagram of voltages and magnetomotive forces for any condition such that E_g leads (or lags) I_a by some angle θ ($0 < \theta < 90$ deg).

hence the difference E_x between these phasors is the phasor voltage change due to armature reaction. It is proportional to the current and leads it by 90 deg.

Armature Resistance. In addition to I^2R loss due to current in the ohmic resistance of the armature winding (as measured by direct currents), there are a number of other components of armature loss that vary approximately with the square of the armature current and are supplied by it. The hysteresis and eddy-current losses due to the slot leakage flux are two of these.

The slot leakage flux (Fig. 16-27) passes through the iron in the armature teeth. This flux, produced by the armature current, is approximately proportional to the current and varies with it. The pulsating flux gives rise to hysteresis and eddy-current losses, principally in the teeth where the flux density is largest. These losses are supplied by the armature current and are roughly proportional to the flux density squared, and hence to the square of the armature current [Eqs. (4-15) and (5-15)]. Moreover, particularly when the armature slots are deep, the number of interlinkages of flux with conductor is larger for the lower or closed end of the slot than for the upper or open end (Fig. 16-27). This results in increasing the current density in the portion of the conductors near the open ends of the slots, thereby increasing the copper losses.

If the sum of all the losses supplied by the armature current is divided by the square of the current, the *effective resistance* is obtained. It may be as much as 50 per cent larger than the ohmic resistance, depending upon the size of the conductors and the shape of the slots. The value of the effective resistance is often estimated by increasing the ohmic resistance by an arbitrary figure of about 40 per cent. It may also be measured approximately, but the method is rather involved and will not be described here.

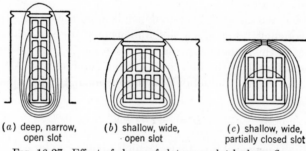

(a) deep, narrow,   (b) shallow, wide,   (c) shallow, wide,
    open slot   open slot   partially closed slot

FIG. 16-27. Effect of shape of slot upon slot-leakage flux.

Leakage Reactance.   Current in a circuit sets up a magnetic flux which links the circuit.   The self-inductance L of the circuit in henrys, due to weber-turns $N\phi$ of self-linkages produced by the current I in the circuit, is defined as the number of weber-turns per ampere of current.   Symbolically, it is

$$L \text{ (henrys)} = \frac{N\phi \text{ (weber-turns)}}{I \text{ (amperes)}}$$

If the current wave is sinusoidal, the emf of self-inductance of the circuit is $E_l = X_l I$, where $X_l = 2\pi f L$ is the inductive reactance of the circuit and f is the frequency.

Armature leakage reactance is difficult both to define and to compute. A full discussion of the subject is beyond the scope of this book.   Roughly, it may be thought of as the reactance due to the flux which links the armature winding but does not interlink the field turns.   A part of such leakage flux exists in the end connections of the armature winding, although this flux contributes less to the armature-leakage inductance than the flux that leaks across the armature slots (Fig. 16-27).

The mmf of the armature ampere-turns in the slots causes local fluxes to be set up along the paths indicated in the figure. These fluxes obviously do not link the field winding. If the slot is deep and narrow, as in (a), the total reluctance of the path is small. The reluctance of the steel portion of the path is very small and may be neglected in comparison with that of the slot itself. Hence, the total reluctance is approximately proportional to the width of the slot. For a given slot mmf, narrow deep slots, as in (a), and partially enclosed slots, as in (c), have relatively large leakage fluxes, while wide shallow slots have small leakage fluxes. It is thus apparent that the leakage inductance is, to some extent, under the control of the designer. Since the methods of computing and measuring leakage reactance are usually somewhat involved, detailed discussions of these topics are omitted. In a later paragraph, however, the Potier-triangle method of approximating the leakage reactance of an alternator is presented.

The leakage reactance $X_l = 2\pi f L$ depends upon the leakage inductance and the frequency. For given slot dimensions, the slot leakage flux is proportional to the ampere-turns in the slot ($\phi_l \propto NI$), and since inductance is proportional to the flux linkages per ampere, $L = N\phi_l/I$, it follows that the leakage inductance is proportional to the square of the number of turns.

$$L = \frac{N\phi_l}{I} = kN^2$$

Accordingly, slow-speed machines, which require a larger number of armature turns to generate a given voltage than do high-speed machines, also have larger reactances. Also, the reactance of a 60-cycle machine is larger than that of a 25-cycle machine of comparable rating.

When the machine is loaded the terminal voltage differs from the generated voltage $\mathbf{E}_g$ by the voltages consumed in armature resistance and reactance. The generated voltage under load cannot be measured, but it may be computed by adding the consumed voltages mentioned to the terminal voltage. If the terminal voltage $\mathbf{E}$ be taken as reference phasor and R is the effective resistance, X_l is the leakage reactance, and I is the effective armature current, one may write

$$\mathbf{E}_g = \mathbf{E} + \mathbf{I}(R + jX_l)$$

This matter will be discussed further presently.

Synchronous Reactance. It has already been shown that in a loaded generator, armature reaction causes a voltage drop $\mathbf{E}_x$ proportional to the current when the current lags the generated voltage 90 deg, a voltage rise proportional to the current when the current leads 90 deg, and a shift in voltage proportional to the current when the current neither leads nor lags. In a synchronous motor, similar voltage changes are experienced.

These voltage changes, brought about by the armature reaction, may be represented as in Figs. 13-27, 14-27, and 15-27. They are proportional to the current, and $\mathbf{E}_x$, representing the voltages consumed by these drops, leads the respective current by 90 deg, or in the same manner as the voltage consumed by leakage-reactance.

Thus, subject to the assumptions previously made, armature reaction affects the voltage in the same manner as a reactance in the armature circuit. Accordingly, a fictitious reactance X_{eq} may be assumed to exist in the armature circuit for the purpose of properly accounting for the effect of armature reaction. The value of this reactance must be such that the product of the armature current and the reactance $jX_{eq}\mathbf{I}$ is equal to the change in voltage $\mathbf{E}_x$ caused by armature reaction. The equivalent reactance may be combined with the armature leakage reactance. The sum X_s is called the *synchronous reactance*. That is, $X_s = X_l + X_{eq}$ and the total voltage drop under load, due to armature reaction and armature leakage reactance combined, is $X_s I$.

While the effect of synchronous reactance is to cause an internal-voltage drop in the machine when loaded, it is not a wholly undesirable property. The amount of synchronous reactance a machine may have is under the control of the designer and is adjusted to meet operating requirements. Alternating-current generators, unlike d-c machines, are not designed to have good inherent regulation; that is, they do not of themselves maintain even approximately constant terminal voltages at all loads.

Maintaining constant terminal voltage in alternators is the function of a separate automatic device called a *voltage regulator* (page 493). This device works just as well on an alternator with high reactance as upon one with low reactance. High reactance protects the armature of a machine against heavy short-circuit currents by increasing the internal-voltage drop and reducing the terminal voltage; hence it serves as a protective measure. At full-rated current the reactance drop may be from 50 to 100 per cent or more of the rated terminal voltage. When this drop is 50 per cent, for example, the machine is said to have 50 per cent reactance.

Synchronous Impedance and Its Measurement. In addition to the voltage consumed by synchronous reactance, there is a much smaller component of voltage consumed by the effective armature resistance. The latter is in phase with current in the phase winding while the former leads the phase current by 90 deg. The sum of these two components is the voltage consumed by the synchronous impedance, $\mathbf{Z}_s$. Referred to the phase current as reference, the phasor voltage consumed is

$$\mathbf{Z}_s\mathbf{I} = \mathbf{I}(R + jX_s)$$

and the synchronous impedance is

$$Z_s = \sqrt{R^2 + X_s{}^2}$$

where R = armature effective resistance

$\quad\quad X_s$ = armature synchronous reactance

$\quad\quad Z_s$ = armature synchronous impedance

The synchronous impedance of a three-phase machine may be measured as follows: Select three similar ammeters of suitable range. Connect one terminal of each meter to a common point (neutral) and the remaining terminal of each to one of the leads of the machine. Drive the rotor at synchronous speed and excite the field with direct current of such value that from 1.5 to 2 times rated current flows in the ammeters. Since the armature is short-circuited, the terminal voltage is zero. Next, remove the short circuit but maintain the same field excitation as before and measure the open-circuit terminal voltage $\sqrt{3}E_o$. Compute the open-circuit voltage to neutral E_o. Since under short circuit the terminal voltage is zero but when the short circuit is removed the voltage to neutral rises to E_o, one concludes that E_o is the voltage consumed per phase (Y connection assumed) by synchronous impedance at the value of current used. Hence, if I is the average of the three ammeter readings, the synchronous impedance per phase is

$$Z_s = \frac{E_0}{I} \tag{5-27}$$

The synchronous impedance is not strictly constant but varies considerably with saturation. At low saturation the effect of a given number of ampere-turns of armature reaction is larger than at high saturation. Under the conditions of the short-circuit test just described, the saturation is usually less than under operating conditions. Accordingly, as large a value of short-circuit current as practicable should be used for making this test in order more nearly to approximate the correct operating impedance.

Example 1. The effective resistance per phase (assumed Y-connected) of a 1,500-kva 60-cycle 2,300-volt three-phase alternator is 0.028 ohm. The armature winding is short-circuited; the rotor is driven at synchronous speed; and the field winding is excited a sufficient amount to circulate 750 amp in the armature. When the short circuit is removed, the excitation remaining unchanged, the terminal voltage rises to 2,060 volts. What is the synchronous impedance of the armature under the conditions of test?

The rated voltage to neutral is $2{,}300/\sqrt{3}$ or 1,330 volts. After the short circuit is removed the voltage is $2{,}060/\sqrt{3}$ or 1,190 volts. The voltage per phase consumed in the synchronous impedance is 1,190 when the current is 750 amp. Hence the synchronous impedance is

$$Z_s = \frac{1{,}190}{750} = 1.59 \text{ ohms per phase}$$

The rated current of the machine is 376 amp, and the percentage synchronous impedance drop at rated load is

$$Z_s I = \frac{100 \times 376 \times 1.59}{1,330} = 45 \text{ per cent}$$

Voltage Diagrams of a Loaded Generator.[1] The voltage consumed in the armature impedance of a generator depends upon the load current and upon the power factor. The influence of power factor is well illustrated in the phasor diagrams of Fig. 17-27. In these diagrams,

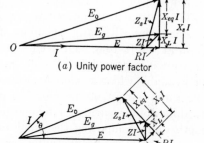

(a) Unity power factor

E = terminal voltage
I = output current
θ = power-factor angle
E_g = generated voltage
E_o = open-circuit voltage

(b) Leading current

At unity power factor [Fig. 17-27(a)] the voltage consumed in the impedance adds nearly at right angles to the terminal voltage, and the latter differs only slightly from the open-circuit voltage. Hence, under load the drop in voltage is small.

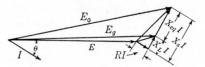

(c) Lagging current

In (b) the current leads the terminal voltage by a large angle. The armature ampere-turns aid the field

FIG. 17-27. Phasor diagrams of a loaded generator. (Synchronous-impedance method.)

ampere-turns and thereby increase the effective excitation. Furthermore, the leakage-reactance causes a rise in voltage as shown in the diagram. Hence, the open-circuit voltage is less than the terminal voltage; to obtain the same terminal voltage as in (a), the excitation must be reduced.

In (c) the current lags the terminal voltage by a large angle. The ampere-turns of the armature oppose the field ampere-turns and thereby

---

[1] The voltage diagrams of Fig. 17-27 employ what is called "the synchronous impedance method" for determining the relationships among the several voltages involved. The effect of changes in saturation with load and excitation is usually neglected, and the synchronous impedance is assumed to have some appropriate constant value which may be determined by experiment in the manner previously described. This method is applicable to round-rotor machines but is less accurate when applied to machines with salient poles. In case of the latter this method has been superseded by the more suitable "two-reaction method" of computation. Space limitations make it impractical to include a full discussion of the "two-reaction method" in this book.

reduce the effective excitation.   Furthermore, the leakage-reactance drop and the resistance drop both cause the terminal voltage to fall.   Hence, to maintain the same terminal voltage as in (a) the excitation must be increased.

Regulation.   The standards of the American Standards Association define the regulation of a synchronous generator as "the rise in voltage when the rated load at rated power factor is reduced to zero, expressed in per cent of rated voltage."

This ratio can be measured directly by a loading test if the machine is small, but with large machines it becomes impractical to make such tests at the factory, and even after the machine is installed in its final location it may be difficult to do so.   A driving motor of some kind must be available which is capable of developing an amount of power equal to the rated output of the machine under test.   Because of the impracticability of measuring the regulation of commercial machines by loading, methods of computing the regulation have been developed which give quite satisfactory results under certain conditions.   For example, in the phasor diagrams of a loaded alternator (Fig. 17-27), if E, I, θ, R, and X_s are known, the open-circuit voltage can be found and from the above definition the regulation can be estimated, for

$$\text{Regulation} = \frac{100(E_o - E)}{E} \tag{6-27}$$

where E_o = open-circuit voltage.

In this method X_s is assumed to have a constant value.   Thus the effect of saturation is neglected as is also the effect of saliency upon the value of X_s in salient-pole machines.   This effect introduces inaccuracies, particularly at low power factors.   The use of the method is illustrated in the following example.

Example 2.   Calculate the regulation of the alternator specified in the example on page 486 for rated load and each of the following power factors: (a) unity, (b) 0.70, current leading, (c) 0.70, current lagging.

At rated load the resistance drop per phase is 376 × 0.028 = 10.5 volts.   The rated voltage to neutral is 2,300/$\sqrt{3}$ or 1,330 volts.   Hence the RI drop per phase is

$$RI = \frac{100 \times 10.5}{1,330} = 0.79 \text{ per cent}$$

By the example on page 486 the percentage synchronous impedance drop at rated current is 45.   This is also approximately equal to the percentage synchronous reactance drop.

(a) Power factor is unity.   Under these conditions the voltage consumed in RI drop is in phase with the terminal voltage and the voltage consumed in X_sI drop leads the voltage by 90 deg, as in Fig. 17-27(a).   The terminal voltage is the phasor of reference and its length is taken as 100 per cent. Expressed in percentage, the open-circuit voltage is

$$\mathbf{E}_o = \mathbf{E} + R\mathbf{I} + jX_s\mathbf{I}$$
$$= 100 + 0.79 + j45$$

The magnitude of the open-circuit voltage is

$$E_o = \sqrt{100.79^2 + 45^2} = 110.4$$

and by Eq. (6-27),

Regulation $= 110.4 - 100 = 10.4$ per cent

(b) Power factor is 0.7, current leading. The voltages consumed in resistance and synchronous reactance have the same values as in (a), but since $R\mathbf{I}$ is in phase with the current and $X_s\mathbf{I}$ leads the current by 90 deg as in Fig. 17-27(b), these voltages must be expressed in terms of their components in phase with and in quadrature with the reference $\mathbf{E}$ before they can be added to $\mathbf{E}$ to find $\mathbf{E}_o$. The cosine of θ is 0.7 and the sine of θ is 0.714. Expressed as phasors in terms of their rectangular components,

$$R\mathbf{I} = 0.79(\cos \theta + j \sin \theta)$$
$$= 0.79(0.70 + j0.714)$$
$$= 0.553 + j0.564$$
$$jX_s\mathbf{I} = 45(- \sin \theta + j \cos \theta)$$
$$= 45(-0.714 + j0.7)$$
$$= -32.1 + j31.5$$

The percentage open-circuit voltage is

$$\mathbf{E}_o = \mathbf{E} + RI(\cos \theta + j \sin \theta) + X_sI(- \sin \theta + j \cos \theta)$$
$$= 100 + 0.553 + j0.564 - 32.1 + j31.5$$
$$= 68.5 + j32.1$$

The magnitude of the open-circuit voltage is

$$E_o = \sqrt{68.5^2 + 32.1^2} = 75.4 \text{ per cent}$$

and

Regulation $= 75.4 - 100 = -24.6$ per cent

(c) Power factor is 0.7, current lagging. The voltage consumed in resistance and synchronous-reactance again have the same full-load values as in (a), but $R\mathbf{I}$ lags the terminal voltage by the angle θ and $jX_s\mathbf{I}$ leads the terminal voltage by the angle $90 - \theta°$, as in Fig. 17-27(c). Hence

$$R\mathbf{I} = 0.79(\cos \theta - j \sin \theta)$$
$$= 0.79(0.70 - j0.714)$$
$$= 0.553 - j0.564$$
$$jX_s\mathbf{I} = 45(\sin \theta + j \cos \theta)$$
$$= 45(0.714 + j0.70)$$
$$= 32.1 + j31.5$$

The percentage open-circuit voltage is

$$\mathbf{E}_o = \mathbf{E} + RI(\cos \theta - j \sin \theta) + X_sI(\sin \theta + j \cos \theta)$$
$$= 100 + 0.553 - j0.564 + 32.1 + j31.5$$
$$= 132.65 + j30.94$$

The magnitude of the open-circuit voltage is

$$E = \sqrt{132.65^2 + 30.94^2} = 136.2 \text{ per cent}$$

and

$$\text{Regulation} = 136.2 - 100 = 36.2 \text{ per cent}$$

Potier Triangle. To draw the Potier triangle it is necessary to take data for (1) a no-load saturation curve, and (2) a zero-power-factor (current lagging) rated-load-current saturation curve. Data for the first curve are obtained by running the machine at rated speed and no load, and recording a series of corresponding values of open-circuit terminal

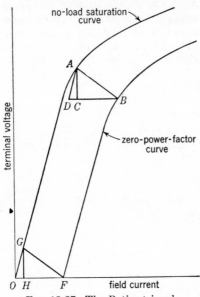

voltages $\sqrt{3}\, E_o$ and field currents. The curve is usually plotted in terms of line-to-neutral voltage E_o vs. field current. To obtain data for the zero-power-factor saturation curve, two similar machines are required both of which are driven mechanically, are connected in parallel electrically, and are run at synchronous speed. One of these is operated as a generator and the other as an underexcited synchronous motor. For each point on the curve, readings of generator field current and terminal voltage are recorded when the relative field excitations and the mechanical power supplied to each of the machines have been adjusted to such values that the generator

Fig. 18-27. The Potier triangle.

delivers rated output current at zero-power-factor, current lagging. A series of such readings is required over a range of generator field currents corresponding to the range of terminal voltage desired. Typical curves taken under the conditions described are illustrated in Fig. 18-27.

From a consideration of Fig. 18-27 it may be seen that the zero-power-factor curve is a duplicate of the open-circuit curve except that it is shifted to the right and downward, and for every point A on the open-circuit curve there is a point of corresponding saturation B on the zero-power-factor curve. Point B is shifted to the right of A because of the demagnetizing effect of the armature reaction and is shifted downward from A because of the voltage drop in the leakage reactance. The IR drop is negligible for currents lagging 90 deg. The right triangle ACB, which is determined by points A and B and the coordinate axes, is called the *Potier triangle*. The line AC in volts is approximately equal to $X_l I$, and hence the leakage reactance may be evaluated. The line BC represents the effect of armature reaction in terms of equivalent field amperes; when multiplied by field turns, it becomes F_a of Fig. 13-27.

It should be recognized that the same Potier triangle determined as above must everywhere fit between the no-load and zero-power-factor saturation curves when the base line HF is kept parallel to the field-current axis. The triangle is designated GHF at the bottom of the curves in Fig. 18-27, and it forms a part of the larger triangle GOF. If G and F are moved up the curves to points A and B, keeping OF parallel to the field-current axis, then the upper triangle lies as shown by ADB. This is the basis for the geometrical construction used to locate a point A on the upper curve corresponding to another point B on the lower curve. Briefly then, to erect the Potier triangle at any point B, lay out a horizontal line BD equal in length to FO, draw the line DA parallel to OG and locate point A, from which the perpendicular AC is dropped to complete the triangle.

When the leakage reactance and the armature reaction (in terms of equivalent field current) are known from the Potier triangle, it is possible to use these values in accordance with the general principles outlined on pages 477 to 482, to make a more precise analysis of the behavior of an alternator under load than that which the synchronous impedance theory provides. To illustrate, assume a condition of loading similar to that which corresponds to the phasor diagram of Fig. 15-27(a). Let the alternator deliver rated load current I, which lags the terminal voltage E by θ deg, as in Fig. 19-27. The phasor voltages consumed in the resistance and the leakage reactance may be added to $\mathbf{E}$ to find the generated voltage $\mathbf{E}_g$. This voltage is the result of some net excitation F_r which may be found in terms of equivalent field amperes by entering the open-circuit saturation curve of Fig. 18-27 at voltage E_g.

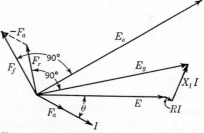

FIG. 19-27. Phasor diagram of a loaded generator.

The net excitation F_r may be laid off as a phasor which leads its voltage $\mathbf{E}_g$ by 90 deg as shown. The sum of the net field amperes $\mathbf{F}_r$ and the negative of the equivalent armature reaction field amperes $\mathbf{F}_a$ must be the actual field current $\mathbf{F}_f$ that is required to establish this condition of voltage. Again, the voltage E_o may be determined by entering the no-load saturation curve with the field current F_f. It should be observed that this method of analysis, unlike the synchronous impedance method, takes the saturation effects of the machine into account.

Obviously, the field-current phasors used above differ from the corresponding field mmf phasors by a constant (the number of field turns), so the equivalent field ampere-turns may just as well be used in place of field current in Figs. 18-27 to 22-27, inclusive.

ASA Method of Voltage Regulation. Since the various approximations which may be made in calculating the alternator regulation are many, it is desirable to have a standard method in order that guarantees of machine performance may have some basis for comparison and checking. Such a method is given in the American Standards Association publication entitled "American Standards for Rotating Electrical Machinery." The ASA method, which is recognized as empirical, is found to yield results that check closely the performance data obtained from load tests; it is

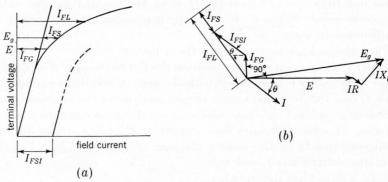

Fig. 20-27. Regulation by method of the American Standards Association.

therefore regarded as a useful method. This method presupposes a knowledge of the voltage consumed by the leakage reactance of the machine such as might be obtained from a Potier triangle. In the ASA method the voltage consumed by leakage reactance is actually accounted for by substituting an equivalent increase in armature reaction mmf. It is necessary, however, to know the leakage reactance in order that the generated voltage and the effects of saturation may be found.

By referring to Fig. 20-27(a) and (b), it may be noted that the air-gap line of the no-load saturation curve has been extended, thus making it possible to pick off the curve at any desired voltage the added increment of field current required because of saturation effects in the steel. The load current is laid off at the correct angle with respect to the terminal voltage **E** (usually rated voltage), which is taken as the reference. If the voltage E be regarded as a generated voltage, the field current I_{FG} required to generate this voltage, if there were no saturation, can be found from the air-gap line. The field current found is then a fictitious net excitation which generates E and is laid off as a phasor leading $\mathbf{E}$ by 90 deg. The equivalent field current representing armature reaction is taken as I_{FSI} from Fig. 20-27(a). A little thought reveals that this current is the field current necessary to circulate rated current in the armature at short circuit. This current differs from CB of the Potier triangle in that it represents a fictitious armature reaction set up to account for the total voltage consumed at full-load current and zero power factor. The total excitation required in an *unsaturated* machine is the sum of $\mathbf{I}_{FG}$ and $\mathbf{I}_{FSI}$ as indicated in Fig. 20-27(b). Phasor $\mathbf{I}_{FSI}$ is parallel to $\mathbf{I}$.

In order to account for saturation, the voltage $\mathbf{E}_G$, corresponding to the flux crossing the air gap, is found by adding $R\mathbf{I}$ and $jX_l\mathbf{I}$ as phasors to the terminal voltage $\mathbf{E}$. Again, if one refers to the no-load saturation curve, it is noted that the increment I_{FS} is required to overcome the effects of saturation; therefore, this increment is added to the sum of $\mathbf{I}_{FG}$ and $\mathbf{I}_{FSI}$ as shown. By referring this value of I_{FL} to the saturation curve, the open-circuit voltage of the machine may be found and the regulation may be determined.

Voltage Control. The necessity of controlling the voltage of generators connected to distribution feeders became apparent when the first Edison systems were put into operation. Because feeder circuits were short and generators were small, simple hand-operated devices would do. As each feeder was customarily supplied by a separate generator, it was possible to control the voltage by means of manually operated field rheostats. The demand for electric energy grew very rapidly, however, and to meet it the size of generating units as well as the number and capacity of feeder circuits were increased year by year. As the complexity of power systems increased, manual control of voltage became progressively less satisfactory and some form of automatic control had to be developed to replace it.

Within rather narrow limits the voltage of a d-c generator can be controlled automatically by the addition of a series-field winding to form the compound generator. With this machine the terminal voltage may be held nearly constant throughout the full range of load, or it may be increased somewhat with increase of load to compensate for line drop. When a-c generators first came into use, attempts were made to apply the same principle of control to these machines by rectifying a fraction of the load current and passing it through a separate field winding. Such alternators were called *composite-wound* alternators. This method of control was found to be unsatisfactory, however, and has long since been abandoned except for occasional minor applications. Automatic *voltage regulators* of the vibrating type have been used quite generally in power stations to control the voltage of a-c generators and synchronous condensers, but other types of improved automatic regulators have largely replaced them. One of these is illustrated in Fig. 21-27 and is described briefly in following paragraphs.

The regulator is designed for the automatic control of voltage of a-c machines. It is direct acting and is arranged for operation in the shunt-field circuit of a self-excited exciter. The principal parts consist of a voltage-sensitive electromagnetic torque element, the pull of which is balanced by a helical spring, and a quickly acting rheostat the resistance of which is capable of being varied from the maximum required value to substantially zero. The rheostat is connected in the exciter shunt-field circuit. Any change in the voltage of the a-c machine produces corresponding changes in the exciting current of the electromagnets of the torque element and thus immediately brings about corrective changes in the resistance of the rheostat. The electromagnets are excited with direct current supplied by a small rectifier from the potential of the a-c machine.

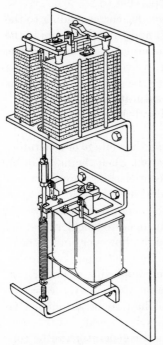

FIG. 21-27. Diactor (direct-acting) generator-voltage regulator. (*General Electric Company.*)

The rheostatic element of the regulator comprises two stacks of special nonmetallic resistance plates (Figs. 21-27 and 22-27). The stacks are formed of resistance plates, metal contact plates, and insulating spacers disposed as shown. At the front end of each resistance plate a silver button, which is slightly thicker than the plate itself, extends through the plate and protrudes on each side. At the back end an insulating spacer is mounted, while in the middle of each is a metal contact plate, which is slightly thicker than either the protruding portions of the silver button or the insulating spacer, thereby providing a fulcrum on which adjacent plates may be tilted slightly either forward or back. By means of fins that fit into slots in adjacent pairs, resistance plates are locked together to form a stack so that, in the manner just described, the entire stack or any part of it may be tilted at one time.

There is no metallic contact between adjacent contact plates, but a resistance circuit exists between them through the material of the resistance plate. When the entire stack is tilted backward, the silver buttons at the front end of the stack are separated and a relatively high-resistance circuit is formed through the center of the stack with all plates in series.

By adjusting the extent of the tilting action the number of resistance plates in series may be varied. The top plate of each stack is made of metal; it acts as contact plate for the entire stack. The stack itself is mounted on a copper bracket that serves to make good electrical connection between the bottom plates of the two adjacent stacks, which are series-connected. Tilting of the plates brings about a change in the resistance of the stack as illustrated in Fig. 22-27. The tilting action is produced by the pull of a spring which is counterbalanced by the force of attraction of an electromagnet for its armature. The resultant force is transmitted through a rod to an equalizer arrangement which presses down upon the top plate of a stack in varying amounts, depending upon the resultant action of the torque element and spring, and produces the

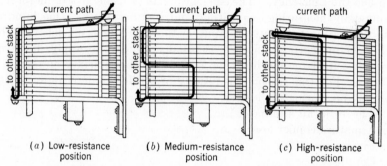

(a) Low-resistance position   (b) Medium-resistance position   (c) High-resistance position

FIG. 22-27. Variation of resistance in Diactor due to tilting: (a) low-resistance position; (b) medium-resistance position; (c) high-resistance position.

tilting motion through the medium of which the change of resistance of the rheostat is brought about.

A number of auxiliary devices that are essential to the regulator include a stabilizer, a rectifier, an external resistance, and, if the voltage of the a-c machine to be regulated exceeds 125 volts, a potential transformer. The stabilizer is an antihunting device which prevents the regulator from over-shooting when it operates to correct changes in voltage, thus eliminating the need for dashpots or similar devices. The rectifier supplies full-wave rectified single-phase current to the coils of the electromagnets. The rectified direct voltage is proportional to the alternating voltage impressed, and hence the regulator action is responsive to changes in voltage of the a-c machine. The rectified current, moreover, is substantially independent of small changes in frequency.

Rating. The ratings of a-c generators include a statement of the number of phases (whether single-phase, two-phase, or three-phase) and the kilovolt-amperes available at the terminals at specified speed, voltage, frequency, and power factor. The rating assumes continuous operation unless a definite short-time rating is specified. The allowable temperature rise is usually 50 C. When special heat-resisting insulation is used, this limit may be increased. Modern machines often have built-in thermocouples or resistance temperature detectors in the windings at points where a knowledge of the temperature is desired. These are connected to a suitable indicating or recording meter by a switching device. When recording meters are used, the switching device is operated by a clock mechanism that makes it possible to record the temperature of each indicator in turn.

Speeds depend upon the nature of the driving unit. Turbo-driven machines employ speeds as high as 1,800 and 3,600 rpm. The standard frequency is 60 cycles and standard generator voltages are those given on page 555.

Losses and Efficiency. The efficiency of an a-c generator or motor may be found by measuring the output and input directly. One hundred times the ratio of output to input is the percentage efficiency. This method of measuring efficiency is usually difficult to apply, however, especially with large machines, on account of the difficulty of absorbing the load. For this reason it is usually preferable to determine the efficiency by measuring the losses.

The losses in an alternator are

1. Armature copper loss
2. Field copper loss
3. Core losses
4. Windage and friction losses
5. Miscellaneous losses

The armature copper loss includes some core loss and eddy-current loss due to stray fields, as well as the ordinary I^2R loss in the winding. The total loss may be expressed as I^2R_{eff}, where R_{eff} is the effective resistance of the armature. This loss is usually found by a short-circuit test. The rotor is driven by a small motor, the output of which may be determined (such as the calibrated d-c shunt motor described on page 237). The armature is short-circuited and the field is excited with sufficient current to cause the desired armature current to circulate. Owing to the low value of excitation, the core losses, other than those due to stray fields, are negligible. The output of the driving motor is found. The armature and field circuits are then opened and the output of the driving motor is again found. The difference between the driving-motor outputs in the two cases is the effective armature copper loss $3I^2R_{eff}$, where I and R_{eff} are the per-phase values.

The field loss may be found from measured resistance and current. It should include the loss in any necessary field rheostats.

The sum of the core losses and friction losses may be measured by driving the motor at rated speed, with field excited to a value such that the voltage generated is the same as that generated at the load and power factor for which the losses are desired. The output of the driving motor is then the sum of the core and friction losses.

When a separate blower is used to supply cooling air exclusively to a single machine, the blower losses are chargeable to the alternator. Likewise, when a separate direct-connected exciter is used exclusively to excite a single alternator, the exciter losses are chargeable to the alternator. These are classed as miscellaneous losses.

The efficiency of a three-phase a-c generator may then be expressed as

$$\text{Efficiency} = \frac{\text{output}}{\text{output} + \text{losses}}$$

$$= \frac{3EI \cos \theta}{3EI \cos \theta + 3I^2 R_{eff} + W_f + W_c + I_f^2 R_f + M} \qquad (7\text{-}27)$$

$$E = \text{terminal voltage per phase}$$
$$I = \text{output current per phase}$$
$$\cos \theta = \text{power factor}$$
$$3I^2 R_{eff} = \text{effective copper loss from short-circuit test}$$
$$W_f + W_c = \text{stray-power loss from open-circuit test}$$
$$I_f^2 R_f = \text{shunt-field loss}$$
$$M = \text{miscellaneous losses, if any}$$

Problems

1-27. Determine the correct speeds for (a) 60-cycle alternators and (b) 25-cycle alternators with 4, 8, 12, and 20 poles.

2-27. (a) Compute the full-load current output of a 2,000-kva 2,300-volt 0.80-power-factor three-phase alternator. (b) What is the current per phase winding if the machine is Δ-connected? (c) If the efficiency is 94 per cent, what is the prime-mover horsepower required to drive the alternator?

3-27. A three-phase four-pole 60-cycle alternator with 48 slots has a double-layer ⅔-pitch lap winding (see Fig. 5-27). Draw the developed wiring diagram of a winding of this kind with one turn per coil.

4-27. Determine the *pitch factor* and the *distribution factor* of the winding in Prob. 3-27.

5-27. If the stator windings of the machine in Prob. 3-27 are Y-connected and the air-gap flux per pole is 2.5×10^6 maxwells, how many turns per coil are required to give a terminal emf of 2,300 volts?

6-27. A three-phase, Y-connected generator is rated to deliver 2,000 kva at 2,300 volts and 0.8 power factor. The effective resistance of the stator winding is estimated to be 20 per cent larger than the ohmic resistance. The latter has an average value of 0.022 ohm measured between two terminals. The field is supplied with 76 amp from 125-volt mains. Friction and windage losses are 15.2 kw and iron losses 33.1 kw. (a) Determine the efficiency of the machine. (b) What is the efficiency of the same machine at rated output and unity power factor if the field current required at unity power factor is 62 amp?

7-27. The rated terminal emf of a 30,000-kva Y-connected three-phase water-wheel generator is 13,200 volts or 7,630 volts per phase. Data for the open-circuit and rated-current, zero-power-factor (current lagging) saturation curves are given in the tabulation below:

DATA FOR OPEN-CIRCUIT SATURATION CURVE

Terminal voltage per phase, kv........	0	2.8	4.6	5.75	7.0	8.5	9.7
Field current, amp..................	0	80	128	165	220	340	500

DATA FOR FULL-LOAD, ZERO-POWER-FACTOR SATURATION CURVE

Terminal voltage per phase, kv........	0	3.2	4.0	5.2	6.1	7.3	8.2
Field current, amp...................	210	300	325	380	460	633	810

Data for both curves were obtained at rated speed. The effective armature resistance per phase is 0.018 ohm. (a) Plot the open-circuit saturation curve and the rated-current zero-power-factor saturation curve, and draw in the air-gap line. (b) Locate the rated terminal voltage-per-phase line, draw in the Potier triangle, and determine the Potier reactance ($X_l \approx E_x/I_a$). (c) Compute the voltage consumed in the armature resistance, compare it with the value of E_x, and judge whether the resistance voltage may be disregarded. Determine the regulation of the generator by the ASA method for 0.80 power factor, current lagging.

8-27. From the full-load, zero-power-factor curve of Prob. 7-27 it is observed that the terminal voltage per phase is 7,630 when the field current is 700 amp. If the excitation is held constant and the armature circuit is opened, the terminal voltage per phase rises to 10.8 kv. (a) Determine the synchronous impedance. (b) Compute the regulation for 0.80 power factor, current lagging, by the synchronous-impedance method and compare the answer with the regulation found by the ASA method in Prob. 7-27.

9-27. The data below apply to the generator of Prob. 7-27 when it operates at 0.90 power factor, current lagging:

Item	Full load	Three-fourths load	One-half load
Terminal voltage.......................	12,600	12,600	12,600
Field current, amp......................	475	414	352
Field terminal voltage..................	184.5	161	140
Windage and friction loss, kw.............	150	150	150
Core loss, kw...........................	180	180	180
Exciter loss, kw........................	15	12.3	10

The effective armature resistance per phase is 0.018 ohm. Determine the percentage efficiency of the generator at each of the three loads and 0.90 power factor.

10-27. The average effective armature resistance measured between two leads of a 500-kva 25-cycle 2,300-volt three-phase generator is 0.242 ohm, and the corresponding synchronous impedance is 3.2 ohms. At unity power factor the field current is 46.5 amp, the field impressed voltage is 120, friction and windage losses are 6.2 kw, and the core loss is 8.7 kw. (a) Find the percentage efficiency at full load and unity power factor. What is the percentage regulation at full load (b) at a power factor of 0.8, current lagging, (c) at 0.70 power factor, current leading?

CHAPTER 28

SYNCHRONOUS MOTORS AND PARALLEL OPERATION OF GENERATORS

Introduction. An alternator may be used to generate electrical power when it is driven mechanically, or to develop mechanical power when it is driven electrically. Hence, although they are discussed separately for convenience, an a-c generator and a synchronous motor may be one and the same machine; the appropriate name is determined only by the way the machine is used. The underlying theory of operation is the same for both generator and motor. The student usually finds his work much simplified if he clearly understands this feature of reversibility in electric machines.

In view of the foregoing, little further need be said concerning the synchronous motor as a physical structure. In most essential details it is built just like the generator. Certain features of its design may be varied best to suit a particular application. The units are usually built for moderate speeds and have projecting or salient rotor poles. Pole faces are usually slotted and have *amortisseur* or *damper windings*. These windings serve to minimize hunting in a manner to be described later. They may also be used to start the motor.

Operating Principle. 1. *Polyphase Motors.* The principle upon which the operation of polyphase synchronous motors depends was discussed briefly on page 476. A somewhat more detailed discussion may now be undertaken, using the three-phase motor as an example.

Consider one pair of poles of a p-pole three-phase alternator like the one in Fig. 9-27; the action of the remaining pairs of poles is identical with the action of the single pair considered. When the stator windings are connected to three-phase mains, the voltages impressed on the three-phase windings are e_{1a}, e_{1b}, and e_{1c} of Fig. 1-28. These cause currents to flow in the armature windings that are distributed over the air gap as represented in (b) of Fig. 1-28. When the power factor is unity, the dots and crosses in (b) may also represent the space distribution of impressed voltage, for then the voltages and currents in the separate phases are respectively in phase with each other.

It was shown in the previous chapter, as well as in the chapter on induction motors, that in a polyphase machine the belts of dots and crosses shown in (b) revolve;[1] they move a distance of one pole pitch in the time of one-half cycle.   When the fields are excited and the rotor is stationary, the reaction between the armature currents and the air-gap field produced by the d-c field winding results in the production of a torque that tends to

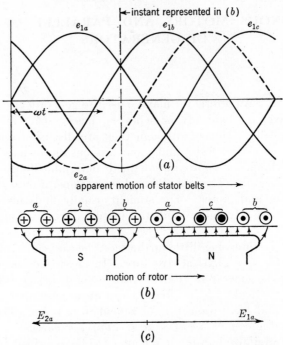

FIG. 1-28. Voltage and current per phase of a three-phase synchronous motor at unity power factor.

drive the rotor first one way and then the other, for the bands of dots and crosses in (b) are constantly slipping past the poles.   The result is that the average torque is zero, and the motor will not run.   A motor of this kind has no starting torque and must be started some other way.   Furthermore, at standstill the current in the armature winding may be large, depending upon the value of X_l; it is limited only by the impedance of the armature, for no counter emf of rotation is generated in the winding.

If in Fig. 1-28, however, the rotor is brought into synchronism with the supply, the poles of the rotor always occupy, with respect to the stator

[1] The conductors, of course, remain stationary, but the impressed voltages and currents rise and fall in such a manner that the effect is the same as though the voltages and currents remained constant, as shown in the figure, and the conductors themselves revolved.

belts, the positions shown in (b), for the stator belts and the rotor poles then move together in time. A torque is produced that is constant in value and is continually in one direction—from right to left on the stator and from left to right on the rotor. This torque keeps the motor going at synchronous speed, even under load. Furthermore, when the field is properly excited, the flux produced by the field cuts the armature conductors and generates therein emfs that are approximately equal and opposite to the impressed voltages. The counter emf of phase a is represented by curve e_{2a}. The counter emfs e_{2b} and e_{2c} are omitted from the figure. These counter emfs limit the currents in the armature conductors to low values, just sufficient to produce the torque required by the load and the losses.

The curves e_{1a} and e_{2a} and the corresponding phasor diagram in (c) represent the impressed and counter emfs of one phase of an ideal (no-loss) motor at no load.

2. *Single-phase Motor.* Let two of the phase windings in Fig. 1-28(b) be removed, and let the remaining phase winding be connected to a single-phase supply. The impressed voltage and current in the armature winding pulsate; the former varies in accordance with the ordinates to the curve e_{1a} in Fig. 1-28(a). At the instant of time corresponding to 1 in Fig. 2-28(a), the impressed voltage is zero; at 2, it has its maximum value and is directed inward in A and outward in B; at 3 the voltage is zero; at 4 it is again maximum, and is directed outward in A and inward in B.

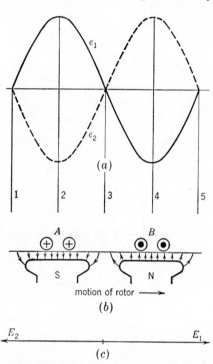

(a)

(b)

(c)

Fig. 2-28. Voltage and current of a single-phase synchronous motor at unity power factor and light load.

When the field is excited and the rotor is stationary, a constantly reversing torque is produced, because the current in the armature is alternating. The average value of the torque in either direction is zero and the rotor will not start. On the other hand, when the rotor is driven at synchronous speed, the poles move forward the distance of one pole pitch in the time of a half cycle. Then if the center line of the pole face S reaches a position coincident with the center line of conductors A at the instant when the impressed voltage is a maximum, as in (b) of Fig. 2-28, the same condition will be repeated each following half cycle. Currents in the armature then react with the field flux to produce an average torque that is always in one direction. Since the strength of the current in the armature windings changes from instant to instant as the rotor turns, the instantaneous torque is not constant as in a polyphase motor but pulsates between zero and a maximum, or it may even be negative for brief periods during each half cycle. After it is properly synchronized, a single-phase

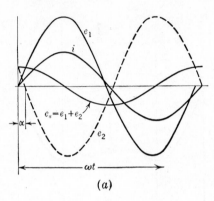

(a)

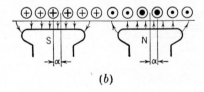

(b)

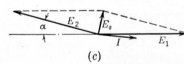

(c)

FIG. 3-28. Diagrams of a loaded three-phase motor.

synchronous motor continues to run at synchronous speed and may be used to carry a load in the same way as a polyphase motor.

The curves of impressed voltage e_1 and generated or counter emf e_2 for an unloaded motor are shown in (a), while the corresponding phasor diagram is that in (c).

Action of Motor under Load. When load is applied to the motor shaft, the resisting torque of the load tends to slow the motor down. There is a momentary drop in speed that causes the rotor to assume a new position with respect to the stator somewhat behind its no-load position, indicated by the angle α in Fig. 3-28(b). The *average speed of the rotor, however, does not change.* The size of α depends upon the load and upon the field excitation. Assume the excitation to be such that the generated voltage or counter emf is equal to the impressed voltage. The waves then have the same maximum ordinates but are shifted out of exact phase opposition by α electrical degrees, as in (a) and (c). These figures show the voltages for one phase only. The sum of the voltage waves is not zero but is the resultant wave $e_s = e_1 + e_2$. In the phasor diagram (c), $\mathbf{E}_s = \mathbf{E}_1 + \mathbf{E}_2$.

If the impedance of the busses is negligible as compared with the synchronous impedance Z_s of the motor, the voltage differential E_s causes a current I to flow in the stator winding of a value such that $E_s = Z_s I$. This current lags the resultant voltage E_s by nearly 90 time degrees, as in

(a) and (c), because the resistance of the armature is small as compared with its synchronous reactance.   The current is therefore nearly in phase with the impressed voltage E_1 and the armature currents are approximately represented by the dots and crosses in (b) of Fig. 3-28.   From an application of the rule for force action, it is apparent that these currents react with the air-gap flux to produce a clockwise torque on the rotor. So long as the load and the excitation do not change, the current belts, the flux, and the torque remain constant.

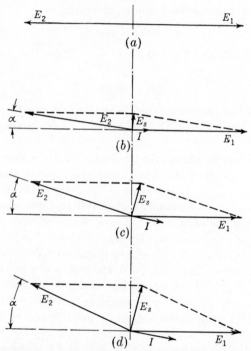

Fig. 4-28. Phasor diagrams for a synchronous motor under constant excitation and for four conditions of load.

For a given excitation the resultant voltage E_s, and therefore the armature current and the torque produced, depend upon the load only.   The more the rotor is loaded, the greater is the angle of rotor shift α, called the *torque angle*, and the greater are the current and the developed power. This is clearly shown in the series of phasor diagrams of Fig. 4-28, in which the load increases progressively, beginning with zero load in (a).   As a matter of fact, the angular shift of the rotor automatically adjusts itself to such a value that the torque developed is just sufficient to carry the load and to supply the rotor losses at synchronous speed, and no more. Should the load become so great that no value of α satisfies this condition, then the motor will break out of synchronism.   The torque developed at the pull-out point is called the *pull-out torque*.

In the diagrams of Fig. 4-28,

E_1 = bus voltage, line to neutral
E_2 = counter emf of motor, line to neutral
I = current input to motor armature
θ = power-factor angle (not shown)
$E_s = Z_sI$, synchronous impedance drop of motor, line to neutral

For the case of a three-phase motor, the input is

$$P_1 = 3E_1I \cos \theta$$

The angle between $\mathbf{E}_2$ and $\mathbf{I}$ is $180 - (\alpha - \theta)$; hence the power developed by the rotor is

$$P_2 = 3E_2I \cos (\alpha - \theta)$$

The power output of the rotor is less than the developed power P_2 by the amount of the rotor losses.   The difference $P_1 - P_2$ is the stator copper loss and iron loss.

Influence of Overexcitation.   In the foregoing discussion the excitation of the motor was assumed to be such that the counter emf generated in the motor armature at no load was approximately equal to the impressed voltage.   This value is commonly called 100 per cent excitation.   The effect of increasing the excitation will now be considered.

The influence of excitation on the behavior of a synchronous motor is conveniently discussed with the help of diagrams like those of Fig. 5-28. Let the motor armature be connected to the busses of a power system, and in (a), (b), and (c) let the input have the constant value $P_1 = 3E_1I \cos \theta$. In these diagrams the in-phase component of current ($I \cos \theta$) is then the same for all.   This assumption neglects slight differences in the losses in the three cases.

In (a) the motor excitation is 100 per cent and the current is nearly in phase with the impressed voltage.   In (b) the excitation is 125 per cent, and in (c) it is 150 per cent.   This means that in (c), for example, the generated counter emf at no load is 50 per cent greater than the impressed voltage, as in (d).   If we neglect the drop in the resistance and leakage reactance of the armature, however, the generated counter emf in the armature must exactly balance the impressed voltage at all loads, just as in a transformer.   Hence, when the motor is overexcited, such internal reactions must be set up as to bring the effective excitation back to the correct value.   The agency which brings this about is the demagnetizing ampere-turns of the armature.

It was shown on page 481 that, when a synchronous motor takes a leading current, the resulting armature ampere-turns demagnetize the field.

Hence, it is clear that in addition to the required load component ($I \cos \theta$) the loaded motor in (b) and (c) must take a leading component of current ($I \sin \theta$) of sufficient amount so that its demagnetizing action will bring the effective excitation back to approximately the same value in each case. The result is that, the further the excitation is increased, the greater is the leading component of current and the lower is the power factor of the motor.

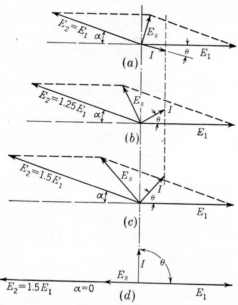

FIG. 5-28. Phasor diagrams for a synchronous motor illustrating the effects of over-excitation.

Constant input $\begin{cases} (a) & 100 \text{ per cent excitation} \\ (b) & 125 \text{ per cent excitation} \\ (c) & 150 \text{ per cent excitation} \end{cases}$

(d) Ideal motor at no load and 150 per cent excitation.

It should be repeated here that, when a generator delivers a leading current, its armature ampere-turns act to increase its effective excitation. Thus the generators that supply power to overexcited synchronous motors receive part of their excitation from the motors. A part of the excitation, at least, of the system consisting of generators and synchronous motors may be shifted from motors to generators, or vice versa, at will by adjusting the excitations of one or more generators and motors of the system.

The condition for no load and 150 per cent excitation is shown in (d). In this case, with losses neglected, the voltage $\mathbf{E}_s$ consumed in the synchronous impedance is in phase opposition to the impressed voltage, and the current $\mathbf{I}$ supplied to the motor leads $\mathbf{E}_1$ by 90 deg. The power input

$3E_1I \cos \theta$ is zero, but the motor takes leading reactive power in the amount of $3E_1I \sin 90 = 3E_1I$ vars.

Influence of Underexcitation. The reasoning developed in the preceding section applies to this condition also. In (a), (b), and (c) of Fig. 6-28 the motor is assumed to have a constant load equal to $3E_1I \cos \theta$. With differences in losses neglected, the in-phase component of current $(I \cos \theta)$

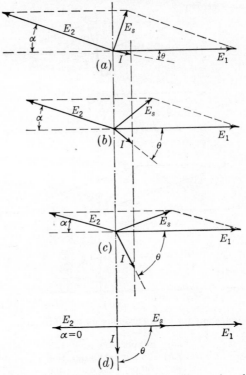

FIG. 6-28. Phasor diagrams for a synchronous motor illustrating the effects of underexcitation.

$$\text{Constant input} \begin{cases} (a) & 100 \text{ per cent excitation} \\ (b) & 75 \text{ per cent excitation} \\ (c) & 50 \text{ per cent excitation} \end{cases}$$

(d) Ideal motor at no load and 50 per cent excitation.

must therefore have a constant value as shown. When the motor is underexcited as in (c), the field excitation is only 50 per cent. In order that the motor may generate a counter emf approximately equal to the impressed voltage, internal reactions must be set up to increase the effective excitation. In a synchronous motor this is brought about by armature reaction when the current supplied to the motor is lagging, as explained on page 481. Hence the motor takes a lagging component of current ($I \sin \theta$) of sufficient magnitude to increase the effective excitation to the appropriate value. The generator or generators that supply lagging current, however, have their effective excitations decreased by armature reaction (page 481). Hence, such generators must be overexcited in order to maintain their voltages. Part of this excitation is transferred to the motor through the medium of armature reaction. The motor may, of course, be made to supply all its own excitation by increasing the current in its field winding until the quadrature component of current ($I \sin \theta$) becomes zero.

At no load, with losses neglected, the voltage consumed by the synchronous impedance is in phase with the impressed voltage and the current **I** supplied to the motor lags $\mathbf{E}_1$ by 90 deg as in (d). The power input ($3E_1I \cos \theta$) is zero, but the motor takes lagging reactive power in the amount of $3E_1I \sin 90$ deg $= 3E_1I$ vars.

Current Locus for Any Load and Excitation. The current input of a synchronous motor under varying conditions of load and for any one of a number of constant field excitations may be visualized with the aid of circle diagrams similar to those of Fig. 7-28. The equations

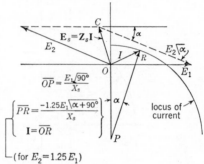

$$\overline{OP} = \frac{E_1 \underline{/90°}}{X_s}$$

$$\overline{PR} = \frac{-1.25E_1 \underline{/\alpha + 90°}}{X_s}$$

$$\mathbf{I} = \overline{OR}$$

(for $E_2 = 1.25 E_1$)

FIG. 7-28. Locus of synchronous motor input current for fixed excitation and varying load.

of which these circles are graphical representations are derived on the basis of the following assumptions:

1. The round-rotor theory applies.

2. The constant bus voltage $\mathbf{E}_1$ is the reference phasor.

3. The effect of saturation of the magnetic circuit is negligible over the range of loads and excitations represented.

4. The total generator capacity connected to the bus is very large in comparison with the capacity of the motor. Hence, the impedance of the composite machine representing the bus (called an infinite bus) is disregarded, and the synchronous impedance Z_s of the motor and the composite generator which represents the bus is the synchronous impedance of the motor and its connecting leads alone.

5. In commercial machines generally, the synchronous reactance is many times as large as the effective resistance, and the following approximations may sometimes be used: $\theta_s = \tan^{-1} \dfrac{X_s}{r} \cong 90$ deg, $X_s \cong Z_s$ and $r = 0$.

In Fig. 7-28 let some constant value of motor excitation voltage E_2 be maintained and let the torque angle α be increased from zero to a maximum by gradually increasing the load applied to the motor.   From the figure it is apparent that

$$\mathbf{Z}_s\mathbf{I} = \mathbf{E}_1 + \mathbf{E}_2 = E_1 - E_2\overline{\backslash\alpha} \qquad (1\text{-}28)$$

or

$$\mathbf{I} = \frac{E_1}{Z_s}\overline{\backslash\theta_s} - \frac{E_2}{Z_s}\overline{\backslash\alpha + \theta_s} \qquad (2\text{-}28)$$

This is the equation of a circle that represents the phasor current input to the motor.   The first right-hand term is the phasor distance from the origin to the center at P while the second right-hand term is the radius

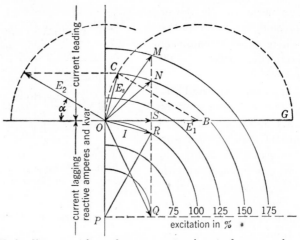

FIG. 8-28. Circle diagrams of synchronous-motor inputs for a number of constant excitations.

phasor of constant length, the angular position of which is $\overline{\backslash\alpha + \theta_s}$. There is a separate circle for each excitation voltage.   If the simplifying assumption is made that the effective resistance is negligible, then $X_s = Z_s$, $\theta_s = 90$ deg, and Eq. (2-28) reduces to

$$\mathbf{I} = \frac{E_1}{X_s}\overline{\backslash90°} - \frac{E_2}{X_s}\overline{\backslash\alpha + 90°} \qquad (3\text{-}28)$$

A family of circles based on Eq. (3-28), each member of which applies to some constant value of excitation voltage E_2, is shown in Fig. 8-28. The theoretical operating range of α for the motor is 90 deg, but as α approaches 90 deg the motor operation becomes unstable.   (It pulls out of synchronism at $\alpha = 90$ deg, but its operation at even considerably smaller angles is impractical because a sudden increase in load may cause the rotor to swing far enough beyond its mean operating angle to pull it out of step.) It may also be pointed out in passing that if Eq. (3-28) is multiplied through by $\mathbf{E}_1^* = E_1/0$, the resulting equation is the phasor power output of the bus (which is the input to the motor). The resulting equation is

$$\mathbf{P}_1 = \frac{E_1^2}{X_s}\overline{\diagdown 90°} - \frac{E_1 E_2}{X_s}\overline{\diagdown \alpha + 90°} \tag{4-28}$$

This equation yields circles exactly like those of Fig. 8-28 to another scale.

The circles in Fig. 8-28 show clearly the effect of excitation upon the phase position of the current drawn by the motor. In general, the motor draws leading current from the bus when it is overexcited and lagging current when it is underexcited. Since adding load results in increasing the torque angle, however, the current at all excitations becomes more lagging as load is added, and if the increase in load is large enough, the current may eventually become lagging no matter what the excitation may be. It should be noted, however, that even at 150 per cent of its rated output the torque angle of a motor usually does not exceed about 40 degrees.

Power Developed by the Motor. The electrical power developed by a synchronous motor is the real part of the product $\mathbf{P}_2 = \mathbf{E}_2^*\mathbf{I}$ (Fig. 7-28). From the figure $\mathbf{E}_2^* = -E_2/\alpha$, and $\mathbf{I}$ is available from Eq. (2-28). It follows that

$$\mathbf{P}_2 = -E_2/\alpha \left(\frac{E_1}{Z_s}\overline{\diagdown \theta_s} - \frac{E_2}{Z_s}\overline{\diagdown \alpha + \theta_s} \right)$$

$$= \frac{E_2^2}{Z_s}\overline{\diagdown \theta_s} - \frac{E_1 E_2}{Z_s}/\alpha - \theta_s \tag{5-28}$$

This equation, with signs reversed, is the equation of the circle in Fig. 9-28. There is a separate circle for each assumed value of E_2. The centers of all circles lie on ON or ON extended. The distance of the center of any given circle is E_2^2/Z_s units of measure from O.

The active power P_2 developed is the real part of Eq. (5-28) or

$$P_2 = \frac{E_2^2}{Z_s}\cos\theta_s - \frac{E_1 E_2}{Z_s}\cos(\alpha - \theta_s)$$

$$= \frac{E_2^2 R}{R^2 + X_s^2} - \frac{E_1 E_2}{\sqrt{R^2 + X_s^2}}\sin(\alpha + \gamma) \tag{6-28}$$

where $\theta_s = \tan^{-1}\dfrac{X_s}{R}$ and $\gamma = (90 - \theta_s)$. If the resistance be neglected $(r = 0)$, γ reduces to zero, Z_s reduces to X_s, and the power developed becomes

$$P_2 = -\frac{E_1 E_2}{X_s}\sin\alpha \tag{7-28}$$

The electrical power developed by the motor is negative since the motor *receives* electrical power from the bus. Thus, if Eqs. (5-28) to (7-28) inclusive are written with reversed signs these equations then represent, respectively, the mechanical power developed by the rotor, and since the speed is constant, they also represent a constant times the electromagnetic torque developed. The power developed at the pulley is obviously the mechanical power developed by the motor less the power consumed in windage and bearing friction.

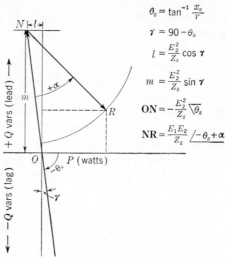

$$\theta_s = \tan^{-1} \frac{x_s}{r}$$

$$\gamma = 90 - \theta_s$$

$$l = \frac{E_2^2}{Z_s} \cos \gamma$$

$$m = \frac{E_2^2}{Z_s} \sin \gamma$$

$$\mathrm{ON} = -\frac{E_2^2}{Z_s} \underline{\diagdown \theta_s}$$

$$\mathrm{NR} = \frac{E_1 E_2}{Z_s} \underline{/-\theta_s + \alpha}$$

Fig. 9-28. Circle diagram of power developed by a synchronous motor.

It should be recalled that E_1 and E_2 in the foregoing equations were defined as the per-phase values and that P_2, therefore, is the power developed per phase. If both sides of the power equation (7-28), for example, be multiplied by 3, however, one obtains

$$3P_2 = \frac{(\sqrt{3}\,E_1)(\sqrt{3}\,E_2)}{X_s} \sin \alpha$$

which shows that the power equations also represent the total power developed by the motor when E_1 and E_2 are taken as line-to-line voltages. Hence, since $3P_2/1{,}000$ is the total kilowatts developed by the motor, it can readily be shown that the electromagnetic torque of the rotor is

$$T = \frac{7{,}040 \ (\text{kw developed})}{\text{rpm}} \qquad \text{lb-perp-ft} \qquad (8\text{-}28)$$

When the more accurate two-reaction method of analysis is used to derive the expression for the mechanical power developed by a salient-pole synchronous motor which is connected to an infinite bus through leads of negligible reactance, the resulting equation obtained is

$$P_2 = \frac{E_1 E_2}{X_d} \sin \alpha + \frac{E_1{}^2 (X_d - X_q)}{2 X_d X_q} \sin 2\alpha \qquad (9\text{-}28)$$

where X_d is the direct-axis reactance (the reactance in the axis of the poles) and X_q is the quadrature-axis reactance (the reactance in the axis midway between poles). The former is approximately equal to X_s, while $X_q \cong 0.60 X_d$.

Since X_s is substantially equal to X_d, a comparison of Eq. (9-28) with Eq. (7-28) with sign reversed shows that the two equations differ by the added term

$$\frac{E_1{}^2 (X_d - X_q)}{2 X_d X_q} \sin 2\alpha$$

of Eq. (9-28). This term is independent of the excitation voltage E_2. Thus a salient-pole motor develops some mechanical power even when the field excitation is reduced to zero. The torque corresponding to this output is called the *reluctance torque*. With saturation neglected, a salient-pole motor that is connected to an infinite bus through leads of negligible reactance, and is so excited that the motor operates at unity power factor at light load, develops, at rated load, a total output of which roughly 30 per cent is due to the reluctance torque.

Small synchronous motors for many applications, including drives for electric clocks, are true reluctance motors. The rotor may be suitably formed of steel plate or punchings and has no field winding. The rotor assumes a position of minimum reluctance with respect to the path of the revolving flux and so revolves with the flux at synchronous speed so long as the resisting torque of the load does not exceed the total reluctance torque developed.

V curves. The so-called V curves of a synchronous motor (Fig. 10-28) show how the armature current varies when the input to the motor is kept constant and field current is increased continuously from the lowest to the highest practical limits. A separate curve may be obtained for each assumed constant input.

The input of a three-phase synchronous motor, for example, is given by the equation $P = 3 E_1 I \cos \theta$, where E_1 is the impressed voltage from line to neutral, I is the line current, and $\cos \theta$ is the power factor. Let E_1 and the input P be held constant. Under these conditions the power component ($I \cos \theta$) of the input current is also constant, although I and $\cos \theta$ both vary with the excitation. Suppose, for example, that the power component of the current is OS in Fig. 8-28. The constant input corresponding to this current, theoretically, may be secured with any excitation between 50 and 175 per cent, although actually operation becomes unstable for the assumed load in the region of 50 per cent excitation. The magnitude of the current varies considerably with the excitation used. It is represented by the length of the current phasor corresponding to a particular load and excitation. The lengths OQ, OR, and ON, for example, represent the currents corresponding to the assumed constant input and the excitations of 50, 100, and 150 per cent, respectively.

The minimum excitation that suffices to carry the assumed load is 50 per cent, and the corresponding current is OQ. Starting with this excitation and increasing the field current gradually, while holding the input constant, causes the armature current to decrease in magnitude and to become less lagging with respect to E_1. The locus of the current phasor for the assumed load is the straight line $QRSNM$. As the excitation is further increased, the current continues to fall off and the power factor continues to improve until the value OS is reached. This is the smallest current that can carry the assumed load, and for this current the power factor is unity. Increasing the excitation further causes the armature current to again increase and the power factor to fall off, but the current now leads the impressed voltage and will continue to lead it at constantly increasing angles until the maximum excitation is reached.

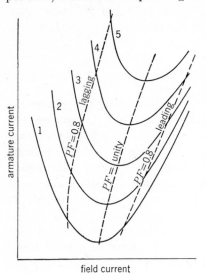

Fig. 10-28. V curves of a synchronous motor. Each curve represents some constant value of motor input.

The V curves may be obtained from the diagram of Fig. 8-28 by plotting the lengths of the current phasors vs. corresponding field currents for a number of assumed constant inputs. Data for the V curves are obtained experimentally by running the synchronous motor from a bus of constant voltage and frequency, maintaining some selected constant motor input, and then taking a series of simultaneous readings of armature current and field current while the latter is increased in suitable steps from the lowest to the highest desired values. The plot of armature current vs. field current yields the V curve for the selected constant input. Other curves may be obtained by repeating the process for several other selected constant inputs. Curves based on the phasor diagram of Fig. 8-28 assume a constant synchronous impedance and are somewhat in error for this reason.

Synchronous Motor Used for Power-factor Correction. A large percentage of motor-driven industrial loads are carried by means of induction motors. Lighting and industrial heating loads are supplied through transformers. Both transformers and induction motors draw exciting currents from the line that lag the impressed voltage by a large angle (pages 399 and 451), and therefore, especially when lightly loaded, the power supplied to them has a large reactive component and the power factor may be very poor. This reactive power, although necessary to operate the equipment, increases the losses in generators and line and reduces the active power output which they are capable of delivering without (usually) increasing the revenue derived from their use.

In large industrial plants and in power systems feeding direct-current loads, it is often possible to use synchronous motors for some of the drives. When this is done, a part or all of the excitation required by the transformers and induction motors may be supplied by overexciting the synchronous motors. In this way the reactive power is supplied locally; the power factor of the load is improved, and the line and generators are relieved of much of the reactive component and supply largely only the active component of the load current. A synchronous motor used in this way is sometimes called a *synchronous capacitor*, for it draws a leading component of current from the line and to this extent acts like a capacitance.

In recent years the design of static condensers for use on power circuits has been greatly improved. Moreover, costs have been reduced to such an extent that it is now usually more economical to supply needed reactive kilovolt-amperes for power-factor correction by means of such static equipment than with synchronous machines. The result has been that static condensers are now quite extensively used in power-distribution applications.

Example 1. An industrial plant has the following loads: (a) 750 kw of induction motor load at 80 per cent power factor, current lagging, (b) 50 kw of unity-power-factor lighting load, (c) 100 kw of load to be carried by a synchronous motor. It is desired to buy a synchronous motor of sufficient rated capacity to carry the 100 kw of synchronous motor load and to serve as a synchronous capacitor to correct the power factor of the entire plant to 90 per cent,[1] current lagging. What must be the rated capacity of the synchronous motor, and what will be its power factor?

[1] The object of power-factor correction is to reduce the current flowing in the circuit connecting the consumer's load with the source of supply. The line current is equal to the square root of the sum of the squares of the active and reactive components. When the power factor is high, the reactive component is a small percentage of the total and so a given change in the reactive component produces only a small change in the total. Accordingly, it is unnecessary to correct the power factor to exactly unity.

A graphical solution of the problem is shown in Fig. 11-28. The corresponding analytical solution follows.

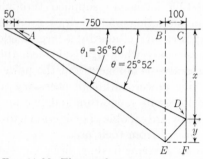

FIG. 11-28. The synchronous motor used to correct power factor (Example 1).

Total active power delivered is 50 + 750 + 100 or

$$P_0 = 900 \text{ kw}$$

The lamps require no reactive power. The reactive power (current lagging) required by the induction motors is

$$Q_1 = BE = 750(\tan \theta = 0.749)$$
$$= 562 \text{ kvars, current lagging}$$

The total net reactive power to be supplied over the line is

$$Q_0 = CD = 900(\tan \theta = 0.484)$$
$$= 436 \text{ kvars, current lagging}$$

The difference between the total required reactive power and that supplied by the line is made up by the overexcited synchronous motor. This difference is

$$Q_3 = FD = 562 - 436$$
$$= 126 \text{ kvars, current leading}$$

Hence the rating of the synchronous motor must be

$$\text{Synchronous motor kilovolt-amperes} = ED = \sqrt{100^2 + 126^2}$$
$$= 161 \text{ kva}$$

and the synchronous motor power factor is

$$\cos \theta_m = {}^{100}\!/_{161}$$
$$= 0.625, \text{ current leading}$$

Synchronous Motor Used to Control Line Drop. When a lagging current flows in a circuit that is inductively reactive, the voltage falls in the direction of flow; if the current is leading, the voltage rises (or tends to rise) in the direction of flow (pages 413 and 572). This principle is utilized, notably in connection with transmission lines, to maintain a constant voltage at the receiver end of the line at all loads. This is accomplished by connecting a synchronous motor to the transmission line at the receiver end. The motor is usually run without load. When the line is delivering a light load, the receiver voltage tends to rise. The synchronous motor is then underexcited and draws a lagging current from the line. This current increases the line drop and thus maintains the receiver voltage. On the other hand, when the load on the line is heavy, the excessive line drop tends to cause the receiver voltage to fall. The synchronous motor is then overexcited and draws a leading current over the line. This leading component of current offsets some of the lagging component taken by the load and makes the current delivered over the line less lagging, or even leading. The line drop is reduced and the voltage at the end of the line is kept from falling. The excitation of the synchronous motor may be controlled by means of a voltage regulator, which automatically holds the receiver voltage at a constant value, regardless of load.

A synchronous motor used in this manner serves as a variable inductive reactance when underexcited (voltage high) and as a variable capacitive reactance when overexcited (voltage low). Synchronous motors applied to the regulation of voltage on transmission lines are therefore called *synchronous reactors*. The rated capacity of synchronous reactors required for voltage control on a line is usually about 50 per cent of the rated capacity of the generators. Thus a line fed by a 30,000-kva generator would require a 15,000-kva synchronous reactor to control the line voltage.

Example 2. A three-phase transmission line 38 miles long, built of 250,000-cir-mil stranded copper cable, delivers a maximum load of 50,000 kw at a power factor of 85 per cent, current lagging. The receiver line voltage is 110 kv or 63.5 kv from one line to neutral. The resistance of one line conductor is 9 ohms, and the reactance is 31 ohms. At the receiver end a synchronous reactor of 23,700-kva capacity is installed. This reactor has its maximum overexcitation at maximum line load and, when so excited, draws from the line 23,700 kva at zero power factor, current leading. When the load on the line is zero, the synchronous reactor has its maximum underexcitation and draws 23,700 kva from the line at zero power factor, current lagging. Show that, when the line is so operated, the supply voltage required to maintain a receiver voltage of 110 kv is the same at no load as at full load.

(*a*) *No load.* When the load is zero, the only current over the line is that drawn by the synchronous reactor. The reactive kilovolt-amperes per phase is then

$$Q = \frac{23,700}{3}$$
$$= 7,900 \text{ kvars, current lagging}$$

Hence the line current is

$$I = \frac{7,900}{110 \div \sqrt{3}} = \frac{7,900}{63.5}$$
$$= 124 \text{ amp at zero power factor, current lagging}$$

The phasor diagram of voltages is then that shown in Fig. 12-28(*a*), in which E_s is the supply or generator-bus voltage on the line side of the transformer, and E_r is the corresponding receiver voltage, both values being from line to neutral (or per phase). In symbolic form, with E_r as reference,

$$\begin{aligned} \mathbf{E}_s &= \mathbf{E}_r + \mathbf{ZI} \\ &= \mathbf{E}_r + \mathbf{I}(R + jX) \\ &= \mathbf{E}_r + I(\cos \theta - j \sin \theta)(R + jX) \end{aligned} \quad (a)$$

This equation has exactly the same form as the equation applying to the transformer. In this case, however, $\theta = 90°$, $\cos \theta = 0$, and $\sin \theta = 1$. Hence, since jX_sI adds directly to $\mathbf{E}_r$, while RI lags $\mathbf{E}_r$ by 90 deg,

$$\begin{aligned} E_s &= 63,500 + XI - jRI \\ &= 63,500 + 3,844 - j1,116 \\ &= 67,344 - j1,116 \end{aligned}$$

The magnitude of this phasor is

$$E_s = \sqrt{67,344^2 + 1,116^2}$$
$$= 67,400 \text{ volts to neutral}$$

The line voltage at the generator end is therefore

$$E_g = \sqrt{3} \times 67,400 = 116,700 \text{ volts}$$

(b) *At full load.* At full load the line delivers to the load 50,000 kw at 85 per cent power factor, current lagging. The receiver voltage to neutral is still 63.5 kv. Hence the load per phase is

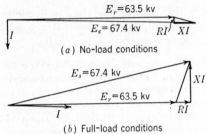

(a) No-load conditions

(b) Full-load conditions

FIG. 12-28. Voltage control of transmission line with synchronous condenser.

$$P_r = \frac{50,000}{3} = 16,667 \text{ kw}$$

The in-phase component of load current is

$$I_1 = \frac{16,667}{63.5} = 262 \text{ amp}$$

Since

$$\cos \theta_L = 0.85$$
$$\sin \theta_L = 0.527$$
$$\tan \theta_L = 0.62$$

the reactive component of load current is

$$I_2 = 262 \tan \theta$$
$$= 162 \text{ amp (lagging 90 deg)}$$

At full load the synchronous reactor acts as a condenser and receives 7,900 kvars per phase (current leading) from the line. Hence the reactor draws a leading component of current equal to

$$I_{sr} = \frac{7,900}{63.5}$$
$$= 124 \text{ amp (leading 90 deg)}$$

The total reactive component of current drawn from the line is the sum of I_2 and I_{sr} or

$$I_q = (162 - 124)\,\backslash\underline{90^\circ}$$
$$= 38 \text{ amp (lagging 90 deg)}$$

Hence, the total current drawn from the line at full load is

$$I = \sqrt{262^2 + 38^2} = 264.7 \text{ amp}$$

and this current lags the receiver voltage by the angle whose cosine is $262 \div 264.7$. Therefore,

$$\cos \theta = 0.99$$
$$\sin \theta = 0.143$$

With Eq. (a), page 515, used as before [phasor diagram Fig. 12-28(b)],

$$E_s = E_r + IZ$$
$$= E_r + RI \cos \theta + XI \sin \theta - jRI \sin \theta + jXI \cos \theta$$
$$= 63,500 + 2,360 + 1,175 - j34 + j8,130$$
$$= 67,030 + j8,100.$$

The magnitude of this voltage is

$$E_s = \sqrt{67,030^2 + 8,100^2}$$
$$= 67,500 \text{ volts}$$

and the generator line voltage is

$$E_g = 116,900$$

This is substantially the same as the generator voltage at no load, which was to be proved.

Hunting. A synchronous motor must run at the exact average speed determined by the frequency of the supply. If the supply frequency is pulsating, as is apt to be the case when the supply generator is driven by reciprocating or internal-combustion engines, the synchronous-motor speed tends to follow the frequency; that is, its speed tends to oscillate about a mean value. Were it not for the kinetic energy of rotation (WR^2), the rotor would follow the supply frequency exactly without difficulty. When the frequency is rising, the motor momentarily has its torque angle α increased. It therefore develops more than enough power to carry the load at the existing speed, so the motor accelerates. Its rate of acceleration is retarded by the inertia of the rotating parts, however, so the motor does not swing so fast, and usually not so far, as it otherwise would. When the frequency again falls, the angle α is momentarily reduced and the motor cannot develop enough power to carry its load at the existing speed, so it drops back. Some of the deficiency is then supplied by the stored energy of the rotor and load, so that the motor does not drop back so fast, and usually not so far, as it otherwise would. When the frequency again rises, the cycle is repeated. If the frequency of oscillation approaches the natural period of the motor, the amplitude of the oscillation may increase with each swing until the motor falls out of step.

The phenomenon described above is known as *hunting*. Hunting also may be caused by momentary changes in frequency or voltage due to suddenly applied loads either on the motor or elsewhere on the system. Oscillations due to such causes, however, are usually soon damped out. When a motor hunts, the power supplied to it is not steady but surges above and below the average value as the rotor swings about its mean position. This surging power causes a pulsation in the line voltage, which is objectionable, especially when lighting loads are operated from the same circuit.

Amortisseur or Damper Windings. The revolving-field structures of synchronous motors are provided with poles with faces slotted parallel to the shaft. Conducting bars are built into these slots (Fig. 13-28), and the ends of the bars are short-circuited to form a structure similar to the squirrel-cage winding of an induction motor. These windings are called *amortisseur* or *damper* windings; they may be used to start the motor and to bring it into approximate synchronism with the line.   After the motor is synchronized, they serve to minimize the oscillations due to hunting.

Damper windings do not entirely prevent hunting, for their operation depends upon the existence of some oscillation.   The speed of the revolving magnetic field is exactly proportional to the frequency of the supply. The rotor tends to follow this speed exactly also.   When the motor hunts, however, the rotor runs periodically slower and faster than the rotating field of the armature (but it always maintains an average speed corresponding to the average frequency of the supply).   When the rotating field of the armature revolves faster than the rotor, the flux from the former cuts the bars of the damper winding, just as in an induction motor, and induces currents therein.   Their reactions with the revolving field

Fig. 13-28. Rotor of a 1,500-kva 0.80-power-factor 720-rpm 2,300-volt 60-cycle synchronous motor showing wound field, collector rings, and damper winding. (*General Electric Company.*)

produce a torque that tends to accelerate the rotor, thus helping to maintain its speed.   When the rotating field revolves less rapidly than the rotor, on the other hand, the bars of the damper winding cut the flux of the rotating field in the reverse direction, as in an induction generator. The induced currents in the damper winding then react with the revolving field to produce a torque that retards the rotor, thus again helping it to maintain its correct average speed.   In this way the damper winding always tends to prevent any change in rotor speed and serves to decrease the amplitude of the oscillations when hunting occurs.   When there is no hunting the damper winding moves synchronously with the rotating field and no currents circulate in it.

Starting Synchronous Motors.   The amortisseur winding may be used to start a synchronous motor, and this is, in fact, the most common method of starting.

During the initial starting period the d-c excitation is removed and the armature winding is connected to the supply circuit.   A compensator may be used to reduce the voltage impressed on the armature, or the full voltage may be impressed, just as in the case of induction motors, depending upon the size of the motor relative to the generating system. The use of a compensator reduces the current drawn from the line during the initial period. The revolving field of the armature cuts the bars of the amortisseur winding and sets up circulating currents therein which react with the armature currents, as in a squirrel-cage induction motor, to produce the necessary starting torque. This starting torque must be sufficient to accelerate the motor and its load to within a few per cent of synchronism. The amount of the starting torque produced is under the control of the designer and depends upon the resistance of the amortisseur winding.

If the field circuit is left open when the motor is started, the revolving armature flux cuts the field winding initially at synchronous speed, and a high alternating voltage is thereby induced in the many turns of the field winding. For this reason the field windings of synchronous motors are usually insulated for much more than the normal d-c exciting voltage. Breakdown of the field insulation during the starting period is thus prevented. When the field winding is short-circuited during the starting period, the voltage in the winding sets up a circulating current, thereby reducing the terminal voltage of the winding. The circulating current, however, produces but a small starting torque, especially because of its low power factor. Introducing the resistance of a field rheostat into the circuit improves the power factor of the circulating current and permits the starting torque to increase. As the motor approaches synchronism, the circulating current in the field winding is related to the armature currents in much the same way as are the currents in the amortisseur winding. They therefore increase the torque during the final stage of synchronizing and help to bring the motor close to synchronism.

After the motor is brought near to synchronism as described above, the d-c field is excited. The motor then develops a large "pull-in" torque as a synchronous motor (owing to the momentary displacement angle α due to the slip) and the motor pulls into step (displacement angle α reduced suddenly to a small value). At the instant of pull-in, the motor draws a large current from the line. When a compensator is used, the fields are excited before the switch is thrown to the full-voltage position. In this way the rush of current is reduced.

Automatic starting and control panels are available for starting synchronous motors. These are designed to perform automatically all the necessary starting operations. All that is required of the attendant is to press a push button.

When a large synchronous motor is to be started from a circuit to which power is supplied by generators with aggregate capacity not greatly different from that of the motor, it may be impractical to start the motor in the manner described above. The same may be true if the large starting current drawn by the motor is objectionable. These objections are less and less apparent each year, however, for power systems have grown very large indeed. Nevertheless, the objection to high starting current may be removed by starting the synchronous motor by means of a separate driving motor. A direct-connected exciter may be used as a starting motor when available, or, if the synchronous motor is used to drive a d-c generator, the latter may be driven as a motor to start the synchronous machine. This method of connecting a synchronous machine to the line is discussed in greater detail in the following section.

Synchronizing. In modern power systems many synchronous machines are connected to the circuits forming the system network. Power is supplied to the system by synchronous generators operating in parallel and is utilized by many types of electrical machinery, including synchronous motors operating in parallel. The behavior of synchronous machines in parallel will be discussed in more detail in a following section. For the present it will suffice to note that all synchronous machines connected to a given system, including generators and motors alike, must run at such speeds that at every instant their generated emfs are approximately equal and opposite to the impressed voltage of the line or lines to which they are connected.

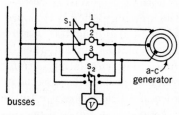

FIG. 14-28. Connections for synchronizing with lamps dark.

Some slight angular displacement α, of course, exists between the generated emf of a machine and its no-load position, depending upon its load. At zero load this displacement angle is zero for both motors and generators.

Before an idle synchronous machine may be properly connected to the lines of a power system, therefore, the operator must be assured that the above conditions are fulfilled. This process of bringing a synchronous machine up to speed and suitably connecting it to the line is called *synchronizing*.

The process of synchronizing is conveniently discussed with the aid of the diagram of connections[1] shown in Figs. 14-28 and 15-28. The three

---

[1] In the present discussion it is assumed, for convenience, that the synchronous machines are small, low-voltage ones which are suitable for operation from 120-volt busses. In the case of the usual generator application, instrument potential transformers would be used to reduce the voltages impressed on the lamps and on the potential coils of meters, while suitable oil circuit breakers would be used in the line in place of the knife switches shown.

terminals of the incoming machine, marked "a-c generator," are connected to one side, and the busses to the other side, of a switch S_1. A double-pole double-throw switch S_2 is connected as shown; by means of this switch and the voltmeter V the bus voltage may be compared with the line voltage by taking alternate readings. Three lamps 1, 2, and 3 are connected across the terminals of switch S_1. The incoming machine is driven by a separate motor (or by its prime mover) and its fields are excited. When the speed of the alternator is such that the frequency of its generated emf is nearly equal to that of the busses, the lamps will go bright and dark together, provided the machine terminals are properly connected to the switch S_1, that is, provided the *phase rotation*[1] is the same for machine and busses. If the terminals are improperly connected, reversing any pair of leads will correct the error. When the connection is correct, the speed of the driver and the excitation of the alternator are adjusted until the voltage of the bus is equal to that of the incoming machine, and the lamps beat dark and light regularly and very slowly.

Equality in the voltages indicates that the effective values of the bus and machine voltages are the same. When the lamps are dark, the bus voltage and the machine voltage are opposite as well as equal; the displacement angle α and the resultant voltage E_s are both zero. When the lamps are bright, the machine voltage and the bus voltage add; α is then 180 deg and the resultant voltage is $E_s = 2E$. The pulsation of the lamps thus has a frequency equal to the difference of the frequencies of the machine and the bus. At the instant when the lamps are dark, the switch S_1 may be closed without causing any disturbance to the line. The alternator is then synchronized and may either be driven as a generator to share the load or be loaded as a motor, receiving its power from the line.

One difficulty with the method of synchronizing just described lies in the fact that the lights go dark even when there is still considerable voltage across their terminals. For this reason it is desirable to let the lights beat slowly when synchronizing, in order better to estimate the correct instant for throwing the switch. If the switch is thrown when the result-

---

[1] When a generator or motor is to be wired to an existing system, its terminals must be so arranged for connection to the bus bars that, when the machine is about to be synchronized, its voltage waves will reach their positive maxima in the same order as the corresponding waves of the bus bars to which the machine terminals are to be connected. Thus if the line potential differences on the bus side of the switch S_1 (Fig. 14-28) reach their positive maxima in the order E_{12}, E_{23}, E_{31}, then the machine terminals must be so connected that the potential-difference waves will reach their positive maxima in the same order. This process is called "phasing out" the machine. When once the machine has been permanently wired in with the correct phase rotation, its phase rotation will always be correct in the future, and the machine may be synchronized without further checking in this respect.

ant voltage E_s is not zero, considerable disturbance may result, especially in large, high-speed machines.

A better way to synchronize is to use the connection of Fig. 15-28, in which two of the lamps are cross-connected. With this connection, 3 is dark while 1 and 2 are bright at the instant of synchronizing. Near synchronism one of the cross-connected lamps is increasing in brilliancy, while the other is decreasing in brilliancy. This makes it possible closely to estimate the exact instant when the switch should be thrown.

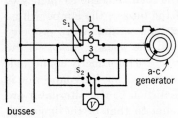

FIG. 15-28. Connections for synchronizing with two lamps bright and one dark.

When the machine voltage is higher than that for which commercial lamps are available, potential transformers must be used to reduce the voltage to a value suitable for the lamps.

In the routine operation of generators, the machines are usually synchronized by means of a device called a *synchroscope*. This device, presently to be described, shows by means of a pointer whether the incoming machine is fast or slow, as well as indicating the proper instant for throwing the switch.

Synchroscope. The principle of operation of the Westinghouse synchroscope may be understood by reference to Fig. 16-28. Two coils A and B are connected in split-phase fashion (page 542) to the busses.

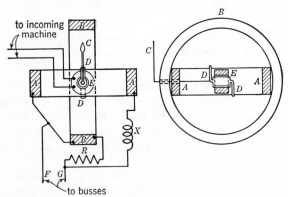

FIG. 16-28. Sketch illustrating principle of operation of synchroscope.

Coil A is connected in series with a reactance, while coil B is connected in series with a resistance R. When the terminals FG are connected to the busses, a rotating field of frequency equal to that of the supply is produced within the coils. Coil E is connected through a resistance (not shown) to the terminals of the incoming machine. Within this coil a soft-iron vane D is mounted on an axle to which a pointer C is fastened. When E is connected to the terminals on the incoming machine, the armature is alternately magnetized, first in one direction and then in the reverse direction. When synchronism is approached, the vane takes up a position such that its axis is parallel to the axis of the revolving field at the instant when the magnetizing force of coil E is a maximum and magnetizes the vane in the same direction as does the revolving field.

So long as the frequencies do not change, the vane maintains a fixed position. When the incoming machine is slow, it has a lower frequency than the revolving field; if the revolving field turns to the right, the position of the vane (in accordance with the above) then shifts constantly to the right. When the incoming machine is "fast," the position of the vane shifts constantly to the left. Obviously, the vane may remain stationary in any fixed dial position (indicating that the frequencies are alike) but there is only one dial position for which the voltages are in phase opposition. This zero position is marked at the top of the scale. When the vane remains stationary in the zero position, the switch connecting the incoming machine to the bus may be closed.

Parallel Operation of Synchronous Machines. Present-day power-supply systems consist of extensive networks of electrical conductors into which power is fed from a considerable number of generating units operating in parallel. The necessary conditions which must be fulfilled in order that machines so operated may perform satisfactorily, together with the influence of various factors upon the performance of the machines, will be considered.

In Fig. 17-28, let 1, 2, and 3 represent the station bus bars to which other generators not shown in the figure are connected, and let it be required to connect to the same set of bus bars another machine A. This connection is made by closing the switch S when A is ready to be synchronized. It has already been shown that at the instant of synchronizing the following conditions should be fulfilled:

1. The machines should be designed to generate waves of approximately the same shape.

2. The excitation of the incoming machine A should be such that the effective voltage E_a is approximately equal to the bus-bar voltage E_b.

3. The relative phase positions of the machines—bus bars and generator—should be such that the voltage wave of A is opposite (or very slightly ahead of) that of the bus bars. This condition is fulfilled when the instantaneous voltages across the three open-switch blades S are at all times zero.

4. The frequency of the incoming machine A should be exactly the same as the bus-bar frequency.

5. The phase rotation of the bus bars and of the incoming machine should be the same.

When the above conditions are fulfilled, switch S may be closed without in any way disturbing the behavior of either machine A or those already connected to the busses. No current will circulate between A and the busses, and no interchange of power will take place until further adjustments are made.

Modern machines are designed to have waves of approximately sine shape. The slight differences in wave shapes that do exist are usually not of sufficient importance to prevent satisfactory parallel operation or to introduce harmonics of any consequence in the current waves. All generators and synchronous motors operating on a given system must operate at exactly the same frequency. Therefore the speeds of all such units are inversely proportional to their numbers of pairs of poles. All machines

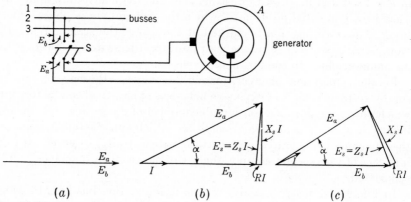

FIG. 17-28. Phasor diagrams for generators in parallel. (E_a = open-circuit voltage; E_b = terminal or bus voltage.)

with a given number of poles obviously run at exactly the same average speed. Any tendency of the prime mover of a generator or the load of a synchronous motor to cause the frequency to pulsate tends to cause the unit to break out of step with the system. For this reason engine-driven generators are provided with sufficient flywheel effect to prevent the considerable fluctuations in speed which would naturally arise from the pulsating driving torque that is characteristic of reciprocating engines. Turbine- and water-wheel-driven machines are propelled by steady torques and are free of the above objectionable feature.

At the moment when the machine is synchronized with the bus, no current circulates between it and the bus bars, as has been pointed out, and the machine neither receives power from the busses nor delivers power to them. From the point of view of the bus bars, the bus voltage $\mathbf{E}_b$ and the machine voltage $\mathbf{E}_a$ are then in phase, as shown by the solid lines in the diagram (a) of Fig. 17-28. So long as the assumed conditions remain unchanged, generator A simply idles. In order to make A share the load, its driving torque must be increased. This is accomplished by adjusting the governor of the driver so as to admit more steam, in case of a steam turbine, or more water, in case of a water-driven unit. Increasing the driving torque does not increase the average speed of the generator, for its speed is fixed by the frequency of the system and cannot change.[1] The instantaneous speed is momentarily increased, however, and the rotor shifts to a new position α deg ahead of its no-load position shown in (b). The generated voltage $\mathbf{E}_a$ is no longer in phase with the bus voltage but is also displaced from it by α electrical degrees. The difference $\mathbf{E}_b - \mathbf{E}_a = \mathbf{E}_s$ is sometimes called the *synchronizing voltage*. If the bus voltage remains unchanged, a current $\mathbf{I}$ will be established in the generator of such magnitude and phase position that the phasor voltage consumed in the synchronous impedance of the armature is exactly equal to $\mathbf{E}_s$. The current lags $\mathbf{E}_s$ by slightly less than 90 deg. The machine now delivers power to the busses in the amount of $\sqrt{3}\,E_b I \cos\theta$, with a three-phase generator assumed. With constant excitation the amount of load delivered is determined by the adjustment of the driving torque, for this alone fixes the torque angle α, which in turn controls the value of E_s and the armature current. When the driving torque is further increased, the load is also increased, as illustrated in (c).

It is obvious that, with a given governor setting of its driver, the generator cannot carry more than a certain definite amount of load because of the action above described. It is therefore impossible for the average generator speed to exceed or fall below the synchronous speed fixed by the bus frequency. If the generator should momentarily overspeed, its output would be more than the prime mover could furnish with the given governor setting. The excess output would then have to be drawn from the rotative energy WR^2 of the rotor, and the latter would therefore quickly fall back to its correct phase position as determined by the load which the driver is capable of delivering continuously at synchronous speed. When the speed momentarily falls below the synchronous value, the driving torque is in excess of that demanded by the generator at its then existing speed. The result is that the excess torque developed by the driver accelerates the rotor until its speed again becomes synchronous. At this speed the propelling torque of the driver and the resisting torque of the load are equal and the speed of the rotor no longer changes.[2] Thus

---

[1] An infinite bus is assumed, that is, the total capacity connected to the bus is assumed to be infinite (very large) in comparison with the capacity of the incoming machine.

[2] This statement is strictly true only for an ideal machine in which the rotating part has no inertia. Actually, the rotor approaches its mean position of synchronous speed by a series of oscillations of diminishing amplitude. The instantaneous speed is alternately higher and lower than synchronous speed and reaches the steady synchronous value only when the oscillations disappear.

generators operating in parallel keep in step by virtue of corrective forces that are set up within the machines themselves when disturbing forces are applied which tend to cause their speeds to vary. They pull out of step only if excessive loads are suddenly applied or if they are gradually overloaded. When the load becomes so great that there is no rotor position at which sufficient torque can be developed to carry the applied load at synchronous speed, the *pull-out* torque is reached.

When a generator is connected to the bus bars of a large system and operates in parallel with a number of other units, changing its field excitation has practically no effect on its power output, for such change cannot influence either the speed of the machine or the driving torque of the

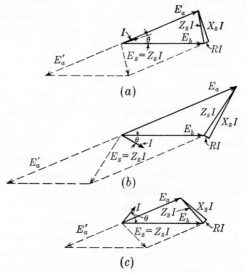

Fig. 18-28. Influence of excitation on voltage diagram.

prime mover. It has been shown that the speed must remain constant and that the torque is fixed by the governor setting. The only important effect produced is a change in the reactive power output of the machine.

The effects produced by changes in the field excitation are illustrated in Fig. 18-28. In (a) the excitation is such that the open-circuit voltage E_a is equal to the bus voltage E_b, and the output current I is delivered at approximately unit power factor. In (b) the excitation is increased 50 per cent, but the load on the machine remains substantially unchanged, as is indicated by the fact that the in-phase component of current is the same as before. Increasing the voltage E_a causes the machine to deliver a lagging component of current which sets up armature reaction that demagnetizes the field poles and brings the effective excitation back to the required value. The change in voltage produced by armature reaction and leakage reactance combined is indicated by the line Z_sI in the figure. When the excitation is reduced, as in (c), the machine supplies a leading component of current. This sets up armature reaction that aids the ampere-turns of the field winding and again restores the effective excitation to the correct value.

It should be remembered in the above discussion, however, that the total amounts of active and reactive powers supplied by the busses are in no way affected by the field adjustments mentioned but are dependent only upon the nature of the connected load. Changing the field excitation of one machine has the effect of redistributing the reactive power output among the several machines while the total which they jointly supply remains the same.

When the load on a system changes, the several machines connected to it should always divide the total output in proportion to their ratings, just as d-c machines operating in parallel are expected to do. For this reason the speed regulations of the prime movers should be alike; that is, the percentage drop in speed for a given percentage increase in load should be the same for the several machines on the system. The drop in speed between no load and full load may be only about 2 per cent, but if all parallel-connected machines have the same percentage drop, they will always divide the total load in proportion to their capacities. Furthermore, the governors of the prime movers should be free from oscillations and should quickly bring the machines to a steady speed. Oscillations of the governors cause a periodic transfer of load between the machines and produce a fluctuation in the voltage.

Problems

1-28. A 1,250-hp 2,300-volt 60-cycle 10-pole three-phase Y-connected synchronous motor has 0.085 ohm resistance and 1.8 ohms synchronous reactance per phase winding. When the motor is run from 2,300-volt mains and is loaded until it draws 250 amp from the line, what is the counter emf when the power factor of the motor is (a) unity, (b) 0.80, current lagging, (c) 0.80, current leading? Draw a phasor diagram for each case.

2-28. With no load on the motor in Prob. 1-28 the excitation is adjusted to a value that will cause the motor to draw minimum current from the line. The excitation is then held constant and the motor is loaded until it draws 300 amp from the line, per terminal. (a) What is the approximate angle of lag of the rotor from its no-load position? Express in mechanical degrees. (b) Using values per phase, draw a phasor diagram showing impressed voltage, counter emf, the voltage consumed in the impedance, and power angle (angle of rotor lag). Disregard field distortion due to armature reaction.

3-28. With the same excitation as in Prob. 2-28, what is (a) the voltage consumed in armature impedance when the rotor lags 0.50 mechanical degree behind the no-load position? (b) the current input?

4-28. Two three-phase generators A and B operating in parallel deliver a combined load of 8,000 kw at unity power factor to a 6.6-kv bus. Machine A delivers 4,230 kw

at 0.8 power factor, current lagging.   Using the bus voltage as reference phasor write
the expressions for (a) the phasor current output of A, (b) the phasor current output
of B.   (c) What is the power factor of B?

5-28. A 1,500-hp 6,600-volt 12-pole 60-cycle Y-connected three-phase synchronous
motor has 0.36 ohm resistance and 14.5 ohms synchronous reactance per phase.
When the excitation and load are such that the motor operates at unity power factor
and draws 104 amp per line from the mains, the field takes 155 amp at 120 volts.
Windage and friction losses are 15.5 kw, while the core losses are 20.2 kw.   Exciter
losses are disregarded.   Determine (a) the mechanical power developed by the rotor,
(b) the speed, (c) the pulley torque in pounds-perp-feet, (d) the output in horsepower,
(e) the efficiency.

6-28. An industrial plant has the following loads:

> 670 hp of induction motors at 0.80 power factor, current lagging
> 400 hp of induction motors at 0.70 power factor, current lagging
> 50 kw of lamp and heating load at unity power factor
> 135 hp of synchronous motor load.

Assume the average induction-motor efficiency to be 85 per cent and the synchronous-
motor efficiency to be 92 per cent.   If the synchronous-motor excitation is such
that its power factor is 0.80, current leading, what is the power factor of the total
load?

7-28. If the synchronous motor in Prob. 6-28, in addition to carrying 135 hp of
useful load, is required to supply sufficient kilovars, current lagging, to bring the
power factor of the entire plant load to 0.95, current lagging, (a) what is the kilovolt-ampere rating of the smallest motor that can be used to accomplish this?   (b) If
a 500-kva synchronous motor were available, how much shaft load could it carry in
addition to supplying the necessary kilovars?   Disregard motor losses.

8-28. An electric arc plant takes 2,400 kw from a 6,600-volt three-phase 60-cycle
line at a power factor of 0.65, current lagging.   Determine the kilovolt-ampere
rating of an idling synchronous motor of just sufficient capacity to correct the plant
power factor to each of the following values, current lagging: 0.8, 0.85, 0.90, 0.95,
and unity.   Plot rating of synchronous condenser as ordinates vs. power factors as
abscissas.

9-28. In Prob. 8-28 assume that the synchronous motor used for power-factor
correction also carries a constant shaft load that requires the motor to draw 350 kw
from the line.   Determine the minimum rating of the synchronous motor that may
be used to carry the given shaft load and, in addition, to correct the plant power
factor to each of the following, current lagging: 0.80, 0.85, 0.90, 0.95, and unity.
Tabulate kilovolt-ampere synchronous-motor rating vs. power factor.

10-28. A 60-cycle 7,200-volt 1,200-kva three-phase synchronous motor has an
effective resistance per phase of 0.42 ohm and a synchronous impedance per phase of
10.2 ohms.   For the condition of 100 per cent excitation and disregarding windage,
friction and core losses, and the effects of saturation, determine (a) the torque angle
and pounds-perp-feet of torque at rated full load, and (b) the maximum or pull-out
torque in pounds-perp-feet.

CHAPTER 29

CONVERSION EQUIPMENT

Introduction. The earliest applications of electric power were those in which street lighting, incandescent lighting, street and interurban railway electrification, and the gradual electrification of industrial drives were the principal objectives. Initially, these applications utilized direct currents exclusively. Electric power was generated as direct current, and in the metropolitan areas, the general power supply was transmitted short distances over three-wire Edison networks. Generation, transmission, and utilization voltages were low, and the distances over which power could be transmitted economically were short.

When the a-c transformer became available and the a-c system was introduced, generation, transmission, and utilization voltages were no longer dependent upon the voltage of generation. By means of transformers higher transmission and distribution voltages could be obtained; it became economically feasible to transmit power over much greater distances than formerly, and gradually power became generally available, often many miles from a generating station. The over-all advantages of the a-c system are so great that primary d-c generation and transmission have disappeared almost completely in the United States.

Direct-current utilization, however, still represents an important power load in such areas as electrolytic processing, urban railways and trolley busses, electrified steam railway service, industrial motor drives, etc. Hence, there is a continuing need for conversion equipment that can transform alternating current to direct current for utilization in these and other applications. The special machines and devices used for this purpose include synchronous converters, motor generators, mercury-arc rectifiers, and several other kinds of electronic and mechanical rectifying devices.

There are two other types of conversion that are sometimes required:

1. The conversion of alternating current of a given frequency to alternating current of some other frequency, as from 60 to 25 cycles. Machines used for this purpose are called *frequency converters*.

2. The conversion of alternating currents of a given number of phases to alternating currents of a different number of phases, as, for example,

from single-phase to three-phase or vice versa. Machines used for this purpose are called *phase converters*.

The remainder of this chapter is devoted to brief discussions of most of the rectifying and other conversion equipment already mentioned. The discussions of electronic rectifiers, however, including the important mercury-arc rectifier, have been deferred to the chapter on electronics for obvious reasons.

Synchronous Converters. In design and construction the synchronous converter is similar in most respects to a d-c generator. It has the same kind of armature core and windings, its field structure is the same, and it has a commutator. The latter is usually considerably larger than the commutator of a d-c machine of the same physical size, owing to the larger amount of power it is designed to handle. In addition to the commutator, slip rings are provided. These are two in number for a single-phase machine, three for a three-phase machine, four for a four-phase machine (usually called a two-phase machine), and six for a six-phase machine. The slip rings are mounted on the end of the shaft opposite the commutator and are connected to the armature winding by means of taps. In polyphase machines there is one tap per pair of poles for each slip ring. All taps connected to a given ring are spaced exactly 360 electrical degrees apart, and adjacent taps of an n-phase machine are $360/n$ deg apart. Thus a three-phase four-pole converter has three rings, to each of which two diametrically opposite taps are connected. Accordingly, there are 3×2 or 6 taps in all. To make this arrangement of taps possible, the total number of armature slots per pair of poles must be a multiple of the number of phases. Synchronous converters usually have commutating poles for the same reason that such poles are used on direct-current machines, and have damper windings to prevent hunting and to serve for starting from the alternating-current side.

Principle of Operation. The emf generated in the armature winding of a d-c generator is alternating, and the current flows continuously in a given direction in the external circuit only because of the rectifying action of the commutator. When the armature winding of a d-c generator is provided with the proper number of suitably connected taps as described in the previous paragraph, and the taps are correctly connected to slip rings, the d-c machine becomes an alternator, when viewed from the slip-ring end. The armature is the rotating element and the field is stationary. When mechanically driven from some outside source, the machine may be used as a synchronous generator to deliver power through the slip rings. If so desired, alternating currents may be taken from the slip rings and direct currents may be drawn from the commutator at the same time, although the machine is seldom used in this manner. When so used, the machine is called a *double-current generator*. The armature may also be driven as a synchronous motor by connecting the slip rings to the mains of a suitable supply in the usual way, while at the same time direct currents may be drawn from the commutator. In this application the machine is a *synchronous converter*. Viewed from the slip-ring end, it receives power in the form of alternating currents and runs as a synchronous motor; viewed from the commutator end, it is a d-c generator. The order of conversion may also be reversed. The armature may be driven as a d-c motor and power may be drawn from the slip rings. When used in this way, the machine is an *inverted synchronous converter* or *inverter*.

The simplified drawing of Fig. 1-29 illustrates the electrical connections of armature, commutator, taps, and slip rings of a ring-wound two-pole, single-phase converter. The single-phase converter, although seldom

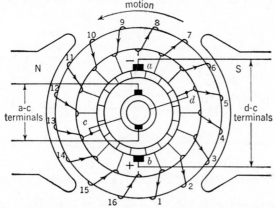

Fig. 1-29. Elementary sketch of a ring-wound single-phase synchronous converter.

built except in small sizes, is chosen here in order to simplify the discussion. Direct-current brushes a and b rest on the commutator at the neutral points. The direct potential difference E_0 between brushes is constant in value, except for the very slight fluctuations that occur from instant to instant as the successive armature coils are commutated. In the illustration there are always eight armature coils under each pole, regardless of the position of the armature. Since these are series-connected between positive and negative brushes, the direct voltage is equal to the sum of the voltages generated in the several coils.

Let the coils under the south pole at a given instant occupy the positions numbered from 1 to 8, as shown. As the armature revolves, these generate alternating voltages. The voltage wave of each coil lags that of the coil just ahead of it by $\pi/8$ electrical time degrees. The individual coil voltages may therefore be represented by the phasors numbered from 1 to 8 in (*a*) of Fig. 2-29, and these, added vectorially, as in (*b*), yield the constant direct voltage E_0. The same value of voltage is generated under the north pole by the other half of the winding. This may be represented by eight additional phasors such as 9, 10, etc., and these, added as in (b), complete the circle. The sum of all the phasors from 1 to 16 is zero, indicating that no circulating current can flow in the armature when all brushes are lifted.

The a-c slip rings are connected to the armature coils 5 and 13 by taps c and d. The instantaneous value of alternating voltage e available between the slip rings varies with the position of the armature. At the instant shown in the figure, the alternating phasor voltage between slip rings may be represented by E_m drawn to connect 13 and 5 in (b), while the instantaneous value of voltage between rings is represented by the length of the vertical projection of this phasor. The vertical component voltages generated in coils 14, 15, and 16 offset the equal and oppositely

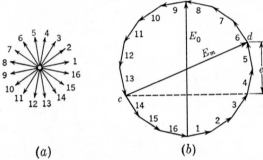

(a)   (b)

Fig. 2-29. Phasor representation of voltages in a single-phase synchronous converter.

directed components generated in 3, 2, and 1, respectively, thus leaving only the sum of the vertical components of coils 4 and 5 as the instantaneous voltage between rings. When the armature has turned to a position such that taps c and d are directly under the direct-current brushes, E_m becomes vertical and coincident with E_0. When the armature has turned 90 deg farther, taps c and d are midway under the poles. The phasor E_m is then horizontal and the instantaneous slip-ring voltage is zero. Thus the alternating voltage is zero when the taps are midway under the poles, is maximum when the taps are under the d-c brushes, and goes through all intermediate values between zero and maximum as the armature progresses from the first position to the second.

Voltage Relationships in Synchronous Converters. The instantaneous values of direct and alternating voltages may be represented by the waves shown in Fig. 3-29. The sine wave represents the voltage impressed on the slip rings, while the rectangular wave is the voltage across the d-c brushes. The two waves are drawn opposite each other, because one is an impressed voltage wave while the other is generated in the winding. The maximum value of the alternating wave is equal to the steady value of the d-c wave for reasons already given. In a synchronous converter there is always a fixed ratio between the alternating voltage impressed and the direct voltage. If the impressed voltage wave is sine-shaped, E_0 is equal to E_m in a single-phase converter, and since the maximum value of a sine wave is equal to $\sqrt{2}$ times the effective value, the effective alternating voltage E_1 of a single-phase converter is

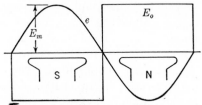

$$E_1 = \frac{E_0}{\sqrt{2}} = 0.707 E_0$$

Fig. 3-29. Instantaneous voltages on the d-c and a-c sides of a synchronous converter.

Similarly, the following comparative effective alternating voltages (E_2, E_3, and E_6) must be applied between adjacent slip rings of two-, three-, and six-phase converters, if it be assumed that all of them deliver direct current at the same terminal voltage E_0: $E_2 = 0.50\ E_0$, $E_3 = 0.612\ E_0$, and $E_6 = 0.353\ E_0$. Special transformers must generally be used to supply the correct alternating voltage to the slip rings. The ratio of transformation in each case depends upon the direct voltage, the voltage of the a-c supply, the number of phases of the converter and of the supply, and the type of transformer connections that are used. The a-c supply is usually three-phase, and converters are usually designed for three-phase or six-phase operation.

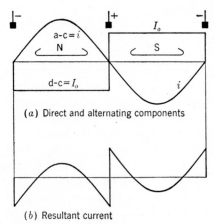

(a) Direct and alternating components

(b) Resultant current

Fig. 4-29. Current in the conductors of a single-phase converter lying midway between taps. Unity power factor assumed.

Heat Loss in Synchronous Converters. The single armature winding of a synchronous converter functions simultaneously as both d-c generator and synchronous-motor windings. The resultant current at any point in the winding is the difference between the alternating (motor) current and the direct (generator) current. The magnitude of the resultant current varies from point to point in the winding and depends upon the power factor. While the armature current varies in a rather complex manner (Fig. 4-29), the effective value of the resultant current is usually very much less than that of the same machine when operated at the same load either as a d-c generator or a synchronous motor.

If the relative armature copper loss of the machine when running as a d-c generator at rated load is taken as unity, the comparative loss of the three-phase synchronous converter delivering the same d-c output is 0.59 and that of the six-phase converter is 0.27. (Unity-power-factor operation is assumed.) Owing to reduced armature copper losses, the approximate relative rated capacities of a given machine, which operates at unity power factor, is 133 when connected three-phase and 195 when connected six-phase, as compared with the rated output of the same machine as a d-c generator, taken as 100. The direct terminal voltage is assumed to be the same in all cases.

Motor Generators. Motor generators may be used in place of converters. They usually consist of a synchronous motor and a direct-connected d-c generator, but the set may be induction-motor-driven if required. Synchronous-motor sets are used on systems which have very poor voltage regulation on the a-c side but which require good direct-voltage regulation, or where it is desired to correct power factor by over-excitation of a synchronous motor. Since the motor winding is on a separate armature and has a separate field as well, the motor may be designed for a larger rating than the generator, and power-factor correction may be had without affecting the generator performance. If the frequency and voltage regulation of the supply are so poor that a synchronous motor cannot be satisfactorily operated, an induction-motor-driven set may be used.

A synchronous converter with its necessary transformers is generally about 5 per cent more efficient at full load than is the equivalent motor generator and, even at light loads, is usually somewhat more efficient. For most applications (voltages below 13,000), synchronous motors may be connected to the supply lines without transformers, while converters always require transformers, as has been noted; but even so, it is usually found that the converter and transformers cost less than the motor generator alone.

Mechanical Rectifiers. The process of rectification, or conversion from alternating to direct current, could conceivably be accomplished by means of a double-pole double-throw switch connected between the source and the load as in Fig. 5-29. If the switch is thrown from one side to the other each time that the voltage starts to reverse, the current may be maintained through the load in the same direction at all times. In the form shown such a device would be practical only at very low frequencies, but by suitable construction this principle can be used at commercial power frequencies. A device which converts alternating to direct current by such means is a *mechanical rectifier*.

One practical form of mechanical rectifier employs a vibrating reed with suitable contacts on its end. The reed is caused to vibrate synchronously

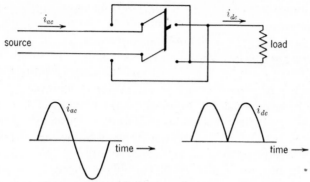

FIG. 5-29. Rectification by means of a switch.

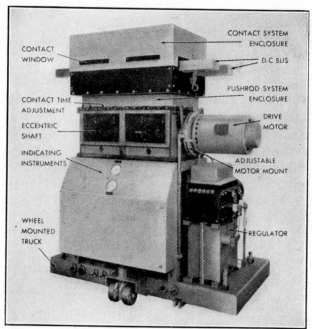

FIG. 6-29. 10,000-amp 12-phase mechanical rectifier. (*I-T-E Circuit Breaker Company.*)

with the applied voltage to perform the desired switching operation at the desired time. Another form of mechanical rectifier uses an arrangement of a commutator and slip rings driven by a synchronous motor. Power is led to the slip rings from the alternating source by brushes and is removed from the commutator as pulsating direct current by means of another set of brushes. Still another form of mechanical rectifier uses a set of contactors to perform the switching operation. The contactors are operated by push rods driven by a cam shaft which, in turn, is driven by a synchronous motor.

The outstanding problem in mechanical rectifiers is deterioration of the contacts owing to arcing at the instant of switching. In the case of lower-power rectifiers this difficulty may be met by using suitably heavy contacts and capacitors for spark suppression. In high-power installations very special means must be provided to minimize sparking and arcing at the contacts. If the voltage and current on the alternating side of the rectifier are sinusoidal, it is extremely difficult to perform the switching operation at the exact zero of voltage and current. In one successful modern mechanical rectifier this problem is met by shaping the wave with a commutating reactor as shown in Fig. 7-29, thus creating a zone of practically zero voltage and current during which the switching operation may

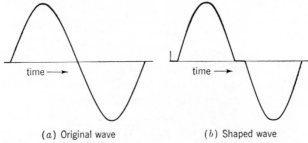

(a) Original wave   (b) Shaped wave

FIG. 7-29. Shaping of sine wave for mechanical rectifier.

be performed. Mechanical rectifiers of the contactor type which use this principle are available in ratings up to 400 volts and 10,000 amperes.

Applications of mechanical rectifiers in the high-power sizes are similar to those of mercury-arc rectifiers (page 589). The voltage drop in a mercury-arc rectifier is nearly a constant at approximately 20 volts, regardless of the rating of the rectifier. Consequently, at the lower voltage ratings this drop is an appreciable part of the rated voltage, and the efficiency of conversion suffers correspondingly. It is in the lower voltage ranges that the advantages of the mechanical rectifier are most apparent, because good efficiencies are obtained down to as low as 50 volts.

Phase Conversion. In cases where polyphase power is available but utilization apparatus requires power of a different number of phases than the source, the conversion is usually accomplished by means of transformers. An example of such a conversion is the conversion from two-phase to three-phase power by means of the Scott-connected transformer bank as illustrated in Fig. 27-25, page 426. If a polyphase energy source is available, the use of phase-shifting transformers makes possible the supply of power in any desired number of phases. In some cases, in feeding a mercury-arc rectifier load, the equivalent of as many as 72 phases has been used.

If only single-phase power is available, and it is desired to supply a polyphase load, a fundamentally different problem is present. Single-phase power pulsates at double frequency as shown in Fig. 1-23, page 361, whereas balanced polyphase power is constant, since the pulsating components of the several phases add to zero. An apparatus for converting from pulsating single-phase power to continuous polyphase power must evidently have provision for alternately storing and releasing the pulsations of energy. Since a transformer is unable to store and release energy as required, it is impossible to find a transformer connection which will supply polyphase load from a single-phase source. Capacitive and inductive reactance elements can be used to provide a phase shift, since these elements are capable of storing and releasing energy, but the use of reactive elements for this purpose leads to poor voltage regulation under conditions of varying load. Rotating machinery provides a much more satisfactory converter from single-phase to polyphase power. The flywheel effect of a rotor is able to smooth the pulsations of single-phase power and deliver energy at a constant rate.

The most obvious rotating phase-converter is a motor generator set, in which a single-phase synchronous or induction motor drives a polyphase generator. It is possible, however, to do the job more simply with a single induction motor. Since a revolving field is set up in a single-phase motor by the combined action of the applied voltage and the rotation of the rotor, the stator conductors are cut in sequence by the revolving field. If the stator winding is uniformly distributed around the circumference of the stator, polyphase voltages may be found by tapping into the winding at the desired positions, and a polyphase load may be supplied. The flywheel action of the rotor again is the energy storage medium which makes the conversion possible.

Phase converters of the induction-motor type have been used in the cab of electric locomotives where it was desired to supply polyphase motors from the single-phase trolley and track circuit.

Frequency Conversion. The problem of converting power from one frequency to another sometimes arises. As examples, in certain sections of the country 25-cycle systems are geographically interlinked with 60-cycle systems and it is desirable to be able to interchange power from one system to the other. In other cases, as in Europe, it may be desired to convert power from the generated frequency of 50 cps to $16\frac{2}{3}$ cps for railway use. Various means have been used to make the frequency conversion, and some of the more important ones are discussed below.

1. *Synchronous-Synchronous Sets.* One of the most common methods of conversion is to use a synchronous motor which is supplied with power

from a bus of one frequency to drive an alternator that generates power at some other frequency. Since each machine must have an integral number of pairs of poles, only certain speeds are possible, which are synchronous speeds for each of the two frequencies. For example, in converting from 60-cycle to 25-cycle power, the highest speed possible for the motor generator set is 300 rpm, which corresponds to a 10-pole 25-cycle machine and a 24-pole 60-cycle machine. Particular attention must be given to load division in frequency changer sets operated effectively in parallel. In some cases it is necessary to provide means to shift the stator of one of the machines relative to the rotors in order to control the direction of power flow.

2. *Induction-motor Frequency Changers.* It has been noted in the chapter on induction motors that the frequency of f_2 of the rotor emfs in an induction motor is equal to the product of the slip s and the stator frequency f_1. If a wound-rotor motor is driven at a speed corresponding to a slip s, then power may be removed from the rotor at a frequency of $f_2 = sf_1$. This is the basis for certain types of frequency converters. Many different variations in this type of frequency converter have been used, differing principally in the details of the drive of the induction motor.

3. *Mercury-arc Converters.* In the chapter on electronics the mercury-arc rectifier is described as a device for converting alternating current to direct current. Mercury-arc sets have also been built to convert power from one frequency to another. These sets utilize resonant circuits made up of inductance and capacitance elements. Effectively, the mercury-arc set converts to direct current and also acts as an oscillator fed from the direct current to supply power of a different frequency. Actually, the conversion takes place in a single step without the direct current being identified as such. Such frequency converters have the advantage that the ratio between the two frequencies need not be exactly maintained as in synchronous-synchronous sets. Also, the output of the mercury-arc frequency converter may be at higher frequencies than are practical for rotating machinery. High-frequency sets find application in induction melting furnaces used for high-purity alloying operations.

CHAPTER 30

SINGLE-PHASE MOTORS

Single-phase Induction Motor. A two-phase induction motor with one phase open will continue to run as a single-phase motor. Such a motor, with one stator phase winding removed, is shown in Fig. 1-30.

1. *Standstill Conditions.* When a sinusoidal potential difference E_1 is impressed on the stator winding, an exciting current flows and a sinusoidal flux ϕ_a is set up along the $A'A$ axis. If the saturation is relatively low,

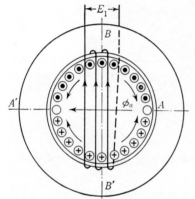

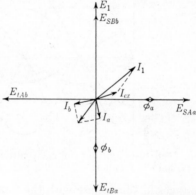

Fig. 1-30. Single-phase induction motor at standstill.

Fig. 2-30. Phasor diagram of voltages. Current and flux of a single-phase induction motor.

the current wave is also approximately sinusoidal. Since the flux is alternating, it induces an emf in the stator winding which is counter to the impressed voltage and differs from it by an amount equal to the primary impedance drop. An emf is also induced in the rotor bars that lie above and below the $A'A$ axis which, if the leakage flux be neglected, is equal per turn to the stator counter emf and, for the instant indicated by p in Fig. 3-30, is *out* at B and *in* at B'. In the phasor diagram of Fig. 2-30, which shows the time-phase relations of currents, voltages, and fluxes, this emf is represented by E_{tBa}, the subscripts of which indicate that the emf is induced by *transformer action* in the *rotor conductors of the region B* and B' by the flux ϕ_a.

Since the rotor circuit is closed and highly reactive, the voltage E_{tBa} sets up a current I_b which lags nearly 90 deg, as shown in Fig. 2-30, or exactly 90 deg for the ideal case represented in Fig. 3-30. At the time indicated by p the rotor emf is at p' and the current i_b at p'', and since the current and voltage are both negative, the current also flows *out* at B and *in* at B', as shown in Fig. 1-30. Thus as in a transformer, the stator and rotor mmfs are almost oppositely directed and together produce the stator flux ϕ_a.

It is apparent from Fig. 1-30 that the torques produced by the reactions of rotor currents and stator flux are equal and opposite in adjacent quadrants, and that the resultant torque is zero and the motor will not start.

2. *Running Conditions.* Assume the motor to be started in a clockwise direction. The rotor conductors to the left and right of the BB'-axis now cut the gap flux ϕ_a in the regions A' and A and thereby generate

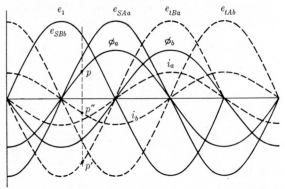

Fig. 3-30. Instantaneous voltages, currents, and fluxes of an ideal (no-loss) single-phase induction motor.

voltages in time phase with the flux and proportional to the speed. By the right-hand rule, these emfs are found to be *in* at A and *out* at A'. They are shown in Figs. 2-30 and 3-30 as E_{sAa}, since they are generated by *speed action in the conductor A by the flux ϕ_a.*

Owing to the speed emf, the conductors at A' and A carry a current I_a which lags the emf nearly 90 deg, as in Fig. 2-30, or, for the *ideal* case, exactly 90 deg, as in Fig. 3-30. The direction of the current at the instant indicated by p of Fig. 3-30 is opposite that of the voltage, as seen from the curves of E_{sAa} and I_a, and accordingly the current flows *out* at A and *in* at A', as represented in Fig. 4-30. The mmf thus set up magnetizes the core at right angles to the stator field and produces the flux ϕ_b in time phase with the magnetizing component of the current I_a which produces it (Fig. 3-30).

An examination of Fig. 4-30 shows that the resultant torque produced by the flux ϕ_b reacting with the current I_a is zero, just as it was for ϕ_a and

I_b in Fig. 1-30. The actions indicated by Figs. 1-30 and 4-30, however, take place simultaneously, and the resultant effect may be visualized by superimposing the figures. One then observes that the current I_b of Fig. 1-30 reacting with the flux ϕ_b of Fig. 4-30 produces a clockwise torque, and that the same is true of I_a in Fig. 4-30 reacting with the flux ϕ_a of Fig. 1-30. The resultant torque is, therefore, in the direction of motion, and the motor continues to run and carry a load.

Had the motor been started in the reverse direction, by modifying the figures for the new situation, one observes that the resultant torque would have been counterclockwise. A single-phase motor thus develops a torque to keep it going in the direction in which it is started.

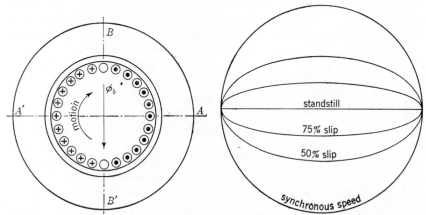

FIG. 4-30. Current in AA' band of con- FIG. 5-30. Loci of revolving flux phasor
ductors due to speed emf e_{sAa} and the of a single-phase induction motor for
flux θ_b. several percentages of slip.

It should be observed that in addition to those already shown, two additional emfs are generated in the rotor windings: one by speed action in the conductors BB' by the flux ϕ_b, represented as E_{sBb}, and the other by transformer action with the same flux in the conductors $A'A$ and represented as E_{tAb}. These are the counter emfs of E_{tBa} and E_{sAa}, respectively, as shown in Fig. 2-30.

Since the two fields ϕ_a and ϕ_b are in space quadrauture as shown in Figs. 1-30 and 4-30, and also in time quadrature as indicated by Figs. 2-30 and 3-30, together they produce an equivalent revolving field for the reasons and in the manner explained on page 437 for the two-phase motor. The behavior of the motor is now readily understood, for in terms of its equivalent revolving field the theory of its performance is quite like that of the polyphase machine.

It may be shown that at synchronous speed the maximum values of the component fields ϕ_a and ϕ_b are equal; at any other speed corresponding to a slip s the maximum value of the component ϕ_b is only $(1 - s)$ per cent as large as that of ϕ_a, since the former is proportional to the speed. The rotating field produced by ϕ_a and ϕ_b is therefore elliptical, as indicated in Fig. 5-30, but approaches circularity under no-load conditions because the slip is small.

Motors Classified on the Basis of Method of Starting. Because the single-phase induction motor has no starting torque of its own, some special provision must be made for starting it. A number of methods have been developed and are in common use. Often the name of the motor is derived from the starting method used. Several single-phase motors of this type are described in the following paragraphs.

1. *Split-phase Motor.* This method of starting utilizes an auxiliary *starting winding* indicated by B in Fig. 6-30, for the case of a two-pole motor, in addition to the main winding A, both excited from the same phase. The starting winding is displaced 90 deg in space from the main winding, as shown, and is provided with a large resistance R for the purpose of bringing the current in the winding nearly in phase with the applied voltage E. The main winding is highly inductive, and hence its current has a large lagging quadrature component. The result is that, when an alternating potential difference E is impressed simultaneously upon the two windings, since the currents in A and B have components which are in time quadrature with each other, while the windings in which these flow are in space quadrature, an elliptical revolving field is produced. A small torque is thus provided which is sufficient to bring the unloaded motor up to speed. By means of a centrifugal device (Fig. 7-30) operated from the motor shaft, the cutout switch S is opened when the motor is nearly up to speed, thus deenergizing the starting winding when it is no longer needed.

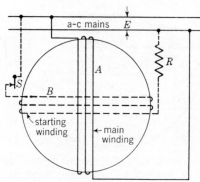

Fig. 6-30. Diagram of circuit connections for split-phase starting of a single-phase induction motor.

Simplicity of construction and reliability of performance are the features of the split-phase motor that have made it popular. A disadvantage is that it has a rather poor starting torque, usually less than 1 oz-ft/amp, and takes a relatively large current from the line at starting. When the motor is connected to a lighting circuit, the large starting current may cause an objectionable flicker in the lights. To avoid this it is necessary to limit such motors on lighting circuits to small fractional-horsepower sizes. They are usually built for ratings of from $\frac{1}{30}$ to $\frac{1}{3}$ hp, for operation on 120-volt circuits.

Fractional-horsepower split-phase motors are admirably suited to applications that require an inexpensive, constant-speed motor with moderate torque. They are simple in construction, are reliable in operation, and require no attention except occasional oiling. They have become the accepted drive for many small appliances found in stores, shops, offices, and homes, such as fans, power tools, office machines, mixers, washing machines, ironers, oil burners, refrigerators, etc.

FIG. 7-30. Centrifugal switch mechanism for disconnecting starting winding after proper speed has been attained. (*Wagner Electric Company.*)

2. *Capacitor Motor.* The capacitor motor is essentially a two-phase induction motor supplied from a single-phase circuit. The stator windings of the two phases may or may not be alike, depending upon the design. The rotor is identical with that of any polyphase induction motor. Usually the rotor is of squirrel-cage design, although, of course, a wound rotor may be used.

In Fig. 8-30(*a*) is illustrated, in principle, the diagram of a simple capacitor motor. Comparison with Fig. 6-30 indicates that the principal difference between the split-phase and the capacitor-start motor lies in the substitution of a capacitor for a resistor as a phase splitter. By selecting the proper size of capacitance for a given motor, the currents in the two-phase windings may be brought into the desired time-phase relation. In this way two-phase operation is secured. If the phase winding which contains the starting capacitance is automatically cut out when the motor has reached about 2/3 of rated speed, the motor continues to run like any single-phase motor with starting winding removed. This motor is called a *capacitance-start* single-phase induction motor. On the other hand, if a part of the capacitance is retained in the circuit after the motor has started as in (*b*) and (*c*) of Fig. 8-30, the motor is a *capacitance-start capacitance-run* motor. The description that follows pertains to this type of motor.

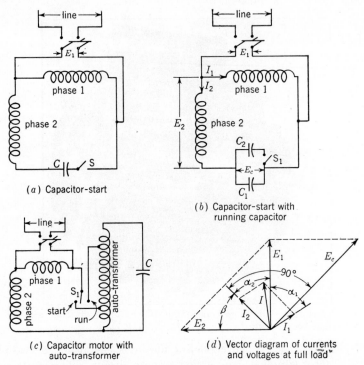

FIG. 8-30. Circuit and phasor diagrams for capacitor motor.

To obtain a large starting torque it is necessary to use considerably more capacitance for starting than for running conditions. This may be done in either of two ways:

1. An additional capacitance may be used when starting, as illustrated in (*b*) of Fig. 8-30. This capacitance may subsequently be removed from the circuit by opening switch S_1. (Starting and running capacitors are usually in a 4:1 ratio.)

2. Since the number of volt-amperes delivered to a capacitance is proportional to the square of the impressed voltage, an autotransformer may be used to increase the voltage applied to the capacitance at starting

[Fig. 8-30(c)] and in this way to increase the leading volt-amperes. By means of the tap switch S_1 the voltage across the condenser terminals may be reduced to a suitable value after the motor has come up to speed.

The motor diagram for full-load operation is shown in (d) of Fig. 8-30. Since phase 1 is inductive, the impressed voltage $\mathbf{E}_1$ sets up a current $\mathbf{I}_1$ in this phase that lags $\mathbf{E}_1$ by some angle α_1, determined by the impedance characteristic of phase 1. The same voltage $\mathbf{E}_1$ is also impressed on the combined impedance of phase 2 and the series-connected capacitance. This circuit is capacitive, so the current $\mathbf{I}_2$ leads $\mathbf{E}_1$ by some angle α_2 which is determined by the impedance characteristic of circuit 2. The voltage $\mathbf{E}_c$ consumed in the capacitance lags $\mathbf{I}_2$ by 90 deg, while the voltage $\mathbf{E}_2$ consumed in coil 2 leads $\mathbf{I}_2$ by the angle $\beta = \tan^{-1}(X_{L2}/r_2)$, where r_2 and X_{L2} are the resistance and the inductive reactance, respectively, of coil 2, and $\mathbf{E}_2 = Z_2 I_2 \underline{/\alpha_2 + \beta}$ with respect to $\mathbf{E}_1$ as reference. The sum of $\mathbf{E}_2$ and $\mathbf{E}_c$ is $\mathbf{E}_1$, and the sum of $\mathbf{I}_1$ and $\mathbf{I}_2$ is the input current $\mathbf{I}$.

For the condition shown, the impressed voltage and input current are nearly in phase, so the power factor is nearly unity. This is due to the retention of the capacitor C_1 in the circuit of phase 2 after the motor has been started. Thus C_1 serves not only as part of the phase-splitting capacitance at starting but also as a source of leading vars to improve the power factor of the motor under running conditions.

Fractional-horsepower capacitor motors are preferred in many applications because of their good starting characteristics and high power factor while running. They are especially well adapted to driving fans. Their use in this application has resulted in substantial increases in efficiencies and reductions in weights. Moreover, since the output torque is far smoother than that of older types of single-phase motors, quieter and smoother operation is secured. They are built with ratings of $\frac{1}{8}$ to 1 hp, usually for operation on 120-volt circuits, and have starting torques per amp of roughly three to four times the corresponding torques of split-phase motors.

3. *Motor with Shading Coil.* The auxiliary windings employed in this case consist of short-circuited coils, one for each pole, which embrace corresponding tips of the pole structures, as illustrated in Fig. 9-30. The short-circuited coils are highly inductive, and because of this the flux densities set up by the stator excitation in the iron embraced by the shading coils are *larger* than in the unshaded portions of the poles when the current in the stator is *decreasing* and are *smaller* when the current is increasing, for the effect of the current induced in the shading coil *is to oppose any change in the amount of flux linking it.* Thus a shifting flux is produced in the air gap, and the region of maximum density moves from right to left over the pole face once during each half cycle. The emf induced in the

rotor conductors by the shifting field sets up a current in the rotor which reacts with the air-gap flux and produces sufficient torque to start the motor when unloaded.

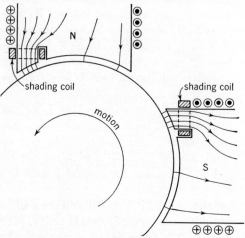

FIG. 9-30. Principle of shading coil applied to the starting of small single-phase induction motors.

Motors of this class have low starting torques per ampere of current and are built in small sizes of about $\frac{1}{20}$ hp or less.

4. *Repulsion-start Induction Motor.* This motor was developed to meet the need for a single-phase induction motor with high starting torque. The principle employed in its operation is discussed on page 552, and a motor that applies this principle for starting is pictured in Fig. 11-30. A d-c armature with radial commutator segments is used. When starting, the brushes normally rest on the commutator segments in an axis somewhat displaced from the neutral axis. The brushes are connected together and thus short-circuit the armature winding. The alternating field induces currents in the armature which in turn react with the flux to produce a net torque (page 553) that turns the motor to the right or left, depending upon which way the brushes are shifted from the neutral axis, and quickly brings the motor up to speed. At some predetermined speed a centrifugal device mounted on the shaft operates a mechanism that forces the brushes away from

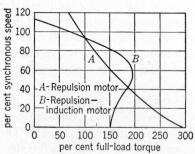

FIG. 10-30. Typical torque-speed curves of repulsion and repulsion-induction motors.

the commutator and at the same time short-circuits all the commutator bars on their under sides. From this point on, the motor runs and behaves like any other single-phase motor.

More recently motors of this type, called *repulsion-induction motors* (page 553), have been built with an induction-motor winding on the rotor in addition to the commutated winding and commutator. This makes it possible to eliminate the centrifugal switch, for the induction-motor winding prevents the speed from rising much above synchronism (Fig. 10-30). Above synchronism the induction motor becomes an induction generator.

Fig. 11-30. Wagner single-phase induction motor with repulsion starting.

The repulsion-start induction motor develops from three to four times full-load torque at starting and draws only from 2½ to 3 times rated full-load current from the line. Hence, this motor starts with small line disturbance. Domestic refrigerators are sometimes supplied with motors of this kind. Most larger single-phase repulsion-start motors have similar characteristics.

Alternating-current Series Motor. On account of its desirable speed-torque characteristic (high torque at low speeds and low torque at high speeds), the series motor is used almost exclusively in railway service. While the d-c motor is entirely satisfactory for this class of service and is generally used on street-railway cars and trolley coaches, the fact that it is more convenient and more economical to transmit power and to transform voltages in a-c systems than with direct currents has led to the development of the a-c series motor for use on some of the important steam-road electrifications.

The principle of operation of this motor is the same as that of the d-c series motor discussed in Chap. 14. The armature and field are wound and interconnected in the same manner as the d-c series motor. When an alternating emf is applied to the terminals, since field and armature windings are connected in series, the field flux and the armature current reverse simultaneously every half cycle, but the direction of the torque remains unchanged. The torque is pulsating, but its average value is equal to that which a d-c motor would develop if it had the same rms values of flux and current. Motor connections, direction of torque, etc., for two successive half cycles are shown in Fig. 12-30. If the field and

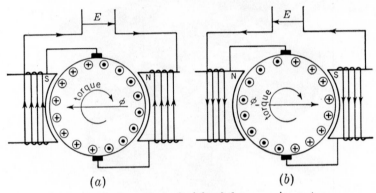

(a)   (b)

Fig. 12-30. Operating principle of the a-c series motor.

armature core are run at low saturation, the air-gap flux is approximately proportional to the current and the torque is approximately proportional to the current squared, for since torque $= k_1\phi_a I_a$ and $\phi_a = k_2 I_a$, by substitution, torque $= k_1 k_2 I_a^2$, where k_1 and k_2 are constants and ϕ_a and I_a are the gap flux and armature current, respectively.

While it is theoretically possible to operate a d-c series motor from an a-c circuit, important structural changes noted below must be made in the motor before it becomes a practical and reasonably efficient machine.

1. *The entire magnetic circuit must be laminated,* and materials with low iron-loss coefficients should be used as in transformers. Since the field flux is alternating, these changes are required in order to keep the hysteresis and eddy-current losses within reasonable limits. The use of a low frequency is also advantageous in this respect. A frequency of 25 cps is used for the railway motors operated in this country.

2. *The field circuit must be designed for a much lower reactance than the corresponding d-c motor field* in order to reduce the reactance voltage drop

of the field to a minimum and to improve the power factor of the motor. Since the reactance depends upon the number of linkages of flux with the turns of the field winding and upon the frequency, it may be reduced by reducing the number of field turns per pole and the flux per pole, and by using a low frequency. All these methods are employed. The reluctance of the magnetic circuit is decreased by using a very short air gap and relatively low flux densities, both of which aid in reducing the field turns per pole. Since the flux per pole is less than in the corresponding d-c machine, the number of poles is usually larger. Furthermore, on account of the lower gap densities employed, the torque per ampere of current is reduced, and hence, to secure a given torque, the number of armature conductors must be increased proportionally. As compared with the d-c machine of a given rating, the a-c motor is considerably larger and has a weaker field and a magnetically stronger armature than the corresponding d-c machine.

3. *A distributed compensating winding is required* to reduce the reactance of the armature winding by reducing the leakage flux, and to neutralize the cross-magnetizing effect of the armature ampere-turns. The first of these effects decreases the armature impedance drop and improves the power factor of the machine, while the second makes satisfactory commutation possible. The distributed compensating winding is similar to that illustrated in Fig. 9-12 (page 168) for the case of a d-c motor. It is embedded in the laminated pole faces and is so wound and connected as to carry a current the magnetizing force of which at all points on the periphery of the armature is always approximately equal and opposite to that of the armature itself.

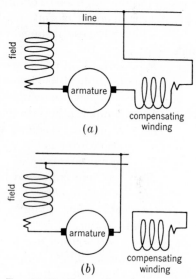

FIG. 13-30. Connections for (a) conductive compensation, (b) inductive compensation.

The compensating winding may be connected in series with the series-field and armature windings, or it may be short-circuited upon itself and receive its excitation voltage by transformer action, since it is inductively coupled with the armature cross field (Fig. 13-30). In the first case the motor is said to be *conductively* compensated, while in the second it is *inductively* compensated. Conductive compensation is required on motors which are intended for operation in d-c as well as a-c circuits.

4. *Special provisions must be made to secure satisfactory commutation.* During the period of commutation the two sides of the short-circuited coil lie in the axis of the brushes.   The coil itself, therefore, links all the flux from a pole.   Since the field is alter-

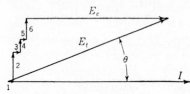

FIG. 14-30. Phasor emfs and voltage drops in a single-phase series motor.

nating, an emf is induced in the coil by transformer action which circulates a current through the coil and thus causes sparking when the coil is commutated.   In order to reduce the amount of the induced voltage, the armature is wound with only one turn per coil.   This requires a large number of commutator segments and thus makes the commutator large and costly.   Commutation is further aided by keeping the impressed voltage between segments low.

A phasor diagram of emfs for this type of machine is shown in Fig. 14-30.   The voltages consumed in the several parts of the circuit are the following:

1. IR_s = series-field resistance voltage
2. IX_s = series-field reactance voltage
3. IR_c = compensating-winding resistance voltage
4. IX_c = compensating-winding reactance voltage
5. IR_a = armature resistance voltage
6. IX_a = armature reactance voltage

E_c = motor counter emf

E_t = terminal impressed voltage

I = armature current

θ = power-factor angle

Universal Motor.   Fractional-horsepower series motors that are adapted for use on either d-c or a-c circuits of a given voltage are called *universal motors*.   These motors were originally developed to fill the demand of the manufacturers of vacuum cleaners for a motor which could be used on either d-c or a-c supply.

The principle of operation and the basic factors which must be considered in the design of these motors do not differ materially from those already discussed in connection with the larger series motors used for traction service.   Cores of field and armature are built of high-permeability sheet-steel punchings to reduce core losses.   High-permeability material permits the use of a field with few turns, which results in a low reactance, since the inductive reactance is proportional to the square of the number of turns.   To keep the field flux as high as possible, the area of the field poles is relatively large and the air gap is as short as mechanical clearance permits.

To develop a good torque with a weak field in large series motors, as already explained, requires a large number of armature turns. This results in an armature winding with a comparatively large inductive reactance. It is possible to reduce the armature reactance by means of a compensating winding or a distributed field winding, and in large machines either one or the other of these methods is employed. In small motors (under $\frac{3}{8}$ hp), however, the number of armature turns is small enough so that satisfactory operation may be secured without resorting to compensation. The commutator has a large number of segments and the number of armature turns per segment is small. In this way good commutation is secured. High-resistance brushes are also used to limit the current in the short-circuited coil and thus to aid in securing sparkless commutation.

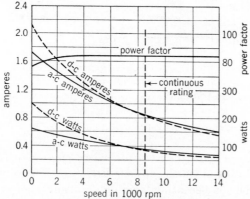

Fig. 15-30. Performance curves of $\frac{1}{16}$-hp a-c 115-volt universal motor on alternating and direct currents. (*The Dumore Company.*)

The performance curves of a $\frac{1}{16}$-hp universal motor are shown in Fig. 15-30. It may be observed that the speed varies inversely with the load. In the motor for which the curves are given, the speed varies from about 15,000 rpm at light loads to 8,500 rpm at rated load. In these motors the torque is proportional, approximately, to the square of the current and is inversely proportional to the speed. The starting torque is high— approximately three times the torque at rated load. The power factor is good and the efficiency at rated load is about 50 per cent. Universal motors built for voltages between 32 and 220 and for frequencies of 60 cycles or less perform satisfactorily and have quite similar characteristics whether run from d-c or a-c circuits.

Because of their very high armature speeds (above 7,000 rpm), universal motors develop very high outputs per unit of weight. This is a great advantage on portable equipment and in applications where space is limited. These motors find wide use in a host of applications. They are used on vacuum cleaners, beverage mixers, grinders, hand drills, dental drills, floor polishers, sewing machines, motion-picture projectors, etc. Many thousands are sold each year.

Repulsion Motor. If the main-field winding and the compensating winding of a series motor be connected in series and at the same time the

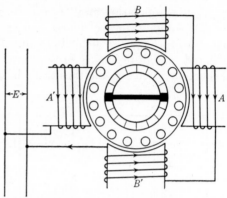

FIG. 16-30. Illustrating the operating principle of a repulsion motor.

brushes be short-circuited, the resulting motor is the so-called *repulsion motor*.

The schematic circuit diagram for a two-pole motor of this kind is shown in Fig. 16-30, in which the coils BB' represent the main-field winding and AA' the compensating winding. Salient poles are indicated for convenience of illustration, although actually nonsalient poles and short

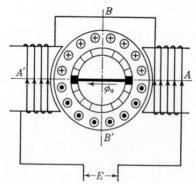

FIG. 17-30. Repulsion motor with winding AA' alone excited.

air gaps are used to provide uniform and minimum air-gap reluctance and thus to reduce the reactance of the windings.

Let the motor be standing still and assume first that the winding AA' alone is excited, as in Fig. 17-30, and that at the instant considered the current flows in the direction indicated but is *decreasing* in value. The emfs induced in the armature conductors by transformer action are then as indicated—*inward* in the upper half of the armature and *outward* in the lower half. Since the circuit is closed through the short-circuited brushes, a current circulates in the winding. This current has a large component in time phase with the flux ϕ_a and reacts with it to produce a torque. It is apparent, however, that equal and oppositely directed torques are produced in the adjacent quadrants of the armature formed by the AA' and BB' axes, and that therefore the net resultant torque is zero.

Next assume that the winding BB' alone is excited, as in Fig. 18-30, and that the exciting current is in the direction indicated and is decreasing as before. The induced emfs of the armature are then as shown in Fig. 18-30—*inward* in the half of the armature to the right of the BB' axis and *outward* in the left half. Thus in each of the two paths through the armature (upper and lower halves) equal positive and negative emfs are induced, and the resultant potential difference between brushes is zero. No potential difference exists between brushes, no current circulates in the armature, and no torque is produced.

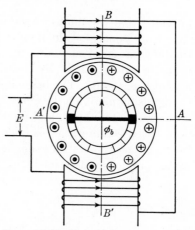

FIG. 18-30. Repulsion motor with winding BB' alone excited.

When both fields are excited simultaneously, the currents set up in the armature by the induced emfs of Fig. 17-30 react with the flux produced by the BB' field and thus produce a large resultant torque continually in one direction, and if the rotor is free to move it will rotate. The direction

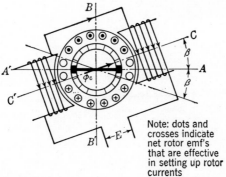

FIG. 19-30. The resultant field CC' is produced by the simultaneous excitation of both AA' and BB' windings.

of rotation may be changed by reversing the direction of current through the field BB'. It is evident that the AA' and BB' windings acting together are equivalent to, and may be represented by, a single winding CC' of Fig. 19-30, which is displaced from the brush axis by an angle β

determined by the relation

$$\frac{\text{Mmf of winding } BB'}{\text{Mmf of winding } AA'} = \tan \beta$$

provided that the mmf of winding CC' is equal to the square root of the sum of the squares of the mmf AA' and mmf BB'. Obviously, the direction of rotation of such a motor may be changed by giving the angle β a negative value, that is, by shifting the brushes backward from the AA' axis of Fig. 19-30. The best angle of brush shift is usually about 20 deg.

Repulsion motors have much the same commutation troubles that the a-c series motors have, and for the same reason, although near synchronous speed commutation is fairly good. These motors are usually built in small sizes. They have much the same characteristics as the a-c series motor previously described.

CHAPTER 31

ALTERNATING-CURRENT TRANSMISSION AND DISTRIBUTION

General Layout of System. The generating, transmission, and distribution network of a large system is usually made up of the elements shown in the single-line diagram of Fig. 1-31. One or more of these elements may be missing in a particular system. When the generating station is near by, for example, the distribution system proper begins at the generator bus bars. Three-phase generation and transmission are used almost exclusively in this country, because of the greater economy they afford. Secondary transmission is three-phase also, while distribution to the ultimate consumer may be three-phase or single-phase, depending upon the consumer's requirements. The ordinary residence receives single-phase power from a 240/120-volt three-wire secondary.

The voltages used in generating, transmitting, and distributing power vary somewhat from system to system and may vary from station to station within a system. Common generator voltages are 2,400, 7,200, and 13,800. Transmission voltages vary widely, depending upon the amount of power to be transmitted and upon the distance of transmission. Lines carrying moderate amounts of power, for distances up to perhaps 30 miles, operate at voltages between 24,000 and 69,000. Lines designed to carry large amounts of power—20,000 kw or more per line, let us say—operate at voltages of 110, 132, 154, 220, and 330 kv. The amount of load to be carried and the distance of transmission are the principal factors that determine the choice of voltage. Secondary transmission (transmission within cities, etc.) is carried out at voltages of 13,200, 22,000, 33,000, and up, depending upon conditions. Primary distribution voltages in common use are 2,400, 4,800, 7,200, and 13,200.

The circuits between the generator and step-down transformers of the secondary transmission (6) are all three-phase circuits. A single line is used to represent the three wires of the circuit, and a single transformer is used to represent the three transformers of a bank, in order to simplify the diagram. The circuits between C and F may be either three-phase or single-phase, depending upon the nature of the consumer's load.

555

The generating station and the high-voltage transmission line are included between A and B.   Since high voltages are required for the economical transmission of considerable amounts of power, these lines usually terminate in step-down transformers in a substation, located on the outskirts of a city, for it is not safe to bring high-voltage overhead lines into thickly populated communities.   High-voltage underground cables are sometimes used to carry these high-voltage lines into large cities, and high-voltage submarine cables are used occasionally to transmit power under water barriers.   From B to C power is transmitted either

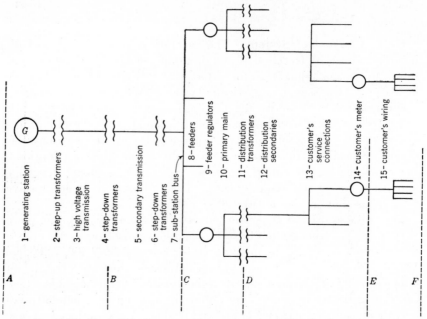

Fig. 1-31. Single-line diagram of transmission and distribution network.

overhead or in underground cables to a transformer substation (6), where the voltage is stepped down to the voltage of the primary distribution bus (7).   The voltage on each feeder (8) leaving the substation is held approximately constant by means of a feeder regulator (9).   Each feeder supplies power to primary mains (10), to which distribution transformers (11) are connected.   In residential districts with overhead distribution these transformers are supported on poles located in the streets or alleys. The secondaries of the distribution transformers supply single-phase power at 240/120 volts to three-wire distribution secondaries (12) for residence lighting, cooking, etc.   Where required, three-phase secondaries are used to supply power for motors at either 240 or 480 volts.   From the low-voltage secondaries (12) customers' connections (13) are made, and

power is supplied through the customer's meter (14) to his local wiring
(15).   A residence customer with only a small lighting load is supplied
from one of the outside wires and the neutral wire of the three-wire secondary.   Customers with range loads in addition to lighting and small
appliances divide their loads between the two sides of the three-wire
secondary.

High-voltage Transmission.   Alternating current is generated at voltages of 2,400 to 13,800 volts, as has been mentioned.   These voltages are
too low to use for economically transmitting large amounts of power over
considerable distances.   For this reason the voltage at the generator must
be stepped up to a value suitable for transmission, while at the receiver end
of the line the voltage must again be stepped down to a value suitable for
secondary transmission.   The step-up and step-down transformers are
therefore necessary in all high-voltage transmission and should be considered as a part of the line when making design calculations.

The selection of the best size of conductor and the best transmission
voltage for a given case depends upon a number of factors in the manner
briefly outlined below.

1. *Effect of Conductor Resistance.*   To simplify the argument, let the
line voltage be assumed to be fixed, and let it be required to find the most
economical conductor of a given kind of metal—say, copper—to transmit
a certain assumed load.   If a small conductor is used, its first cost is low,
but its resistance is high.   A large percentage of the generated power is
wasted in the line conductors as heat and the efficiency of transmission is
low.   If a somewhat larger conductor is selected, its cost is greater, its
resistance is less, the line loss is less, and the efficiency of transmission
is higher.   Evidently, one can go on increasing the size of conductor to
advantage just so long as the saving annually made thereby, in the money
value of the reclaimed line loss, is greater than the corresponding annual
outlay chargeable to the increased cost of conductor.   When the condition has been reached where further increasing the size of conductor shows
a loss instead of a saving, then, if the conductor be satisfactory in other
respects, the most economical conductor will have been found.   For average conditions, and for lines between 50 and 100 miles long, the resistance
of a copper conductor that gives best economy is such that at full load the
RI drop in one line conductor is roughly between 30 and 40 volts/mile.
The best value to use for a given case depends upon a number of factors
which cannot be discussed to advantage here.

2. *Minimum Conductor Size.*   There is a minimum size of conductor
that may be used with any given voltage.   Reducing the conductor size
to a smaller value (or increasing the voltage) results in producing a
sufficiently high voltage gradient at the surface of the conductor to
ionize the air about the conductor.   A glow discharge, called *corona*, then

forms about the conductor, and the insulation of the line is endangered. Roughly, the minimum conductor permissible is one the diameter of which in inch units is equal to the line voltage in kilovolts divided by 220.   In other words, a 110-kv line requires a conductor at least ½ in. in diameter, while a 220-kv line demands a conductor at least 1 in. in diameter, *regardless of how little power is to be transmitted over the line.*

3. *Effect of Raising the Voltage.*   The discussion in 1, above, assumed the line voltage to be fixed.   There is no assurance that the voltage selected, however, is the best voltage to use.   It may be possible to make further savings by increasing the voltage, for by so doing the line current is proportionally reduced and, since the line loss is proportional to the square of the current, the loss is in inverse ratio to the voltage squared. This explains why high voltages are used.   To offset the advantage of low loss, however, is the fact that the cost of transformers and high voltage switches increases approximately in proportion to the square of the voltage.   Furthermore, it has already been shown that the size of conductor, and hence its cost, also increases with increase of voltage.   A limit is soon reached, therefore, beyond which it is uneconomical further to increase the voltage.   The voltage to be selected depends more upon the load to be transmitted than perhaps upon any other single factor.   This is illustrated in Table V.   In this table it is assumed that, with each transmission voltage listed, the minimum permissible conductor diameter is used.   It is assumed further, that all conductors carry the same current per unit of cross-sectional area.   This table forcefully illustrates the advantage of using high voltages for large amounts of power.   It is not intended to indicate, however, that it is always possible, regardless of length of line, to transmit the amounts of power indicated in the last column.

TABLE V

Line voltage, kv	Cross-sectional area of conductor (aluminum steel), cir mils	Line current, amp	Load per three-phase line, kw, at unity power factor
110	211,000	106	20,200
132	266,800	133	30,400
154	336,000	168	44,800
220	715,500	358	136,000
330	1,590,000	795	454,000

4. *Effect of Distance of Transmission.*   In short and moderately long lines, a modified form of Kelvin's law is the principal factor that determines the conductor area and the voltage to be used, for such lines are

usually electrically stable at all loads likely to be encountered during normal operation. With these lines, other factors remaining unchanged, the voltage is roughly proportional to the distance. As the length of line, increases however, this factor has less influence on the choice of voltage, because for short lines the cost of terminal equipment per mile of line is a large percentage of the total cost, while for long lines this item is much less. In long lines with heavy loads considerations of stable operation have an important bearing upon line design. Such lines may have higher voltages than are found from an application of the modified Kelvin's law, owing to stability requirements. The factors affecting stability are too complex to be discussed to advantage here.

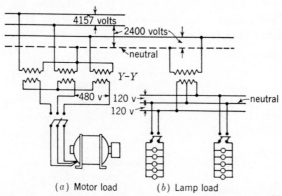

(a) Motor load   (b) Lamp load

FIG. 2-31. 4,157-volt primaries with motor and lighting loads supplied through transformers.

Distribution. A number of different types of distribution systems have been used, although here, as elsewhere, there is a tendency toward standardization. While some two-phase systems are still in use, primary distribution systems are now generally three-phase. They are somewhat cheaper, and they supply power to three-phase motors without the use of special transformers. Formerly 2,400 volts (approximately) was quite generally used as the primary distribution voltage, but some systems operated with voltages as low as 1,100. More recently systems have grown rapidly and they have been extended more and more into the thinly settled fringes surrounding the load centers and into rural communities. For these reasons many larger systems have found it desirable to change to a higher voltage, and many of them have adopted the three-phase four-wire system illustrated in Fig. 2-31. This system has now become common, for it has a number of advantages, especially where an old 2,400-volt system is to be changed over to a higher voltage. Y-connected transformers provide the neutral connection, and the neutral is usually grounded. An existing 2,400-volt three-wire system may be changed to a four-wire system by simply adding a fourth wire, and without changing the line insulation. The 2,400-volt equipment of the old system may still be used on the new one. Single-phase loads are supplied with 2,400-volt transformers connected between one line wire and neutral, while three-phase loads may be served from Y-connected 2,400-volt transformers. Motor load and lamp load may both be supplied from the same transformer if desired. The loads on the three phases are kept balanced as well as possible, so that current in the neutral wire is held to a minimum. In this way the advantage of distribution at the comparatively high voltage of 4,157 volts is secured, while the voltage between line and neutral (or between line and ground) does not exceed 2,400, just as in the old system.

Industrial plants using large amounts of power are generally supplied over three-phase circuits connected directly to the secondary transmission

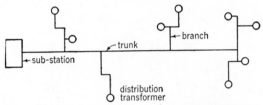

FIG. 3-31. Trunk and branch system of distribution.

system. The customer distributes power throughout his plant at whatever voltages may best suit his needs. Standard voltages for the medium-sized motors are 240, 460, 600, and 2,300 volts. Large industrial motors may operate at voltages such as 2,300, 7,200, and 13,800. Such plants often require some direct current for running adjustable-speed motors on machine tools, or series motors for operating cranes, elevators, etc. Direct current is obtained by rectifying alternating current.

Feeder Systems. A number of different arrangements of feeder circuits may be used to supply power from a substation to a distribution area. The type to be used in a given case depends largely upon the character and distribution of the load. Any one system usually employs several types. Figure 3-31 illustrates the type of system commonly used to feed a number of small scattered loads in a thinly populated section, such as one finds in a small town or in a rural district. In the more thickly populated areas, such as the built-up sections of a large city, the system shown in Fig. 4-31 is used. In this system the area to be fed from a given substation is blocked out into more or less equal parts. Each area is fed by a single feeder. This feeder runs directly to the center of the area from the substation without connecting to any loads on the way and is there connected to the *mains*. The mains are circuits operating at

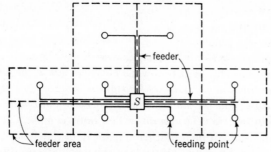

FIG. 4-31. Feeder and main system (mains not shown).

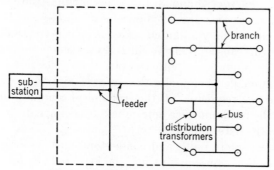

FIG. 5-31. The straight-bus system.

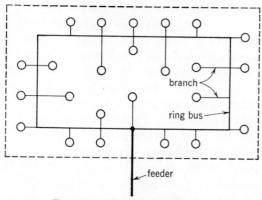

FIG. 6-31. The ring-bus system.

the potential of the feeder and distributing power over the area assigned to the feeder, from the feeding point.   Sometimes a *straight feeder bus* is carried down the middle of an area to be served, as in Fig. 5-31.   Lateral branches from the bus are used to distribute the circuits over the area to be served.   An alternate system is the *ring-bus* system shown in Fig. 6-31.

Size of Feeder Conductors.   Three factors influence the choice of conductor size for feeder circuits.   These are

1. Economy
2. Voltage drop
3. Mechanical strength

The principle of *conductor economy* is essentially the same for all types of circuits and may be stated as follows: *That conductor is the most economical for which the annual outlay chargeable to all items of investment that vary with the conductor area, plus the money value of the energy annually wasted as line loss in the conductor, is a minimum.* The most economical conductor to use for a given load can be found from a study of line losses and construction and maintenance costs. Details of the method would be out of place in this book. Factors 2 and 3 above permitting, the conductor used should be chosen as near the economical size as possible.

In a given circuit, only a limited *voltage drop* is permissible at full load. Too great a drop causes too large fluctuations of the voltage at the terminals of lamps, motors, and other appliances. Therefore, voltage drop determines the smallest conductor that may be used, for satisfactory service is always a first requisite. If the economical conductor happens to be smaller than the minimum size determined by voltage drop, then voltage drop must be the determining factor.

Lines must be safely built, and conductors must be strong enough to carry any load that (reasonably) may be expected to come upon them. The most severe conditions of loading are experienced during times of low winter temperatures when ice and sleet loads cover the wires, and high winds are blowing. These conditions are the limiting factors in the mechanical design of overhead circuits. Small wires are too frail to carry ice loads. As a general rule, in districts where heavy ice loads are encountered, it is found to be undesirable to use any wires smaller than No. 6 medium hard-drawn copper. Too large a wire or cable, on the other hand, is awkward to handle and cannot be supported on the ordinary pole line without special provisions. For this reason it is not desirable to use cables larger than No. 0000 in distribution circuits.

Transmission and Distribution Conductors. Conductors and their characteristics were briefly discussed in Chap. 17. At this point some further discussion seems to be desirable particularly with reference to the use of conductors in transmission and distribution systems.

The important characteristics of conductors useful for this service are high electrical conductivity, high tensile strength, availability, and reasonable cost. In addition, the conductor should be easily handled, spliced, and soldered, if possible. Conductor materials with these characteristics in sufficient degree to make them useful in transmission and distribution circuits are

1. Copper
2. Aluminum

3. Steel

4. Alloys of copper and aluminum

Copper. Copper is the most commonly used conductor material. It has the advantages of high conductivity and moderate strength; it is hard enough to stand handling without injury and is easily spliced and soldered. It is manufactured in three grades of hardness—hard-drawn, medium-hard-drawn, and soft-drawn. *Hard-drawn* wire is not annealed after drawing down to size. It is considerably stronger then either of the two other grades but is stiff and hard to handle and is used only for lines with relatively long spans and where high strength is especially desired. If, in the process of drawing, wire is annealed when it is partly drawn and is then subsequently drawn to the desired dimensions, it has a degree of hardness intermediate between soft-drawn wire and hard-drawn wire. It is then called *medium-hard-drawn.* Medium-hard-drawn wire is used for average conditions of transmission and distribution. *Soft-drawn* wire is annealed after the drawing process is complete and is softer than either of the two other grades. It is used for interior and underground wiring, where high strength is not important, and for service wires and tie wires. All copper conductors have a high scrap value, which is an additional advantage.

Aluminum. Aluminum conductors are available in two forms—as all-aluminum wires and cables, and as aluminum cable with a steel core. The latter are designated as A.C.S.R., meaning "aluminum cables, steel reinforced." Aluminum has a conductivity of about 62 per cent, a weight of about one-third, and a tensile strength of about two-thirds that of soft-drawn copper. The tensile strength of an aluminum conductor is therefore roughly the same as that of soft-drawn copper conductor with the same conductance. The diameter of the aluminum is larger, however, and this is a disadvantage because sleet and ice load is proportional to the square of conductor diameter. Aluminum is a soft metal and requires careful handling to prevent injury that may affect its mechanical strength. Nevertheless, aluminum is a strong competitor of copper, particularly in the form of steel-core aluminum cables. Aluminum conductors of this type are much used in transmission circuits, and for the distribution of power through thinly populated rural areas. The steel core gives the cable as a whole high tensile strength and makes it possible to use longer spans than could be used with either copper or all-aluminum cables. A saving in the cost of pole or tower line may therefore be effected. In distribution circuits where short spans prevail, copper is generally used.

Steel. The conductivity of steel is only about one-ninth that of copper, and while its cost per pound is much less it is generally uneconomical to use steel. Steel has a high tensile strength, and for this reason steel cables are occasionally (although infrequently) used in extra-long-span construction. Generally speaking, steel can scarcely be considered as a useful conductor in electrical circuits, except in combination with other metals, and in that case it is used because of its strength and does not serve as an electrical conductor.

Copper-clad Steel. Copper is used in combination with steel in copper-clad steel conductors. These are made from mild-steel billets around which copper has been cast. In the subsequent rolling and drawing process the original relative thickness of the two metals is approximately retained. Copper-clad steel conductors are made in two grades, one with 30 per cent and the other with 40 per cent of the conductivity of a hard-drawn copper wire of the same size. Wires of 40 per cent conductivity are sometimes used in distribution and telephone circuits. Those of 30 per cent conductivity are used for guys and messengers. When the copper covering is uniform, as it should be, copper-clad wires have the advantage that they may be soldered and otherwise connected like copper wires, while in addition they have high strength and are noncorrosive.

Alloys. Copper alloys in the form of brass or bronze are sometimes used where high strength is desired. To be useful as a conductor, the alloy must be such that the conductivity is not greatly reduced from that of copper. Alloys of aluminum (containing silicon, iron, copper, etc.) have found some application as conductors in Europe.

Circuit Constants. It is necessary to calculate the voltage drop in transmission and distribution circuits to make sure that the voltage at the end of the line does not go too low at heavy loads or too high at light loads. There are two components of voltage drop that always have to be considered, namely, *resistance drop*, which is in phase with the current, and inductive *reactance drop*, which is in quadrature with the current.

Resistance. The resistance R of a solid round wire is given by the equation

$$R = \frac{\rho l}{d^2} \tag{1-31}$$

where ρ = resistivity of conductor material at desired temperature, ohms circular mils/ft

l = length of wire, ft

d = diameter of wire, mils ($= 1,000 \times$ diameter in inches)

Usually it is not necessary to make the resistance calculation indicated by Eq. (1-31), for tables of resistances giving the results of such calculations are generally available.

Inductive Reactance. The inductive reactance of a circuit depends upon the frequency and is given by the equation

$$X_L = 2\pi f L \tag{2-31}$$

where f = frequency, cps

   L = inductance, henrys

In overhead electric circuits, parallel wires or cables form the outgoing and return leads.   When the wire is made of a nonmagnetic material such as copper or aluminum, as is usually the case, the inductance of 1 mile of wire depends only upon the diameter ($d = 2a$) of the wire and upon the spacing D between the wires of the circuit.   It can be shown[1] that for two

[1] Consider the two parallel round wires A and B of a single-phase 60-cycle power circuit shown in Fig. 7-31.   Let D m be the distance of separation and $d = 2a$ m be the diameter of each conductor.   The wires are assumed to be made of nonmagnetic material, and the current $+I$ is assumed to flow away from the observer in A and to return in B.   Since $D \gg a$ and the frequency is low, skin effect and proximity effect

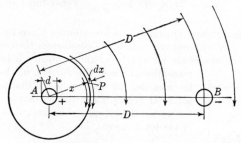

FIG. 7-31. Linkages of flux with a parallel-sided return loop.

may be disregarded.   The magnetizing force of the current in A sets up a cylindrical magnetic field about A as shown.   At any point P, x m from the center of A, the field intensity due to the current in A is $H = I/2\pi x$ amp-turns/m in a clockwise direction, and the flux density at the same point is $B = \mu_r\mu_0 I/2\pi x$, by Eq. (5-6). The flux linking A that lies between the walls of a hollow cylinder of radius x, of width dx, and 1 meter long is

$$d\phi = B \, dx = \frac{\mu_r\mu_0 I}{2\pi x} \, dx \qquad \text{webers}$$

But since $\mu_r \cong 1$ for air and $\mu_0 = 4\pi \times 10^{-7}$, this reduces to

$$d\phi = \frac{2I \times 10^{-7}}{x} \, dx \qquad \text{webers}$$

The total flux per meter passing between the walls of a hollow cylinder of outer radius $D - a$ and inner radius a is

$$\phi = 2I \times 10^{-7} \int_a^{D-a} \frac{dx}{x} \qquad (a)$$

$$= 2I \times 10^{-7} \log_\epsilon \frac{D - a}{a}$$

$$= 2I \times 10^{-7} \log_\epsilon \frac{D}{a} \qquad \text{webers} \qquad (b)$$

since, in this application, $D \gg a$ and $D - a \cong D$.

Flux lines linking all of both A and B cannot exist, for the resultant mmf within such a hypothetical line is zero.   From symmetry it is evident that the number of round nonmagnetic parallel wires suspended in air, the inductance of one wire of a single-phase circuit is

$$L = \left(741.13 \; \log_{10} \frac{D}{r}\right) 10^{-6} \quad \text{henrys/mile} \qquad (3\text{-}31)$$

In Eq. (3-31) it is necessary to express both D and r in the same units of measure, where r is the gmr of the conductor.

---

lines linking B due to the current in B is likewise given by Eq. (b). Each such line links the conductor once and therefore represents one linkage, so the total number of external linkages $N\phi_1$ per meter of one conductor is

$$N\phi_1 = 2I \times 10^{-7} \log_\epsilon \frac{D}{a} \quad \text{weber-turns} \qquad (c)$$

In addition to the external linkages of each conductor given by Eq. (c), there are partial linkages of flux with current within the conductors themselves. When outgoing and return conductors are far apart and the frequency is low, as in overhead transmission lines, the current in the conductors may be regarded as uniformly distributed over the cross-sectional area. Then the current I_x (Fig. 8-31) that lies within the cylinder of radius x m is the fraction x^2/a^2 of the total current, or

$$I_x = \frac{x^2 I}{a^2} \qquad (d)$$

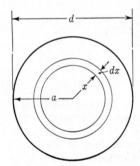

By Eq. (5-6), this current sets up a flux density within the hollow cylinder of radius x and width dx of $B_x = \mu_r\mu_0 I_x/2\pi x$ webers/sq. m. By Eq. (d) this reduces to $B_x = \mu_r\mu_0 I x/2\pi a^2$ webers/sq. m. But since, by assumption, the relative permeability of the conductor material is unity, and $\mu_0 = 4\pi \times 10^{-7}$, the expression may be further reduced to $B_x = 2 \times 10^{-7} I x/a^2$. The

FIG. 8-31. Flux linkages within a round wire.

flux embraced by the walls of a meter length of the hollow cylinder is

$$d\phi_x = B_x \; dx = \frac{2 \times 10^{-7} I}{a^2} \; x \; dx \quad \text{weber} \qquad (e)$$

This flux links only the fraction x^2/a^2 of the current I, however, and so the linkages represented by $d\phi_x$ are

$$d(N\phi_2) = \frac{2 \times 10^{-7} I}{a^4} \; x^3 \; dx \qquad (f)$$

and

$$N\phi_2 = \frac{2 \times 10^{-7} I}{a^4} \int_0^a x^3 \; dx$$

$$= \frac{10^{-7} I}{2} \quad \text{weber-turns/m} \qquad (g)$$

By taking the sum of the external and internal linkages, Eqs. (c) and (g), the total linkages per meter of one conductor is found to be

It can also be shown that when the conductors of a three-phase circuit are supported at the apices of an equilateral triangle, as in Fig. 9-31(a), the inductance per mile of one wire of the three-phase circuit is the same

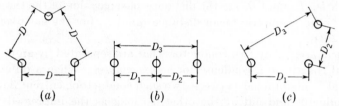

FIG. 9-31. Spacing arrangements of three-phase lines.

as the inductance per wire mile of a single-phase circuit with equal conductor separation. For any other arrangement of the conductors of a three-phase circuit [Fig. 9-31(b) and (c)], Eq. (3-31) may still be used to calculate the inductance per mile of one wire, provided

1. The conductors are transposed so that each conductor occupies each of the possible three positions for a total of one-third the length of the line.

$$N\phi = 2 \times 10^{-7}I \left(\log_\epsilon \frac{D}{a} + \frac{1}{4}\right)$$

By definition the inductance of one conductor is $L = N\phi/I$ or

$$L = 2 \times 10^{-7} \left(\log_\epsilon \frac{D}{a} + \frac{1}{4}\right) \qquad \text{henrys/m} \qquad (h)$$

Equation (h) can be simplified by introducing a new concept r called the *geometric mean radius* (gmr) of the conductor. Suppose that the conductors A and B are replaced by two similar very thin-walled, hollow, cylindrical shells, each of radius r, such that the inductance per meter of each shell is exactly equal to the inductance per meter of one of the solid wires as shown by Eq. (h). The shell has no internal linkages, so the inductance per meter of shell is

$$L = 2 \times 10^{-7} \log_\epsilon \frac{D}{r} \qquad (i)$$

This equation is identical in form to the first right-hand term of Eq. (h), which defines the component of inductance due to the external linkages of the solid wire.

From the conditions stated it follows that the above value of L and the value given by Eq. (h) are equal, so that $\log_\epsilon D/r = \log_\epsilon D/a + \frac{1}{4}$. By combining the $\log_\epsilon$ terms, writing the resulting equation in exponential form and solving, one obtains

$$r = a\epsilon^{-0.25} = 0.7788\,a$$

Thus is the gmr of a solid round wire determined in terms of the radius of the wire. Equation (i) also may be used to compute the inductance of any stranded cable, subject to the restrictions stated, for which the gmr is known. The gmrs of stranded cables of various kinds are available in handbooks for electrical engineers.

Upon converting to $\log_{10}$ and multiplying by the number of meters per mile, Eq. (i) becomes

$$L = \left(741.13 \log_{10} \frac{D}{r}\right) 10^{-6} \qquad \text{henrys/mile} \qquad (j)$$

2. The value of D in Eq. (3-31) is defined by the relation

$$D = \sqrt[3]{D_1 D_2 D_3}$$

in which D_1, D_2, and D_3 are the distances of separation of the three wires, and D is the geometric mean distance (gmd). For the flat spacing (b), $D = 1.26D_1$.

Capacitance. Any two conductors that are separated by an insulating material constitute a condenser or a *capacitance*. When a difference of potential is maintained between two such conductors, current flows in at one conductor and out at the other, so long as the impressed voltage changes. The conductors of a transmission or distribution circuit fulfill these conditions. They are supported on insulators at the poles, while elsewhere they are insulated by the air between them. When an alternating potential difference is impressed across the conductors, a leading component of current that is independent of the load exists in the circuit. This current is called the *charging current*. The amount of charging current in a circuit depends upon the capacitance of the circuit, the impressed voltage, and the frequency.

It can be shown that the capacitance per mile of one wire to neutral of a single-phase circuit with widely separated conductors is given by the equation

$$C = \frac{3.883 \times 10^{-8}}{\log_{10} D/a} \qquad \text{farads} \qquad (4\text{-}31)$$

The capacitive reactance per mile of one wire to neutral is

$$X_c = \frac{1}{2\pi f C}$$

and the corresponding charging current per mile is

$$I_c = \frac{E}{X_c} = 2\pi f C E \qquad (5\text{-}31)$$

where E = voltage to neutral.

The capacitance to neutral per mile of one wire of a three-phase circuit may be calculated from Eq. (4-31) above for all cases,[1] subject to the same restrictions with respect to transposition and the use of an equivalent value of D that apply to the calculation of inductance.

Since the charging current depends upon the impressed voltage and upon the length of line, charging current is always negligible in short distribution circuits and is usually negligible in transmission lines under 50

---

[1] This statement applies only to overhead construction in which the conductors are separated by considerable distances. When the conductors are close together as in a cable, Eq. (4-31) does not give the correct value of C.

miles in length as well.   In long high-voltage lines, however, its effect must be carefully calculated.

Single-phase Circuit Calculations.   Single-phase circuits are always relatively short and operate at relatively low voltages.   The charging current may be neglected.   The circuit therefore consists of two wires, each with a resistance and an inductive reactance, as in Fig. 10-31. The line impedance drop per wire consists of two components—one the resistance drop RI and the other the reactance drop XI. Since the wires are in series in the circuit, the total resistance drop is $2RI$ and the total reactance drop $2XI$.

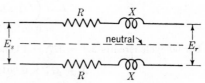

FIG. 10-31. The electric circuit of a single-phase line.

The voltage E_r at the load end is called the *receiver* voltage, while the voltage at the input end is called the *supply* voltage E_s. The numerical difference between the values of E_s and E_r is the *line drop*, and this difference expressed in percentage of the supply voltage is the *percentage line drop*.   The line drop for a given load on the line varies considerably with the power factor.   When the power factor is unity as in Fig. 11-31(a), the resistance drop largely determines the difference between the values of E_s and E_r.   When the current is lagging, however, as in Fig. 11-31(b), the impedance drop ZI may be nearly in phase with

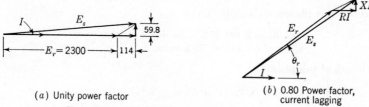

(a) Unity power factor

(b) 0.80 Power factor, current lagging

FIG. 11-31.   Single-phase circuit phasor diagrams.

E_s, in which case the reactance may influence the drop as much as the resistance.   In three-phase lines carrying large currents, the reactance is usually several times as large as the resistance and is often the principal factor influencing the drop.

The method of making single-phase calculations is illustrated in the following example.

Example 1.   A single-phase 60-cycle feeder circuit supplies a load of 175 kw over No. 4 copper wires spaced 2 ft apart.   The load is 3,000 ft from the substation, and the load or receiver voltage is 2,300.   What is (a) the supply voltage, (b) the percentage line drop, (c) the percentage line loss, when the load power factor is unity, and when the load power factor is 0.80, current lagging?

No. 4 copper wire has a diameter of 0.204 in., and a resistance per 1,000 ft of 0.25 ohm. The resistance of one feeder wire is therefore 0.75 ohm.

From Eq. (3-31) the inductance per mile of wire is found as follows:

$$a = 0.102$$

and

$$r = 0.7788a = 0.0794 \text{ in.}$$

$$L = \left(741.1 \log_{10} \frac{24}{0.0794}\right) 10^{-6}$$

$$= 0.00184 \text{ henry/mile}$$

For 60-cycle circuits $2\pi f = 377$, and hence the reactance per mile of one conductor is

$$X = 377 \times 0.00184 \text{ or } 0.693 \text{ ohm/mile}$$

and the reactance of one feeder wire (3,000 ft) is

$$X = \frac{3,000 \times 0.693}{5,280} = 0.394 \text{ ohm}$$

At unity power factor the load current is

$$I = \frac{175}{2.3} = 76.1 \text{ amp}$$

while at 0.80 power factor the current is

$$I = \frac{76.1}{0.80} = 95.1 \text{ amp}$$

1. *Unity power factor.*

$$RI = 0.75 \times 76.1 = 57 \text{ volts drop per wire}$$
$$XI = 0.394 \times 76.1 = 29.9 \text{ volts drop per wire}$$

Expressed as a phasor, the supply voltage is

$$\mathbf{E}_s = 2,300 + 2 \times 57 + j(2 \times 29.9)$$
$$= 2,414 + j59.8 \text{ volts}$$

The length of this phasor is

$$E_s = \sqrt{2,414^2 + 59.8^2} = 2,414 \text{ volts}$$

The line drop is $2,414 - 2,300$ or 114 volts, and

$$\frac{114 \times 100}{2,414} = 4.73, \text{ the percentage line drop}$$

$$\begin{aligned}
\text{Line loss} &= 2 \times 76.1^2 \times 0.75 \div 1,000 \\
&= 8.7 \text{ kw} \\
\text{Supply power} &= 175 + 8.7 \\
&= 183.7 \text{ kw} \\
\text{Percentage loss} &= \frac{8.7 \times 100}{183.7} \\
&= 4.73
\end{aligned}$$

2. 0.80 *power factor, current lagging.*

$$RI = 0.75 \times 95.1 = 71.4 \text{ volts drop per wire}$$
$$XI = 0.394 \times 95.1 = 37.5 \text{ volts drop per wire}$$

The receiver voltage is displaced from the receiver current by an angle θ, and $\cos \theta$ is 0.80 [Fig. 11-31(b)].   Before the receiver voltage can be added to the drops above computed, its horizontal and vertical components must be found.   Expressed as a phasor, the receiver voltage is

$$\begin{aligned}
\mathbf{E}_r &= 2{,}300(\cos \theta + j \sin \theta) \\
&= 2{,}300(0.80 + j0.60) \\
&= 1{,}840 + j1{,}380
\end{aligned}$$

Accordingly, the supply voltage is

$$\begin{aligned}
\mathbf{E}_s &= 1{,}840 + 2 \times 71.4 + j(1{,}380 + 2 \times 37.5) \\
& \quad 1{,}983 + j1{,}455
\end{aligned}$$

while the numerical value of the supply voltage is

$$E_s = \sqrt{1{,}983^2 + 1{,}455^2} = 2{,}460 \text{ volts}$$

The line drop is $2{,}460 - 2{,}300$ or 160 volts, or

$$\begin{aligned}
\text{Percentage drop} &= \frac{160 \times 100}{2{,}460} \\
&= 6.5 \\
\text{Line loss} \quad &= \frac{2I^2R}{1{,}000} \\
&= 13.6 \text{ kw} \\
\text{Supply power} \quad &= 175 + 13.6 \\
&= 188.6 \text{ kw} \\
\text{Percentage loss} \quad &= \frac{13.6 \times 100}{188.6} \\
&= 7.2
\end{aligned}$$

Three-phase Circuit Calculations.   Three-phase circuit calculations are no more difficult to make than single-phase calculations if the circuits are comparable as to length, voltage, power, etc.   A balanced three-phase circuit may be subdivided into three exactly similar parts, for convenience, each part consisting of one of the line wires and an imaginary neutral return, as in Fig. 12-31, and carrying one-third of the total three-phase load.   The same neutral return is assumed to

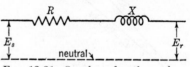

FIG. 12-31. One leg of a three-phase line.

serve for each of the three wires, and so the current in it is the phasor sum of the three line currents.   The phasor sum of the three line currents in a balanced three-phase line is zero, however, and the imaginary neutral has no current in it.   It has no impedance drop and is used only as a convenient reference for the voltages at the two ends of the line.   The resistance and the inductive reactance of each line wire are computed, just as for the single-phase circuit, and the corresponding voltage drops per wire are calculated.   These are then added in correct phase relation to the receiver voltage *from line to neutral* to find the line-to-neutral value of the supply voltage. An example will illustrate the method.

Example 2. A 35-mile 60-cycle three-phase line has three No. 0000 stranded copper cables of 0.528 in. diameter, supported in a single plane (flat spacing), with 6 ft between centers of conductors 1 and 2 and conductors 2 and 3, and 12 ft between conductors 1 and 3. The cables are transposed to balance phases. The resistance of each conductor is 0.26 ohm/mile. The receiver voltage is held constant at 50 kv, and the receiver load is 12,000 kw at 0.85 power factor, current lagging. What is (*a*) the supply voltage, (*b*) the percentage line drop, (*c*) the percentage line loss?

Consider an element of the line consisting of one conductor and an imaginary neutral, as in Fig. 12-31. From the definition of equivalent spacing, the value of D to use in calculating the line inductance for the condition of flat spacing is

$$D = 1.26 \times 6 \times 12 = 90.7 \text{ in.}$$

The diameter of a 19-strand No. 0000 copper cable is 0.528 in., the radius is 0.264 in. and the gmr is $r = 0.7577 \times 0.264 = 0.2000$ in. or 0.0167 ft. By Eq. (3-31),

$$L = \left(741.13 \log_{10} \frac{90.7}{0.20}\right) 10^{-6}$$
$$= 0.00197 \text{ henry/mile of one conductor}$$

and

$$X = 377 \times 0.00197 \times 35$$
$$= 26 \text{ ohms per conductor}$$

The resistance per conductor is

$$R = 35 \times 0.26$$
$$= 9.1 \text{ ohms per conductor}$$

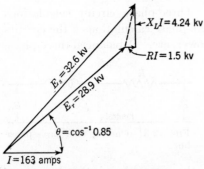

The receiver voltage to neutral is $50 \div 1.732$ or 28.9 kv, while the receiver load per conductor is $12,000 \div 3$ or 4,000 kw. The current in a line conductor is therefore

$$I = \frac{4,000}{28.9 \times 0.85} = 163 \text{ amp}$$

Expressed as a phasor (Fig. 13-31), the receiver voltage between line and neutral is

$$\mathbf{E}_r = 28.9(\cos \theta + j \sin \theta)$$
$$= 28.9(0.85 + j0.527)$$
$$= 24.6 + j15.2 \text{ kv}$$

Fig. 13-31. Phasor diagram for three-phase line of Example 2. One line to neutral.

The resistance and reactance consumed voltages per conductor are

$$RI = \frac{163 \times 9.1}{1,000} = 1.5 \text{ kv}$$
$$XI = \frac{163 \times 26}{1000} = 4.24 \text{ kv}$$

The voltage at the supply end is $\mathbf{E}_s = \mathbf{E}_r + \mathbf{ZI}$ or

$$\mathbf{E}_s = 24.6 + 1.5 + j(15.2 + 4.24)$$
$$= 26.1 + j19.4 \text{ kv}$$

The magnitude of the supply voltage per phase is

$$E_s = \sqrt{26.1^2 + 19.4^2} = 32.6 \text{ kv}$$

The line-to-line voltage at the supply end is 1.732×32.6 or 56.5 kv.

$$\text{The line drop} = 32.6 - 28.9 = 3.7 \text{ kv}$$

$$\text{The line drop} = \frac{3.7 \times 100}{32.6}$$
$$= 11.35 \text{ per cent}$$

$$\text{The loss per conductor} = \frac{163^2 \times 9.1}{1,000}$$
$$= 242 \text{ kw}$$

$$\text{The line loss} = \frac{242 \times 100}{4,000}$$
$$= 6.05 \text{ per cent}$$

In the above example the charging current was neglected. It may be of some interest to show that the results would have been approximately the same had the charging current been included.

The capacitance of one wire to neutral may be computed from Eq. (4-31) thus:

$$C = \frac{3.883 \times 10^{-8}}{\log_{10} D/a}$$
$$= \frac{3.883 \times 10^{-8}}{2.595}$$
$$= 1.5 \times 10^{-8} \text{ farad/mile}$$

The susceptance (b per mile) of one conductor is the reciprocal of the capacitive reactance per mile, or

$$b = 2\pi f C$$
$$= 377 \times 1.5 \times 10^{-8}$$
$$\doteq 5.65 \times 10^{-6} \text{ mho per mile}$$

and the total susceptance of one conductor is

$$b = 35 \times 5.65 \times 10^{-6}$$
$$= 198 \times 10^{-6} \text{ mho}$$

The charging current is the product of voltage to neutral and susceptance, or

$$I_c = bE_0$$
$$= 28,900 \times 198 \times 10^{-6}$$
$$= 5.7 \text{ amp}$$

Figure 14-31 shows how the line capacitance is connected in the circuit in short lines.[1] The circuit now consists of the resistance and the react-

---

[1] When the line capacitance is assumed to be connected to the end of the line (as here assumed for the sake of illustration), the computed values of supply current and voltage are still in error by about the same amounts as before. A much better approximation is obtained for short lines if the capacitance is assumed to be connected between line and neutral at the middle of the line.

ance of one line conductor in series, as before, but in addition the capacitance of one conductor to neutral is assumed to be connected between the

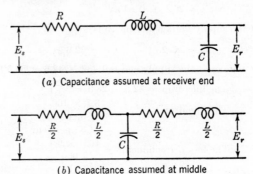

(a) Capacitance assumed at receiver end

(b) Capacitance assumed at middle

FIG. 14-31. Transmission circuit with line capacitance included.

line conductor and the imaginary neutral at the receiver end of the line, and in parallel with the load.

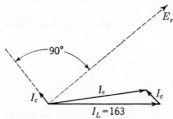

FIG. 15-31. Diagram showing phasors of receiver load current, line charging current, and supply current.

To find the current in the line now, the charging current must be added as a phasor to the load current. This addition is shown in Fig. 15-31.

A condenser takes a charging current that leads the impressed voltage by 90 deg. The voltage impressed on the condenser in this case is the receiver voltage between one line and neutral. Therefore I_c must be drawn 90 deg ahead of E_r. The phasor addition of 5.7 amp charging current and 163 amp of load current yields the current I_s in the line.

In the present instance, however, the difference between the 163 amp and the true line current is so small that the error made by neglecting the effect of the 5.7 amp of charging current is quite negligible.

Problems

1-31. Compute the 60-cycle reactance of a single-phase circuit 5 miles long composed of No. 000 copper wires spaced 50 in. apart.

2-31. The voltage at the receiver end of the circuit in Prob. 1-31 is 2,300, the current is 110 amp, and the receiver power factor is unity. The resistance of the conductor is 0.34 ohm per mile. Determine (a) the phasor impedance of the circuit, (b) the phasor impedance drop, (c) the phasor supply voltage, (d) the scalar value of the supply voltage. Use receiver voltage as reference phasor and disregard the line capacitance.

3-31. Solve for (b), (c), and (d) of Prob. 2-31 on the assumption that the receiver load power factor is (a) 0.80, current lagging, (b) 0.80, current leading. Neglect the line capacitance.

4-31. A 60-cycle 110-kv three-phase transmission line 80 miles long is built of three 212,000-circ-mil copper cables 0.528 in. in diameter. The resistance of the cable is 0.059 ohm per 1,000 ft. The cables are strung 10 ft between centers [flat spacing as in Fig. 9-31(b)] and are suitably transposed to balance phases. Calculate (a) the inductance of one conductor, (b) the capacitance of one conductor to neutral in microfarads. (c) Assume the entire capacitance of each conductor to be concentrated at the receiver end of the line between the corresponding line wire and neutral; under these conditions, when the receiver line voltage is 110 kv, what is the charging current?

5-31. The receiver line voltage of the line in Prob. 4-31 is 110 kv. Determine (a) the supply voltage, (b) the supply current, (c) the supply power input, and (d) the percentage efficiency of transmission under the following assumptions: Receiver load = 18,000 kw at 0.90 power factor, current lagging; the capacitance of each conductor to neutral is concentrated at the mid-point of the line.

6-31. A 110-kv three-phase 60-cycle line 50 miles long delivers 30,000 kw to the receiver at unity power factor. Assume the following:

1. Copper is worth 28 cents/lb.
2. The value of energy is 0.35 cents/kwh.
3. Annual interest, depreciation, and taxes on the conductor material are computed on the basis of 8.5 per cent of the cost.
4. The annual energy loss in the line copper is substantially equal to the loss resulting when the line is considered to operate at rated full load for 65 per cent of the total number of hours in a year.
5. The line capacitance can be disregarded.

Find the most economical size of copper cable for the line. Express in circular mils of the nearest standard size of cable. (See Kelvin's law, page 266.)

7-31. Determine the area in circular mils of the most economical conductor for the line in Prob. 6-31 when the line is operated at 132 instead of 110 kv. All other conditions remain as stated.

CHAPTER 32

ELECTRON TUBES AND RECTIFIERS

Methods of Producing Electronic Emission. There are four principal methods of producing electronic emission: by the action of an electric field; by bombardment; by thermal agitation, called *thermionic emission;* and by the action of light, called *photoelectric emission.*

Emission by Action of an Electric Field. It is possible to draw electrons from a material by a positive electric field maintained at its surface if the field is sufficiently strong. In general, however, such a field must be very intense—on the order of millions of volts per centimeter—before any electrons are drawn from the material.

Emission by Bombardment. When electrons strike a solid material with sufficient velocity, they are able to knock other electrons out of the material. This method of freeing electrons, called *secondary emission,* is utilized in some vacuum tubes, notably the *dynatron,* and is present in some degree in all tubes.

Thermionic Emission. Ordinarily the free electrons and atoms of a material are in random motion. At a given instant the velocities of individual electrons and atoms may vary widely, but their average velocity has a definite value, depending upon the absolute temperature. Because of their much smaller mass, electrons move with much higher velocities than do the atoms. In solids the atoms and electrons are held within the limits of the material by a potential barrier at the surface. It is this barrier that maintains the shape of the solid. In liquids there is much less surface restraint than in solids, and in gases there is no surface restraint whatever.

Since the velocities of the electrons and atoms depend upon the absolute temperature, one would expect that if a metal were heated to a high enough temperature some of the electrons would acquire sufficient velocity to break through the surface barrier and escape into the surrounding space. If the temperature were further increased, it would seem natural to suppose that the number of escaping electrons would increase rapidly until a temperature was reached at which the atoms also would acquire velocities high enough to enable them to escape, and the metal would begin to disintegrate. This is actually found to be the case. The phenomenon of "boiling electrons out of a metal," called *thermionic emission*, here described, was observed and first studied by O. W. Richardson about 1901.

In order further to clarify the mechanism of thermionic emission, assume that a tungsten filament is sealed in a glass bulb from which the air has been exhausted as completely as possible (Fig. 1-32). Evacuation is necessary to prevent oxidation of the filament and interference with the electrons as they escape. If the filament is heated to a high temperature, say 2400 K[1] some of the electrons in the filament have a sufficient component of velocity normal to the filament surface so that their kinetic energies carry them completely through the surface barrier and out into the surrounding space. When an electron escapes it gives up energy. The amount of energy given up, called the *work function*, is a characteristic of the material and is measured in volts. For example, the work function of tungsten is 4.53 volts. This function represents the potential difference through which a freely falling electron would have to drop in order

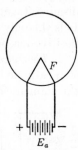

FIG. 1-32. A filament in an exhausted glass bulb.

to acquire a velocity (10^8 cm/sec for tungsten) large enough to enable it to escape through the surface barrier of the metal.

As emission continues, the space about the filament becomes filled with a cloud of electrons and acquires a negative charge known as the *space charge*. Any additional electrons that are being urged to leave the filament are repelled by the space charge. They are also attracted by the filament itself because it has a positive charge since it has lost electrons. The net result of these two forces is that some electrons that would otherwise be emitted are not able to leave the filament. Moreover, some of those that have already escaped, particularly those that are in close proximity to the filament, are forced back into it. Equilibrium is reached when the number of electrons leaving the filament in a given time is just equal to the number returning in the same interval.

The power used to heat the filament of a vacuum tube serves no useful purpose other than to make thermionic emission possible. It represents a loss which, in order to keep the efficiency high, should be kept small. The heat energy radiated by a hot body is proportional to the fourth power of the absolute temperature. Hence to keep the power expended in heating the filament as small as possible, it is desirable to use materials that give good emission at relatively low temperatures. The principal emitting materials used as cathodes in vacuum tubes are

[1] The Kelvin (K) scale of temperature is the absolute temperature in centigrade degrees.

1. Tungsten
2. Thoriated tungsten
3. Oxide coatings

1. *Tungsten Cathode.* Because tungsten has a large work function, it must be operated at a very high temperature (about 2500 K) if useful emission is to be obtained. This makes it necessary to supply a considerable amount of power to the filament for heating which, in itself, is a disadvantage, because most of the energy delivered to the filament is lost. It is the only type of cathode that is capable of withstanding the severe positive-ion bombardment present in high-voltage tubes.

2. *Thoriated-tungsten Cathode.* It has been discovered that if a tungsten cathode is covered with a thin layer of thorium—for the best results the filament should be entirely covered with a layer of thorium exactly one molecule deep—the emission for

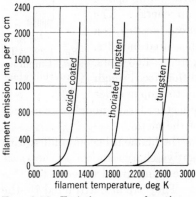

FIG. 2-32. Emission as a function of temperature for three types of cathodes.

a given temperature is increased manifold. This type of cathode permits the use of a much lower operating temperature than is possible with pure tungsten. A modern thoriated-tungsten cathode, operating at about 1900 K, produces a much larger emission than does pure tungsten operating at 2500 K (Fig. 2-32). The saving in power required to heat the cathode, due to the lower operating temperature, results in a marked improvement in efficiency over that of the pure tungsten cathode. The thoriated-tungsten cathode is used extensively for medium-voltage medium-power tubes, but is unsuitable for very-high-voltage tubes because it disintegrates under the positive-ion bombardment.

3. *Oxide-coated Cathode.* The emission efficiency can be still further improved by coating tungsten or other suitable material with certain oxides, notably those of barium, strontium, and calcium. A properly constructed oxide-coated cathode operating at 1100 K produces a much larger emission than can be obtained from a pure tungsten cathode operating at a temperature of 2500 K. This cathode uses even less energy for filament heating than the thoriated-tungsten cathode. It is this low energy consumption that makes possible the modern indirectly heated cathode with an a-c heater. This cathode utilizes a metal sleeve, coated with emitting material, surrounding but insulated from a small filament or heater. The heater is supplied with alternating current, while the

cathode sleeve is heated indirectly by conduction and radiation from the heater element. These cathodes are used in low-voltage low-power tubes —principally receiver tubes.

Two-electrode Tube or Diode. To the tube of Fig. 1-32 let a second electrode be added and let this electrode—usually in the form of a plate surrounding the filament—be connected to the negative side of the filament through a galvanometer and potentiometer, as shown in Fig. 3-32. If the potential of the second electrode or plate be made zero with respect to the negative end of the filament, the galvanometer G indicates zero[1] current. On the other hand, if the plate is made positive with respect to the filament, the galvanometer indicates a current flowing from plate to filament. In general, this

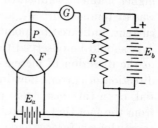

Fig. 3-32. The two-electrode vacuum tube.

current increases as the plate voltage is increased. If the plate potential is made negative with respect to the filament, however, the galvanometer indicates no current regardless of the amount of the negative potential.

When readings of plate currents are plotted against corresponding plate voltages for some constant value T_1 of filament temperature, a curve like the one indexed T_1 in Fig. 4-32 is obtained. If similar additional sets of readings be taken for other higher constant filament temperatures T_2 and T_3, corresponding curves like those indexed T_2 and T_3 may be secured. These curves resemble magnetic saturation curves. The reason for this shape should be clear from the explanation that follows.

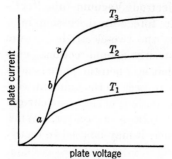

Fig. 4-32. Plate current vs. plate voltage for temperatures T_1, T_2, and T_3.

When the plate is made positive with respect to the filament, it attracts some of the electrons that are being emitted. As the plate potential is steadily increased, more and more electrons are attracted to the plate. This has the effect of neutralizing the space charge about the filament more and more completely as the plate potential rises. At some value, such as that represented by a on curve T_1, the plate potential is high enough to draw to it almost all the electrons that the filament can emit at

---

[1] Actually there is a very minute plate current at zero plate potential, due to the initial velocity of the electrons as they come from the filament. This current is so small, however, that it is not indicated by a galvanometer of appropriate size for measuring the normal emission current.

the operating temperature.   Consequently, any further increase in plate potential results in only a slight increase in plate current.   This accounts for the fact that the curve (T_1, for example) bends over rather sharply at a and for higher plate voltages becomes flat.   The condition represented by this portion of the curve is known as *temperature saturation*.   At some higher filament temperature T_2 the emission, of course, is larger than it was at temperature T_1, and saturation occurs at a larger value of plate current, indicated by point b on curve T_2.

It should be observed that *the flow of electrons is from filament to plate*, in the direction of increasing positive potential, while the conventional direction of current flow in a circuit is the direction of decreasing potential, or in this case, from plate to filament.   This paradox comes about from the fact that the positive direction of current flow was chosen arbitrarily long before we had any knowledge of electrons.   It so happens that the direction selected as positive is opposite to the direction in which electrons move when subjected to the directing force of an electric field.   If this fact is kept in mind, no trouble should be experienced in determining the direction of current flow in a circuit.

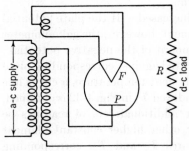

FIG. 5-32. The single-phase half-wave rectifier.

Two-electrode Vacuum-tube Rectifier. The foregoing discussion indicates that the two-electrode vacuum tube is strictly a unidirectional conductor, that is, when the plate is positive with respect to the filament, current flows in the plate circuit, while when the plate is negative no current flows.   Fundamentally, then, this type of tube is a *rectifier*.   When properly connected by means of a transformer, it may be used to rectify alternating currents.

The circuit connections for the simplest case of a single-phase half-wave rectifier are found in Fig. 5-32 while Figs. 6-32(a) and 6-32(b) show the corresponding voltage and current waves.   Current flows during one-half cycle only [Fig. 6-32(b)], that is, during the interval when the plate is positive.   The current in the load is always in one direction and consists of a series of positive loops which, because of the nonlinearity of the tube, are not quite half-sine waves.   There is one-half cycle of current for each positive half cycle of voltage.

The single-phase half-wave rectifier has a number of limitations.   Its output is hard to filter (see following topic); the inverse voltage—the voltage impressed on the tube in the nonconducting direction—is high in comparison with the direct voltage; the d-c component in the secondary winding tends to saturate the transformer core; and the utilization efficiency of the transformer and tube is poor. Much better results are obtained if both halves of the wave are rectified by using either two separate tubes or, as is done in low-voltage low-power circuits, a single tube that has two plates with a single cathode. If the rectifier (Fig. 7-32) is supplied with a sinusoidal alternating current and is operated with a pure resistance load, the voltage and current waves are like those of Fig. 6-32(c). The d-c components in the secondary windings of the transformers supplying a full-wave rectifier cancel out, and therefore there is no tendency to saturate the core.

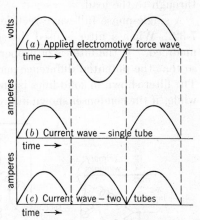

FIG. 6-32. Waves of applied voltage and rectified current.

Two-electrode high-vacuum tubes are built for a wide range of voltages and currents. They are designed to withstand as high as 200,000 volts with power outputs up to 250 kw. The ultra-high-voltage tubes are at present used principally in applications requiring relatively small amounts of direct current at high voltages, such as cable testing, smoke and dust precipitation, and X-ray equipment. The medium-voltage tubes are used in the power supply of radio transmitters, while low-voltage tubes of this type find wide application in the power-supply circuits of radio receivers.

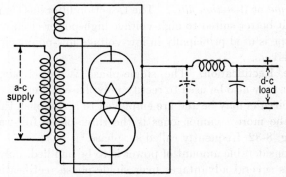

FIG. 7-32. The single-phase full-wave rectifier with filter circuit.

Filters. It can be shown by suitable analysis that the series of approximately half-sine waves [Fig. 6-32(b)] consists of a d-c component, equal to the average value of the wave, on which is superimposed a series of sine waves of successively decreasing amplitudes and increasing frequencies.

In order to obtain a smooth direct current in the output circuit it is necessary to use a *filter* in the output of the rectifier.   A filter is usually a combination of inductances and capacitances that by-passes or suppresses the a-c components in the output and allows the direct current only to pass through to the load.

A single-phase full-wave rectifier circuit with a filter is shown in Fig. 7-32.   When a filter is used the shape of the current wave is decidedly modified.   If the filter is of proper design, it smooths the output voltage so that the potential difference across the load is substantially constant. The filter shown in solid lines is known as a *choke-input* or *L-section filter*, while, if the condenser shown in broken lines is added, the filter becomes a

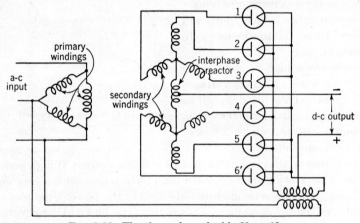

FIG. 8-32. The three-phase double-Y rectifier.

condenser-input or Π-*section filter*.   The L-section filter has characteristics that render it better suited to high-voltage high-power circuits, while the Π-section type is used principally in low-voltage low-power circuits, such as radio receivers.

Polyphase Rectification.   The single-phase two-electrode, vacuum-tube rectifier may also be used to rectify polyphase currents.   A number of different circuits may be and are employed to accomplish this purpose. Typical of the more common ones is the three-phase full-wave circuit shown in Fig. 8-32, frequently called six-phase.[1]

When a considerable amount of power is to be handled, polyphase rectification has several advantages over single-phase rectification despite the increased complications involved.   Consequently, for high-voltage high-power rectification, polyphase power is almost always used.   Its principal advantages over single-phase rectification are better utilization

---

[1] For a more detailed discussion of rectifier circuits the student is referred to any standard text on vacuum tubes or rectifiers.

of transformers and tubes, lower inverse voltage on tubes, higher ratio of the d-c output to the a-c input voltage, and much greater ease of filtering.

X-ray Tubes. The Coolidge X-ray tube is a highly evacuated two-electrode tube, similar in some respects to the Kenotron. The filament F (Fig. 9-32) is heated from a low-voltage source of either alternating or direct currents. The target T is a solid tungsten electrode about ¾ in. in diameter. A high-voltage direct potential difference (usually supplied by a high-vacuum rectifier) is impressed between the filament and the target. Electrons are liberated from the filament and are directed toward the target in a very fine stream by an electrostatic shield S in the form of a molybdenum cylinder surrounding the filament. The emitted electrons are speeded up or accelerated by the steep voltage gradients in their paths due to the high impressed voltage and strike the target at high velocities —proportional to the ½ power of the applied voltage. As a result of the

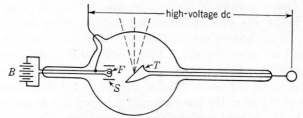

Fig. 9-32. The Coolidge X-ray tube.

impact of electrons on the target, the protons and electrons of the tungsten atoms are set in violent vibratory motion, and waves of extremely short wave lengths and great penetrating power are emitted.

Scientists are continually striving to produce X-ray tubes of higher and higher voltages and hence to secure X rays of greater and greater penetrating power. Devices such as the betatron produce X rays corresponding to potentials of up to 100,000,000 volts, which have extreme penetrating power.

X rays are extensively used in medical, dental, and surgical work, in ways more or less familiar to all; in industry for detecting flaws in iron, steel, and other solids, and in the scientific laboratory for revealing the internal structures of crystalline substances, etc.

Two-electrode Gas-filled Tubes. The two-electrode high-vacuum tube discussed in a previous section has a relatively large internal voltage drop. In the high-voltage diode the drop at full-current output may be several thousand volts. The drop is approximately proportional to the ⅔ power of the current through the tube and is due to the presence of the space charge which makes it necessary to apply a considerable voltage in order to pull the electrons over to the plate. The product of the drop in the tube and the current through it is the power loss. The power loss in the tube reduces the efficiency and heats the plate.   This makes it necessary to have a plate structure that can dissipate considerable heat and may even require that the tube be water-cooled.   Moreover, because of the large drop in the tube, which results in severe positive-ion bombardment of the cathode, it is necessary to use a tungsten filament.   Accordingly, the maximum current that the tube can pass is not more than a few amperes.

By introducing a gas into the tube, its characteristics are radically changed and are dependent upon the kind and pressure of the gas used. As the plate voltage on a two-electrode gas-filled tube is steadily increased from zero, conduction starts and follows the same laws as for the high-vacuum tube until a voltage is reached at which the electrons in passing to the plate have sufficient velocity so that when they strike a gas molecule they cause the gas to be ionized.   When this voltage is reached the conduction characteristics of the tube become similar to those of an arc, the current in the tube suddenly increases, and thereafter the voltage drop in the tube remains approximately constant at about 15 volts, irrespective of the amount of current passed.   This effect is due to the neutralization of the space charge in the tube.

When an electron is emitted from a cathode and strikes a gas molecule with sufficient velocity, the gas molecule gives up one or more electrons and a positively charged gas atom or ion remains.   The electrons thus released, like those in the cathode, are attracted toward the plate, while the positive ions are attracted toward the cathode.   The number of these ions, and therefore the number of electrons formed by the ionization process, is small as compared with the emission from the cathode.   Owing to their relatively large mass, however, the positive ions move at very low velocities and thus remain in the tube for a much longer time than do the electrons.   For this reason, if a sample of the gas within the tube could be taken, one would find that the number of positive ions and the number of electrons present per unit volume of gas would be approximately the same.   This means that the space charge of the tube has been largely neutralized and the space about the filament is almost neutral electrically. Thus, the plate is able to draw to it the complete emission of the cathode with a plate voltage of only 15 or 20 volts.

Tungar[1] or Rectigon Rectifier.   The Tungar rectifier is a gas-filled tube that is used primarily to charge storage batteries.   The cathode con-

---

[1] *Tungar* is a trade name applied to a tube manufactured by the General Electric Company.   A similar tube manufactured by the Westinghouse company is sold under the name of *Rectigon*.   There are a number of other trade names which are applied to vacuum tubes, such as *Kenotron*, *Phanotron*, etc.   These names are commonly used to designate certain types of vacuum tubes and are familiar to engineers. For this reason it seems desirable to use them in this text.

sists of a concentrated-coil tungsten filament, while the plate is a small graphite button or target mounted close to the cathode. After being thoroughly evacuated, the bulb is filled with argon gas to a pressure of about 5 cm.

The use of gas in the tube is advantageous in a number of ways. When conduction starts, the gas is ionized and the space charge is neutralized. In addition, with the gas pressure employed in this type of tube, large numbers of secondary electrons are produced, which add to the plate current. Moreover, as in a gas-filled lamp, the presence of the gas inhibits the evaporation of the filament. Accordingly, for a given filament life the filament of a Tungar or Rectigon tube may be operated at a much higher temperature than is feasible in a vacuum tube. At the high temperatures permissible in these tubes, the emission of the tungsten filament is approximately ten times as much as it would be if operated in vacuum at the maximum safe temperature. Accordingly, a large increase in emission is obtained for a very moderate increase in filament power.

The tube circuit commonly used for charging storage batteries is shown in Fig. 10-32. In the 5-amp tube, for example, the filament is supplied with approximately 14 amp at low voltage from a heavy section of the transformer winding. During the half cycle when a is positive, the electrons emitted by the filament move toward the anode, for they are attracted by the plate and repelled by the cathode. If the plate voltage is about 15 volts or more, the electrons have sufficient velocity to knock other electrons off the gas molecules when they strike them, thus leaving positively charged ions. The new electrons thus liberated are also attracted toward the plate, while the positive ions travel toward the cathode. By reason of their low velocities the positive ions remain in the space between anode and cathode for a considerable period of time and so

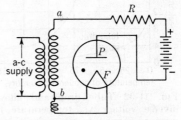

Fig. 10-32. The two-electrode gas-filled tube used to charge a storage battery.

are able to neutralize completely the space charge produced by a very much larger number of electrons emitted by the cathode. Thus one positive ion, in moving toward the cathode, can neutralize the charge of only one electron at a time, but the much higher velocity of the electrons permits each ion to neutralize the charges of several electrons, one after another, as they pass from cathode to anode.

A ballast resistance R is shown in Fig. 10-32. This is necessary because the tube drop decreases slightly with increasing current, and if the battery were connected directly to the output terminals of the tube and transformer, the current would tend to increase to excessive values. More commonly, the necessary ballast is provided by building the transformer with a high reactance.

Normally, during the negative half of the cycle, the plate repels the electrons emitted from the filament and the tube becomes nonconducting. If the negative voltage is too high, however, some of the free electrons may be urged toward the cathode with a velocity high enough to cause the gas to ionize and the tube becomes conducting in the reverse direction. For this reason the inverse voltage of the Tungar must be limited to not much more than 100 volts.

The circuit of Fig. 10-32 rectifies only half the wave. Full-wave rectification may be had by using a circuit like the one in Fig. 7-32. Owing to the ballast resistance, the regulation is poor, but this is not objectionable in a battery-charging circuit. Tungar rectifiers are built for outputs up to 300 watts. While the energy efficiency is low (not over 30 per cent), Tungar rectifiers nevertheless compare favorably with motor generator sets of like capacity for battery-charging service, particularly when first cost and operating expense are considered.

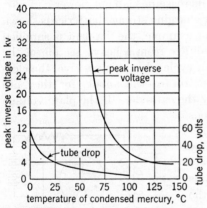

Fig. 11-32. Tube drop and allowable inverse voltage vs. temperature for a mercury-vapor tube.

Mercury-vapor Two-electrode Tube. This tube is essentially a high-vacuum diode within the bulb of which a few drops of mercury have been introduced. The vapor pressure within the tube, which is determined by the temperature of the coolest part of the bulb, is very much lower in the mercury-vapor diode than it is in the Tungar rectifier. Accordingly, while the cathode must be operated at a lower temperature than that of the Tungar tube, the permissible inverse voltage of the mercury-vapor tube is comparable with that of the high-vacuum tube. The relationship between the temperature of the condensed mercury and the flash-back voltage is given in Fig. 11-32.

The conduction phenomenon of the tube is similar to that of the Tungar, which has already been explained. When the plate reaches a positive potential of 10.4 volts, the ionization potential of mercury, ionization starts, because of the collisions between the emitted electrons and mercury molecules. By the time the plate potential has increased to 15 volts, ionization has become so intense that the space charge of the tube has been almost completely neutralized. The positive ions formed in the process of ionization are drawn toward the cathode, but compared with electrons, they are relatively heavy and move with far less velocities—for mercury, about one six-hundredth of the velocity of the electrons. As in the Tungar tube, these slow-speed ions are capable of neutralizing the space charge of a much larger number of electrons emitted from the cathode, so that the space charge of the tube may be and usually is positive instead of negative as in the high-vacuum tube. This makes it possible for the plate to draw the full emission of the cathode with a tube drop of only about 15 volts.

The positive ions formed when the mercury molecules are ionized are attracted to the cathode and strike it with considerable velocity. It has been found that, if the potential drop in the tube is less than about 22 volts,[1] the bombardment of the cathode by the positive ions is not severe enough to prevent the use of an oxide-coated cathode with a reasonably long life. The use of this type of cathode results in an improvement in tube efficiency owing to the reduction in the power required to heat the cathode.

The cathode is made in several forms. In tubes of small rated current it is frequently a flat ribbon that is coated with emitting material and wound in either spiral or zigzag form. In larger tubes the cathode is indirectly heated. In one form of cathode a spiral heater is surrounded by concentric cylinders of metal, coated on both sides with active material. In another form the heater is located at the center or hub of a wheel-like structure. Radial flat spokes connect the hub to a cylinder at the rim (Fig. 12-32). Both surfaces of the spokes and cylinder are coated with active material. The entire structure is enclosed by one or more heat-shielding cylinders that serve to prevent the heat from leaving the cathode and thus to reduce the power required for cathode heating to a minimum.

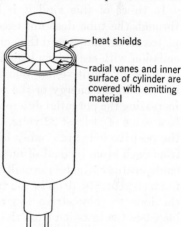

heat shields

radial vanes and inner surface of cylinder are covered with emitting material

Fig. 12-32. Heat-shielded cathode.

Small *Thyratons*[2] employ indirectly heated cathodes very similar to the one illustrated in Fig. 12-32. This type of cathode could not be used successfully in a high-vacuum tube because the space charge within the cathode structure would make it impossible for the plate to draw electrons from any except the end surfaces near the plate, even if it be assumed that

---

[1] At 22 volts mercury molecules become doubly ionized (lose two electrons), which leaves the ion with a double positive charge.

[2] Thyratron is the trade name for the three-electrode gas-filled tube.

the oxide coating could withstand the severe positive-ion bombardment to which it would be subjected. It has been previously noted that, to prevent destructive bombardment, it is necessary to keep the tube drop below 22 volts. The tube drop depends upon the vapor pressure in the tube, as shown in Fig. 11-32. The lower the vapor pressure, the higher is the potential difference between cathode and plate that is required to produce positive ions in sufficient quantity to neutralize the space charge. Consequently, the tube temperature must be kept above a certain minimum, otherwise rapid disintegration of the cathode takes place. For this reason it is necessary to preheat the tube, that is, the filament power must be supplied to the filament for some time before potential is applied to the plate. The time of preheating may vary from a few seconds, in the case of small tubes, to 30 min or more for the larger, more efficient tubes with indirectly heated cathodes.

In tubes of this kind it is important, also, that the current drawn through the tube does not exceed the emission from the cathode. The plate current can exceed the normal emission only by augmenting thermal emission with secondary emission and by raising the temperature of the cathode by positive-ion bombardment. This requires a considerable increase in the energy of the positive ions, which energy is obtained by increasing the potential difference applied between the cathode and anode to a value of at least 22 volts. With a difference of potential of 22 volts the positive ions are doubly ionized; that is, two electrons are knocked from each atom instead of one. Ions of this energy quickly destroy the oxide-coated cathodes normally used. If an attempt is made to draw still more current, the drop in the tube will exceed 22 volts and the energy of the ions as they strike the cathode will be further increased. This increases the emission from the cathode by producing secondary emission and, to a lesser extent, by raising the temperature of the cathode. The increased emission needed to supply the larger current demand persists until the cathode is so damaged that emission ceases.

From the foregoing discussion one readily concludes that the gas-filled tube must be operated within very definite limits of temperature and load. It is much less rugged than the high-vacuum tube. Overloads of short-circuit proportions may heat the plate of a high-vacuum tube to a cherry-red temperature, but loads of this character, even if of very short duration, would completely destroy the tube under discussion. The efficiency of the mercury-vapor tube is much better than that of the high-vacuum tube, however, owing partly to the much smaller tube drop (approximately 15 volts at all loads as compared with, perhaps, from 100 to several thousand) and partly to the much more efficient type of cathode, which results in a saving in filament power. In the larger sizes these tubes are competitive with the synchronous converter for changing alternating to direct current, even on low-voltage circuits.

Two-electrode mercury-vapor tubes are available in a wide range of capacities. Current outputs may be had varying from a fraction of an ampere to as much as 100 amp or more, continuous, while inverse voltage ratings presently available run up to approximately 30,000 volts. Because of the small tube drop and resulting low plate loss, nearly all tubes of this kind are air-cooled.

Mercury-arc Rectifiers. The amount of power that a mercury-vapor rectifier can handle is limited. This is particularly true in heavy-duty work, for in such applications short-time overloads frequently occur which are apt to result in damage to the cathode from positive-ion bombardment. This difficulty is largely overcome by employing a liquid-mercury cathode in rectifiers which are designed for high-power applications. This form of construction permits heavy power loads to be supplied under rugged service conditions. Rectifiers of this general class have largely supplanted rotating machinery as a-c-to-d-c conversion equipment for electrolytic processing and even for railway service. These rectifiers take many forms, but usually each rectifier is enclosed in a metal tank which may be permanently evacuated and sealed or which may be supplied with a vacuum pump that runs continuously while the rectifier is in service. A single-phase unit comprises one mercury pool or cathode and one anode per tank. For polyphase service a number of single-phase units may be used or a single cathode and tank may be fitted with multiple anodes.

When an arc is initiated between the anode and the cathode, mercury is vaporized and the arc current enters the cathode at a single spot, the temperature of which quickly rises to the very high value of about 3000 C. This spot, called the *cathode spot*, shifts from point to point about the mercury pool. A large number of electrons are emitted from the cathode spot. While some of this emission may be due to the high temperature, experiments indicate that most of it is caused by very high voltage gradients. Gradients of the order of millions of volts per centimeter are produced in a very thin sheet of positive ions close to the surface of the mercury, which causes electrons to be extracted from the cathode by electrostatic forces. In a multianode tank the electrons are attracted to the anode that is most positive and are repelled by the anodes that are negative. Since the negative space charge is completely offset by the positive ions present within the tube, the electrons move easily toward the positive anode. The anode is heated by the electrons striking it, but in normal operation its temperature is much lower than that of the cathode. The temperature of the anode is normally about 400 to 600 C. Under certain abnormal conditions the anode may become white-hot or be contaminated by deposits of mercury or dirt, thus causing the arc to strike back and become conducting in both directions.   This backfire represents a short circuit on the power supply to the rectifier in the case of full-wave or polyphase rectifier circuits.   It must be cleared at once by fast-acting circuit breakers.

The internal voltage drop in a mercury-arc rectifier varies somewhat with the current, but at normal loads it has an average value of about 20

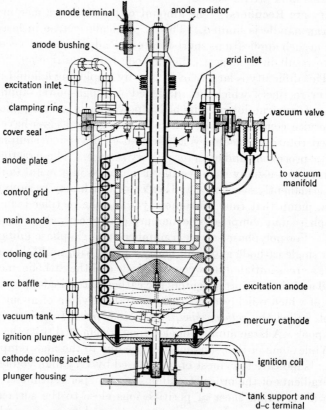

Fig. 13-32. Cross section of single-anode mercury-arc rectifier. (*Allis-Chalmers Manufacturing Company.*)

volts.   The power loss in the rectifier therefore increases almost directly with the load current instead of with the square of the load current as in the case of constant resistance devices.   Accordingly, the rectifier is very efficient at high currents.   Since the internal voltage drop is substantially the same for a high- as for a low-voltage rectifier, the efficiency of the higher voltage unit is correspondingly greater.   For all but the lowest voltages and currents the efficiency of the mercury-arc rectifier is higher than that of a corresponding rotating machine which would normally be employed for the same purpose. Rectifiers have large overload capacities for short periods of time, but they cannot be operated for long periods (1 hr or more) much in excess of their ratings. Long overloads result in overheated anodes, which in turn may bring about backfiring or short-circuiting.

Establishing the Arc. All mercury-arc rectifiers require a method of starting the arc and initially establishing the ionization required to conduct the load current. This is usually accomplished by means of an auxiliary electrode. In the case of a simple single-phase rectifier, the current exists only during positive half cycles as shown in Fig. 14-32(a), and therefore the arc is extinguished during alternate half cycles.

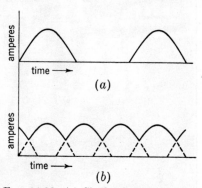

FIG. 14-32. (a) Single-phase half-wave rectification; (b) three-phase half-wave rectification.

In some rectifiers an auxiliary "keep-alive" electrode is supplied with direct current from a supplementary source to maintain ionization in the tank at all times. In one very successful form of rectifier the arc is reestablished each half cycle or as desired by an auxiliary electrode known as an *ignitor*, which is supplied with currents in pulses of proper timing and short duration. This type of rectifier is known as an *ignitron*. In a multianode tank rectifier supplied with polyphase power, the current never goes to zero, but instead the arc keeps transferring to the most positive electrode as illustrated in Fig. 14-32(b) for a simple three-phase rectifier. In this case the keep-alive arc is not strictly necessary; periods of light load may allow the arc to go out, however, and so, from a practical standpoint, some form of keep-alive mechanism is desirable.

One form of circuit connection used with an ignitron half-wave rectifier, is shown in Fig. 17-32. The circuit operates as follows: When the upper terminal, line *a*, becomes positive by approximately 26 volts, the small hot-cathode control tube *C* breaks down and passes current through the ignitor and the mercury pool. The arc is immediately transferred to the anode *A* of the ignitron. The voltage impressed on tube *C* and ignitor in series then immediately falls to about 15 volts, the normal drop of the ignitron. This potential difference is not enough to maintain the control tube *C* in a conducting condition when in series with the ignitor electrode. Hence tube *C* deionizes and the current in the circuit falls to zero. The ignitron continues to conduct current during the remainder of the half cycle, when it also deionizes. The tube is then in a position successfully

FIG. 15-32. A 1,500-kw 250-volt ignitron rectifier.   (*General Electric Company.*)

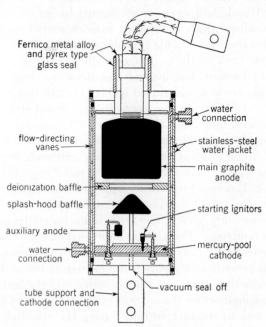

Fernico metal alloy
and pyrex type
glass seal

water
connection

flow-directing
vanes

stainless-steel
water jacket

main graphite
anode

deionization baffle

splash-hood baffle

starting ignitors

auxiliary anode

water
connection

mercury-pool
cathode

vacuum seal off

tube support and
cathode connection

FIG. 16-32. Cross-sectional view of sealed ignitron.   (*General Electric Company.*)

to withstand a high inverse voltage.   Tube C also prevents current from flowing in the ignition circuit during the inverse half cycle and thus helps to maintain the insulation of the main tube.

The current required to initiate the arc is about 10 amp, but it flows for only a very short time, so the power loss in the ignition circuit is small.

Difficulty is sometimes experienced in getting the arc to transfer from ignitor to the main anode.   A resistance placed in the circuit as indicated improves conditions by increasing the drop in the ignitor circuit, thus delaying ignition until later in the cycle when the main anode potential is higher and the transfer is more readily made.   Delaying the ignition, however, reduces the current output of the main tube. Accordingly, it is desirable to keep the value of resistance used as small as satisfactory operation will permit.

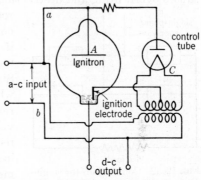

FIG. 17-32. Schematic diagram of ignitron with ignition circuit.

By using a grid-controlled rectifier or Thyratron for the control tube C, it is possible to vary the current output over very wide limits by controlling the point on the cycle at which conduction starts.   This is similar to the *phase-shift* method of controlling the output of a Thyratron, to be explained later on.

The ignitron is particularly suited to resistance-welding control.   In resistance welding a very large current—as much as several thousands of amperes—may be required for a period of time as short as one-half cycle.

Contact Rectifiers.   Under certain conditions a *barrier* layer may be set up at the junction of two substances of vastly different conductivities. This layer causes the combination to exhibit the properties of a rectifier. The mechanism by which the action occurs is a matter for discussion in more specialized texts.   Let it suffice to say that the net result is that a device of this sort offers a much higher resistance to the passage of current in one direction than in the other. Common examples of this type of rectifier are the *copper oxide rectifier* and the *selenium rectifier*.

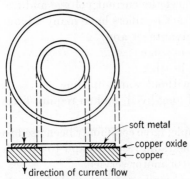

FIG. 18-32. Contact rectifier.

The copper oxide rectifier is formed as a disk or plate of copper with a layer of copper oxide on one side and a lead washer placed in contact with the copper oxide as in Fig. 18-32. The selenium rectifier is formed of an iron or aluminum disk or plate with a thin layer of selenium on one side, covered with a thin layer of solder.

The amount of current that can be passed by one of these contact rectifiers is a function of the surface area of the plates. Too large a current causes overheating and destruction of the rectifier. In applications that require large current ratings and hence correspondingly large total area of plates, it is common practice to employ the requisite number of units in parallel. Similarly, since the maximum voltage which the rectifier can withstand in the reverse direction is of the order of 25 volts, when higher voltage ratings are required several disks may be connected in series. Series-parallel connected units may also be used as needed. Contact rectifiers have been built to furnish several hundred amperes on the one extreme and to withstand several thousand volts on the other.

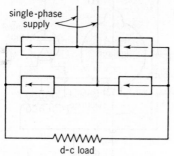

FIG. 19-32. Connections for single-phase rectification.

Just as in the case of the high-vacuum and gas-filled rectifiers, contact rectifiers may be connected in half-wave, full-wave, or polyphase circuits. A common full-wave circuit is illustrated in Fig. 19-32.

Where it is economically possible to meet the current voltage and frequency requirements of the service, contact rectifiers have many advantages over other types. Among these advantages are

1. They are compact and inexpensive in some sizes.
2. They require no power for cathode heating.
3. They are always ready for service without warm-up time.
4. They are mechanically rugged and long-lived, and so require little maintenance or supervision.

The newer selenium rectifiers, for example, have commonly been used to provide the low-power supply for portable radio receivers and to furnish the higher-power direct current for elevator-motor service.

Germanium Diodes and Transistors. Certain materials including germanium, silicon, and lead sulfide, among others, from the standpoint of their resistivities, lie within the region that separates ordinary metallic conductors from insulators. These materials are called *semiconductors*. (In ohm-centimeter units the volume resistivity of copper, for example, is 1.724×10^{-6}, that of germanium is about 60, while the resistivity of fused quartz is 5×10^{18}). Adding to pure germanium an impurity that has a larger number of valence electrons than germanium itself, called a *donor* impurity, results in greatly increasing the number of free electrons in the material and thereby in enhancing its ability to pass negative charges. Adding a small amount of an impurity that has a smaller number of valence electrons than germanium, called an *acceptor* impurity, results in the production of a large number of "holes" which allow the passage of positive charges. At the junction formed by two sections of germanium which contain donor and acceptor impurities, respectively, marked directional effects with respect to the passage of current may be observed. These effects may be employed to form rectifiers and *transistors*.

One common form of diode utilizes a small piece of germanium crystal with an exceedingly fine point contact formed between the wire electrode and the crystal. A localized discontinuity in the metal structure is produced by the pressure of the contact together with the effects of a high-temperature forming process. Other types of germanium diodes use a diffused junction between two sections of germanium with different impurities, thus obtaining a rectifying action.

It is possible, also, to build a three-element device whereby the current in one electrode may be controlled by the current in another, thereby performing an amplifying function analogous to that of a three-element high-vacuum tube or triode. Such devices are known as *transistors*. The construction and application of these devices are still changing very rapidly.

Germanium diodes and transistors have the advantages over their high-vacuum-tube counterparts in that they are mechanically rugged and require no cathode heater supply. Compared with high-vacuum tubes, they have the disadvantage that applications must be confined to the lower frequencies at the present time.

Three-electrode High-vacuum Tube or Triode. So far as its mechanical structure is concerned, the three-electrode tube is exactly similar to the two-electrode tube, except that an additional electrode is provided. This electrode, called the *grid*, usually consists of a grating of fine wire with adjacent turns quite widely separated. It is mounted near the cathode, between cathode and anode, and is so placed that the emitted electrons must pass through the grid on their way to the plate.

The arrangement of grid, cathode, and plate of such a tube is shown symbolically in Fig. 20-32. The cathode is heated by means of a heater element supplied by current from an external source, either alternating or direct current. The potential of the plate is kept positive with respect to the cathode by the B battery. If an additional battery, the C battery, be interconnected between the cathode and the grid as shown in the figure, the potential of the grid with respect to the cathode will be positive when the slider S contacts the resistor between the points O and L, negative when between points O and R, and zero when at point O. When S

is to the left of O, the grid is said to have a *positive bias*, and when S is to the right of O a *negative bias*. If S is connected to the plate, the tube operates exactly like a two-electrode tube; the emitted electrons are repelled by the cathode, attracted by the anode, and move to the plate unopposed. When the grid is given a small negative bias the grid, being negative, opposes the action of the plate by assisting the space charge in repelling the electrons coming from the cathode. The grid now acts as a barrier to the passage of electrons through it, and because of its advantageous position near the cathode, a small negative bias is sufficient to offset the influence of a much higher plate voltage and completely stop the flow of current. When the grid is given a small positive bias, the grid is positive and, being located in the midst of the space charge, serves to

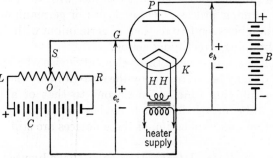

FIG. 20-32. Triode with indirectly heated cathode.

neutralize a part or all of it. The existing plate voltage therefore experiences greatly reduced opposition from the space charge and is thus enabled to maintain a much larger current than would be possible without the help of the grid.

It is then apparent that in the three-electrode tube or triode described above a change in the potential of the grid produces a change in plate current. If the grid potential is increased (made less negative), the plate current increases, while if it is made sufficiently negative, the plate current falls to zero. The point on the grid-potential curve for which the plate current is zero is called the *cutoff point*. It is thus possible completely to control the plate current of the tube simply by adjusting the impressed grid potential.

When the plate potential e_b is held constant and the grid potential e_c is varied, the plate current i_b varies in the manner indicated by the curves of Fig. 21-32. These curves are called the *static characteristic curves* of the tube. To obtain experimental data from which the curves may be drawn, adjust the voltage of battery B in the figure to some convenient value, 100 volts for example, and hold it constant. Vary the impressed potential of the grid in steps throughout a suitable range, as from $+5$ to

— 10 volts, and read corresponding values of grid voltage and plate current. The upper curve of the figure may be drawn from the readings taken. Adjust the plate voltage to a new constant value and repeat the process for another curve, etc.   When the grid is made positive, electrons are attracted to it and current flows in the grid circuit.   Provision must therefore be made to supply a small amount of power to a grid which is operated in the positive region.   When the grid is negative, electrons are

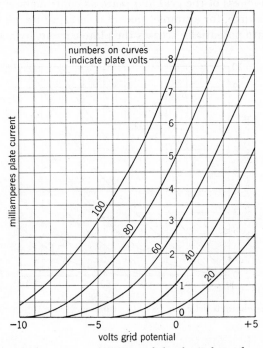

Fig. 21-32. Static characteristic curves of the three-electrode vacuum tube.

repelled, no current is passed by the grid, and no power is required from the grid-voltage source.

The triode has another useful set of static characteristic curves.   Data for these curves are obtained by holding the grid at some predetermined constant potential while a series of corresponding readings of plate current and plate voltage is taken as the plate potential is varied in steps over the normal range of the tube.   Adjust the grid potential to some new constant value and repeat.   Curves like those in Fig. 22-32 are obtained from these readings.   The two sets of curves in Figs. 21-32 and 22-32 are, of course, simply two different presentations of the relations among the same three variables: plate potential e_b, plate current i_b, and grid voltage e_c.   If the one set of curves is available the other may be plotted from it.

Vacuum-tube Constants. Three constants are of fundamental importance in the study and use of vacuum tubes: (1) *amplification factor*, (2) *plate resistance*, and (3) *mutual conductance*. While, for any given tube, values of these quantities vary somewhat depending upon the operating point, they usually do not vary greatly over the working range when the tube is used as a linear device.

1. *Amplification Factor.* The amplification factor μ is a measure of the relative effectiveness of the grid and plate as controllers of the plate current. Thus assume, for example, that in a certain tube an increase of 10 volts in the plate potential increases the plate current by a given amount,

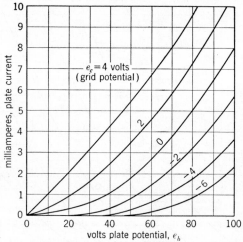

Fig. 22-32. Static characteristic curves of the three-electrode tube with grid potential e_c constant.

while a decrease of 1 volt in the grid potential is required to bring the plate current back to the original value. The grid is then ten times as effective as the plate in controlling the plate current and the amplification factor is defined in terms of infinitesimal increments as the ratio of the increase in plate voltage ∂e_b to the corresponding increase in grid voltage ∂e_c for constant plate current. Since the grid voltage decreases (increases negatively), as we have seen, the ratio is negative, and symbolically the amplification factor becomes the partial derivative

$$\mu = -\frac{\partial e_b}{\partial e_c} \tag{1-32}$$

The negative sign is used because it is customary to consider μ as a positive number.

2. *Plate Resistance.* The plate resistance r_p is the resistance of the plate circuit to the flow of alternating current. It is defined mathematically as

$$r_p = \frac{\partial e_b}{\partial i_b} \qquad (2\text{-}32)$$

That is, it is the reciprocal of the slope of the static characteristic curve of Fig. 22-32 taken with constant grid voltage. The plate resistance is generally not equal to the d-c resistance of the plate circuit.

3. *Mutual Conductance.* The mutual conductance g_m is the limiting value of the ratio of the incremental change in plate current to the corresponding incremental change in grid voltage (with plate potential constant) as the increment of grid voltage approaches zero. Mathematically it is expressed by the partial derivative

$$g_m = \frac{\partial i_b}{\partial e_c} \qquad (3\text{-}32)$$

From a comparison of Eqs. (1-32) and (2-32) one observes that the mutual conductance is equal to the ratio μ/r_p or

$$g_m = \frac{\mu}{r_p} \qquad (4\text{-}32)$$

Mutual conductances of commercial tubes range, roughly, from 500 to 25,000 micromhos or more.

Triode Amplifier. The ability of the vacuum tube to amplify electrical impulses is its most useful and most commonly used characteristic. The vacuum-tube amplifier, in short, is one of the most important electrical devices ever developed. It is used extensively in long-distance telephony, sound movies, radio, television, and a host of other less familiar and less spectacular applications. Without it these developments could probably not have been made.

The amplifying property of a vacuum tube is due to the fact that any change produced in the grid potential results in a corresponding change in the anode current. Accordingly, an input voltage with a small amount of associated power is enabled completely to control a relatively large amount of power in the output circuit. The method of operation is explained in more detail in later paragraphs.

The basic circuit connection of a triode amplifier with resistance load is illustrated in Fig. 23-32. The source of power for heating the cathode is not shown. It may be either a battery or an a-c supply connected to the tube through a transformer, depending upon the type of tube. The plate battery, also called the *B battery*, furnishes the power for the plate circuit, while the bias battery, also called the *C battery*, gives the grid an initial potential or bias. The grid bias fixes the point on the characteristic curve at which the tube operates. The grid is normally given a negative bias because, in this condition, it does not attract electrons, and hence draws no current and no power from the input circuit. Moreover, it is then possible for the input voltage and an extremely small amount of associated input power to control completely a very much larger power in the output circuit. If the potential of the grid is allowed to become positive, the grid is still able to control the space current, but some power is required from the input circuit, and some changes in the circuit design may be necessary. The output power is supplied by the plate battery; the tube serves merely as a valve to control its flow.

If the static characteristic curves of the tube in Fig. 23-32 are known, as in Fig. 22-32, the performance of the amplifier may be predicted by

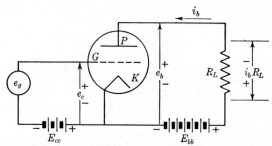

FIG. 23-32. Circuit diagram for triode with resistance load.

means of a simple graphical construction. It may be noted from the figure that the plate voltage at the tube is the source voltage minus the voltage consumed in the load resistor, or

$$e_b = E_{bb} - i_b R_L \tag{5-32}$$

Equation (5-32) is the equation of a straight line and it is convenient to draw this line directly on the static characteristic curves as in Fig. 24-32. The line may be located by recognizing that its intercepts are E_{bb} and E_{bb}/R_L on the axes of abscissas and ordinates, respectively. The line thus drawn is known as a *load line*, and operation of the tube must satisfy both this line and the characteristic curves of the tube. Apparently, for any given value of grid voltage e_c the only point that satisfies both the load line and the tube characteristic is the intersection of the load line and the tube characteristic for the particular grid voltage at hand. This intersection is known as the *operating point*. The application of the data contained in the characteristic curves together with the load line is perhaps best illustrated by a specific example, as in the following paragraph.

In the case of the tube described by Figs. 23-32 and 24-32, let the voltage E_{bb} be taken as 100 and let the load resistance R_L be 10,000 ohms.

The load line is then determined as in the preceding paragraph. If the grid voltage E_{cc} is set at -4 volts, then the operating point is the intersection of the load line and the characteristic curves of $e_c = -4$ volts. At this point the plate current I_b is read as 1.9 ma. If, in addition to the direct grid potential E_{cc} an alternating potential $e_g = 2 \sin \omega t$ be applied to the grid, the total grid voltage becomes

$$e_c = E_{cc} + e_g = -4 + 2 \sin \omega t$$

The grid voltage then varies between the limits of $e_c = -2$ volts and $e_c = -6$ volts, and by referring to the load line, it may be seen that the plate current i_b varies between the limits of 2.6 and 1.3 ma. For each

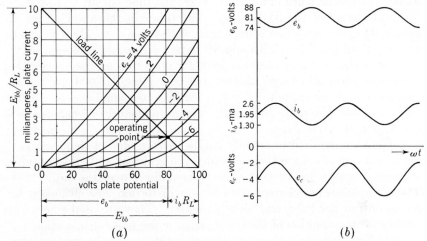

FIG. 24-32. (a) Use of load line to determine resistance-coupled amplifier characteristics; (b) instantaneous voltage and current waves.

instantaneous value of e_c there is a corresponding value of plate current i_b, as illustrated by the waves of grid voltage and plate current of Fig. 24-32(b). If the static characteristic curves were equally spaced parallel lines, the plate current would pulsate sinusoidally when a sinusoidal grid voltage was applied. In practice these curves are never exactly ideal; the plate-current wave is distorted somewhat and does not reproduce exactly the grid-voltage wave. The distortion can be minimized by operating over only a limited portion of the curves and by using as high a value for R_L as practical.

It may be seen that as the plate current i_b pulsates the voltage $i_b R_L$ pulsates also. This voltage then contains an alternating component. In the example, reference to the curves shows that the peak value of the alternating component of voltage is approximately 7 volts. This compares with a peak input grid voltage of 2 volts, and the input has therefore been amplified 3.5 times.

Classification of Amplifiers. Amplifiers may be classified on a functional basis as *voltage* and *power amplifiers*, on the basis of the frequency range covered in normal operation as *audio-frequency, video-frequency,* and *radio-frequency amplifiers,* and on the basis of the amount of the tube bias as *class A, class B,* and *class C amplifiers.*

Voltage amplifiers are used in the lower stages of a train of cascaded amplifiers. Starting with a weak signal, the signal strength is increased through successive stages until it is great enough to be put on the grid of a power tube, the output of which is supplied (in radio reception) to a loud-speaker. The last stage only is required to produce any considerable amount of power, since in all other stages the tube output is supplied to the grid circuit of the next stage. The tubes in the lower stages are adjusted to give maximum voltage gain, while the last one gives maximum power output consistent with approximately distortionless operation.

Audio-frequency amplifiers are built for operation on frequencies that fall within the audio range, roughly, between 15 and 16,000 cps, but the frequency band or range usually covered by audio amplifiers is substantially less than the range indicated. Radio frequencies include frequencies above the audio range. In the usual application radio-frequency amplifiers are required to amplify only a narrow band of frequencies.

Class A amplifiers are those in which the grid bias and grid-excitation voltages are so adjusted that plate current flows over the entire cycle. These amplifiers are characterized by low distortion, low efficiency, low power output per tube, and high plate loss. They are used where high quality of reproduction of the input signal is the first consideration.

Class B amplifiers are those in which the grid bias is adjusted to approximately cutoff so that plate current flows only during approximately one-half of the cycle of signal voltage. When a sinusoidal voltage is impressed on the grid, the plate current is a series of pulses of approximately half-sine wave form. The Class B amplifier has higher efficiency and larger output per tube than the Class A amplifier, but it is not distortionless. It is used in applications where distortion is not objectionable or in a circuit (such as the push-pull circuit) in which the most objectionable distortion components are eliminated.

The Class C amplifier is one in which the tube is biased considerably beyond the cutoff point. Consequently, the plate current flows in pulses of considerably less than one-half cycle duration. It has still higher efficiency, more distortion, and larger output per tube than the Class B amplifier. It is used primarily for amplifying signals of a single frequency when the distortion components can be eliminated by the associated circuit.

Equivalent Circuit of an Amplifier. While proof of the statement is beyond the proper scope of this text, it can be shown that, so far as the alternating components of current and voltage are concerned, applying a small voltage e_g to the grid has the same effect on the output as would be produced by impressing a voltage $-\mu e_g$† on the plate circuit of the tube.

Accordingly, the tube may be replaced by an equivalent alternator supplying power to the load (Fig. 25-32). The alternator has a generated voltage $-\mu e_g$ and an internal resistance r_p. *The parameters μ and r_p are assumed to be constant.* Usually only alternating components are of interest, but if actual currents are required, the direct component must be added to the alternating component.

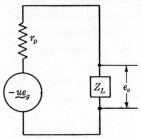

Fig. 25-32. The equivalent circuit of a vacuum-tube amplifier.

The voltage gain, power output, etc., are readily computed from the equivalent circuit. For example, assume that a signal of effective value E_g volts is impressed. The effective alternating component of plate current, expressed as a phasor quantity, is

$$\mathbf{I}_p = \frac{-\mu\mathbf{E}_g}{r_p + \mathbf{Z}_L} \qquad \text{amp} \qquad (6\text{-}32)$$

where $\mathbf{Z}_L = R_L + jX_L =$ impedance of load. The alternating voltage impressed on the load is

$$\mathbf{E}_0 = \mathbf{Z}_L\mathbf{I}_P \qquad \text{volts}$$

and the voltage amplification is the ratio of the scalar values of output to input voltage, or

$$A = \frac{E_0}{E_g} = \frac{\mu\sqrt{R_L{}^2 + X_L{}^2}}{\sqrt{(r_p + R_L)^2 + X_L{}^2}} \qquad (7\text{-}32)$$

If the impedance is a pure resistance, A becomes

$$A = \frac{\mu R_L}{r_p + R_L} \qquad (8\text{-}32)$$

and the power output to the pure resistance load is

$$P = I_p{}^2 R_L = \frac{\mu^2 E_g{}^2 R_L}{(r_p + R_L)^2} \qquad (9\text{-}32)$$

When the load impedance is not purely resistive the power is calculated by taking account of the angular displacement between the current and voltage phasors.

† The minus sign is necessary to take proper account of the relative directions of current and voltage in the grid and plate circuits.

It is apparent from Eqs. (7-32) and (8-32) that the larger the load impedance Z_L the more nearly does the voltage gain approach the amplification factor. Hence when a tube is used as a voltage amplifier the load impedance should be as large as practicable. Moreover, a large value of R_L tends to produce a straight-line dynamic characteristic and distortionless operation. Both considerations point to the desirability of using a large load resistance.

When maximum undistorted power output of a triode is desired, as in a power amplifier, the load resistance should be about twice as large as the plate resistance. Values of r_p and R_L may vary, however, from equality to $R_L = 4r_p$ and the tube will still deliver approximately 90 per cent of the maximum possible undistorted power.

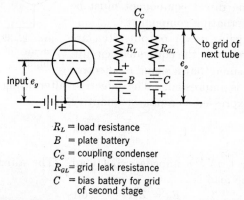

R_L = load resistance
B = plate battery
C_c = coupling condenser
R_{GL}= grid leak resistance
C = bias battery for grid of second stage

FIG. 26-32. Circuit diagram for a resistance-coupled amplifier.

Multistage Audio Amplifiers. A single tube and its associated circuit usually do not yield the required voltage gain. It then becomes necessary to operate two or more amplifiers in cascade. Multistage amplifiers are classified on the basis of the type of coupling used to connect successive stages together as (1) *resistance-coupled*, (2) *impedance-coupled*, and (3) *transformer-coupled*.

1. *Resistance-coupled Amplifier.* The circuit diagram for this type is shown in Fig. 26-32. The coupling condenser C_c should be of high quality to keep the high potential of the B battery off the grid of the following tube. The *grid-leak* resistance R_{gl} serves to conduct away any current that may leak through the condenser and provides a grid return circuit to the cathode. The amplifier performance may be computed from an analysis of the equivalent circuit.

The curve of voltage amplification vs. frequency falls off at low frequencies (Fig. 27-32) because the amplified voltage developed across the load resistance R_L is impressed on the coupling condenser C_c and the grid leak R_{gl} in series. The potential difference across the grid leak is impressed on the grid of the following tube, but as the frequency diminishes the impedance of the coupling condenser increases and a decreasing proportion of the voltage appears across the grid leak. At zero frequency the voltage gain is zero. The gain also falls off at high frequency owing to the capacitance between plate and cathode of the driving tube, that between the grid and cathode of the following tube, and that due to the

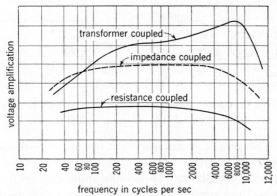

FIG. 27-32. Variation in amplification with frequency for typical resistance-, impedance-, and transformer-coupled amplifiers.

wiring. This capacitance shunts R_L and R_{gl} with an impedance that varies inversely with frequency, and approaches zero at high values. This type of amplifier is characterized by a moderate gain per stage, excellent frequency response, and low cost.

2. *Impedance-coupled Amplifier.* This type (Fig. 28-32) uses an inductive impedance or choke Z_L in place of the coupling resistance and gives

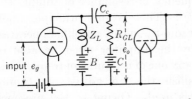

FIG. 28-32. Circuit diagram for impedance-coupled amplifier.

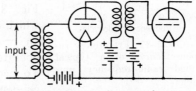

FIG. 29-32. Circuit diagram for transformer-coupled amplifier.

a response curve as indicated in Fig. 27-32. In a resistance-coupled amplifier large gain per stage demands a large value of load resistance which, in turn, necessitates high B-battery voltage (page 599). In order to limit the battery voltage to that of a standard power supply, R_L must be reduced and some gain must be sacrificed. In the impedance-coupled amplifier the choke coil makes high battery voltage unnecessary, and at the same time the gain at intermediate frequencies is improved. The high-frequency response is generally poorer owing to the capacitance of the choke-coil winding.

3. *Transformer-coupled Amplifiers.* This type (Fig. 29-32) gives a larger gain per stage than either of the other types and is capable also of handling larger amounts of power. A typical response curve is shown in

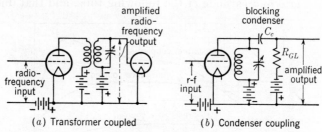

(a) Transformer coupled   (b) Condenser coupling

FIG. 30-32. Typical radio-frequency amplifier circuits.

Fig. 27-32. With proper design, excellent frequency response is obtained over a limited range in frequency.

Radio-frequency Amplifier. The simple amplifier circuits described in the foregoing sections are useless for frequencies much above the audio range (Fig. 27-32) unless very special design techniques are employed, as

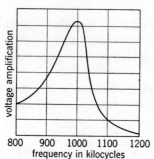

FIG. 31-32. Frequency-response curve of a typical tuned radio-frequency amplifier.

in the case of video amplifiers for television signals. This is so because the gain falls off rapidly at high frequencies as shown by the curves. If, however, a resonant parallel circuit that is tuned to the frequency to be amplified is inserted in the plate circuit (Fig. 30-32), the amplifier again becomes effective at the frequency of resonance or tuning (see Fig. 31-32).[1] This is the principle upon which the radio-frequency amplifier operates. In practice the amplifier must be able to operate at any one of a number of frequencies. To accomplish this an adjustable tuning condenser is used. Owing to the presence of the tuned circuit, the amplification is selective, that is, the circuit amplifies the frequencies at or near resonance more than others. This is desirable in radio circuits, for by this means desired signals are selected and amplified without producing a corresponding amplification in undesired signals.

---

[1] Radio-frequency amplifiers use pentode tubes almost exclusively rather than the triodes shown in Fig. 30-32. The circuits used are the same, however, except for the potentials required for the additional electrodes in the tube. See p. 620 for a note on the pentode.

Magnetic Amplifiers. The nonlinear nature of the magnetization curve of iron causes the effective inductance of an iron-core coil to vary if the degree of saturation is changed. If a d-c winding is placed on the core of an a-c reactor, the alternating quantities may be controlled to some extent by varying the direct current and hence the effective inductance of the reactor. If two such cores are arranged with the d-c windings connected in opposition, it is possible to balance out the reaction of the alternating power circuit upon the d-c control circuit. If a portion of a-c output is rectified by means of small selenium rectifiers and "fed back" into the input or control circuit, the over-all sensitivity of the device may be increased. A device employing principles such as these is known as a *magnetic amplifier*.

If the control winding is energized from an a-c source, the frequency of which is much lower than that of the a-c winding, then over one cycle of the higher frequency the control winding has essentially a constant excitation and the amplifier behaves as though it were controlled by direct current for that instant. As the high-frequency cycles progress, the effective "direct current" of the control winding changes, and hence the output follows the amplitude of the input signal. Amplifiers of this type have been built which amplify signals up through the audio-frequency range.

Magnetic amplifiers, as contrasted with electron-tube amplifiers, possess the advantage of being rugged and long-lived. They have been used in applications where they are subject to the shock of gunfire, as well as in other kinds of rugged service where conventional electron tubes might be damaged and so become inoperable. In further contrast with electron-tube amplifiers, it is noteworthy to observe that magnetic amplifiers are in the infancy of their development and that great future progress in this development may be expected.

Electronics in Instrumentation. Many sensitive devices, known as *transducers*, have been developed which convert mechanical quantities such as force, velocity, acceleration, strain, etc., into proportional electrical quantities such as voltage or current. Examples are quartz-crystal pickups to measure vibration, resistance-wire strain gages, and a vast number of other devices that have been used to solve various special measuring problems. Unfortunately, if the transducer is small enough to have negligible effect on the apparatus to which it is applied, the output is too small to actuate an indicating or recording instrument. Vacuum tubes may then be used to amplify the weak signal and in turn drive an instrument which requires a moderate amount of power.

Vacuum-tube Oscillator. A portion of the output of a vacuum-tube amplifier may be fed back into the input circuit to make the amplifier self-exciting. When operated in this way the tube becomes an *oscillator*. Amplifiers operating at radio frequencies, owing to interelectrode capacities in the tube itself or to inductive or electrostatic coupling between input and output circuits, may feed back sufficient energy from output to input circuit to cause undesired oscillations to take place. Some form of neutralization or other special device may be necessary to make the amplifier stable in its operation.

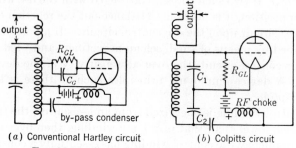

(a) Conventional Hartley circuit   (b) Colpitts circuit

FIG. 32-32. Commonly used oscillator circuits.

The two oscillator circuits most frequently used are the Hartley and Colpitts circuits (Fig. 32-32). They differ principally in that the first uses inductive coupling to feed back energy from plate to grid, while the second employs capacitive coupling.

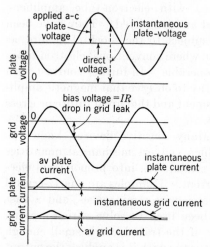

FIG. 33-32. Voltage and current relations in a typical oscillator.

The bias may be obtained either from a bias battery in the grid circuit or by the use of a grid leak and condenser as in the figure. The latter method has the advantage of making the oscillator self-starting. Moreover, the bias is more or less self-adjusting with changes in load. Because of the better efficiency obtainable by so doing, oscillators are usually operated class C, although class A or class B operation may, of course, be used.

Curves showing the current and voltage relations of the oscillator (Fig. 33-32) facilitate an understanding of the tube's operation. Once each cycle the grid becomes positive, during which time it draws current and the grid condenser becomes charged. During the remainder of the cycle the grid condenser discharges through the grid-leak resistance, thus automatically producing a bias on the grid equal to the grid-leak RI drop. If the bias is insufficient the grid potential becomes more positive and the charge on the condenser is increased, which, in turn, increases the grid-leak RI drop and, therefore, the grid bias.   In this way the grid bias is automatically maintained at its proper value.

A pulse of plate current flows for a period of time slightly longer than the interval during which the grid is positive.   While this occurs, the plate voltage passes through its minimum value; hence plate loss is low and efficiency good.   While energy is fed to the oscillating circuit in a series of pulses, it is delivered to the output circuit in approximately sinusoidal fashion, owing to the energy-storage capacity of the circuit.

The action of an oscillating circuit and tube is similar to that of the balance wheel and escapement of a watch.   The balance wheel corresponds to the oscillating circuit and the escapement permits energy from a spring to be delivered in pulses to the balance wheel, the pulses coming at just the correct time to keep the wheel running smoothly and containing enough energy to supply the losses incurred during a cycle.   Similarly,

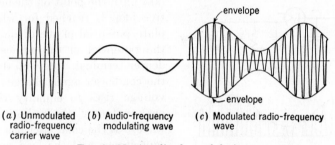

(a) Unmodulated   (b) Audio-frequency   (c) Modulated radio-frequency
radio-frequency   modulating wave   wave
carrier wave

FIG. 34-32. Amplitude modulation.

the vacuum tube is a valve which, once each cycle, operates to pass a pulse of energy from the battery into the oscillating circuit, where it is used up in overcoming the losses and supplying the useful output of the oscillator.

Oscillators, usually quartz-crystal-controlled to give frequency stability, are used as the source of carrier frequency for all radio stations. They also have a large number of other applications.

Vacuum-tube Detectors.   In wire telephony and telegraphy the number of effective circuits can be increased by using waves of frequencies just beyond the usual audible range as *carriers* of audio-frequency currents.   In radio telephony and telegraphy, electromagnetic waves of frequencies above 10,000 cps are used as audio-frequency carriers.   The process of superimposing audio-frequency currents on carrier waves is known as *modulation*.   Discussion of the technique of modulation may be found in any standard radio text.   It is sufficient to say here that, in practice, modulation is brought about by varying the amplitude of the carrier-wave oscillations in accordance with the amplitude of the impressed audio-frequency wave as illustrated in Fig. 34-32.   This is called *amplitude modulation*. Since the frequency of the carrier wave is beyond the audible range, it cannot be used to operate any sound-producing device such as a telephone receiver or radio loud-speaker. Before the intelligence carried on the wave can be made audible the wave must be *demodulated*, that is, signals like the original impressed audio signals must be restored. This is the function of the *detector*.

Generally speaking, any rectifying device may be used as a detector. A diode detector circuit, together with a graph of the rectified wave, is found in Fig. 35-32. The incoming modulated radio-frequency signal, after amplification, if necessary, is passed into the detector. On the positive half cycle the tube conducts current and the condenser C charges until a potential difference equal to the crest value of the positive loop is reached, after which current flow into the condenser ceases. The condenser discharges through the load resistance R, however, so its voltage

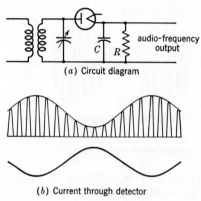

(a) Circuit diagram

(b) Current through detector

Fig. 35-32. The diode detector.

falls until the point on the next positive loop is reached for which the plate potential of the diode exceeds the potential of the adjacent condenser terminal. Beyond this point the condenser again charges and its voltage rises to equality with the peak value of the radio-frequency wave. If the condenser has suitable capacitance and the load resistance is properly selected, the condenser does not have time to discharge appreciably during the time of one cycle of the carrier wave, and its potential follows the potential of the crests of successive half cycles of the radio-frequency wave. Hence the potential of the condenser varies in accordance with the envelope of the modulated wave, which is the original audio-frequency wave (speech or music) that was used to modulate the carrier wave, and the original sounds may be recovered.

In addition to the diode other types of detectors are used, such as the *grid-leak* and *grid-bias* types. The diode detector is used in high-quality radio reception, but it has the disadvantage of producing no amplification. The other types mentioned amplify as well as rectify. They are discussed in more detail in standard radio texts.

Three-electrode Gas-filled Tube. The three-electrode gas-filled tube, commonly known as a Thyratron, is similar to the two-electrode gas-filled tube already described except for the addition of a grid. It has the same type of cathode and is subject to the same limitations of operating temperature, inverse voltage, tube drop, etc. In the high-vacuum three-electrode tube the grid exercises complete control over the plate current at all times. When the potential of the grid is changed, the plate current changes correspondingly. By introducing into the tube a gas, such as mercury vapor, for example, the control of the grid over the space current is changed to a marked degree. The grid no longer exercises complete control over the plate current but is able only to determine the time of starting. The grid exercises no control after the current is started.

Let a Thyratron be connected as in Fig. 36-32. When the grid potential is made sufficiently negative, no current flows to the plate, but if the grid is gradually made less negative, a grid potential, called the *starting voltage*, is soon reached for which the tube suddenly becomes conducting. After the tube is started the grid potential may be made either positive or negative without appreciably affecting the plate current, indicating that the grid no longer controls the amount of conduction. A rather large current, either positive or negative, may be drawn from the grid, how-

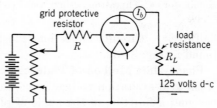

Fig. 36-32. Control circuit for a Thyratron.

ever, depending upon the grid potential. Unless it is protected by a resistance R, the grid may be damaged. If the grid is made more negative than the starting voltage, and the plate circuit is momentarily interrupted, it is found that the grid has regained control. The behavior of the tube here outlined is explained in the following paragraph.

At the beginning of the action described the grid potential is sufficiently negative so that very few of the electrons emitted by the cathode can reach the plate. As the grid potential becomes less negative and the starting voltage is reached, the number and velocity of the electrons passing to the plate are great enough to ionize the gas, thus neutralizing the space charge. After conduction starts the negative grid merely attracts positive ions from the gas. These form a so-called *sheath* around the grid, which its field is unable to penetrate. Hence the grid loses control, for it exerts no influence over the current in the tube. When the plate circuit is interrupted, conduction stops and the gas deionizes. If, when conduction stops, the grid potential is more negative than the starting or critical voltage, the tube remains nonconducting even if the plate voltage is reestablished.

The starting voltage is a function of the plate voltage. The higher the plate voltage, the more negative the starting voltage becomes. The starting voltage is also affected by the gas pressure and hence by the tube temperature, but it may be either negative or positive, depending upon the tube construction.

It may be seen from what has been said that, if direct potential is applied to the plate, means must be provided for momentarily interrupt-

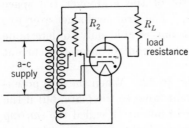

ing plate current so the grid may regain control. Usually this is inconvenient. When simple on-and-off control is required, as in relay operation, it is usually more satisfactory to use alternating potential difference on the plate and usually on the grid also. Since with alternating voltage the plate voltage passes through zero twice each cycle, the grid regains control at the end of each conducting

FIG. 37-32. Relay type of control circuit for a Thyratron using a-c supply.

half cycle. Circuit connections illustrating this type of application are found in Fig. 37-32.

Phase-shift Method of Plate-current Control. By shifting the phase of the grid-excitation voltage wave, the average value of the plate current becomes a function of the angle of phase shift (Fig. 38-32). Curves g_1, g_2, and g_3 are three assumed grid-excitation curves; e_p is the impressed plate voltage; and the broken-line curve is the curve of starting potential,

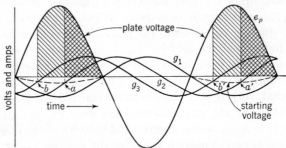

FIG. 38-32. Curve illustrating control of Thyratron plate current by the method of phase shifting.

assuming a tube with negative control. When the grid-excitation curve is g_1 (larger than the starting voltage and 180 deg out of phase with the plate voltage) no plate current flows during any portion of the cycle. This follows because, whenever the plate is positive, the grid is more negative than the critical voltage and conduction cannot start. When the phase of the grid excitation is advanced to g_2, however, the grid becomes more positive than the critical starting voltage at point a, hence conduction starts at this point, continues to the end of the half cycle, and then stops. Conduction begins again at a' on the following half cycle and continues until the plate voltage falls to zero. This cycle of events is repeated indefinitely.

The average plate current for grid excitation g_2 is proportional to the double-crosshatched area under the plate-voltage curve. When the grid excitation is shifted still farther forward to g_3, conduction starts at b and b' and the average output current becomes proportional to the area included under the plate-voltage curve between b and b' and the end of the corresponding half cycle. Thus the current output of the tube can be controlled by simply shifting the phase of the grid voltage.

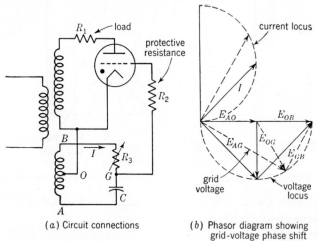

(a) Circuit connections

(b) Phasor diagram showing grid-voltage phase shift

Fig. 39-32. Circuit and phasor diagrams illustrating method of controlling Thyratron current by shifting the phase of the grid voltage.

The circuit of Fig. 39-32 may be used for phase-shift control. If the circuit is accidentally so connected that either the grid voltage or the plate voltage is reversed, no grid control is possible. The current comes up to full value and remains there. The connection is corrected by reversing the terminals of either the grid or the plate transformer coils.

The phase-shift method may also be applied to ignitron tubes to control the point on the cycle at which ignition takes place. A small auxiliary grid-controlled Thyratron is used in the ignition circuit for this purpose, and the time of ignition is controlled by shifting the phase of the grid excitation of the auxiliary tube. Electric welders employing ignitrons use this method of control.

Thyratrons and ignitrons are now being used in applications such as dimmers for theater lighting, for converting direct to alternating currents (inverters), for generator-voltage regulators, and in a great variety of relay applications. A great deal of experimental work employing vacuum tubes has been carried out in d-c power transmission. Power is generated as alternating current, rectified by vacuum tubes, transmitted as direct current, reconverted to alternating current at the receiver end of the line, and then distributed as alternating current in the usual way.   The commercial importance of this development is a matter of the future.

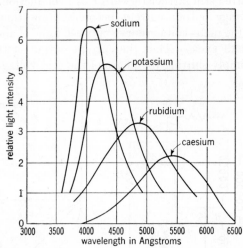

Fig. 40-32. Color sensitivity of several photoelectric materials.

Photoelectric Cells.   Photoelectric cells are classified as

1. Photoemissive cells
2. Photoconductive cells
3. Photovoltaic cells

Each of these has individual characteristics that render it most suitable for particular applications.

1. *Photoemissive Cells.*   Certain materials, notably the alkali metals and their oxides, have the power to emit electrons when light[1] shines upon

TABLE VI

Material	Work function, volts
Lithium	2.36
Sodium	1.82
Potassium	1.55
Rubidium	1.45
Cesium	1.36

them.   Experiment shows that the number of electrons emitted per unit of time is proportional to the intensity of the incident light, while the maximum velocity of the electrons depends upon the frequency or color

[1] Light, as here used, includes ultraviolet and infrared radiations as well as the visible spectrum.

of the light used. The limiting frequency below which the material does not emit electrons is called the *threshold frequency*.

The work functions of different materials are not alike, and therefore their threshold frequencies are different also (Table VI). Thus one would expect cesium, for example, to emit electrons at a much lower frequency than lithium or sodium, and such, in fact, is the case (Fig. 40-32). Sodium and potassium emit electrons only under the influence of ultra-violet light, while cesium has its maximum sensitivity at a much lower frequency. Certain composite layers like cesium oxide, for example, have threshold frequencies that are still lower than those of the corresponding pure metals. The emission does not depend upon the excess of the frequency of the incident light over the threshold frequency, as one might suppose. For each material there is a frequency at which the maximum emission occurs, and emission falls off at frequencies both above and below this value.

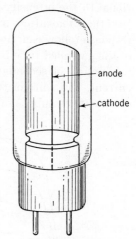

FIG. 41-32. Sketch of a photoelectric cell.

The usual commercial photoelectric tube (Fig. 41-32) has a cathode consisting of a semicircular plate coated with active material, and an anode, usually in the form of a straight wire rod or a metallic ring, both suitably mounted inside a highly evacuated bulb. It is important that anode and cathode be very well insulated from each other because even a very minute leakage current partly masks the small current produced by the cell.

The circuit connections of a photoelectric cell and amplifier are illustrated in Fig. 42-32. A battery connected in series with a load resistance

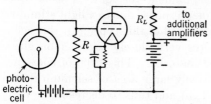

FIG. 42-32. Typical photoelectric cell with associated amplifier.

R furnishes potential to the anode. When light shines on the cathode, electrons are emitted and current flows in the circuit. The drop produced by the tube current flowing in the resistance is the useful output of the cell. If the plate potential is high enough so that the anode is able to draw over all the electrons emitted, the tube is said to be saturated. The plate current is then proportional to the intensity of incident light [Fig. 43-32(b)]. This is the way these tubes are normally operated when used for sound movies, television, etc., where good response to light intensity is desired. The electronic emission of a high-vacuum photoelectric cell seems to respond instantly to variations in light intensity.   Certain it is that the response is proportional to such variations of intensity up to millions of cycles per second.

By introducing an inert gas into the bulb of a high-vacuum photoelectric cell the response may be increased, but it is then no longer proportional to the intensity of the incident light except for anode voltages so low that ionization of the gas cannot take place.   Neither does the response follow exactly rapid variations in intensity.   The larger current of the gas-filled tube is due to ionization by collision and the consequent production of secondary electrons and positive ions, which add to the current.   In spite of the nonlinearity introduced by the gas, the output of a gas-filled tube is several times larger than that of a high-vacuum tube

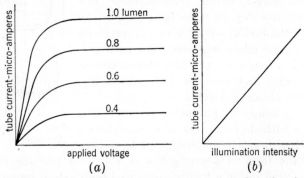

FIG. 43-32.   Characteristic curves of a high-vacuum photoelectric cell.

and a slight distortion is tolerated in many instances, in the interest of high output.

2. *Photoconductive Cells.*   A number of materials such as selenium, rock salt, cinnabar, and some others have the peculiar property of changing their electrical resistance under the influence of light.   *Photoconductive cells* employ this principle to obtain a response due to a light stimulus.

The selenium cell is the most common cell of this type.   In this cell a grid is made by winding two fine wires very closely together on glass, porcelain, or other suitable insulating material.   This type of construction makes it possible to have a relatively large area of selenium in the form of a very thin sheet exposed to light and thus to decrease the light resistance of the tube.   The selenium is painted or distilled on the wire grid and is later heat-treated to form crystalline selenium, the only form of this metal which possesses photoconductive properties.   The assembly is then mounted in a tube filled with inert gas.

Selenium is a poor electrical conductor.   The resistance of the grid construction described is about 1 megohm when illuminated with a light intensity of 100 ft-c, while the resistance when dark runs up to approximately 6 megohms. The current obtained from the tube with normal impressed potential difference is, therefore, very small indeed. Neither is the current output exactly proportional to the intensity of illumination. Because the selenium cell has its maximum color response in the red end of the spectrum, it may be used in burglar alarms employing invisible infrared radiation.

Other types of photoconductive cells are available, but owing to space limitations, they cannot be described here. Descriptions may be found in standard texts on vacuum tubes.

3. *Photovoltaic Cells.* This type of cell converts light energy into electrical energy directly. In one form of cell a cathode of copper, covered with cuprous oxide, and an anode of lead are immersed in an electrolyte of lead nitrate. The cell is provided with a glass window through which light is admitted. When light shines on the cuprous oxide surface a small emf is set up between the electrodes. If the resistance of the external circuit is zero, the current output is substantially directly proportional to the applied light-intensity. With an applied intensity of 80 ft-c, a current output of approximately 100 μa is produced.

The *Photox* light cell employs a copper disk, which is oxidized on one side, as one electrode, and a thin translucent metallic film covering the oxide, as the other. No electrolyte is necessary, so the cell is dry. Light, admitted through a window, passes through the translucent film and onto the barrier layer separating the copper oxide and mother copper. This layer seems to be the seat of the photovoltaic action. The cell has characteristics similar to those of the lead nitrate cell except that it is more sensitive and its color response more closely approximates that of the human eye.

A third type of cell (*Photronic*) is very similar in construction and appearance to the copper oxide cell, but uses iron and iron selenide in place of copper and copper oxide, and has very similar characteristics.

The dynamic response of photovoltaic cells is very poor. Roughly, it varies inversely with the frequency. At a frequency of only 2,000 cps the response has fallen off seriously. Moreover, it is difficult to amplify the output of this type of cell. For these reasons they are not suitable for use in sound movies. They are used principally as light meters (for measuring illumination intensities) and with low-resistance relays for control purposes. They have the advantage that no external power, other than light, is required to operate them.

Cathode-ray Tubes. When it is desired to make measurements of electrical quantities in a circuit under steady-state conditions, voltmeters, ammeters, wattmeters, etc., are used. These instruments are useless, however, for studying rapidly changing, transient phenomena. If the rate of change is not too rapid, a moving-coil oscillograph may be used, but for frequencies much above 5,000 cps, the inertia of the moving element is sufficient to prevent the coil from following the driving force, so the instrument fails to respond. For studying very-high-frequency phenomena, therefore, an instrument with a still lighter moving element is required. Such an instrument, called the *cathode-ray tube*, using a beam of electrons as the moving element, has been developed (Fig. 44-32). It responds accurately to frequencies of millions of cycles per second. The cathode-ray tube, together with amplifiers, sweep circuit, etc., is manufactured under the name of *Oscilloscope*.

The beam-producing (electron-gun) section of the tube consists of an indirectly heated cathode, a grid that controls the intensity of the beam, a first anode that draws the electrons into the beam, and a second anode that accelerates the electrons and focuses them on a fluorescent screen.

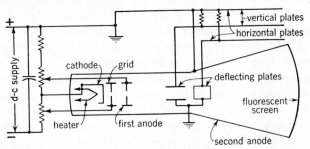

FIG. 44-32. Cathode-ray tube and associated circuit.

The electron beam may be deflected electrically by an electric field produced between two plates, as in the figure, or electromagnetically by means of a magnetic field produced by a pair of coils. The first method is sometimes the more advantageous, because it takes very little power from the circuit under investigation to produce the desired deflection. Two pairs of parallel deflecting plates are used. They are arranged in planes at right angles to each other, one producing horizontal and the other vertical deflection. Usually one plate of each pair is connected to a common junction point that is grounded. The remaining terminal of the horizontally deflecting pair is connected to the sweep circuit, while the other terminal of the vertically deflecting pair is connected to the circuit under investigation.

The *sweep circuit* consists of a condenser that is charged through a current-limiting device (a saturated triode or a pentode), which is connected in parallel with a small Thyratron or similar tube. When current is supplied to the condenser at a constant rate, the condenser voltage builds up at a constant rate also, as indicated by the sloping lines of Fig. 45-32. At some definite value of voltage determined by the grid potential, the Thyratron breaks down and the voltage across the condenser terminals falls to a considerably lower value very quickly (along the almost vertical line of the figure). When the condenser voltage is impressed on the horizontally deflecting plates of the Oscilloscope, the electric field of the plates causes the electron beam to move across the screen at a uniform rate—corresponding to the sloping lines—with a speed determined by the capacitance of the condenser and the amount of current fed to it. When the Thyratron breaks down, the spot is brought back to the starting point so rapidly that the trace of the beam on the screen during the return period is not visible. The sweep action is synchronized with the phenomenon under observation, hence the electron beam moving horizontally across the screen provides a linear time axis for the instrument.

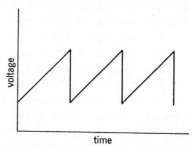

FIG. 45-32. Saw-tooth wave of sweep circuit for cathode-ray oscilloscope.

It is the function of the vertically deflecting pair of plates to produce a deflection of the electron beam at right angles to the time axis, the amount of the deflection being proportional to either the voltage or the current of the circuit that is being studied, as the case may be. The combined action of the two sets of plates, therefore, is to produce on the fluorescent screen the trace of a curve of voltage or current vs. time of the phenomenon under consideration.

Oscillographs of this kind are used extensively in work of a research or investigational nature. If the observed phenomenon is repetitive, the curve produced on the screen can usually be photographed; if not, the trace of the beam on the screen may be so dim that photographing is impossible unless a special type of fluorescent screen with long persistence is used.

Cathode-ray tubes are commonly used in television receivers to form the received image. Cathode-ray tubes that are used for this purpose are usually of the magnetic-deflection type. Controlled sweep circuits move the spot over the entire surface of the tube in horizontal lines. As the spot is moved over the surface of the tube, the intensity of the beam is varied by a control grid in the electron gun. The intensity of the beam is so coordinated with the sweep circuits that an image is formed on the screen. The entire process is repeated many times per second, and the combination of persistence of the image on the screen plus the persistence of vision of the human eye creates a continuous moving picture for the observer.

Screen-grid Tube.   Because of the interelectrode capacitance of the triode when it is used in an amplifier, there is sometimes sufficient feedback of energy from output to input of the tube to cause sustained oscillations.   The *screen-grid tube* or *tetrode* was developed to prevent this. In this tube a second grid is placed between the control grid and the plate. The screen grid is operated at a positive direct potential but is connected to the cathode through a condenser and hence is at cathode potential, dynamically.   Accordingly, the control grid is effectively shielded from the plate, so variations in plate potential do not appreciably affect the grid potential, and feedback is avoided, even at radio frequencies.   The amplification factor of the screen-grid tube is quite high (300 to 1,500), but the plate resistance is correspondingly large, so the mutual conductance of the tube is, after all, comparable with that of the triode.

Other Multiple-element Tubes.   The *pentode* is a screen-grid tube to which a third grid, called a suppressor, has been added.   It represents a considerable improvement over the screen-grid tube, which it has largely replaced in the radio-frequency stages of radio receivers.   It is also used in the audio stage, particularly as a power tube, in which application the large power output per tube is a distinct advantage.

The *beam tube* is a screen-grid tube which has the characteristics of a pentode but does not use a suppressor grid.   Secondary emission is prevented from reaching the screen grid by forming the electrons into beams, thereby producing a region in which the density of electrons is sufficient to provide a retarding potential for any electrons that attempt to leave the plate.   These beams are formed by proper design of the tube and by insertion of beam-forming electrodes at either side of the plate.

APPENDIX A

Metal or alloy	Resistivity	
	Microhm-cm	Ohms/cir mil-ft
Advance (copper nickel)..........................	48.8	294
Aluminum (at 20 C).............................	2.83	17.0
Climax (nickel steel).............................	87.2	525
Constantan (copper nickel).......................	50	300
Copper at (20 C)................................	1.72	10.37
German silver [copper, nickel (18 per cent), Zn]......	48.2	290
Iron:		
Cast.......................................	74–98	446–590
Electrolytic..................................	9.96	60
Telephone wire...............................	11.3	68.1
Lead...	18.4–19.6	111–118
Mercury..	95.8	576
Nickel..	10.7–12.4	64.5–74.8
Nichrome (nickel chromium)......................	99.6	600
Phosphor bronze.................................	33.95	23.7
Platinum..	9–15.5	54.3–93.4
Silver..	1.5–1.7	9.0–10.3
Steel:		
Cast.......................................	19.1	115
Silicon steel................................	51.15	308
Transformer sheets...........................	11.09	66.9
Tin..	9.5–11.4	57.3–68.7
Tungsten.......................................	5.6	33.7
Zinc...	5.5–6.0	33.2–36.2

APPENDIX B

(Solid conductors)

A.w.g. (B. & S.) number	Diameter, mils	Area, cir mils	Area, sq mils	Resistance, ohms per 1,000 ft (25 C)		Weight, lb per 1,000 ft	
	d	d^2	$0.7854d^2$	Copper	Aluminum	Copper	Aluminum
0,000	460.0	211,600	166,200	0.0500	0.0820	641.0	195.0
000	409.6	167,800	131,800	0.0630	0.103	508.0	154.0
00	364.8	133,080	104,500	0.0795	0.131	403.0	122.0
0	324.9	105,530	82,890	0.100	0.164	320.0	97.1
1	289.3	83,690	65,730	0.126	0.207	253.0	77.0
2	257.6	66,370	52,130	0.159	0.261	201.0	61.1
3	229.4	52,630	41,340	0.201	0.330	159.0	48.4
4	204.3	41,740	32,780	0.253	0.506	126.0	38.4
5	181.9	33,100	26,000	0.320	0.524	100.0	30.4
6	162.0	26,250	20,620	0.403	0.661	79.5	24.2
7	144.3	20,820	16,350	0.508	0.833	63.0	19.2
8	128.5	16,510	12,970	0.641	1.05	50.0	15.2
9	114.4	13,100	10,280	0.808	1.33	39.6	12.1
10	101.9	10,380	8,153	1.02	1.67	31.4	9.55
11	90.74	8,234	6,467	1.28	2.11	24.9	7.57
12	80.81	6,530	5,129	1.62	2.66	19.8	6.00
13	71.96	5,178	4,067	2.04	3.36	15.7	4.76
14	64.08	4,107	3,147	2.58	4.22	12.4	3.78
15	57.07	3,257	2,558	3.25	5.33	9.86	2.99
16	50.82	2,583	2,029	4.09	6.72	7.82	2.38
17	45.26	2,048	1,609	5.16	8.48	6.20	1.88
18	40.30	1,624	1,276	6.51	10.7	4.92	1.495
19	35.89	1,288	1,012	8.21	13.5	3.90	1.185
20	31.96	1,021	802.3	10.4	17.0	3.09	0.940
21	28.46	810.1	636.3	13.1	21.4	2.45	0.745
22	25.35	642.7	504.8	16.5	27.0	1.94	0.590
23	22.57	509.5	400.1	20.8	34.1	1.54	0.469
24	20.10	404.0	317.3	26.2	42.9	1.22	0.372
25	17.90	320.4	251.6	33.0	54.2	0.970	0.294
26	15.94	254.0	199.5	41.6	68.4	0.769	0.234
27	14.20	201.5	158.3	52.5	86.1	0.610	0.185
28	12.64	159.8	125.5	66.2	108.1	0.484	0.147
29	11.26	126.7	99.53	83.4	136.7	0.384	0.117
30	10.03	100.5	78.93	105.0	172.0	0.304	0.0924
31	8.93	79.71	62.60	133.0	217.0	0.241	0.0733
32	7.95	63.20	49.64	167.0	274.0	0.191	0.0582
33	7.08	50.13	39.37	211.0	346.0	0.152	0.0461
34	6.30	39.74	31.21	266.0	437.0	0.120	0.0365
35	5.61	31.52	24.76	335.0	551.0	0.0954	0.0290
36	5.00	25.00	19.64	423.0	694.0	0.0757	0.0230

α_{25} for copper = 0.00385 per degree centigrade. ρ_{cu} = 10.6 at 25 C.
α_{25} for aluminum = 0.00396 per degree centigrade. ρ_{al} = 17.3 at 25 C.
Note.   The resistance of hard-drawn copper may be found approximately by multiplying the values in the table by 1.027.

APPENDIX C

(Standard annealed copper)

Circular mils	A.w.g. num- ber	Resistance, ohms per 1,000 ft.		Weight, lb per 1,000 ft	Standard concentric stranding		
		25 C. (77 F.)	65 C. (149 F.)		Number of wires	Diameter of wire, mils	Outside diameter, mils
2,000,000	....	0.00539	0.00622	6,180	127	125.5	1,631
1,800,000	....	0.00599	0.00692	5,560	127	119.1	1,548
1,600,000	....	0.00674	0.00778	4,940	127	112.2	1,459
1,400,000	....	0.00770	0.00889	4,320	91	124.0	1,364
1,200,000	....	0.00899	0.0104	3,710	91	114.8	1,263
1,000,000	....	0.0108	0.0124	3,090	61	128.0	1,152
900,000	....	0.0120	0.0138	2,780	61	121.5	1,093
850,000	....	0.0127	0.0146	2,620	61	118.0	1,062
800,000	....	0.0135	0.0156	2,470	61	114.5	1,031
750,000	....	0.0144	0.0166	2,320	61	110.9	998
700,000	....	0.0154	0.0178	2,160	61	107.1	964
650,000	....	0.0166	0.0192	2,010	61	103.2	929
600,000	....	0.0180	0.0207	1,850	61	99.2	893
550,000	....	0.0196	0.0226	1,700	61	95.0	855
500,000	....	0.0216	0.0249	1,540	37	116.2	814
450,000	....	0.0240	0.0277	1,390	37	110.3	772
400,000	....	0.0270	0.0311	1,240	37	104.0	728
350,000	....	0.0308	0.0356	1,080	37	97.3	681
300,000	....	0.0360	0.0415	926	37	90.0	630
250,000	....	0.0431	0.0498	772	37	82.2	575
212,000	0000	0.0509	0.0587	653	19	105.5	528
168,000	000	0.0642	0.0741	518	19	94.0	470
133,000	00	0.0811	0.0936	411	19	83.7	418
106,000	0	0.102	0.117	326	19	74.5	373
83,700	1	0.129	0.149	258	19	66.4	332
66,400	2	0.162	0.187	205	7	97.4	292
52,600	3	0.205	0.237	163	7	86.7	260
41,700	4	0.259	0.299	129	7	77.2	232
33,100	5	0.326	0.376	102	7	68.8	206

APPENDIX D

ALLOWABLE CARRYING CAPACITIES OF COPPER CONDUCTORS[1]
(Single conductor in free air)

Size of conductor			Carrying capacity, amp	
Gage number	Diameter of solid wires, mils	Area, cir mils	Rubber insulation	Varnished cambric insulation
14	64.1	4,170	20	30
12	80.8	6,530	25	40
10	101.9	10,380	40	55
8	128.5	16,510	55	70
6	162.0	26,250	80	100
4	204.3	41,740	105	135
3	229.4	52,630	120	155
2	257.6	66,370	140	180
1	289.3	83,690	165	210
0	325.0	105,500	195	245
00	364.8	133,100	225	285
000	409.6	167,800	260	330
0000	460.0	211,600	300	385
		250,000	340	425
		300,000	375	480
		350,000	420	530
		400,000	435	575
		500,000	515	660
		600,000	575	740
		700,000	630	815
		750,000	655	845
		800,000	680	880
		900,000	730	940
		1,000,000	780	1,000
		1,250,000	890	1,130
		1,500,000	980	1,260
		1,750,000	1,070	1,370
		2,000,000	1,155	1,470

[1] Allowable continuous current-carrying capacities of copper wires and cables of 98 per cent conductivity. For aluminum wire the allowable carrying capacities shall be taken as 84 per cent of those given in the table for the same sizes of copper wire with the same kind of covering.

APPENDIX E

Quantity	Symbol	Equation in mks (r) units	Name of Mks (r) unit	Name of Practical unit	Equivalent number of practical (cgs) units per unit mks (r)
Length..............	l	....	meter	centimeter	10^2
Mass................	m	....	kilogram	gram	10^3
Time................	t	....	second	second	1
Force...............	F	$F = ma$	newton	dyne	10^5
Work, energy........	W	$W = Fl$	joule	joule	1
Power...............	P	$P = W/t$	watt	watt	1
Electric charge.......	q	....	coulomb	coulomb	1
Electric field intensity.	$\mathcal{E}$	$\mathcal{E} = F/q$	volts/m	volts/cm	10^{-2}
Permittivity..........	ϵ	$F = q^2/4\pi\epsilon l^2$	farads/m	....	$4\pi \times 10^{-9}$
Displacement.........	D	$D = \epsilon\mathcal{E}$	coulombs/m^2	....	$4\pi \times 10^{-4}$
Displacement flux.....	ψ	$\psi = DA$	coulomb	....	4π
Emf, electric potential.	E	$E = \mathcal{E}l$	volt	volt	1
Current..............	I	$I = q/t$	ampere	ampere	1
Resistance...........	R	$R = E/I$	ohm	ohm	1
Conductance.........	G	$G = 1/R$	mho	mho	1
Resistivity...........	ρ	$\rho = RA/l$	ohm-meter	ohm-cm	10^2
Conductivity.........	γ	$\gamma = 1/\rho$	mhos/m	mhos/cm	10^{-2}
Capacitance..........	C	$C = q/E$	farad	farad	1
Elastance.............	S	$S = 1/C$	daraf	daraf	1
Magnetic charge.......	m	....	weber	....	$10^8/4\pi$
Magnetic field intensity	H	$H = NI/l$	amp-turns/m	oersted	$4\pi \times 10^{-3}$
Permeability..........	μ	$F = m^2/4\pi\mu l^2$	henrys/m	gauss/oersted	$10^7/4\pi$
Induction.............	B	$B = \mu H$	webers/m^2	gauss	10^4
Flux of induction......	ϕ	$\phi = BA$	weber	maxwell (line)	10^8
Mmf, magnetic potential.	M	$M = Hl$	amp-turn	gilbert	$4\pi \times 10^{-1}$
Reluctance...........	R	$R = M/\phi$	amp-turns/weber	gilberts/line	$4\pi \times 10^{-9}$
Permeance...........	P	$P = 1/R$	webers/amp-turn	lines/gilbert	$10^9/4\pi$
Inductance...........	L	$L = \phi/I$	henry	henry	1

INDEX